The 'production processes' of crops and pastures – photosynthesis and use of water and nutrients in fields – provide the unifying theme of this new text on the ecology of crop production. The book provides a unique combination of great breadth and depth in its treatment of production processes and systems problems. The approach is explanatory and integrative, with a firm basis in environmental physics, soils, physiology, and morphology. Systems concepts are introduced early and expanded as the book proceeds, giving emphasis to quantitative approaches, to management strategies and tactics employed by farmers, and to environmental issues. The systems approach is brought together in the final chapters, where production and nutrient cycling are analyzed, drawing on examples from American and Australian farms. The concluding chapter looks at trends in population growth and food supply and considers how the challenges of an uncertain future can be met.

Crop Ecology is based on courses taught by the authors in the United States and Australia, and is designed for use as a text for an introductory course in crop ecology (advanced undergraduate and graduate level). It is more than a text, however. Given the wide range of subjects, the authors have integrated reference and background material to create a 'stand-alone' reference work useful to a wide audience among agriculturalists.

Crop ecology:
productivity and management in agricultural systems

# Crop ecology: productivity and management in agricultural systems

R. S. LOOMIS

*Department of Agronomy*
*University of California, Davis*

D. J. CONNOR

*School of Agriculture and Forestry*
*University of Melbourne*

CAMBRIDGE
UNIVERSITY PRESS

Published by the Press Syndicate of the University of Cambridge
The Pitt Building, Trumpington Street, Cambridge CB2 1RP
40 West 20th Street, New York, NY 10011-4211, USA
10 Stamford Road, Oakleigh, Victoria 3166, Australia

First published 1992

Printed in Great Britain by Redwood Press Limited, Melksham, Wiltshire

*A catalogue record for this publication is available from the British Library*

*Library of Congress cataloging in publication data*

Loomis, R. S.
Crop ecology: productivity and management in
agricultural systems / R.S. Loomis, D.J.
Connor.
  p.  cm.
Includes bibliographical references and index.
ISBN 0-521-38379-X. – ISBN 0-521-38776-0 (pbk.)
1. Agricultural ecology.  2. Agricultural systems.  I. Connor, D.
J.  II. Title.
S589.7.L66  1992
631 – dc20 91-29201 CIP

ISBN 0 521 38379 X  hardback
ISBN 0 521 38776 0  paperback

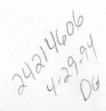

# Contents

# Preface

Humans make extensive use of land, water, energy, labor, and other resources in the production of crops and pastures. We do this because it is essential to our survival and well-being. As world population grows so does the demand for continuing success in agriculture, and as more land is used in agriculture, concern for loss of natural ecosystems increases. The conflict between production and conservation can best be resolved with cropping systems that are both efficient and sustainable.

Agricultural management is engaged with fields of plants and areas of land. This requires knowledge of whole-plant behavior under crowded conditions and of the interactions of plant communities with aerial and soil environments. These organismal and higher levels of biological organization are the subject fields of ecology, but explanation of behavior at these levels depends upon integration of relevant knowledge spanning lower levels from molecules and cells to organs. Ecology thus can be characterized as an integration of other disciplines. In turn, however, it provides specialist disciplines with context and relevance and, further, explains that in isolation they rarely effect system outcome. Crop ecology has additional dimensions in agricultural technology that interface with engineering, the social sciences, and perspectives provided through history.

The tools of crop ecology (strong basic physics, chemistry and mathematics) are not different than those of other biological disciplines. Mathematical models are especially useful in integration and are generally appropriate to crop ecology. Perhaps more than anything, ecological thinking derives from an eagerness to understand the whole and a willingness to maintain a broad appreciation of component disciplines.

We have designed this book as a text and reference for advanced undergraduate and postgraduate students and for practicing professionals. It derives from our experiences in teaching over many years and from our frustration with the great breadth and diffuse nature of appropriate readings. We especially want to encourage young scientists to use information in orderly ways to expand our understanding of crop ecology, and to develop new ways in which it can be applied to the changing problems of plant production. We do not, however, see the book limited to agriculturalists. It can also provide an ecological context for courses in environmental science that would benefit from an agricultural perspective.

Our approach is explanatory and integrative. Although we review many topics, and introduce some new topics slowly, the text generally builds quickly on basic

xiii

plant biology, soil science, and environmental physics and chemistry. Integration is apparent in systems themes introduced at the beginning and is brought to a focus in two case studies (Chapters 16 and 17) that can serve as models for analyses of other farming systems.

We wish to record our appreciation to colleagues and friends who have helped us in discussion and by critical evaluation of various chapters: A. Bloom, K. Cassman, M. Demment, D. Munns and R. Pearcy of the University of California, Davis; L. Malcolm and R. Simpson of the University of Melbourne; D. Coventry, Rutherglen Research Institute, Victoria; E. Fereres and H. Rapoport, University of Cordoba, Spain; H. Holmes, Renewable Energy Council, Melbourne; G. Morris and J. Morris, farmers, Kellogg, Iowa; A. Plowman, grazier, Devenish, Victoria; W. Stern, University of Western Australia; and E. Walton, MAFTech, Ruakura, New Zealand; and many students, in particular J. Brady, J. Real, and M. Vayssieres.

'Plowing Scene' by the Grant Wood rural life project is reproduced courtesy of the Special Collections Department, Iowa State University Library. Acknowledgements to the sources of other figures are given in their legends.

Finally, we thank the University of California and the University of Melbourne, and most importantly, Ann and Katharine, for their patience and support for us in this project.

R. S. Loomis
D. J. Connor

# ONE

# Farming systems and their biological components

A view from space gives emphasis to areal dimensions of vegetation and agriculture at the thin interface between atmosphere and solid earth. It is only by spreading plants across the landscape that they efficiently intercept fluxes of limiting resources such as $CO_2$, water, and sunlight. Tillage, rates of crop growth, and accumulation of yield all relate to the areas of land involved. In farming, land is divided into individual fields as the units of management and production. In ecological terms, the plants that occupy those fields constitute a **community** of cohabiting organisms. A community considered together with the chemical and physical features of the environment form a further fundamental grouping, the **ecosystem**.

Farmers' efforts in crop and pasture management aim at beneficial control over the structure of crop communities and physical and chemical aspects of the environment. Establishment of plant communities dominated by desirable species is presented in Chapter 1 as the basic strategy of agriculture.

This is followed by discussions of community structure (Chapter 2), stability (Chapter 3), genetic resources (Chapter 4), and plant development (Chapter 5). All are important topics relating to the biological materials used in agriculture.

# 1

*Agricultural systems*

## 1.1 INTRODUCTION

Production of organic materials in farmers' fields depends upon the physiological abilities of plants and on the environment within which they grow. These matters are subject to ecological analyses in terms of biological, chemical, and physical principles. What crops are grown and how they are grown are human decisions, however, depending also upon the usefulness of products, costs of production, and risks involved. Agriculture thus engages technology, economics, and the skills of farmers as well as principles from natural science.

Decisions about cropping practices for individual fields within a farm rest, at one level, on factors such as the field's unique soil characteristics and topography. At the farm level, those considerations must be rationalized with the farm's need for animal feeds, with the availability of labor, and with needs for crop rotation to control disease or erosion. Additional constraints imposed, for example, by market forces and by the availability of capital and technology also influence the strategies and tactics employed by farmers. Through integration into this large scheme of farm management, each field comes to have its own history of use and capability in production.

An understanding of the production ecology of crops and pastures thus extends beyond the boundaries of individual fields to embrace the farming systems of which the fields are a part. This chapter introduces several ideas about farming systems followed by overviews of plant production and the roles played by animals.

## 1.2 ON THE NATURE OF AGRICULTURAL SYSTEMS

**Terminology**

Individual fields are the fundamental units for studies in crop ecology. A crop or pasture community, together with management practices such as tillage methods and rotations used in its production, is termed a **cropping system**. It is here that we can examine the production processes of plants, soil processes, and their dependence upon environment. By observing a field over years, effects of crop rotation, tillage practices, soil amendments, and removal of harvested material on states of soils and subsequent yields can be seen and analyses made of the use of resources such as nutrients and water. Economic budgets of costs and returns and assessment of labor requirements are also usually done on fields.

At a higher level, fields are components of farms under the management of particular farmers. The principal crops and management practices employed on a particular farm constitute a **farming system**. Ruthenberg (1980) makes the point that because farms are organized to produce a net economic return they are the fundamental units for economic and sociological analyses. Other goals such as supplying food for the farm family (subsistence agriculture) and perpetuating the farm for later generations are also important. A farm, then, is a goal-oriented system in which the goals dictate how capital and labor are committed to production activities. The availability of capital and labor plus the need to manage risk impose constraints on which crops are grown, the rotations used, and the intensity of farming. Some aspects of agricultural ecology are analyzed best at the farm level. Examples include integration of livestock with crops and pastures and cycling of nutrients from one field, through manure, to another.

Attempts at classifying farming systems encounter the problem that no two farms are exactly alike. Soil types, crops, areas of land, financial resources, and skills and opinions of farmers about best practices vary from farm to farm. Ruthenberg (1980) found it useful, however, to assume that farmers are always rational: that there are good reasons why farms are similar or different. When most farms within a region are organized in a similar way, we can appy a descriptive phrase that characterizes regional farming practices. Chapters 16 and 17, for example, deal with 'ley farming' (small grains in rotation with legume pasture) in Australia and 'mixed farming' (with both crops and livestock) in Iowa. It is convenient to use the term **agricultural system** when talking about the regional organization of farming systems. The regional basis opens additional avenues for analysis, including matters such as drainage and air and water pollution. At this level, economic and sociological studies also may include service roles (e.g. grain purchase, storage, and transport) of towns and villages within the region.

### Important attributes

Productivity is perhaps the most important property of a farming system but it is not the only important one. Marten (1988) provided the definitions used in this book for five main system properties:

| *Ecological attributes* | *Social attributes* |
| --- | --- |
| Productivity (efficiency) | Equitability |
| Stability (variation, persistence) | Autonomy |
| Sustainability | |

**Productivity** is explicitly defined by the yield of useful product per unit land area. Expression per unit land area is multidimensional because various natural and human inputs, such as radiation, water, nutrients, or labor, also occur per unit land. Yield measures therefore have the property of also measuring **efficiency** relative to

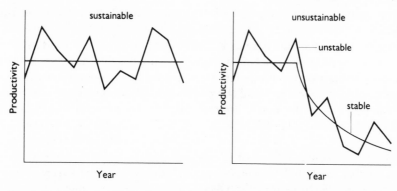

**Fig. 1.1. Marten's (1988) views of the meaning of stability and sustainability of production.**

such inputs. Yields vary over years with weather and other causes. Marten used the term **stability** in reference to the degree of such variation; **sustainability** is concerned with whether the production level can be maintained over years at the same site. The simplicity and clarity of these terms commend them for our purposes. Stability and sustainability are broad terms, however, and sometimes carry other definitions, so it is important to be explicit about the contexts in which they are used. As discussed in Chapter 3, ecologists who work with natural plant communities give a different emphasis to stability, and sustainability can be abused in reference to a specific *type* of farming system rather than as a variable *attribute* of all farming systems. 'Sustainable agriculture', for example, is sometimes taken as a synonym for 'organic farming', implying (incorrectly) that other types of farming are not sustainable.

**Equitability** (evenness of benefits within an agricultural system and between it and the larger society) and **autonomy** (the degree that agriculture is independent of the larger society) are important in social and economic analyses. Subsistence farmers, for example, have a high degree of autonomy but contribute little to urban economies.

Productivity, stability, and sustainability are principal themes throughout this book. The relationships among these terms are illustrated in Fig. 1.1. We would add to this list of important attributes that agriculture must also be **sufficient** in supplying food for humans. Given the continuing rapid increase in human population, agriculture must continue to expand in area and/or yield per unit area.

The interactions between agriculture and the rest of society deserve comment before proceeding with more ecological questions. Farming is generally an extension of the larger society in which it exists. The larger society supplies markets for produce as well as sources for necessary inputs. In this context, most agricultural systems, particularly those of developed countries, have a low degree of autonomy. Within a nation, farm and urban populations are usually exposed to the same general rules of existence. If labor and capital are free to move between the two sectors, they compete for those means of production and come to have similar standards of living. That process usually leads to a reasonable degree of equity. Government regulation has important influences on equity, however. Price controls on the inputs or outputs of farming, for example, can change the balance sharply.

Economists analyze the complex and diverse interactions involved in common units of currency. It is difficult (and in many cases impossible), however, to interpret economic findings or to extrapolate them to the future without also having an understanding of the biology and chemistry of production processes: of knowing, for example, about the finite, limiting relationships that exist between solar radiation, water use, and nutrient supply on one hand and agricultural production on the other.

In addition to essential flows of information, goods, and services that take place between urban and rural sectors, economic dislocations in one sector invariably affect the other. Each sector also affects the other's environment. Air pollution orginating in urban centers affects farm production; soil erosion as dust from fallow fields, and sediments and solutes in streams, affect the quality of life for all. Agriculture's need for goods and services stimulates the growth of urban communities within the food-producing region with the result that urban sprawl may remove productive lands from agriculture.

## Farming regions

Farmers choose the crops and pastures they produce from the range of species that will grow on their farms. Given the possibilities for modifying the environment by tillage, drainage, fertilization, and other means, numerous options exist. Practices that combine high productivity with safety and efficient use of scarce resources define ecological optima for individual fields. Very commonly, however, what is grown is not the most productive, safest, or efficient even when such information is available to the farmer. Subsistence farmers, for example, who consume all they produce, must pay attention to traditional foods of their culture, nutrition, and the need for a year-round supply of food. All farmers must view the whole farm as an integrated activity, considering factors such as labor and capital requirements of particular crops, need for rotation of crops, best use of marginal lands, and feed requirements for animals. Considerable variation also arises because farmers differ in personal objectives and energy as well as in technological and business skills. Increasingly, both farming and its markets are subject to extensive economic and political controls imposed by governments. Decisions about what will be grown are then influenced by those rules and real economic and agricultural efficiencies are given less attention.

What generally happens in practice is that regions of good soil and favorable climate are able to produce crops more economically than other regions. Farmers in those regions concentrate on crops that provide the best return for their investment and labor, at an acceptable level of risk. The balance of the market is then open to other, less-favored regions where farmers choose from lower-valued crops and farm larger areas with less intensive and less costly systems of management. As a result, land values come to reflect the capitalized return for their most economic use.

Geographical zones have probably been evident in agriculture from the begin-

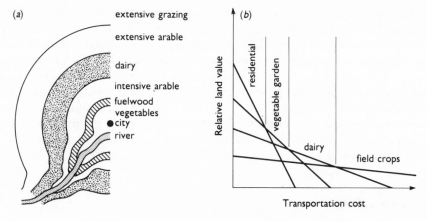

Fig. 1.2. (*a*) Thunen's concept of concentric land use around an imaginary urban center based on the cost and frequency of transporting agricultural products. Also shown in his view of how a river providing easy transport would modify the zones. (*b*) Competitive land values based on transportation costs. Concentric zones result because activities with a greater need for closeness to the center are able to value land higher than those with less need. (After Haggett (1979).)

ning, with cropping close to home and grazing more distant. The phenomena are recognized in geographers' concept of central places (urban centers) and 'Thunen zones' of agriculture (Haggett, 1979). In 1826, J. von Thunen noted that farms close to cities concentrated on high-value, perishable commodities (fruits and vegetables) whereas those distant from markets favored non-perishable, transportable products such as grains. Even today with many alternative forms of transportation and food processing, market gardeners are found near cities, with relatively small, intensive operations. Substantial investments in labor and technology are needed there to ensure high returns from the limiting resource, high-valued land. Where competition for land is not so great, production is more economically increased by putting more land into production than by employing more labor or technology to increase yield per unit area. The grain belts of North America, the Ukraine, Argentina, and Australia fit that concept of Thunen zones. These ideas are illustrated in Fig. 1.2. In general, farmers who wish to pursue a particular type of enterprise do well to move to a region where the infrastructure exists to support it and where land values and markets are appropriate to that form of production.

All of this determines that farming in most regions tends to focus on a limited number of crops and types of pasture. In developed societies, attempts at achieving a high diversity in a single farm commonly lead to mediocrity and failure because high diversity requires more information and management skills and more equipment than can be manipulated by a single manager. California, with its great diversity of horticultural crops, might seem an exception. With irrigation and a range of mild climates, California is able to achieve high yields and high quality of horticultural crops and farmers there supply over 50% of the fresh and processed fruits and vegetables consumed in the USA despite large distances to principal markets. In this case, the diversity of crops applies to the region rather than to individual farms. Perishable crops can be very risky because their markets are inelastic: prices vary considerably with supply and demand and thus with timing. In addition, more is at risk because they generally require considerable labor as well as special machinery. As a result, individual farms in California are generally rather specialized in the crops they produce. A high diversity of cropping per farm is more common in densely populated regions of India and Japan where household gardens, horticultural production, field crops, and pastures become geographically inter-twined on small farms. In those places, household needs and the advantage of an even distribution of labor over the year are important factors favoring diversity.

**Continuing change**

A fundamental feature of agriculture is its continuing transformation through changes in markets and through technological innovation. Market size depends mainly on population size but it also is affected by transportation modes, changes in processing, and shifts in diet preference. The current popularity of Italian cuisine in the USA has increased the use of durum wheat and tomato products, and concerns about cholesterol have favored an increased market share for poultry relative to beef. New technology was a factor in both changes. A machine-harvestable, determinate tomato, for example, sharply lowered production costs for tomato paste and new methods of broiler poultry production increased its efficiency in the use of feed. On a broader scale, expanded use of nitrogen fertilizer has sharply lowered production costs for most crops.

Farmers are the source of most innovations related to production, but ideas also flow freely between urban and agrarian domains. Diffusion of new technology is sometimes very rapid (hybrid maize and short-stature wheat) and sometimes very slow (combine harvesters). Ruttan (1982) concluded that the general education level of farmers (communication skills and arithmetic, for example) are much more important than research and advanced education in the creation and spread of technology. In some cases, new innovations force immediate changes in farming practices and crop regions; in others, crises due to changes in climate and markets stimulate change. Chapter 16 explains how the use of phosphorus fertilizer and legume rotations in Australia were delayed until wool prices increased sharply. In the USA, drought during the 1930s forced a retreat from extensive arable farming in the American Great Plains and the adoption of different tillage methods. Similarly, irrigation and the development of harvesting machines resulted in a shift of cotton production in the USA from the southeastern portion of the country to the arid southwest.

## 1.3 MANAGEMENT OF FARMING SYSTEMS

The strategy in agriculture is to manipulate the environment and the plant community in ways that result in optimum production and transfer of useful materials to humans. This involves creation of crop and pasture communities dominated by desirable species that partition a maximum portion of their primary production into useful organs and materials. It is also important to minimize losses from the system during production (e.g. losses due to weeds or diseases) and afterwards during processing and distribution.

The number of relationships that exist between organisms and their environment, and among and within organisms, is very large. Some have very little influence on overall performance whereas others exert strong control. The key to success in farming is to be able to identify and tactically adjust major control loops. The decision process is not as complex as it might seem. Once the decision about what crop to grow is made, choices of cultivar, planting date, land preparation, spacing, and fertilization follow in sequence.

Farmers have a wide array of management tools to control events in their fields, including tillage method, choice of species, time and density of planting, weed control measures, and soil amendments. Because weather and markets are uncertain, flexibility in operations is important. Consider some of the tactical options open to graziers. If an imbalance exists between stocking rate and pasture production, excess animals can be harvested or the breeding rate can be reduced. Alternatively, pasture production might be increased by applying fertilizer or water to increase the number of animals that may be grazed, or the amount of land involved could be extended by supplying the animals with hay or grain produced in other fields. Conversely, if the number of animals was insufficient to stay abreast of production, an increase in stocking rate or a harvest of excess forage as hay would achieve a balance. In practice, considerable managerial skill and experience are required in such decisions.

The use of different lands for pasture and feed in the preceding example illustrates that non-uniform treatment of land in time or space can be an important tool in management. We refer to this as the **non-uniformity principle** (Noy-Meir 1981). The principle applies particularly well to situations where soil resources are limiting to production. Those resources can sometimes be concentrated to a crop by farming in non-uniform ways, or, as in the pasture example, through allocation of fertilizer only to the pasture.

We use the phrase 'optimum' management (rather than maximum or minimum) deliberately. The reason is that the extra efforts in management required to achieve maximum biological performance generally return less than they cost. Minimum efforts are also inefficient because cropping involves a significant overhead in land preparation, planting, and other operations. Unless other inputs such as fertilizer and weed control are also made, the returns per unit input may be very small. The continued existence of a farm enterprise, i.e. its sustainability, is heavily dependent upon continued profitability. Maximum production and low-input production seldom equate to maximum economic efficiency. To provide an extreme example, it is quite feasible technologically to cultivate crops in the Antarctic (in controlled environments) or on barges in mid-ocean, but it would hardly be economic to do so. With competition for other uses for land, labor, and capital, and other regional sources of commodities, farmers generally must follow the basic rule that uneconomic practices are unsustainable in the long run.

Criteria of economic practice vary from one farming region to another. In Australia and the USA, where farm land is abundant relative to human population, and commodity prices are low, management practices tend to optimize net return per unit of labor. Capital expenditures for machines and fertilizer are made to ensure a high productivity of labor. In Japan, where land is the limiting resource and commodity prices and wages are high, heavy investments in fertilizer aim at high productivity per unit area. These situations contrast sharply with those in many developing nations where labor is abundant and capital is scarce.

Production per unit land is maximized in only a few farming regions (e.g. Japan, N. Europe); therefore, current yields of an agricultural system are usually a poor indicator of potential performance. Observed yields may fall anywhere on a continuum between crop failure and potential yield. Terminology used by the Food and Agriculture Organization of the United Nations (FAO) is useful in describing that continuum. The average yield of a district is defined as **actual yield**. This represents the current general state of soils and climate, average skill of the farmers, and their average use of available technology. **Attainable yield** corresponds to the best yields achieved through skilful use of the best available technology. High yields reported by experiment stations and the best growers serve as measures of attainable yield.

**Potential yield** defines what might be obtained for particular plant species when not limited by technology, i.e. when the best cultivars, fertilizer, machinery and labor including 'knowledge' are all available and applied in the best possible ways. Where water supply is a limiting resource and the opportunity for irrigation exists, knowledge of potential yields with and without supplemental irrigation is useful. Potential yield is commonly assessed by using theoretical models as restrained by climate and by physiological and morphological attributes of the plant species. In practice, potential yield models must be validated against reality with record yields (highest observed yields) serving as one standard.

The concepts of actual, attainable, record, and potential yields assist in assessments of farming systems and help to identify opportunities for improvement. They also serve to define the **intensity of farming**. Where actual yields are close to the attainable level, as is the case in Japan or northern Europe, agriculture may be described as intensive. In contrast, that of North America is of only moderate intensity and opportunities exist there and elsewhere for large yield advances. The intensity of farming also increases as the proportion of time in crop relative to fallow increases.

## 1.4  PLANT PRODUCTION

Growth of crops and pastures depends on the synthesis of organic compounds from $CO_2$ absorbed from the atmosphere and on inorganic nutrients and water absorbed from soil. The major component of biomass is carbon (40–45% of plant dry matter) and the major chemical compound is a carbohydrate, cellulose [$(CH_2O)_n$], but many other more complex compounds are found in the structures of living cells.

Production processes begin with the assimilation of $CO_2$ from the atmosphere

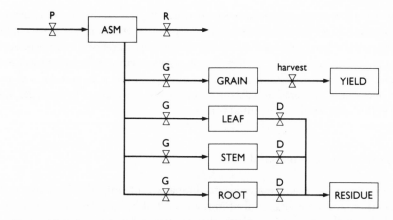

**Fig. 1.3. Scheme for the path of carbon and energy in production of an annual grain crop. Gate symbols represent processes: P for photosynthetic production of new ASsiMilates in leaves; R for respiration related to maintenance, biosyntheses, and growth; G for growth of various plant parts; and D for the death of parts.**

through the process of photosynthesis. The initial products are mainly simple sugars. These serve as chemical building blocks and, through respiration, provide energy needed for biosyntheses of new compounds and for maintenance of existing tissues. A simple scheme of the flow of energy and carbon in these processes is presented in Fig. 1.3. The format of the figure follows conventions used for 'state-variable models' (Forrester 1961) and is easily expanded with additional detail on control variables. The term **partitioning** describes the distribution of new assimilates to growth of various plant parts and to respiration. The total dry mass accumulated by a crop is **biomass**, and that portion useful to humans directly or indirectly as animal feed is **economic yield**, or just yield. The fraction, yield/total plant mass, is termed the **coefficient of economic yield**. It is difficult or impossible to measure the mass of crop roots in many cases, however, and **harvest index**, denoting useful fractions of just the above-ground biomass, is common in agronomic studies.

Photosynthesis is examined in Chapter 10 and partitioning and respiration are the subjects of Chapter 11. Partitioning patterns change over the course of a plant's annual cycle, and in response to environment, resulting in important changes in production. The control of development (what grows and when) is discussed in Chapter 5. In addition to carbon, hydrogen, and oxygen, nitrogen and several other elements have essential roles in the chemistry of growth (Chapters 8 and 12). The metabolic apparatus of plants is rich in nitrogenous compounds, phosphorus, and metal ions associated with enzyme function. Management of supplies of these elements is critical to the productivity and sustainability of agriculture.

Water provides a liquid milieu in which metabolism operates and it also participates in many metabolic reactions. The challenge of terrestrial existence is protection of the plant's internal aqueous environment from the dry, and thus hostile, external environment. Absorption of $CO_2$ depends on an open diffusion pathway from atmosphere to chloroplasts inside the leaves; this pathway inevitably allows evaporation of large amounts of water from wet, interior surfaces of leaves (transpiration). As a result, plants transfer vastly more water to the atmosphere than is ever involved in their metabolism. In ecological terms, photosynthesis involves exchanging water for $CO_2$. The physics of evaporation (Chapter 6), soil–plant–water relations (Chapters 7 and 9), and management of water resources (Chapters 13 and 14) join our family of essential topics.

## Composition of plant material

The usefulness of plant materials to humans and animals depends on their composition and on energy stored in the chemical bonds of their organic constituents. The cellular nature of plants dictates that a degree of stoichiometry must always exist among proportions of basic biochemical substances found in the **structural** components of biomass. Each cell is enclosed by a rigid cellulosic wall and its dimensions are fixed once its growth ceases. Because growth involves an increase in size, mass, or number of cells, wall materials including cellulose, hemicellulose, pectin, and lignin normally constitute 70–80% of the organic matter in vegetative parts of plants. The balance is composed mainly of proteins and nucleic acids found in the nucleus, various organelles, and cytoplasm, and of lipids that form membrances around those compartments.

Plant cells also contain varying amounts of **non-structural** material. Assimilates such as starch, sugars, and free amino acids not incorporated into walls or protoplasm are classified as non-structural materials. Temporary accumulations of non-structural material can usually be mobilized and used elsewhere in the plant. Such accumulations are sometimes referred to as 'reserves' but one needs to be careful about teleological implications. Plants do not accumulate non-structural material with some 'intent'; rather, possession of that trait has conferred an advantage in evolution. Storage of non-structural materials in fruits and specialized storage organs such as tubers is more permanent and the materials are generally available only to the next generation. In contrast to moderate concentrations of non-structural materials found in vegetative tissues, starch, oil, protein, or sugar can account for up to 75% of the dry mass of storage organs and seeds.

For a plant cell to expand during growth and maintain its size and shape thereafter, a positive hydrostatic pressure (turgor) must be exerted against the cell wall. Accumulation of solutes (osmotica) by cells lowers the water potential below that of soil water (see Chapter 7). That gradient assures a flow of water from soil and thus a positive turgor despite a continuing loss through transpiration. Cell vacuoles are the principal place where non-structural osmotica accumulate. Osmotica can be almost any soluble substance of convenience: sugars or amino acids not currently needed in metabolism, by-products such as organic acids that provide pH buffering, and mineral ions such as $Na^+$, $K^+$, $NO_3^-$, and $Cl^-$.

The composition of biomass is constrained by inclusion of structural components, yet it can vary over a considerable range depending on types and amounts of various tissues involved, on cell size (which determines the surface:volume ratio and thus amount of wall material), and on type and amount of non-structural material. In leaves, chloroplasts add a large amount of protein to the structural component; the principal carboxylase enzyme of photosynthesis accounts for about 25% of the leaf protein in many plants. Xylem tissues on the other hand contain large amounts of specially differentiated vessel and tracheid elements with lignified wall thickenings. Those cells are dead and thus nearly free of nucleic acid, protein, and lipid. Vascular strands and schlerenchyma, another tissue in which lignified walls are common, contribute stiffness that aids the display of stems and leaves and hence the plant's ability to intercept light.

**Methods of analysis** The composition of biomass in terms of the major biochemical classes is important information for ecological studies. The need of animal scientists for a better understanding of animal rations was a major force behind the development of simple methods for the analysis of plant material. By 1900, agricultural chemists and animal feeders had established that energy (carbohydrates and lipids) and nitrogenous compounds (e.g. protein) were the main factors in animal nutrition, and **proximate analyses** involving solvent extractions had emerged as a standard method for distinguishing broad biochemical classes. The extensive tables of feed analyses constructed by that method (e.g. National Research Council 1982) are useful in ecological work.

To use such feed composition tables, one must know something about the methods of analysis. The fraction soluble in petroleum ether (oils, fats and waxes) is taken as **lipid**. Kjeldahl analysis is used to measure total nitrogen. Proteins and amino acids comprise most of that (nucleic acids are a very small component) and total $N \times 6.25$ is taken as an estimate of **crude protein** (Table 1.1). The factor 6.25 comes from the observation that $0.16 \pm 0.01$ of the mass of plant proteins is nitrogen and $1/0.16 = 6.25$. Smaller, species-specific, factors are used for estimating the protein contents of grains, and corrections for nitrate–nitrogen content are needed with some vegetative materials. In the proximate method, the residue after extractions with acid and alkali is defined as wall material (**crude fiber**, CF). Treatment with acids and alkalis dissolves some wall material, however, and the CF fraction lacks validity for some purposes. An alternative method (Van Soest 1982), in which wall material is the residue after extraction with neutral detergent solution, gives better results. This wall fraction is called **neutral detergent fiber** (NDF). None of the wall is dissolved and its contents of cellulose, hemicellulose, lignin, and protein are open to further analysis.

It is very difficult, even by highly refined methods of analysis, to account for 100% of the composition of biomass by any method of analysis. The proximate method takes the remainder after subtracting lipid, crude protein, CF or NDF, and ash from the beginning mass as **nitrogen-free extract** (NFE), i.e. as non-structural carbohydrate. With the CF method, dissolved wall material is included in NFE. The scheme of analysis presented in Table 1.1 employs the NDF determination. In this case, the remainder is due to incomplete extraction and to the presence of other classes of compounds such as pectin and tannin. Analyses of feeds are now

Table 1.1 A *scheme for the analysis of major biochemical classes in dry plant material*

This approach borrows from the proximate scheme and from the neutral detergent fiber (NDF) scheme of Van Soest (1982).

| Class | Procedure | Major components | Comment |
|---|---|---|---|
| Nitrogenous compounds | Kjeldahl N × 6.25 | Proteins, amino acids, nucleic acids | 6.25 converts to crude protein |
| Lipids | Extraction with petroleum ether | Fats, oils, waxes | |
| Wall material | Residue after boiling with neutral detergent | Cellulose, hemicellulose, lignin, wall protein (NFE) | Wall protein; may deserve further analysis |
| Non-structural carbohydrates | Extraction with ethanol, followed by gas or liquid chromatography | Sugars | Treatment with amylase for starch analysis |
| Organic acids | As for non-structural carbohydrates | Organic acids | |
| Minerals | Ignition at 500–600°C | Mineral oxides | Actual minerals = *ca.* 0.6 × ash |
| Remainder | By difference | Pectin, tannin | May deserve specific analysis |

commonly done with physical methods in which spectral distribution of reflected near-infrared radiation (NIR) provides information on moisture, starch, protein, lipid and fiber contents.

**Examples of composition**   Some examples of biomass composition are presented in Table 1.2. Large differences in the content of wall material are evident between vegetative biomass (sorghum at anthesis, bluegrass, and alfalfa) and the grains and soybean seed. The sharp increase of non-structural carbohydrate in sorghum with maturity is due to grain growth; note how the protein content of the whole plant is diluted to 7.4% (1.2% N) by the increase in starch.

**Energy storage in plant material**   The substrates for photosynthesis, $CO_2$ and $H_2O$, are fully oxidized compounds. By contrast, the organic constituents of plants are all reduced to some degree and will release their chemical bond energy as heat energy upon oxidation. **Gross heat content** ($\Delta H_c$, the heat of combustion) is determined easily by ignition of a plant sample or chemical substance under an oxygen atmosphere in a 'bomb calorimeter'. The released heat is measured from the rise in temperature of a surrounding water bath. Engineers distinguish between 'higher heating values', obtained when the water product of combustion is condensed to liquid, and lower values found when water remains as vapor. The higher values are used in this book and in biological studies in general because liquid water, not vapor, is the product in metabolism.

Table 1.2 *Approximate biochemical composition of several plant materials (% dry matter)*

| Class | Grain sorghum biomass (anthesis) | (mature) | Bluegrass forage (early bloom) | Alfalfa hay (midbloom) | Maize grain | Wheat grain | Soybean seed |
|---|---|---|---|---|---|---|---|
| Nitrogenous compounds[1] | 12 | 7 | 17 | 18 | 11 | 15 | 43 |
| Lipids[2] | 3 | 3 | 4 | 3 | 4 | 2 | 19 |
| Wall materials[3] | 59 | 42 | 65 | 46 | 9 | (11) | (10) |
| Cellulose | 27 | 18 | 28 | 26 | 2 | | |
| Hemicellulose | 29 | 21 | 16 | 10 | 6 | | |
| Lignin | 3 | 3 | 4 | 9 | 1 | | |
| Non-structural carbohydrates[4] | 9 | 33 | na | (15) | (74) | (68) | (13) |
| Sugars | 9 | 3 | | | (2) | (2) | (11) |
| Starch | 0 | 30 | | | (72) | (66) | (2) |
| Organic acids | 2 | 1 | na | na | — | — | — |
| Minerals[5] | 6 | 4 | 4 | 5 | 1 | 1 | 3 |
| Remainder | 9 | 10 | 10 | 13 | 1 | 3 | 12 |
| Total | 100 | 100 | 100 | 100 | 100 | 100 | 100 |

*Notes:*
[1] $N \times 6.25$.
[2] Petroleum ether extract.
[3] Values in parentheses are 'acid-detergent fiber'; all others are by the neutral detergent method.
[4] Values in parentheses were gleaned from other sources.
[5] Ash $\times 0.6$.
na, Not analyzed.
*Sources:* Sorghum data from Lafitte & Loomis (1988*b*); other crops from National Research Council (1982).

Heats of combustion indicate the maximum amount of energy that might be derived from a material in metabolism and thus serve as crude measures of its value as a food source. They also provide a measure of the cost for the biosynthesis of the material. Characteristic $\Delta H_c$ values (in MJ kg$^{-1}$) for the major biochemical classes are: organic acids, 4–11; carbohydrates, 15.6 to 17.5; proteins, 22–25; lipids, 35–40. Vegetative biomasses of most crop and pasture species, with their relatively small content of lipid and protein, average 17–17.5 MJ kg$^{-1}$. Woody materials contain more lipid (e.g. waxes) and their $\Delta H_c$ values are nearer 18–19 MJ kg$^{-1}$; oil seeds, such as soybean and sunflower, yield 21–25 MJ kg$^{-1}$. Only a portion of the heat content of protein can be released in metabolism because amino groups ($-NH_2$) cannot be oxidized by higher plants and animals. Energy yields from metabolism of proteins for those organisms, about 17 MJ kg$^{-1}$, are similar to what they obtain from carbohydrates. Soil microorganisms that can metabolize reduced nitrogen perform the important function of recycling reduced nitrogen to atmospheric $N_2$ (Chapter 8).

It is sometimes convenient to represent the costs of plant biosyntheses in terms of the amounts of a simple sugar, glucose, consumed in the process (cf. Chapters 8 and 11). For comparison with other substances, the heat of combustion of glucose at 20 °C is 15.6 MJ kg$^{-1}$.


## 1.5    TROPHIC SYSTEMS IN AGRICULTURE

Humans and other animals differ in their capabilities in digestion. Animals are included in farming systems because they thrive on plant materials unsuited for human consumption while converting it to high-quality food for humans. The biological values of milk and meat as human food are superior to those of most plant materials, and wool and hides are enormously useful. Further, some animals harvest their own feed thus saving human labor. The biochemical composition of plant material and the capabilities of animal digestive systems are therefore pivotal determinants of farming systems.

World-wide, domestic animals graze an area of land more than 2.5 times that given to crops. In addition, the majority of the production from arable lands goes directly to animals. More than 5 billion humans now inhabit Earth; they are accompanied by 1.6 billion large mammals (principally cattle), 2.5 billion smaller mammals (sheep, swine, and goats) and 9 billion chickens (FAO Production Yearbook). The feed requirements of these animals are more than 2.5 times those of humans.


### Trophic chains

Despite the great diversity found among the soils, climates, crops, and animals employed, all farming systems can be classified within four basic **trophic chains** (Fig. 1.4). These food chains serve as maps of 'who eats what'. They begin with the crop and follow some attribute such as energy, nitrogen, or dry mass through the animals that consume it. Agricultural systems, in contrast to some natural systems, have short trophic chains. In addition to food, agriculture also provides organic raw materials for industry. Fibers (e.g. cotton, hemp, flax, and wool), hides, and lipids (waxes and oils) are among the more obvious examples. The heavy emphasis given to soybean in world trade is based as much on industrial uses of its oil in alkyd resin paints as it is on food and feed values of that oil and of the high-protein oil-seed cake that remains after oil extraction. The trophic pathways of Fig. 1.4, then, are paralleled by a crop→industry path.

Trophic chains are transformed into complex webs when weeds, insects, birds, and soil flora and fauna are included in the schemes (Fig. 1.5). Various organisms in the web can be grouped into functional classes according to their principal role and level as producers or consumers. Autotrophic green plants of crops and pastures are termed **primary producers**, and their important characteristic is the **net primary**

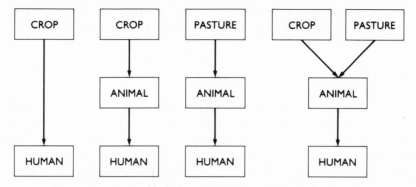

Fig. 1.4. The four basic trophic chains found in agriculture.

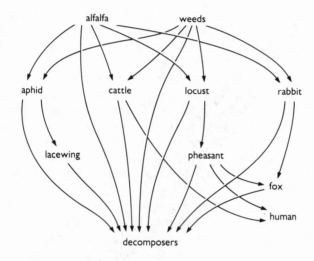

Fig. 1.5. The chain alfalfa→cattle→human expanded into a trophic web.

**production** of dry matter that they achieve through photosynthesis, associated metabolism, and nutrient uptake. Consumers of green plants are considered **primary consumers**, or more simply, herbivores; carnivores dominate as **secondary consumers** of other animals. Waste and dead material from each of these levels are ultimately decomposed by microbial populations, and trophic chains and webs are terminated by a decomposer level. Decomposers perform the critical role of recycling chemical elements; without their activities, C, H, N, O and essential mineral elements would simply accumulate in dead material.

The real world is not quite as simple as this trophic classification suggests. Many species including man are omnivores, consuming both plant and animal material, and an alternative scheme might arrange animals according to the anatomy and capability of their digestive systems. Microbial populations participate in more than just a terminal role. In particular, they are important in the digestive tracts of animals (and insects) and thus could be considered primary consumers.

### Biological efficiency in trophic chains

Production of organic materials is only the first step in bringing food to our tables in palatable forms. Losses of energy and carbon occur during plant growth (Fig. 1.3) and in subsequent stages of harvest and consumption, particularly where domestic animals are involved. One of our concerns is to minimize such losses.

Some rather broad principles emerge from Fig. 1.5 that serve as a foundation for farm management. The web makes the point that only a portion of the production of one trophic level passes to the next level while the balance eventually passes to decomposers. In plant-to-herbivore transfers, for example, some of the plant material is inaccessible to grazers (e.g. roots), or indigestible by them (lignin). Additional losses occur at each level through respiration and senescence. Therefore, short trophic chains can pass more of the initial primary production to the last consumer than can long chains. A second point is that crops and pastures usually include a number of plant species of little utility to ourselves or our animals. Such plants are weeds; they occupy 'space' and utilize resources of light, nutrients, and water that would have supported additional crop production. Deficiencies of plant nutrients also result in lost production. Grazers such as rabbits, birds, and insects consume production that could have gone to domesticated animals, while parasites and imbalances in animal diet lessen production per unit feed consumed. Each of these problems represents a drain of organic material and associated nutrients from the trophic flow to humans and are therefore targets of management strategies that might reduce them.

Only rarely does wildlife consume enough to be a significant issue in production and most farmers view the presence of wildlife as a fringe benefit of farming. Predation of sheep by carnivores, attacks on ripening grain by birds, and devastation of pasture by rabbits (Australia) are examples where control measures may be required.

Measurements of the efficiency with which materials transfer from one trophic level to another (**trophic efficiency**) define how well a system is working. Trophic efficiency is calculated as the net production by animals per unit feed input. This can be expressed in energy terms $(J J^{-1})$ or, for example, as the mass of nitrogen in eggs per unit grain or grain nitrogen consumed. Trophic efficiencies vary with amounts of feedstuff supplied, how it is presented to the animals, biochemical composition of the feed, type and size of animal, ambient temperature, and other factors.

Theoretical charts of energy and material fluxes through a population of consumers become more complex when heat production from voluntary and involuntary work, digestion, and thermoregulation are included. Measurement of total heat production can be done in a whole-animal calorimeter, an elaborate and expensive apparatus, but the problem remains of identifying the proportions of heat that come from digestion, metabolism, and thermoregulation. In addition, measuring the growth of cattle in other than live-mass terms is a significantly difficult task, compared with measuring dry matter growth of plants with an oven and a balance. Live-mass measures are in fact subject to considerable variation because gut fill for ruminants can vary between 10 and 50% of the empty-body mass (Agricultural Research Council Working Party 1980). Lactation efficiency (milk production/feed intake) also seems simple until associated changes in the animal's mass and composition are considered.

## 1.6  ANIMAL AND HUMAN NUTRITION

### Digestive systems of animals

Through evolution, higher animals have arrived at a divergence of designs for gastrointestinal tracts that allow existence on various types of vegetation. All animals including humans can digest simple proteins, fats, and sugars, but they differ greatly in digestion of complex carbohydrates such as starch and cellulose. Digestion of cellulose is important, first because cellulose is the most abundant biochemical constituent of plants, and second because cellulosic wall materials enclose and protect cell contents. Some wall material is digested by acid and alkaline digestive secretions but a serious attack on cellulose requires cellulase enzymes produced by microorganisms. Anaerobic bacteria that exist through fermentation have a principal role in cellulose digestion. Gastrointestinal tracts that provide a place and opportunity for bacterial fermentation of wall material gain access to the resulting products (bacterial protein and byproducts such as volatile fatty acids) as well as released cell contents.

Digestion of plant material increases as the time between intake and elimination ('passage time') increases. Passage time increases with length of the digestive tract and thus with body size. Most animals depend on the large intestine (colon) and its appendages for fermentation (Fig. 1.6). The human colon, for example, is 'sacculated', allowing an opportunity for some fermentation. Our body size and passage time are small, however, and we gain little from fermentation. Dietary fiber is beneficial to our digestive activity but, despite the sacculated colon, humans are dependent mainly upon readily digestible carbohydrates, fats, and proteins that can be released (by cooking or chewing) from constraining influences of plant cell walls. In some animals, an appendage of the colon located near the junction of the small and large intestines, the **cecum**, increases the capacity for fermentation. The human cecum is small. That of swine is larger but it does not circumvent entirely the need for relatively high-quality feed. In contrast, the horse has a very large and well-developed cecum. Coupled with a large body size and long passage time, the cecum allows the horse to subsist solely on forages. In poultry, the gizzard grinds cellulosic fibers, increasing their surface area and the subsequent rate of digestion in a small cecum. The rabbit overcomes the passage-time problem by ejecting separate feces from the cecum and the rectum. Nutrient-rich cecal pellets are reingested for a second passage.

A multichamber stomach, the **rumen** (Fig. 1.6), serves as the principal site for fermentation in ruminants including cattle, sheep, goat, and buffalo. Cattle and

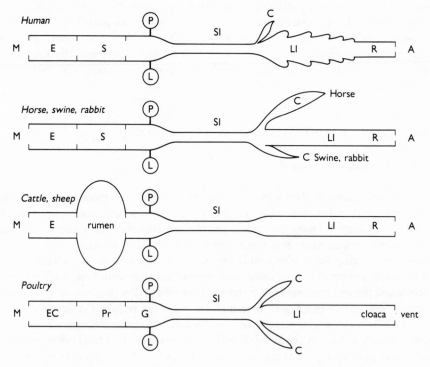

**Fig. 1.6. Digestive tracts of humans and various domestic animals. Code: M, mouth; E, esophagus; S, stomach; P and L, pancreas and liver, respectively; SI and LI, small and large intestine, respectively; R, rectum; A, anus; C, cecum; EC, esophagus–crop; Pr, proventriculus; G, gizzard.**

sheep possess a complex, four-chamber rumen. This organ can retain fiber for continued attack while screening and passing digested materials to the intestine. The fermentation capacities of rumens are impressive. Most cellulosic materials except those intimately linked to lignin can be digested. The differences in digestion are evident from an examination of the resulting fecal matter. Horse dung contains a considerable amount of undigested wall material and associated protein, whereas that of cattle is much lower in fiber and protein (Azevedo and Stout 1974). One consequence is that horse manure, because of its greater nitrogen content, has a greater value as fertilizer than that of cattle.

Differences in digestion cause animals to vary in their roles in agricultural systems and in their competitiveness with man for foodstuffs. Fowl and swine, although competitive with humans because of their dependence on grain, are used in places where the ratio of humans to arable land is large and pasturage is scarce. Their utilization of excess grain gives them a role in buffering human food supplies. Populations of poultry and swine can be reduced by consumption during food shortages and their high reproductive rates allow them to be restored rapidly when grain is abundant. Ruminants are less competitive with humans. They greatly extend human food supplies through use of grazing lands, forages, and coarse grains unsuited as sources of human food. Their reproductive rates are small, however, and their numbers cannot be adjusted quickly in response to variations in food supply.

## Feeds and feeding

Despite difficulties in determining the fate of mass and energy after ingestion by animals, a number of important concepts emerge from feeding trials. These serve in calculating dietary requirements and expected yields of domestic animals.

**Digestible nutrients**   The apparent digestibility of a feedstuff is determined by acclimating animals to the feed, collecting the fecal mass produced over a period of time, and subtracting it from feed mass. The difference equals the **total digestible nutrients** (TDN) in the feedstuff. Digestibility of attributes such as nitrogen and energy can be assessed from the same samples. Sufficient trials have been done with domestic animals that TDN can be calculated from proximate analyses as the sum of protein, lipid, and fiber, with the latter adjusted according to the digestive abilities of the animal.

TDN has been used as a basis for the formulation of animal rations mainly in America, where tables of TDN values for most feedstuffs along with daily TDN requirements of various sizes and kinds of animals were developed. Europeans have used an equivalency approach in which a feedstuff's merit was expressed relative to some standard feed such as starch, barley, or hay.

**Nutritional energetics**   TDN accounts for digestibility but it does not account for energy losses in digestion, thermoregulation, and later metabolism. Those costs are considered in a set of energy concepts summarized in Table 1.3. The **gross energy** (GE) content of a feedstuff is its heat of combustion ($\Delta H_c$, usually about 17 MJ kg$^{-1}$). Additional energy categories define the fate of energy within an animal. **Digestible energy** (DE), for example, is the $\Delta H_c$ of TDN and is near 18.4 MJ kg$^{-1}$ in most cases. Like TDN, DE is calculated from composition with an allowance for the greater heat content of lipids. In ruminants, significant portions of digested energy are lost in urine, as heat during fermentation, and in gaseous products such as methane. In cold climates, digestive heat contributes to maintenance of body temperature, but in hot climates animals must expend additional energy to cool themselves and production efficiency is less. **Metabolizable energy** (ME) is the energy remaining from DE after accounting for gas production and urinary losses; **net energy** (NE) is the remainder after correcting ME for heat losses.

NE is a measure of the residual energy yield from a feed that can be used in maintenance, growth, or lactation. An amount of feed energy sufficient to maintain the animal without change in body mass, is the first requirement. NE$_m$ satisfies the animal's 'basal metabolism' (energy expenditure while fasting and resting) and voluntary work such as standing and eating. The basal metabolism of warm-blooded animals is roughly proportional to their surface:volume ratio and thus to $W^{0.75}$ ($W$ = body mass) and to the temperature gradient. When the supply of net

Table 1.3 *Definitions used in analyses of the nutritional energetics of domestic animals*

| Energy category | Fate of energy or measurement | Source |
|---|---|---|
| Gross Energy (GE) | Heat of combustion | Total feed intake |
| | → Fecal energy (FE) | Undigested fraction and dead bacteria |
| Digestible Energy (DE) | DE = GE − FE | |
| | → Gaseous products of digestion (GPD) | Mainly methane |
| | → Urinary energy (UE) | Mainly urea from protein turnover in body maintenance |
| Metabolizable Energy (ME) | ME = DE − GPD − UE | |
| | → Heat production (H) | Heat produced in digestion through fermentation + heat loss from metabolism |
| Net Energy (NE) | NE = ME − H | |
| | → Maintenance ($NE_m$) | Basal metabolism + voluntary work + cost of temperature regulation |
| | → Production ($NE_g$) | Growth (gain) or work |
| | → Lactation ($NE_l$) | Milk production |

*Source:* National Research Council 1981.

energy exceeds the maintenance level, additional NE will support growth or lactation. Growth is measured as the 'gain' in live mass, including, for example, the gain in wool produced by sheep. Calculations of the $NE_g$ (gain) and $NE_l$ (lactation) produced by a feed take account of the metabolism required for production.

Both ME and NE have powerful applications in animal management. The British have developed equations for feed requirements of cattle and sheep from ME (Agricultural Research Council Working Party 1980); Americans generally employ NE for those purposes. The American system has been reduced to tables giving the nutrient requirements of domestic animals (National Research Council 1984; and various handbooks) for use in ration formulation. Data from large numbers of carefully conducted feeding trials are summarized in the regression equations used to calculate such tables.

The NE method is outlined in Box 1.1. As shown in that example, $NE_g$ (2.4 MJ $kg^{-1}$) supplied by a feed is significantly smaller than its $NE_m$ value (5.3 MJ $kg^{-1}$). That occurs because some feed mass is converted into the structural material of the growing animal rather than being respired. (This effect is explained by the growth–yield concept introduced in Chapter 11.) Production of milk also has a smaller cost than growth: $NE_l$ from alfalfa hay, for example, is 5.4 MJ $kg^{-1}$. The effectiveness of hay in milk production explains in part why milk is a cheaper source of protein for humans than beef meat and why hay (which costs less to produce than grain) is a common feed for dairy animals and for maintenance of breeding cattle. The low bulk density and slow digestion of **roughages** such as hay can be limiting to daily intake in some cases. In contrast, feeds such as grains, with their greater bulk density and greater feeding value per kilogram, are termed **concentrates**.

Calculations presented in Box 1.1 illustrate how it is now possible to manipulate diets of confined animals in ways that make best use of available feedstuffs while optimizing animal performance and minimizing waste. The NE system is available in computer programs used by feeders to determine the 'least-cost' diet for a given rate of production. Those programs compare current prices and net energy values of feeds to arrive at a feed mixture and rate of feeding that provide the best economic return. The main problems with the NE system lay with the expense of experiments conducted to obtain NE values.

**Influence of work**  Exercise requires food energy; animals in sparse or hilly pastures have smaller trophic efficiencies than those in level, lush, pastures and in lots or barns. For sheep and cattle, the cost of level walking is $2–3 \, J \, kg^{-1}$ body mass $m^{-1}$ traveled, and for climbing, $27–32 \, J \, kg^{-1} \, m^{-1}$ vertical lift (Agricultural Research Council Working Party 1980). Effects of exercise are readily apparent even in feedlots: trophic efficiencies are greater in level than in sloping lots. Exercise has a similar effect on food requirements of humans.

When animals are used for work, their energy requirements increase sharply. Brody's (1945) discussion of the horse and other animals is instructive. It turns out that humans and horses are rather similar. Their maximum net efficiency (work accomplished/DE expended in muscle activity) increases asymptotically to about 0.25 as the rate of doing work increases. Much of the work done by humans goes to lifting of the body, however, and the effective work is considerably less than 0.25. In lifting a pencil from the floor, for example, we must also lift all of our upper body. By contrast, animals are used mainly for pulling or carrying, which are relatively efficient activities. Large (700 kg) workhorses can generate as much as 10 kW (13.3 HP) but for only a few seconds at a time. At that rate, the animal would need to consume 4.3 kg of good hay per hour to obtain the necessary 36 MJ of DE! (Horse rations are usually done on a digestible energy basis; good hay is about 45% digestible.) The maximum sustained effort of a horse for a 10 h day is nearer 0.75 kW (1 HP) resulting in 27 MJ of work accomplished, corresponding to 40 km travel with a draft equal to about 10% of body weight (about 70 kg). Net efficiency is still near 0.25, but when the maintenance requirement is added the overall efficiency drops to 0.16. The total digestible energy requirement is 174 MJ $d^{-1}$ (66 MJ for maintenance + 108 MJ for work). That could be met with 21 kg of good hay per day, but that quantity is too bulky to be consumed and digested in a day so a portion of the diet is fed as concentrate. The efficiency of work accomplished to gross energy ingested is 7% (27 MJ work/ (174 MJ DE/0.45 digestibility)).

Work animals are still used in many areas of the world. Cattle perform better on low-quality feedstuffs such as straw than do horses and mules but they also work at a slower rate. As a result, their maintenance overhead per unit work is greater and more human labor is required while the animals perform a given task. In the USA,

Box 1.1 *An example of rations based on net energy*

Example calculations of the daily feed requirement for a half-grown, 250 kg steer with data drawn from the NRC tables (National Research Council 1984) help in understanding NE concepts and differences in the merits of feedstuffs. From the tables, the animal's NE maintenance requirement is:

$NE_m = 20.2$ MJ d$^{-1}$

Possible rates of growth are linked with feeding beyond the $NE_m$ level:

$NE_g$ for a gain of: 0.4 kg live mass d$^{-1}$ = 5.4 MJ d$^{-1}$
0.8 kg d$^{-1}$ = 11.5 MJ d$^{-1}$
1.2 kg d$^{-1}$ = 17.9 MJ d$^{-1}$

Therefore the total NE required for 0.8 kg gain per day is $20.2 + 11.5 = 31.7$ MJ d$^{-1}$. That could be met by various feeds. NE yields from alfalfa hay (National Research Council 1982; composition shown in Table 1.2) are $NE_m = 5.3$ MJ kg$^{-1}$ and $NE_g = 2.4$ MJ kg$^{-1}$. Hay requirements for 0.8 kg gain d$^{-1}$ therefore are:

for maintenance   20.2 MJ d$^{-1}$/5.3 MJ kg$^{-1}$ = 3.8 kg d$^{-1}$
for gain       11.5 MJ d$^{-1}$/2.4 MJ kg$^{-1}$ = 4.8 kg d$^{-1}$
_____

Total hay = 8.6 kg d$^{-1}$

For comparison, NE yields from flaked maize grain (composition shown in Table 1.2) are $NE_m = 8.9$ MJ kg$^{-1}$ and $NE_g = 6.1$ MJ kg$^{-1}$. Feed requirements with grain are only one-half that with alfalfa:

for maintenance   20.2 MJ d$^{-1}$/8.9 MJ kg$^{-1}$ = 2.3 kg d$^{-1}$
for gain       11.5 MJ d$^{-1}$/6.1 MJ kg$^{-1}$ = 1.9 kg d$^{-1}$
_____

Total grain = 4.2 kg d$^{-1}$

The smaller amount of feed required with grain compared with hay explains why it is referred to as concentrate.

This example demonstrates the variable nature of trophic efficiency. At 17 MJ kg$^{-1}$ feed in each case, gross energies for the two diets are 146 and 92 MJ for alfalfa and maize, respectively. The efficiency of the system is limited by the large loss of energy between GE and NE and by the maintenance requirement. With 11.5 MJ retained in the animal body as gain, the feeding efficiencies are $11.5/146 = 0.078$ for alfalfa and $11.5/92 = 0.125$ for maize grain. Trophic efficiency declines if intake is reduced because a larger fraction of NE is then expended on maintenance. From this example, it is clear that feeding grain is a more efficient practice for growing beef than feeding hay. Efficiencies with either feed are reduced sharply, however, when feeding requirements of the steer's parents are included in the budgets.

The steers in this example need 0.66 kg digestible protein d$^{-1}$ (0.1 kg N d$^{-1}$) (National Research Council 1984). The alfalfa diet would supply 0.93 kg digestible protein (1.57 kg total protein), resulting in considerable waste to manure, whereas maize grain with only 0.43 kg digestible protein (0.46 kg total protein) would have to be supplemented with a protein source such as oil-seed meal.

where horses and mules predominated over oxen in earlier times because of shortages of farm workers, nearly $4 \times 10^7$ ha of farmland (20% of the total) was once given to their grazing and feed production. Conversion to tractor power released that land for general farming. The world-wide population of horses, mules, asses, and buffalo is nearly 260 million (FAO Production Yearbook). Assuming that they consume an average of 10 kg feed per day, the annual feed requirement is near 1 Gt of dry matter containing 15–20 Mt nitrogen.

## Trophic efficiency in animal production

The efficiency of trophic transfers through an animal population is not calculated easily. In addition to the variable nature of animal production, problems arise from the different bases of measurement used by plant and animal scientists. Crop ecologists emphasize dry-matter yield per unit area and, in some cases, heat of combustion ($\Delta H_c$) or nutrient content. Given the non-linear nature of feeding responses, animal scientists prefer to view animal intakes in the derived concepts of DE, ME, and NE. The situation is further confused by variations in live mass, dressed carcass, and edible parts under different feeding systems, by measurement of output as fresh masses of gain, milk, egg, and wool yield per animal, and by maintenance costs of breeding animals. Readers are referred to Leitch and Godden (1953), Agricultural Research Council Working Party (1980), and Bywater and Baldwin (1980) for insights into data on 'usual' trophic efficiency. The ARC publication provides the most complete information on body composition but fails to translate that to human-edible fractions.

Table 1.4 illustrates the levels of trophic efficiency that can be achieved with good management. These calculations include feed requirements of the entire herd in addition to the milking cow or the animal grown for slaughter. The three beef systems employ different proportions of grazing. All have low efficiency in use of total feed compared to dairy, swine, and poultry because of greater overhead in breeding animals. Feed requirements of breeding cattle, however, are derived entirely from roughages unsuited for human consumption. In constructing this table, the authors considered grain portions of the feed supply to be 'human-edible' on the basis that crops such as wheat or potato could have been grown instead of feed grains. The efficiency of the systems in converting these 'human-edible' inputs ($DE_h$) to human-edible output declines as the proportion of human-edible material in diets increases. All of the systems are quite efficient in returning human-edible output per unit human-edible input, however. Contrary to popular notions that grain feeding of cattle is inefficient, cattle have a clear advantage over swine and poultry, returning significantly more human-edible material than they consume.

## Human nutrition

Energy sources and protein are also the main components of proper diets for humans. Early nutritional standards were drawn from surveys of eating habits of

Table 1.4 *Efficiencies of various animal production systems in the conversion of feedstuffs to human-edible food*

Inputs of human-edible digestible energy ($DE_h$) and corresponding amounts of digestible protein ($DP_t$ and $DP_h$) per GJ total animal-digestible energy ($DE_t$) fed. The efficiencies for human-edible outputs of energy ($E_h$) and protein ($P_h$) are given for both total (t) and human-edible (h) inputs. The amounts of feed required for the breeding population are included with that needed for the slaughter or milking animal.

| System | Product | Inputs per GJ $DE_t$ | | | Efficiencies (%) in output of human-edible food | | | |
| | | $DE_h$ (GJ) | $DP_t$ (kg) | $DP_h$ (kg) | $E_h/E_t$ | $E_h/E_h$ | $P_h/P_t$ | $P_h/P_h$ |
|---|---|---|---|---|---|---|---|---|
| Dairy[1] | Milk, meat | 0.23 | 35 | 2.8 | 23 | 101 | 29 | 181 |
| Beef[2] A | Meat | 0.07 | 35 | 1.4 | 4.9 | 73 | 5.8 | 139 |
| B | Meat | 0.07 | 35 | 1.7 | 4.3 | 60 | 6.0 | 126 |
| C | Meat | 0.09 | 40 | 1.9 | 5.2 | 57 | 5.3 | 108 |
| Swine | Meat | 0.40 | 44 | 19.3 | 23 | 29 | 38 | 86 |
| Poultry | Meat | 0.48 | 52 | 20.9 | 15 | 31 | 30 | 75 |

*Notes:*
[1] Principal product is milk; some meat production from calves and cows.
[2] Three common management systems varying in amounts of grazing are compared.
*Source:* Adapted from Bywater & Baldwin (1980).

well-fed people rather than from exhaustive feeding trials. As a result, a high intake of protein ($85$–$100\,\mathrm{g\,cap^{-1}\,d^{-1}}$) was thought necessary and debates ensued about the undesirability of low-protein carbohydrate sources (grains, sugar, potato, and cassava were labeled 'empty calories' by critics), and a need for protein sources with a high content of the amino acid lysine. These questions were settled in the 1970s with findings from nitrogen balance experiments. The daily requirement for an average healthy adult is now set at $0.6\,\mathrm{g}$ of high-quality (animal) protein $\mathrm{kg^{-1}}$ body mass. It was also found that any balanced diets, even those depending mainly upon grains and potato, are adequate in all essential amino acids providing enough is eaten to satisfy energy requirements (Payne 1978).

As is the case with animals, required food intakes of humans vary with body mass, age, sex, activity, and other factors. Our knowledge of energy and protein requirements is now embodied in regression equations fit to the mean needs of various groups of people. In contrast to these daily 'requirements', 'safe levels' of intake and 'recommended dietary allowances' (RDAs) are set at a somewhat higher level (e.g. the mean $+2$ standard deviations) to include population extremes. The FAO/WHO committee thus uses $0.75\,\mathrm{g}$ protein $\mathrm{kg^{-1}}$ body weight as the *safe level* of daily intake whereas only $0.6\,\mathrm{g}$ is *required*. Readers are referred to the most recent consultative reports (FAO/WHO/UNU 1985; National Research Council 1989b) for equations and detailed tables of requirements and allowances. Those publications also include information on other aspects of diet and food quality.

Table 1.5 presents a summary of current American RDAs for energy and protein

Table 1.5 *Recommended dietary allowances (RDAs) of energy and protein for median adults in the USA*

| Category | Age (y) | Median mass (kg) | Energy allowance (MJ d⁻¹) REE[1] × | Activity factor[2] = | Energy RDA | Protein RDA[3] (gd⁻¹) |
|----------|---------|------------------|------|----------|--------|---------|
| Males    | 19–24   | 72 | 7.4 | 1.67 | 12.4 | 58 |
|          | 24–50   | 79 | 7.5 | 1.60 | 12.0 | 63 |
|          | 51+     | 77 | 6.4 | 1.50 | 9.6  | 63 |
| Females  | 19–24   | 58 | 5.6 | 1.60 | 9.0  | 46 |
|          | 25–50   | 63 | 5.8 | 1.55 | 9.0  | 50 |
|          | 51+     | 65 | 5.4 | 1.50 | 8.0  | 50 |

*Notes:*
[1] REE is the resting energy expenditure, i.e. basal metabolism.
[2] Activity factors range from 1.0 for resting, 1.5 with very light activity, 2.5 with light work, 5.0 with moderate work, and 7.0 with heavy work. The factors given here are integrated daily values for the US population.
[3] Protein allowances are calculated as body mass × 0.8 g protein kg⁻¹ body mass.
*Source:* Adapted from National Research Council 1989*b*.

intakes of adults. In contrast to the relative constancy of the protein requirement, daily energy requirements can vary for the same individual by more than a factor of 2 as is explained in the footnote to the activity multiplier. Requirements and allowances for children are larger per unit body mass but smaller in total than for adults. Although these numbers should apply generally to western nations, the allowances are larger than for small people (Asians). People with high-fiber diets (as in India and Africa) need a somewhat higher intake of protein to offset reduced absorption of amino acids in the presence of fiber.

It is useful to have numbers representing the energy and protein allowances for an 'average' human. Table 1.5 serves to illustrate, after allowing for children and the large size of Americans, that 10.5 MJ (2500 kcal) of digestible energy and 50 g of digestible protein (8 g N) would serve as reasonable estimates of adequate daily allowances. For comparison, FAO/WHO (1973) estimated that the average human needs 9.1 MJ and 30 g protein per day. The average American allowances translate to annual requirements of:

$$10.5 \text{ MJ energy d}^{-1} \times 365 \text{ d y}^{-1} = 3.8 \text{ GJ y}^{-1};$$
$$50 \text{ g protein d}^{-1} \times 365 \text{ d y}^{-1} = 18.2 \text{ kg protein (2.9 kg N) y}^{-1}.$$

With 17 MJ kg⁻¹ as the average energy yield from plant materials, 3.8 GJ could be obtained from 224 kg of digestible dry matter. Ingestion of this amount of even low-protein sources (9% protein) would satisfy protein and amino acid needs (0.09 × 224 kg dry matter = 20.2 kg protein or 3.2 kg N). It appears that the present world population of 5.2 billion people could be adequately fed for a year with 1200 Mt of digestible grain or its equivalent containing at least 16 Mt of nitrogen.

## 1.7   CARRYING CAPACITY

Knowledge of food requirements allows one to calculate the **carrying capacity** of a particular farming system. Carrying capacity is defined as the number of animals (or people) that can be supported by the primary production from a given area of land. Carrying capacity is a very old and important concept that relates to the sufficiency of agriculture. It is apparent that carrying capacities depend upon performance of producer communities and thus on the environment and intensity of cultivation. Calculations of carrying capacity follow the Conservative Law based on dietary energy terms (GE, DE, or NE) or some component such as protein. The approach is illustrated with DE as follows:

$$K = \frac{k_c k_d \text{GE} \, P}{\text{DE}_d \text{ or } \text{DE}_y},$$
[Eq. 1.1]

where:

$K$ = carrying capacity (animals ha$^{-1}$);
$k_c$ = fraction consumed;
$k_d$ = fraction digested;
GE = Gross Energy content of the feed (MJ kg$^{-1}$);
$P$ = net production (kg biomass ha$^{-1}$ y$^{-1}$); and
$\text{DE}_d$ and $\text{DE}_y$ = daily and annual energy requirements (MJ cap$^{-1}$).

Carrying capacity is illustrated in Box 1.2 with production from an intensively managed pasture. In that example, the forage is indigestible by humans but, after conversion by dairy cattle, 7 humans can be fed. A wheat crop with a similar 15 000 kg ha$^{-1}$ of above-ground production and a harvest index of 0.4 would supply 6000 kg of human-edible grain. Only about 80% could be consumed because some grain is needed as seed and there are losses in storage and processing. The digestibility of whole wheat grain for humans is about 0.85 (compared with 0.96 for refined flour) and an energy content of 17 MJ kg$^{-1}$ would again apply. Our average annual dietary allowance for energy could be met by the production of 329 kg grain [3.8 GJ cap$^{-1}$ y$^{-1}$/ (0.8 consumed × 0.85 digested × 17 MJ kg$^{-1}$ grain) = 329 kg cap$^{-1}$ y$^{-1}$]. The hectare of wheat would therefore support the energy requirements of 18 humans (6000/329 = 18.2) or twice what is accomplished by dairying.

The nitrogen content of wheat grain ranges from 2 to 3% of dry matter depending on cultivar and environment. The composition of wheat protein is sufficiently different from the average that 5.9 rather than 6.25 is used as the factor for conversion to protein from nitrogen content. On that basis, the wheat crop would supply humans with at least 453 kg crude protein ha$^{-1}$ y$^{-1}$ (6000 kg grain × 0.8 consumed × 0.8 digested × 0.02 N × 5.9 kg protein/kg N). That would be sufficient for 25 humans (453 kg protein/18.2 kg protein cap$^{-1}$ y$^{-1}$ = 24.9).

A simpler approach serves in rough assessments of national and world food budgets. Grains dominate in world food supplies (*ca.* 60% of both energy and protein) (Table 4.1) and the protein and energy of other foods can be expressed in equivalent amounts of grain. The wheat example illustrated the need to allow for

Box 1.2 *Carrying capacity of a grazing system*

Ryegrass is an important pasture species in the cool climates of Europe, New Zealand, and elsewhere. With intensive management, annual production of 15 000 kg forage ha$^{-1}$ is common. Taking 17 MJ kg$^{-1}$ as the gross energy of forage, a total of 255 GJ ha$^{-1}$ is available for grazing. With $k_c = 0.7$ and $k_d = 0.7$, 125 GJ of that energy would be obtained as DE by ruminants. The annual DE requirement per milking cow of the Holstein–Friesian breed is near 64 GJ and an additional 19 GJ is needed to support replacement heifers (when 1/3 of the cows are replaced each year) (Bywater & Baldwin 1980). Total DE$_y$ per cow unit is thus 83 GJ; and 125/83 = 1.5 cow units (1.5 cow and 0.5 heifer) could be supported per hectare. An output of 28 GJ ha$^{-1}$ y$^{-1}$ in the form of fat and protein in 9525 kg milk would be obtained. This corresponds to 11% of the total energy in forage and 22% of the grazed, digestible, part. Using the average energy allowance developed in the section on human nutrition, and ignoring losses that occur in transportation and distribution, each hectare would support a population of 7 humans (28 GJ in milk/3.8 GJ cap$^{-1}$ y$^{-1}$ = 7.4).

The high protein content of milk is perhaps as significant for human nutrition as the energy. The 9525 kg of milk produced would contain about 314 kg protein or enough to sustain 17 people (314 kg protein/18.2 kg protein cap$^{-1}$ y$^{-1}$ = 17.2).

losses in harvest, storage, distribution, and food preparation chain, as well as to cover variations in production, seed supplies, and diet diversity. One measure of a desirable level of 'original' (on-farm) production is the **standard nutritional unit:**

$$1 \text{ SNU} = 23 \text{ MJ cap}^{-1} \text{ day}^{-1} \times 365 \text{ days} = 8.4 \text{ GJ cap}^{-1} \text{ y}^{-1}. \qquad \text{[Eq. 1.2]}$$

This amount of gross energy is contained in 500 kg grain. A convenient feature of this number is that each tonne of a system's production expressed in grain equivalents can be equated with the generous nutrition of two humans.

The SNU is large enough (more than twice the necessary human intake of digestible energy) to accommodate significant diversity in diets since portions of the farmland can be given to the production of fruits, vegetables, and animal products rather than to grain. Year-to-year variations in yields can be accommodated through grain storage and increased animal production in abundant years which can be consumed in poor years. Animal populations can be increased or decreased according to the feed supply but this strategy is not viable with humans. Two of the points made in this chapter are that domestic animals insulate us from variations in primary production and that they do so with reasonable efficiency.

**The yield–area relationship**

Production of a farm, region, or country is the mathematical product of area harvested and yield per unit area. This is such an obvious relationship that its significance is often overlooked in discussions of carrying capacity and input–

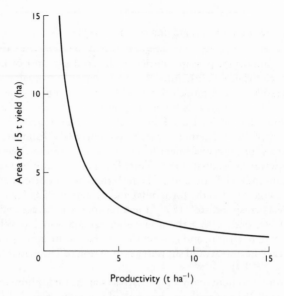

**Fig. 1.7. Area of land required for production of 15 t grain as a function of yield per hectare.**

output relationships of agricultural systems. There are two basic reasons why yields may be small. One is that climate, through shortness of season, limited rainfall, or other factors, may be restrictive. The other is that farming is not intense and actual yields are small relative to attainable yields. Limits arise from factors such as poor management of nutrient supply or weeds, i.e. from things that are preventable through human effort and technology. Intensity thus depends as much on increased inputs of knowledge as it does on material resources. The important point is that the area required to achieve a given production is inversely related to yield (Fig. 1.7). With small yields, the area required to meet the production goal is much larger than with a more productive agriculture. This is a critical non-linear component of calculations of carrying capacity. Options for increasing food supply are therefore simple: increase yields and/or the area under cultivation.

## 1.8  SUMMARY

This introduction to agricultural systems has emphasized the central role that farming plays in providing food and fiber for humans. Agriculture can be viewed as a hierarchy of systems beginning with individual fields (cropping systems) and extending to the integration of fields into farms (farming systems) and regions (agricultural systems). Biological, environmental, and social questions can be identified for each level in the hierarchy. Yield is the basic ecological attribute of such systems; time trends in yield serve in defining stability (variation in yield) and sustainability (maintenance of yield over time).

Agricultural systems interact strongly with the larger society that consumes the products of agriculture and in turn provides goods and services needed by farmers in production. The demand for products depends upon the size of the population and its wealth. As a result, how and where farming is conducted are determined as much by economic issues of prices of inputs and products as by the dependence of biological activities of crops on environment.

As is the case in the larger society, agricultural systems are subject to continuing evolution and change. In capitalist societies, capital and labor move freely between urban and rural sectors of the economy with the result that agriculture exists as a continuum of the larger economy. Climate and soil determine what crops can be grown in a farming region but the crops actually grown and the intensity of production depend upon access to markets and upon availability of labor and other means of production. Transportation costs are an important factor in access to markets. Intensive systems such as market gardening and dairying tend to be located close to urban centers. Production of low-value bulk commodities such as grain and pastoral farming is accomplished by much less intensive methods and in more remote regions.

Cropping systems differ from natural systems in that they are managed so that the greatest proportion possible of production is diverted away from competing consumers and decomposers to yield. The level of production is important, not only because it determines efficiency of resource use and the economic viability of farming, but also because it is the basis of carrying capacity for domestic animals and humans per unit area of agricultural land.

Domestic animals are major consumers of plant production. Their efficiency in trophic transfers to man vary with type of digestive system and with the level and quality of feed supplied. Animal nutritionists recognize feed materials in terms of their digestibility and ability to supply net energy, first for maintenance and then for work, lactation, or gain. Differences in those traits help explain the roles played by different animals in agricultural systems.

## 1.9  FURTHER READING

Duckham, A. N. and G. B. Masefield. 1970. *Farming systems of the world*. Praeger, New York. 542 p.

Haggett, P. 1979. *Geography: a modern synthesis*. Harper & Row, New York. 627 p.

National Research Council. Committee on Animal Nutrition. Subcommittee on Biological Energy. 1981. *Nutritional energetics of domestic animals*. (Second Revision.) National Academy Press, Washington, D.C. 54 p.

National Research Council. Subcommittee on the Tenth Edition of the RDAs. 1989b. *Recommended dietary allowances*. National Academy Press, Washington, D.C. 283 p.

Pearson, C. J. and R. Ison. 1987. *Agronomy of grassland systems*. Cambridge University Press. 169 p.

Ruthenberg, H. 1980. *Farming systems in the tropics*. Clarendon Press, Oxford. 424 p.

# 2

*Community concepts*

## 2.1 INTRODUCTION

The main features of crop communities can be described in simple terms. Species and cultivar define genetic content while density, spacing pattern, plant size, and stage of development define structure. The type of community is termed a **monoculture** when only one crop species is grown in a field at a time; the terms **polyculture** and **mixed cropping** apply to communities with two or more cohabiting crop species. Other definitions exist (see, for example, Francis 1989; Vandermeer 1989) but these are the traditional ones employed by agronomists. Most arable farming involves rotations of monocultures over time whereas pastures are mostly polycultures.

## 2.2 COMMUNITY CHANGE

Current views of community structure have evolved from complementary work by agronomists who study managed communities and by botanists concerned with natural communities. In agriculture, small differences in production are important and agronomists make intensive studies of how production rate, competition, limiting factors, and genetic expression influence the behavior of simple communities. Botanists, faced with highly diverse, natural systems give greater attention to species composition of communities in relation to adaptive traits and evolution. A background in plant ecology is useful for agriculturalists. Properties of soils employed in agriculture, for example, derive in part from the natural vegetation under which they developed. Thorough understanding of complex matters such as competition between neighboring plants requires an understanding of the contrast with events in natural communities.

Natural communities are subject to continuing change as different species of plants invade a site and displace earlier occupants. This process is termed **succession** and the sequence followed, the **sere**. Annual species capable of aggressive occupation of space are usually the pioneer invaders of unvegetated sites. If soil organic matter is scarce, the ability to exist on scant supplies of available nitrogen or to obtain nitrogen through symbiosis are important traits for pioneers. With time, organic detritus and soil organic matter accumulate, soil water relations

32

change, and plants compete more intensely for resources as their density increases. Where rainfall and nutrients are not strongly limiting, height growth becomes a critical factor for competitive success. Taller perennial shrub and tree species invade, shading out pioneer herbaceous species. Persistence of a species within the community becomes increasingly dependent on the ability of replacement seedlings to develop in the shade of their maturing parents. The community eventually approaches equilibrium with the environment and change slows. That more stable condition is termed the **climax**.

Climate strongly controls the results of succession. To take an example, succession on upland sites in Wisconsin (USA) with abundant rainfall leads to a climax association dominated by maple (*Acer* spp.) and basswood (*Tilia americana*) trees (Curtis 1959). With beech (*Fagus grandifolia*) instead of basswood, similar associations once spread across much of northeastern North America. These climax communities are relatively simple but the course of succession can be quite complex with many different species taking temporary residence in the community. West of Wisconsin, along a gradient of decreasing rainfall, tall-grass and then short-grass prairies are the climaxes in Minnesota and the Dakotas. In many cases, wildfire once served as an important factor, 'arresting' succession at an intermediate grassland stage. North of Wisconsin, with a colder climate, conifer trees dominate the great boreal forests and beyond them, in very cold climates, tundra is the principal vegetation. Each of these vegetation types can be characterized by its general appearance and structure (physiognomy) and by the dominant species. **Dominance** relates to a species' relative importance in terms of numbers, size, or activity in ecosystem processes. Other species within the community may be strongly suppressed by dominant ones.

Succession in similar climates around the globe leads to similar vegetation; hardwood and boreal forests and tundra are found in comparable latitudinal sequences in Europe and Asia. The dry mid-latitudes of Asia support grasslands similar to those of the North American plains. Control by climate is so strong that when vegetation is destroyed, as by fire or agriculture, recovery is generally by the same sequence and towards the same climax. Climate and vegetation together control soil formation (Chapter 7) and the areas where agriculture is now practiced correspond in important ways with the original vegetation. The rich, subhumid grasslands of Ukraine, Argentina, and Iowa (Chapter 17), for example, have all become major centers of agriculture.

Widespread occurrence of vegetation with similar general appearance and with the same or similar species led early botanists to ideas about communities as 'superorganisms' with a relatively fixed complement of participating species. Gleason (1926) challenged that proposition with evidence that community structure was more the result of fortuitous immigration of plants. It is now clear that cohabitation involves a large measure of randomness in accord with Gleason's 'individualistic' view: communities are composed, from the available species, of those able to persist at the site. Survival within a community, however, requires adherence to social rules imposed by competitors. This occurs because all plants use the same resources. If one species adjusts osmotically and takes the soil towards dryness, all would-be cohabitors must escape that condition or have a similar ability. If some species grow tall or are aggressive in the uptake of nitrogen, only those able to accommodate to that new environment will persist. The explanation, then, for similar endpoints to succession is that only a limited range of physiological tactics are possible for dominants in each climate.

Because cohabiting species experience similar selection pressures, they frequently come to similar evolutionary solutions for survival under a given set of conditions ('convergent evolution'). Dry Mediterranean climates, whether in Chile, Australia, or California, lead to grasslands generally composed of annual grasses and forbs, and perennial species found in those communities usually have some form of summer dormancy. With greater rainfall, chaparral vegetation composed of a floristically highly diverse group of shrubs predominates. Those diverse shrubs, however, are sometimes remarkably similar in physiological and morphological traits that lend adaptation to life with severe summer drought.

## 2.3  BIOMASS ACCUMULATION

### Biomass dynamics

Primary production by plant communities results in the accumulation of biomass with time. Within a season, accumulation generally follows a sigmoidal (S-shaped) curve. Trees continue to accumulate biomass (as dead xylem) for many years. In that case, the sigmoidal pattern for each year is superimposed with a larger one for the entire life of the trees. The simplest pattern of biomass ($W$) accumulation per unit area occurs with communities of annual plants (Fig. 2.1a). The slope is the **crop growth rate** (CGR) (Fig. 2.1$b$), defined as the rate of change of $W$ with time, $\Delta W/\Delta t$, with units of $kg\,ha^{-1}\,d^{-1}$ or $g\,m^{-2}\,d^{-1}$. The curve can be established by sampling the crop periodically over the season. CGR then can be calculated as the increase in biomass, $\Delta W$, between two dates divided by $\Delta t$. More accurate values are obtained by taking the first derivative ($dW/dt$, the value of $\Delta W/\Delta t$ as $\Delta t \rightarrow 0$) of an equation fitted to the data.

It is easy to sample above-ground and tuberous underground portions of annual crops but proper sampling of fine roots is difficult. Most data on $W$ and CGR reflect only above-ground material. When soil resources are not limiting, roots constitute only about 10% of crop biomass and the error is small. Where water or nutrients are limiting, however, the root fraction may be much larger and the error becomes significant.

Sigmoidal curves can be divided into an early 'exponential phase' of production, a 'grand period' during midseason, and a final 'senescent phase'. Those periods are indicated in Fig. 2.1$a$. Growth rates of seedlings are limited by leaf area and light interception and the exponential phase results from positive feedback of expanding leaf area on growth rate. As leaf area increases, light interception and photosynthesis increase, and so CGR, which includes leaf growth, increases. That continues up to the time when the foliage canopy closes in 'complete cover' of the land area and thus complete light interception. The term **cover** denotes the fraction of land area obscured by leaves when viewed from above; it can be measured experimentally

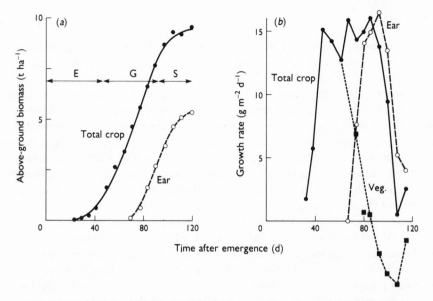

**Fig. 2.1.** (*a*) Accumulation of total biomass and ears over time by an average crop of maize. (*b*) Growth rates of total crop, ears, and vegetative parts of the maize crop. Grain growth exceeds crop growth late in the season as materials are transferred from vegetative parts. (Data from Bair (1942).)

from photographs, by noting the frequency with which a 'point quadrant' (a thin needle) encounters leaf or ground when projected vertically into the community, or indirectly with radiation meters.

During the exponential phase, the absolute growth rate, $dW/dt$, is proportional to $W$ (and through $W$ to leaf area):

$$dW/dt = \mu W, \qquad\qquad \text{[Eq. 2.1]}$$

where $\mu$ is the **specific growth rate** (or **relative growth rate**, RGR). After rearrangement:

$$\mu = 1/W \; dW/dt \qquad\qquad \text{[Eq. 2.2]}$$

and

$$RGR = 1/W \; \Delta W/\Delta t.$$

These equations express growth rate per unit (i.e., 'specific' or 'relative' to) existing biomass. Units for $W$ cancel and the units for $\mu$ and RGR reduce to $t^{-1}$. Parameter $\mu$ assumes its largest value during the seedling phase but declines rapidly as the plants increase in size and as the canopy closes. During the exponential phase, $\mu$ relates closely to leaf area and photosynthetic activity. Values of $\mu$ for full-cover crops are essentially meaningless because $dW/dt$ is then largely independent of $W$ and leaf area.

The integrated form of Eq. 2.2 defines $W$ at any time $t$ after beginning exponential growth at time 0 with an initial biomass of $W_0$:

$$W = W_0 \, e^{\mu t}.$$ [Eq. 2.3]

With complete cover, the crop enters the grand period during which light interception and photosynthesis are maximum. CGR then varies mainly with changes in solar radiation. With determinate annuals such as maize (Fig. 2.1*b*) and sunflower, the declining phase of crop growth is due to maturation and senescence. These are synchronized phenomena in annual crops; all members of a field obey the same phenological rules (Chapter 5) and die at the same time. CGR also declines as radiation and temperature decrease towards the end of summer and also when the standing crop of biomass becomes so great that the requirement for maintenance respiration usurps most of the photosynthate supply. Thus, sigmoidal patterns are also seen over the season in pastures and sugarbeet crops even though no senescence or death of the plants occurs.

Seasonal production is greatest when full cover is achieved early in the growing season and is then maintained as long as weather is favorable. Perennial plants have an advantage over annuals in that the lag of the exponential phase is bypassed: cover is established very quickly by the growth of new leaves supported by reserves from perennial portions. A price is paid, however, through the costs of producing and maintaining perennial parts such as the underground rhizomes of pasture grasses. Other than tree and vine crops and forage species, there is little agricultural use of long-lived species. Some perennials such as cotton are in fact grown as annuals and in some cases the storage organs of perennial and biennial species form the basis for annual crops (e.g. tubers of potato and tuberous roots of beet and carrot).

### Leaf area and light interception

CGR depends on the photosynthetic activities of leaves; relationships exist between CGR and the area of leaves involved in the foliage cover. The term **leaf-area index** (LAI or $L$) describes the sum of the area of all leaves (only one surface is counted) per unit area of ground. The most common procedure for measuring the area of individual leaves is with a light-cell planimeter (the leaf is passed over an array of light cells to integrate the area of leaf between the cells and a source of light). Alternatively, leaf area may be established from a regression on the product of leaf length ($l$) and width ($w$): area $= blw$ where $b$ is the regression coefficient.

Because of mutual shading among leaves, light interception by a foliage canopy is a diminishing-returns function of LAI. Japanese workers were among the first to develop techniques for examining light penetration into foliage canopies in relation to leaf area. By comparing leaf area and light interception in successive horizontal strata beginning at the top of canopies, they found that the light flux at any level ($I$) could be related to the leaf area above it and the light flux incident to the top of the community ($I_0$) with a simple analytical expression, the Bouguer–Lambert Law (Monsi & Saeki 1953):

$$I = I_0 \exp\left(-k_L L\right)$$

and

$$\ln(I/I_0) = -k_L L$$ [Eq. 2.4]

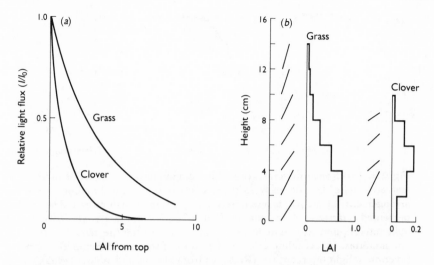

Fig. 2.2. (*a*) Attenuation of sunlight in stands of clover and ryegrass as a function of leaf-area index penetrated. (After Stern and Donald (1962).) (*b*) Typical patterns of leaf display by clover and ryegrass. Clover leaves tend to horizontal display (noted by the angled line) and to cluster some distance above the soil surface. Ryegrass leaves are more erect and the distribution with height is pyramidal. (After Warren Wilson (1959).)

where $k_L$, the **extinction coefficient**, relates to the fraction of the light intercepted per unit LAI (*L*). The equation has the same form as the familiar Beer's Law for light absorption by homogeneous media but canopies are not homogeneous, hence the Bouguer–Lambert name. The diminishing returns relationship is illustrated in Fig. 2.2*a* for clover and grass canopies. When these curves are plotted as $\ln(I/I_0)$ versus LAI, straight lines of slope $-k_L$ are usually obtained. The $k_L$ values of grass and clover differ because of differences in canopy architecture. Clover, with a tendency towards horizontal leaf display (Fig. 2.2*b*), is very effective in light interception. It has a large $k_L$ whereas grass, with vertical leaves, has a small $k_L$. With $k_L$ equal to 0.7 (clover), near 90% interception is achieved with LAI = 3. With $k_L$ equal to 0.5 (grass), a similar approach to full cover requires LAI = 4. The $k_L$ also varies with solar altitude and azimuth and thus with time of day and year (Chapter 10).

Light interception is particularly useful as an index of canopy development. In contrast to measurements of LAI and $k_L$, interception is measured easily as the ratio of readings from appropriate light sensors exposed horizontally above the vegetation and at ground level. Interception (like $k_L$) varies with leaf display and solar angle, and observations taken near solar noon correlate best with cover and CGR. The daily average obtained from continuous measurements is needed for some purposes.

Examples of the relationships between CGR and LAI and between CGR and relative interception ($I/I_0$) are presented in Fig. 2.3. The plateau response of CGR with increasing LAI is explained by the diminishing relationship between light interception and LAI. The linear relationship between CGR and light interception, first reported by Shibles & Weber (1965), is now known to occur with most crops

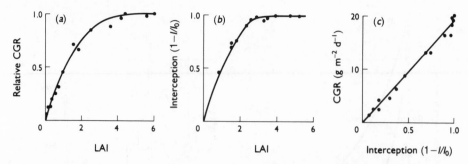

Fig. 2.3. (*a*) Crop growth rates of soybean communities as a function of total leaf area. The data come from three communities with different spatial arrangements of the plants and different maximum growth rates and so are presented relative to the maximum CGR of each community. (*b*) Relative light interception as a function of leaf-area index for the same soybean communities. (*c*) Absolute crop growth rates of soybean communities as a function of light interception. (Redrawn from Shibles and Weber (1965).)

(Monteith 1977). The slope of that relationship, using absolute rather than relative interception, embodies the non-linear relationship between CGR and LAI and defines **radiation-use efficiency** in units of g dry matter $MJ^{-1}$ sunlight intercepted.

### Growth analysis

CGR, LAI, and interception (or cover) define the main features of a community relating to primary production. CGR, RGR, and LAI are concepts and terms developed by early English crop ecologists. They also developed mathematical methodologies for estimating these and other variables from periodic sampling of a crop. That approach is sometimes termed Growth Analysis (Radford 1967; Hunt 1978). In contrast to the usefulness of CGR and LAI, we find little meaning or use in net assimilation rate (NAR; crop growth rate per unit leaf area) and leaf area duration (LAD; sum of LAI × time). LAD recognizes that the duration of LAI is important to seasonal production but study of Fig. 2.3*a* reveals that a non-linear relationship rather than a simple sum must be used because CGR is not a linear function of LAI. LAI greater than that needed for full cover increases LAD but has no effect on CGR and seasonal production because light interception is not increased. In contrast, the linear relation between CGR and interception offers a sound foundation for a linear relationship between *W* and summations of interception over time (Monteith 1977).

### Productive structure

Leaves are the key elements in light interception and crop productivity but leaves cannot exist alone. They must be displayed appropriately on stems and petioles and they must be supplied with water and nutrients. The **productive structure** of a crop thus includes stems and roots as well as leaves. Definitions from Growth Analysis for **specific leaf area** (SLA; leaf area/g dry mass leaf) and its inverse, **specific leaf mass** (SLM) are useful here. As an example, SLM for sugarbeet is near 400 kg leaf mass ha$^{-1}$ leaf area. A roughly equal amount of dry matter is required for supporting stem and petioles, and each kg of leaves needs about 0.15 kg of fine roots to supply water and nutrients. Thus, production of about 3000 kg dry matter ha$^{-1}$ is required to achieve a full-cover display of LAI = 3.

Annual plants follow characteristic partitioning patterns in which early growth is given to productive structure while growth of fruit and vegetative storage organs is delayed until later in the season. That was illustrated in Fig. 2.1 by the patterns of dry matter accumulation in maize. Nutrient uptake occurs mainly during vegetative growth when large amounts of nutrients, in particular nitrogen, are needed to create the photosynthesis apparatus in leaves. Later, as the grain fills and the leaves die, that nitrogen may be transferred to grain. In most crops, as much as 70% of the whole-crop nitrogen is found in grain or seed at the end of the cycle. That pattern accounts for changes in the composition of sorghum biomass presented in Table 1.2 and for the small amounts of nitrogen generally found in crop residues.

Factors that limit growth or photosynthesis rate, such as temperature and water and nutrient supplies, also limit leaf expansion and development of cover. Temperature constraints can be manipulated to some extent through choice of genotype or with tillage practices that influence soil temperature (Chapters 7 and 12). Time to full cover is less for dense plantings than for wide-spaced plantings and for large-seeded plants (large initial leaf area) than for small seeded ones. Those practices have the effect of increasing $W_0$ in Eq. 2.3. Shortening the period of incomplete cover also is important in limiting opportunities for development of weed competition.

Above-ground productive structures form the useable yield of forage grasses and legumes but, in contrast to reproductive organs, the amount of biomass that can accumulate in fine stems and leaves is relatively small. As a result, CGR for such plants declines after a brief period at full cover, owing to maturity or to 'feedback inhibition' of photosynthesis (Chapter 10). The solution to that problem is to graze or mow forage crops periodically to allow the production of new stems and leaves. Another problem with forages is that older stems generally have a greater content of lignin and digestibility therefore declines with age. For these reasons, the sum of repeated harvests of pastures and forage crops during a growing season is generally much greater and more useful as feed than the biomass obtained in a single, end-of-season harvest. Regrowth after each harvest follows lag and grand phases as leaf area expands.

## Production rates

The main portion of seasonal yield accumulates during the grand period of growth and it is useful at this point to consider the magnitude of production rates during that period.

**Potential production rate**   Photosynthesis is driven by energy absorbed in light quanta. The amount of sunlight incident on a crop therefore sets an upper limit to its production. Assuming that nutrients and $CO_2$ are abundant, the potential gross (before respiration) and net (after respiration) productivity of a crop with complete cover can be estimated. To do that, we need to borrow information about the spectral characteristics of solar radiation from Chapter 6 and about the photosynthetic ability of leaves from Chapter 10. The steps in the estimate are presented in Table 2.1 for a full-cover canopy of leaves during the grand period of growth. Each MJ of incident solar radiation contains about 2 mol quanta in the photosynthetically active region of the spectrum (0.4 to 0.7 $\mu$m wavelengths; Chapter 6). Some of the radiation intercepted by the crop is lost by reflection and through absorption by non-photosynthetic structures, leaving 1.69 mol quanta available for photosynthesis. The maximum observed quantum yield of photosynthesis is near 0.10 mol $CO_2$ assimilated per mol quanta reaching the chloroplast. Gross photosynthesis is therefore 0.169 mol (5.07 g) carbohydrate $MJ^{-1}$ radiation. If a third of that production is then used in dark respiration, the net increase in dry matter with 1 MJ sunlight is 3.4 g $MJ^{-1}$. That ratio of organic production to radiation defines potential radiation-use efficiency. With a moderate daily total radiation of 20 MJ $m^{-2} d^{-1}$ (40 mol quanta $m^{-2} d^{-1}$), 68 g carbohydrate $m^{-2} d^{-1}$ would be produced.

The amount of chemical bond energy stored in dry matter can be determined from the heat energy released when the material is combusted to $CO_2$. The heat of combustion of carbohydrate (glucose) is near 15.6 kJ $g^{-1}$, therefore the potential energy efficiency of net photosynthesis in the use of total radiation is 3.4 g $MJ^{-1} \times 15.6$ kJ $g^{-1} = 0.053$. Because photosynthetically active radiation amounts to only about 45% of the total energy in sunlight, the potential energy efficiency in that band is near 0.12. By contrast, the best artificial solar cells with double layers of gallium compounds now approach 0.4 efficiency.

**Record rates of production**   It is instructive to compare these estimates of potential production with record performances of crops under conditions of adequate water and nutrients. Considerable care is needed in assessing such records because many estimates in the literature do not meet essential standards of sampling or attention to cultural conditions (Loomis & Gerakis 1975; Monteith 1978). Data on the daily productivity of crops presented in Table 2.2 were selected as valid measurements against which fair comparison of potential productivity can be made. The largest daily crop growth rates shown there belong to a group of crop plants of the family Gramineae distinguished by a 'C4' system of photosynthesis and a high content of carbohydrates. C4 plants are capable of very rapid rates of photosynthesis. None of the record observations of dry matter production rates by C4 crops (30–54 g $m^{-2} d^{-1}$; 300–540 kg $ha^{-1} d^{-1}$) exceed our estimated potential daily net production (68 g $m^{-2} d^{-1}$) despite the fact that some of those crops experienced radiation levels as great as 30 MJ $m^{-2} d^{-1}$. Broad-leafed species with the 'C3' type of photosynthesis (characterized by smaller rates of photosynthesis than in C4s) and those that accumulate compounds such as oil and protein had smaller daily rates of production (20–30 g $m^{-2} d^{-1}$; 200–300 kg $ha^{-1} d^{-1}$). The C3 and C4 systems of photosynthesis are examined in detail in Chapter 10.

Table 2.1 *Daily potential productivity of a crop surface*

| | |
|---|---|
| *Incoming solar radiation* | 1 MJ m$^{-2}$ |
| *Incoming photon flux density*[a] | 2.06 mol m$^{-2}$ |
| Loss by reflection (8%) | $-0.16$ mol m$^{-2}$ |
| Loss by inactive adsorption (10%) | $-0.21$ mol m$^{-2}$ |
| *Quanta for photosynthesis* | 1.69 mol m$^{-2}$ |
| *[CH$_2$O] produced at quantum yield of 0.10* and as carbohydrate | 0.169 mol m$^{-2}$ 5.07 g m$^{-2}$ |
| *Average loss to respiration (33%)* | 1.67 g m$^{-2}$ |
| *Net production per MJ*[b] | 3.40 g m$^{-2}$ |
| *Daily net production at 20 MJ m$^{-2}$* | 68 g m$^{-2}$ |

*Notes:*
[a] Based on the spectral composition of average sunlight in the photosynthetically active range, 0.4 to 0.7 μm.
[b] With glucose as the product, 5.3% of the energy in total radiation and 12% of that in the photosynthetically active range is conserved in biomass.
*Source:* Adapted from Loomis & Williams (1963).

Table 2.2 *Some high daily rates of dry matter increase (CGR) and radiation-use and photosynthetically active radiation (PAR) conversion efficiencies for various cultivated crops and forages*

| Crop | PS type | CGR (g m$^{-2}$ d$^{-1}$) | Irradiance[a] (MJ m$^{-2}$ d$^{-1}$) | Radiation use (g MJ$^{-1}$) | PAR conversion (%)[b] | Location |
|---|---|---|---|---|---|---|
| Sugarbeet | C3 | 31 | 12.3 | 2.52 | 9.5 | United Kingdom |
| Potato | C3 | 23 | (16.7) | 1.38 | 5.4 | Netherlands |
| Maize | C4 | 29 | (18.8) | 1.54 | 6.1 | New Zealand |
| Maize | C4 | 52 | 30.8 | 1.69 | 6.4 | California |
| Maize | C4 | 52 | 20.9 | 2.49 | 9.8 | New York |
| Sudangrass | C4 | 51 | 28.9 | 1.87 | 6.7 | California |
| Millet | C4 | 54 | 21.3 | 2.53 | 9.5 | Australia (NT) |
| Napiergrass | C4 | 39 | (16.7) | 2.34 | 9.3 | El Salvador |

*Notes:*
[a] Daily total solar irradiance; estimated values in parentheses.
[b] Energy content of organic production/energy in PAR; MJ/MJ × 100.
*Source:* Adapted from Cooper (1970).

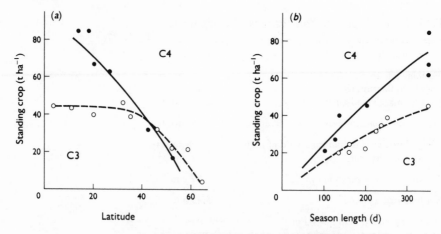

Fig. 2.4. (*a*) **Latitudinal distribution of annual aboveground production by record crops. (Data sources are given in Loomis & Gerakis (1975).) (*b*) Dependence of record yields on length of growing season. (After Monteith (1978).)**

There are several possible explanations for the difference between the calculated potential rate and record daily rates of production: the 0.1 quantum yield is optimistic; 30% respiration is conservative; and real plants encounter limitations in $CO_2$ diffusion, non-optimum temperatures, and mid-day stresses for water.

Annual yields of 50 t ha$^{-1}$ or greater are achieved by real crops but only over long periods of time. Length of season and a sensitivity of C4 plants to low temperature (high latitude) are revealed in Fig. 2.4 as major restrictions of annual production. The best C4 crops outyield the best C3s at low latitudes where they receive abundant radiation, but above latitude 40°, C3 crops are more productive. Differences in short-term productivity also persist into seasonal yields. The mean growth rates of the best crops in Fig. 2.4*b* are $22 \pm 4$ and $13 \pm 2$ g m$^{-2}$ d$^{-1}$ (mean $\pm$ SE) for C4 and C3 crops respectively.

## 2.4   RESPONSES TO CROWDING IN MONOCULTURE

### Concepts of competition

Leaf-area index, light interception, and production rate are functions of the entire plant community. Within the community, plants are crowded and very strong interactions occur among them. Controlling variables include the number of different species involved, plant density ($\rho$, plants ha$^{-1}$ or m$^{-2}$) and plant size ($w$, kg plant$^{-1}$). Because of their small size, seedlings have little or no interaction with neighbors. As the plants grow in size, they overlap to an increasing extent in both aerial and soil environments. Average space per plant is $1/\rho$ and the area of sunlight per plant at full cover declines with increasing density. As a result, growth rates and morphologies of individual plants differ dramatically with density.

Crowded plants interact with each other in a number of ways. Clearly, they interfere with each other for light. The evaporative demand leading to transpiration per plant is less for dense stands than for sparse ones but at the same time the area for receipt of rainfall and $CO_2$, and the soil volume supplying stored moisture and nutrients, are also less. The terms **interference** and **competition** are used interchangeably in reference to crowding phenomena. The usual basis for interference is that the supply of resources at a site is less than the collective ability of closely spaced plants to use them. Interference may also occur because chemical substances released from a plant or its residues affect the growth of neighbors. That type of interference is termed **allelopathy** (Putman & Tang 1986). Although relatively common in natural systems, allelopathy, particularly self-allelopathy, is unusual in crop plants. Agriculturally relevant examples occur mainly with pasture species. It may be that allelopathic compounds are expensive in synthesis (Chapter 11), or toxic to humans and animals, and have therefore suffered under selection by humans.

Regardless of whether resources limit, or whether allelopathy is involved, interference among plants is largely **indirect** (passive) through changes in the surrounding environment. For example, as one plant depletes the levels of soil nitrogen and water, a second plant then finds less of those resources available to it. Interference is easily demonstrated when plants grown at a low density achieve a larger size than those at greater density, or when crowded plants respond with expansive growth after thinning or receiving fertilizer.

In contrast, crowding responses of animals may be either indirect (one animal reduces forage supply below the amount needed for a second animal) or **direct** (active) as occurs when two animals contest physically for territory. Although the phrase 'competition for resources' is acceptable in crop ecology, its use should not imply direct physical contention as can be the case with Darwin's 'struggle for existence'. The passive nature of plant competition led to use of the term interference (Harper 1977).

## Density effects

The general nature of crowding responses in a monoculture (intraspecific competition) is illustrated in Fig. 2.5*a*, where the usual exponential pattern of biomass accumulation is modified sharply by changes in density. In particular, the 'lag' associated with the exponential phase is shortened as density increases: ten apical meristems m$^{-2}$ can provide new leaves and increase light interception and growth rate much more rapidly than one. As a result, crop growth rate (the initial slopes of the curves in Fig. 2.5*b*) increases with increasing density during the period of incomplete cover. CGR at full cover, however, is affected little by density. The denser crop has significantly greater biomass early in the season but the relative magnitude of that advantage declines as the season progresses. The curve for low density in Fig. 2.5*a* fails to reach full cover and is fated to a small final yield.

During the early stages of growth in a community, seedling plants grow without interference and all plants have similar mass ($w = W/\rho$). Thereafter mass per plant is

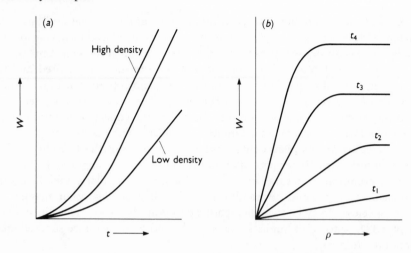

Fig. 2.5. (a) Time course of biomass (*W*) accumulation beginning at emergence by crop communities with different plant densities. (b) Biomass accumulation as a function of plant density (*ρ*) at different times after emergence.

affected according to the intensity and duration of interference and *w* varies as a reciprocal of density. Curves of this shape suggest analysis on a logarithmic or reciprocal basis that would tend to straighten the relationship (Fig. 2.6a) (Kira *et al.* 1953). As plants increase in size, the onset of interference is evident as a break from constant *w*. In this case, the plants grew within the space allotted them at planting, adjusted their growth accordingly, and none died.

Planting densities chosen for field and vegetable crops result in the pattern of behavior illustrated in Fig. 2.6a. The aims are to have mature plants sufficiently crowded to use all resources efficiently, yet not so crowded that some plants die or are unproductive. Each plant then produces less than it would with unlimited space but production from the community is optimized. Plants of large final size must be sown with wide spacing; as a consequence, achievement of full cover is delayed. As noted above, wide spacing allows opportunity for invasion by weeds. That problem can be offset with large seeds, which enter the exponential phase with a large initial leaf area, but weed control measures are usually needed.

### Self-thinning

Some variation in space and mass per plant is usual even with precision planting, and quite large variations occur with broadcast (random) seedings. When crowded, the smallest plants with the least resources become further disadvantaged and die, and the open space allows expanded growth of neighbors. In this case, competition leads to winners and losers.

Where mortality occurs, Kira plots of log mean *w* against log *ρ* show the interesting relationship illustrated in Fig. 2.6b. Individual plant masses in closed

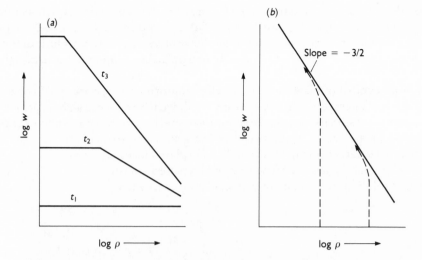

Fig. 2.6. (a) Log of individual plant mass (w) displayed against log density (ρ) for various times after emergence in a Kira plot. (b) Kira plot of the self-thinning phenomenon. The dotted tracks depict the course of log w up to, then along, the –3/2 limit.

stands eventually reach a limit defined by $w = a\rho^{-3/2}$, where $a$ is a proportionality factor. That leads to the linear relation, $\log w = \log a - 1.5 \log \rho$. Dotted lines in Fig. 2.6b depict time-course trajectories for two stands, differing in initial density, towards and then along the 3/2 limit line. Communities apparently reach a ceiling in the amount of biomass that can be supported per unit area; individual plant masses can then increase further only as space is created by the death of neighbors. The relationship has been observed with a wide range of plants, including annual crops and trees, and is termed the **self-thinning rule**. One explanation is that as plants increase in size they need larger areas of sunlight to supply enough carbohydrate for maintenance respiration. The 3/2 term then comes from a correlation between plant mass (proportional to volume occupied, length³) and sunlit area (length²). Other theories are discussed by White (1981).

Self-thinning is of great importance in natural systems and in forestry. In agriculture, we attempt to avoid it because the dead plants tie up nutrients and carbon that would have benefitted the survivors. Self-thinning is common, however, during the early stages of growth with heavy seedings of forage legumes and grasses.

## Plasticity

Optimum density for a crop is influenced by many factors including resource levels and length of growing season. Potential plant size and the degree of **morphological plasticity** for successfully occupying varying amounts of space are also important. Branching (including tillering of grasses) is a basic feature of plasticity. Tillering allows small grain crops to reach the same number of heads and final yield per unit area over a wide range of densities (Fig. 2.7*a*). By contrast, maize can be precision-planted to final stand and modern cultivars have been selected to tiller little or not at all. As a result, that crop has a relatively narrow range of optimum densities (Fig. 2.7*b*).

Precise control of plant density as well as uniform spacings are easily achieved with plate planters using large, uniformly sized, seed. Small seed can be coated with clay or other materials to form a large, uniform size. Precision planters allow control not only of the average space per plant but also of the spatial arrangement. The foliage of a sugarbeet plant, for example, is displayed in a circle around the axis; for that shape, the hexagon ('French orchard') pattern illustrated below is a more efficient solution than square or rectangular arrangements.

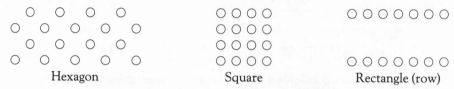

| Hexagon | Square | Rectangle (row) |

In the hexagon, each plant encounters six equidistant neighbors and circular foliage packs efficiently. The yield advantage gained by that arrangement is small, however, and it is not used with crops. It seems that most plants have sufficient plasticity to adjust to whatever space they are provided above or below ground. Row patterns

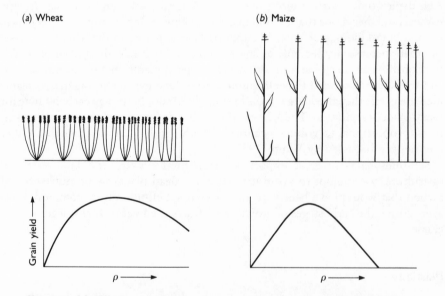

Fig. 2.7. (*a*) Tillering of wheat varies over a broad range of plant densities. That results in a wide range of optimum densities for grain production. (*b*) Tillering is suppressed in maize and plasticity rests mainly with variations in ear number and grain number per ear. The optimum plant density occurs over a narrow range.

reduce the number of planter and harvester passes needed and fertilizer can then be distributed efficiently in bands (Chapter 12). A longer time is required for canopy closure but weeds then can be controlled by cultivation or directed sprays. Row culture can also serve as a means to conserve and ration a limiting supply of soil moisture (Chapter 13).

Many crops are sown with drills. That gives reasonable control of row width and seed per meter of row, but spacings between plants within the row are variable and a degree of morphological plasticity is required. Broadcast sowing is much less precise. In that practice, seeding rates are denoted in kg of seed ha$^{-1}$ and the seed are broadcast on the surface and then incorporated with soil by harrowing. Seed distribution is random and each plant encounters variable amounts of space between itself and neighbors. A high degree of morphological plasticity is needed and $w$ is variable. Given such plasticity, a wide area can be occupied by aggressive tillering; with close spacing, tillering is suppressed by crowding and self-thinning is common.

## 2.5   COMPETITION IN MIXTURES

The main features of competition for resources by mixtures are examined here; stability is considered in Chapter 3 and aspects of genetic diversity within species in Chapter 4.

### Niche concept

Competition in mixed stands among unlike genotypes of the same or different species (interspecific competition) can differ from competition in monoculture as is seen by considering competition between unlike animals. If animals eat different things and do not prey on each other, there is very little interference between species. Such animals are considered to occupy different **niches** (places) in the community. Definitions of niche vary. The issue can be kept relatively simple by saying that the habit or functions that an organism *might use* and perform represent its **fundamental niche**, and those which it *actually uses* and performs constitute its **realized niche**.

Some experiments with animals indicate that the intensity of competition between two species is greatest when their niches are similar. Those studies support the view that species with overlapping niches may compete so intensely that they cannot continue to coexist within a community. That hypothesis, known as Gause's exclusion hypothesis, is of particular interest in evolution and animal ecology and has been used as a basis for theories about mixed crops (Vandermeer 1989).

Whether Gause's hypothesis applies as well to plants remains to be established. The theory suggests that interference in mixtures will be more severe among closely similar plants (i.e. monocultures) than with plants differing in growth habit. Opportunities for use of different space or different resources (**niche differentiation**), however, are much less with plants than with animals. All plants require the same resources of light, carbon dioxide, water, and nutrients. Except for legumes, which are capable of using atmospheric as well as soil nitrogen, there is near-perfect overlap among plant species in their resource requirements. Crop species do differ in development and in tolerance of environmental factors such as temperature, soil pH, salinity, or aluminum levels, but niche differentiation with those traits apply at different times or with different soils (i.e. in different places).

A key feature of agricultural monocultures is that all plants grow similarly and in unison. As a result, they are more or less equally affected by crowding and thus more or less equal in size, particularly when interference is balanced by precision planting, selection for uniform seed size, or by thinning so that each plant has the same amount of space (and thus resources) as its neighbors. Competition is intense but it does not affect survival or reproductive success, i.e. competition is not 'important' in an evolutionary sense (Weldon & Slauson 1986).

The example in Fig. 2.8 illustrates two plant species cohabiting in time, but differing in size. In the pure stands of A and B, interference may become intense; indeed it must if the crops are to achieve maximum yield or efficiency of resource use, but it is equal among all plants, and all individuals perform well. When A is interplanted with B having a quite different size, the result is very different. Placed in the understory, A is suppressed strongly by shading and perhaps also by interference for nutrients and water unless B is widely spaced. If A is unable to reduce the nutrient or water supply to a level limiting to B, the large B plants may respond almost as if they were competing only against themselves. In this case, competition is severe and 'important' for A and 'unimportant' for B. Unlikeness has led to winners and losers. That, of course, is exactly what we hope will happen when a crop encounters competition from weeds.

The most-limiting resource in a competitive situation is easily diagnosed in extreme cases, for example, where nutrients and water are abundant, competition for light may be inferred. Interactions occur, however, where more than one resource may be in marginal supply (Donald 1958). Such situations are not so easily diagnosed. A species that has an advantage in light capture will have a greater supply of substrates for root growth. As a result of a larger root system, it may capture

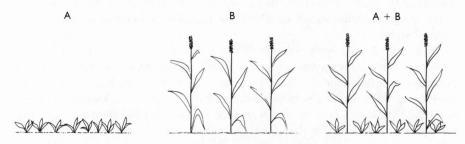

Fig. 2.8. Pure and mixed stands of hypothetical species A and B. The understory niche in a community of B has very limited light resources for the growth of A; when the crops are mixed, little production can be expected from A.

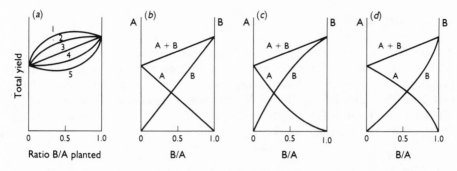

Fig. 2.9. (*a*) Possible outcomes of total yield of binary communities created by replacement of species A with species B. (*b*) Total yield and component contributions with neutral interference. A and B respond to each other as they do to themselves. (*c*) B wins. (*d*) A wins (the Montgomery effect).

more of the limiting soil resources, enhancing leaf growth and light capture. Competing species are then distressed in their access to soil resources as well as to light. Conversely, a primary advantage in root display or nutrient uptake can have a secondary effect through greater leaf display. In these situations, competition for one factor induces increased competition for other factors. The effects can be additive and therefore stronger than expected from the primary competition alone.

### Replacement experiments

Competitive interactions among unlike plants can be tested in **replacement experiments** with treatments consisting of a series of communities with varying proportions of two cohabiting species (de Wit 1960). Fig. 2.9*a* depicts the range of possible total yields (biomass or economic) that might be obtained as a pure stand of species A is progressively diluted by species B. Over-yielding (line 1) indicates that the species in combination exploited the environment more thoroughly than either alone. If both species perform better in the mixture than in pure stand, they **complement** each other, perhaps through the use of different space. Conversely, a total yield less than either pure stand (line 5) indicates the possibility of mutual **antagonism**. The straight line (3) indicates the possibility of a neutral interaction.

The separate yields of the components must be examined in each of these cases for proper interpretation of the interactions involved. That is done in Fig. 2.9*b–d* for the case where total yield suggested a neutral interaction. Component analysis reveals that interference may indeed be neutral (Fig. 2.9*b*), or that B, which is superior in pure stand, wins (Fig. 2.9*c*), or that A, the poorer yielding in pure stand, wins (Fig. 2.9*d*). The last case is common in crops and is sometimes termed the 'Montgomery effect' after an early agriculturalist in Montana (USA) who first observed it with small grains. It fits the case of a wild-type plant (A) with vigorous vegetative habits but only a small harvest index competing against a productive, small-stature, cultivar (B) having a large harvest index.

## Relative yield total

Yields of mixtures may also be compared on a relative basis. If each component of a 50:50 mixture yielded 0.6 times as much as it does in pure stand, 1 ha of the polyculture would provide the same total yield as the sum of 0.6 ha A and 0.6 ha B, or 1.2 ha. The ratio, 1.2 ha/1 ha = 1.2, is termed the **land equivalent ratio** (LER). The same result, termed the **relative yield total** (RYT) (de Wit and van den Bergh 1965), is obtained from the sum of the relative yields:

$$RYT = \sum_{i=1}^{n} Y_{m_i}/Y_{p_i} \qquad\qquad\qquad \text{[Eq. 2.5]}$$

where $Y_{m_i}$ and $Y_{p_i}$ represent the yields of the $i$th species in mixture and pure stand respectively. Some workers prefer the name LER to RYT for its implication of optimization per unit area land. LER or RYT > 1 indicates that the mixture is superior in yield to the sum of the pure stands, i.e. that complementation exists. Serious mistakes about management practices can be made from experiments on mixed cropping unless the pure stands and the mixtures both are formulated independently in optimal ways (i.e. with spacings and ratios of plant numbers that provide the best performance of the communities). Most reports on the performance of polycultures involve this error and the reported RYT (or LER) values are meaningless. In addition, RYT is affected strongly by environment: values from the same mixture may be < 1 or > 1 depending upon fertility or water supply.

## Complementation in mixtures

Complementation in the use of resources by mixtures can arise in two ways: through the use of different space while cohabiting; and through partial cohabitation in time. Each approach deserves separate discussion.

**Different space**   The only way that cohabiting crops might achieve niche differentiation is by acquiring resources from different spaces. There is little opportunity for complementary use of aerial resources because $CO_2$ and light can be fully intercepted by any canopy at full cover. Full cover is just as easily achieved with monocultures as it is with polycultures. In addition, the lower leaves of sun plants adapt to the low light levels within the canopy as well as a 'shade' plant might. With less than full cover, as frequently is the case when soil resources are limiting, it makes little difference what canopy is displayed because all leaves are then in bright sun. Then, final yield is determined largely by limiting soil resources.

Complementation through the use of different space is sometimes possible when soil resources are limiting and the species have marked differences in rooting habit (Fig. 2.10). With a mixture of species A and B, soil resources not accessed by shallow-rooted A could be captured by deep-rooted B. The two species might complement each other and the yield of the mixture could be expected to exceed that of pure stands of either species (i.e. RYT > 1). In this case, spatially non-

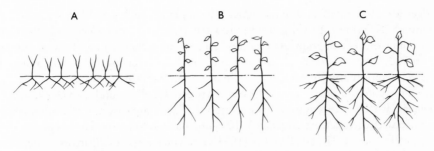

**Fig. 2.10.** Shallow-rooted species A and deep-rooted species B could complement each other in a binary mixture but species C, with both shallow and deep roots, could fully exploit the soil profile in monoculture. Species A and B can be viewed as phenotypic defects that might be corrected by selection for type C plants in a breeding program.

uniform treatment of the land through mixed cropping increases the use of scarce soil resources.

Possibilities for complementation based on different use of soil resources clearly depend upon resource level. Spitters (1980) and Ofori & Stern (1987) both make the point that situations with limited soil resources offer the best opportunities for complementation. Surface layers of soils generally have the greatest supply of nutrients (Chapter 7) and can be accessed by most species, whereas water resources are distributed throughout the profile. As a result, niche differentiation for water resources is more likely than for nutrients in mixtures not involving legumes. Supplied with adequate nutrients and water, however, each species easily acquires all of its needs from its usual rooting zone and the basis for complementation vanishes (RYT declines). When the limiting resource is non-mobile (P or stored moisture), advantage goes to the species that, through rapid or directed root growth, reaches it first. Where the limiting resource is mobile (nitrate ions or a downward flux of soil moisture), advantage passes to the species best displayed for interception.

A plant breeder could view the existence of complementation (RYT > 1) of A and B at low fertility as an indication of a genetic defect. For the example in Fig. 2.10, versions of A and B might be selected that, like species C depicted there, would each be capable of exploring the entire soil profile. With limited soil resources, yields of both pure stands would be improved by more expansive rooting but the advantage previously shown by the mixture would disappear because a mixture of the improved strains would find no more nutrients or water than are accessed by either alone. Alternatively, instead of altering A and B through plant breeding, they could simply be replaced with a monoculture of C that already possesses the desired rooting habit.

Interactions between legumes and non-legumes can be viewed as involving the use of different space because non-legumes depend on soil nitrogen whereas legumes can obtain much of their nitrogen from air (Chapter 8). Maize–bean polycultures, common on infertile soils in tropical regions, are a principal example with crops. A situation with RYT > 1 is illustrated in Table 2.3 with an approximate nitrogen budget for a low-nitrogen site in Kenya. Maize plants, each provided with 1 m² of catchment (7.5 times the value used in Iowa) (Chapter 17), obtain enough nitrogen to produce one ear of grain. At that low density, abundant light and water remain for an understory bean crop. In the polyculture, the bean crop and its companion of nitrogen fixation appear twice in a cycle of two polycultures compared with only once in rotated monocultures. Given nitrogen fertilizer and dense plantings, however, RYT for this system drops below 1. For comparison, maize adequately supplied with nitrogen easily yields 5–10 t grain ha⁻¹ in Kenya and 2–3 t ha⁻¹ can be expected for beans. The small yield of the Kenyan maize monoculture in Table 2.3 is explained by nitrogen deficiency; the poor yield of the bean monoculture indicates problems with disease, other nutrients, or acid soil.

**Different time**   Long growing seasons create opportunities for niche differentiation in time. When a single species is unable to utilize the full season, growth duration may be extended by adding other species. The most common examples are pasture communities constructed by sowing mixtures of cool- and warm-season grasses and legumes. That not only extends the growing season but also may provide a more even distribution of green forage over the season than could be obtained with monocultures. RYT values seldom exceed 1 (Trenbath 1974), however, so the principal advantages seem to come from improved animal nutrition (high-protein legume forage balances the more productive, cellulosic grasses), nitrogen fixation, and from a more even distribution of forage.

### Advantages and limitations in the use of polycultures

Any advantage from polycultures compared with monocultures depends on achieving a RYT > 1. As we have seen, that is most likely where soil resources are limiting, and rooting habits differ, or one of the species is a legume. Considerable attention has also been given to whether RYT > 1 can also result through less disease or insect problems than occur in monocultures. The basis for this is that some insects and diseases can be limited in their dispersal and spread when susceptible host plants are interspersed with resistant plants. With insects, it is also possible that one species may serve as a trap for insects, reducing infestations of the other, or that it may serve as a breeding place for predators. Evidence on these possibilities is equivocal. Examples of both increased and reduced insects and disease have been observed but they have not been linked well with yield effects. In general, the greater number of hosts in the polyculture generally also means a greater diversity of pests and diseases. That problem can be particularly severe with soil-borne organisms. Since host plants are present in every crop, the sanitizing effects obtained with rotated monocultures are lost. The maize–bean complex is reasonably successful in the tropics because neither species is faced with severe attack by soil-borne organisms. The system would not work in the American Corn Belt, however, where corn rootworm (*Diabrotica longicornis*) builds up quickly when maize is present in the same field every year.

Polycultures are not widely employed with arable crops in the agriculture of

Table 2.3 *Estimated RYT for yield and nitrogen for one cycle of rotated maize and*
*bean monocultures and two crops of maize–bean polyculture per year in Kenya*

Yields[1]:

| | Monoculture | Polyculture |
|---|---|---|
| Maize | 1200 kg grain ha$^{-1}$ | 800 kg grain ha$^{-1}$ |
| Bean | 800 | 600 |
| Yield/cycle | 2000 | 2800 |

$RYT_Y = 800/1200 + 600/800 = 1.42$.

Estimate of N harvested per crop cycle with 1.5% N in maize grain and 3% in bean[2]:

| | Monoculture | Polyculture |
|---|---|---|
| Maize | $1200 \times 0.015$ $= 18$ kg N ha$^{-1}$ | $800 \times 0.015 \times 2$ $= 24$ kg N ha$^{-1}$ |
| Bean | $800 \times 0.03$ $= 24$ kg N ha$^{-1}$ | $600 \times 0.03 \times 2$ $= 36$ kg N ha$^{-1}$ |
| Total N harvested | 42 kg N ha$^{-1}$ | 60 kg N ha$^{-1}$ |

$RYT_N = 12/18 + 18/24 = 1.42$.

*Sources:* [1] Yield formation came from local farmers. [2] N content of maize grain and bean seed are from National Research Council (1982).

developed countries because of two reasons in addition to the loss of rotation benefits. First, fertility levels are higher and RYT > 1 is rare and, second, improved performance, if it occurs, generally does not compensate for the difficulties encountered in balancing competition, planting and harvesting, and optimizing management (e.g. weed control and supplies of nutrients and water). Optimal management of two or more crops in a polyculture in terms of planting date, water and nutrient supplies, and other factors is more complex or even impossible compared with monocultures. Possibilities for mechanical harvests and for controlling weeds with herbicides also are greatly restricted.

Management of pasture polycultures (e.g. grass–legume mixtures) faces several of those issues as well as the question of how to insure persistence of the desired species over time. With an adequate supply of soil nitrogen for grasses, legumes languish; with nitrogen deficiency, grasses perform poorly while legumes and weeds (unpalatable or toxic species) increase. In some systems, rotation of pastures through a cropping phase allows them to be reconstructed periodically with suitable species. In Europe, the legume component has in many cases been abandoned as a source of nitrogen for intensive pastures (see Table 8.2) which are now managed as pure stands of grass supplied with fertilizer or manure nitrogen. Management of the extensive grasslands found in semiarid regions is usually limited to timing grazing activity and stocking rates in ways that favor dominance by the best species. Efforts are sometimes made to introduce legumes and to supply them with needed soil amendments (e.g., P, S, or Mo) but that approach is generally expensive.

### Polyculture variants

Agricultural polycultures with cohabitation in time and space involve varying degrees of niche differentiation and serious competition. Some variants, such as **intercropping** (planting one crop within open areas of another), may actually have little or no competitive interaction. During the early years of a new orchard, for example, spaces between young trees can be planted to an annual crop.

**Overlap** systems (two or more species overlap for portions of their life cycles) are sometimes used to extend growth duration in mild climates. That can be done by interplanting a monoculture nearing maturity with a second monoculture. Inter-planting maize with beans in some tropical regions is an example. Another practice involves placing rows of early-maturing beans between widely spaced rows of cassava. Cassava is a long-season crop; it is planted with wide spacings because the plants ultimately occupy a large amount of space in the aerial environment. Very little interspecific competition occurs in these systems unless the overlaps continue for an extended period of time and the beans are overtopped by the cassava (Cock 1987).

**Companion cropping** is a special case of overlap cropping. The most common case involves seeding a small grain as a companion crop with forages. The grain crop serves to reduce soil erosion in the seedling forage stand while smothering weeds and providing an economic return as the forage crop becomes established. The forage crop is also smothered, however, and little or no hay is harvested in the first year. Selective herbicides are now available for weed control and forage crops can be established without a companion crop. The advantage of herbicide, in addition to smaller cost, is that significant hay production, and significant nitrogen production, are obtained from legumes in the first year.

As the length of overlap is shortened, overlap systems grade into **relay cropping**, in which two (double cropping) or more monocultures are grown in sequence in the same year. This is sometimes defined as a polyculture technique but is actually just a form of crop rotation. No interspecific competition occurs. Relay cropping is found in vegetable gardening, with rice production in Asia, with wheat–soybean (winter–summer) double cropping in the southern USA, and in many other forms.

## 2.6   COMMUNITY RESPONSE TO LIMITING FACTORS

Yield is a community property that reflects the collective ability of crowded plants to capture light and access soil resources. How a community responds to additions of a limiting resource is important.

### Single-factor responses

Returning to the sigmoidal growth curve seen in an annual monoculture (Fig. 2.1), consider what may happen when the supply of a resource such as nitrogen or water is less than adequate. Two patterns of behavior over time are possible. In Fig. 2.11a,

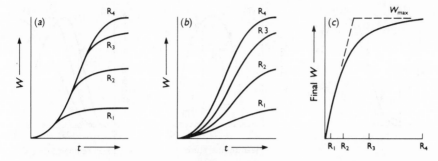

Fig. 2.11. (*a*) Time course of biomass accumulation by crops with different initial supplies of a limiting resource ($R_1 \rightarrow R_4$). Growth slows as the resource is exhausted. (*b*) Time course of biomass accumulation with varying degree of limitation by a resource whose supply is never adequate. (*c*) Total biomass ultimately produced by the crops in (*a*) or (*b*) as a function of resource level. The broken lines indicate initial slope and asymptotic yield, $W_{max}$.

the resource is exhausted after a varying period of normal growth with an adequate supply; thereafter, growth is restricted. This pattern is common with nitrogen and water resources. The second pattern is illustrated in Fig. 2.11*b*. In this case, the resource is always limiting as occurs, for example, when mineralization of nitrogen from soil organic matter proceeds at a rate slower than the plants could use it. An unfavorable soil pH or toxicity (aluminum for example) has a similar effect.

Response functions of biomass yield (*W*) versus resource level (*R*) can be obtained for the examples in Fig. 2.11*a*,*b* using *W* values observed late in the season after treatment differences are fully developed. Both of these examples produce a plateau response function (Fig. 2.11*c*). The same general curve is found when growth rate is graphed against resource level. Plateau curves can be fitted empirically by several expressions including the negative exponential:

$$W = W_{max} (1 - e^{-cR}),$$ [Eq. 2.6]

where $W_{max}$ is the asymptotic yield, unlimited by resource level (*R*), and *c* is a constant. The slope ($dW/dR$) defines the **sensitivity** of yield to changing levels of *R*:

$$dW/dR = c(W_{max} - W).$$ [Eq. 2.7]

For practical purposes, it is sometimes convenient to simplify the curve to two intersecting straight lines (Fig. 2.11*c*), one reflecting the initial slope of the response (equal to $W_{max} c$ at $R = 0$), and the asymptote ($W_{max}$) (Cerrato & Blackmer 1990). That concept was first applied by J. Liebig to soil nutrient responses and by G.E. Blackman to photosynthesis rate with increasing light. The terms 'Liebig' or 'Blackman' response are still in common use.

The diversity of response functions encountered in crop ecology is relatively small. Examples of plateau responses (Fig. 2.3*a*) and exponential decay (Fig. 2.2*a* and Eq. 2.3) have already been presented. The observed dependence of growth and development rates on temperature in controlled environments (Fig. 2.12*a*) has a different shape. Whereas a plateau response is explained reasonably well by the

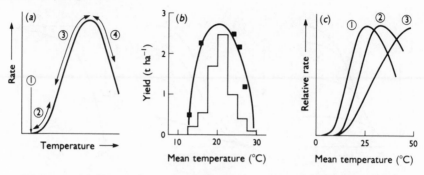

Fig. 2.12. (*a*) Shape of the complex response function observed with most plants for growth rate or development rate as a function of temperature. The numbered portions are explained in the text. (*b*) Curve of cardinal temperatures for bean production defined from observed yields and mean growing-season temperature at five locations (filled squares) in Latin America. The histogram describes the present distribution of bean yields in Latin America. (Redrawn from Laing *et al.* (1983).) (*c*) Generalized growth and development responses for (1) temperate grasses and legumes, (2) tropical legumes, and (3) tropical grasses. (Adapted from Fitzpatrick & Nix (1970).)

initial slope and asymptote, responses to temperature apparently integrate several processes. A set of hypotheses can be proposed to account for the numbered regions in Fig. 2.12*a*: the threshold (1) could involve the activation energy for a limiting enzyme; an increase in the frequency of collisions between enzymes and substrates would account for region (2); enzyme saturation or substrate limitation would slow the increase (3); and injury to critical enzymes could explain region (4).

The fine detail of growth response to temperature is difficult to see under field conditions but 'cardinal temperatures' corresponding to minimum, optimum range, and maximum temperatures for growth can usually be drawn from field data. The example given in Fig. 2.12*b* explains the distribution of bean production in Latin America. Optimal responses are also seen with factors such as soil pH. As with temperature, species may differ significantly in the threshold and maximum and in the general breadth of the response. Such response functions give quantitative definition to the term **tolerance**. The wide range between the minimum (12.2 °C) and maximum (29.1 °C) temperatures for bean in Fig. 2.12*b* give it a 'broad' (in contrast to 'narrow') tolerance to temperature. Fitzpatrick & Nix (1970) make the useful point that crop plants can be classified into the three broad crops characterized by the growth responses to temperature illustrated in Fig. 2.12*c*.

## Multiple-factor interactions

The curvilinear nature of many single-factor responses offers the possibility that two or more factors can simultaneously limit crop performance. Consider a simple example with plateau responses to N and P as nutrients. Through construction of a three-dimensional diagram (Fig. 2.13*a*; visualize this in the corner of a room), the

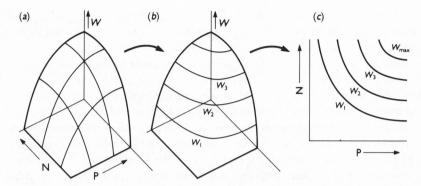

**Fig. 2.13.** (*a*) **Response surface of yield to variation in levels of N and P constructed from intersecting plateau functions. (*b*) The same surface shown with elevation (yield) contours. (*c*) The contour lines transferred as isoquants to the two-dimensional, N–P plane.**

interaction of two factors results in a response surface that can be shown with contour lines of equal yield (Fig. 2.13*b*). Reduced to a two-dimensional drawing of yield isoquants (Fig. 2.13*c*), it depicts the yield obtained with any combination of the two factors. An important point derived from this figure is that field situations can always be analyzed as single-factor responses. The response to nitrogen alone is qualitatively similar at all levels of phosphorus; the principal difference is that maximum yield differs with P level.

Graphical presentation of more than two simultaneously limiting factors is more difficult. Yield response to factors X, Y and Z can be represented by:

$$W = W_{max} f(X, Y, Z). \qquad \text{[Eq. 2.7]}$$

A multiplicative function [$f(\ )$] is appropriate in most instances. The most widely used approach employs a series of negative exponential responses:

$$f(X,Y,Z) = (1 - b_1 e^{-k_1 X})(1 - b_2 e^{-k_2 Y})(1 - b_3 e^{-k_3 Z}). \qquad \text{[Eq. 2.8]}$$

At the other extreme is Liebig's Law:

$$W = W_{max} \, min[f_1(X), f_2(Y), f_3(Z)], \qquad \text{[Eq. 2.9]}$$

where the *min* function indicates selection of only the most limiting factor. Applied this way, Liebig's Law effectively circumvents the interaction of factors.

Care is needed in the application of equation Eq. 2.8. Suppose that factors X, Y, and Z are each present at levels that give $0.5 W_{max}$ when the others are not limiting. Eq. 2.8 leads to the trap: $0.5 \times 0.5 \times 0.5 = 0.125 W_{max}$, whereas Liebig's Law (Eq. 2.9) predicts $0.5 W_{max}$, a more realistic result for most cases with simultaneously limiting factors. The reason that Liebig's Law generally works better than more elaborate equations can be explained with an example involving nutrient limitations. With nitrogen supply sufficient for $0.5 W_{max}$, the amounts of other nutrients such as phosphorus needed to support that yield are also much less than are needed for $W_{max}$ and therefore less likely to limit growth. Eq. 2.8 works well only when the coefficients are adjusted to each specific situation; in this example, predicted yield is near $0.5W_{max}$ if each term is near 0.8. The need for empirical tuning of this sort is a common problem in crop simulation models constructed with multiplicative response functions.

Solutions are also more difficult when independent factors limit sequentially. That is illustrated in crop simulation models that advance time on a daily or weekly basis using numerical methods. Multiple limiting factors then must be included with situation-specific response functions in multiplicative fashion. With a shorter, hourly time advance and internal feedback control, selection of just one most-limiting factor for each hour provides realistic interaction over time in crop models using pure response functions (Ng & Loomis 1984; Denison & Loomis 1989). The most-limiting factor then changes hourly as temperature, water, or substrate become limiting in turn (an example is presented in Fig. 11.6; see also Loomis *et al.* (1990)).

The real world of the farmer is manageable by simpler approaches providing one is alert to what factors limit crop performance. With nitrogen and phosphorus both limiting, for example, capital additions of phosphorus in excess of that needed by a single crop may be possible because phosphorus is not readily leached from soils. The farmer has simplified the management decision to questions of how much and when to apply the more-labile nitrogen (Chapters 8 and 12). Good farmers know their land and rotations well enough to define the minimum level of N required to bring their crops towards maximum yield with Liebig's Law.

In general, most multifactor issues in farming can be simplified into a series of simple single-factor decisions: which species, then which cultivar, then what spacing and planting date, then what kind of fertilizer, then how much, and so on.


## 2.7  SUMMARY

Crops and pasture are grown as communities of closely spaced, interacting plants. Sunlight, rainfall, and yield are all properties of areas of land. Communities, then, rather than individual plants, are the focus of farm operations.

The increase in biomass of the community follows a sigmoid pattern during the growing season. During the early lag phase, growth of new seedlings is proportional to the leaf-area index of the crop. Biomass increases exponentially with time while the specific growth rate (or RGR) remains constant. As plants increase in size, adjacent plants interfere (compete) with each other for limiting resources of light, water, nutrients, and $CO_2$. After the canopy closes in full cover of the ground (LAI 3–4), the biomass increase rate (CGR, crop growth rate) of well nourished crops is limited by the flux of light for photosynthesis. As a consequence, CGR is a plateau function of LAI.

Interception of sunlight determines production rate. The potential production rate of full-cover crops corresponds to more than 3 g biomass $MJ^{-1}$ solar radiation and the maximum efficiency of energy storage in chemical bonds of biomass is near 5% of total radiation. Record crops approach those rates of production. Examination of sigmoidal seasonal growth curves reveals two important principles about community productivity. Seasonal production will be greatest when (i) the duration of growth extends over the available growing season (whether set by temperature or some resource such as water) and (ii) duration of full cover is maximized.

The result of crowding within the community is that each plant is restrained to less than its potential growth rate and final size. In monocultures, interference between plants can be controlled by density and spacing pattern. Competition is then equal for all plants and all plants survive and contribute equally to community yield. Precise spacing is not always possible, however, and varying degrees of morphological plasticity are needed. Planting densities employed with crops are designed to reach full cover quickly but with a level of interference that optimizes the output of economic yield.

Achieving balanced competition in mixed stands (polyculture) is more difficult. All plants require similar resources from air and soil and the possibilities that mixtures can exploit an environment more thoroughly than a monoculture requires niche differentiation in time or space. When that occurs, the relative yield total (RYT; or land equivalent ratio, LER) of a mixture can exceed the combined yields of the component monocultures. Those cases are found where soil resources are limiting and the species differ markedly in rooting or nitrogen nutrition and where crops overlap in time so as to extend the growing season.

The community properties of biomass and yield respond in characteristic ways to variations in the levels of limiting factors. Response functions to temperature, pH, and plant nutrients, for example, follow different patterns. Species differ in the ranges of temperature and other factors over which they perform best. Those differences define a species' adaptation.

## 2.8 FURTHER READING

Donald, C. M. 1963. Competition among crop and pasture plants. *Adv. Agron.* **15**:1–118.

Harper, J.L. 1977. *Population biology of plants*. Academic Press, New York. 892 p.

Hunt, R. 1978. *Plant growth analysis*. Studies in Biology No. 96. Edward Arnold, London. 67 p.

Monteith, J. L. 1977. Climate and the efficiency of crop production in Britain. *Phil. Trans. R. Soc. Lond.* **B281**:277–94.

Ofori, F. and W. R. Stern. 1987. Cereal-legume intercropping systems. *Adv. Agron.* **41**:41–90.

Vandermeer, J. 1989. *The ecology of intercropping*. Cambridge University Press. 237 p.

Whittaker, R. H. 1975. *Communities and ecosystems*. 2nd Edition. MacMillan, New York. 385 p.

# 3

*Stability*

## 3.1 INTRODUCTION

We define stability (Chapter 1) as the variation in yield over time, i.e. as relating to repeatability and predictability in farming. This is a narrower definition than those used by ecologists who work with natural systems and focus more on changes in community structure than on variations in production. For them, stability also embraces continued existence of genetic information within the community, i.e. persistence of particular species or genes. Similar questions arise with the genetic structure of agricultural populations (Chapter 4) and for persistence of species in pasture polycultures. Persistence of crops within a farming system, however, is largely a human decision and thus more an issue in sustainability. It depends upon whether production can be sustained and whether it is worth sustaining.

An overlap evidently exists between concepts of stability and sustainability. Large yield variations and persistence of crops both affect sustainability but maintenance of soil resources is the key issue because soil degradation has the effect of gradually lowering the potential of a site until farming is no longer a viable proposition. This chapter focuses on several aspects of yield variation and their causes as features of stability. Causes and controls of soil degradation are discussed in later chapters: acidification (Chapter 7), salinization (Chapters 13 and 14), and nutrient exhaustion and erosion (Chapter 12).

### The nature of variations in farming

In addition to fluctuations in markets, farming is affected by weather, pests, and diseases as well as by human errors. Considerable variation in yield is normal because weather varies year-to-year and because fields differ naturally in their history, production potential, and spatial uniformity. Additional irregularity is introduced through variations in moisture level during tillage or planting, tool condition and settings, and operator alertness. Crop variation and losses also occur with unusual sequences of weather and with epidemics of weeds, pests, or disease.

Complete failure is generally a local event resulting from weeds or a local occurrence of disease, soil crusting, frost, or flood. Repeated too often, such events threaten continuation of the farm as an enterprise and indicate the need for changes in farming practice. Farmers have many options that help to temper or avoid problems. Resistant cultivars, seed treatment with fungicides, tillage, and selection of planting dates that avoid normal outbreaks are simple methods that reduce exposure to pests and disease. Other practices include the use of fallow, crop rotation, and burning or incorporation of residues.

## Economic aspects

The social causes and consequences of variations and changes in crop production can be examined at several levels of aggregation and from several points of view. Perspectives on variation differ for individual farmers, for a region or nation, and the world as a whole.

Prices and costs of production are significant factors in the risks associated with variations in production. Farmers are numerous and competitive and thus are price-takers rather than price-makers; further complexity is added by the degree of price elasticity of crops. Our need for food is relatively fixed, and prices for sugar, fresh fruit, and vegetable crops, in particular, are inelastic; small surpluses can cause large declines in price whereas a shortfall in supply can cause a large increase. Feed grains and other bulk commodities such as hay, oil seeds, and cotton, on the other hand, are stored more cheaply and can be used in variable amounts. Prices for those commodities are more elastic and change moderately with supply because market demand increases as price declines.

Farmers worry mainly about a positive flow of income (area × yield × price) and whether productivity of the land can be sustained during their lifetimes and for their children. They respond to price in assessments of risk and in their choices of crops, area planted, and intensity (i.e. costs) of production. When prices for a particular commodity are high, farmers may expand its area at the expense of less favored crops not only on higher-quality lands where yield variation is small, but also on those with marginal climates and soils where yield variation may be greater. Changes in the area distribution of crops have the effect of altering the boundaries of the Thunen zones (Chapter 1). For farmers, overall risks must be balanced by the value of the crops being grown.

Nations are concerned more with variations in the total supply from all farms and with whether production from one region may buffer variations or decline in supply from another. Changes in area distribution and intensity of production can result in either an increase or a decrease in the variation of total production. Governments influence the operation of markets, imports, and exports, and engage in efforts at price and area stabilization. The European Community and Japan, for example, presently limit imports while supporting high internal prices that stimulate production. Those actions tend to isolate and thus protect their farmers from the variations and lower prices found in world markets. As a result, exporting nations have lost significant portions of their traditional markets. The response of the USA and Australia has been to work towards reopening such markets while taking actions to curtail production and to support minimum prices for their farmers. In the 1930s, many countries attempted to protect internal markets with restrictive tariffs. In retrospect, those actions seemed to have contributed to the intensity and duration of the world-wide depression of that era.

## 3.2  YIELD VARIATION

### Measures of variation

**Coefficient of variation**  One of the simplest means for expressing yield variation is illustrated in Fig. 3.1*a*, where observations over years and locations are distributed 'normally' around the mean yield ($\overline{Y}$). The width of the distribution is defined by the standard deviation (SD) and $\overline{Y} \pm 1$SD includes two-thirds of the observations. The ratio SD/$\overline{Y}$, termed the **coefficient of variation** (CV), is a useful measure of variation. A large CV reflects a wide distribution of yields relative to the mean, i.e. low stability, whereas a small CV indicates constancy and thus high stability. The frequency of extreme yields can be calculated with the aid of a $z$ table from a statistics reference. It turns out that one observation in 20 (5%) lies outside $\overline{Y} \pm 1.96$ SD and one in 100 is outside $\overline{Y} \pm 2.57$ SD. This simple approach defines variation well in most cases but in others the distribution of yields departs from a normal distribution, as is illustrated in Fig. 3.1*b*. The excess of small yields in this figure occurs because many factors can reduce yields from an upper boundary imposed by solar radiation and water supply. Field observations are required to identify the cause.

**Sensitivity to resource level**  A common cause of yield variation is apparent from examination of Figs 2.11 and 2.12. Those figures reveal regions where factors such as temperature and nutrients strongly limit growth and the slopes ($dY/dx$) of the responses to changes in temperature or nutrients are large, and other regions where those factors are not limiting to growth and $dY/dx = 0$. The slope defines the **sensitivity** of yield to variations in the factor. When crops are grown outside the optimal range of weather, resource factors, or soil pH, small variations in the environment can cause large variations in yield.

Consider a cereal crop grown in a field where response to added nitrogen is similar to the curve illustrated in Fig. 2.11*c*. The initial slope of such curves for cereal yields can be as great as 30–50 kg grain kg$^{-1}$ N. That results from the low concentration of N in grain (1.5 to 2.5%) and a large harvest index for N (about 70% of N generally goes to grain). The supply of available N can easily vary by 50 kg ha$^{-1}$ from field to field or year to year depending upon management and weather. With a legume forage as the previous crop or where manure is used, the supply may be large but its availability is even more uncertain (Chapter 8). With nitrogen limiting yield to, say, 3000 kg ha$^{-1}$, a 50 kg ha$^{-1}$ variation in nitrogen could cause grain yield to vary over a wide range: (0.7 harvest index for N × 50 kg N ha$^{-1}$)/ (0.02 kg N kg$^{-1}$ grain) = 1750 kg grain ha$^{-1}$. The observed CV would be quite large. With an adequate supply of nitrogen, however, yield approaches the asymptotic limit shown in Fig. 2.11*c* and variation in yield due to variation in nitrogen drops to zero.

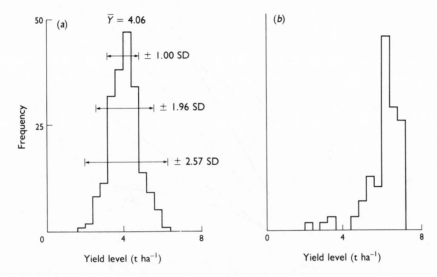

Fig. 3.1. (*a*) A normal distribution of yields around the mean with the ranges for ± 1, ± 1.96, and ± 2.57 SD units that include 67%, 95%, and 99% of the observations, respectively. (*b*) A skewed distribution of yields.

**Stability coefficient** Effects of weather and management on yield variation depend in part on the species and cultivar employed. Consequently, plant breeders are concerned about the stability characteristics of cultivars. Breeders routinely compare new germplasm selections with standard cultivars in simple nursery trials over years and locations but they seldom have time for the careful experiments needed for sensitivity analyses. Simple tests of stability are possible with nursery trials, however, using the yields of standard cultivars, or the mean yield of a whole nursery, as an index of environment (*E*) (Finlay & Wilkinson 1963; Eberhardt & Russell 1966). This approach requires that nursery trials be conducted over a range of environments or years. As illustrated in Fig. 3.2, mean yields of a standard cultivar are arrayed on a linear scale along the abscissa as the independent variable. This array represents a gradient of all factors affecting yields at the sites where the cultivar was grown. Yields of other entries in the trials are plotted on the ordinate and the slope (*b*, d*Y*/d*E*) of their response to the gradient is taken as their **stability coefficient**. The 1:1 lines (*b* = 1) represents the performance of the standard. An entry with a larger slope varies more than the standard over those environments and therefore is less stable; a smaller slope indicates greater stability.

Cultivar trials are usually distributed over representative production regions and the gradient is then complex because limiting factors (soil condition, weeds, disease, rainfall, or temperature) usually differ among the locations. When the tests are carefully distributed at locations that offer a gradient in some factor such as temperature or rainfall, researchers gain more insight into causes and effects.

One must be careful about giving too much weight to *b* in identifying superior cultivars. Although stability is desirable, greater yield is usually more important because it generally represents a more efficient use of environment and greater

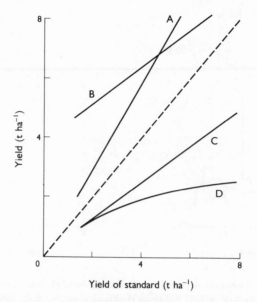

Fig. 3.2. Yields of specific cultivars plotted against yields of a standard cultivar over a range of environments. Abscissa values serve as indices of environment. The slopes of the lines ($b$ values) for individual entries relative to the 1:1 line define their stability.

return for labor and resources expended in production. Values of $b$ are relative to a standard, or to the mean, of particular trials and therefore change as environment changes or as entries forming the mean change. Entry A in Fig. 3.2, for example, is superior to the standard at all locations. It therefore has a larger stability coefficient, $b$, and is judged to be less stable than the standard. Its CV, however, would equal the standard's because its yield is always a simple multiple of the standard. Entry B is also superior at all locations but its $b$ and CV are less. If A was used as the new standard, the old standard would behave like entry C. Some cultivars give nonlinear results like entry D. Yields of standards change over years at the same locations: if the weather becomes less variable, or cultural practices improve, the range is smaller and $b$ values for all lines under test also change.

Cock (1987) offered an insightful analysis of how plant breeders can improve stability in cassava cultivars. Of interest here is that he distinguishes between the perspectives of farmers and plant breeders. Farmers have the most concern for temporal stability (over years) and cropping system stability (change in yields when cultural practices or rotations change) whereas breeders must emphasize stability within and across broad edaphoclimatic zones.

### The influence of technology

It is important to know whether stability of production increases or decreases with particular changes in technology. Drainage for control of excess moisture in wet regions (Chapter 12) and for salinity control in dry regions (Chapters 13 and 14) has major beneficial effects in both in increasing yield and in reducing yield variation. Other important changes have come through plant breeding, improved nutrition, and the use of biocides. Treatment of planting seed with fungicides and the use of herbicides, in particular, have major benefits in stability. In addition to advances in yield potential and harvest index, plant breeding has contributed much greater insect and disease resistance. Machinery has contributed improved quality, uniformity, and timeliness of tillage and harvest with major improvements in stability as a result.

Most of these changes can also serve as sources of increased variation. Machinery, for example, has permitted farming in more risky environments, leading to less stability, and cultivars that take advantage of fluctuations in resource supplies are less stable than unresponsive lines. Weeds, pests, and diseases sometimes adapt through evolutionary change to selection pressures imposed by new control measures such as biocides and resistant cultivars. Stability is improved while controls are effective. When they break down, variation increases requiring attention to new solutions.

Increased use of fertilizers is perhaps the most significant recent technological change. The sensitivity to added nutrients is large with limiting levels of resources and small at high levels where they are not limiting. The variation observed with small additions of fertilizer can actually be greater than without external inputs because natural inputs of nutrients by rainfall, although strongly limiting to yield, may be relatively even in supply over time. The experience in developing countries seems to be that CV at first increases with increasing use of fertilizer and modern cultivars and then decreases as growers become more experienced and inputs are brought to optimal levels. Evidence exists that farmers in developed nations view fertilizer application as a risk-avoidance measure and, in some cases, tend to over-fertilize as a result (Legg *et al.* 1989).

One way to examine the influence of technological changes on stability is through the historical patterns of yield variation in developed nations that have made the transition to higher yields. Stanhill (1976), for example, analyzed trends in English wheat yields over a 700 y period. 'National' yield was estimated for the early periods by clustering Abbey records for as many fields as possible. Yields progressed from near 500 kg ha$^{-1}$ in AD 1200, reflecting a very small nutrient supply (Section 8.8; Loomis 1978), to over 6000 kg ha$^{-1}$ in recent years with fertilizer additions, legume rotations, and improvements in cultivars and tillage methods. Surprisingly, the CV was small (near 0.07) and varied little over that period.

Hazell (1989) examined wheat yields around the world during the period 1971–83. He found small ($< 0.1$) interannual CVs for national average yields of cereals in humid and irrigated areas, whereas those for dryland farming in semiarid regions were much larger (0.14–0.23). The interannual CV for total grain production of the world (excluding China because of the lack of data), however, was only 0.034. World production is near 1.5 Gt y$^{-1}$ (see Table 4.1) and while few aspects of human endeavor vary as little, CV = 0.034 corresponds to $\pm 50$ Mt of grain. In addition, that CV is significantly larger than 0.028 observed during an earlier period (1961–71) and is thus a basis for concern.

The possibility has been raised that present cultivars are increasingly similar in genetic structure, which might allow them to respond similarly to weather over large regions. That point was addressed by several authors in Anderson & Hazell (1989) but little correlation with cultivars was found. Duvick (1989), for example, found that variation in American maize yields per hectare are little different now than 60 y ago (CV near 0.1 in both periods). During those 60 y, yields increased more than threefold as open-pollinated cultivars were replaced by highly developed hybrids, planting densities doubled, tillage systems changed and planting became more timely, weeds were controlled with herbicides, and nutrient deficiencies were alleviated with fertilizer. Some change in the geographical distribution of production also occurred. To distinguish how each of these factors has contributed to gains in national and regional average yields per hectare is difficult (see discussion of genetic advances in Chapter 4); to partition their influence on variation is nearly impossible.

Several other hypotheses can be outlined to explain the slight trends in recent years for increasing national and global yield variation. One is that yield variation due to nutrient deficiencies, weeds, and pests has declined and that crops now respond more clearly to weather variations. Another is that part of the trend may be due to increasing variation in planted area due to fluctuations in supply and demand since variations in planted area may include changes in the proportion of the crop grown with marginal soils and climates.

Individual farmers experience greater interannual and field-to-field variation in yield than occurs on national and global scales. Variation in individual fields, however, is now much less with modern methods than was observed in the medieval period, or even during the past century when CV = 0.3 was common in Europe. CVs for individual fields in England (humid climate) in recent years range between 0.14 and 0.19 (Austin & Arnold 1989). Those authors also examined interannual data from individual fields in the Broadbalk experiment at Rothamsted, where crops well supplied with nitrogen from either fertilizer or legume rotations had CVs near 0.10 whereas those for unfertilized fields (0.17) and manured fields (0.18) were considerably larger. Manure, even in large amounts, has variable effectiveness depending on composition and time of application (Chapter 8).

## 3.3   ACCOMMODATING VARIATION

### Adjustments to normal variations

Most agricultural practices have the aim or effect of limiting yield variation. Variation cannot be avoided entirely, however, and many practices are designed to accommodate it or even exploit it. Storage facilities, for example, allow surpluses to be carried forward to years of low production. Coupled with expansion and contraction of production (by change in area or intensity), storage now accommodates large variations in production. The costs of such inventories (figured at the discount rate on the value of facilities and grain) is significant and is borne ultimately by consumers. The buffering role of animals discussed in Chapter 1 represents the

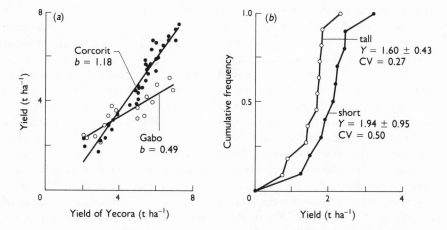

Fig. 3.3. (*a*) **Stability of long-season 'Corcorit' and early maturing 'Gabo' wheats plotted against the standard, 'Yecora', over a range of water supplies. Gabo offers greater stability and greater yield under drought but it responds poorly as water supply increases. (Adapted from Fischer & Maurer (1978).) (*b*) Cumulative frequency of observed wheat yields on an Australian farm with tall cultivars grown during the period 1964–74 and improved, short cultivars during the period 1975–84. The coefficient of variation nearly doubled with the change but that was offset by greater average yield. (Adapted from Anderson *et al.* (1989).)**

major means for expanding or contracting grain consumption and is a principal factor in the greater price elasticity for feed grains than for foods.

Income stabilization can be achieved in several ways. It is now common for perishable fruits and vegetables to be produced for processors and shippers under contracts that guarantee price and supply arrangements. In addition, farmers, like processors, are increasingly involved in futures markets and forward contracting for grain and other bulk commodities. Government and private sources of insurance are also available against hazards such as hailstorms.

Circumstances arise where it is better to exploit than to suppress the causes of yield variation. Examples occur in areas with variable rainfall (see Chapter 13). In the sensitivity analysis depicted in Fig. 3.3*a*, short-season 'Gabo' and long-season 'Corcorit' were compared over a controlled gradient of increasing moisture supply. From these results, one can predict that Gabo would always have a better chance of finding enough moisture to complete its life cycle than Corcorit and that its yield would fluctuate less over years. Even though Gabo gives greater yield with a small water supply, and its yields are more stable, it would fail to take full advantage of years with greater rainfall. Late-maturing Corcorit, however, is able to exploit the additional water resource. That, in fact, is the reason for its large variation in yield with water supply. Fixed costs of land preparation, seed, and overhead are the same for the two cultivars. Because fertilizer and harvesting costs will be only slightly greater with the long-season crop, it provides greater average return despite its greater variability (larger *b*).

   That yield can be more important than stability is illustrated with data for a historic series of wheat yields under ley-farming with limiting rainfall in Australia (Fig. 3.3b) (see Chapter 16 for a discussion of ley-farming). The CV on this farm for the period after the change to short-stature cultivars (0.50) was nearly twice that for the earlier period (0.27) but the mean yield was also 20% greater. Most Australian farmers adopted the new, more efficient cultivars and the CV for national production has also increased. Because the years during which the cultivars were used are different, it is not clear how much of the yield differences in Fig. 3.3b can be assigned to weather, to cultivars, or to other changes in management. None the less, the greater yield in every year more than compensated for the greater variability. Risk associated with farming declined but, because of elasticity in wheat prices, the decline was not as much as we might suspect from the increase in yield. The yields displayed in Fig. 3.3b were for the second crop of wheat in rotation sequence of clover–clover–wheat–wheat. Wheat after clover produced larger yields than wheat after wheat and with less difference in variability between tall and short cultivars. It seems with short cultivars that the first crop may reduce the supply of nitrogen and/ or water to a greater extent than did the older, tall, cultivars resulting in greater variation in the second crop.

   It is worth looking ahead to Fig. 13.6 as an example of the stability improvement that can be achieved through farming practice. For the period 1940–70, the mean yield with continuous wheat at that Nebraska (USA) site was $0.73 \pm 0.43$ t ha$^{-1}$ (CV = 0.70) with many years of crop failure. By contrast, the wheat–fallow rotation produced $2.48 \pm 0.74$ t ha$^{-1}$ (CV = 0.30). In this case, extended fallow increased the crop's supply of water through non-uniform treatment of the land in time.

   Many situations with variable length of growing season, due to variations in temperature or rainfall, are farmed more safely with indeterminate species than with determinate ones. The reason is that indeterminate plants tend to begin reproduction early and then to continue flowering until the season is terminated (Chapter 5). That allows good performance in both short and long seasons at the expense of a somewhat smaller harvest index and larger CV.

   Perennial crops and pastures differ from annual crops in their exposure to weather and other hazards. The short periods of time that annuals occupy the land can be chosen so as to reduce risks. Growth and yield of perennial crops, on the other hand, reflect weather for the entire season rather than only a portion. The effect is seen clearly with variable rainfall. Analogous to the Gabo example in Fig. 3.3a, an annual crop might always find sufficient moisture to complete a short life cycle independent of rainfall variation whereas production of a perennial pasture would vary over a wide range.

   This raises important questions about how graziers choose the stocking rates they employ in their pastures. A conservative rate, closer to the minimum performance of the pasture than to the maximum, is clearly necessary unless the pastures are supplemented by feed supplies such as hay produced in other fields. For this reason, most graziers in developed countries try to carry large reserves of hay, grain; or cash. The area planted to forage crops then can be varied according to carry-over supplies of hay. One can also adjust consumption. Accelerated culling of breeding stock and early sales of young animals are means for reducing feed requirements. Movement of livestock along gradients of productivity, from regions of low to high rainfall, for example, is another alternative (an example is presented in Chapter 16).

## Extreme variations and famine

Failures in agriculture arising from both human error and natural causes provide insights about present vulnerabilities and necessary preventive measures. Human errors involve mistakes in business management as well as in management of crops and livestock. Few guarantees exist against business failure in Western countries but the rate of failure is significantly less than in other endeavors. Among the reasons is that most land is closely held in family businesses with its capital value being passed by inheritance. In the USA, the proportion of farm land operated by family owners (now near 90%) has increased steadily since 1900. Operating capital is under greater risk than land ownership, and the circumstances of farming force most farmers to handle that prudently.

The greatest concern with natural causes is for failure of individual fields over wide areas due to uncommon regional weather or disease epidemics. Economic disruption and, in severe cases, famine due to food shortages may result. Famine has been a frequent event throughout history. Cox & Atkins (1979) make the point that most famines have occurred in regions with highly variable annual rainfall. Famines in India, for example, have occurred with deviations in the normal pattern of the monsoon rains. Subsistence populations without adequate reserve stores or means for imports are generally at the most risk. Stated another way, famine is a danger where human populations strain the carrying capacity of the land and supporting infrastructures. Problems in the African Sahel occur in this way. During this century, global communications and rapid dispatch of relief supplies from grain-surplus areas have helped reduce the impact of famine. Unfortunately, disruption of farming by war and social unrest, as occurred in the USSR during the 1920s and more recently in East Africa, have been as common a cause of food shortage as weather.

The European potato famine of the 1840s, although much less severe than many Asian famines, is the best known example to the western world. Potato, with its ease of culture and high merit as food, was one of the most important of the new crops that came to Europe from the New World. Introduced in the 1500s, it spread gradually through Europe and around the world. In Ireland, it became the staple food of tenant farmers engaged in grain production for export. With potato from their own garden plots providing abundant, high-quality food, the human population expanded rapidly. The land was subdivided to smaller and smaller plots with exorbitant rents and about 40% of the population were landless workers with no secure food supply (Woodham-Smith 1962). By 1845, the situation was ripe for disaster. European potato crops succumbed to a succession of epidemics of late blight fungus (*Phytophthora infestans*). The consequences in Ireland were particularly severe. By some estimates, 1.5 million Irish people died of starvation and 1–2 million emigrated during the next 6 y. On the continent, grain supplies helped meet food needs but, in Ireland, an oppressive and unresponsive political system offered no mechanism for diversion of wheat and oat supplies from export contracts, and imports of maize grain from America were too small and too late.

Late blight fungus is carried over winter in unharvested tubers and seed potatoes. In spring, fungal mycelia grow into the new shoots and sporulate. Germination of wind-blown spores and infection of new plants are favored by cool, wet, weather. The infection–sporulation cycle is short, allowing the disease to increase rapidly to epidemic proportions. Late blight now is controlled to some extent with plant resistance, crop rotation, and production of disease-free seed potatoes, but the fungus remains the most serious disease of potato.

## 3.4   DIVERSITY AND STABILITY

### The diversity–stability hypothesis

Charles Elton (1958), a prominent English ecologist, drew on circumstantial evidence to theorize that complex communities with high species diversity ought to be more stable in species numbers than simple ones because loss of a single species has only a small relative effect. Ramón Margalef (1969) of Spain, and others, considered this in relation to plant communities and added the hypothesis that net primary production should be inversely correlated with species diversity. A corollary theory, that diversity *causes* stability (stability in a broad sense of both variation and persistence), emerged from these concepts. Extended to agriculture where diversity is small, mostly in monocultures, and productivity high, the prediction was that agriculture is, *a priori*, unstable.

That diversity is the basis of productivity, species persistence, or stability is now rejected by ecologists (including Margalef; Goodman 1975). Failure of the diversity–stability theory is seen from examining species diversity over the course of plant succession in natural systems. Seral stages generally have the greatest diversity but species persistence is low (most exist only as passing actors during those stages) and the communities are unstable in the persistence sense. By contrast, many climax communities such as the Coast Redwood (*Sequoia sempervirens*) association of California, brigalow (*Acacia harpophylla*) shrublands of Queensland, and salt marshes have very high persistence in species numbers, but low species diversity. The present view of ecologists is that there is little or no evidence that diversity serves as an important basis for community stability in natural systems.

The 'diversity-lends-stability' theory was intuitively attractive. Because it seemed to provide a theoretical basis for a multitude of issues, it became a tenet of alternative agriculturalists. Diversity arguments, based vaguely in the Elton–Margalef theory, continue to appear about income stability, monoculture vs. polyculture, diverse habitats for insect predators and biological control, and about slowing the spread of foliar diseases (see multilines, Chapter 4). Those supposed advantages have been demonstrated only rarely in practice, however. On the other hand, within-field diversity (polyculture) creates a number of obstacles to stability in addition to the problem of balancing competition (Chapter 2). In particular, soil-borne diseases and insects may increase because susceptible host species are always present in polycultures whereas continued monoculture or rotation through a sequence of monocultures (a different type of diversity) can bring a decline in inoculum levels.

### Diversity and risk in agriculture

Persistence of arable crops within a farming system depends on very different principles than operate in natural communities. As long as a crop continues to be relatively free of problems and is successful in economic terms, farmers will continue to plant it, and the species will persist within the system. Freedom from problems means that control of weeds, pests and diseases has been gained with resistant cultivars, tillage, rotation, biocides, or other means. Economic success depends on markets and thus on events in the larger society as well as on costs of production.

With greater return, greater economic risk can be accepted. Winter frosts have devastated citrus orchards in Florida (USA) twice during the past century, most recently in the 1980s. Resilience is evident because growers have re-established plantings at great expense after each disaster. Competition from lower-cost producers in Brazil and North Africa, and fears about future weather, are slowing the current replant, but the rewards are apparently still sufficient to justify long-term investments in trees. Other pursuits such as forestry or grazing on permanent pastures would be more stable ecologically in this region but, with much smaller economic returns, the economic risks might actually be greater. A greater frequency of severe frost or lower prices for citrus would shift the balance sharply.

Wheat production in the American Great Plains is at risk to both drought and cold. Farming there was not successful until the 1880s, when Mennonite immigrants from Russia introduced winter-hardy Crimean wheats (Quisenberry & Reitz 1974). Arable farming expanded throughout the area, much of it in marginal areas and with unsafe methods. Droughts during the 1930s ('dust bowl' years) brought a significant contraction in farming accompanied by a major emigration of people. Farming there is now by safer methods (see 'stubble mulching', Chapter 12) but yields still vary greatly with weather and complete crop failure due to drought is not uncommon. The capital cost of replanting annual crops is much less than for tree crops, however. Using conservative, low-cost methods, Plains farmers tolerate failure as frequently as one in five to one in ten years. As in Florida, the alternative of cattle ranching is less attractive.

The distribution of dominant crops along a transect of increasing rainfall (but similar temperatures) in the USA from Colorado through Illinois is depicted in Fig. 3.4. Maize and soybean are dominant in eastern areas with high rainfall but are replaced by wheat in drier regions. Drought is a greater risk to maize and soybean than to wheat at the western margins of their zones, whereas wheat is at an economic disadvantage to maize and soybean further east. Variations in the proportions of maize and soybean in regions with more than 700 mm annual rainfall are related to topography: maize offers greater protection against erosion on sloping land. Types of wheat differ along the spectrum: hard red wheats are grown west of Iowa and soft

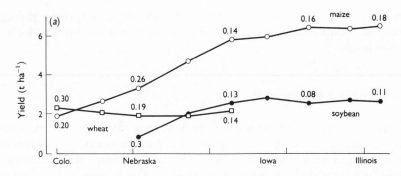

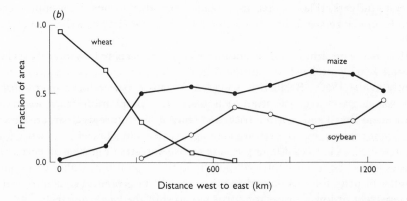

**Fig. 3.4.** (*a*) **Distribution of mean grain yields in the USA (during the 1980s) for wheat, maize, and soybean under dryland conditions along a transect of increasing annual rainfall with mean July temperatures near 24 °C. The transect extends from eastern Colorado (long. 103° W) through Nebraska and Iowa to eastern Illinois (long. 88° W). The numbers are interannual coefficients of variation for representative groups of counties.** (*b*) **Areas cropped to wheat, maize, and soybean as fractions of the total non-irrigated land given to these crops along the transect described in** (*a*)**.**

red wheats to the east, with their peak production further east in Ohio. Oat is grown on 5–10% of the arable lands receiving more than 600 mm of rainfall; grain sorghum is found along the entire spectrum but is significant only in the 500–600 mm zone, where it accounts for up to 20% of the dryland crops. Transects with July temperatures greater than 24 °C (Oklahoma) reveal increasing substitution of sorghum for maize; with lower temperatures (Canada), wheat replaces maize. All of these crops have been tried along the entire spectrum but they persist only where adaptation, economic return, and a present lack of superior alternatives combine to determine the safest choice for farmers. The ratio of grain prices, maize:wheat:soybean, is generally near 1:1.5:3. Fig. 3.4 reveals the important point that high economic return and sustainability (erosion control) are more important than stability (small variation in yield) in American farmers' choices among crops.

Agricultural systems involving continuous culture of rice in Southeast Asia and wheat and barley in the Middle East have persisted for many thousands of years. Among the reasons are that those crops are not highly demanding of nutrients or, except for barley, particularly sensitive to soil pH. We can assume that farming was attempted during earlier times on most lands within those regions and that some areas did fail owing to salinization, erosion, or other problems. Those problems have been corrected in areas that continue in farming, or they are less subject to such hazards. The continuing existence of those farming systems is comforting but it does not mean that side consequences such as soil erosion or disease will not subvert farmers' efforts, or that future climate and economic changes will not bring an end to certain cropping practices. Yet through history, dramatic changes in agriculture have been due more often to the appearance of superior new alternatives than to the failure of older systems. Potato, for example, is still an important crop in Ireland because we now know something about controlling the extent and severity of late blight.

**Diversity and increased risk**  Questions arise about whether greater species diversity among fields within a farm (a greater number of monocultures) might better insulate the enterprise from variations in markets and natural hazards, giving economic stability. We can analyze this concept by assuming that farmers choose their crops from among those that are 'safest' for their region. In one sense, diversity of cropping increases the risk of farming; in another, it may reduce it. Let us examine each of these propositions in turn.

Safest must be defined in economic terms as well as by vulnerability to weather and other factors. If the first crop chosen for a farm is the safest, then the second by definition is less safe, and the third and fourth even less so. The simple result of adding more crops is that a greater range and degree of risks are encountered, and the economic–ecological stability of the enterprise is most likely less. Consider a simple case where economic returns for several crops are the same and their weather vulnerability can be ranked. If the chance of failure for the first crop is 0.1, for the second 0.2, and for the third 0.3, the weighted mean risk of crop failure with $\frac{1}{3}$ of the farm planted to each is twice that of the safest crop:

$$R = 0.33(0.1 + 0.2 + 0.3) = 0.2.$$

A rebuttal to this argument, that all crop is lost when disaster strikes the safest, in contrast to only a portion of the crop when greater diversity is employed, does not change the fact that increased diversity has increased risk. The real problem with our argument is that farmers seldom have perfect information about differences in risk factors for their crops. In addition, farmers differ in their need to avoid variations in income, and in their access to storage, insurance, bank financing, and other means of accommodating income variation. Farmers with marginal finances have greater need than those with secure finances for a flow of produce and income in every year despite the smaller average return.

Concentration on just a few crops provides greater safety in other ways as well. Farmers recognize that the knowledge and skills needed for farming differ between crops and that specialization permits one to reach a high level of competence. The Renaissance person who can master all at hand is rare. Also, a smaller range of equipment and facilities is needed when crop diversity is limited, resulting in less capital investment per farm.

**Diversity and risk reduction**   On-farm diversity is commonly a response to needs unrelated to weather variation and markets. Included here are needs for crop rotation (e.g. for disease control), for a variety of feeds for livestock, and for an even flow of labor. The concept of 'labor', including that required in management, opens several interesting issues. An even distribution of labor allows a single farmer to farm a larger area and thus achieve a larger annual return for labor. On large farms, some diversity of crops reduces exosure to adverse weather by allowing operations for each crop to be completed in a timely manner. If most of the land is given to the safest crop, it may be difficult to concentrate the work of land preparation, planting and harvest into the necessary small windows of time. Some operations may not be completed in time thus increasing variability and risk, with the result that the 'safest crop' is no longer so safe. In mechanized systems, and in labor-intensive agriculture as well, moderate diversification allows most tasks to be performed at the right time with family labor (Chapter 15). In developed countries, machines substitute for labor in the achievement of timeliness over larger areas of land. Recent trends towards larger tractors seem to be driven as much by the safety and yield advantage found in timeliness, and by the desire for increased time for leisure, as by a need for larger farms. An example coupling diversity and timeliness is given with the maize–soybean rotation for Iowa agriculture in Chapter 17.

Crop rotation is an important tool for risk management, particularly where crops are plagued with soil-borne diseases or insects. Rotation with a non-susceptible crop or fallow allows a period of sanitation during which inoculum declines through starvation, decay, or predation. Most plant pathogens are poor saprophytes and suffer from competition and attack by superior decay organisms when hosts are absent. Best control occurs when crop residues are burned or incorporated with soil.

Crops that 'trap' pathogens, for example, by stimulating their germination from resting stages but failing as a host for reproduction, would be ideal in rotation. Unfortunately, few trap crops are known for plant diseases. Their use is more common with insect problems. An example occurs in California with lygus bug (*Lygus hesperus*) where alfalfa and cotton are grown in rotation (Flint & van den Bosch 1981). Lygus has a strong preference for alfalfa but it has little effect on forage yields because it feeds on flowers and flower buds. When the forage is harvested, however, the lygus migrate and take temporary residence in cotton fields with devastating effects on reproductive yields. Two 'integrated pest-management' alternatives to applying insecticides to alfalfa have emerged. One involves cutting alfalfa in alternating strips so that lygus remain with the crop; the second approach is to interplant cotton with sacrificial rows of alfalfa which 'trap' migrating lygus away from cotton.

Take-all fungal disease of cereals (*Gaeumannomyces graminis*) offers insights into biological control of soil-borne agents (Cook & Baker 1983). This disease destroys the roots and crowns of wheat and other grasses. No source of resistance has been found in wheat, and take-all can be a serious problem when wheat is grown after wheat or when certain grasses remain as weeds in intervening crops. 'Suppressive' soils, leading to abatement of the disease, can form when wheat is grown every year, however. In those cases, take-all is suppressed through antibiosis and competition for iron by populations of pseudomonad bacteria, which increase with continuous wheat. Control by development of suppressive soils is not uncommon with continuous monoculture. Suppression of common potato scab (*Streptomyces scabies*) occurs in a similar way. Alternatives to continuous wheat for control of take-all include long fallow, rotation, and development of an acid soil. Take-all does not form resistant spores and survives for only a short time when hosts are absent. In Australian winter-rainfall zones, take-all on wheat is controlled effectively with fallow and through rotation with crops (lupin, field pea, or rapeseed) or annual pasture (subterranean clover or medic), providing grasses are controlled with herbicides or, for pasture, through intensive grazing by sheep.

Control of diseases through rotation reveals something of the subtle effects that can arise through crop sequences and it is tempting to view rotation as a panacea for any ill. Detecting and unraveling such effects are difficult tasks, however, requiring long-term studies (Cook & Baker 1983). Survey research of farmers' fields subjected to particular rotations is a better source of clues than costly station experiments because rotation effects are often site- or situation-specific: what works at one place is not effective at another. Take-all, for example, is more severe with alkaline soils and problems may be exacerbated by liming to permit rotation with certain legumes. Common potato scab is less severe in moist soils, owing perhaps to competition by non-pathogenic bacteria. This seems to be one reason why potato is commonly grown with irrigation. Not only do rotation effects on take-all and potato scab differ with soil condition, including fertility, but other problems including other diseases, dictating different approaches, then come into play.

Few universal axioms can be proposed for the practice of crop rotation. Possibilities for disease control and benefits from legumes (nitrogen fixation) are among them. We can also list benefits from weed control through rotation of crops with different cultural practices, occasional scavenging of deep moisture and nutrients with a deep-rooted crop, and reduction of erosion with sod crops. Trade-offs are always involved since income may be reduced and weeds and diseases may increase with rotation. Successful rotations are those that offer, on balance, more benefits to income and risk reduction than they cost.

## 3.5  SOME UNCERTAINTIES ABOUT THE FUTURE

Lacking long-range forecasts for weather, markets, and disease, farmers make choices about crops and risks based on past experience. Inevitably, this leads to a degree of caution and conservatism, with preservation of the enterprise taking precedence over possible gains from radical changes in practice. An example in Chapter 16 demonstrates how use of phosphorus fertilizer in Australia began only when high prices for wool served to finance the practice. 'Watching-the-neighbor' try new things is a game played by most farmers. Two time-constants constrain changes on individual farms: the lifetime of machinery and tools (5–10 y) and the lifetime of farmers as decision-makers (*ca.* 25 y). These properties are randomized among farms, however, and change within a region tends to be evolutionary with time. Even though the experiments may be small, and only a small fraction of farmers may engage in innovation, the number of farmers is large and change in farming is surprisingly rapid. Let us consider two uncertainties about the future, weather and biocides, and how they may force adjustments in agricultural practices.

### Uncertain weather

Identifying whether a weather event is a short-term aberration – the $\frac{1}{100}$ y drought sequence, for example – or a sign of a more permanent change is very difficult. Most cropping practices are conservative in the sense that they accommodate significant year-to-year variation in weather while minimizing down-side risks. If a weather event is just an aberration, farmers can stay with proven methods, but if the change is permanent, different crops and cultural practices may be needed. Agriculture may soon face major decisions of that sort due to changes in global climates. Several factors, including natural fluctuations in Sun–Earth geometry and solar activity, could change climates significantly. Of immediate concern are changes in the composition of the atmosphere owing to rising concentrations of 'greenhouse gases' such as $CO_2$ (Chapter 6). One prediction is that an increase in greenhouse gases could cause a rise in global mean temperature and a redistribution of rainfall. Such forecasts are hampered by gaps in our understanding of past climate changes and because general circulation models (GCMs) designed to simulate atmospheric circulations and climate are not yet entirely equal to the task (Mearns *et al.* 1990). Lack of knowledge about the roles of oceans, and lack of computer capacity, are key problems.

Rough estimates of the consequences of a global warming are possible, starting with the present distribution of crops. Optimal cropping systems for each region would change following the principle of substitution seen in Fig. 3.4. Because annual crops occupy the land for only a portion of the year, simple adjustments in planting date may suffice to place a crop in a suitable environment. Some crops will be displaced geographically, however. With warmer climates, cropping zones will shift to higher latitudes. Prognosis is complicated by the fact that rising $CO_2$ will have a beneficial fertilizing effect (Chapter 10) and will also improve the water-use efficiency of crops (Chapter 9). Crop simulation models that might be used to make quantitative predictions about these effects are not yet adequate for the task.

How agriculture might respond to an actual climate change depends very much on how rapidly the change occurred. With a slow transition to a predictable end-point, present agricultural systems could evolve to a new state through gradual changes in crops and methods of production. Rapid change, on the other hand, could cause enormous dislocation (Bryson & Murray 1977).

### Biocides: from rats to men

Herbicides, fungicides, and insecticides have a large stabilizing effect on crop production. Herbicides, for example, are credited with 23% of the threefold increase in maize yields in Minnesota since 1930 (see Table 4.5) and fungicidal treatment of seed has given enormous improvements in stand emergence. Biocides receive significant credit for the continuing improvements in human nutrition and longevity but they also may be hazards to human health through residues in food and contamination of water supplies. Benefits to farming can be quantified but assessments of risks and benefits to health are more complex. Given this uncertainty, and examples of careless and unnecessary use of poorly designed biocides, it is not surprising that biocide residues in food became a widespread public concern.

Governments responded with examinations of risks to health, registration procedures, and bans on some biocides. In the USA, efforts by the Environmental Protection Agency (EPA) to establish tolerance levels for biocide residues in food have been a source of controversy (National Research Council 1987). EPA gives major attention to whether or not a biocide may be 'oncogenic' (capable of inducing a benign or malignant tumor). This therefore includes all 'carcinogenic' materials that cause malignant tumors, i.e. cancers. Birth and mutagenic effects are also considered. Cancer can occur when normal cells are exposed to mutagenesis during cell division. In addition to chemicals, natural oxidants, viruses, and radiation have been implicated as mutagenic agents. Cancerous events are normally arrested by immune systems but those systems decline in effectiveness with age and as other causes of death are eliminated or reduced, the frequency of cancer must inevitably increase. The background level of significant cancers in the USA is 0.25 per lifetime; if one lives long enough, the chance approaches 100%.

The possibility that food contaminants may increase the frequency of cancers in humans is not testable by any direct measurements, and epidemiological evidence for the occurrence of problems has not been found. Given our inability to conduct experiments with humans, tolerances are established in tests with animals such as rats. The tests involve chronic exposure of the test organisms to toxic doses and then scaling down the effective dose to a small tolerance level that humans might safely receive in a standard diet over a period of 70 y. Tolerances are set conservatively to insure that risks are 'negligible' despite local variations from the standard diet.

Current US laws allow that tolerances set for *unprocessed commodities* may balance risk with benefit (importance in production or assurance of food quality). For those commodities, EPA normally approves tolerance levels with maximum oncogenic risks < 0.000 001 per lifetime, and in a few cases as large as 0.000 1 per lifetime. By contrast, no oncogenic residues are permitted in *processed foods* unless the risk is zero; the only way to have zero risk from an oncogen is to avoid residues completely by banning use of that material. The difference between 'negligible' and 'zero' is important because a law based on the neglible-risk concept would permit further lowering of risks by changing to safer chemicals whereas zero-risk inhibits substitution.

NRC (1987) considered a group of oncogenic materials accounting for more than half of the total biocide use in the USA. Their study found, if all foods carry *maximum* tolerances of *all* approved biocides and risks are additive, that the upper bound for the risk of cancer is < 0.001 per lifetime. In other words, cancer risk might be increased from 0.250 to 0.251 by those biocides. This risk is by definition 'negligible' because 0.001 is not detectably different from 0, or even from a negative risk (positive benefit) to health; however, 0.001 times the current USA population (250 million) equals 250 000 persons. Fungicides account for 59% of the risk, herbicides for 27%, and insecticides for 14%. A large share of the total risk was laid to only a few chemicals and crops.

Actual residue levels generally are very much less than EPA tolerances and 0.001 is thus a generous overestimate of real risks. Archibald & Winter (1989) found that only a few of the biocides registered for use with each crop are actually employed in any one field and many crops are not treated at all. Because a majority of samples from treated fields have no residues, and the average residue level from treated fields is only about 0.1 of tolerances, Archibald & Winter set the additive risk of cancer due to major biocides at 0.000 000 2 to 0.000 000 01 per lifetime. Ames & Gold (1990) challenged the entire approach to setting tolerances. Their point is that feeding toxic levels causes injury and thus stimulates cell division. Dividing cells reveal, as tumors, mutagenic defects arising from any source, including natural oxidants and radiation. In other words, it is toxicity at massive doses rather than oncogenicity that is being tested by EPA. They note that approximately the same proportion (50%) of the biochemicals naturally present in foods are oncogenetic in rat tests as is the case for biocides. The content of natural products in foods is vastly greater, however. Only a few biochemicals have been tested but 1.5 g of these are found, mainly in fruits and vegetables, in a standard daily diet compared with only 0.1 mg of biocides (a ratio of 15 000:1). A single cup of coffee, for example, contains 100 times the daily dose of biocides. It seems that the only certain thing about food is that not eating is more dangerous to health than eating!

The negligible risk from biocides is not easily explained to a public that tends to differentiate strongly between small hidden risks extended through 'common' resources (air, water, food) (Hardin 1977) and personal decisions to engage in far greater risks, such as riding in automobiles. Whether the public might accept 'negligible risk' as a substitute for 'zero risk' in parts of current laws is problematic. An ironic aspect of this dilemma is that our expanding food needs are due to an exploding population brought about by control of human diseases with another group of chemicals (pharmaceuticals) that includes many oncogens.

Diminished access to fungicides for seed treatment would have serious impacts for most crops. Loss of herbicides would probably create the most difficulty for field crops, which, because of their low value, cannot support the more expensive alternatives of hand- or machine-cultivation for weed control that are possible with high-valued fruits and vegetables. Insecticides and post-emergence fungicides are seldom used with field crops although exceptions occur with cotton (control of lygus and bollworm insects) and in Europe with wheat production (control of aphids and leaf pathogens). In contrast, production of fruits and vegetables is more dependent upon biocides and at some locations (e.g. humid regions) it would no longer be competitive without the use of fungicides and insecticides.

The search for alternative methods is clearly important. Most of those proposed for weed control by another NRC panel (National Research Council 1989a) (rotation, high density, and tillage) are widely employed at present, however, and not particularly effective. Cultivation, for example, has significant costs in fuel, labor, compaction, and soil erosion and some rotations actually make weed control more difficult. Others methods, including weed-specific diseases and phytophagous insects, have been given many years of research with little success. It seems that the future may hold more molds and weeds and thus smaller and more variable yields.

## 3.6  MAINTENANCE OF AGRICULTURAL SYSTEMS

Agricultural systems depend on human effort for maintenance of the essential biological, soil, and human resources. Off-farm, maintenance takes form in provision of drainage and irrigation systems, regulation of markets and biocides, scientific and technological research, and the education of farmers. On-farm, the principal concerns are for maintenance of soil fertility, proper drainage, weed control, and protection from erosion.

The need for scientific effort is seen clearly with diseases and insects. Weaknesses in the resistance of existing cultivars and the continued evolution of diseases and insects necessitate major efforts in plant breeding just to maintain a *status quo*. Similar problems occur when weed species develop tolerance to current herbicides. Competent diagnosis and correction is also needed in dealing with inevitable changes in soils and soil fertility. Much of the world's arable land is still new to farming, and nutrient deficiencies continue to appear as original supplies are exhausted. In addition to efforts toward erosion control, drainage is needed to insure yield in humid areas and to prevent salinization in semiarid regions.

Maintenance of human resources is perhaps less obvious. The skill levels of young farmers are developed mainly in traditional ways through apprenticeship with parents and others, but education, particularly basic literacy to facilitate continued learning, is essential (Ruttan 1982). Business affairs and the technology of farming in developed nations are now complex, and advanced education is increasingly beneficial for success in farming.

A significant portion of the benefits from research and education accrue to the larger society, through lower cost and safer supplies of food, and through assurance of future supplies. Recognition of those relationships has led to government-sponsored programs including research and extension in most countries. In the developed nations, those commitments have weakened in the face of adequate food and declines in the agrarian population and there is now little support for maintenance research in many countries. What difficulties may result remain to be seen. Real professional competence in breeding, pathology, and economic entomology requires years of experience. Plant breeders, for example, must become familiar with a wide range of germplasm. Without continuing activity in those fields, society may lack the technological skills necessary for response to future crises.

Government policy can affect the viability of agriculture in other ways. A farmer's sense of land stewardship, no matter how strong, can be subverted by social rules, such as price controls that place returns below costs, subsidies that distort markets, or oppressive taxes, that place farming at a disadvantage. Special problems occur with maintenance activities such as terracing for erosion control.

There, the present worth of future benefits accruing during a farmer's lifetime is generally much less than costs. Continued farming without preventive practices may allow erosion at greater than tolerable rates, degrading the land's production potential. Off-site consequences of erosion include silting of lakes and streams that are common resources for all. Some governments share costs with farmers for such conservation projects in recognition of both farmers' responsibility for externalities and the public's benefit from future productivity and from protection of the commons.

Issues with the commons also arise from off-farm flows of nutrients and agricultural chemicals, and with pollution of the common air by wind-blown soil and by smoke from agricultural burning. Some of those issues are examined in later chapters. Difficulties with the commons take a different form in fishing, and in pastoral cultures of Africa and Asia where animals owned by individuals graze the common pasture. In those cases, no 'fences' exist to delineate an individual's share of the common resource. In fishing, the share depends upon the numbers of hours spent fishing and number and size of boats employed. In grazing, it depends on the number of animals owned. Inevitably, the commons is overgrazed to the detriment of all.

## 3.7   SUMMARY

Farming is a variable and thus a risky business. In contrast to natural systems, where species persistence is the focus of concerns about stability, agricultural stability is evaluated more from year-to-year and field-to-field variations in yield. Variable weather, weeds, disease, and markets are the major sources of risk. Impacts of climate are greatest with dryland farming in semiarid regions with large variations in rainfall. The coefficient of the interannual variation of wheat production in Australia (CV = 0.22), for example, is more than three times that in Germany (CV = 0.06). Small variation in yield is generally perceived as desirable, yet farming is most efficient when the best use is made of current weather, i.e. when production expands and contracts with temperature and rainfall.

Yield variation is now much less than in the 1800s and earlier but it is not clear which technological changes should be given credit. Fertilizer, biocides, drainage, and machinery are important factors. The greater disease resistance of modern cultivars also is clearly important but other components of genetic stability are probably much less important.

The future holds numerous uncertainties for farming. Climate change, further restrictions of biocides, and increased demand due to population growth will perhaps have the greatest impacts. While it is certain that people will continue to need food, much of the future stability of farming will depend on the course of these factors and on the ability of farmers and supporting services to respond. The continuing education of farmers and the existence of competent programs in plant breeding, entomology, plant pathology, and soils are examples of components needed to maintain a viable agriculture.

## 3.8 FURTHER READING

Anderson, J. R. and P. B. R. Hazell (ed). 1989. *Variability in grain yields.* Johns Hopkins University Press, Baltimore, Maryland. 384 p.

Bryson, R. A. and T. J. Murray. 1977. *Climates of hunger: mankind and the world's changing weather.* University of Wisconsin Press, Madison. 171 p.

Finlay, K. W. and G. N. Wilkinson. 1963. The analysis of adaptation in a plant breeding programme. *Aust. J. Agric. Res.* **14**:742–54.

Goodman, D. 1975. The theory of diversity-stability relationships in ecology. *Quart, Rev. Biol.* **50**:237–61.

# 4

## Genetic resources

### 4.1  INTRODUCTION

Crop plants carry information acquired during their evolution and breeding that defines their performance in agricultural fields. That information is held in the genetic material of living plants and is subject to change through mutation and through recombination into new patterns, and can be lost. Proper management of this resource involves knowing the capabilities of germplasms, maintaining and improving their genetic constitution, and employing them advantageously in farming.

Terminology relating to genetic resources is in a state of flux. Here we use **germplasm** to denote the totality of genes and genetic combinations found in a species, or a major portion of it. A **genetic population** (sometimes 'line' or 'strain') describes a smaller group of individuals (plants or seed) that share common ancestry and genes, and thus common traits. This use of the term population differs from that of population ecologists, who use it to denote closely related individuals that cohabit in time and space.

### 4.2  GENETIC DIVERSITY IN AGRICULTURE

**Species diversity**

Genetic diversity in farming must be defined at several levels. At the species level, thousands of plant species have been cultivated by humans at some time or place, and several hundred are currently employed as crops, yet the great majority of crop production is derived from only a small number. Data presented in Table 4.1 account for most of the production from the arable lands and permanent crops. The production shown there equals about 640 kg dry matter (*ca.* 7.9 GJ) for each of the present world population, compared with 500 kg and 8.4 GJ of the SNU (Section 1.7). More than 60% of that production is grain, large portions of which are fed to animals and reach us indirectly in animal products. Major contributions to food supply are derived through other sources of animal feed (residues, forages grown on arable lands, and permanent grazing lands) but good data about those sources are not available. The 1989 FAO Production Yearbook estimates that animal

Table 4.1 *World areas and production of principal crops, 1988*

Cereal and pulse production values have been adjusted for an assumed 0.86 dry matter fraction. Values in parentheses are estimated.

| Crop | Area (Mha) | Production (Mt dry matter) |
|---|---|---|
| Wheat | 220 | 438 |
| Rice (paddy) | 146 | 416 |
| Maize | 127 | 349 |
| Barley | 76 | 145 |
| Sorghum & millet | 86 | 80 |
| Other (oat, rye, etc.) | 47 | 70 |
| Total cereals | 702 | 1498 |
| Potato | 18 | 57 |
| Cassava | 14 | 48 |
| Sweet potato, yam, etc. | 14 | 49 |
| Total root and tuber | 46 | 154 |
| Sugarcane | 16 | 99 |
| Sugarbeet | 9 | 41 |
| Total sugar crops | 25 | 140[1] |
| Total pulses[2] | 68 | 47 |
| Soybean | 55 | 92 |
| Peanut (in shell) | 20 | 23 |
| Cotton (seed) | 34 | 53 |
| Sunflower | 15 | 21 |
| Rapeseed | 17 | 22 |
| Other oilseed | 13 | 5 |
| Total legume & oilseed | 222 | 263 |
| Total vegetables & melons | (27) | 46[3] |
| Total fruits & berries | na | 31[3] |
| Total nuts | na | 2[3] |
| Total all crops | (1022) | 2380 |
| Arable land[4] | 1373 | |
| Permanent crops[4] | 100 | |
| Permanent pasture | 3214 | |
| Total ice-free land | 13080 | |

*Notes:*
[1] Sugar production.
[2] Includes dry beans, pea, chickpea, and broad bean.
[3] Vegetables, melon, fruits, and berries assumed to have 20% dry matter; nuts in shell assumed to have 50% edible dry matter.
[4] Total 'arable land' given to temporary crops is 1022 Mha; the balance (1373 − 1022 = 351 Mha) includes temporary meadow and fallow; 'permanent crops' includes all tree and vine crops (fruits, nuts, berries, grapes, rubber, cocoa, coffee, and tea).
*Source:* 1989 FAO Production Yearbook.

production supplies about 16% of the energy in our diets and about 34% of the protein. Additional amounts come from fish and home gardens but, again, information about those sources is poor or non-existent.

Four species from the family Gramineae – wheat, rice, maize, and barley – account for more than half the total production shown in Table 4.1. Even discounting amounts fed to animals, cereals are clearly the major sources of energy and protein in our diets. The number of agricultural species expands considerably only when forage, pasture, and horticultural species are included.

Very great diversity is available in horticultural species (see *Bailey's Hortus*; Staff of the L. H. Bailey Hortorium 1976). Fruits and vegetables are important sources of vitamins, minerals, and roughage, and they add desirable diversity to our tables, but their place in agriculture and their contribution to food supplies are small. Less than 8% of the world's plant production comes from vegetables, melons, fruits, berries, and nuts; white potato alone accounts for more than 30% of that. Some produce is also obtained from household gardens.

Limited species diversity is not a recent phenomenon in agriculture; rather, it seems always to have been that way. The archeological evidence is that domestication was a gradual process and that a small number of crops satisfied basic food needs within each region where agriculture developed (Smith 1990). Movement of species around the globe results in a much greater diversity of crops for each region than was available to earlier cultures. In the USA, for example, maize, sorghum, wheat (several species), oat, barley, rice, beans, potato, sugarcane, and sugarbeet all serve as carbohydrate sources whereas native Americans cultivated mainly maize, beans, and squash.

There are several reasons why cereals continue as dominant crops: they satisfy basic dietary needs; as annual generalists they fit well in a broad range of environments; and they can be grown easily and safely. As noted in Chapter 1, human and animal nutrition rests mainly on dietary requirements for protein and energy. To be useful as a staple food, a plant must contribute those, or supply a material such as cellulose that can be converted by animals into a basic food. Cereals, with high digestibility and 8–14% protein content and 60–80% carbohydrate, supply protein and energy as well as or better than other groups of plants. In addition, dry grain has high bulk density and is easily transported and stored.

The relative safety of cereals from disease and insects is perhaps unexpected until we recall that resistance is the common trait while susceptibility is rare. We have yet to observe wheat succumb to measles, for example (or to encounter humans infected by the rust fungus of small grains). Insects and disease are in fact serious problems in agriculture but in any one region, the number of such hazards facing cereal crops is generally small, allowing focused efforts for relief through breeding ('maintenance' research) and management.

Considerable research effort has been given to the development of new crops, and to resurrecting old ones, but the number of successes in those efforts is small. Grain amaranths, for example, were once a staple crop in the Americas and, to a limited extent, elsewhere. In comparison to cereals, amaranths offer similar protein and carbohydrate but they suffer disadvantages in their small seed (with a large proportion of indigestible seed coat) and small harvest index. Those factors perhaps contributed to their displacement from Meso-America in prehistoric times by maize. The high content of lysine in amaranth seed proteins has been cited as justification for making efforts to improve their potential as crops, but cereal grains are already nutritionally adequate in that regard. One of the difficulties for 'new crops' such as grain amaranths is that a large investment in research is needed just to evaluate whether they might be brought to a level of performance competitive with existing crops.

Sugarbeet is one of the crops that have been advanced to new roles through plant breeding research. French scientists developed it as a sugar crop for temperate zones after the French navy's defeat by the British at Trafalgar in 1805 deprived France of West Indian sugar. Although successful, the crop lacks both wide resistance and a large germplasm bank and requires intensive maintenance research to continue as a competitive crop. More recently, the roles of soybean, sunflower, rapeseed, narrow-leafed lupin (Australia), and safflower as oil crops, and a cereal, triticale (derived from hybrids of wheat and rye), have been significantly advanced by plant breeding. Despite the small number of successful new crops, the present importance of these examples to agriculture justifies continuing efforts with other species.

**Agricultural cultivars**

During domestication with selection by man, and more recently through breeding, the genetic diversity of the wild ancestors of our crops has been segregated and maintained in populations with relatively narrow genetic bases. In earlier times, when farmers simply saved the best and brightest seed from their own fields as planting stock, distinct local populations emerged through natural selection to local environments and farming practices. Coupled with removal of undesirable plant types and/or positive selection of desirable types, such populations differentiated regionally into **landraces**. In modern times, landraces have gradually been displaced by more carefully bred populations possessing distinctive traits. These are given names as **cultivars**. The term cultivar (*culti*vated *vari*ety) is used in preference to **variety**, which applies in botanical taxonomy to morphologically and geographically distinct subgroups of species. Varieties are given Latinized names whereas cultivars are not.

A cultivar's genetic structure depends on how it is propagated, the mating system of the species, and on tactical choices about the type of matings to allow. **Clonal lines**, for example, are propagated vegetatively without sexual reproduction and the opportunities that reproduction offers for genetic exchanges. As a result, clonally propagated cultivars of crops such as potato, asparagus, bermudagrass, and sugarcane generally consist of a single genotype. The same is true for most tree and vine crops and many ornamental species. One of the advantages of clonal propagation is that a superior genotype, even a highly heterozygous one, can be propagated indefinitely without change. By contrast, hybridization, segregation, and recombination can occur with each generation of seed production and considerable attention must be given to controlling changes in genetic structure. Recombination of genes on a particular chromosome occurs through breakage of

Table 4.2 *Reproduction and planting methods, and types of cultivars used with several important crops*

The order of the crops follows that in Table 4.1. HYB, hybrid; IB, inbreeding; IBL, inbred line; IBOB, inbreeder with some outbreeding; OB, outbreeding; OPP, open-pollinated; PP, polyploids; SYN, synthetic.

| Crop | Reproduction | Propagation | Cultivar types |
|---|---|---|---|
| Wheat | IB | seed | IBL |
| Rice | IB | seed | IBL |
| Maize | OP | seed | HYB, OPP |
| Barley | IB | seed | IBL |
| Sorghum | IBOB | seed | HYB, OPP–IBL |
| Oat | IB | seed | IBL |
| Potato | OB | clone | HYB[1] |
| Cassava | OB | clone | HYB[1] |
| Sugarcane | OB | clone | HYB[1] |
| Sugarbeet | OB | seed | HYB, PP |
| Dry bean | IB | seed | IBL |
| Soybean | IB | seed | IBL |
| Peanut | IB | seed | IBL |
| Cotton | IBOB | seed | IBL |
| Sunflower | OB | seed | HYB, OPP |
| Alfalfa | OB | seed | SYN, OPP |
| Clover | OB | seed | SYN, OPP |
| Ryegrass | OB | seed | OPP |

*Note:*
[1] These species flower weakly.
*Source:* Adapted in part from Simmonds (1979).

the chromosome and reassembly with portions of the analogous chromosome from another parent.

**Open-pollinated species** (reproduction with pollen from any nearby plant) are normally outbreeding and even selected populations are highly heterogeneous unless pollen source and seed parent are controlled by isolation from other sources. **Self-pollinated species** (reproduction with pollen from the same plant) such as barley, cotton, and wheat, on the other hand, are largely inbred and thus homozygous at most gene loci (but not completely, since outbreeding rates of 1–2% are common). The mating systems of several important crops and tactics employed for cultivar development and propagation are summarized in Table 4.2.

## 4.3   CHANGE IN GENETIC STRUCTURE

### Selection

The genetic structure of an agricultural population is defined by the particular genes, their relative frequency in the population, and by their combination with other genes. Structure is subject to change during reproduction through natural or induced mutation of genes, through loss of genes, by introduction of genes from other populations, and through recombination or sorting of genes into new patterns. **Selection** is the key process affecting the relative frequency of genes. Plant breeders artificially select for new populations composed of progeny from individual plants found to possess certain traits. Artificial selection is fundamental to all efforts at crop improvement. Selection also occurs naturally in seed-propagated plants in response to pressures imposed by the environments in agricultural fields.

**Artificial selection**  Artificial selection is conceptually simple. A 'screen' (test or standard) is established that allows identification of phenotypes possessing a particular trait and individual plants that meet that criterion are accepted or rejected. The aim is to isolate favorable or unfavorable genotypes from the balance of the population. The screen (or standard) might be very simple: for example, plant height, flowering date, or response when inoculated with disease. Devising screens for improvement of integrative traits such as partitioning pattern or efficiency in the use of nitrogen can be much more complex.

Success in selection depends on many factors including whether the desired trait is controlled by a single dominant or recessive allele, or is polygenic. The term polygene refers to traits under the influence of many gene loci, each with only a small control over the trait. The mating system of the species is also important. With highly homozygous, inbreeding species, selection of individual plants can be effective with both single and polygenes if they are evident in the phenotype but repeated cycles of mass selection of many individuals may be necessary to capture a desired trait from a highly heterozygous population.

A danger to be avoided in selection is that a screen may lead to the inadvertent loss of desired traits. This can be illustrated with selection for virus tolerance in sugarbeet. The sugarbeet industry of the USA during its early years depended on seed imported from Germany. In the 1920s, curly top virus transmitted by leaf hoppers from surrounding desert vegetation reduced sucrose yields by half in the western states and the industry nearly collapsed. The problem was solved by collecting plants that escaped disease symptoms in farmers' fields. These then were grown for seed at a USDA station near Aberdeen, Idaho. The screen for true resistance or tolerance involved plantings during the summer when the seedling plants would be exposed to massive flights of viruliferous hoppers from adjacent desert vegetation. The program was highly successful in the development of resistant cultivars. In yield trials, these gave superior performance in the western states where the disease is always present. Many years later when the selected populations were compared with the original German lines under disease-free conditions in controlled environments, it was found that the important ability to grow rapidly in cool weather of spring had been lost under the conditions set for the screen (Ulrich 1961). In the field, loss of a cool-climate ability had been offset by the greater benefit of disease resistance. Yields and production efficiencies would have been even greater, however, if the cool-climate ability had not been lost.

Successful selection is only a part of plant breeding. Captured genes must then be placed into combinations that result in agronomically useful phenotypes. This is usually done by making specific crosses ($F_1$ generation) and then testing for desirable recombinants in the segregating $F_2$ and later generations. The frequency of recombination between chromosomes from closely related parents is great enough to serve reliably in transferring genes. When chromosomes come from distant parents, special chromosome manipulations including radiation treatment may be needed to effect recombination. The great promise of biotechnology is that it will greatly facilitate intraspecific transfers of genetic information. Included here are possibilities for using genes from sources as distant as bacteria and animals.

**Natural selection and genetic shifts**   Heterogeneous agricultural populations are subject to natural selection. That occurs because of differences among genetic combinations in their reproductive success. Phenotypes that are well suited to a particular environment achieve a greater reproductive rate than poorly suited phenotypes, and their genes increase in frequency in the population over generations. This process is termed **genetic shift**. The successful genotypes generally have greater 'fitness' to local conditions including crop management practices. Climatic adaptation, for example, may involve changes in phenology or tolerances to extreme temperatures. Adaptation to factors such as disease, soil pH, aluminum or heavy metal toxicities, and nutrient deficiencies also occurs. A gradual divergence between the original and selected populations is observed in most cases, but with intense selection, as can occur when a non-dormant cultivar of alfalfa is transferred to a region with severe winters, selection can result in rapid and dramatic genetic shifts. Subterranean clover has undergone shifts of this sort during its movement around Australia (Gladstones 1967). The same phenomenon is seen with **ecotype formation** in natural populations. Ecotypes are subpopulations of wild species with a set of common traits lending fitness to a local environment.

Data presented in Table 4.3 reveal a genetic shift in a rye cultivar grown as a winter cover crop and forage in the Mississippi basin. The original cultivar was released in Tennessee but was adopted widely in other states. Seed production was done in each locale. After 10–20 y of reproduction in other locations, this comparison made in Tennessee with seed from several sources reveals a strong shift in growth habit related to flowering. This seems to have involved changes in the vernalization requirement (requirement of a cold period for flowering; see Chapter 5) through natural selection at locations with more severe winters.

Natural selection involves selection for *individual* fitness rather than for performance of the entire *community*. This is a major problem for agriculturalists. The point was made in Chapter 2 that vigorous individuals (e.g. tall, rank plants) may acquire above-average shares of local resources and thus achieve a larger reproductive rate than their suppressed neighbors. Such selection for competitive ability represents a reversion towards 'wild type', however, causing a decline in harvest index and community yield per unit area as the fraction of the population with those traits increases. Reversion is combatted in agricultural populations by careful management and roguing of seed fields. One difficulty is that we have only a poor understanding of the traits that cause individuals to give superior performance as a community. This is addressed in more detail under the topic of ideotypes in Chapter 11.

Detailed analyses of natural selection in crops are found in Allard's (1988) long-term studies with composite crosses of barley. Composite Cross II (CCII) popula-

Table 4.3 *Genetic shift in scorings for spring growth habit of 'Balboa' rye*

Seed from various sources were planted in Tennessee (origin of the cultivar). An erect habit, due to culm elongation and indicating earliness in flowering, was scored as 1; scores ranged to 10 for continued prostrate growth and lateness in flowering.

| Seed source | Iowa | Kansas | Illinois | Tennessee |
|---|---|---|---|---|
| Erectness score | 10.0 | 7.4 | 5.6 | 1.9 |

*Source*: Data from Hoskinson & Qualset (1967).

tion, for example, was synthesized in 1928 by Harlan & Martini (1929) from seed of all possible crosses of 28 barley cultivars. It has been grown at Davis, California, since 1930 with standard agricultural practices. The level and stability of community grain yield for the population have improved markedly (relative to earlier generations) owing to increases in average number of grain per spike and individual grain mass. An important point is that certain clusters of genes lending adaptedness tended to be selected as a group.

Although the yield of CCII remains less than that of the best local cultivars, it is significant that natural selection among individuals was beneficial to community performance. This lends support to the idea that population methods can be used in development of new cultivars. An increase in yield was to be expected, however, because many of the original parent cultivars were poorly suited to the Davis environment. A discouraging point is that while the original cultivars were mostly tall, there has been some increase in plant height, a sign of increased competitive ability. Had the composite been constructed with less competitive, short-stature, locally adapted materials, the most likely result would have been a significant increase in height and a yield decline.

Natural selection is also seen in the loss of genes relating to insect and disease resistance in the absence of those pests, and in the increase in frequency of resistance genes in their presence. Selection pressures imposed on pests, diseases, and weeds by farming practices are very strong and those organisms also adapt to new circumstances. Weed populations, for example, commonly shift towards greater tolerance of herbicides and cultivation practices employed in a farming system. When the selection screens are very strong, evolutionary changes may occur rather rapidly. In Arkansas (USA), wild-type red rice with phenology, stature, and grain size similar to those of domestic rice is a problem. In California, barnyardgrass (*Echinochloa crus-galli*) adapted quickly to changing depths of water used for its control in flooded rice. It is interesting, on the other hand, that no obvious patterns of coevolution of forage grasses and legumes have been reported despite hundreds of years of use in pasture polycultures.

**Relative reproduction rate**

Natural selection occurs because individual plants that do well in a particular environment have high reproduction rates and contribute more progeny to subsequent generations. The example presented in Fig. 4.1 with simple populations of two genotypes helps in understanding relationships between reproductive rate and natural selection. Fig. 4.1a depicts seed yields of two genotypes of an inbreeding species grown together in a replacement series (Section 2.5). The reproductive rate of each genotype can be calculated directly as the ratio of seeds harvested to seeds planted and the ratio of those rates for the two components is termed the **relative reproduction rate** ($\alpha$). For component A relative to component B:

$$\alpha_{AB} = \frac{(Y_A/P_A)}{(Y_B/P_B)} = \frac{Y_A P_B}{Y_B P_A}, \qquad \text{[Eq. 4.1]}$$

where $Y$ and $P$ represent, respectively, numbers of seed harvested and planted. When seed harvested from the last generation is used as planting stock for the next, and $\alpha_{AB} > 1$, the frequency of A in the mixture increases over generations. That corresponds to a left-to-right progression in planting ratio in Fig. 4.1a. If $\alpha_{AB}$ were $< 1$, A would decline in frequency over generations. Eq. 4.1 assumes a useful linear character after conversion to logarithmic form and rearranging (de Wit 1960):

$$\log \alpha_{AB} = \log (Y_A/Y_B) - \log (P_A/P_B). \qquad \text{[Eq. 4.2]}$$

Plots of log (harvested ratio) versus log (planted ratio) (Fig. 4.1b) make it easier to understand how a mixture changes over generations. With $\alpha_{AB} > 1$, the mixture is unstable and proceeds towards pure A; the reverse is true with $\alpha_{AB} < 1$. In some situations, $\alpha_{AB}$ changes as proportions of A and B in the mixture change. Such mixtures may be either stable or unstable (Fig. 4.1c).

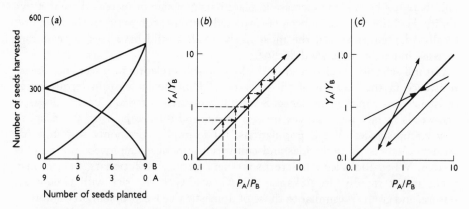

Fig. 4.1. (a) A hypothetical example of numbers of seed harvested from genotypes A and B, grown in a replacement series, as a function of numbers of seed planted. The figure is similar to that presented in Fig. 2.9d. (b) Data from (a) displayed in a log–log plot of the ratio of harvested seed ($Y_A/Y_B$) as a function of the ratio of seed planted ($P_A/P_B$). The 1:1 line corresponds to cases where no selection for A or B occurs over generations. In the example from (a), however, A increases in frequency in each planting cycle (the dotted line) because $\alpha_{AB} = 1.2$. The course of selection is seen in the solid line. (c) Stable (converging to an equilibrium value $\alpha = 1$) and unstable patterns of selection.

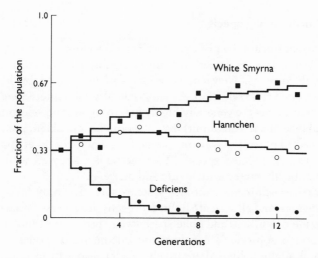

Fig. 4.2. Changes over generations in the frequency of three barley cultivars grown in a blend at Aberdeen, Idaho. Data points are from Harlan & Martini's (1938) experiment; lines are de Wit's (1960) predictions based on relative reproductive rates observed in the first year. (Redrawn from de Wit (1960).)

This method of analysis is applicable to any mixture, whether of genotypes within a particular population or of different species. It can also be used to follow the course of marker genes in successive generations of an outbreeding species. The power of this approach is seen in Fig. 4.2 where the 25 y course of an unstable cultivar mixture of barley is fit (explained) by $a$ values measured in the first year. This example involves a rather stable environment (Idaho, USA) and rather large phenotypic differences in an inbreeding species, however. Most genetic changes, particularly those in outbreeding species, are not so easily seen or predicted. Spitters (1979) extended de Wit's basic model into a powerful stochastic treatment that can deal with more complex examples of competition and selection for phenotypes and gene frequencies.

## 4.4 CULTIVAR DEVELOPMENT

Superior, predictable performance in the field is the principal feature of any cultivar, and thus the main objective in plant breeding. Adaptations to the local environment, including tolerance of normal stresses, appropriate pest and disease resistance, yield performance, and suitable quality for the intended uses, are attributes that determine superiority. There are many different approaches to the development of new cultivars, dictated in part by mating habits and genetic structure of the species. A further narrowing of genetic structure so that all individuals display the desired phenotypic traits is involved in most cases.

### Cultivars of out-breeding species

Selection and isolation are the principal means used to limit diversity in outbreeding open-pollinated species. Isolation from foreign pollen is used in maintaining open-pollinated cultivars. New combinations can be created by hybridization followed by repeated mass selection. A major difficulty encountered with outbreeding species is that plants are generally highly heterozygous and selection efficiency (i.e. the heritability of a selected trait) may be poor. That problem is circumvented easily when selected phenotypes are propagated as clones, but other approaches are required for seed-propagated species. Two methods employed with open-pollinated crops can be illustrated with alfalfa and maize.

Alfalfa possesses self-incompatibility systems such that only foreign pollen is accepted by stigmas, and all seed are hybrid. Progeny are diverse because of gamete sorting during meiosis in seed and pollen parents and because pollinating bees visit a diversity of pollen sources. When bees are uncontrolled, pollen sources may include all local alfalfa fields. Alternatively, alfalfa plants from specific superior sources, e.g. from seed of clonal lines, can be brought together for open pollination in isolated fields. Bulked seed from such fields, although also highly diverse genetically, represents a more controlled result that is released as a **synthetic cultivar**. Synthetics are usually reconstituted at regular intervals from their original parental lines, in this case clones. Without reconstitution, synthetics eventually become ordinary open-pollinated cultivars. Most of the more advanced cultivars of alfalfa and various clovers used in forage production are synthetics or began as such.

Given their heterogeneous nature, many changes can occur in a synthetic when seed is increased. Data presented in Table 4.4 illustrate natural selection in a synthetic cultivar of Ladino clover grown for seed production outside its region of adaptation. This cultivar was created with seed from 21 clonal lines having high biomass production and good forage quality under conditions of the Atlantic coastal plain of eastern USA. Seed production, however, was in western states where seed yield and quality are much greater. The frequency of several marker traits changed considerably during a single cycle of reproduction at different latitudinal locations. This occurred because the original clones differed in flowering response to photoperiod (Chapter 5), a trait that did not affect forage production. Although California farmers were pioneers in production of Ladino clover seed, this cultivar now is increased in Idaho (Aberdeen in the table) because less divergence of genetic structure occurs there than in California.

Maize, in contrast to alfalfa and clover, is grown for its grain, and uniformity in reproduction is important. Maize plants are wind-pollinated and self-compatible, accepting their own as well as foreign pollen. Prior to 1930, cultivars of maize were all open-pollinated. Some were landraces while others, as a result of isolation and repeated selection, formed distinctive cultivars. Mass and individual selection techniques, however, were frustratingly inefficient. The problem of how to further narrow open-pollinated populations to the most desirable genotypes was solved through inbreeding, which fixes genes into homozygous combinations, followed by the production of **specific hybrids**. Crossing two highly homozygous inbred lines leads to genetically and phenotypically uniform (and heterozygous) $F_1$ hybrid seed

Table 4.4 *Frequency of several marker traits in 'Pilgrim' Ladino clover and seed production by component clonal lines when grown at several locations in western states*

| Location | Davis | Aberdeen | Tulelake | Prossor |
|---|---|---|---|---|
| Latitude: | 38.5 N | 43.9 N | 41 N | 46.2 N |
| *% total progeny having:* | | | | |
| Leaf fleck | 0.02 | 2.7 | — | 18.1 |
| Linamarase enzyme | 21.4 | 3.0 | — | 4.1 |
| Cyanogenic glucoside | 19.8 | 12.4 | — | 9.7 |
| Petiole mark | 86.3 | 90.2 | — | 85.1 |
| *% total seed from:* | | | | |
| Highest-yielding clone | 22 | — | 13 | 9 |
| Highest 7 clones | 80 | — | 61 | 52 |
| Lowest 7 clones | 5 | — | 9 | 15 |

*Source:* Data from Laude & Stanford (1960).

that can be used directly as planting stock or as parents in additional crosses for more complex cultivars such as 'double crosses' ($F_1 \times F_1$).

Seed production for $F_1$ hybrids of maize is done in fields planted with alternate strips of male and female parent inbreds. In earlier times, contamination by pollen from the tassels of female parents [maize is 'dioecious' with separate male (tassel) and female (ear) inflorescences] was avoided by removing those tassels from the plants before they shed pollen. Female inbreds are now made male-sterile through genetic means, eliminating the need for hand work. $F_1$ hybrids are preferred as planting stock and with the cost of seed production contained through use of vigorous inbreds and male-sterile female parents, most cultivars are now $F_1$s. Because genetic segregation in $F_2$ and later generations results in less uniformity and lower yield, farmers buy newly constituted, hybrid seed for each crop. Grain yields obtained with segregating $F_2$ populations of maize are 20–30% less than for the corresponding $F_1$ hybrid (G. Benson, personal communication).

In the USA, hybrid maize quickly displaced open-pollinated cultivars: the transition was complete in the state of Iowa in only 10 y. While 'hybrid vigor' is often credited for the rapid adoption, the principal reasons were that the new hybrids solved several long-standing problems through resistance to fungal stalk rots and greater uniformity.

**Heterosis or hybrid vigor** Unlike cotton and some other crops, inbred lines of maize are not used in commercial production because they are generally smaller and less vigorous than their open-pollinated parents owing to 'inbreeding depression'. That occurs because maize germplasms carry many inferior recessive genes. These appear as deleterious double recessives in inbred lines, and those lines therefore are generally weaker plants than their open-pollinated parents. In hybrids and open-pollinated populations, the inferior genes are masked by dominant alleles, or have additive effects with unlike alleles. A key step in hybrid development is the search for superior 'combining ability' in specific crosses between inbred lines. A favorable combination of genes in the $F_1$ offspring restores plant vigor to the same or greater level than in the open-pollinated parents, a phenomenon known as **heterosis**, or hybrid vigor.

Some researchers believe that gene interactions as well as genetic dominance and additivity contribute to hybrid vigor in maize but that point remains unproven (Sprague & Eberhart 1977; Simmonds 1979). By eliminating inferior genes, breeders may eventually find homozygous inbred lines that are equal to hybrids for each use or environment. Inferior genes are exposed to elimination through selection among inbred lines. Significant advances in the vigor of maize inbreds have been achieved in that way but they are not yet equal in productivity to hybrids. Because inbred lines still tend to be small in stature, proper comparisons of inbreds and hybrids depends on the inbreds being grown at a higher density than hybrids. Few such trials have been conducted properly.

Specific hybrids offer a rapid and very efficient way to generate superior cultivars of several open-pollinated species. Another reason for the wide use of hybrids has been that inbreds, and their specific combinations, represent an information system with proprietary opportunities for commercial plant breeding. Hybrid efforts continue with many crops, mainly by private breeders. Hybrid breeding is particularly suited to clonally propagated crops because they retain their genetic structure over vegetative generations. Methods now exist (Simmonds 1979) for the development of open-pollinated synthetics of maize and other species that could be equal or superior to specific hybrids. Whether inbreds or superior open-pollinated cultivars may some day replace hybrids remains to be seen. Farmers could then save their own seed as they do with small grains. The breeding work then would probably have to be done with public financing, however, because seedsmen and private breeders would not be able to capture a return for breeding as they are able to do with hybrids.

## Cultivars of inbreeding species

Examination of Table 4.2 reveals that inbreeding is the common pattern in annual plants whereas out-breeding is more prevalent in perennials. Selection of plants from an inbred population can lead directly to a true-reproducing, **pure-line** cultivar. The tasks in breeding, then, relate mainly to the transfer of genes between pure lines by crossing. New pure lines are developed from segregating populations through repeated selection. 'Back-cross' breeding, involving repeated crossing to the desirable parent, is a useful tool. In this, selection is made for recombinants having the desired parent's phenotype coupled with the transferred trait. With a constant phenotype, farmers need to make only small adjustments in production practices when using the new cultivar.

Pure lines are employed widely in agriculture. Most possess a degree of genetic heterogeneity as is demonstrated by responses to selection pressures. Continuing gene mutation and small amounts of out-crossing are the basis for the heterogeneity. In some cases, heterozygotes have an advantage in competition and thus a greater reproductive rate, which helps perpetuate the diversity. Such heterogeneity is usually not a problem in production, and farmers can use their own crops as seed for several generations.

## Multilines and blends

There are instances where genetic diversity is deliberately included in agricultural communities in the form of population-based cultivars or physical mixtures of genotypes or cultivars. The example in Fig. 4.2 resulted from a simple physical mixture, or **blend**, of several existing cultivars. More sophisticated blends composed of cultivars or lines chosen for similarity and compatibility in the mixture find occasional use in agriculture. Blends of closely related isolines of the same cultivar, differing only in disease-resistance genes, are termed **multiline** cultivars. These are more interesting and more widely used than common blends of cultivars.

The basis for developing population cultivars and blends is found in several theories. One theory is based on the fact that fields are seldom uniform throughout their area in soil type, fertility, drainage, slope, or other features. The idea is that a population with an array of genotypes differing in adaptation might better exploit such spatial variability. It is also thought (Marshall & Allard 1974; Simmonds 1979) that genetically heterogeneous cultivars may provide increased stability by evening out yield over even small microsite differences and through less variation in yield owing to year-to-year variation in weather. The achievement of superior yield through genotype selection over microsites is unlikely with annual crops, however, and at present no means exists for matching genotype and microsite at planting. The tactic is suited better to perennials (e.g. pastures) because there is then sufficient time for selection and persistence of the best genotype at each microsite. It also may be useful in Mediterranean climatic regions where pastures are dominated by annual species (Rossiter & Collins 1988). Those pastures reseed themselves each year from their own production. When the pastures are established with genetically diverse seed sources, the best adapted genotypes come to dominate the stands even at the microsite level.

Although genetically diverse crop cultivars sometimes achieve relative yield totals $> 1$ (Section 2.5) compared with some of their components, they seldom provide greater yield than their best component. One reason is that most narrow-based cultivars are capable of considerable physiological and morphological plasticity and thus satisfy the goal of adjusting to spatial variability. In addition, large gains in yield and stability have been achieved more easily with other breeding methods, through changes in farming practices (e.g. improved tillage, drainage, and fertility) and by choice of field boundaries that reduce or restrict habitat variation. Spatial variability of arable fields also can be controlled to some extent through seedbed preparation, fertilization, drainage, and other means.

A theory relating to the use of genetic diversity in multilines revolves around the possibility for slowing the secondary spread of diseases from epicenters within a field by presenting pathogens with mosaic patterns of plants varying in resistance genes. The theory is supported by observations that disease problems seem to decrease with increased diversity of a cultivar (clone $>$ inbred $>$ outbred). Similar evidence has been developed with epidemiological models (Kampmeijer & Zadoks 1977). The approach appears well suited to air-borne pathogens, such as black stem rust of wheat, having numerous races (pathotypes). Van Der Plank's (1963) terminology for **horizontal resistance** (HR; general resistance) and **vertical resistance** (VR; specific resistance) is useful in this case. Host resistance to stem rust is centered on major genes at single loci. A particular VR gene provides resistance to only a few of the hundreds of races of the pathogen. A wheat cultivar can thus be completely resistant to some pathogen races but not to all. In the absence of a single source of general resistance (HR) to all races of a disease, the usual tactic is to release new cultivars carrying the major gene for specific resistance (VR) to the currently dominant pathogen races. Other races will then increase in frequency over years, however, and unless we again change to a new wheat cultivar carrying appropriate VR, a disease epidemic and drastic yield decline may occur. To avoid 'boom and bust' cycles in crop production, pathogen races must be monitored to allow timely release of cultivars and advice to farmers.

Use of multilines for disease control aims at reducing the pattern of secondary infections within a field. Infection by stem rust, for example, can be described by a sigmoidal disease-progress curve in which the fraction of diseased leaf or stem area is plotted against time. Sigmoidal curves can be fit with the **logistic equation** obtained as an extension of Eq. 2.3 by including a limiting term, $1-F_d$, that diminishes to 0 as the fraction diseased area, $F_d$, approaches 1:

$$dF_d/dt = \mu F_d(1 - F_d) \qquad\qquad\qquad \text{[Eq. 4.3]}$$

and integrated:

$$F_d = 1/[1 + (1 - F_d)e^{-\mu t}]. \qquad\qquad\qquad \text{[Eq. 4.4]}$$

Logistic equations are not useful for prediction because they require advance knowledge of the endpoint, $F_d$. In this case, we circumvent that problem by using a relative endpoint of 1.0 corresponding to complete coverage of leaves. The point with multilines is that each host–pathogen combination will have a different specific rate of disease increase, $\mu_i$. By mixing isolines with different VR genes, the effective $\mu$ for the community can never be as great as $\mu_i$ for the most susceptible line in the mixture. As a result, disease progress is slowed relative to that in susceptible lines and the outbreak is held to a tolerable level. Multilines thus are 'dirty' in the sense that some members will be susceptible to whatever races are present (Marshall 1977). Disease may occur each year and yields are less than for cultivars with complete resistance (either HR or VR to the prevailing races) as was shown by Kølster *et al.* (1989) with barley multilines exposed to powdery mildew (*Erysiphe graminis*).

Multilines of oat (Iowa) (Browning & Frey 1969; Frey *et al.* 1977) and barley (Europe) (Wolfe 1985) are now used in agriculture. The oat multilines used in Iowa consist of collections of isolines carrying combinations of VR genes for resistance to different races of stem rust. These multilines have yet to be tested under epidemic conditions, however. It is unclear whether the lack of epidemics is due to the use of multilines or to employment of cultivars with improved resistance in mild-climate regions, south of Iowa, that are the overwintering source of the disease. Trenbath

(1984) has shown theoretically that there may, in fact, be little practical difference over the long term between the use of multilines, the currently most-resistant component, or a rotation of lines with various VR genes. It seems that the 'jury is still out' on the value of multiline use.

Ross (1983) found a different mechanism operating in a soybean blend exposed to mosaic virus. In this case, resistant plants compensated for the reduced performance of infected plants and in that way had a buffering effect on yield. Compensatory growth by healthy plants did not occur, however, in sugarbeet fields infected with yellows virus (Loomis & Bennett 1966). That virus blocks phloem transport. As a result, leaf area and cover were unchanged by the disease, blocking opportunities for expanded growth by the healthy plants. Root yield declined in direct relation to the percentage of diseased plants in the field.

## Biotechnology

New methods for gene transfer based in a variety of molecular techniques are now being used to supplement traditional methods of plant breeding. These 'biotechnology' methods should prove particularly useful for interspecific transfer of single genes, for example, for resistance or tolerance to a disease or herbicide, once these genes are known. (A point of caution, however, is that care is needed to insure that the resulting genotypes are not also then 'cow-' or 'human-resistant'!) Traits such as disease and herbicide tolerance generally depend upon only one or at most a few genes. By contrast, quantitative aspects of plant growth and development such as yield and vigor are integrative attributes of the whole plant. Control of such traits is usually highly polygenic and poorly understood. We have only a limited ability (mainly with simulation models) to predict the performance of communities with new genetic combinations of that sort. Progress through directed gene transfer is likely to be no more effective than induced mutations have been. Therefore, each new genetic combination will have to be evaluated over a wide range of climates and cultural practices before its potential usefulness can be known. These ecological and morphogenetic considerations will limit application of the new molecular methods.

## Seed production

Advances in plant breeding have made farmers' choices of genetic material increasingly important. Modern cultivars are generally greatly superior to earlier cultivars and landraces and they also may differ greatly from each other in adaptation to local conditions and in the quality of their yield. This leads to the problem of how farmers can be well informed in their choice of cultivars. A cultivar's traits can be defined through field trials and farmer experience and that knowledge is generally available from local seedsmen and extension agencies. Most technologically developed nations now have specific legal requirements surrounding the naming and release of new cultivars and production and sale of agricultural seed. The rules are designed to help farmers in choosing the cultivars best suited to their needs. Such regulations generally provide that seed produced and processed with independent inspection may be sold with a 'certification' as to the genetic purity, germinability, and contamination by weed seed. The requirements are demanding and most seed is now produced by specialized growers who are able to produce high-quality seed while maintaining genetic purity.

Many farmers still save their own seed, however, particularly of inbreeding species that remain reasonably true over generations (small grains and grain legumes), returning to the certified sources as superior cultivars are released or when their own stocks deteriorate. Uncertified seed, with or without a cultivar designation, is also used. In the USA, landraces of some species still enter the seed trade under a designation of 'common' seed (e.g. 'Arizona Common' alfalfa).

Special circumstances for the production of seed arise when regions where a crop is grown are climatically unsuited for seed production. An example with Ladino clover was considered earlier. Sugarbeet is also interesting. This species is biennial, flowering in the second year after vernalization during a period of low temperatures during the winter. The danger exists that plantings for sugar production made in early spring (or in the fall in areas with mild winters) will flower prematurely and adversely affect sugar yield. In that case, 'bolting-resistant' cultivars having a strong vernalization requirement are employed to avoid premature flowering. Seed production is conducted in other localities where winters are sufficient for strong vernalization yet mild enough for the plants to survive. Similar problems occur with alfalfa production in temperate zones. Strong winter hardiness is required but the seed yields in those regions are usually much less than can be obtained in milder climates. Seed yields of alfalfa amount to perhaps 100 kg ha$^{-1}$ in Wisconsin compared with the 800 ka ha$^{-1}$, of much better quality, that is obtained with irrigation in California's Central Valley. As a result, much of the USA's supply of alfalfa seed comes from California. Seed fields of winter-hardy cultivars come under inspection and certification routines designed to minimize the genetic shift towards non-dormant, non-hardy, types that occurs with California's mild winters. Production is limited to one generation in California, and volunteer (second-generation) plants are rogued from the seed fields.

## 4.5   GENETIC ADVANCE AND MAINTENANCE OF DIVERSITY

### Genetic advance

Agricultural productivity in developed nations has increased several-fold during the past 150 y. It would be useful to know how much of that advance is due to genetic improvement and how much to improvements in management including changes in nutrition and planting density. These are not easy questions to answer. The simplest approach is to compare present cultivars side-by-side at the same time and place with the earlier cultivars that they have displaced (de Vries *et al.* 1967; Donald & Hamblin 1976; Austin *et al.* 1980; Fehr 1984; Tollenaar 1989; see also Duncan *et al.* (1978) as discussed in Section 11.3).

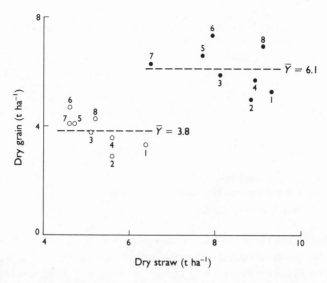

**Fig. 4.3.** **Grain yields of eight English wheat cultivars released between 1908 and 1978 plotted against their straw yields. Cultivar no. 1 is the earliest release, no. 8 the most recent. Open circles, Paternoster Field, 38 kg N applied ha$^{-1}$, mean yield = 3.8 t ha$^{-1}$, range 1.7 t ha$^{-1}$; filled circles, Camp Field, 104 kg N applied ha$^{-1}$, mean yield = 6.1 t ha$^{-1}$, range 2.3 t ha$^{-1}$. (Data from Austin *et al.* (1980).)**

Surprisingly, such trials reveal little or no genetic advance in the photosynthetic abilities of crops. New and old cultivars generally have very similar abilities in biomass production. The genetic component of yield advances has come mainly through advances in harvest index due to more conserving patterns of partitioning. Less stem growth, for example, leaves more assimilate for reproductive activities. Benefits from improved resistance to lodging are also important. Not so obvious in those trials are significant improvements in insect and disease resistance. All of these traits should contribute to more efficient use of scarce resources of nutrients, water, land, and labor, and they should provide greater safety and stability.

Progress with English wheats during the past 80 y is illustrated in Fig. 4.3. As has been found in other studies with wheat, most of the genetic gain came from improvements in harvest index. Total above-ground biomass produced by these cultivars varies over only a small range (about 10%) but cultivars released before 1950 had harvest indices near 0.35 whereas more recent releases approach 0.45 to 0.50. This is demonstrated in Fig. 4.3 by small yields of straw. Plant height has been reduced sharply, in line with the smaller amount of biomass partitioned to straw.

This example provides a good test of the role of nutrition in yield improvements. The genetic advances were made during the same period of time that farmers were increasing their use of nitrogenous fertilizers. Many claims of genetic advance ignore this point and credit all yield increases to breeding. In this case, the mean yield increase due to an additional 66 kg N ha$^{-1}$ was 2.3 t grain ha$^{-1}$ (35 kg grain kg$^{-1}$ N). This is the same amount as can be ascribed to the genetic yield advance

Table 4.5 *Contributions of various changes in production practices to the net increase (4280 kg ha$^{-1}$) in maize yield 1930–79 in Minnesota*

| Sources of increase | Magnitude (%) | Sources of decrease | Magnitude (%) |
|---|---|---|---|
| Genetic gains | +59 | Less manure | −15 |
| Fertilizer N | +47 | Less organic matter | −13 |
| Plant density | +25 | Erosion | −8 |
| Herbicides | +23 | Insects | −8 |
| Machinery | +21 | Rotations | −6 |
|  |  | Other factors | −25 |
| Total | +175 |  | −75 |

*Source:* Adapted from Cardwell (1982).

demonstrated by the range of yields within the +N field. Austin *et al.* (1980) found that these wheat crops accumulated considerably more nitrogen than was applied as fertilizer (total uptake was 60–75 kg N ha$^{-1}$ in the low-N field and 161–215 kg N ha$^{-1}$ in the +N field) indicating that wheat is an effective scavenger of nitrogen released from soil organic matter. The recent releases not only had greater nitrogen uptake, but they also partitioned a larger fraction (nearly 80%) of that to grain. 'Nitrogen-use efficiency' can be said to have improved.

Cardwell (1982) took a different approach in his elegant analysis of the contributions of various changes in farming practice to maize yield increases in Minnesota (USA) from 1930 to 1979 (Table 4.5). During that 49 y period, the state's average yield increased by 4280 kg ha$^{-1}$, from 2010 to 6290 kg ha$^{-1}$. By regressing the time-course of state-average yields against information on farming practices and cultivars, he was able to assign 59% of the yield gain to cultivars, 47% to fertilizer, and 25% to increased plant density and closer rows. Herbicides and machinery contributed 23% and 21%, respectively. Those gains total more than 100% but they were offset during the same period by less input of organic nitrogen, continuing soil erosion, and other factors.

Cardwell's study demonstrates the difficulty of distinguishing between genetic and management components of gain, since 2525 kg ha$^{-1}$ (59% of 4280) of genetic gains could never have been achieved without at least 60 kg additional N ha$^{-1}$. Positive contributions from drainage and from P and K fertilizers were not included in the analysis and it seems that Cardwell may have overestimated genetic gains by perhaps the −25% shown for 'Other factors'. Tollenaar (1989) was able to link genetic advance over the period from 1959 to 1988 with other aspects of technology. His field experiments in Ontario, Canada, were conducted in a way that allowed each cultivar to be grown at its optimum density. Machine-harvestability (machine-harvested yield/hand-harvest yield) improved dramatically with year of introduction, owing to advances in lodging resistance even as optimal density increased.

The disturbing point that emerges from these studies is that the easy genetic gains, such as advances in harvest index, may have been achieved already with most crops. We use the word 'easy' but the advances were not necessarily obvious or easy for plant breeders to accomplish. Some breakthrough in photosynthetic or metabolic efficiency (both unlikely) may be needed for further quantum jumps of similar magnitude. Other possibilities do exist, however, for designing plants that are better suited to community conditions, and questions relating to more efficient use of nutrients, for example, have hardly been explored. We examine some of those issues in Chapters 5 and 11. In the meantime, yields are not likely to stagnate at present levels. Present differences between attainable and actual yields indicate that considerable opportunity remains for improvements in management, and significant increases can be expected from rising atmospheric $CO_2$ levels.

## Germplasm collections

Most crops are supported by germplasm banks that can be searched for alternative sources of resistance and other traits. The size of genetic bases available for various species differ greatly. Those for cereals are generally very large, whereas those for fruit and vegetable crops are generally small. The principal genetic bases of clonally propagated species such as sugarcane and asparagus, and most tree and vine crops, can be traced to a few individual plants. Seed propagation allows greater opportunity for continuing generation of new diversity through mutation and recombination. Even there, however, modern breeding may rest on only a small number of truly excellent lines. Concern about whether our genetic bases are broad enough to embrace resistance to new diseases, or traits suitable to unknown, future technologies (National Research Council 1972), has prompted greater efforts to expand and conserve genetic materials. As landraces disappear, it is increasingly important to have programs for the preservation of the diversity resident in older strains, special lines, and their wild relatives.

Plant breeders generally maintain their own small germplasm collections centered around entries useful in their breeding programs. Sharing information and seed with other plant breeders is a tradition in that profession. That does not insure the preservation of a wide range of germplasm, however, because maintenance of large collections is expensive. Collections for some inbreeding species have as many as 30 000 to 50 000 entries. Outbreeding species, by contrast, can generally be managed in a smaller number of populations. Certain elite lines may be kept as clones or, as is the case for maize, as inbred lines. Typical germplasm bases for horticultural crops are much smaller but it is clear that simply cataloging a collection is a major task. Cooperative, government-funded systems have been established to maintain the collections of some species.

One of the problems of germplasm collections is that seeds have finite lifetimes in storage and seed-propagated plants are subject to mutation and selection with every generation. Debate continues on how best to deal with the problem of collection size and genetic change. One solution is to treat inbreeders in the same way as outbreeders by compositing diversity in heterogenous populations. CCII barley, discussed above, provides a model of that approach. The collections can be stored as seed for extended periods before reproduction, and changes in gene frequency can be controlled to some extent through reproduction in different environments. Maintenance of diversity is greatly simplified then, but searching composites for a desired trait can be much more difficult than searching through a collection of pure lines because phenotypic control becomes dispersed by genetic exchange. Clonally propagated materials present special problems because they cannot be stored as seed. Some can be maintained in plantings indefinitely (asparagus and bermuda-grass) or for very long periods (fruit trees) with little care. Others, such as sugarcane and potato, are burdensome because they require frequent propagation. Alterna-tive methods for cryogenic storage of vegetative material and DNA are being explored.

Genetic collections are of little value unless plant breeders have time to explore that diversity, since maintenance of genetic resources takes meaning only as new cultivars are developed through breeding. One of the ironies of today is that at the very time that more attention is being given to preservation of germplasm and to creation of new diversity through biotechnology, research administrators, particu-larly in universities and government agencies, are increasingly reluctant to support plant breeding. It is strange, and potentially dangerous to the sustainability of agriculture, to see one of our most sophisticated forms of technology viewed as too mundane. The main effect of biotechnology may be to increase the diversity of germplasm collections: for manipulation by an extinct species, the plant breeder.

## 4.6  SUMMARY

Knowledge of cultivar characteristics and their proper employment is increasingly important for success and safety in farming. The principal attributes of a cultivar, its adaptation and morphological features, are more important than is its degree of genetic variation. Clear expression of advanced traits by a cultivar, however, generally depend on it having a relatively narrow genetic structure. This provides a degree of predictability of response to climate and management as well as high performance. How narrow remains an open question. Broad genetic diversity is vital in agriculture but increasingly the diversity is being kept in nurseries as most plant breeders strive towards a high degree of genetic purity in their cultivars. Monogenotypic communities perform very well in agriculture but it is also clear that a degree of heterogeneity is not necessarily damaging to performance, and many outbreeding species may always be handled as heterogeneous populations (e.g. synthetics). It is also important to continue exploring the use of multilines. In the absence of effective horizontal or vertical resistance to air-borne disease, multilines through their potential for limiting the expression of disease offer an alternative to cultivar substitution. Complete resistance is obviously to be preferred.

Genetic populations are subject to change. Natural selection is a strong force even within inbreeding populations and may have both positive and negative effects on cultivar performance. Adaptation to prevailing climate, disease, and management is beneficial to performance but resistance to diseases and insects not present may be lost, and positive selection for crop yield and quality may not occur. Natural selection operates on individual plants, through the reproductive success of individuals, rather than of the community. Where reproductive success is increased through an increase in competitive ability, more of the community resources may be expended on vegetative growth to the detriment of economic yield.

While many of the easy changes for genetic advance of productivity may already be past, important opportunities remain for advances in efficiency for the use of scarce resources of water and nutrients. In the meantime, continuing progress in disease and insect resistance and exploration of germplasm banks are 'maintenance' activities that need renewed commitments.

## 4.7 FURTHER READING

National Research Council. Committee on Genetic Vulnerability of Major Crops. 1972. *Genetic vulnerability of major crops*. National Academy of Sciences, Washington, D.C. 307 p.

Donald, C. M. and J. Hamblin. 1976. The biological yield and harvest index of cereals as agronomic and plant breeding criteria. *Adv. Agron.* **28**: 361–405.

Donald, C. M. and J. Hamblin. 1983. The convergent evolution of annual seed crops in agriculture. *Adv. Agron.* **36**: 97–143.

Simmonds, N. W. 1979. *Principles of crop improvement*. Longman, London. 408 p.

Simmonds, N. W. (ed.) 1976. *Evolution of crop plants*. Longman, Burnt Mill, Essex, UK. 339 p.

# 5

## Development

### 5.1 INTRODUCTION

In plants, the numbers and types of organs produced are not defined in the embryo, as is the case in animals, but are determined later in variable response to environmental conditions. There are two parts to this. On the one hand, specific responses to temperature and daylength control the initiation of new organs, and on the other, more general environmental conditions determine the assimilate supply and hence the capacity for growth. The continuing change in plant form and function that results is called **development**.

Development involves the coordination and timing of the initiation, growth, and longevity of new vegetative and reproductive parts. Those new organs are initiated in meristems where their appearance is signaled by the formation of primordia, which are localized collections of meristematic cells. The subsequent change in size and form of those primordia (**morphogenesis**) to produce mature leaves or fruit, for example, is determined by the patterns of growth through cell division and enlargement and by specialization through differentiation of the cells and tissues.

The apical meristems of shoot and root have the capacity for unlimited growth and produce the continuously elongating body of the plant. The shoot meristem progresses in a special way with periodic production of new leaves at stem nodes separated from each other by internodes. Intercalary meristems in the internodes also contribute to shoot elongation, new apices in the leaf axils (axillary meristems) provide branching while lateral meristems, mainly vascular cambia, increase girth.

In agriculture, particular attention is paid to reproductive development because fruit and seed comprise the economic yield of most crops. Shoot apices usually convert from the production of leaves to the production of flowers in response to environmental conditions. The timing and extent of reproductive development is critical to the determination of yield. Crops must complete their reproductive development within the available growing season, avoid stresses at vulnerable stages and, for maximum yield, must balance the available time and resources between vegetative and reproductive growth.

The anatomical and physiological bases of organ formation are important background for crop ecology, requiring integration of information from plant physiology (e.g. Wareing & Phillips 1981; Salisbury & Ross 1985), morphology

Table 5.1 *The decimal scale for*
*phenological description of cereals*

A second digit is used to divide each
phenophase in up to 10 further steps

| Value | Phenostage |
|-------|-----------|
| 0 | germination |
| 1 | seedling growth |
| 2 | tillering |
| 3 | stem elongation |
| 4 | booting |
| 5 | inflorescence emergence |
| 6 | anthesis |
| 7 | milky grain |
| 8 | doughy grain |
| 9 | ripe |

*Source:* From Zadoks *et al.* (1974); see also
Tottmann *et al.* (1979).

(Williams 1975) and development (Steeves & Sussex 1972). This chapter deals with
timing aspects of development, especially flowering, and with seed germination.

## 5.2   DEVELOPMENTAL TIME

**Developmental stages**

Through evolution, plants have arrived at a variety of timing mechanisms for
controlling their development. These confer selective advantage by improving the
chance that germination and reproduction occur while conditions for growth
remain favorable. Analysis of crop development is helped by the recognition of
distinctive developmental events, termed **phenostages**, such as 'emergence',
'flower initiation', and 'first flower', that signal changes in the pattern of development. The rate of advance within the intervening **phenophases** is the **developmental rate**, and the study of the progress of crop development in relation to
environmental conditions is called **phenology**.

Numerical phenological scales have been devised for many crops, permitting
quantitative description of crop development. The Feekes' Scale (Large 1954) is still
widely used for wheat and related cereals. The Decimal Scale summarized in Table
5.1 is a recent improvement of it. Most phenostages are recognized by observation,
but some (the most important is flower initiation) can be detected only by dissection
and microscopic examination. It is frequently critical that such detailed observations of development be made if the response of a crop is to be understood.
Illustrated descriptions of meristem differentiation (e.g. Bonnett 1966; Kirby &
Appleyard 1984; Moncur 1981) are often helpful in focusing on the importance of

'hidden' stages of development, such as the sensitivity of reproductive yield to environmental stresses during early flower development.

Individual plants in a crop vary in development rate because of differences in genotypes and microsites, so it is usual to record the occurrence of a phenostage when 50% of the individuals in the population have achieved it. In some crops, synchronized development permits critical management operations such as application of herbicides or fertilizer to be made near the optimal time for most individuals. However, tight synchrony usually occurs only with cultivars having a narrow genetic base, such as $F_1$ hybrids of maize and homozygous pure lines of self-pollinated crops such as pea and small grains.

## Developmental rate

The rate at which a plant proceeds through the stages from germination to maturity varies with environment. Active meristems produce organs faster or slower depending upon the supply of assimilate and general chemical activity that is positively linked with temperature. Thus it is necessary to distinguish the 'physiological' time of an event or age of an organ from the corresponding chronological time or age.

The concept of physiological time is evident in the initiation of new leaves by a stem meristem. The time interval between the **initiation** of successive leaves is the **plastochron** and the accumulated number of leaves at any time is the **plastochron index**. These terms define the developmental stage (physiological age) of the shoot and each leaf by the plastochron index, and their developmental rates as the reciprocal of the plastochron.

A practical difficulty with the application of the plastochron concept is that initiation of new primordia can be seen only after destructive dissection of meristems. In most plants, the rate of appearance of organs lags behind their initiation rate so that primordia accumulate within apical buds. Primordia have little influence on the production or use of assimilate, however, and so in studies of plants in the field it is appropriate and more convenient to use the number and type of visible organs in defining the developmental stage (e.g. leaf number or the presence of flowers) and developmental rate (rate of organ appearance) of crops.

The influence of temperature on physiological processes is nonlinear (Fig. 2.12) but workable linear approximation can be established for individual regions of the response. This is shown in Fig. 5.1, constructed from various measurements of the growth response of maize to temperature. The central response of development, the rate of organ initiation, appears to be closely related to growth by a common response of cell division to temperature. Therefore, the same form of optimal response also describes the rate of development of the crop, included in the figure as the reciprocal of the duration from sowing to flowering. Three ranges are evident in the response to temperature: in the range AB, growth and developmental rate increase positively with temperature; the range BC is optimal; while in CD, temperature is supra-optimal and both growth and developmental rate decrease as temperature increases. This non-linear response of development to a wide tempera-

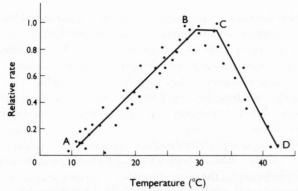

**Fig. 5.1.** Rate of growth and of development to flowering in maize in response to temperature (after Coehlo & Dale 1980; see also Warrington & Kanemasu (1983).

ture range is often overlooked in the application of simple phenological indices to the analysis of crop development (Section 5.5).

The cardinal temperatures (A, B, C and D) differ for species and cultivars and for individual phenophases but the form of the response has general application to all species. Individual response functions can be derived from field data provided a sufficient environmental range is included. Otherwise, they must be established through experiments in controlled environments.

The aging rates of mature organs towards senescence may depart from the pattern shown in the CD range of Fig. 5.1. Although few data are available, it seems that senescence is not delayed by high temperature.

## Determinate and indeterminate crops

Flowering is perhaps the single most important phenostage in crop development because it signals change to the growth of fruit and seed essential for the yield of most crops. A useful operational distinction can be made between crops depending upon the timing of flowering relative to vegetative growth. In **determinate** crops, including most cereals and sunflower, flowering occurs over a period of a few days following the end of vegetative growth. Typically, vegetative growth ceases because flowering involves conversion of the apical meristem of the shoot to the reproductive structure.

In **indeterminate** crops, including cotton and many grain legumes such as soybean, flowering overlaps with vegetative growth and can be prolonged for weeks or even months. This occurs because flowering progresses from axillary meristems while the apical meristem continues to produce new leaves and new axillary positions. Under certain conditions, reproductive growth in some indeterminates so monopolizes the assimilate supply that apical activity ceases. Such crops behave as facultative determinates with a single flush of fruit. Cotton behaves in this way but, given a sufficiently long season, may subsequently resume vegetative growth after the initial 'cutout', leading to a second flush of flowering and yield.

This distinction between determinate and indeterminate crops has great significance to crop adaptation and management. Indeterminate cultivars of fruit and vegetables such as tomato are frequently chosen for home gardens and fresh markets because a single planting provides produce daily over extended periods. That is a disadvantage with processing crops, however, for which repeated harvests are expensive and some fruit become too ripe. An alternative strategy, common with crops processed to frozen or canned products, is to employ staggered plantings of determinate cultivars.

Progressive ripening is especially disadvantageous to mechanical harvesting and facultatively determinate cultivars with a flush of flowering and fruiting over a short period have been selected for the indeterminate processing tomato and lima bean to allow harvest in a single pass by machine. Yields of those cultivars are actually greater with a single harvest than with repeated harvest of indeterminates. Indeterminate field crops grown for dry seed or grain must be selected against losses from shattering of the first-maturing fruit. Pods of most wild-type *Phaseolus* beans, for example, spring open at maturity, scattering their seed. Pods of domesticated types remain closed, and mature, dry pods accumulate on the plant as flowering progresses.

The two flowering habits have different significance in stressful environments. The prolonged flowering of indeterminate crops permits compensation for flower loss or seed abortion caused by transient stresses such as occur with high or low temperature and water shortage. In contrast, determinate crops are vulnerable to isolated periods of stress that occur during flowering. In wheat, for example, a single stress from frost or heat at flowering can abort the majority of flowers, so that grain yield is negligible, regardless of the potential of the crop at that stage or the environmental conditions during grain-filling.

Determinate crops do, however, have a yield advantage under resource-limiting conditions provided they avoid such devastating, transient stresses. The sharp transition in growth pattern provides the basis for an 'optimum switchover' from vegetative to reproductive growth (Paltridge & Denholm 1974). Harvest index (HI) increases during seed-filling because there is no further vegetative growth. An optimum balance is achieved, and HI and yield are greatest when the assimilatory capacity of the shoot just matches the yield capacity of the seed. In indeterminate crops, each additional flowering unit comprises the leaf and stem portion that subtend it. As a result, the amount of vegetative material increases with yield. HI remains low and the allocation of growth between vegetative and reproductive parts is not optimal (Paltridge *et al.* 1984).

## 5.3   DEVELOPMENTAL SWITCHES

### The importance of switches

Shoot meristems of some species switch from the initiation of leaves to flowers at a certain developmental age as determined by temperature. In others, the switch occurs as a specific response to daylength (photoperiodism) and/or low temperature (vernalization). Daylength and low temperature operate as inductive switches that change the type of organs initiated and are important factors in crop adaptation. Daylength is precisely and invariably related to latitude and day of the year (Fig. 6.5) and it is not surprising that plants have evolved adaptive responses to it. Because daylength is repeated twice annually outside the tropics, each followed by progress-ively more distinct seasons in the move from the equator to higher latitudes, the combination of photoperiodic and vernalization responses has proven particularly successful in selecting appropriate seasons for growth and reproduction.

### Photoperiodic control of flowering

The flowering response of plants to daylength is called **photoperiodism** and is one of a number of **photomorphogenic** responses of plants that also include initiation of tubers and root thickening in some crops.

Some plants (**day neutral plants, DNP**) are insensitive to daylength and for them time to flowering is controlled by temperature. Most plants, however, respond to various combinations of changing photoperiod. These can be divided into two broad groups: those that flower in response to lengthening days are termed **long day plants (LDP)**, while **short day plants (SDP)** flower in response to shortening days. In a few plants, such as Italian ryegrass, a single inductive cycle can cause an irreversible shift to reproductive behavior but, more commonly, several consecu-tive cycles are required.

The distinction between SDP and LDP lies in their responses to shortening or lengthening days (lengthening or shortening nights) and not to some absolute daylength, particularly 12 h as has often been inferred from the terminology of LDP and SDP. Some LDPs flower at daylengths well below 12 h while some SDPs respond at longer daylength. Thus a cultivar of chickpea (LDP) flowers only when daylength exceeds 8 h, whereas one of soybean (SDP) flowers only at daylengths less than 14 h (Roberts & Summerfield 1987).

Recognition of daylength depends on the ability of the phytochrome pigment system in leaves to measure the duration of night (rather than duration of day) through the ratio of red and far-red light received. The importance of the dark period is evident because interruptions of a few minutes, even less in some species, are just as effective in promoting flowering of LDPs as is increasing daylength. Manipulation of photoperiod with artificial lighting is useful in commercial horticulture and to some extent in plant breeding.

Fig. 5.2 presents several photoperiodic responses recognized in agricultural species. It records the developmental rate (DVR) from emergence to flowering at constant temperature, i.e. the reciprocal of the duration of the phenophase. Some responses (e.g. 3, 4 and 5) are **facultative** in that flowering is promoted by changing daylength but proceeds at all daylengths. Other plants have **obligate** photoperiodic responses because there are daylengths above (e.g. 1, a SDP) or below (e.g. 2, a LDP) in which they will not flower. Most plants respond to daylength over a finite range but in a few species (e.g. 5, a SDP) the responsive range is narrow enough that it can be expressed practically by a single value. The former response has been described as quantitative and the latter as qualitative.

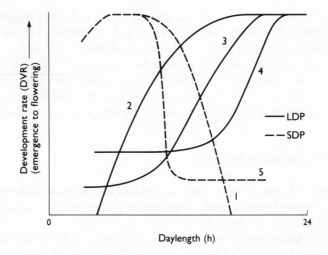

**Fig. 5.2. Examples of photoperiodic responses found in agricultural species (LDP, long day plant; SDP, short day plant; see text for explanation of symbols) (after Salisbury 1981).**

As is shown in Fig. 5.2, LDPs commonly maintain high DVR at daylengths above that required for most rapid development. With very short days the response of all plants is more complex and DVR usually declines. In such cases it is difficult to separate the inductive effects of short days from the associated small supply of assimilate for growth.

Cultivar response needs to be defined as a basis for breeding and selection and for predicting crop development in the field. Linear approximations of the response functions are frequently adequate for that purpose (Fig. 5.3). That is done by establishing the **maximum** and **minimum DVRs** occurring, respectively, at the **critical** and **threshold daylengths**. **Photoperiodic sensitivity** is the slope of DVR versus daylength within that responsive range, as shown in Fig. 5.3. For plants with an obligate response, minimum DVR is zero, but is finite for facultative plants. In species of high photoperiodic sensitivity, threshold and critical photoperiods coincide and the responsive range approaches zero.

The photoperiodic responses of a range of agricultural species are presented in Fig. 5.4. These responses correspond with the generalized linear models of Fig. 5.3. They also show how closely related plants may differ in the range and sensitivity of their photoperiodic responses, offering potential for manipulation in breeding programs.

**Soybean** Soybean, in which the mysteries of photoperiodism were first seen by Garner & Allard (1920), provides the most elaborate example of the use of photoperiodic response to match cultivar to environment. Ten phenological 'maturity' groups serve to identify the zone of adaptation of soybean cultivars in Canada and USA. Groups OO, O and I are adapted to the longer days and cooler temperatures of Canada and northern USA, while groups II to VIII are adapted

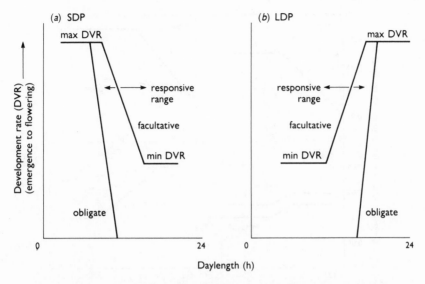

Fig. 5.3. **Linear models for obligate and facultative photoperiodic responses of short-day (SDP) and long-day (LDP) plants.**

progressively further south. A reference cultivar chosen from each group serves as a maturity standard against which other cultivars are rated. The differences between the photoperiodic responses of the groups are small as is the difference in daylength across the distribution of the crop. For example, for a May 20 planting there is a difference of only 2 h between 25° and 45° N. Nevertheless, cultivars grown outside their zone of adaptation flower too soon if planted to the south and too late if planted to the north. As short-day plants, northern cultivars (groups O, OO, I) have narrower geographic adaptation than those adapted to the shorter daylengths of the south (V, VI, VII). The North American cultivars flower just 30 days after planting under the short days of tropical regions.

## Natural distribution of photoperiodic responses

As a generalization, plants from tropical regions are either DNP or SDP without vernalization and those from higher latitudes are DNP or LDP, often with a vernalization response. There are notable exceptions to those rules including strawberry and soybean that are SDP from midlatitudes, and the pasture legume stylo (*Stylosanthes guianensis*), a LDP from the tropics (Roberts & Summerfield 1987). Sunflower is a species of temperate origin that now has SDP, LDP, and DNP cultivars (Goyne & Schneiter 1987). Such a wide range of responses is more common in species that are naturally widely distributed, as is seen in the photoperiodic and vernalization responses of the ryegrasses from Europe and North Africa. In those and other species, such variation is readily manipulated by selection and breeding to suit the specific production requirements of many regions.

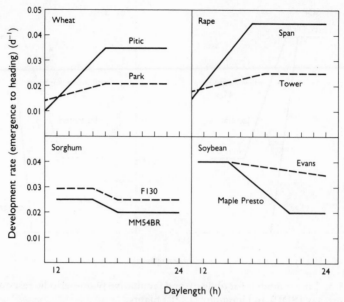

Fig. 5.4. Photoperiodic responses of wheat and rape (LDP) and sorghum and soybean (SDP) cultivars (after Major 1980).

## Vernalization

In some species, germination of seed, initiation of flowering, or bud break require or are hastened by prolonged exposure to temperatures down to −4 °C. The process involved in these varied responses in called **vernalization**. This section concentrates on the flowering response, a subsequent section deals with seed dormancy. Many winter annuals, biennials, and perennials have a vernalization requirement for flowering. As with responses to daylength, vernalization responses, may also be **absolute** or **facultative**. Winter cereals, for example, follow the form of response presented in Fig. 5.5 for 'Petkus' rye. During exposure to low temperatures, the stimulus is recognized and 'accumulated' by shoot apices but the mechanism is not understood. Exposure to high temperatures (> 30 °C for wheat) reverses the process. That is called **devernalization**.

## Interaction of daylength and vernalization

A wide range of vernalization requirements is found in commercial cultivars of oat, barley, rye, and especially of wheat. Wheat cultivars (LDPs) can be classified into three phenological groups according to environmental controls over development as summarized in Table 5.2. The differences are controlled by four genes (Pugsley 1971, 1982) and are now readily manipulated in breeding programs. **Winter wheats** have an absolute requirement for vernalization before they can develop beyond the vegetative phase. These cultivars are used in continental climates with moderate

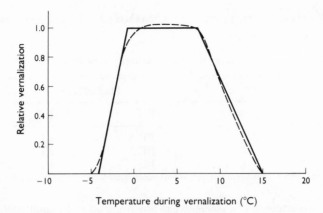

**Fig. 5.5. Vernalization response of flowering in winter cereals (based on data for 'Petkus' rye from Salisbury (1963); see also Weir *et al.* 1984).**

winters, such as Kansas and Ohio, England, and Ukraine. The crops experience prolonged cold following sowing in autumn but the winter climate is not so intense that the crops do not survive.

**Spring wheats** have no vernalization requirement and develop reproductively in response to increasing temperature and photoperiod. Such cultivars are sown in spring in regions where winters are too severe for the survival of wheat (e.g. Canada) but they are also sown in autumn in milder climates (e.g. southern Australia, Argentina, Chile, South Africa and Pacific coastal regions of North America). The distinction between winter and spring wheats is thus a phenological one based on a requirement for vernalization rather than the season when they are usually sown.

**Intermediate wheats** exist between these two extremes. They display a wide range of facultative vernalization responses in which exposure to cold enhances but is not essential for reproductive development.

An example of the interaction between temperature and daylength is presented in Fig. 5.6 with leaf production by 'Pitic' wheat over a range of daylengths at constant temperature. This cultivar is LDP with a facultative vernalization response. The plants had previously received varying degrees of vernalization by subjecting imbibed seed to temperatures in the range 2–4 °C for six weeks. Vernalization promoted flower induction except at daylengths less than 12 h. The number of leaves produced by the vegetative apex varied from 6 to 14. Leaf initiation ceased when the apex switched to production of flowers. The apex produced most leaves without vernalization, especially under short days. These results emphasize the role of developmental responses in canopy formation.

Intermediate wheats find many applications. The incorporation of some 'winterness' ensures that crops sown under warm temperatures in the autumn following early rains in Mediterranean environments (the break) do not develop prematurely in early spring. In this way flowering is delayed until after the last destructive frosts. Also, as with winter wheats, they can be safely used for winter grazing because flower initiation and stem elongation are delayed, thereby protecting the reproductive organs.

Table 5.2 A *summary of the thermal (T), photothermal (PT) and vernalization (V) responses of wheat cultivar types*

All responses are facultative except for the vernalization response of winter wheat

| | Phenophase | | | |
|---|---|---|---|---|
| Type | S–E | E–I | I–A | A–M |
| Winter | T | PT, V | PT | T |
| Intermediate | T | PT, V | PT | T |
| Spring | T | PT | PT | T |

*Note:*
S–E, sowing to emergence; E–I, emergence to flower initiation; I–A, initiation to anthesis; A–M, anthesis to maturity.

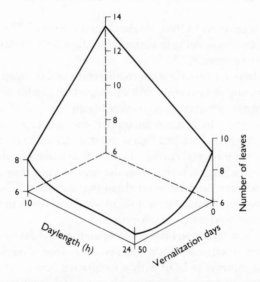

**Fig. 5.6. Effect of duration of seed vernalization on leaf number in wheat grown at constant temperature over a range of daylengths (after Levi & Petterson 1972).**

**Summary of interactions**   Table 5.3 records the interaction of photoperiod and vernalization in the control of flowering in a number of agricultural species. More elaborate classifications of the interactions of photoperiod and temperature have been made. Salisbury (1981), for example, distinguishes 25 groups.

## 5.4  CROP IMPROVEMENT

The complex developmental responses of crop plants derive from their long evolutionary history before and since domestication. Under natural selection,

Table 5.3 *Photoperiodic and vernalization responses of some agricultural species*

|  | SDP | DNP | LDP |
| --- | --- | --- | --- |
| Obligate photoperiodic response | soybean rice dry bean maize coffee | soybean cotton potato rice sunflower tobacco | oat annual ryegrass canary grass red clover timothy grass spinach radish |
| Facultative photoperiodic response | soybean cotton sugar cane rice potato sunflower |  | cabbage spring barley spring wheat spring rye potato sunflower red clover |
| Positive vernalization requirement | onion | onion carrot broadbean | winter oat winter barley perennial ryegrass winter wheat sugarbeet |

*Source:* After Vince Prue (1975) and other sources.

adaptation is generally restricted to local environments. Wide geographic distribution of individual species is achieved by the evolution of phenological populations each adapted to distinct local conditions. An important question in crop ecology is what developmental responses (wide or restrictive) are consistent with the managed conditions we might now create in agriculture?

Some crops are generalists, finding roles in a wide range of environments. Typically, that is achieved by having a growth duration less than the available season so that planting and harvest can be fit to a suitable portion of the year, or by having a range of cultivars with different phenological responses. Identification of phenological patterns has been an important aspect of crop improvement. This has been achieved by screening wide ranges of germplasm in time-of-sowing experiments, at a range of sites, to identify the best cultivar–time-of-sowing combinations. Such experiments have also contributed to our understanding of development as well as helping to identify methods for quantitative analyses of the responses.

Interesting contrasts are evident in the solutions reached by plant breeders for controlling development. Many crops, the prime example being soybean, are bred with attention to carefully tuned photoperiodic responses for local environments. A common thrust with others such as wheat has been to simplify developmental response through suppression or elimination of photoperiodic controls resulting in wide geographic adaptation of improved cultivars. In those cases, temperature remains the principal control over developmental rate (Fig. 5.1). The task is often straightforward because relatively few genes are involved (Wallace 1985).

## 5.5    QUANTIFYING PHENOLOGICAL RESPONSE

The complexity of phenological development can be quantified most easily with mathematical models. This section presents a model structured to allow easy incorporation of functional relationships between developmental rate and controlling environmental factors. The model is also used to explain the utility of two well-established phenological indices, **thermal** and **photothermal units**, often used to provide simple analyses under more restricted conditions. The two units are shown to be subsets of the general model.

### A model of developmental rate

This model is adapted from Robertson (1973). Chronological progression through a phenophase depends upon the accumulation of daily development (DVR, $d^{-1}$). The phase is complete after $d$ days when $\Sigma DVR = 1$. DVR is set as a multiplicative function of responses to temperature ($f_1(T)$), vernalization ($f_2(V)$), and daylength ($f_3(L)$):

$$DVR = f_1(T)\, f_2(V)\, f_3(L). \qquad \text{[Eq. 5.1]}.$$

This form allows easy, but effective, representation of the independent controls that vernalization and photoperiodism exert on development. The function $f_1(T)$ holds the units of DVR ($d^{-1}$), while $f_2(V)$ and $f_3(L)$ are scalar functions (range 0 to 1) that modify the expression of $f_1(T)$. Species lacking vernalization or photoperiodic responses are represented by setting $f_2(V)$ or $f_3(L) = 1$. The three functions are linear or non-linear depending upon particular phenophase–cultivar combinations as established by experiment. Observations made in controlled environments are valuable because they widen the combinations of temperature and daylength that are available at individual field sites.

Hammer *et al.* (1982) used this model to define the phenological development of 'Sunfola 68–2' and 'Hysun 30' sunflowers. Observations made in a phytotron suggested functional forms for $f_1(T)$ and $f_3(L)$ during the phenophase emergence-to-'head visible' as presented in Fig. 5.7. Data from time of sowing experiments in a number of locations were then used to estimate the parameters of the quadratic response to temperature and the switch function used to portray the influence of photoperiod. Vernalization plays no role in development through any phenophase of sunflower so $f_2(V) = 1$. Both cultivars had the same temperature response but whereas 'Sunfola 68–2' was day-neutral, 'Hysun 30' responded as a facultative LDP within the daylength range 12.5 to 15 h. The model explained 96% of the variation in independent observations of heading date over a wide range of temperature and daylength.

The model presented in Eq. 5.1 has also been applied to the analysis of the phenological development of winter wheat (Weir *et al.* 1984) by including a vernalization response in the phenophase emergence-to-flower initiation (Table 5.2).

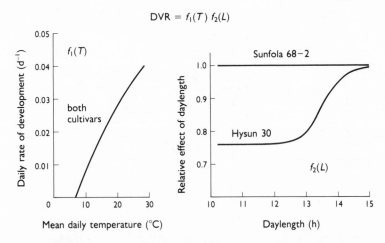

$$\mathrm{DVR} = f_1(T)\, f_2(L)$$

Fig. 5.7. Daily rate of development (DVR) of two cultivars of sunflower from emergence to head-visible in response to temperature ($T$) and daylength ($L$) in the form of the general phenological model (Eq. 5.1) (after Hammer *et al.* 1982).

## Thermal units

The dependence of developmental rate on temperature was recognized by the French naturalist Reaumer in 1735 when he invented a linear temperature model (and a thermometer scale!) for the analysis of development. Thermal models have since been used widely in the analysis of crop development and in applications such as the scheduling of planting dates for vegetable crops.

In its simplest form, thermal analysis relates DVR directly to mean daily temperature ($T_d = (T_{max} + T_{min})/2$)) in excess of a base temperature ($T_b$):

$$\mathrm{DVR} = f_1(T) = (T_d - T_b)/\mathrm{TU}. \qquad [\text{Eq. 5.2}]$$

If $T_d < T_b$, no thermal time is accumulated.

The daily accumulation ($\Sigma(T_d - T_b)$; units are 'day degrees,' d deg) serves as an estimate of physiological time expressing development through a phenophase rather than chronological time. The summation of thermal time corresponding to the completion of a phenophase (i.e., in the $d$ days when $\Sigma\mathrm{DVR} = 1$) defines the **thermal unit (TU)** for that phenophase.

A comparison of the method of calculating thermal time with the response of DVR to temperature (Fig. 5.1) shows that it describes the linear approximation, line AB, to the rising part of the curve. Eq. 5.2 is successful only when $T_d$ remains within that linear range. Some modifications have been made to improve the scope of TU. Thus the Canadian Corn Heat Unit calculates the daily accumulation of thermal time to a maximum $T_d$ of 30 °C, acknowledging that DVR does not increase beyond that temperature (line BC). Gilmore & Rogers (1958), also for maize, included a reverse linear function in their calculations of thermal time (line CD) to account for decreasing DVR when $T_d > 30$ °C.

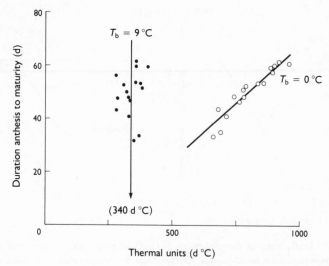

Fig. 5.8. Thermal analysis of the duration of the phenophase anthesis to maturity in four cultivars of wheat. For each cultivar, thermal units calculated to a base temperature ($T_b$) of 9 °C explain the duration of all times of sowing. Calculations to $T_b = 0$ °C do not (after Weir *et al.* 1984).

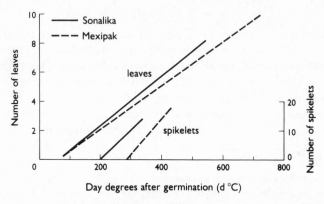

Fig. 5.9. Thermal dependence of leaf and spikelet formation in two cultivars of wheat (adapted from Stapper 1984).

The duration of the phenophase anthesis-to-maturity in wheat is determined by temperature and is relatively constant for various cultivars. The thermal analysis presented in Fig. 5.8 shows that TU calculated against $T_b = 9$ °C provides a common description of the thermal duration of that phenophase (340 d deg) for four cultivars. Calculation against $T_b = 0$ °C does not.

Thermal analysis may also be used to describe developmental advance within phenophases. Fig. 5.9 presents field data on the rate of appearance of leaves and spikelets of two wheat cultivars. The data illustrate that rate of organ appearance was linearly related to temperature in that experiment. Spikelets were produced faster than leaves and the two cultivars had different DVR for both organs.

## Caveats on the use of thermal units

The use of daily mean temperature ($T_d$) introduces a confusing empiricism into the determination of TU. TU for a particular phenostage of a cultivar can be different at locations with the same mean temperature but differing in diurnal amplitude. The problem is particularly evident in comparisons between arid (large amplitude) and humid (small amplitude) regions. The reason for that is seen in the response presented in Fig. 5.1. There, a wide amplitude around the optimum temperature results in a smaller daily advance than at the optimum because the crop spends many hours at temperatures that limit development. As a result, most published TU values are useful only in environments with similar diurnal amplitude to those in which they were established. TU can be made more generally applicable, however, by accumulating it from hourly temperature, which if necessary can be estimated by sinusoidal interpolation from daily maximum and minimum values. Suitable equations for interpolation of diurnal temperature are included in various crop simulation models, e.g. that of Denison & Loomis (1989).

Finally it is important to re-emphasize that success of TU does not demonstrate that development, unlike growth, has a linear response to temperature. The basic calculation remains a linear approximation to one part of the non-linear response of development to temperature (Fig. 5.1). The modifications referred to previously in the calculation of thermal units for maize (Gilmore & Rogers (1958), and the Canadian Corn Heat Unit) and the use of hourly rather than daily time steps seek to account for that non-linearity of response. Given the more general model of phenological development (Eq. 5.1), restrictions to linear approximations can be avoided.

## Photothermal units

A second important phenological index, the **photothermal unit (PTU)**, finds utility in the definition of phenological development of LDPs. In this model, DVR is made proportional to the product of mean daily temperature ($T_d$) and daylength ($L$), above base values, $T_b$ and $L_b$, respectively:

$$\text{DVR} = f_1(T)\, f_3(L) = (T_d - T_b)(L - L_b)/\text{PTU}. \hspace{2em} \text{[Eq. 5.3]}$$

If $T_d < T_b$ or $L < L_b$, no photothermal time accumulates. As with TU, a species or cultivar is characterized by the PTU (units, d deg h) required for completion of a phenophase. $L_b$ is the extrapolation of the photoperiodically responsive phase to DVR = 0 (Fig. 5.3). For obligate LDPs, $L_b$ will approximate the threshold photoperiod, but for facultative LDPs it is merely a mathematical extrapolation. For species with a facultative response, PTU analyses will be most successful when daylength remains above the threshold for sensitivity. PTUs work best for all species when daylength does not exceed the critical photoperiod.

PTU, like TU, is established empirically by iterative regression from field and/or laboratory data. It leads to descriptions of the phenological development of cultivars, such as is presented in Table 5.4 for the spring wheat cultivar Olympic.

Table 5.4 *Thermal (TU) and photothermal (PTU) units for the development of the spring wheat cultivar Olympic*

| Phenophase | Unit | Value | | $T_b$ (°C) | $L_b$ (h) |
|---|---|---|---|---|---|
| Sowing–emergence | TU | 78 | d deg | 3 | — |
| Sowing–stem extension | TU | 315 | d deg | 4 | — |
| Stem extension–booting | PTU | 6600 | d deg h | 4 | 0 |
| Sowing–anthesis | PTU | 6846 | d deg h | 2 | 6 |
| Anthesis–maturity | TU | 416 | d deg | 8 | — |

*Source:* Adapted from O'Leary *et al.* (1981).

An analysis of crop phenological development from the pioneering work of Nuttonson (1955) (Fig. 5.10) compares TU and PTU for the phenophase sowing to heading for 'Marquis' wheat, sown at 11 sites along a transect from Mexico (lat. 19° N) to Alaska (lat. 64° N). For each site, the diagram records the deviation from mean behavior across all sites. The comparison demonstrates that chronological duration

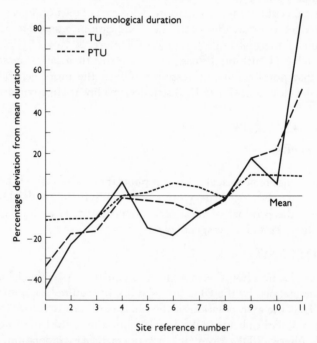

Fig. 5.10. Thermal (TU) and photothermal (PTU) analysis of development from emergence to heading in the wheat cultivar Marquis for plantings at 11 sites on a N–S transect from Alaska (site 1, 64° N) to Mexico (site 11, 15° N). The deviation at each site from mean behavior across all sites is shown for chronological, thermal and photothermal duration of the phenophase. Photothermal duration provides the most consistent descriptor (±10%) of the duration of the phenophase across all sites (after Nuttonson 1955).

varies widely and that PTU provides a better descriptor of phenological development across all sites than does TU.

PTU analysis has been used formally to describe only the promotive effects of increasing temperature and daylength on the development of LDPs but the general model (Eq. 5.1) is readily adapted to short-day plants as well. For example, Kiniry *et al.* (1983) investigated the interaction between temperature and daylength on the development of a number of maize cultivars. The response of one of them, 'TX60', from emergence to tassel initiation is presented in Fig. 5.11. It shows, for this SDP, that development can be described by a constant TU (290 d deg > 8 °C) for optimal daylengths between 10 and 12.5 h. Above 12.5 h, development slows linearly to 17.5 h, the maximum daylength studied. At 17.5 h, TU for tassel initiation is 450 d deg (> 8 °C).

This developmental response of 'TX60' can be expressed in the form of Eq. 5.1, namely:

$$DVR = f_1(T) = (T_d - 8)/290; \quad (10 < L < = 12.5)$$

$$DVR = f_1(T) f_3(L) = [(T_d - 8)/290] [1 - 0.074(L - 12.5)]. \quad (12.5 < L < 17.5)$$

## 5.6  SEED GERMINATION AND DORMANCY

Seed are key organs of propagation and dispersal. They preserve the genetic resource of the species and also serve to disperse the genetic diversity that is generated during sexual reproduction. In nature, this requires that seed do not germinate prematurely under transiently favorable conditions, and further, that germination is synchronized with conditions most favorable for subsequent growth and reproduction. An understanding of the range and action of the environmental factors and physiological conditions that determine the germination of seed are important to the successful storage of seed and establishment of field crops. It is also important to the management of species composition of crops and pastures by attention to the seed banks that accumulate under them.

This section considers the physiological and anatomical conditions that render seed dormant and the environmental factors that control the establishment of germinable seed. It also discusses the soil seed banks and their management for community productivity and persistence.

### Storage

Dry seed have low metabolic rates and consequently can survive in that state for considerable periods on their generally small reserves. Longevity is increased at low temperature and oxygen concentration that further depress metabolic activity. For that reason, farmers avoid high-temperature locations for the storage of seed; and scientists, concerned with the long-term maintenance of germplasm, carefully dry seed and store them at low temperatures. The National Seed Collections that have

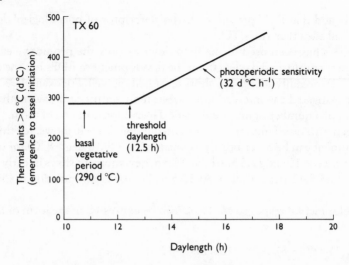

Fig. 5.11. **Dynamic nature of temperature and photoperiod response of tassel initiation in maize. Below the threshold daylength of 12.5 h, the thermal duration (basal vegetative period) is 290 d deg ( > 8 °C). The photoperiodic sensitivity between 12.5 and 17.5 h daylength is 32 d deg h$^{-1}$ ( > 8 °C) (adapted from Kiniry *et al.* 1983).**

been assembled in a number of countries store seed to around 5% moisture and − 15 °C. Germinability is tested every five years or so; most species can be maintained in that way for 15–20 years before there is a need to return seed to the field and regrow the collection.

## Germination and establishment

Seed germination, defined by the emergence of the radicle from the seed coat (testa), can be studied in the laboratory or field. In contrast, seedling establishment relates only to field performance, occurring when seedlings have grown sufficiently to emerge from the soil and establish functional shoot and root systems.

The major environmental factors that determine germination are moisture, temperature and aeration. The first step, the imbibition of water by seed, is a physical process dependent upon the colloidal properties of seed and the permeability of seed coats. For seed with permeable coats, the rate of imbibition is determined by the water content of the medium and degree of contact with it. For that reason, the imbibition of seed is less predictable in the field than in the laboratory. Contact between seed and soil is critical to continued uptake of water and depends upon relative sizes of seed and soil particles and, for recently sown seed, the subsequent repacking of the soil.

Imbibition of water initiates metabolic activity leading to the mobilization of reserves, growth of the embryo and ultimately germination of the seed. The rate of embryo and seedling development is then determined by the prevailing temperature and supply of oxygen for respiration. Consequently, the initial stages of imbibition can proceed with seed immersed in water, but germinating seed or growing seedlings cannot persist under such conditions.

Seedling establishment requires continued development after germination. Provided there is sufficient moisture to maintain hydration and oxygen for respiration, the rate of establishment depends largely on temperature. Development during that time continues to depend upon the mobilization of reserves to meet the growth requirements of root and shoot systems. Size of seed reserves thus sets limits to the duration of the period and hence to a major practical issue also, the maximum depth in the soil from which seed can successfully establish. Complex environmental responses of some seed to light, oxygen and carbon dioxide concentrations, and alternating temperatures have evolved as adaptations that restrict germination at locations from where establishment is improbable. However, most responses of that type have been bred out of crop plants, so provided moisture and aeration are adequate, the rate of germination and ultimate establishment depends largely upon temperature.

The rate of germination of individual species provided with adequate water and aeration shows the same form of optimal response to temperature presented in Fig. 5.1. Provided the temperature range is not extreme, laboratory measurements of the time to 50% germination can usually be explained by such linear approximations. The response of seedling establishment to temperature is more complex, but in general seed that germinate rapidly will establish most rapidly and successfully also. Physical conditions favorable for germination and establishment are more likely maintained for short rather than long periods and also there is less chance of seed and seedling loss by predation and particularly by fungal infection. Seed germinating from depth may exhaust reserves regardless of the rate of germination.

Table 5.5 presents an analysis of crop establishment, i.e. the duration of the phenophase sowing-to-emergence, for monthly sowings of a number of species over two years. It applies the thermal unit (TU) analysis (Section 5.5). The base temperature ($T_b$) was derived from the data by iterative regression to find the TU sum with the least variation over sowing dates. In most cases the degree of fit, shown by the $R^2$ values, is good. The failures indicate either that TU is not an adequate index of response to temperature for those species, perhaps because temperatures varied beyond those for which a linear approximation is appropriate, or that factors other than temperature influenced germination.


## Dormancy

Dormancy is detected when seed will not germinate under conditions of moisture and temperature known to be suitable for the species. It may arise in a variety of ways in either the seed coat or the embryo. Many crop plants have been selected during domestication to remove such impediments to ready germination but seed of most species exhibit some degree of dormancy, varying from year to year in response to environmental conditions during seed-set. In contrast, most weed and many pasture species, particularly self-regenerating annuals, rely on environmental

Table 5.5 *Thermal units (TU) calculated above base*
*temperature (T_b) for the establishment of various*
*agricultural species*

| Species | TU | $T_b$ | $R^2$ (%) |
|---|---|---|---|
| Wheat | 78 | 2.6 | 46 |
| Barley | 79 | 2.6 | 39 |
| Oat | 91 | 2.2 | 32 |
| Maize | 61 | 9.8 | 91 |
| Sorghum | 48 | 10.6 | 96 |
| Pearl millet | 40 | 11.8 | 97 |
| Field pea | 110 | 1.4 | 10 |
| Soybean | 71 | 9.9 | 87 |
| Peanut | 76 | 13.3 | 99 |
| Navy bean | 52 | 10.6 | 86 |
| Rapeseed | 79 | 2.6 | 45 |
| Safflower | 70 | 7.4 | 68 |
| Sunflower | 67 | 7.9 | 73 |
| Linseed | 89 | 1.9 | 37 |
| Buckwheat | 37 | 11.1 | 90 |
| Amaranthus | 32 | 11.7 | 86 |

*Source:* Adapted from Angus *et al.* (1981).

cueing for successful establishment and some form of distributed germination for persistence in the soil **seed bank**. They achieve this by a variety of dormancy mechanisms.

**Hard seed** are those in which the seed coat restricts the uptake of water or the exchange of gases. Low $[O_2]$ or high $[CO_2]$ can prevent or delay germination but low permeability to water is the most common limitation. This morphological condition is general in important families such as the Leguminosae, Chenopodiaceae, and Malvaceae. In the field, hard seed are isolated from their external environment and germinate only as seed coats break down under the action of the soil solution, temperature and moisture fluctuations, and digestion by soil microorganisms. Hard seed with no other impediment will germinate following treatment to break the impermeability of the seed coat. This can be achieved physically or chemically in various ways but the easiest technique, used routinely by seedsmen with clover seed, is 'scarification' (abrasion). Seed of many clover cultivars have high germinability only after such treatment.

**Immature embryos**   Some seed are unable to germinate when formed because the embryos are immature. There are two forms of this condition. Embryos of some species complete development only following imbibition of water. These combined processes of maturation and germination take between several days to weeks in various species. In others, embryos are unable to germinate at maturity but can develop further ('after-ripen') in dry storage without imbibition. This is an important characteristic for all seed crops. Germination in the head ('shot grain') can be a persistent problem in wheat and other small grains exposed to rainfall after maturity. An after-ripening requirement has been deliberately bred into cultivars for regions where such problems occur.

**Embryo dormancy** Completely developed embryos may be incapable of germination because of true physiological dormancy or the presence of a chemical inhibitor. In wild oat the inhibitor resides in the seed coat but in other species it is in the embryo itself. Seed of some species have this form of dormancy at formation; in others, it develops later (**secondary dormancy**). These forms of dormancy are induced and 'broken' by a seemingly bewildering array of responses to environmental signals including light, temperature, vernalization, nitrate concentration, and various alternating patterns of these factors.

Dormant seed are undesirable for the sowing of crops because farmers rely on full germination to achieve a crop stand of appropriate density and spacing (Chapter 2). Seed-bed preparation and planting are done carefully and at the 'right' time. The situation is different in pastures. The main reason is that seed bed preparation and placement are usually less precise so that some proportion of dormant (usually hard) seed helps overcome losses due to variable conditions during establishment.

### Seed banks

Seed in surface litter and soil make up the seed bank. Seed are added to it intermittently but lost gradually by germination, death due to exhaustion of reserves, decay, consumption, and physical transport by wind and water. Because of dormancy, the seed of each species exist in a range of age classes and states of germinability. A large part of the germplasm of a species may reside in the seed bank; for this reason, input–output dynamics (Fig. 5.12) of the seed bank are a focal point in the study of weed ecology and the persistence and productivity of pastures (Roberts 1981).

Not surprisingly, the seed bank is commonly comprised of thousands of seed $m^{-2}$. Most species rely upon annual additions to maintain their place in plant communities. Under rapidly changing vegetation, the species composition of the seed bank may be quite unlike that of the existing plant community. In crop-pasture rotations this is almost always the case. Tillage during the cropping phase incorporates seed of arable weeds, pasture weeds, and pasture species into the soil. This can be detected by comparing their relative numbers in the seed bank before and after each annual seed-set. For such species, attempts at control by preventing annual seed-set have good chances of success. Seed of other species, however, are extremely persistent in soil with examples of arable weeds persisting in soil for as long as 40 y.

Seed are formed in a range of positions above and below ground, at various seasons and with varying degrees of dormancy. Seed of some species exist in the hazardous surface litter where special adaptations, such as mucilaginous seed coats, are required to provide adequate contact with water for germination. Others, such as those of subterranean clover, are produced in the safer environment of the surface soil, and some have special adaptations, such as the hygroscopic awns of

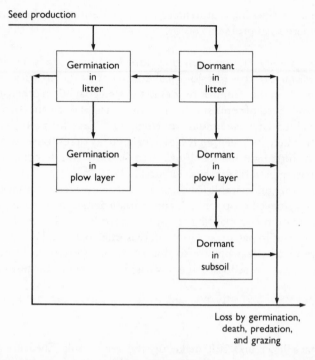

Fig. 5.12.  **A compartment model of the soil seed bank emphasizing location and dormancy. Seed passes between soil layers by natural movement and predators, but mainly by cultivation. Losses occur by consumption, death, and germination. Seed may gain and lose dormancy in response to environmental factors and internal physiological activity. Although single compartments are shown, seeds of individual species have different responses and dormant seed may include a range of dormancy states.**

wild oat and many grasses, that assist entry into the soil. Others rely on ingestion or gathering by animals and insects or more simply upon the formation of surface cracks, to enter the soil.

The microenvironment of the soil attenuates rapidly from the surface (Chapter 7). Water penetrates the most effectively, temperature less so (there is little diurnal variation below 0.5 m), and light does not penetrate at all. The vertical distribution of these factors and of $[O_2]$ and $[CO_2]$ determine the induction or breaking of dormancy and germination. The depth at which seed germinate and the level of their remaining reserves determine the chance of successful emergence and establishment.

**Managing seed banks**  Under cropping, the disposition of seed banks is dominated by tillage, which rearranges seed, burying some and uncovering others. Tillage also incorporates the surface litter into the soil, changing the energy balance and hence the temperature and moisture regimes of the surface soil. Seed buried to the depth of the plow layer (15–20 cm) experience a subdued diurnal and seasonal temperature range, low $[O_2]$, and high $[CO_2]$. Those conditions are conducive to the induction or maintenance of dormancy. However, the redistribution of seed by tillage also presents previously buried seed to fluctuating environmental conditions near the surface that encourage germination. On balance, tillage is an effective way to reduce the weed-seed load of soil, even though seed burial contributes to persistence.

In pastures, the seed bank is closely associated with the soil surface. The regeneration of annual pastures requires special attention to the seed bank. Seed production is managed through variations in the timing and intensity of grazing, mowing, herbicides, fertilizer, and fire. Sufficient seed must be retained to establish a competitive pasture of the desired composition each year and to accommodate losses that arise when conditions suitable for germination do not persist sufficiently long for establishment.

In the case of annual pastures (Chapter 16), the continuing production of some degree of hard seed aids in regeneration of the pasture in subsequent years by accommodating false breaks which lead to the death of that cohort of seed whose germination they caused. A high degree of dormancy ensures the persistence of pasture species but there are circumstances in which they thwart efforts at pasture improvement through the introduction of new species or cultivars. Beale (1974) measured the persistence of subterranean clover seed in self-regenerating annual pastures on Kangaroo Island, South Australia. Attempts to renovate the pastures with more productive cultivars of lower estrogen content (estrogen causes infertility in sheep) were commonly unsuccessful. A survey of 10 pastures (age 9–19 y) established a mean seed bank of this species of 243 kg ha$^{-1}$ (range 36–2260 kg ha$^{-1}$). The new cultivars established in the first year but were soon lost to competition and the pastures reverted to dominance by the original cultivars. Observations on pastures where seeding was prevented showed that 20% of the seed bank remained viable after three years, leaving considerable reserves for continued reestablishment of the old cultivars. Interestingly, only 11% of the seed bank decline was due to germination. Other losses, particularly consumption by mice, were dominant; sheep were excluded from these plots.

Fire is commonly used in the management of crops and pastures. It removes litter, controls disease, modifies the microenvironment of the soil surface, and also has a major effect on the size and disposition of the seed bank. Fire destroys most seed in the litter but conditions others, particularly hard seed in the surface soil, for germination. The species composition of many natural systems is determined by the role of fire in exposing the mineral soil and providing a seed bed. In such communities there is a wide range of adaptation of seed to survive fire and to germinate after it, including loss of dormancy due to heat treatment and mechanisms that release seed, protected from heat in bulky fruit.

## 5.7 SUMMARY

Development involves a close interrelationship between the differentiation and growth of new organs that change the form and reproductive status of plants. The rate of organ production depends upon temperature and the supply of assimilate. Stem meristems switch from the formation of leaves to flowers in response to daylength and temperature. There are many combinations of these photoperiodic and vernalization responses. With them, plants have adapted successfully to most environmental combinations.

Crop productivity relies upon the continual provision of new organs as sites for the utilization or storage of assimilate. It also requires a balance between the production and activity of vegetative (leaves and stems) and reproductive organs (seed and fruit). Successful crops are those which complete reproductive development within the available growing season. In environments of variable growing season, this involves developmental responses that allow complete use of both long and short seasons for maximum yield. Adaptation also requires that the pattern of sexual reproduction does not expose the crop to environmental stresses at vulnerable stages.

The control of development by photoperiodism and vernalization has enabled plants to cue their reproductive development to favorable environmental conditions. In agriculture, these responses are manipulated to provide cultivars best suited to specific environments, or they can be suppressed to provide cultivars of wide adaptation.

Much has been achieved in the production of new cultivars and the development of cropping practices without detailed quantitative understanding of developmental responses. Work with crop simulation models has encouraged quantitative analyses, and models of phenological development have improved considerably. There remains, however, much work to be done in defining the phenological response of agriculturally important cultivars. Quantitative analyses of the responses of crop development to environmental factors will play an increasingly important role in the design of cultivar-management combinations, particularly in variably stressful environments where optimum combinations require the assessment of crop performance over more years than traditional field experimentation can sustain.

## 5.8   FURTHER READING

Aitken, Y. 1974. *Flowering time, climate and genotype.* Melbourne University Press, 193 p.

Atherton, J. G. (ed.) 1987. *Manipulation of flowering.* (Proc. 45th Easter School, Univ. Nottingham.) Butterworths, London. 438 p.

Heydecker, W. (ed.) 1973. *Seed ecology.* Butterworths, London. 578 p.

Leck, M. A., Parker, V. T., and R. L. Simpson (eds.). 1989. *Ecology of soil seed banks.* Academic Press, London. 462 p.

Mayer, A. M. and A. Poljakoff-Mayber. 1982. *The germination of seeds.* 3rd edn. Pergamon Press, Oxford. 211 p.

Salisbury, F. B. 1981. Response to photoperiod. p. 135–167. In O. L. Lange, P. S. Nobel, C. B. Osmond and H. Ziegler (eds.), *Physiological plant ecology.* I. *Responses to the physical environment.* Encylopedia of Plant Physiology, NS. Vol. 12A. Springer-Verlag, Berlin.

Steeves, T. A. and I. M. Sussex. 1972. *Patterns in plant development.* Prentice-Hall, Englewood Cliffs, NJ. 302 p.

Vince-Prue, D. 1975. *Photoperiodism in plants.* McGraw Hill, New York, NY. 444 p.

Wareing, P. F. and I. D. J. Phillips. 1981. *Growth and differentiation in plants.* 3rd edn. Pergamon Press, Oxford. 343 p.

Williams, R. F. 1975. *The shoot apex and leaf growth.* Cambridge University Press. 256 p.

# Physical and chemical environments

Animals with thermoregulatory abilities and mobility can seek or avoid certain features of current weather. In contrast, terrestrial plants are rooted in place and must accept that rates of their metabolic processes are determined by ambient conditions. Crop ecology gives special emphasis to environment as the main determinant of what will grow, how rapidly, and for how long.

Crop communities extend a strong influence over their local microenvironment. Nearly all cropping practices are directed toward, or have the effect of, modifying chemical and physical aspects of that environment. The next two chapters deal specifically with these issues, beginning in Chapter 6 with the aerial environment, giving emphasis to radiation, and continuing in Chapter 7 with properties of soils.

# Physical and chemical environment

# 6

## *Aerial environment*

### 6.1  INTRODUCTION

Electromagnetic radiation is a central feature of the crop environment; its energy is the factor that determines soil and air temperatures, wind movements, evaporation, and photosynthesis. Two types of electromagnetic radiation, distinguished by their sources and spectral distributions, are important in crop environments. Solar radiation from a very hot thermal radiator, the Sun, is termed **short-wave radiation** (SW) because the majority of the energy is received in relatively short wavelengths, 0.3 to 3 $\mu$m. Thermal radiation from objects on our planet, including soils, plants, and the atmosphere, on the other hand, occurs at longer wavelengths because the radiating bodies are at much lower temperatures. Such **long-wave radiation** (LW) is found mainly between 5 and 100 $\mu$m.

This chapter examines these radiation sources and their roles in the macro- and microclimates of crops. When long- or short-wave radiation is absorbed by objects in our environment, the temperature of the absorber is increased. That heat energy may remain in the object or it may be radiated as new long-wave radiation, transferred to another object, or dissipated in the evaporation of water. All of these subjects are covered here. We begin with a review of several physical laws important in radiative transfers of energy among plants, soil, and the atmosphere, as well as from the Sun.

### 6.2  RADIATION CONCEPTS

**Thermal radiation**

All objects with a temperature greater than 0 K are sources of a continuous spectrum of electromagnetic radiation which, because of its source, is termed **thermal radiation**. The intensity and spectral distribution of thermal radiation may be compared with those from a reference 'black body'. Black body is a physicists' term for a perfect emitter of thermal radiation, represented by a hollow sphere pierced by a pinhole. The term black body is used because such spheres are also perfect absorbers of radiation: light entering the hole has essentially no chance of being reflected out again.

131

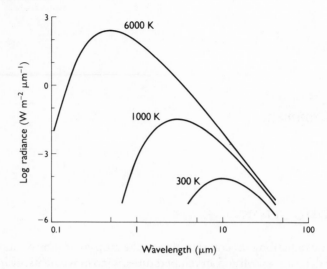

**Fig. 6.1. Spectral distribution of black body radiation as calculated with Planck's distribution for bodies at 300, 1000, and 6000 degrees Kelvin (K).**

The intensity and spectral distribution of radiation from a black body vary with temperature as illustrated in Fig. 6.1. Wavelengths of the maxima of the curves ($\lambda_{max}$) in Fig. 6.1 are predicted by **Wein's Displacement Law**:

$$\lambda_{max} = 2897/T, \quad (\mu m) \qquad \text{[Eq. 6.1]}$$

where T is the absolute temperature (K). Total energy emitted over the entire spectrum (E) can be calculated with the **Stefan–Boltzmann Law**:

$$E = \epsilon \sigma T^4, \quad (W\ m^{-2}) \qquad \text{[Eq. 6.2]}$$

where $\epsilon$ is **emissivity** (effectiveness as a radiator relative to the black-body standard) with values between 0 and 1, $\sigma$ is the Stefan-Boltzmann constant ($5.67 \times 10^{-8}$ W $m^{-2} K^{-4}$), and $T$ is absolute temperature (K). Although the tails of the distributions shown in Fig. 6.1 extend beyond infrared regions to very long wavelengths in the radio spectrum, the majority of energy is emitted around $\lambda_{max}$. The energy flux calculated with the Stefan-Boltzmann Law is the **radiance** per unit area of the source (sometimes also referred to as intensity) whereas **irradiance** is the amount of energy received per unit area some distance from the source. **Flux density** is also used to describe the strength of a beam of radiation in either energy or quantum terms.

Most Earth objects, including crops and soils, are near 300 K. At this temperature, $\lambda_{max}$ is 9.6 $\mu m$, i.e. at a long wavelength in the infrared region (LW). At this temperature, emissivities of crops and soils are all near 0.95, indicating that they are nearly as effective as a black body in emission. By contrast, the surface temperature of the Sun is near 6000 K and $\lambda_{max}$ is near 0.5 $\mu m$. This is a short wavelength in the visible portion of the spectrum. Radiation from Sun and Earth thus differ markedly in spectral properties (Table 6.1).

Thermopile pyranometers of Kipp (Europe) and Eppley (USA) designs are

Table 6.1 *Characteristics of thermal, black-body, radiation from objects at various temperatures*

| Temperature (K) | $\lambda_{max}$ ($\mu$m) | Range for 95% of energy ($\mu$m) | Emission with $\epsilon = 1.0$ (W m$^2$) |
|---|---|---|---|
| 0 | — | — | 0 |
| 300 | 9.6 | 3–100 | 459 |
| 1000 | 2.9 | — | $56.7 \times 10^3$ |
| 6000 | 0.48 | 0.3–3 | $73.5 \times 10^6$ |

standard instruments for measurements of SW irradiance. Because they depend on differential heating of a black absorber and a white reflector, thermopiles are equally sensitive over a very wide range of wavelengths. The receivers are protected from convection by domes of special glass. Photoelectric cells constructed of layered semiconductors (e.g. silicon) provide an electric current proportional to the number of quanta (or 'photons', if visible to the eye) received rather than to energy. Silicon photocells are sensitive only to particular wavebands. They can be calibrated to measure SW irradiance, however, providing the spectral properties of the radiation remain constant. Fitted with appropriate filters, silicon cells are used to measure the number of quanta of **photosynthetically active radiation** (PAR, 0.4 to 0.7 $\mu$m). (Human eyes are sensitive to this same band so we also refer to it as 'visible' radiation.) The usual units for PAR are mol m$^{-2}$ s$^{-1}$; a mole of quanta also may be termed an Einstein.

### Kirchhoff's Law

**Kirchhoff's Law** states that the effectiveness of a body in absorbing radiation of a given wavelength is the same as its emissivity at that wavelength. Crops and soils vary considerably in their absorption and reflectance of SW radiation but they all have LW emissivities near 0.95; therefore, they also absorb nearly all the LW radiation they receive. LW absorptivity and emissivity of air also obey Kirchhoff's Law but they occur in complex spectral bands and are not generalized easily.

### Cosine Law

Irradiance of a surface depends upon its display relative to the source of radiation. A surface such as a leaf displayed normal to the Sun's rays (at a right angle to them) receives the maximum radiation per unit area. If the surface is inclined to the beam, the energy is distributed over a larger area and the irradiance is less. Irradiance of that larger surface (I) can be calculated with the **Cosine Law**:

$$I = I_0 \cos \theta,$$

[Eq. 6.3]

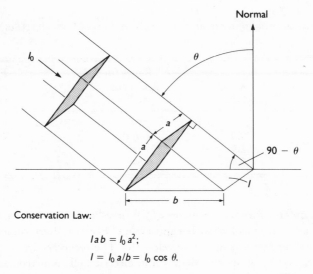

Conservation Law:

$$Iab = I_0 a^2;$$
$$I = I_0 a/b = I_0 \cos \theta.$$

**Fig. 6.2.** Derivation of the Cosine Law beginning with a beam of radiation with flux density of $I_0$ normal to the beam. The energy in this beam ($I_0$ times the area $a^2$) is distributed over a larger surface, also of width $a$ but with length $b$, having an angle of incidence $\theta$ to the beam. Because the energy is distributed over a larger area $ab$, the irradiance $I$ is less than $I_0$. From the Conservation Law, $I_0 a^2$ must equal $Iab$.

where $I_0$ is the irradiance normal to the rays and $\theta$ is the **angle of incidence** formed between the normal to the inclined surface and the rays (Fig. 6.2). The law can also be expressed in terms of the surface's inclination angle: $I = I_0 \sin(90 - \theta)$. When the beam of radiation lies outside the plane of the surface's normal, two angles, one for incidence and one for azimuth (A), are needed to define the three-dimensional geometry: $I = I_0 \cos \theta \cos A$.

## 6.3   THE SW SOURCE

Our Sun is a rather ordinary celestial body, one among an estimated $10^{16}$ thermonuclear stars of various sizes and ages in the Universe. The Sun is of moderate size and is composed almost entirely of fluid gases. It probably formed about $4.6 \times 10^9$ years ago from dust and gas dispersed at the 'beginning' of the Universe approximately $15 \times 10^9$ years ago. What is remarkable and exciting to us is the vastness of space and energy relations involved. The Sun's diameter is 540 000 km; its mass, $2.1 \times 10^{27}$ t, comprises 99.9% of all the mass in our solar system. That mass generates enormous gravitational force, leading to low-grade thermonuclear reactions in the solar core where hydrogen and neutrons fuse to helium. During that process, mass is lost and energy is released as radiation: $E = mc^2$ (energy emitted = mass loss × velocity of light$^2$). The Sun emits energy at the rate of $4 \times 10^{26}$ W; the corresponding loss of mass is $4.6 \times 10^6$ t s$^{-1}$. Even at that enormous rate, less than one-billionth of the Sun's mass will be converted to energy before it collapses to a cooling white dwarf about $5 \times 10^9$ y from now.

The outer surface of the Sun, the photosphere, is the principal source of sunlight. Through telescopes, the photosphere appears as a granulated surface composed of very large, gaseous, convection cells, broken periodically by long-lasting eruptive storms called sunspots, and by short-lived flares. The 6000 K spectrum of radiation from the photosphere is modified slightly by atomic absorption of solar gases, and by radiation from coronal streamers that extend millions of kilometers into space. As a result, the temperature of the Sun calculated with the Stefan–Boltzmann Law (5760 K) differs slightly from that obtained by using the measured peak wavelength and Wein's Law (6170 K).

## 6.4  SUN–EARTH GEOMETRY

Radiation from the Sun diverges in all directions but our distance from it is so great ($1.5 \times 10^8$ km) that we generally consider that the radiation arrives in parallel beams from a point source. In fact, the angular difference between light from opposite edges of the Sun's photosphere is 0.2° to an Earth observer (the angle is larger when the coronal streamers are included). This means that solar shadows are not really sharp but have a diffuse boundary (penumbra) between light and dark as is illustrated in Fig. 6.3. As a result, canopies composed of small leaves distributed over a large vertical distance (e.g. in a pine forest) cause unintercepted light to appear as diffuse shade rather than as shadows and sunflecks.

The amount of solar energy received by Earth can be measured with a radiation sensor displayed outside our atmosphere and normal to the Sun's rays. The amount varies slightly with sunspot activity, which affects X-ray, ultraviolet, and radio portions of the spectrum. A larger variation of several per cent occurs over the

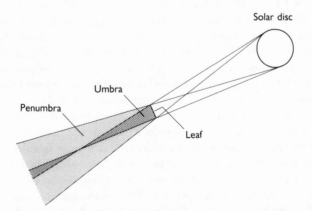

**Fig. 6.3.** Diffusion of a leaf's shadow owing to penumbral effects caused by the finite size of the Sun. A full shadow from direct beam radiation occurs only within the umbra. The distance *d*, beyond which shadows are fully diffuse, equals approximately 100 times leaf width. (Not drawn to scale.)

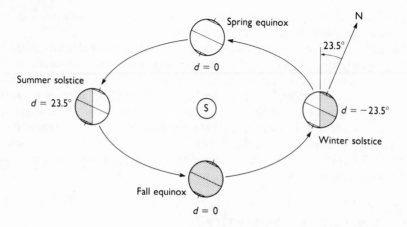

Fig. 6.4. Sun–Earth geometry during Earth's annual progression around the Sun. Solstices and equinoxes are labeled according to seasons in the northern hemisphere; the declination angle, *d*, is indicated for each position.

course of a year because Earth follows a slightly elliptical orbit around the Sun and the Sun–Earth distance varies accordingly. For practical purposes 1360 W m$^{-2}$, the radiant energy received at the mean Sun–Earth distance, is taken as the **solar constant**.

The average amount of solar radiation received by Earth is affected by its rotation and curvature. The amount can be calculated by considering that the area of sunlight intercepted is equal to the projected area of Earth and, owing to Earth's rotation, that the radiation is spread over the total area of our globe. Earth has a diameter of 6365 km and thus a projected area ($\pi r^2$) of $3.18 \times 10^{13}$ m$^2$ and a total surface area ($4\pi r^2$) of $1.27 \times 10^{14}$ m$^2$. The mean input of energy to Earth's atmosphere is thus $1360(\pi r^2/4\pi r^2) = 340$ W m$^{-2}$; and the annual receipt of energy is $1360$ W m$^{-2} \times 1$ J s$^{-1}$ W$^{-1} \times 3.15 \times 10^7$ s y$^{-1} \times 3.18 \times 10^{13}$ m$^2 = 1.36 \times 10^{24}$ J y$^{-1}$. The cosine effect causes an unequal distribution of this energy between equatorial and polar regions, and Earth's rotation causes it to be unequally distributed between day and night. The resulting circulation and mixing of air and ocean currents between regions are the driving force behind weather systems.

As is depicted in Fig. 6.4, unequal distribution of radiation over Earth's surface is further modified by inclination of Earth's axis of rotation at about 23.5° to the plane of its orbit. During the annual circuit of the Sun, inclination of the axis combined with progress in orbit leads to variations in daylength and to alternation of seasons as Earth's poles are alternately inclined towards and away from the Sun. At one **solstice**, near December 22, the north pole is inclined away from the Sun. In the northern hemisphere, days are short and it is midwinter; in the southern hemisphere, days are long and summer prevails. The situation is reversed 6 months later near June 22 at the other solstice. **Equinoxes** (near March 21 and September 24) mark times of the year when Earth's axis lies in a plane normal to the Sun's rays. Both poles are irradiated then and daylength is 12 h at all latitudes. The equinox between winter and summer is referred to as the vernal or spring equinox; the autumnal or fall equinox comes between summer and winter. Dates of these events vary slightly year to year because Earth completes a revolution around the Sun in 365.256 days and our Gregorian calendar adjusts for the odd 0.256 days with an extra day on leap years. The Nautical Almanac is a useful reference for exact times of events for any given year.

The shape of Earth's orbital ellipse is not constant but varies with periods of about 97 000 y. In addition, Earth precesses its axis like a top, turning slowly through a cycle every 26 000 y. Polaris and Crux, the present guides to the north and south poles, therefore are useful beacons for only portions of the precession. Sun–Earth geometry also changes over time, owing to cyclic variations with a period of 41 000 y in the tilt of Earth's axis of rotation (presently 23.5°). These matters vex calendar makers and high priests who must have things on proper dates. They are a source of excitement to geologists, however, who find in them explanations for past climates, including glacial cycles, and a basis for predicting future climates. Fortunately, these changes occur too slowly to influence agricultural ecology within a human lifetime.

Knowledge of where the Sun is in the sky relative to an Earth observer (or crop) is useful for many purposes not only in crop ecology but also in landscape and building design and for navigation. The Sun's position relative to an Earth observer can be calculated from latitude ($L$ in degrees), day of the year ($D$ in degrees = 360(day number/365)), and the changing **declination angle**, $d$. Declination is the angle formed by intersection of the plane of Earth's orbit and Earth's extended equatorial plane. In practical terms, it is the latitude on Earth where the Sun appears directly overhead at solar noon. As indicated in Fig. 6.4, $d$ varies over the course of a year between $+23.5°$ on June 22 (the Sun is directly overhead 23.5° N) and $-23.5°$ on December 22 (overhead 23.5° S). Values of $d$ (deg) for particular days can be computed from:

$$d = -23.5 \cos (D + 9.863). \tag{Eq. 6.4}$$

Because Earth's orbit is elliptical, actual values of $d$ deviate slightly from this smooth cosine wave. More accurate values of this and other solar parameters can be obtained with series equations developed by Spencer (1971).

Observed from Earth's surface, the Sun reaches its highest **altitude** at local solar noon ($a_{noon}$) (degrees) when the azimuth is 180° for someone at a northern latitude (0° in the southern hemisphere). The geometry of these situations is summarized in Eqs. 6.5 and 6.6.

$$a_{noon} = 90 - (L - d), \tag{Eq. 6.5}$$

where $L$ is latitude and $d$ is declination. Altitude ($a$) at any hour of the day is found from:

$$\sin a = \cos L \cos d \cos h + \sin L \sin d, \tag{Eq. 6.6}$$

where h is the **hour angle** from solar noon ($h = 360(\text{hour} - 12)/24$). The Sun's azimuth ($A$) from due south is found from:

$$\sin A = \cos d \sin h / \cos a. \tag{Eq. 6.7}$$

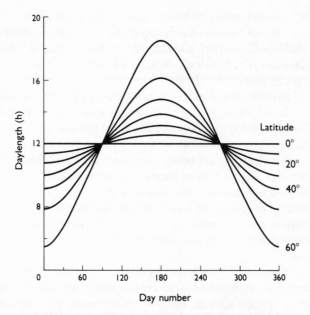

**Fig. 6.5. Length of day (sunrise to sunset) in northern latitudes as a function of day of the year as calculated with Eq. 6.8. The pattern is shifted by 182.5 d for the southern hemisphere.**

It is useful to remember that Earth turns 15° each hour (360°/24 h) and to know that the **sunset hour angle**, $h_0$, may be found from:

$$\cos h_0 = -\tan L \tan d. \qquad \text{[Eq. 6.8]}$$

The sunrise angle is $-h_0$. Daylength, then, is $2h_0$ in degrees and $0.1333h_0$ in hours. Distributions of daylength with latitude and day of the year are presented in Fig. 6.5. A twilight period lit only by diffuse skylight precedes sunrise and follows sunset but is not included in $0.1333h_0$. Length of the twilight period increases with latitude.

## 6.4   SW PENETRATION OF THE ATMOSPHERE

Solar radiation is strongly modified during passage through the atmosphere, owing to absorption in the ultraviolet and blue regions by ozone ($O_3$), in the visible by $O_2$, and in the infrared by $CO_2$, water vapor, and other gases. Absorption spectra for various atmospheric gases, illustrated in Fig. 6.6, have enormous influence on the radiation balance of Earth. Absorption by gases in the infrared region, beyond 1 $\mu$m wavelength, occurs in 'bands'. Each band is composed of many individual lines relating to vibrational and rotational frequencies of gas molecules. $CO_2$ and water vapor have the strongest absorption bands.

Small molecules and dust also scatter light out of the direct beam. Scattered light may be rescattered several times in other regions of the sky before leaving the atmosphere or reaching Earth's surface as **diffuse skylight** from all portions of a

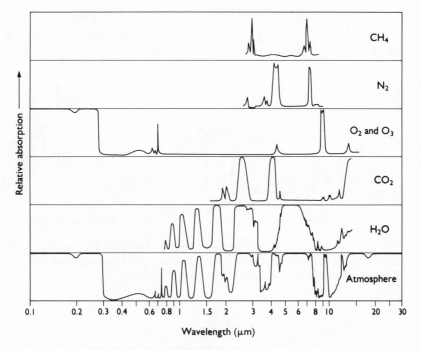

**Fig. 6.6. Absorption spectra of normal air and various component gases. (After Fleagle & Businger (1980).)**

luminous sky. Blue light is scattered more strongly than are longer wavelengths, so skylight appears blue to our eyes.

Absorption and scattering of solar radiation in the atmosphere are proportional to the amount of air through which the radiation passes. The mass of air between an observer and the Sun when it is near the horizon is much greater than when the Sun is directly overhead. The 'air mass' ($m$) is defined as 1.0 when the Sun is directly overhead; $m = 1/\cos\theta$ (where $\theta$ is the zenith solar angle), therefore a solar altitude of $30°$ ($\theta = 60°$) corresponds to an air mass of 2. At that altitude and with clear skies, irradiance on a horizontal surface is reduced by 50% owing to the cosine law (cos $60 = 0.5$) and by an additional 15–20% through absorption and scattering.

Spectral distributions of solar irradiance at Earth's surface with air mass 2 and air mass 6 (solar altitude of $10°$) are presented in Fig. 6.7. In Fig. 6.7*a*, irradiance is plotted in the conventional way against wavelength, $\lambda$. PAR portions of the spectrum with air mass 6 are much more strongly depleted of short wavelengths (0.4 to 0.5 $\mu$m) than of wavelengths between 0.5 and 0.7 $\mu$m. This effect is known as the 'red shift'. The absorption bands in infrared regions (0.7 to 2.5 $\mu$m) match the absorption bands of water shown in Fig. 6.6. In Fig. 6.7*b*, irradiance is plotted versus frequency, $\nu$ ($\nu$ is the velocity of light, $3 \times 10^8$ m s$^{-1}$, divided by $\lambda$). The areas under the curves in Fig. 6.7*b* are proportional to number of quanta in the radiation because energy per mole quanta ($E_q$) is proportional to frequency $\nu$:

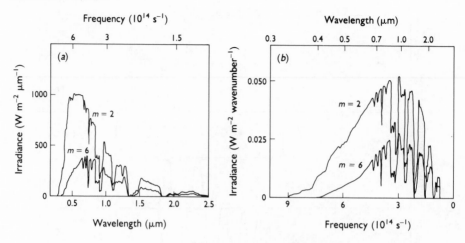

Fig. 6.7. (*a*) Wavelength distribution of short-wave irradiance of Earth's surface for air masses (*m*) of 2 and 6. (*b*) The same spectra as in (*a*) plotted as a function of frequency. (Adapted from Gates (1980).)

$$E_q = nh\nu \qquad (J\ mol^{-1}),\qquad\qquad\qquad\qquad [Eq.\ 6.9]$$

where *n* is Avogadro's number and *h* is **Planck's constant** $(6.63 \times 10^{-34}\ J\ s)$.

Distributions of direct and diffuse irradiances and their sum, **global** irradiance, as functions of solar altitude are illustrated in Fig. 6.8*a*. The measurements were made under clear skies near Melbourne (38° S) at various times of the year. Skylight contributed more than 30% to global radiation with low solar altitudes but it was less than 10% with high angles.

Total irradiance decreases and diffuse radiation increases as atmospheric turbidity increases with greater content of water vapor and/or dust. Absorption and reflection of radiation by clouds also have important effects on the irradiance at ground level. With overcast skies, the radiation is completely diffuse and much less reaches the surface. Fifty per cent cloudiness seems to be an average condition in the midlatitudes during summer, therefore only about half the hours approach the clear-sky condition. As a result, average daily insolation in humid regions is commonly 20–30% less than in arid and semiarid regions. Latitudinal distribution of daily total global irradiance with clear skies is presented in Fig. 6.8*b* as a function time during the year. This figure was based on 70% transmission through the atmosphere (humid conditions): maximum values there are near 24 MJ $m^{-2}$ $d^{-1}$ compared with more than 29 MJ $m^{-2}$ $d^{-1}$ received in midsummer at Davis, California (38° 30′ N), and other semiarid locations.

The fraction of the total SW flux received in the photosynthetically active region (0.4 to 0.7 $\mu$m) varies from about 0.44 in semiarid regions with clear skies and small air mass to about 0.50 where a greater proportion is received as diffuse skylight. The great abundance of energy in this narrow band fits with the evolution of our eye and photosynthetic pigments in their sensitivity to PAR rather than to infrared. Those pigments absorb on a quantum rather than energy basis, however, and the number

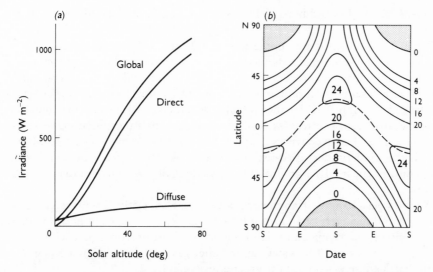

Fig. 6.8. (a) Hourly global, direct, and diffuse radiation observed with clear skies over the course of a year near Melbourne, Australia. (Calculated with regressions given by Paltridge & Platt (1976).) (b) Latitudinal distribution of expected daily total of short-wave radiation over the course of the year. The units are MJ m$^{-2}$ d$^{-1}$. Sun's zenith position at solar noon (broken line) are also shown. (Adapted from Neiburger *et al.* (1982).)

of quanta is greater in the infrared (Fig. 6.7b). A compromise was apparently reached during evolution among the necessary amount of energy per quantum for activating a pigment, quantum abundance, and interference from absorption by $CO_2$ and other atmospheric gases.

## 6.6   RADIATION BALANCE

The mean temperature of Earth varies little year-to-year because the average receipt of solar radiation calculated earlier as 340 W m$^{-2}$ is balanced by a similar LW flux to space. Examination of the fate of SW radiation and how it is balanced through LW radiation to space illustrates several important principles. These principles apply not only to Earth as a whole but also, as will be developed later, to individual crops.

### The 'greenhouse effect'

The atmosphere is relatively transparent to SW radiation but it is almost opaque to LW radiation from Earth owing to strong absorption by water vapor, $CO_2$, and other gases. The $\lambda_{max}$ for terrestrial radiation is near 9.6 $\mu$m, however, and an '**atmospheric window**' to LW radiation exists at 8–14 $\mu$m (Fig. 6.6). This window is an important route for LW loss to space. Radiation emitted at shorter or longer wavelengths (i.e. 4–8 and beyond 14 μm) is completely absorbed by a few meters of air.

When air is warmed by absorption of SW and LW radiation (and also by condensation of water in clouds and by contact with warm objects) its emission of LW increases. Atmospheric emission of LW is directionally random and Earth's surface receives a portion of it as a large downward flux. That flux amounts to as much as 15–20 MJ m$^{-2}$ d$^{-1}$ in the mid-latitudes and is a major factor in maintaining a warm Earth. Earth's surface is usually warmer than the atmosphere, however, and it is the source of an even stronger upward flux of LW (as much as 30–40 MJ m$^{-2}$ d$^{-1}$ in the midlatitudes). Because very little LW comes from outer space (its temperature is near 0 K), a gradual, net 'upwelling' of LW radiation to outer space occurs.

Window glass behaves in an analogous way. It is also relatively transparent to SW radiation and relatively opaque to infrared. That plus entrapment of warm air are the principles underlying use of glass houses for culture of crops in cold climates. By analogy, the roles of $CO_2$, water vapor, other gases, and clouds in maintaining a warm Earth are referred to as the **greenhouse effect**.

### Radiation balance

Fig. 6.9 provides a summary of SW and LW fluxes averaged for the globe. The magnitude of greenhouse effects is indicated in the figure by the large downward flux of LW radiation from the atmosphere. A **radiation balance** based on conservation of energy can be constructed at any level of the atmosphere. At the top of the atmosphere:

$$SW_{incident} - SW_{reflect} - LW_{emit} = 0.$$

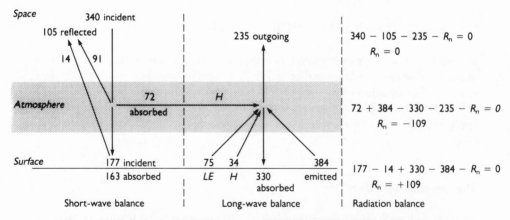

Fig. 6.9. **Global average short-wave and long-wave radiation fluxes and balances. The units are W m$^{-2}$. The radiation balances are constructed following Eq. 6.10 (LW reflectance at the surface is ignored, i.e. LW absorbance is taken as 1.0). (Adapted from Frölich & London (1986).)**

For Fig. 6.9:

$$340 - 105 - 235 = 0 \text{ W m}^{-2}.$$

There is a good reason why incoming and outgoing radiant fluxes balance at the surface of the atmosphere; if they failed to balance, Earth's temperature would simply increase or decrease until they did. At the surface of Earth, additional terms must be included in the balance. One is the downward flux of LW from the warm sky:

$$SW_{incident} - SW_{reflect} + LW_{incident} - LW_{reflect} - LW_{emit} \neq 0.$$

As is indicated by $\neq$, the radiation terms seldom balance to 0 at the surface. The reason is that radiation absorbed or emitted by objects at the surface may be exchanged with other fluxes of energy including evaporation or condensation of water and heating or cooling of crops and soils. For the example in Fig. 6.9, the average short-wave flux incident to the surface is 177 W m$^{-2}$ (340 – 91 reflected by the atmosphere – 72 absorbed by the atmosphere). Reflection from the surface is 14 W m$^{-2}$, so 163 W m$^{-2}$ is absorbed there. Earth's absorptivity for LW is near 0.95 and reflection of LW from the surface is ignored in this example. Due to the greenhouse effect, the sum of short- and long-wave fluxes absorbed at the Earth's surface (163 + 330 = 493 W m$^{-2}$) is much greater than the amount of SW entering the atmosphere. It is also greater by 109 W m$^{-2}$ than LW emitted (384 W m$^{-2}$):

$$163 + 330 - 384 = 109 \text{ W m}^{-2}.$$

This difference in radiant fluxes, termed **net radiation** ($R_n$), represents exchanges with other forms of energy. Inclusion of $R_n$ as an additional term in the radiation balance brings the result to zero:

$$(SW_{in} - SW_{out}) + (LW_{in} - LW_{out}) - R_n = 0. \qquad \text{[Eq. 6.10]}$$

$R_n$ at Earth's surface (109 W m$^{-2}$) is partitioned (Fig. 6.9) between evaporating water (75 W m$^{-2}$) and heating of air (34 W m$^{-2}$). By convention, $R_n$ is positive when the absorbing surface or plane dissipates radiant energy to other forms (temperature increase, evaporation) and negative when the LW flux is increased by loss of energy from other forms (cooling, condensation). In Fig. 6.9, $R_n = +109$ W m$^{-2}$ at the surface is seen to be balanced by $R_n = -109$ W m$^{-2}$ within the atmosphere where air cools and water condenses to clouds. The released energy is further dissipated in LW fluxes.

Similar imbalances in radiant fluxes occur at all levels above the ground within crops and in the air above them. The magnitude of the imbalance varies with time of day, atmospheric conditions, and status of the crop. In practice, $R_n$ can be measured with net radiometers which are simple, flat-disc, differential thermopiles shielded by polyethylene domes transparent to both SW and LW. One surface of the sensor is exposed horizontally to down-welling SW and LW while the other receives upwelling fluxes. Hot and cold thermocouple junctions are attached to the upper and lower surfaces, respectively, so the difference in heating is proportional to the net of the radiant fluxes. Alternatively, the net LW portion of Eq. 6.10 can be estimated with empirical formulae such as those evaluated by Jensen (1974). The net SW part can be estimated with data on incoming SW if we know the albedo of the crop (**albedo** is the term for reflectance from a complex surface). Monteith & Unsworth (1990) indicate that crops generally have albedos in the range 0.18 to 0.25, so net $SW_{absorbed} \approx 0.8SW_{incident}$. Albedos of wet and dry soils and snow may differ considerably from 0.2, however. The small value used as a world average in Fig. 6.9 (14 reflected/177 incident = 0.08) is due to the low reflectivity of oceans.

SW radiation changes dramatically between day and night whereas LW fluxes change only moderately as can be seen by introducing day and night temperatures into the Stefan–Boltzmann relation. Consequently, diurnal and seasonal patterns of $R_n$ are coupled rather closely with receipt of SW radiation. In tropical regions, daily and annual $R_n$ totals are strongly positive whereas those in polar regions are strongly negative. At mid-latitudes, daily $R_n$ is positive in summer and negative in winter.

## 6.7　ENERGY BALANCE

Net radiation is an important concept because it accounts for energy exchanges by crop communities that influence soil and air temperatures and rates of production and water loss. The objective of this section is to construct an **energy balance** for $R_n$ that identifies how energy is partitioned within the crop environment.

### Components of $R_n$

Three forms of energy are involved in $R_n$ exchanges. The most obvious are **sensible heat fluxes** related to increases or decreases in temperatures of air ($H$) and soil, plants, or water ($G$). Such thermal energy is termed sensible because it can be 'sensed' with a thermometer. Also involved are **latent-heat fluxes** related to changes in the states of water. Ice↔liquid water entails input or release of the **latent heat of fusion** of water ($F$; 334 J $g^{-1}$ $H_2O$), and liquid water↔vapor (evaporation and condensation) involves the **latent heat of vaporization** ($L$; 2442 J $g^{-1}$ at 25 °C). Large amounts of energy are exchanged in these processes but the temperature of water does not change and the energy cannot be 'sensed' with a thermometer; it therefore is considered hidden or 'latent'. Radiant energy also is converted to **chemical-bond energy** in photosynthesis ($P$) and then released during respiration ($R$) as sensible heat or thermal radiation.

Sensible and latent heat contents of air are transported with the air by convection. Through mixing into higher altitudes and transport to polar regions, the excess energy of the lower latitudes is eventually lost to space as LW radiation. Clouds, with their very large exchanges of latent heat, are an especially complex component of these processes. Ocean currents also transport enormous quantities of sensible heat between tropical and polar regions.

**The energy balance**

The Conservation Law can be used to construct an **energy balance** for $R_n$ exchanges at the crop surface in terms of the energy forms defined above:

$$R_n - H - G - LE - P - R = 0. \qquad \text{[Eq. 6.11]}$$

Latent heat of vaporization ($L$) is multiplied by the amount of water evaporated or condensed ($E$) to equal the energy flux involved. Each term in the energy balance deserves attention: $H$ and $G$ are important determinants of ambient temperatures in the crop environment; $LE$ is a central issue in water relations; and $P$ and $R$ are determinants of primary production and carbon cycling. Our convention in signs is to consider a flux to one of these components positive ($+$) as it gains energy and negative ($-$) as it loses energy.

Exchanges occur among terms in the energy balance as well as between the terms and radiation. A soil surface, for example, can be warmed ($+G$) through contact with warm air (and the air is cooled, $-H$), or through condensation of water ($-LE$). Conversely, soil may be cooled ($-G$) by transfer of heat energy to air ($+H$) or by evaporation of soil water ($+LE$). Similar exchanges among the energy terms occur on plant surfaces. It is important to note that while SW radiation is the original source of the energy (geothermal fluxes are very small), $R_n$ terms can be quite divorced from it in time. Heat energy lost from soil during winter ($-G$) probably represents energy gained during the previous summer ($+G$). Similarly, energy consumed in melting glacial ice today ($+LE$) is restoring that lost many thousands of years ago during the freezing process ($-LE$). The enormous amount of water on the Earth's surface and the very large amounts of energy involved in phase changes combine to give water a strong buffering role in global temperatures.

In crops, the $G$, $P$, and $R$ terms are generally small (*ca.* 1–5% of $R_n$). Discussion of $G$ will be delayed to Chapter 7; its magnitude is limited by the small ability of soils to conduct heat and because soils are protected from radiant exchanges by crop cover. $P$ and $R$ are considered in Chapters 10 and 11 respectively. Over an annual cycle, $G \approx 0$ (no net change in soil temperature) and $P$ approximately equals $R$ because production of organic material is balanced by decay. That means that $LE$ and $H$ are the main exchanges between the crop surface and the atmosphere and, for climatological analyses, the energy balance can be simplified to:

$$R_n - H - LE = 0. \qquad \text{[Eq. 6.12]}$$

$LE$ dominates in wet systems and $H$ in dry ones. Global averages for $LE$ and $H$ are included in Fig. 6.9; in that example, Eq. 6.12 is satisfied by $109 - 34 - 75 = 0$ W m$^{-2}$. Examples of diurnal patterns of $R_n$, $LE$, and air temperature are presented in Fig. 6.10$a$. Peak $R_n$ fluxes in this figure are near 700 W m$^{-2}$ and the daily average is 195 W m$^{-2}$. Close coupling in time between incident solar radiation, $R_n$, and LE is demonstrated here.

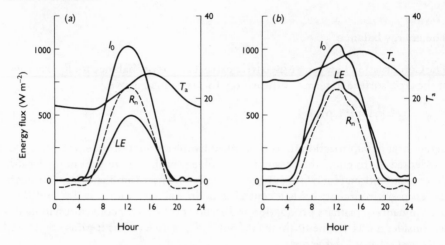

Fig. 6.10. (*a*) Hourly distribution of solar radiation, $R_n$, and latent heat exchanges (*LE*) of a ryegrass crop on a clear day in late spring at Davis, California. Air temperature ($T_a$) is also shown. The daily totals of SW radiation ($I_0$) and $R_n$ were near 31 MJ m$^{-2}$ and 19 MJ m$^{-2}$, respectively; winds were light all day. (*b*) The same crop 2 d later with similar conditions except that winds were strong. In this case, $LE > R_n$. (Adapted from Pruitt (1964).)

## Sensible heat flux to air

Air is a poor absorber of SW radiation and is heated and cooled mainly by contact with the surfaces of soil and plants and by absorption and emission of LW radiation. Changes in the heat content of air are determined by air's specific heat ($c_a$), density ($\rho_a$), and by the change in air temperature, $\Delta T_a$ (deg K):

$$H = \rho_a c_a \Delta T_a.$$

(The analogous equation for soil heat flux is $G = \rho_s c_s \Delta T_s$.) The specific heat of air ($c_a$) is only 1 kJ kg$^{-1}$ deg$^{-1}$ at 27 °C and 1 bar where density is 1.17 kg m$^{-3}$ (1.2 kJ m$^{-3}$ is a convenient value to remember for $\rho_a c_a$ as the volumetric heat capacity of air). The heat capacity of air therefore is only about 0.0003 that of liquid water (4.184 MJ m$^{-3}$ deg$^{-1}$). For air to carry large quantities of heat as it does, very large volumes of air and large temperature changes are necessary.

Air warmed (or cooled) through contact with crop and soil surfaces is moved away from a surface by convective action of prevailing winds and by the buoyancy of warm air (or denseness of cold air). Warmed air is less dense than the surrounding cool air and it rises away from a surface as a bubble even in the absence of wind. The reverse occurs as air is cooled. The basis for density changes is found in the Gas Law:

$$PV = nRT_a \quad \text{(liter bar),} \qquad \text{[Eq. 6.13]}$$

where $P$ is air pressure in bars (or Pascals; 1 bar or 0.1 Pa = 0.987 mean atmospheric pressure), $V$ is its volume in liters, $n$ is moles of gas (air has a mean molecular mass of

29 g mol$^{-1}$), $R$ is the universal gas constant (0.0831 bar mol$^{-1}$ K$^{-1}$), and $T_a$ is air temperature (K). At sea level and 300 K (27 °C), 1 mole of gas occupies 24.9 liters, so the average density is 1.17 g l$^{-1}$ (29/24.9). As $T_a$ increases, $V$ increases because $P$ is fixed by the general mass of air. As a result, $n/V$ decreases, and the air becomes buoyant relative to cooler air. Rising bubbles of light air are replaced by downward fluxes of cooler and thus denser air. Buoyant movements of air are observed most easily in the up-slope and down-slope winds common to mountainous areas, in desert mirages, and in the rough air encountered by small airplanes.

## Latent heat exchanges

Within a crop, the principal latent heat exchanges involve evaporation of water from leaves (transpiration) and soil, and condensation (dew formation). The collective evaporation (or condensation) of water by both leaves and soil is termed **evapotranspiration**, with symbol ET. As long as a surface remains wet (wet soil or freely transpiring leaves), evapotranspiration dominates over sensible heat flux. In temperate climates, latent heat exchanges involved in freezing and thawing of water are also important since the length of growing season is reduced by the time required for thawing of soils in spring.

Latent heat of vaporization can engage very large amounts of energy. With $R_n = 500$ W m$^{-2}$ of ground surface and 2442 J g$^{-1}$ as the latent heat of vaporization at 20 °C, $R_n$ could (potentially) be dissipated by evaporation of 500 W m$^{-2}$/2442 J g$^{-1}$ = 0.205 g H$_2$O m$^{-2}$ s$^{-1}$ or 737 g m$^{-2}$ h$^{-1}$. Given 10$^4$ cm$^2$ m$^{-2}$ and the density of water as 1 g cm$^{-3}$, a depth of water equal to 0.074 cm would evaporate per hour. Energy balance terms are commonly expressed in equivalent mm of evaporation. In this case, the evaporation rate is 0.74 mm h$^{-1}$.

Six millimeters of water is a typical daily total ET at mid-latitudes during the summer. That would require an $R_n$ flux near $+ 14.7$ MJ m$^{-2}$ d$^{-1}$ (14.7 MJ m$^{-2}$ d$^{-1}$/ 2442 kJ g$^{-1}$ H$_2$O $\rightarrow$ 6020 g H$_2$O vapor m$^{-2}$ d$^{-1}$). Six millimeters of water seems like a small amount but the latent heat involved in its evapotranspiration (or condensation and precipitation) is equal to the energy content of about 15 t dynamite per ha! The latent heat exchange through condensation in a typical rain storm can equal many megatonnes of dynamite.

Six millimeters of water occupies a large volume as vapor. Using the Gas Law (Eq. 6.13 with $P = 1.013$ bar (1 atm) and 18 g mol$^{-1}$ as the molecular mass of water), 8060 l of pure water vapor, filling a column 8.1 m high, would accumulate over each m$^2$ land. Unless the vapor mixed quickly with a large volume of air, we would have considerable difficulty breathing! The solution to this problem of air pollution is dilution through mixing with the bulk atmosphere. As was the case for sensible heat flux to air, mixing occurs through wind action and buoyancy. Buoyant transport occurs because moist air is less dense than dry air (molecular mass of water is 18 g mol$^{-1}$ compared to 29 g mol$^{-1}$ for air).

This situation actually requires a very large amount of mixing because a limit, termed **saturation vapor pressure** ($e^*$), exists to the amount of water vapor that can be held in air. This $e^*$ varies with temperature as depicted in Fig. 6.11$a$. Values of $e^*$

as a function of temperature can be found in handbooks of physics and chemistry or calculated from an empirical equation as:

$$e^* = 6.11 \exp[(17.27T)/(T + 237.3)] \quad \text{(mbar)}, \qquad \text{[Eq. 6.14]}$$

where $T$ is in °C. The value of $e^*$ at 20 °C is 23.4 mbar (0.0234 bar). Returning to the example with 6 mm evaporation d$^{-1}$ at 20 °C, mixing into dry air must extend to at least $(8.1 \times 1.013)/0.0234 = 350$ m. Even greater mixing is involved in the real world because air is never completely dry and ambient vapor pressure ($e_a$) seldom approaches saturation.

### Vapor pressure and evaporation

Evaporation depends not only on the rate of energy input to a system but also on the gradient in vapor pressure between the water surface and surrounding air ($e^* - e_a$). As a result, evaporation into unsaturated air differs from that into saturated air. It is convenient to consider these points now before returning to the question of how vapor is mixed with air. Normal air is usually less than saturated with water vapor and is found to the right of the $e^*$ curve in Fig. 6.11a. Air at point P, for example, is at 30 °C and $e_a = 21.2$ mbar water vapor pressure (15.1 g m$^{-3}$). The value of $e^*$ at that temperature (point S) is 42.4 mbar. The air therefore is only 50% saturated, i.e. $e_a/e^* = 0.5$ and the air is said to be at 50% 'relative humidity'. If air at point P is cooled without change in water content, it reaches saturation at point D, corresponding to its **dew point temperature**, $T_d$, of 18.4 °C. The vapor status of air can therefore be characterized by $T_d$ as well as by $e_a$.

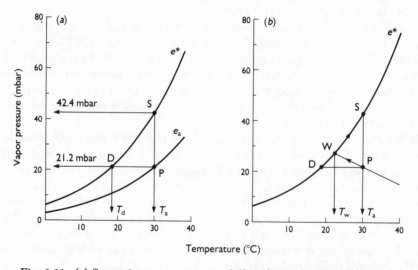

Fig. 6.11. (*a*) Saturation vapor pressure ($e^*$) and actual vapor pressure ($e_a$, 0.5 saturation) in air as a function of temperature calculated from Eq. 6.14. S is the saturation point for the air at P; D is the corresponding dew point. (*b*) Wet-bulb diagram for air at P following Eq. 6.15. The slope of line P–W is $-\gamma$.

**Evaporation into unsaturated air** 'Adiabatic' exchanges can take place between $H$ and $LE$ within a volume of air. In adiabatic processes, total energy content in the volume remains constant ($-H = +LE$, and *vice versa*, independent of $R_n$). When evaporation occurs, $T_a$ and thus the air's heat content declines; with condensation, $T_a$ rises. In such closed systems, evaporative cooling occurs along the sloping line from P in Fig. 6.11b towards saturation at point W and ceases when the air is saturated ($e_a = e^*$).

Similar cooling takes place when the bulb of a thermometer is enclosed in moist cloth and exposed to rapidly moving air as in a 'sling psychrometer'. When the air in the cloth reaches saturation at point W, the thermometer registers the **wet bulb temperature**, $T_w$. This serves as one way to measure actual vapor pressure of water in air, $e_a$. At any point along the line PW:

$$e_a = e^*_{T_w} - \gamma(T_a - T_w) \quad \text{(bar)}, \qquad\qquad \text{[Eq. 6.15]}$$

where $\gamma$ is the slope of line PW. This is the **psychrometric equation** and $\gamma$ is the psychrometric parameter; $\gamma$ varies with atmospheric pressure and with heat capacity of air but remains close to 0.66 mbar deg$^{-1}$ over the range of 20–30 °C. Psychrometers now are generally constructed with electrical humidity sensors (rather than wet and dry bulbs).

Progress forward and backward along line PW in Fig. 6.11b describes adiabatic evaporation and condensation in unsaturated air. Both adiabatic and non-adiabatic processes occur under field conditions. The system becomes open (non-adiabatic) if air within the canopy is exchanged with outside air. A warm, dry wind, for example, can supply energy for evaporation of water from plant leaves and from soil; $LE$ can exceed $R_n$ then because additional energy comes from cooling air. In Chapter 9, this concept is introduced into equations that estimate water loss by crops into unsaturated air.

**Evaporation into saturated air** Interior to a leaf, the air is saturated and **equilibrium evaporation** takes place. If $e^*$ within the leaf equals $e_a$, no evaporation occurs because no gradient $e^* - e_a$ for vapor movement exists. In that case, $R_n$ goes to $H$ and to heating the leaf ($+G$). As leaf temperature ($T_l$) increases, $e^*$ in the interior spaces increases, a vapor pressure gradient is restored, and evaporation ($LE$) continues. Beginning at point W in Fig. 6.11b with saturated air in equilibrium with free water, an input of radiant energy causes evaporation to proceed along the $e^*$ curve. For equilibrium evaporation, the ratio of $H/LE$ is given by $\gamma/s$, where $s$ is the slope of the $e^*$ curve at $T_l$. Because $R_n = LE + H$, $LE$ can be written:

$$LE = R_n s/(s + \gamma) \quad \text{(W m}^{-2}\text{ or mm)} \qquad\qquad \text{[Eq. 6.16]}$$

and

$$H = R_n \Gamma/(s + \gamma) \quad \text{(W m}^{-2}\text{ or mm)}. \qquad\qquad \text{[Eq. 6.17]}$$

As $T_l$ increases, an increasing proportion of $R_n$ goes to $LE$ because the value of $s/(s + \gamma)$ increases: it is 0.50 at 7 °C and 0.75 at 27 °C.

An important difference between evaporation into unsaturated air and saturated air is that unsaturated air can cool and contribute heat energy to evaporation whereas the temperature of saturated air must rise, if it is to hold more water vapor, thus robbing heat energy from evaporation.

## 6.8   TURBULENT TRANSPORT

Our calculation of the volume of water vapor produced through evaporation demonstrated the need for means by which vapor is mixed with very large volumes of air. Diffusion processes are simply much too slow and such mixing can occur only with convection. Buoyancy, involving rising bubbles of light warm or wet air countered by a downward flux of dense cold or dry air, is one type of convection. Another type occurs with turbulence created by the interaction between a lateral wind and vegetation. Together, buoyancy and wind turbulence can involve a great depth of atmosphere in mixing. The eddies of air thus created carry all the properties of air (temperature, water vapor, $CO_2$, and $O_2$) characteristic of their source (crop or atmosphere) and these properties are mixed (transported) between higher and lower altitudes.

The wind profiles illustrated in Fig. 6.12 serve as a starting point for discussion. The surface exerts a 'drag' on air, due to friction, so the wind speed ($u$) near the ground is less than at greater heights; right at the surface it is essentially zero. Smooth surfaces create only small eddies while rough surfaces create larger ones. Coarse vegetation such as a forest is quite rough to a wind while a closely grazed pasture is smooth. Topographical features such as hills and valleys, as well as isolated trees and hedgerows, add additional dimensions of roughness. Eddies near

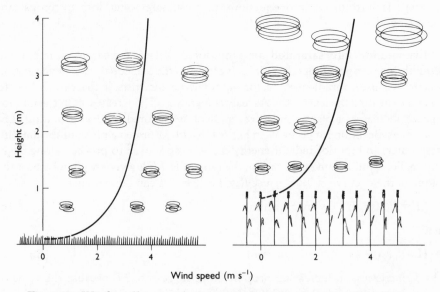

Fig. 6.12.  **Wind profiles over short-grass and small-grain crops. The profiles fit Eq. 6.18.**

the surface tend to be small and have rapid circulation; eddy size increases and the intensity of circulation declines with height above the surface. The effect of wind, then, is to create a mixing zone of turbulent air above a crop.

Mean wind speed increases logarithmically with height for several meters above a **zero plane** near the top of the crop. Wind speed ($u_z$) at height $z$ above that plane is:

$$u_z = a \ln(z - d) - \ln(z_0) \quad (\text{m s}^{-1}), \qquad \text{[Eq. 6.18]}$$

where $a$ is a proportionality constant, $z$ is height above the soil surface, $d$ is **displacement** of the zero plane above the soil, and $z_0$ is a further correction for **roughness**. $d$ is normally between 0.6 and 0.8 of crop height. The layer of air that obeys the logarithmic relationship constitutes a 'crop boundary layer'. Because wind speed is proportional to $\ln(z-d)$, measurement of $u$ at any two heights above the crop and within this layer establishes most of the profile.

A **transport coefficient**, $k$, calculated from the wind profile, describes its effectiveness in transport of sensible heat, water vapor, and $CO_2$ between crop and atmosphere. Lessened wind speed near (and within) the crop demonstrates that friction is extracting kinetic energy from the moving air. Height gradients of horizontally imparted kinetic energy ($0.5\rho_a u^2$ where $\rho_a$ is the density of air), or more simply, momentum ($M = \rho_a u$), are calculated directly from measurements of horizontal wind speed and air density. Existence of a concentration gradient (in this case a gradient of momentum) in a fluid system subject to mixing and diffusion results in transport between regions of unequal concentration. The **general transport equation** describes net flux ($F$) of that property between regions and can be used to find the value of the transport coefficient for momentum, $k_m$. For momentum transfer in turbulent air:

$$F_m = k_m(M_1 - M_2)/\Delta z,$$

where $(M_1 - M_2)$ is the momentum gradient over a vertical distance $\Delta z$. The equation is commonly presented as a simple differential equation:

$$F_m = k_m \rho_a (du/dz), \qquad \text{[Eq. 6.19]}$$

where $du/dz$ is the gradient of wind speed with height. Values of $k_m$ derived from such measurements define the effectiveness of wind in vertical transport of, in this case, the property of momentum; $1/k_m$ is then the resistance to momentum transport. The $k_m$ increases with increasing wind speed. The transport parameter $k$ is given various names depending upon the flux involved and the units employed. It is also known as the 'eddy diffusivity coefficient' and when the gradient is expressed in concentration units (i.e. mass $m^{-3}\, m^{-1}$), $k$ has dimensions of m s$^{-1}$. The physics of turbulent transport in fluid media can become rather complex; references such as Monteith & Unsworth (1990), Rosenberg *et al.* (1983) and Woodward & Sheehy (1983) can be consulted for more detail on theory and applications.

An important point about atmospheric transport is that the same eddies of air that transport momentum also transport sensible heat, water vapor, and $CO_2$ between the crop and a deep layer of the atmosphere. Analogous transport equations can be written for those fluxes:

$$F_H = k_H \rho_a c_a (dT_a/dz);$$ [Eq. 6.20]

$$F_w = k_w (de_a/dz);$$ [Eq. 6.21]

$$F_c = k_c (dC/dz),$$ [Eq. 6.22]

where $\rho_a$ and $c_a$ are respectively the density and specific heat of air, $T_a$ is air temperature, $e_a$ is the concentration of water vapor, and $C$ is the concentration of $CO_2$. Subscripts H, w, and c refer to sensible heat, water vapor, and $CO_2$. The values of all of the $k$ parameters are roughly equal (the '**similarity principle**' or Reynolds analogy), differing slightly owing to buoyancy and to molecular diffusion within the eddies. In principle, we can obtain $k_m$ from wind speed, and then use the same value for $k_c$ and $k_w$. Evaporative and photosynthetic fluxes of a crop can then be calculated from measurements of $CO_2$ and $H_2O$ concentration profiles. In practice, however, wind movements often are too variable and too confounded with buoyancy for accurate measurements.

## $CO_2$ transport

A calculation of $CO_2$ depletion from the air due to crop growth is presented in Box 6.1. This is similar to our earlier calculation for water vapor and helps in understanding the significance of turbulent transport and the great depth of air involved in supplying a crop with carbon. Actual patterns of $CO_2$ depletion over a maize field during calm and windy days are illustrated in Fig. 6.13.

The necessary mixing height in the $CO_2$ example (550 m) is greater than the minimum height we calculated earlier in the evapotranspiration example. Measurements from airplanes reveal that the turbulent mixing zone (or 'crop boundary layer') is frequently as much as 1500 m thick. Thickness of the layer and rates of transport within it increase with wind speed. It is clear that turbulent transport could be limiting to crop performance. With little wind, $CO_2$ supply could become

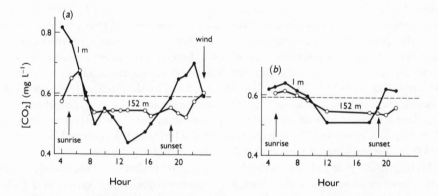

Fig. 6.13. Diurnal changes in $CO_2$ concentrations in the air 1 m above ground within an Iowa maize field and at 152 m height. (After Chapman *et al.* (1954).) (*a*) A still day. (*b*) On a day with light winds of 4–10 m s$^{-1}$.

Box 6.1 *The growing crop as a sink for* $CO_2$

A crop with a moderate growth rate of 30 g biomass $m^{-2} d^{-1}$, and a carbon content of 0.44, has a net uptake of 13.2 g C or 48.4 g $CO_2$ $m^{-2} d^{-1}$. (The molar mass of $CO_2$ is 44 g.) To support this growth and also make up for night-time respiratory losses of 12%, the crop must acquire at least 55 g $CO_2$ $m^{-2} d^{-1}$. The present concentration of $CO_2$ in our atmosphere is near 0.6 g $m^{-3}$ or about 340 ppm, v/v. To acquire 55 g $CO_2$, the crop must completely exhaust $CO_2$ from 92 m of air (55 g $m^{-2}/0.6$ g $m^{-3} = 92$ m) during daylight hours. Some $CO_2$ comes from within the crop by soil and plant respiration but $[CO_2]$ is seldom depleted by more than 1/6 (55 ppm), so the mixing height must be at least $92 \times 6 = 550$ m.

limiting to photosynthesis while water vapor concentration and air temperature within the crop would increase. Vertical transport would then be governed by buoyancy processes.

**Bowen ratio**

The need for estimating $k_m$ from the wind profile can be circumvented by comparing the ratio of two aerodynamically transported fluxes. As we will see in a moment, the transport coefficients then cancel. The ratio $H/LE$, known as the **Bowen ratio** ($\beta$), for example, now finds extensive use in estimating $LE$ from measurements of $R_n$ and profiles of temperature and water vapor. Simplifying Eq. 6.11 by omitting $P$ and $R$, and then rearranging:

$$LE = \frac{(R_n - G)}{(1 + H/LE)} = (R_n - G)/(1 + \beta).$$ [Eq. 6.23]

The value of $\beta$ can be estimated from profile gradients and transport equations as follows:

$$\beta = \frac{H}{LE} = \frac{k_H \rho_a c_a (dT_a/dz)}{k_w (de_a/dz)}.$$ [Eq. 6.24]

Equation 6.24 is further simplified with the assumption that $k_H = k_w$, i.e. that they cancel each other. This approach allows estimation of $LE$ with simple sensors for $R_n$, $G$ (using a soil heat flux plate), $T_a$, and $e_a$. The sensors can be combined with a microprocessor in a single instrument as in EPER, the Energy Partition Evaporation Recorder (McIlroy 1971).

## 6.9 ADVECTION

Crops grown in arid regions sometimes encounter environments that cause $LE$ to be greater than is predicted from the amount of energy supplied in $R_n$. An example is

Table 6.2 *Energy balance of irrigated sudangrass on a summer day in Tempe, Arizona*

Advected sensible heat flux from air supports a rate of *LE* greater than would occur with $R_n$ alone; *u* is wind speed and $\beta$ is the Bowen ratio.

| Hour | $R_n$ | *LE* | *H* | *G* | $u$ (m s$^{-1}$) | $\beta$ |
|---|---|---|---|---|---|---|
| | | (kJ m$^{-2}$ h$^{-1}$) | | | | |
| 0–2 | − 100 | 150 | − 113 | − 138 | 1.3 | − 0.75 |
| 2–4 | − 100 | 150 | − 126 | − 126 | 1.0 | − 0.83 |
| 4–6 | − 88 | 126 | − 75 | − 138 | 0.9 | − 0.71 |
| 6–8 | 163 | 439 | − 351 | 75 | 1.0 | − 0.87 |
| 8–10 | 1260 | 1330 | − 176 | 100 | 0.9 | − 0.13 |
| 10–12 | 1160 | 2310 | − 276 | 113 | 3.2 | − 0.12 |
| 12–14 | 2450 | 2640 | − 264 | 75 | 3.6 | − 0.10 |
| 14–16 | 1920 | 2350 | − 364 | − 63 | 3.5 | − 0.16 |
| 16–18 | 715 | 1730 | − 904 | − 113 | 4.6 | − 0.54 |
| 18–20 | − 151 | 715 | − 703 | − 163 | 5.2 | − 1.00 |
| 20–22 | − 151 | 326 | − 326 | − 151 | 2.8 | − 0.98 |
| 22–24 | − 163 | 251 | − 289 | − 126 | 1.9 | − 1.15 |
| *Daily totals:* | | | | | | |
| | 15 770 | 25 020 | − 7950 | − 1300 | (kJ m$^{-2}$ d$^{-1}$) | |
| | 6.44 | 10.2 | − 3.25 | − 0.53 | (mm) | |

*Source:* Data adapted from Penman *et al.* (1967).

presented in Fig. 6.10*b* with irrigated ryegrass, where $LE > R_n$ throughout the daylight hours. As an indication of the evaporative demand imposed by the wind, $e_a$ at 1600 h was 13 mbar compared with $e^*$ near 65 mbar ($T_a = 38$ °C). Data from irrigated sudangrass (Table 6.2) illustrate a similar condition. In these cases, additional energy for the evaporation of water came from the surrounding unirrigated landscapes where, because of the lack of water, $R_n \rightarrow H$. As warm, dry air moved across the crops, energy was extracted by the crop and the air cooled ($H \rightarrow LE$); as a result, the Bowen ratio ($\beta$) was always negative (Table 6.2). Lateral transfers of energy of this type are termed **advection**. Without a wind for a continuing supply of warm air, the leaves would cool by evaporation, $e^*$ within the leaf would decline, and *LE* would be restricted. When prevailing winds are either drier or warmer than air within the crop, moving air serves as a continuing source of additional energy for evaporation. Advection also occurs with vertical transfers of air.

Advection contributes to 'border effects' that cause plants at the margins of fields to grow differently from those in the center. At a border between short and tall plants, the tall plants are exposed to greater evaporative demand through side-lighting and advection. Other factors such as reduced competition for aerial and soil resources are also involved in border effects.

Most of the microclimate transition is complete within a few meters from the edge of the crop, but the distance needed for a truly steady-state wind profile and pattern of microclimate factors may be several hundred meters and is not achieved

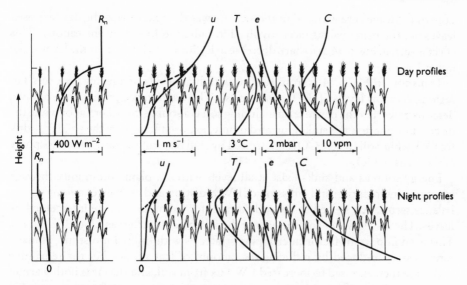

**Fig. 6.14.** Idealized profiles of $R_n$, wind speed ($u$), $T_a$, $e_a$, and $CO_2$ concentration ($C$) in a small-grain crop during day and night. (Adapted from Monteith & Unsworth (1990).)

within the size of fields common in most farming systems. The distance from a change in vegetation is called the wind **fetch**. Deserts have large wind fetches over dry vegetation. In humid regions, the mosaics of pastures, crops, and woodlands are similarly supplied with moisture and transitions between fields are not as dramatic as in dry regions.

## 6.10 MICROCLIMATE

### Microclimate profiles

Radiation and energy budgets and turbulent transport are all involved in the strong control that crops extend over their own microclimates. Microclimates are defined by vertical distributions of air properties within the crop and are driven by $R_n$ exchanges on leaf and soil surfaces. With water present, water vapor and cool temperatures dominate the profiles; without water, temperatures increase. Idealized day and night profiles of various microclimate variables within a wet crop are illustrated in Fig. 6.14.

The $R_n$ flux measured at any level within a canopy is the balance of upward and downward radiant fluxes across the plane. A positive value (daytime) means that radiant energy is going to various terms of the energy balance. In the full-cover crop shown in Fig. 6.14, exposed leaves account for most of the $R_n$ exchange. During daytime, the exposed-leaf plane is also the region where air is being cooled by contact with transpiring leaves. The night sky is a poor source of LW radiation compared with a crop that has warmed during the day, and $R_n$ is negative during the night. Leaves within the canopy are surrounded by warm objects whereas the uppermost leaves are exposed to the sky. As was the case during the day, exposed leaves are the principal surfaces involved in radiation loss from the canopy. This effect is seen in Fig. 6.14 as a sharp decrease in $R_n$ flux and a lower $T_a$ at the level of the upper leaves.

Transport in Fig. 6.14 is from regions with high levels of a factor ('sources') to regions with low levels of the factor ('sinks'). The water vapor profile, for example, demonstrates that the entire crop including soil is a source for water vapor while the drier atmosphere is the sink. During daytime, exposed leaves are the principal sink for $CO_2$ while soil (where $CO_2$ is generated by 'soil respiration') and the atmosphere are sources of $CO_2$.

Energy sources and sinks exist at all levels within a plant community through repetitive interception and emission of LW radiation and exchanges among energy balance terms. Air heated at the soil surface, for example, may be intercepted by leaves. The leaves warm and the energy then disperses further as *LE* or LW fluxes. This is an important factor in cropping strategies with limited moisture. Transpiration can be reduced by reducing the amount of leaf surface but the remaining leaves are then exposed to increased LW flux from soil, and the air is both warmer and drier. These factors increase transpiration per unit leaf area, somewhat offsetting the intended savings of water (see Chapters 9 and 13).

### Dew and frost formation

At night, exposed leaves are colder than other parts of the canopy because they emit more energy than they receive. This explains why frost and dew accumulate on exposed leaves rather than on leaves lower in the canopy. Dew formation is illustrated in Fig. 6.14 where upper leaves are sinks for water vapor during the night. With night-time $R_n = -50$ W m$^{-2}$ (LW$_{out}$ = 350 and LW$_{in}$ = 300 W m$^{-2}$), the maximum rate of dew formation would be $-0.020$ g H$_2$O m$^{-2}$ s$^{-1}$ ($-50$ W m$^2$/2480 J g$^{-1}$, the latent heat of vaporization near 10 °C). This corresponds to 72 g m$^{-2}$ h$^{-1}$ or a depth of about 0.07 mm h$^{-1}$. LE is given a negative sign here because the latent heat content of air within the crop is declining. With leaf temperature at 0 °C, the same rate of cooling would freeze a larger amount of water because its latent heat of fusion is only 335 J g$^{-1}$. Thus $-50/335 = -0.149$ g ice m$^{-2}$ s$^{-1}$.

High rates of dew or frost formation can occur for only a few hours each night because unsaturated air must first cool to the dew or frost point by contact with cold leaves. Dry air, with a low dew point, must cool to a lower temperature than is necessary with moist air, and dew formation occurs over fewer hours of the night in dry climates. The total amount of dew or frost may be as much as at a more humid site, however, because the cooling rate of dry air is greater than for humid air: dry air is more transparent to LW$_{out}$ and a poorer source of LW$_{in}$.

Moisture supply also limits dew formation. Without wind, air near a leaf can be depleted quickly of vapor. Resupply by diffusion is very slow and dew formation is greater when light winds provide turbulent transport. By contrast, freezing damage is greatest on still nights because temperatures can drop rapidly once the supply of moisture for freezing is exhausted.

Strong winds prevent both dew and frost formation because leaf cooling is prevented by advection of warm air from above the crop. Wind machines employed for frost protection in orchards work on that principle. Other methods for frost protection include heaters, which create vertical mixing by buoyancy as well as line-of-sight radiation heating, and sprinkler irrigation. Protection with sprinklers depends on the latent heat released through freezing of irrigation water; water in plant tissues is protected from freezing by the presence of solutes, which lower its freezing point 1–3 deg below 0 °C.

## 6.11  WEATHER AND CLIMATE

### Global climate

Interactions between radiation, the atmosphere, and Earth's surface establish the average temperature of Earth. Unequal heating across latitudes results in continuous motion and mixing of the atmosphere and oceans that give rise to daily weather and long-term patterns of climate.

Atmospheric motion takes form in large circular eddies around centers of high and low barometric pressure. Warm air rising in the tropics spreads away from the equator in both directions. As it is cooled at high altitude by LW losses, it sinks to the surface near 30° latitude, forming subtropical high-pressure cells. Earth's rotation imparts momentum to the air, which causes these high-pressure cells to rotate in the horizontal plane (clockwise in the northern hemisphere and counter clockwise in the southern hemisphere). The descending high-pressure cells are linked at intermediate latitudes with low-pressure cells of ascending air (with a rotation opposite to that of adjacent highs). Strong west-to-east (westerly) movement of the cells occurs at 30 to 70° latitude in both hemispheres; easterlies dominate at the equator and poles.

At intermediate latitudes, frontal systems develop where cold and warm air masses are forced together. The continuing progression of highs and lows with warm and cold air results in daily weather. These patterns are strongly modified by oceans and continents. $R_n$ exchanges on land are controlled by the limited supply of water and by the small heat conductivity of land masses. During summer, continents tend to be dominated by $+H$ and ascending low-pressure cells and during winter by $-H$ and descending highs. Mountain ranges have a strong effect on weather, particularly on the distribution of rainfall. As moisture-laden surface winds are lifted over mountains, they cool adiabatically to the dew point, clouds form, and rain falls. This 'orographic' effect contrasts to frontal and thunderstorm rainfall in areas without mountains. One consequence is that downwind of mountains the air has less moisture, and cloudiness and rainfall are less. That effect contributes to the semiarid and desert nature of many parts of the world. In western North America, for example, much of the moisture content of prevailing westerlies is deposited on the Pacific slopes of the Cascade and Sierra Nevada mountains and in the Rocky Mountains. Ocean currents also have a marked effect. The Gulf Stream of the North Atlantic ocean brings warm water and moderate climates to high latitudes in Europe. Similar currents from the Philippines moderate the climates of Japan and Alaska. The coasts of California, Chile, Morocco, and southwest Africa, by contrast, are influenced by cold currents. There, equilibrium vapor pressures are low and the coastal climates are dry.

## Topographical influences

Hills and mountains influence weather and microclimate in ways other than through orographic rainfall. Temperature declines with altitude, for example, due to adiabatic expansion of air. The barometric pressure at 5500 m is approximately 0.5 bar or only half that at sea level (1.01 bar). As a result, rising air expands adiabatically and from the Gas Law, Eq. 6.13, its temperature declines. The normal **'lapse rate'** of $T_a$ for an unsaturated atmosphere is $-1$ °C per 100 m rise in altitude. Water is condensed from saturated atmospheres on cooling, and the lapse rate then is only about $-0.6$ °C per 100 m owing to release of latent heat in cloud formation. The temperature lapse has an effect on climate similar to increasing latitude so that in the tropics one can progress from a wet tropical climate at sea level to a polar one and see their characteristic vegetations, simply by climbing a high mountain. Lapse rates are also involved in desertifying effects of orographic rainfall. Moist air rising on one side of a mountain range cools at about 0.6 °C per 100 m but after losing its moisture in rainfall it warms at a rate near 1 °C per 100 m during its descent on the opposite side. The result is that downwind air is not only drier but also hotter.

Sites at the same altitude but with different slope and aspect have different climates. Sun-facing slopes receive greater insolation than reverse slopes (from the Cosine Law) and thus are warmer and have greater evapotranspiration. That is seen in Fig.6.15 where annual insolation on a 10°, north-facing slope in the southern hemisphere is nearly 30% greater than for the reverse slope. Sharp differences in natural vegetation and in farming are common between north and south slopes. The effect is particularly evident in France and Germany where vineyards and orchards are generally placed on south-facing slopes. Temperature differences also occur between valley bottoms and surrounding hillsides. During night, with $-R_n$, air is cooled by contact with surfaces and dense, cold, air drains from hillsides into valleys. As a result, crops grown in the valley bottom are more subject to damage from frost than are those higher on the slope. Accumulation of cold air near the ground whether due to advective drainage or to LW cooling of the surface results in an **inversion** of the normal lapse rate. Inversions eliminate buoyancy as a component of turbulent transport at night.

## Climate classification

The continuous motion of the atmosphere results in a seasonal progression of daily weather. That weather, while highly variable, follows general circulation patterns characteristic for each place on the globe. Climate, the 'cumulative expression of daily weather' (Trewartha & Horn 1980), is defined by long-term averages of weather. Weather and climate both influence the practice of agriculture. Farming

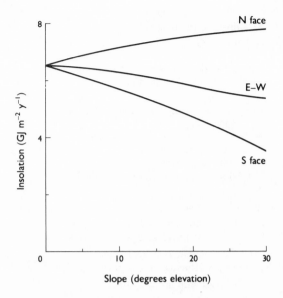

Fig. 6.15. **Effect of slope and aspect on annual insolation at 35° S latitude.** (Adapted from Jacobs (1955).)

systems can be designed for climates with, for example, dry summers, but variations in the beginning of the dry season due to year-to-year variations in weather can strongly influence the results (Chapters 13 and 16).

Several systems have been developed for the classification of land climates. These start either with basic principles of atmospheric circulation (the 'genetic' approach) or, empirically, with long-term weather observations. The best-known system is that devised by W. Köppen in 1931, based mainly on weather observations. Trewartha & Horn (1980) offer a modified Köppen classification that gives emphasis to seasonal temperature and thus to types of vegetation that occur while retaining Köppen's ingenious way of labeling regions of the globe having similar climates. Seasonal patterns of the rainfall-evapotranspiration balance are the first climate element considered, temperature the second, and degree or distribution the third. A simple summary of their approach is given in Table 6.3. Specific criteria are used in establishing boundaries for various climate regions. For example, Tropical–Humid (A) regions divide from Subtropical (C) regions where average temperature for the coolest month is $\leq 18$ °C, whereas Subtropical regions are distinguished from Temperate ones by having at least 8 mo with average temperatures $\geq 10$°C. The resulting maps correspond in general with global patterns of crop production.

## Climate change

Future climates are likely to be different from those we now experience, for two reasons. One is that climates are always subject to variation and change, owing to many factors including systematic variations in Sun–Earth geometry (the 'Milanko-

Table 6.3 *The modified Köppen climate-classification scheme of Trewartha & Horn (1980)*

The dry climates (B) are found at all latitudes while the humid climates (A, C, D, E, and F) tend to rank latitudinally by temperature.

| Climate group | Climate type |
| --- | --- |
| B  Dry | BS, steppe climate |
| | BSh, hot, tropical and subtropical |
| | BSk, cold, temperate and boreal |
| A  Tropical humid | Ar, tropical wet |
| | Aw, tropical wet–dry |
| C  Subtropical | Cs, subtropical with dry summer |
| | Cf, subtropical, rain in all seasons |
| D  Temperate | Do, oceanic, rain in all seasons |
| | Dc, continental, snow in winter |
| E  Boreal | E, cool with limited rainfall |
| F  Polar | Ft, tundra with limited rainfall |
| | Fi, icecaps |

*Source:* Adapted from Trewartha & Horn (1980).

vich theory'), solar activity, continental drift, and the long time-constants associated with ocean–atmosphere equilibria for temperature, sea-level, $CO_2$, and other gases (Lamb 1977). Over very long time-scales, continental drift not only changes the latitudinal position of land masses but also sea level and the avenues for ocean circulation. Some of the most dramatic changes in weather occur when explosive volcanism introduces large amounts of dust and sulfuric acid into the atmosphere. These agents lead to a reverse greenhouse effect by reducing the penetrance of SW. The explosion of Mt Tambora in Indonesia in 1815, for example, lowered temperatures in the northern hemisphere by 1 °C in 1816. In New England (USA), temperatures were 3 °C below normal in a 'year without a summer' (Bryson & Murray 1977). Crop failures were widespread and commodity prices increased dramatically. The natural range of Earth's temperature is quite large. During recent geological times, global mean temperature has been as much as 10–15 °C warmer than the present 15 °C. During the past million years, however, it has generally been much cooler than 15 °C; 18 000 y BP at the peak of the last ice age, for example, global mean temperature was about 5 °C cooler than now and the northern hemisphere was perhaps 15 °C cooler (Schneider *et al.* 1990). Accumulation of ice during that period caused sea level to be nearly 120 m below present. One current theory is that ice ages may be triggered by volcano eruptions.

The second reason that climates may change holds more immediate concern for scientists and decision-makers. The concern is that current trends in concentrations of greenhouse gases, particularly the continuing increase in $[CO_2]$, will affect transparency of the atmospheric window (Fig. 6.6) and cause an increasing feedback effect on atmospheric and surface temperatures. Methane ($CH_4$) from fermentation in wet lands and digestive systems of animals and insects, and chlorofluorocarbons from refrigerants and aerosol products, also affect transparency of the window. Increased [$CO_2$] would narrow the effective width of the window through increased absorption at 10–15 $\mu$m; increased [$CH_4$] would have an even greater effect on the other side near 7–8 $\mu$m. Methane is about 15 times more absorptive in the window area on a molar basis than $CO_2$.

Recent increases in [$CO_2$] result in part from burning of fossil fuels and from disturbance of biospheric carbon pools in soils and forest biomass (Trabalka & Reichle 1986). Expansion of agriculture has been a significant factor in soil disturbance. Reconstruction of past [$CO_2$] from gas trapped in ice cores and from ratios of carbon isotopes in tree rings indicates that [$CO_2$] seems to have remained below 300 ppm (v/v) during the 100 000 y prior to 1850. Since then, it has increased steadily to a present value near 350 ppm and it is expected to peak near 500 to 600 ppm during the next century.

Atmospheric [$CO_2$] is normally stabilized through equilibrium with the oceans where it is sequestered as $HCO_3^-$ and $CO_3^{2-}$. Time-constants for atmosphere–ocean exchanges are too large (1000s of years), however, to accommodate the present surge in $CO_2$. Only a shallow (about 600 m) mixing-layer of the ocean is involved in the annual cycles of temperature and $CO_2$. Major movements of $CO_2$ into ocean storage occur only at high latitudes where dissolved $CO_2$ is carried into the deep ocean by descending cold water. Dissolved $CO_2$ is eventually released through upwelling water in mid-latitudes. The capacity for transport of $CO_2$ into deep waters is small with the result that oceans accommodate large changes in biospheric carbon cycling very slowly. The solubility of $CH_4$ in cold waters and ice can be as great as 0.5 mol $CH_4$ mol$^{-1}$ water so those pools represent an enormous reservoir of another potent greenhouse gas.

Predicting the effects of increases in greenhouse gases is extremely difficult. One reason is that only about 6% of the LW emitted by the surface escapes directly through the window. In recent years, several general circulation models (GCMs; very large computer models), constructed from physical principles, have been employed in efforts to predict long-term climate changes. These models were developed originally for short-term predictions of weather and have a number of limitations for long-range predictions. The small capacity of present computers dictate that the world is modeled in modest number of 'pixels' (areas) for calculation of radiation and energy balances, but the pixels are too large for accurate simulation of cloudiness, solar radiation, and $e_a$. Water vapor concentrations are highly variable and they seem to have a greater direct effect on radiation balances and climate through variable cloudiness than do changes in the atmospheric window. (Fig. 6.6 reveals that water vapor also is a major factor in the transparency of the window.) In addition, present GCMs do not adequately include roles of ocean currents. Another approach to prediction of future climates depends on analysis of past climates using geological and paleobotanical techniques and then, by analogy, extrapolation to the future.

The various methods of analysis generally predict, if the trends in greenhouse gases continue, that the planet will warm by several degrees during the twenty-first

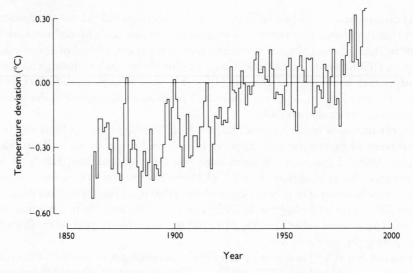

**Fig. 6.16.  Time trend in deviations of global mean temperature from a long-term mean. (Data from Jones *et al.* (1990).)**

century. Several degrees is a very large change in comparison to the pattern of global temperature changes during the past century (Fig. 6.16) but small in comparison with Earth temperature variations during past geologic time.

Warming of Earth due to greenhouse gases would be accompanied by changes in rainfall but there is less agreement on the direction and magnitude of those changes and no predictions yet about the degree of variability. Restructuring our use of fossil energy to reduce releases of $CO_2$ would require many years of effort and a large portion of the wealth of the world to accomplish. Industrialized nations and others now industrializing face the difficult decision whether to begin that effort in the face of uncertain knowledge. Agriculture may be strongly affected if climates do change (see section 3.5 for a brief summary of impacts). M. Budyko (personal communication) concludes that the greatest changes will be in winter temperatures and at high latitudes and such trends are evident in temperature changes that have occurred during the past century (Schneider *et al.* 1990). If that is the case, snow pack in mountainous regions and thus supplies of irrigation water in many arid regions could be strongly affected. Although the predicted warming in tropic and temperate regions during the growing season is less than present interannual variations of temperature, agriculture there could be impacted significantly. It seems that the next century could prove a very challenging period for agriculture.

## 6.12  SUMMARY

The climate of Earth is determined by atmospheric effects on the radiation environment at the surface and by an abundance of water subject to latent heat transformations. Because Earth is a sphere, and spins on a tilted axis in an elliptical orbit around the Sun, receipt of SW radiation varies diurnally and seasonally with latitude, setting up strong vertical and horizontal motions in the atmosphere. The resulting variations in temperature and rainfall constitute our weather; averaged over years the general patterns define climates suitable for agriculture.

Analysis of climate processes begins with the SW-LW radiation balance and its residual, net radiation, $R_n$. $R_n$ is partitioned in the energy balance to sensible- and latent-heat exchanges and to exchanges of chemical-bond energy through photosynthesis and respiration. $R_n$ exchanges within a crop canopy lead to distinctive microclimates depending upon whether the system is wet or dry. As long as crops are well supplied with water, $R_n$ is expended mainly in evapotranspiration with the result that large amounts of water are used during crop production. Enormous quantities of $CO_2$ and water vapor are exchanged between crops and the atmosphere. Simple calculations and direct measurements reveal that turbulent transport engages a great depth of air in those exchanges. Wind turbulence and buoyancy due to warm and/or wet air are both involved. The same eddies of air that transport those gases also transport sensible heat. Lateral and vertical transfers of sensible heat (advection) to a crop sometimes support evapotranspiration rates greater than those predicted from the radiation balance alone.

The climate of a location is defined by its long-term average weather. Different regions of the globe have different climates because of their positions and topography relative to the Sun and because of patterns of atmospheric and oceanic circulation. Those circulations are driven by large, latitudinal differences in radiation balances. The general distribution of climates relative to the possibilities for vegetation is summarized in Köppen climate-classification systems. Climates are subject to change due to natural variations in Sun–Earth geometry and other factors. The possibility exists that increases in greenhouse gases due to natural and anthropogenic causes will significantly alter climates during the next century. How agriculture might respond remains to be seen.

## 6.13 FURTHER READING

Barry, R. G. and R. J. Chorley. 1987. *Atmosphere, weather and climate.* 5th edn. Metheun, London. 460 p.

Jones, H. J. 1983. *Plants and microclimate: a quantitative approach to environmental plant physiology.* Cambridge University Press. 232 p.

Monteith, J. L. and M. H. Unsworth. 1990. *Principles of environmental physics* 2nd edn. Edward Arnold, London, 291 p.

Paltridge, G. W. and C. M. R. Platt. 1976. *Radiative processes in meteorology and climatology.* (*Developments in Atmospheric Science* No. 5.) Elsevier Scientific, Amsterdam. 318 p.

Rosenberg, N. J., B. L. Blad, and S. B. Verma. 1983. *Microclimate, the biological environment.* 2nd edn. John Wiley, New York. 495 p.

Woodward, F. I. and J. E. Sheehy. 1983. *Principles and measurements in environmental biology.* Butterworth, London. 263 p.

# 7

## Soil resources

### 7.1   ON THE NATURE OF SOIL

Soils are formed *in situ* over long periods of time under the influence of climate and vegetation and they come to have vertical distributions (profiles) characteristic of their genesis. Inorganic materials are the major component of soils. These include partially weathered parent materials, secondary minerals, and dissolved salts. Other components are air, water, organic matter in various stages of decay (with the most reduced form being termed humus), and living organisms including plant roots. Typical agricultural soils have a bulk density (dry mass per unit volume) near 1.3 g $cm^{-3}$ (1300 kg $m^{-3}$ or $13 \times 10^6$ kg $ha^{-1}$ $m^{-1}$. Organic matter ranges by mass from 1 to 5% in mineral soils to 80% or more in peaty soils. In typical mineral soils, water accounts for 0.1 to 0.4 of the soil volume but some organic and volcanic soils hold much more. Soil is much more than a single mixture of these components, however.

### 7.2   SOIL CHEMISTRY

Soil chemistry is dominated by the abundance of insoluble compounds of aluminum, silicon and calcium, and centers on interactions between solutions and solids. We begin with a review of several basic concepts essential in advanced work with soils and crops. Although we take a simpler approach in this book, familiarity with these concepts is important.

**Solutions**

Many of the ions in soil solutions are in equilibrium with sparingly soluble minerals and with ion-exchange complexes discussed later. Concentrations range between 1 $\mu$M and 1mM for various ion species in well-drained soils. By contrast, soils in semiarid regions may contain 50 mM or more of soluble $Na^+$ and $Cl^-$, leading to a saline condition.

Except in very dilute solutions, the concentration of an ion is not the best measure of its chemical potential. The ability of an ion to enter into reactions is limited by association with water or other ions and its true **activity**, *a*, is *less* than its molar concentration, M. The relation between activity and concentration is summarized in an activity coefficient, $\gamma$, having values 0 to 1, and $a = \gamma M$. Activity is denoted with ( ) while [ ] are used for concentration. Because $\gamma$ is usually near 1 in dilute solutions, concentration suffices in approximate calculations.

Many reactions in soil solutions depend upon mass action. A dynamic equilibrium is reached in which forward and backward reactions occur at the same rate. In the reaction $A + B \rightleftharpoons C + D$, the quotient of the product of activities of products to the product of reactant activities at final equilibrium defines the **equilibrium constant**, $K_b$:

$$K_b = (C)(D)/(A)(B).$$

For the dissociation of $KNO_3 \rightleftharpoons K^+ + NO_3^-$ in water, as an example:

$$K_b = (K^+)(NO_3^-)/(KNO_3).$$

Where solutes are in equilibrium with a sparingly soluble solid, activity of the solid is taken as 1 and the equilibrium constant is termed the **solubility product**, $K_s$. For solution of $CaCO_3$ (calcite) $\rightleftharpoons Ca^{2+} + CO_3^{2-}$ in water:

$$K_s = (Ca^{2+})(CO_3^{2-})/1 = 4 \times 10^{-9} \text{ at } 25 \,°C.$$

### Oxidation–reduction reactions

Oxidation involves loss of an election by an atom thereby increasing its valence whereas reduction occurs when an atom gains an electron. Oxidation and reduction are always coupled, with one partner serving as electron donor and the other as acceptor. All elements can exist at several oxidation–reduction levels. Oxidized ferric iron ($Fe^{3+}$) and reduced ferrous iron ($Fe^{2+}$) are examples. In soils, reduced C, N, and S from organic compounds are the principal electron donors.

In aerated soils, organic compounds in dead plant material are oxidized in microbial metabolism with oxygen as the electron acceptor ($O_2 \rightarrow 2\,O^{2-}$) leading to the formation of water. When $O_2$ is not available, a 'reducing environment' is created in which oxidized forms of iron ($Fe^{3+}$), manganese ($Mn^{4+}$), nitrogen ($NO_3^-$ and $NO_2^-$), and sulfur ($SO_4^{2-}$) serve as electron acceptors for bacteria. Iron and manganese are also subject to reduction at low pH without biological catalysis. Reduced forms of all of these elements can be toxic to plants.

Each half of an oxidation–reduction couple represents one-half of an electrolytic cell, i.e. an electrode. The electrical potential (voltage) of a half cell serves as a measure of its tendency to donate or accept electrons. In solution under standard conditions, the half reaction $O + 2e^- + 2H^+ \rightleftharpoons H_2O$ at equilibrium generates 1.23 volts. $Fe^{3+} + e^- \rightleftharpoons Fe^{2+}$, by comparison, generates 0.77 volts. When the two reactions are coupled, ferrous iron is oxidized to ferric and oxygen is reduced. Individual potentials cannot be isolated in soil systems but an average value for the whole soil can be measured. Redox potentials of 400 to 600 mv are found in well-aerated soils; values of 0 to $-200$ mv may occur with anaerobic conditions.

**Equilibrium thermodynamics**

Whether a chemical reaction will occur, its direction, and endpoint at equilibrium depend on activities of products and reactants, temperature, and tightness of bonding in products. The science of thermodynamics expresses these factors in energy terms to predict final endpoints of chemical and physical processes from initial states.

The key thermodynamic concepts involve changes in **enthalpy** ($\Delta H$), **entropy** ($T\Delta S$), and **free energy** ($\Delta G$) that occur between initial and final equilibrium states of a reaction system. Enthalpy, $\Delta H$, is the heat energy released or absorbed in reaction; we met it earlier as $\Delta H_c$ from combustion of organic materials. The First Law of thermodynamics holds that total energy of an isolated system is constant. If heat is absorbed in a reaction ($+\Delta H$), the temperature of the surroundings must decline. Entropy ($S$) is a measure of randomness in a system. Degree of randomness is seen in crystalline solids < liquids < gases, and in the tendency of a dye to diffuse throughout a solution. Chemical and physical reactions are driven strongly by a universal tendency for components to become more disordered. That entropy always tends to increase is the Second Law of thermodynamics. The product $T\Delta S$, where $T$ is temperature in K, expresses entropy change in energy units.

Free energy change represents the amount of work that might be done by a system by drawing on changes in enthalpy and entropy. It is defined by the relation:

$$\Delta G = \Delta H - T\Delta S. \tag{Eq. 7.1}$$

The great importance of $\Delta G$ is that it tells us the direction and magnitude that a reaction will take. If $\Delta G$ is negative (e.g. if the reaction releases heat energy ($-\Delta H$) and/or randomness increases ($+\Delta S$)), the reaction may occur spontaneously and continue until $\Delta G$ equals 0 at equilibrium. A positive $\Delta G$ indicates that the reverse reaction may occur. Changes in concentrations of reactants or products, or in temperature (an exchange of heat between the system and its surroundings), may change $+\Delta G$ situations to $-\Delta G$ and allow a reaction to proceed. Negative $\Delta G$ does not insure reaction, however. $\Delta G$ equals $-16.6$ kJ mol$^{-1}$ N for the reaction $N_2 + 3H_2 \rightleftharpoons 2NH_3$ but the reaction must be catalyzed in order to bring $N_2$ to a reactive state. In soils, microorganisms catalyze many processes.

Obtaining quantitative values of $\Delta G$ for a particular reaction can be complex. Fortunately, $\Delta G$s for the formation of many compounds from their elements, and for principal biochemical processes, are tabulated in handbooks. These are denoted $\Delta G°$ for 'standard conditions' (reactants and products at 1 molal, 25 °C, and 1 atm) and can be adjusted to actual concentrations and temperature of a particular system. Several relations are helpful:

$$\Delta G° = \Delta G°_{products} - \Delta G°_{reactants};$$

$$\Delta G° = -2.3RT \log K_b;$$

$$\Delta G = \Delta G° + 2.3RT \log Q,$$

where $R$ is the gas constant, $T$ is temperature (K), and $Q$ is the quotient of product of reactants to product of products at their actual activities. Redox potential is related to $\Delta G$ by the relation:

$$\Delta G = nF\epsilon^\circ + 2.3RT \log Q,$$

where $n$ is the number of moles of electrons involved, $F$ is Faraday's constant, and $\epsilon^\circ$ is the redox potential for the standard state.

## 7.3   SOIL FORMATION

Ideas about soil genesis seem to have begun with observations in the 1800s by V. V. Dokuchaev that the humus content of blackland soils in Russia varied with rainfall, and by E. W. Hilgard that soils from the humid southeastern and semiarid western portions of the USA differed greatly in the type and amount of their secondary clays. Soils in humid areas experience greater leaching than those in semiarid areas and Hilgard found that their content of acid-soluble materials was strikingly lower than in soils from semiarid regions. Dokuchaev, Hilgard, and other early workers demonstrated that climate and vegetation generally dominate processes of soil formation. Hans Jenny later combined these ideas with new ones of his own in *Factors of Soil Formation* (1941).

### Parent material and secondary minerals

Development of soils begins with a **parent material** consisting, usually, of fragmented bits of one or more **primary minerals** (principal ones are augite, feldspar, hornblende, mica, olivine, and quartz). Those minerals originate as igneous, sedimentary, or metamorphic rock under influences of heat and pressure and are subdivided to the size of gravel, sand, silt, and clay (Table 7.1) through weathering. The relative proportions of various particle size classes found in a given soil determine its **texture**. Weathering may occur *in situ* or the materials may have been transported and deposited as wind-blown loess, stream alluvium, or glacial till.

The primary minerals consist of crystalline lattices of oxygen ions ($O^{2-}$) arranged in tetrahedra and octahedra (Fig. 7.1). The oxygens are held together by metal ions, principally $Si^{4+}$ and $Al^{3+}$, that have a small size and large charge density. The six primary minerals are distinguished by having silica ($SiO_2$) and alumina ($Al_2O_3$) arranged in ribbons or plates bonded together or substituted with varying proportions of other metals such as $Ca^{2+}$, $Mg^{2+}$, $Fe^{3+}$, $Na^+$, and $K^+$. Quartz is pure $SiO_4$ in tetrahedra bounded into cubes (its formula is $SiO_2$ because oxygens are shared by adjacent tetrahedra). Augite, hornblende, and olivine are also tetrahedral silicates with $Fe^{2+}$ and $Ca^{2+}$ and/or $Mg^{2+}$ acting to hold the units together while mica and feldspar are aluminosilicates. Micas are composed of flaky layers of aluminum and silicon oxides generally arranged in tetrahedra; $Mg^{2+}$ and $Fe^{2+}$ substitute for Al and Si within the tetrahedra and $K^+$ is involved in binding layers together. Feldspar is composed of aluminum and silicon oxides in a fixed 1:3 ratio; $K^+$, $Na^+$, and $Ca^{2+}$ are found in the lattices.

Table 7.1 *An international classification*
*of particle sizes in soil texture*

| Class | Size range (mm) |
|---|---|
| Gravel | $>2$ |
| Coarse sand | 2 to 0.2 |
| Fine sand | 0.2 to 0.02 |
| Silt | 0.02 to 0.002 |
| Clay | $<0.002$ |

*Note:*
The U.S. Department of Agriculture
classifies five grades of sand covering the
range 2 to 0.05 mm, three silts between
0.05 and 0.002 mm, and divides clays into
coarse (0.002 to 0.0002 mm) and fine
($<0.0002$ mm) categories.

In the presence of water, primary minerals weather slowly through a variety of chemical transformations. Hydrogen ions from water ($H_2O \rightleftharpoons H^+ + OH^-$), for example, may displace base cations from silicates while reacting with oxygen to convert the lattices to $OH^-$ forms. Primary minerals may be altered *in situ* to new forms or solubilized to hydroxides such as silicic acid ($Si(OH)_4$) and $Al(OH)_3$. Silicate hydrolysis is accelerated when solution pH is lowered by dissolved $CO_2$ (from the atmosphere and from respiration of soil organisms; $CO_2 + H^+ + OH^- \rightleftharpoons H^+ + HCO_3^-$) and by organic acids. The hydrolysis products, including swarms of metal ions released from lattice and ribbon structures, may migrate in the soil before recrystallizing as new, **secondary minerals**. Secondary minerals are similar to primary minerals in their silica and alumina lattices and metallic inclusions.

The small size of secondary mineral particles places them in the clay range (Table 7.1). Those less than 0.2 $\mu$m in size behave as colloids, forming sols (stable suspensions) when dispersed in water. In that form, clays may be carried away in surface runoff or leached downward in the soil profile. Solubilization, recrystalization, and sol movement are continuing processes. Secondary clays form throughout the profile but clay particles and dissolved minerals are leached gradually from the surface layer transforming it into a distinctive 'A horizon' (Fig. 7.2). This layer is also characterized by the accumulation of organic matter. Leached clays tend to accumulate in lower 'B horizons'. Soil morphologists sometimes distinguish special subgroups of the A and B horizons. An E horizon, leached of clay minerals but with little accumulation of organic matter, sometimes occurs between the A and B zones. The B horizon is underlain by a C horizon of relatively undisturbed parent material.

The type of secondary minerals formed depends upon the metal ions present, and thus on the kinds of primary minerals, pH of the soil solution, and the amount of leaching. The 'stability diagram' presented in Fig. 7.3 illustrates something of the

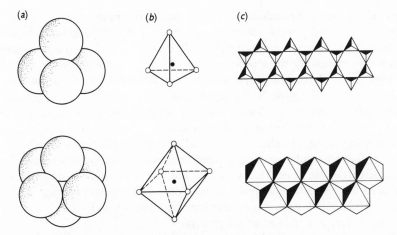

Fig. 7.1. Structural aspects of the aluminosilicate minerals found in soils. (Adapted from Jenny (1980).) (*a*) Basic tetrahedron (4-sided) and octrahedron (6-sided) units formed of either four or six $O^{2-}$ ions surrounding and concealing an $Al^{3+}$ or $Si^{4+}$ ion. (*b*) Schematic views of the tetrahedron and octrahedron. The open and filled circles represent oxygen and aluminum or silicon ions, respectively. (*c*) Top: Arrangement of tetrahedra into ribbons or plates; each shaded triangle represents a tetrahedron. Bottom: Plate formation from octrahedra; one surface of each octrahedron has been shaded.

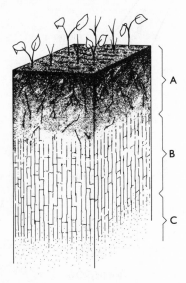

Fig. 7.2. Soil profiles showing the A layers with accumulations of organic matter, B layers with accumulations of secondary minerals, and undeveloped parent material, C.

range of clay transformations that may occur beginning with feldspar. Such diagrams are based on the solubility products of the clays in equilibrium with important ions at various concentrations. In this case, silicic acid activity increases along the abscissa while the activity ratio of $Na^+$ to $H^+$ increases along the ordinate. The lower left of the diagram represents an acid, leached, situation in contrast to the alkaline, unleached region in the upper right. Above a solid line, solutions are supersaturated and the indicated material precipitates under those conditions. Below the line, the solution is unsaturated for that mineral and it dissolves. Beginning in the upper right: as $(Na^+)$ and/or $(Si(OH)_4)$ declines, albite (a form of feldspar) dissolves and montmorillonite forms; montmorillonite is replaced in turn by gibbsite when silicic acid is low and by kaolinite when $Na^+$ is low. This stability diagram represents a very simple case with only a few species of ions. The pattern changes with temperature, when other ions are present (e.g. $K^+$ or $Ca^{2+}$), and when other secondary minerals enter the picture.

Clays form amorphous, gluey gels with small amounts of water and clayey soils become stiff and intractable to tillage when moist. Montmorillonite (in Fig. 7.3) is of special interest in this regard. It and other 'smectite' clays shrink and swell with changes in water content. In montmorillonite, the silica plates are bound together poorly by $Mg^{2+}$ and the clay hydrates and dehydrates strongly during a wetting–drying cycle. When dried, soils containing smectite clays tend to shrink to massive structures and large cracks appear at the surface.

The characteristics of secondary clay minerals, including their very fine particle

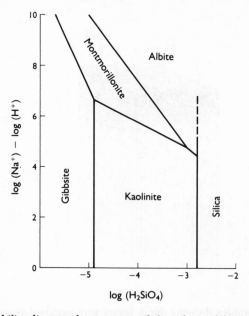

Fig. 7.3. Stability diagram for a system of clays derived from albite feldspar in equilibrium with various solutions. The diagram was constructed from solubility products and ion activities, denoted by ( ), for a system containing $Na_2O$, $Al_2O_3$, $SiO_2$, and water at 25 °C. The text offers additional explanation. (Redrawn from Huang (1989).)

size, determine many soil properties. In addition to their role as nutrient sources, their surfaces contribute to soil structure, ion exchange, and water retention. More on each of these topics will emerge as we proceed. The properties of clay are so dominant in soil processes that soils with as little as 20 or 30% clay particles by mass are classified as clay soils.

Vegetation has a strong influence on clay mineralogy through recycling of elements to the soil surface and through its influence on soil water content. Grasses and deciduous trees, for example, are effective in recycling $K^+$, $Mg^{2+}$, and $Ca^{2+}$ to the surface from deep in the profile. These ions participate in clay formation each time they leach through the profile. Residues of conifers, on the other hand, are low in those metals and serve, upon decay, as a strong source of $H^+$. Acid, leached soils having only a small clay content are formed in that case. $Na^+$ is not recycled effectively by plants and it leaches from the profile over time (sea water is therefore high in $Na^+$). Leaching and recycling patterns result in different secondary minerals being formed under different climate–vegetation regimes even though the starting material may be the same. Conversely, the same class of secondary clays may form under grasslands from different starting materials. Under appropriate conditions, portions of the profile may develop into very rich sources of silicon, aluminum, or iron oxide minerals providing man with abundant sources of those metals for industrial purposes.

## Organic matter in soils

Soil organic matter (SOM) is as complex chemically as clay minerals. Higher plants serve as the original source of organic material and inputs to soil include litter and residues from the aerial portions of plants, supplied to the surface, and from underground organs, mainly roots. In natural systems and managed grasslands, the above-ground material decays in place and only a small portion of it is carried into the profile by rain or by insects. Roots and other underground organs are then the principal substrates for the formation of SOM. When crop residues are incorporated by plowing, decay takes place throughout the plow layer whereas no-till systems (Chapter 12), without incorporation, behave much like grassland.

Decay processes are considered in detail in Chapter 8. Fungi and bacteria do the bulk of the work but they are accompanied and subject to grazing by a wide range of fauna including protozoa. As Jenny (1980) put it: '... invertebrates act as mechanical blenders [in the soil]. They break up plant material, expose organic surfaces to microbes, move fragments up and down, and function as homogenizers of soil layers.' Each type of animal from earthworms to protozoa is open to predation and their residues offer new chemical combinations and new opportunities for bacterial and fungal attack. Jenny estimated (his Table 5.1) that soil might contain 2000 kg ha$^{-1}$ of dry microbial biomass and 600 kg of invertebrates.

Soil organic matter can be divided into several principal fractions: microbial biomass; plant residues; biochemical compounds (sugars, tannins, proteins, and amino acids) recently freed from decaying material; and humus. **Humus** is the final end product of decay. It consists mostly of long-chain condensate polymers of aromatic phenols, sugars, and nitrogenous compounds. These polymers have many free –OH groups that are important in soil properties. The polymers are chemically stable and resistant to further attack, particularly when physically stabilized by adsorption to clays or entrapment by soil particles. Some old organic matter, perhaps the portion that is not physically stabilized, has a life-time in soil in the order of decades and can be classified as 'active'. Another portion is much more resistant. Carbon dating reveals that the oldest fractions in many North American soils date from the last glacial cycles, 10 000 to 20 000 y ago.

The simplest method for determining SOM content is to remove roots and small debris from the soil by sieving and then to analyze the soil for organic carbon or nitrogen. Humus is the major component of SOM in cultivated soils compared to partially decayed material and microbial and faunal biomass; because humus is near 60% C, C/0.6 provides a crude estimate of the organic matter content of a soil. The C/N ratio of humus in agricultural soils is near 10 to 13. If we assume that the ratio is 12, N × 20 provides an additional rough estimate of humus content. Soils from untilled systems commonly have larger C/N ratios because they contain larger amounts of partially decayed material. The C/N ratios of fresh residues commonly range between 25 and 100.

Soil organic matter is usually distributed within the soil profile in about the same pattern that decay occurs, i.e. the content is greatest near the surface and declines more or less exponentially with depth. Some small-molecular-mass fractions of humus may leach gradually within the profile as sols. In some soils (termed podzols), an organic layer forms low in the profile where humus, solubilized from the surface zone, precipitates as salts of iron and other metals.

## Equilibrium level of soil organic matter

The amount of organic matter present in a soil reflects the past balance between rates of humus formation and loss. Loss occurs because humus is oxidized slowly when exposed to air or attacked by microorganisms. Nitrogen and other elements are released in mineral forms and the process is termed **mineralization**. Mineralization is a first-order process, i.e. the rate is proportional to the amount of humus present. Because it depends on microbial activity, the rate of mineralization is near zero at 0 °C and increases to a maximum between 40 and 50 °C. By contrast, the rate of humus formation depends mainly on the annual input of plant residues. The greatest amounts of residues are produced with a long growing season, intermediate temperatures (15–30 °C), and abundant rainfall. In a soil that is treated in the same way year after year, covered with native vegetation or farmed in a certain way, rates of humus formation and loss eventually are equal and humus content comes to steady-state.

The grasslands of the American Great Plains present an outdoor laboratory for the study of temperature and rainfall influences on the steady-state level of soil organic matter. Mean annual temperature decreases from south to north while a humidity index (mean annual rainfall divided by reference evapotranspiration) increases from west to east. By sampling the soil under native grasslands along north–south and east–west transects across the plains, Jenny (1930) uncovered the important generalizations illustrated in Fig. 7.4. Soil organic matter content

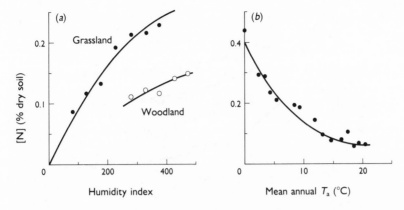

**Fig. 7.4.** (*a*) **Average total nitrogen content in soils along a transect of increasing rainfall relative to evaporation. Data for grassland and woodland sites extending from Colorado (semiarid) to New Jersey and with the same mean annual temperature (near 10 °C) are depicted.** (*b*) **Average total nitrogen in grassland soils along a transect from Canada to Texas. Semiarid sites having similar annual humidity indices are shown. (Adapted from Jenny (1930).)**

increased in a diminishing-returns relationship with rainfall and declined in a negative exponential relationship with increasing temperature.

The greatest amounts of soil N (and C) accumulate under grasslands in cool environments (e.g. Canadian prairie provinces) because good levels of production with a high content of lignin are coupled there with the depressing effects of low temperatures and short season on mineralization. The amounts of carbon and nitrogen involved are impressive: over 30 t N and 330 t C per hectare have accumulated in the profile under good conditions. In contrast, humus N contents near 1 t ha$^{-1}$ are not uncommon in desert regions because biomass production is small and high temperatures favor humus oxidation. For Earth as a whole, it is estimated that between 1500 and 3000 Gt C are sequestered in soils. If C/N = 12, 125–250 Gt of nitrogen are also held there. The sensitivity of the humus equilibrium to temperature and rainfall mean that large changes will occur with a climate change.

Marked differences are evident in Fig. 7.4 in organic matter content of soils that develop under grasslands and deciduous woodlands. Grasses have greater production and turnover of roots and their leaf and stem residues have a greater lignin content than is found in leaves of deciduous trees. In addition, nutrient cycling is tighter with grasses. Dead leaves of deciduous trees begin decaying in fall when the trees are dormant whereas those of grasses remain erect. Grasses mat down during winter and decay in spring when the plants are again active in uptake.

## Influence of farming on soil organic matter

One of the consequences of tillage is an accelerated breakdown of humus. That, coupled with removal of nitrogen in harvested crops usually results in smaller

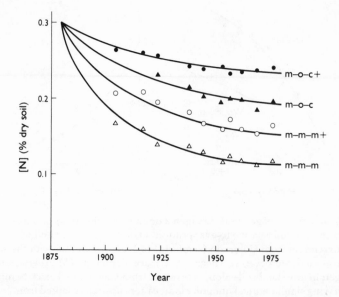

**Fig. 7.5. Changes in organic N content in a Mollisol at the University of Illinois under two crop rotations (m–m–m, continuous maize; m–o–c, maize–oat–clover) with (+) addition of manure, lime, and phosphorus. Farming began in 1876. (Adapted from Stevenson (1982).)**

steady-state levels of SOM in cultivated soils than are found under natural vegetation. Exceptions occur where desert soils are brought under irrigation and where crops are supplied with fertilizer or manure. In those situations, greater inputs to humus formation can offset the increased rate of mineralization due to tillage. Examples of the effects of agriculture on SOM levels in an American soil are presented in Fig. 7.5. New steady-state conditions were reached 60–70 y after the original prairie was put to the plow. Long-term plots in Kansas, Ohio, and England have behaved in a similar way. Final equilibrium levels of SOM reflect farming practice. Lower levels result after continuous grain production than with rotations involving forage crops and manure. As has been demonstrated in long-term plots at Rothamsted (UK), SOM levels in continuous-grain treatments increase again if they are given nitrogen amendments. Nitrogen stimulates crop productivity and larger amounts of residues are available as substrate for humus formation.

## 7.4   SOIL TYPES

### Soil classification

Systems for identifying and naming soils allow information about their characteristics and behavior to be shared over the regions where they occur. Profile characteristics (chemistry and morphology) and the circumstances of formation (genesis) provide bases for classification schemes. The genetic basis is used in many classification systems to assign soils into one of several great soil groups. The groups usually are distinguished by whether formation was dominated by regional climate and vegetation leading to a **zonal** soil or by local topography (e.g. wetlands) or parent material resulting in an **azonal** soil.

Most soils fall into one of several zonal groups. The grasslands of Eurasia, North America, and Argentina provide examples. All generate zonal 'Chernozem' soils, Dokuchaev's name for a large group of black grassland soils characterized by a dark-colored A horizon, rich in organic matter and base metals, with accumulations of $Ca^{2+}$ in the B layers. The Chernozem name is still in common use around the world. Profile characteristics vary continuously within and between main groups such as Chernozems and may be further differentiated by variations in age, drainage, and parent material. As a result, a large number of specific soils are recognized within the Chernozems.

Soviet classification placed an emphasis on soil genesis; the first USDA schemes followed the Russian approach. Western Europeans, on the other hand, have emphasized chemical characteristics of the profile in classification. They encounter young soils on glacial till with indistinct horizons, and 'gley' soils with poor drainage and characterized by zones of reduced iron. Australian soils fit poorly into any of the European or American schemes (Northcote *et al.* 1975). Most Australian soils are very old paleosoils that are typically acid and low in nutrients. In some, shallow surface horizons reflecting genesis under recent semiarid conditions overlay and contrast sharply in texture and structure with lower layers. Such 'duplex' soils may have unfavorable water infiltration and holding characteristics. One theory is that the lower layers formed millions of years ago under vastly different climates.

The new USDA Soil Taxonomy (Soil Survey Staff 1988) emphasizes profile description while retaining some attention to genesis. The system is pragmatic, focusing on what a soil is more than on how it formed. Soils are given a common 'series' name as well as complex scientific names, based on specific quantitative criteria, that define their place among the 'families' and 'subgroups' of 11 great 'orders'. A soil of the Webster series in the US Corn Belt, for example, could be classified in family 'fine-loamy, mixed, mesic' soils of subgroup 'Typic Hapla-quolls'. 'Mixed' indicates that no one clay family dominates the profile; 'mesic' refers to its occurrence in a moderate temperature regime. 'Typic' indicates that is is a central member of the subgroup Haplaquolls. The Haplaquolls name combines the names of its order (**Mollisols**, ending -olls) and its great group (Hapla- for simple horizons and -aqu- for wetness). Mollisols include the Chernozems and other soils with a dark-colored A horizon, considerable organic matter, moderate base saturation, and good structure. They generally develop under grassland.

Detailed soil maps are now available for most developed countries at scales of 1:15000 to 1:30000 (an example is presented in Fig. 12.10). Such maps reveal a high degree of spatial variability in the distribution of soils. Direct comparisons among various systems of soil classification are difficult (see Buol *et al.* 1989; Sanchez, 1976). The usefulness of the USDA taxonomy has recently been improved through extensions to some African soils and through addition of an **Andisol** order for soils that originate from volcanic ash. The USDA names for soil orders are used in this book.

## Soils used in agriculture

Level soils with deep, well-drained profiles provide the best circumstances for agriculture. High fertility and near neutral pH are also useful traits. Only a small portion of world's land area satisfies these criteria; currently, about 11% of the ice-free area is cultivated. In retrospect, it is not surprising that many of the early agrarian centers developed on soils formed from young alluvium (e.g. Nile Delta), wind-blown loess (Chinese and North American sites), volcanic ash (Indonesia, Meso-America), and in semiarid and arid regions (Near East), which have not been leached of their rich base metal fertility. Many arid-zone soils are found in the order **Aridisols**. As human populations increased in Europe, agriculture spread slowly into deciduous woodlands. Two groups of soils came into importance: **Inceptisols**, immature soils with poorly developed profiles and high in base metals; and **Alfisols**, older soils with high base saturation and clayey B layers. Alfisols generally develop under deciduous woodland with favorable moisture.

Special knowledge or technology was needed with many soils before they could be farmed successfully. Cultivation of Mollisols formed under tall grasses is a recent phenomenon aided by the invention of steel plows. **Histosols**, highly organic peat and muck soils formed in boggy places and swamps, require drainage, while the extensive **Vertisols** of India, Australia and Texas (USA), characterized by shrinking and swelling clays, can be cultivated only over a limited range in moisture content. (The prefix *verti-* refers to the turning or churning mixture of A and B horizons that occurs on wetting and drying of smectite clays.) **Ultisols** cover large areas of India, Brazil and southeastern USA; **Oxisols** are common in the humid tropics. Both orders present special problems to agriculture. They occur in mild to warm climates with generous rainfall. That would seem to suit them well for agriculture but the soils are very old. The profiles are highly leached of silica and thus are rich in Fe and Al oxides (hence Oxisol) that in some cases can harden irreversibly to 'laterite' (brick-like structure) on drying. Aluminum acidity and toxicities from aluminum and manganese also occur with these soils.

## 7.5   SOIL PROPERTIES

### Surface area and aggregation of soil particles

The surfaces of clays and humus are very active. Because clay particles are very small, they possess enormous surface area per unit soil volume. One cubic centimeter of parent material has a density near $2.65 \text{ g cm}^{-3}$ and a surface (if cubic) of $6 \text{ cm}^2$. Subdivided to 1 nm cubes (coarse clay), density drops to near $1.3 \text{ g cm}^{-3}$ because cubes do not pack tightly and about 50% of the volume now occurs as pore space. There are then $5 \times 10^{20}$ cubelets per $cm^3$, each with a surface area of $6 \text{ nm}^2$. Total surface area per $cm^3$ of this 'soil' is $3000 \text{ m}^2$! The surface area of real soils is less, but still an impressive $500-1000 \text{ m}^2 \text{ cm}^{-3}$. Part of the mass of real soils is due to larger particles (sand and silt) with much less surface area per unit weight and clay particles are usually aggregated into larger structures, termed **aggregates** or **peds**, with less surface area. Aggregated soils have granular texture with greater porosity between the peds and thus better aeration and water infiltration rates than poorly aggregated ones. In addition, they are more easily tilled.

Linkage of clay platelets and ribbons into large aggregates can occur through cation-bonding by calcium ($Ca^{2+}$) and 'gluing' by humus. Calcium ions, with their small radius and large charge density, flocculate clays by binding negatively charged clay platelets and ribbons into larger particles.

Porosity and aggregation are important factors in soil structure. Structure can be evaluated through measures of soil strength (i.e. ease of tillage), air porosity, and water infiltration rate. Humus content enhances each of these aspects of structure. Farm operations affect soil structure in several ways. Traffic by animals and vehicles on wet soil, for example, compacts clays into massive structures and is to be avoided except with flooded culture of rice where an impervious clay pan helps prevent loss of water by drainage. Structure generally deteriorates with tillage because increased aeration promotes oxidation of organic matter. On the other hand, incorporation of animal manures, green manures, and crop residues through tillage help in maintaining SOM and thus structure. **Green manures** are crops grown specifically for incorporation with soil; grasses high in lignin are the most effective in maintaining SOM.

Freezing and thawing, and wetting and drying aid in maintaining soil structure in most climates. In hot, dry climates, where organic inputs are small and oxidation of humus is rapid, soils are naturally low in humus, and massive structure is common. Tillage of the soil when dry is one means by which massive structures are fractured into granules.

## Ion exchange by clays and organic matter

The oxygen lattices of clay minerals endow them with important surface properties. Shortages of metal ions within the lattices, exposure of oxygen surfaces, and conversion of some oxygens to hydroxyls ($-OH \rightleftharpoons -O^- + H^+$) leave the clay particles with negatively charged surfaces which are highly effective in binding cations and water molecules.

Cation bonding is ionic (e.g. $Ca^{2+}$:$clay^{2-}$). Various cations can be 'exchanged' for one another through mass action. The strength of the bonds depends upon the charge density of the cation. Protons ($H^+$) are very small and thus have a high charge density. $Na^+$, with its small charge density, is weakly held by clay and easily leached from the profile. Cations can be ranked in a **lyotropic series** according to their decreasing charge density and thus decreasing strength of binding to clay: $H^+ > Ca^{2+} > Mg^{2+} > K^+ \approx NH_4^+ > Na^+$. Ion exchange and lyotropic position can be demonstrated by eluting a column of sodium-saturated clay with a dilute potassium solution (e.g. KCl). Sodium is displaced to the eluent solution, leaving a K-saturated clay. Exchange depends upon mass action, therefore an ion low in the series but present in sufficient concentration can displace a higher one.

The amount of cations that can be held by a soil defines its **cation exchange capacity** (CEC, in milliequivalents of cations per 100 g of dry soil). A small CEC means that the soil can hold only small quantities of essential nutrient cations. With a high proportion of $H^+$ or $Al^{3+}$ on the exchange sites, the soil will be both acid and infertile regardless of CEC.

Soil organic matter is even more effective in cation exchange per unit mass than are clay minerals. Metal cations exchange readily with protons of the amino $(-NH_2)$, carboxyl (–COOH), and hydroxyl (–OH) groups of soil organic matter. Representative CEC values for clay range from 30 to 100 meq 100 g$^{-1}$ while humus may be as great at 300 meq 100 g$^{-1}$. Although humus usually constitutes only 2 to 5% of the weight of agricultural soils, it makes a significant contribution to the CEC.

In arid regions, soils have high levels of $Na^+$ on the exchange complex. $Na^+$ hydrates to a large ion with a charge density too small to aggregate clays. That allows clays to disperse and seal the soil surface. Sodium-saturated clays collapse into dense ('massive') structures when dry and disperse as sols when wet. The proportion of CEC occupied by $Na^+$ depends upon amounts of divalent cations present. An alkaline condition (pH > 8.5) develops when $Na^+$ is abundant and balanced by a weak anion such as $HCO_3^-$. Sodium status is evaluated with the **sodium adsorption ratio** (SAR) calculated from the concentrations of soluble $Na^+$, $Ca^{2+}$, and $Mg^{2+}$ in the soil solution:

$$SAR = \frac{[Na^+]}{\sqrt{([Ca^{2+}] + [Mg^{2+}])/2}}.$$  [Eq. 7.2]

Soil and plant problems generally begin with SAR values > 10. Such sodic soils can be reclaimed by leaching (providing the water has a low sodium concentration) and through additions of gypsum ($CaSO_4$). $Ca^{2+}$ from gypsum displaces $Na^+$ and flocculates clays into aggregates while the acid anion helps in lowering pH. Amendment with elemental sulfur is a common treatment for alkali soils. S oxidizes to $SO_4^{2-}$ and in association with water provides $H^+$ for $Na^+$ displacement. Salinity and alkalinity are considered further in Chapters 13 and 14.

Both clay and organic matter can also hold and exchange anions. In humus, amino groups ($-NH_2$) that become positively charged through the attraction of a proton ($-NH_3^+$) are important in anion exchange. The basis of anion exchange by clay may relate to locally dense positive charge centers around $Fe^{3+}$ and $Al^{3+}$. Anions are also held by clays and organic matter in weak, 'double-layer' arrangements. When the primary negative sites of exchangers are satisfied by cations, the exchange complex then presents a positively charged layer. The positive charges are partially neutralized by clay or humus, but enough remain to attract and hold a second layer of anions. This significantly reduces mobility and thus leaching of important anions such as nitrate ($NO_3^-$).

## Nutrient availability

Factors affecting the solubility of phosphate ions ($PO_4^{3-}$) offer insight into the complexity of soil solutions. The ion has a dense negative charge which causes it to form salts with calcium, iron, and aluminum which are only sparingly soluble. In addition, the oxygens of phosphate can fit tightly into clay lattices. Phosphate 'fixed'

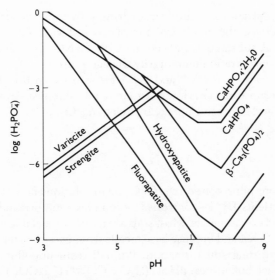

Fig. 7.6. **Stability diagram for phosphate minerals in equilibrium with $10^{-3}$ M $Ca^{2+}$, $Mg^{2+}$, $K^+$, $Na^+$, and $Cl^-$. $Al^{3+}$ and $F^-$ are in equilibrium with gibbsite and kaolinite clays and $Fe^{3+}$ with iron hydroxide. Free phosphate ions occur below the limiting mineral lines. See text for further explanation. (Redrawn from Lindsay *et al.* (1989).)**

or 'bound' in soils by these processes is not available to higher plants. Fig. 7.6 is a stability diagram of phosphate ions in equilibrium with several minerals over a range in pH. The figure is similar to that presented in Fig. 7.3. Above a particular line, the solution is saturated for that mineral and it tends to precipitate; below its line, the mineral dissolves. At pH 4, the solubilities of iron phosphate (strengite) and aluminum phosphate (variscite) restrict free phosphate ions to less than 1 $\mu$M. Formation of these minerals also contributes to iron deficiency in plants. Above pH 6, phosphate solubility is increasingly restricted by precipitation with calcium. Hydroxyapatite is the important calcium phosphate in most soils since activity of $F^{-1}$ and thus formation of flourapatite is restricted by precipitation of fluoride as $CaF_2$. The stability pattern is altered significantly when other ions, in particular $CO_3^{2-}$ and $SO_4^{2-}$, are present.

Plant uptake also helps to restrict the amount of phosphate in solution. About 400 g P are needed daily to support a crop growth rate of 200 kg ha$^{-1}$ d$^{-1}$ (0.002 is a conservative value for the concentration of P in dry biomass; see Table 12.1). With 2000 m$^{-3}$ (2 Ml) of soil solution in the surface 0.5 m of 1 ha of drained clay soil, and phosphate at 1 $\mu$M, the solution contains only 124 g P. Plant nutrition therefore depends on continued dissolution of phosphate minerals as the soil solution is depleted of P by uptake.

Nitrogen availability is also very dynamic. A typical crop demand is 4 kg ha$^{-1}$ d$^{-1}$ (0.02 of a daily growth rate of 200 kg ha$^{-1}$ d$^{-1}$). The concentration of nitrate ions in soil solutions depends mainly on the balance between rates of mineralization of organic matter and use of nitrate and ammonium by plants and soil microorganisms

(Chapter 8). Concentrations of nitrate range from 1 $\mu$M with low fertility to 1 mM in fertile soils. At 100 $\mu$M, the supply in 0.5 m of clay soil with 2000 m$^3$ water ha$^{-1}$ is only 2.8 kg ha$^{-1}$. A substantial application of 100 kg $NO_3$–N with that amount of water raises the concentration temporarily to near 4 mM.

Typical concentrations for $K^+$ and $Ca^{2+}$ range between 0.1 and 1 mM. The concentrations of those metals is low due to mineral solubility, strong retention by cation exchange, and aggressive uptake by living organisms.


**Soil acidity**

High concentrations of protons on the CEC and in solution affect plant growth and availability of nutrients. [$H^+$] is controlled by complex equilibria and buffering with organic matter and clay minerals. Most soils are naturally acid due to exchangeable protons found in SOM and because base metals from parent materials are leached from the profile during soil formation. Rainfall from unpolluted air contains dissolved $CO_2$ which buffers near pH 5.7 ($H_2O + CO_2 \rightleftharpoons H^+ HCO_3^-$). $H^+$ is balanced by $HCO_3^-$ but with heavy leaching $K^+$ is lost from the soil, $H^+$ is retained, and soil pH declines to an equilibrium near pH 5.2 (Helyar & Porter 1989). With less leaching, reactions involving calcium and carbonates dominate and the soil is neutral to alkaline. Acidity is evaluated with pH measurements made on slurries or extracts of soils using salt solutions to release exchangeable $H^+$ and $Al^{3+}$.

There are two important points to make about soil acidity. First, few plants grow well in soils that test outside the range of pH 5–8. Legumes are particularly sensitive to low pH. Bacterial activity also suffers at low pH. Second, soils acidify naturally under vegetation and the process is accelerated in pastures and fields used for production agriculture.

Soil pH has a direct effect on plant roots, but in most cases that is overshadowed by pH-dependent toxicities and deficiencies of specific elements. In alkaline soils, high levels of sodium cause toxicities. As we noted above, deficiencies of iron and phosphorus occur at both extremes of high and low pH. The main problem at low pH, however, is that aluminum minerals are hydrolyzed and soluble $Al^{3+}$ reaches toxic levels near 10 $\mu$M. Given the reducing environment, $Mn^{2+}$ toxicities are also common. Although soils may differ markedly in buffering capacity at other pH ranges, most buffer well near pH 4 to 4.5 owing to aluminum hydroxides released through dissolution of clays. As the clays dissolve, an infertile E horizon composed of sand and silt particles develops between the A and B layers.

Acidification occurs under vegetation in part from accumulation of exchangeable protons of SOM but mainly from changes in cation and anion populations due to biological activity and leaching. The central event, linked with cycles of both carbon and nitrogen, is the addition or subtraction of $H^+$ to the soil-plant system through changes in base cations.

The carbon cycle is involved with soil pH through the accumulation of biomass by plants. Plants accumulate more base cations than anions from soil; within the plant, the difference is balanced electrochemically with organic anions. In terms of equivalents of inorganic cations ($C_i$), inorganic anions ($A_i$), and organic anions

(OA): $C_i - A_i - OA \approx 0$ in biomass. The combination of inorganic cations (mainly $K^+$ and $Ca^{2+}$) with organic anions (weak acids such as malate and citrate) buffers the internal pH of plants in a physiological range near pH 6.5. One consequence of the $C_i$-$A_i$ imbalance in biomass, however, is a surplus of $A_i$ relative to $C_i$ in soil: for each organic anion created in plant metabolism, one $H^+$ accumulates in soil.

$C_i$-$A_i$ imbalances in plant material can be determined from organic acid content or, more simply, from 'ash alkalinity' (a sample is ashed, dissolved in water, and titrated to neutrality with acid). When $C_i$-$A_i$ imbalances are exported in harvested crops, $H^+$ ions remain behind in the soil. Harvest of vegetative material (hay or silage) results in considerably more soil acidification than does the harvest of grain. Using ash alkalinity data from Helyar & Porter (1989), removal of 10 t legume forage $ha^{-1}$ adds 10 kmol $H^+$ $ha^{-1}$ to soils whereas production of 10 t grain $ha^{-1}$ adds only 0.5 kmol $H^+$ $ha^{-1}$.

Events in the nitrogen cycle also contribute to soil acidification because the mineralization and nitrification steps in the cycle (see Fig. 8.2) produce nitrate ions that are subject to leaching from the root zone. $NO_3^-$ is a strong acid but it is accompanied mainly by $K^+$ and other base cations when it leaches because metallic cations are far more abundant than protons at pH 4 to 7. The increased $[H^+]$ in the soil is balanced by the weak acid $HCO_3^-$. With $K^+$ as the accompanying ion in leachates, 1 mol $H^+$ accumulates in soil $mol^{-1}$ N lost.

The magnitude of acidification effects that occur with nitrate leaching depends on the form in which nitrogen originally entered the soil–plant system:

|  | mol $H^+$ gained per mol N leached |
|---|---|
| Nitrogen enters as: |  |
| Nitrate ion ($NO^{\overline{3}}$) | 1 |
| Ammonia, urea, protein (residues or manure), or by nitrogen fixation | 2 |
| Ammonium ion ($NH_4^+$) (ammonium sulfate fertilizer or composted manure) | 3 |

The important messages in these data are (1) that addition of nitrogen in any form will contribute to acidification when it leaches from the system as nitrate and (2) that addition of the more reduced forms of nitrogen cause more acidification than occurs with nitrate alone.

Changes of 0.02 to 0.2 pH units $y^{-1}$ have been observed in agricultural soils (Williams 1980; Helyar & Porter 1989). Cropping practice obviously influences the rate. In grazed pastures, most nutrients and thus the $C_i$-$A_i$ imbalance recycle within the pasture. Milk production results in modest removals (principally N, Ca, and P); exports with grazing by sheep or beef cattle are less. Despite small removals, grazed lands acidify rather rapidly, owing, apparently, to the large amount of forage consumed and to spatial variability in deposits of urine and dung. Localized concentrations of nitrogen (at rates up to 700 kg $ha^{-1}$) result in localized nitrate leaching and acidification. The deposits are not distributed uniformly over a pasture in proportion to grazing but tend to be greater near resting and watering places. In swidden agriculture, vegetation is burned and its nitrogen and organic acid components are combusted. The $C_i$-$A_i$ imbalance is returned to the soil where it has an alkalizing effect. The same phenomenon occurs with the burning of cereal stubbles. Recycling of crop residues and animal manures to the soil also has the virtue that they tend to restore $C_i$–$A_i$ balance but that may be offset by an acidifying effect from the exchangeable $H^+$ of organic compounds.

Concern exists, particularly in the northern hemisphere, about the influence of 'acid rain' due to contamination of air by oxides of sulfur and nitrogen. The pH of acid rain is near 4 and in extreme cases may be < 3. At pH 4, 1 kmol $H^+$ $ha^{-1}$ $y^{-1}$ is added to the soil with 1 m rainfall. The effect is small relative to those of forage production but, continued for a long time, equilibrium soil pH will decline.

Correction of soil acidity is done through applications of lime. The Romans recognized the benefits from liming and today it is a widespread practice in Europe and North America. The ley-farming system of southern Australia (Chapter 16) has acidified significantly and farmers there are now beginning to use lime. The ley system performs reasonably well with low pH because acid-tolerant strains of subterranean clover are used, although rhizobial activity is reduced. Without lime, however, it seems likely that clay dissolution is occurring and that the depth of the acid profile may be deepening to an extent that liming will become uneconomic. In the long run, use of acid-tolerant plants instead of lime can only exacerbate such problems.

Ground calcite limestone is the most common source for pH amendment but marl and other materials high in $CaCO_3$, including waste lime from paper mills, sugarbeet factories and other industries, are also used. Lime requirements are determined in several ways. The simplest approach is to slurry the soil in neutral salt solution and titrate it to a conservative endpoint (pH 7–8) with $Ca(OH)_2$. The reason for the high endpoint is that equilibration of calcium with clay minerals to a true pH endpoint may require several months. Where $Al^{3+}$ toxicity is a problem, exchangeable cations must also be eluted from the soil and titrated so that both $H^+$ and $Al^{3+}$ are considered.

Acidification processes are amplified by spatial differences in wetness, drainage, and nitrogen supply as well as by grazing. As a result, buffering capacity differs spatially and liming may lead to further increases in variation as some places are neutralized and others stay buffered at a low pH. In some cases, it pays to map the lime requirement and apply amendments accordingly.

## 7.6   WATER AND AIR COMPONENTS

### Water in soils

The water molecule is a very strong dipole with separate, strong centers of positive and negative charges (Fig. 7.7). A proton pole of water can associate with oxygen in another water molecule or with clay and humus. Water binding by clay and humus depends on the same principles as ion exchange. Association of a water proton with the negative surface of clay leaves a negative ($-OH^-$) tail of the water molecule extending into the soil solution. That tail links and thus binds with a second layer of water. Carboxyl and hydroxyl groups of humus act on water in a similar way. Such

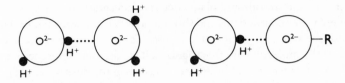

Fig. 7.7. H-bonding in water. (*a*) Oxygen atoms of two water molecules share the same proton. Such linkages extend throughout aqueous media. (*b*) One oxygen (O–R) belongs to a ligand such as humus or clay. This is the basis of matrix potential. Oxygen in R–OH, R–COOH, and in lattices of clays can enter into H-bonding.

'adsorbed water' is held very tightly to the surface matrix restricting its mobility and the possibility for uptake by plants. Chains of H-bonding extend throughout an aqueous solution, imparting a 'structure' to water that is seen in phenomena such as surface tension and viscosity.

Texture and structure determine the portions of a soil volume ($V$) that are pore space ($V_p$) and solid material ($V_s$). 'Porosity' ($V_p/V$) and 'packing density' ($V_s/V$) serve as relative measures of pore space. Soil bulk density, the mass of dry solids per unit volume ($W_s/V$; g cm$^{-3}$) is a more common measure of solids content. Values of bulk density range from 0.5 (volcanic ash) to 2.0 (compacted soils) g cm$^{-3}$; most agricultural soils have values near 1.3 g cm$^{-3}$. As noted earlier, the density of soil minerals is 2.65 g cm$^{-3}$ so a bulk density near 1.3 indicates 50% porosity. The same space can be variously filled with water or air and these important components of soil are reciprocally related.

Large macropores and spaces created by earthworms, past root growth, burrowing animals, and shrinking clays are the major routes for root, water, and air movements. It is not uncommon, for example, to find plant roots descending through decaying residues of earlier roots. Macropores drain freely, retaining only films of water adsorbed by H-bonding. Small capillary pores, and voids within aggregated soil particles, on the other hand, are important holding spaces for water. Pores $< 30$ $\mu$m diameter fall in the capillary range and can hold water against the force of gravity. Most capillary water is held weakly and is easily removed by plants but the final film of adsorbed water is held very strongly. As a consequence, there are two basic ways to characterize soil water: **water content**, $\theta$ (expressed as a fraction of dry mass or volume); and **soil water potential**, $\Psi_s$, in pressure or energy units, which characterizes the activity of water associated with surfaces and solutes.

## Water potential

Water potential describes the activity of water in a particular system. Individual water molecules have a velocity of movement proportional to their temperature and tend to diffuse or to escape as vapor. The collective free energy of all of the water molecules in a unit volume (in units of J m$^{-3}$) is termed water potential, $\Psi$. J m$^{-3}$ is dimensionally the same as force per unit area (1 J m$^{-3}$ = 1 Newton m$^{-2}$ = 1 Pascal), and $\Psi$ is commonly expressed in either Pa or bar (1 bar = 0.1 MPa = 0.987 atm).

Water movement in soils and plants occurs along gradients of free energy, from regions where water is abundant, and thus has a high free energy per unit volume, to those where the free energy of water is less. The potential of pure water is high because all of the molecules are free to move; it is taken as a reference state with the symbol $\Psi_0$. $\Psi$ of water diluted by solutes is less than for pure water. The activity of water is further restricted by hydration reactions and by H-bonding to clays and organic matter in soils and to cell walls and proteins in plant cells. These factors have an additive effect in lowering the potential of water in a soil or plant system relative to $\Psi_0$:

$$\Psi_{\text{system}} = \Psi_0 + \Psi_m + \Psi_\pi + \Psi_p + \Psi_g. \qquad \text{[Eq. 7.3]}$$

By definition, $\Psi_0$ is set to 0 Pa and all other terms, except $\Psi_p$, the hydrostatic potential, are therefore negative (i.e. $<0$). $\Psi_g$, the gravitational term results from differences in height. It decreases 10 kPa m$^{-1}$ height and thus is important in 80 m *Eucalyptus regnans* and redwood trees but can be ignored in crop systems. $\Psi_p$, due to hydrostatic pressure, is positive in turgid plant cells but is 0 in soils. $\Psi_m$, matrix potential, results from adsorption on surfaces. $\Psi_\pi$, solute or osmotic potential, can be approximated for dilute solutions from the Van't Hoff relation derived from the Gas Law:

$$\Psi_\pi = -CRT, \qquad \text{[Eq. 7.4]}$$

where $C$ is the concentration of solutes (mol l$^{-1}$), $R$ the gas constant (0.0831 l bar mol$^{-1}$ K$^{-1}$), and $T$ is Kelvin temperature. Simplifying Eq. 7.3 by ignoring $\Psi_g$, $\Psi_m$ and $\Psi_p$ when appropriate:

Soil:   $\Psi_s = \Psi_0 + \Psi_m + \Psi_\pi;$ $\qquad \text{[Eq. 7.5]}$

Plant: $\Psi_{pl} = \Psi_0 + \Psi_\pi + \Psi_p.$ $\qquad \text{[Eq. 7.6]}$

$\Psi_m$ and $\Psi_\pi$ are negative and $\Psi_p$, although positive, is never greater than the magnitude of $\Psi_\pi$. As a result, $\Psi_s$ and $\Psi_{pl}$ are always less than $\Psi_0$, and for plants to take up water from soil, $\Psi_{pl}$ must be less than $\Psi_s$.

Total $\Psi_s$ and $\Psi_{pl}$ can be determined on samples in the laboratory with psychrometric measurements of equilibrium vapor pressure ($e$ in mbar; Eq. 6.15). Water adsorbed to soil colloids or diluted with solutes has a low equilibrium vapor pressure compared with the saturation vapor pressure of water ($e^*$). The water potential of soils and plant materials is related to vapor pressure as follows:

$$\Psi = \frac{RT \ln (e/e^*)}{18} \quad \text{(J g}^{-1}\text{)}, \qquad \text{[Eq. 7.7]}$$

where $e^*$ is saturation vapor pressure over pure water and 18 is the relative molecular mass of water. The temperature of psychrometers must be controlled precisely so measurements are generally performed in the laboratory. An alternative method used with soils involves squeezing water from the soil in a 'pressure-membrane' apparatus. The soil is compressed in a cylinder against a porous membrane and a graph is constructed of pressure applied (taken as $\Psi_s$) and water content ($\theta$) remaining in the sample as determined gravimetrically. Examples of

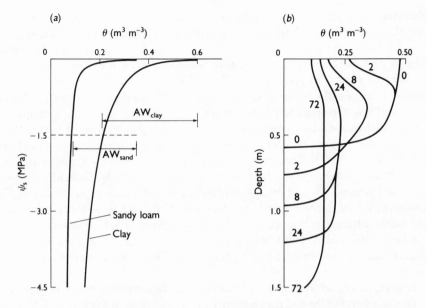

Fig. 7.8. (*a*) Moisture release curves for sandy loam and clay soils. Initial volumetric water contents ($\theta$), near 0.35 for the sand and 0.6 for the clay, provide a maximum estimate of field capacity. (*b*) Infiltration and redistribution of moisture with time in a homogeneous medium (slate dust). The number of hours after the beginning of the experiment are indicated for each curve. (Redrawn from Miller & Klute (1967).)

such **moisture-release curves** are presented in Fig. 7.8*a*. In practice, a standard curve is constructed for a soil in the laboratory. This curve can then be used to translate field data gathered with gravimetric samples or neutron gauges.

## Water and plant growth

Several aspects of the moisture-release curves of Fig. 7.8*a* deserve emphasis. The upper limit of $\theta$ after free drainage is termed **field capacity** (FC) or just 'upper drained limit'. $\Psi_s$ at FC varies from −10 to −35 kPa depending upon several factors including soil compactness. A more consistent number, **moisture equivalent** (ME) corresponding to $\theta$ at −30 kPa can be obtained with a pressure membrane or after centrifuging wet soil at 1000 *g*. Near FC, loosely held capillary water can be removed from soil with only a small decline in $\Psi_s$. As a result, estimates of FC are never very accurate. An empirical relationship, $\Psi_s = a\theta^b$, fits the curve well over most of the range of $\theta$ except near FC.

A second point from Fig. 7.8*a* is that clay, with its much greater surface area and capillary volume, holds more water than sand and its $\Psi_s$ declines gradually as capillary water is removed. After capillary water is removed, the remainder is held very tightly in both sand and clay and $\Psi_s$ drops dramatically with further drying due to the decreasing value of $\Psi_m$. It is obvious that plants must make dramatic adjustments in $\Psi_{pl}$ if they are to continue to extract moisture to low values of $\Psi_s$. For most plants, the practical limit beyond which water uptake and growth cease is near $\Psi_s = -1.5$ MPa. The soil water content at $-1.5$ MPa has been termed the **wilting point** (WP). **Available-water** (AW) capacity of a soil, FC $-$ WP, defines the amount of water that plants can access easily.

How plants are affected near WP depends mainly on the relative rates of water uptake and loss. Growth and photosynthesis of plants with poor root systems and/ or under high evaporative demand are restricted at higher $\Psi_s$ than $-1.5$ MPa (WP). Given time for adjustment (i.e. small evaporative demand), most plants can lower $\Psi_s$ well below $-1.5$ MPa. Cotton plants grown in pots of soil with limited supplies of water will wilt and their stomata close at $\Psi_s$ near $-1.5$ MPa. In the field with much greater soil volume, the soil dries slowly and plants have time to adjust through an increase in solute content causing a decrease in $\Psi_\pi$ and thus $\Psi_{pl}$. Under those conditions, wilting may not occur until $\Psi_s$ drops below $-3$ MPa. Extreme examples have been observed of plant adjustment to $\Psi_s = -7$ MPa. Variation in the true wilting point, plus uncertainties in FC, mean that AW capacity of a soil is never well defined.

Plants extract water from soils in proportion to the distribution of fine roots. As a result, some parts of the soil may remain near FC as others approach WP. $\Psi_s$ varies accordingly while $\Psi_{pl}$ reflects an integration of $\Psi_s$ over all parts of the rooted volume. During the day, $\Psi_{pl}$ varies among plant parts depending upon their position in the transpiration stream. At night, with stomates closed, plant water content is restored and $\Psi_{pl}$ comes to equilibrium with the soil. Predawn values of $\Psi_{pl}$ therefore serve as a useful indicator of integrated soil water status.

### Infiltration of water

Fig. 7.8*b* illustrates the advance of a wetting front from a saturated zone at the surface. Wetting progresses at close to field capacity so there is generally a sharp transition in water potential between wet and dry soil. Infiltration of water influences more than just replenishment of soil moisture. Erosion (Chapter 12), leaching, and soil aeration are also affected. If the rate that water is added to the surface exceeds the infiltration rate, water will pond or run off (with the danger of erosion).

Pore size controls water movement in soils. In a dense soil without macropores, water flux is limited by capillary flow. The hydraulic (water) conductivity of a saturated clay, with very small pore sizes, is only about 0.5 mm h$^{-1}$ at 20 °C. Temperature is specified because the viscosity of water decreases (and conductivity increases) as temperature increases. Conductivity increases approximately one order of magnitude for each step in the textural series, clay→loam→sand. The 'soil' in Fig. 7.8*b* is homogeneous with depth whereas clay content increases with depth in most soils. Lower layers therefore have smaller hydraulic conductivities than those near the surface and rapid infiltration of the A layers is followed by slower wetting of the B layers. Sand, on the other hand, may drain so rapidly that frontal wetting does not occur.

Wetting characteristics are affected dramatically by soil structure. Organization into structural peds leaves macrochannels that allow rapid, deep wetting followed by slower frontal advance into peds. Marked structural organization of B layers is rare, however, so replenishment of deep moisture is slow except with shrinking clays where macrochannels extend there as well. As the clays are wetted, they swell, closing the major pores and wetting continues through saturated flow.

Hydraulic conductivity declines when a soil dries because the remaining water is held strongly by matrix forces. The change is dramatic: conductivity declines by a factor of $10^4$ between FC and WP, sharply restricting capillary flow to plant roots.

### Soil aeration

**Respiration in soils**   Respiration in soils includes the activities of animals and living roots as well as decay organisms. Trophic chains of soil organisms begin with crop residues and their respiration can be estimated from the amounts of organic matter added to soils. The requirements for soil aeration are considerable. A wheat crop with $15\,t\,ha^{-1}$ of above-ground production would return perhaps 9 t straw and 2 t fine roots to the soil at the end of the growing season. Assuming that residues contain 44% carbon, $4.84\,t\,C\,ha^{-1}$ ($11\,t \times 0.44$) are released during complete decay. This is converted to $4.0 \times 10^5$ mol $CO_2$, or 1 $m^3$ gas $m^{-2}$ land (Eq. 6.13, 27 °C). A somewhat greater amount of $O_2$ would be consumed. Averaged over a year, that amounts to 13.3 kg C (28 $m^3$ $CO_2$) $ha^{-1}\,d^{-1}$. The flux would occur mainly during periods with favorable temperature and moisture.

Respiratory activities of roots represent an additional source of $CO_2$ that can amount to 10 kg C or more $ha^{-1}\,d^{-1}$ (21 $m^3$ $CO_2$). As a result, soil atmospheres generally have less $O_2$ (18 to 20% v/v) than normal air (21%) and more $CO_2$ (up to 1% compared with the normal 0.035%). Distinguishing the portions of total soil respiration that come from plant roots, various animals, and decay organisms is impossible without isotopic labels or antibiotic treatments that suppress microbial populations.

**Gas exchange by soils**   Soil aeration is closely linked to soil water content. The capillary pores are open to diffusive exchange of gases only after a soil has drained following a wetting event. Oxygen diffusion through macropores and channels, while more significant than in capillaries, is inadequate to support the potential biological activities of most soils. 'Activated' diffusion driven by pressure changes due to atmospheric turbulence helps exchange gases between the atmosphere and soil. Wetting and drying are also important. Stale air (low in $O_2$, high in $CO_2$) is displaced on wetting and fresh air is drawn into the soil as the macropores drain. The solubility of oxygen and its diffusion rate in water are both small causing wet soils to become anaerobic as oxygen is exhausted by roots and microorganisms. The centers of small clay aggregates as well as large peds may remain anaerobic for extended periods after the soil drains. The relative activities of aerobic and anaerobic bacteria change accordingly. Decay is slowed under anaerobic conditions and the large organic accumulations found in Histosols are one result. Rice is one of the few crops that tolerate flooded soils, in part because oxygen reaches rice roots through specialized aerenchymatous tissues of the stem and roots.

## 7.7   SOIL TEMPERATURE RELATIONS

Soil temperature varies complexly with depth, and over daily and annual cycles, owing to gains and losses of heat energy. Soil heat flux, $G$, was defined in Eq. 6.11 as a term in the energy balance at the soil surface. Contributions of heat energy to the soil surface come from radiative, convective, and latent heat exchanges. Those are not the only sources of heat energy, however. A small, upward flux of about 50 nW m$^{-2}$ resulting from radioactivity and cooling of Earth's core ensures that temperatures deep in the profile (beyond 10 m) are warm (10–15 °C), thus limiting the freezing depth during cold winters. Respiratory activities of plant roots and soil organisms add a much larger source of heat. In the example involving decay of wheat residues, 11 t residues ha$^{-1}$ × 17 GJ combustible heat energy t$^{-1}$ = 187 GJ ha$^{-1}$. The average flux would be 50 kJ m$^{-2}$ d$^{-1}$ (0.6 W m$^{-2}$). Although small compared with $LE$ and $H$ terms in surface energy budgets, heat from decay of large amounts of organic matter will serve to warm protected beds of garden soil.

Surface exchanges, as modified by the character of the soil surface, are important components in soil heat flux. Cover provided by living plants, stubble, and residue mulches insulates the soil, and the color, wetness, and texture of the soil surface affect reflectance of short-wave radiation. Dark soils absorb well; wet soils are usually more reflective than dry soils; and a granulated surface is more absorptive than a smooth one. Wetness is particularly important because $+R_n$ then is dissipated in evaporation rather than as soil heat flux. Slope and aspect of a surface also influence its radiation balance through the Cosine Law (e.g. Fig. 6.15). Daily and seasonal patterns of soil temperature at various depths are influenced further by the thermal conductivity of the soil and its heat capacity, both of which vary depending on the content of minerals, organic matter, air, and water (Table 7.2).

The magnitude of the heating pulse from $R_n$ to soil varies sinusoidally over daily and annual cycles (Fig. 7.9). Peak soil temperature lags behind peak radiation, however, because soils continue to gain heat energy from air and radiation even as the radiation load declines in the afternoon. The daily maximum in soil temperature at 10 cm depth generally occurs 2–3 h after solar noon, and the annual maximum may be 4–6 weeks after the summer solstice. In temperate regions, a similar lag in soil warming following the winter solstice delays planting of crops in spring. In those regions, few warm-season crops achieve full cover by the time of the peak irradiance near the summer solstice.

With full cover, only about 5% of $R_n$ goes to $G$, and soil temperatures under crops tend to be rather stable and cool. Energy exchanges by bare soil are much larger. In both cases, the heat pulse is propagated downward with $+R_n$ and towards the surface during periods with $-R_n$. The heat pulse penetrates slowly, owing to insulating effects of air-filled pores, and the lag time to maximum temperature increases with soil depth. When pores are filled with water, thermal conductivity increases dramatically (Table 7.2) and the lags are smaller. The pulse of heat energy is depleted in proportion to the soil's heat capacity causing diurnal temperature

Table 7.2 *Thermal properties of soils*

| Material | Water content ($m^3 \, m^{-3}$) | Thermal conductivity $W \, m^{-1} \, C^{-1}$) | Heat capacity ($MJ \, m^{-3} \, C^{-1}$) | Thermal diffusivity[1] ($10^{-6} \, m^2 \, s^{-1}$) |
|---|---|---|---|---|
| Sand | 0.0 | 0.29 | 1.2 | 0.24 |
|  | 0.2 | 1.76 | 2.1 | 0.84 |
|  | 0.4 | 2.18 | 2.9 | 0.75 |
| Clay | 0.0 | 0.25 | 1.2 | 0.21 |
|  | 0.2 | 1.17 | 2.1 | 0.56 |
|  | 0.4 | 1.59 | 2.9 | 0.55 |
| Peat | 0.0 | 0.06 | 1.5 | 0.04 |
|  | 0.4 | 0.29 | 3.1 | 0.09 |
|  | 0.8 | 0.50 | 4.8 | 0.10 |

*Note:*
[1] Diffusivity = conductivity/volumetric heat capacity.
*Source:* Calculated from van Wijk and de Vries 1963.

amplitude to decrease with depth; little diurnal variation in temperature is evident below about 0.5 m. Thermal conductivity and heat capacity both increase with increasing water content (Table 7.2); the combination of these changes is seen in the parabolic change in thermal diffusivity (thermal diffusivity = thermal conductivity/ volumetric heat capacity). The situation is confounded further by latent heat exchange and vapor transfer within the soil: water evaporates in one region of a soil and condenses in another.

**Influence of temperature on soil and plant processes**

Temperature affects physicochemical as well as biological processes in soils. The solubility of calcium phosphates (Fig. 7.6), for example, shows a marked dependence on temperature. Phosphorus deficiencies are common during the cool season in plants grown on the Holtville soil illustrated in Fig. 7.10 but generally disappear when soils warm because solubility products of phosphate minerals increase with temperature. Nutrient uptake and root growth generally follow the temperature response presented earlier in Fig. 2.12a, and root permeability and thus water uptake are restricted by low temperatures.

   The phase differences in the times of temperature maxima and minima in air and soil present an interesting problem for plants. Photosynthate is gained as a daytime pulse following the pattern of short-wave radiation. At a particular time, user tissues, such as the apical meristems of shoots and roots may be at different positions on their temperature response curve for growth. Some may be limited by temperature (too high or too low) while others may be in an optimum environment. As a result, phase and amplitude differences between air and soil exert control over the pattern of plant development. This topic is considered further in Chapter 11.

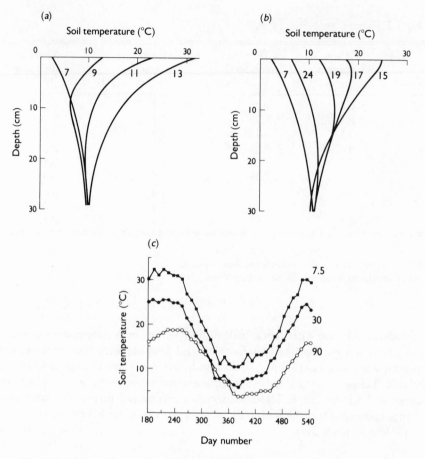

Fig. 7.9. Soil temperature patterns. (Adapted from F.A. Brooks, *ca*. 1960, *An introduction to physical microclimatology*, Mimeo., University of California, Davis.) (*a*) Daytime and (*b*) nighttime soil temperature patterns in bare soil at Riverside, California (34° N) for a day in late February. Numbers on the curves indicate the hour of the day. (*c*) Ten-day running means of temperatures under bare soil (Yolo fine-sandy loam) at Davis, California (38.5° N). Depths in cm are indicated. Measurements began July 1 (Day 182) and continued until June 30 of the next year.

## 7.8 SUMMARY

Soil formation is dominated by climate and vegetation; similar soils are found in similar climates around the world. During formation, surface layers are leached, organic matter accumulates, and primary minerals weather and recrystallize as secondary minerals (clays). The minerals are only sparingly soluble. They consist of lattices and ribbons of silicon and aluminum oxides held together by metallic ions. Soil classification systems are structured on genetic processes and on profile characteristics.

Clays and organic matter influence soil properties. Organic matter is active in

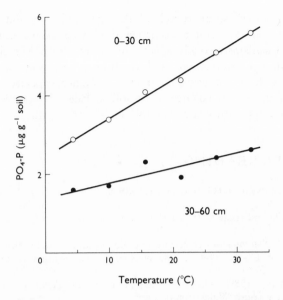

**Fig. 7.10. Phosphorus content of Holtville clay loam soil that is soluble in dilute bicarbonate solution as a function of temperature. The two soil strata differ markedly in phosphorus release. (Previously unpublished data from R.S. Loomis, A. Ulrich, and G.F. Worker, Jr.)**

carbon and nitrogen cycling and it serves to bind soil particles into aggregate structures. Old organic matter (humus) consists of stable products of decay with C/N ratios near 12. The organic content of soils results from an equilibrium between humus formation (favored by high input of residues and thus by climates favorable for plant growth) and humus loss (favored by high temperatures).

Clay and organic matter provide immense areas of negatively charged surfaces that attract and hold water and swarms of ions. Their abilities to exchange ions are measured as cation exchange capacity (CEC). An abundance of $H^+$ on the CEC and in solution results in an acid soil. Soils acidify naturally under any vegetation and more rapidly with cropping or grazing. Base cations and organic acids are lost from the system in harvested material leaving protons in the soil. Addition of nitrogen to a system by any means including biological fixation also leads to acidification because nitrate that leaches from the profile carries metallic cations with it. To avoid deleterious effects of low pH, including aluminum toxicity, and to sustain productivity, pH is corrected towards neutrality with lime.

Attraction of water to negative surfaces results in the matrix term ($\Psi_m$) of total soil water potential ($\Psi_s$). Solutes and gravity also contribute to lowering the activity of soil water below that of pure water. The ability of a soil to hold and deliver water to plants is defined in moisture release curves. The difference between an upper limit of water content after drainage, field capacity (FC), and a practical lower limit at $-1.5$ MPa, the wilting point (WP), serves as a measure of plant available water (AW). At WP, water remaining in soil is held so tightly by matrix forces that little additional water can be extracted.

Soil water content and air alternately fill the same soil pores and thus are linked reciprocally. Macropores facilitate exchange of both air and water. Respiration by roots and soil organisms strongly affects the composition of soil atmospheres. Water, in addition to cooling effects through evaporation at the surface, has a reciprocal effect with air on thermal conductivity and heat capacity of soil. Soil heat flux is driven by the energy balance at the soil surface. The amplitude of diurnal variations of soil temperature is damped strongly with depth.

## 7.9   FURTHER READING

Bohn, H. L., B. L. McNeal, and G. A. Connor. 1985. *Soil chemistry* 2nd edn. John Wiley, New York. 341 p.

Jenny, H. 1980. *The soil resource.* (*Ecological Studies* no. 37.) Springer–Verlag, New York. 377 p.

Kittrick, J. A. 1986. *Soil mineral weathering.* Van Nostrand–Reinhold, New York. 271 p.

Paul, E. A. and F. E. Clark. 1989. *Soil microbiology and biochemistry.* Academic Press, San Diego, California. 273 p.

Robson, A. D. (ed.). 1989. *Soil acidity and plant growth.* Academic Press, Australia, Marrickville, New South Wales. 306 p.

Singer, M. J. and D. J. Munns. 1987. *Soils: an introduction.* Macmillan, New York. 492 p.

Stevenson, F. J. (ed.). 1982. *Nitrogen in agricultural soils.* Agronomy No. 22. Am. Soc. Agron., Madison, Wisconsin. 940 p.

THREE

# Production processes

The adequacy of agriculture as our source of food depends upon production rates in crops and pastures. This section considers the important 'production processes'. It begins with production and cycling of nitrogen (Chapter 8). Nitrogen has key roles in the structure of proteins and nucleic acids and thus can be considered, along with carbon, as one of the central elements of life. Nitrogen is subject to complex cycling and its supply is frequently limiting to the performance of plant communities. Water is also commonly in scarce supply. Uptake of water from soils and its movement along the soil–plant–atmosphere continuum is the focus of Chapter 9, which gives particular attention to losses that occur through evaporation and transpiration. Acquisition of atmospheric carbon dioxide and its fixation and reduction (Chapter 10) are the central production process. Photosynthesis is closely coupled with partitioning (pattern of use) of reduced carbon in respiration and growth (Chapter 11).

Achievement of significant rates of photosynthesis depends upon large investments in the construction and maintenance of a foliage canopy supported by stems and roots. Photosynthesis further depends upon the existence of rapidly growing 'sink' tissues capable of utilizing large supplies of new organic substrates. The aim in farming is to find and culture plant materials in ways that tend to optimize partitioning for efficient use of scarce resources such as sunlight, water, nitrogen, and human effort.

# 8

## Nitrogen processes

### 8.1 INTRODUCTION

Nitrogen is unique among the essential nutrients of higher plants in terms of its roles in biological systems and its complex cycling. In addition, it is the element most commonly limiting to crop production and the one most demanding of management skills. Soil organic matter has a pivotal role in cycling nitrogen contents of crop residues and animal manures to the mineral forms that are used by higher plants. In Chapter 7, we found that the level of organic matter reflects the relative rates of carbon and nitrogen inputs and decomposition on the one hand and mineralization on the other. This chapter is concerned with several microbiological and physical processes important in nitrogen cycling and management of nitrogen in agriculture.

### 8.2 THE NITROGEN CYCLE

#### Oxidation–reduction states of nitrogen

Nitrogen is present in soil–plant systems at stable oxidation states ranging from $+5$ (oxidized) to $-3$ (reduced). Arrows in Fig. 8.1 indicate the transformations, most of which require biological catalysis, that occur in nitrogen cycles. Nitrogen in soil organic matter and in proteins and nucleic acids of living organisms is reduced at the $-3$ level. Most plants produce protein and other reduced nitrogen compounds beginning with mineral nitrogen absorbed from soil as nitrate ($+5$) or ammonium ($-3$) ions. Ammonium ions enter directly into biosyntheses of amino acids and other compounds while nitrate must first be reduced to that level (**nitrate reduction**) through the addition of 8 electrons. Respiration supplies energy and reducing power required in nitrate reduction; glucose, $C_6H_{12}O_6$, a representative substrate for respiration, yields 24 electrons as carbon goes from the 0 to $+4$ oxidation state (see Chapter 11). By contrast, humans, like most animals, are dependent upon finding reduced nitrogen in their diets.

Soil microorganisms have evolved ways to utilize each of the forms of nitrogen found in soils. They participate in release of ammonium nitrogen from soil organic matter (mineralization) but they also compete with plants for the use of nitrogen in

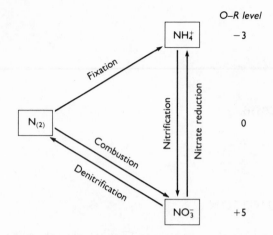

Fig. 8.1. Oxidation–reduction levels of nitrogen in nitrate ($NO_3^-$) and ammonium ($NH_4^+$) ions and dinitrogen gas ($N_2$) and the transformations between these important levels. Nitrite ($NO_2^-$) lays at $+3$ in most pathways to and from nitrate but has been omitted for simplicity.

growth. Microbial processes for oxidation of ammonium to nitrate (**nitrification**, removal of $8\,e^-$) and reduction of nitrate to gaseous $N_2$ (**denitrification**, addition of $5\,e^-$) are also identified in Fig. 8.1. Denitrification to $N_2$ (or to gases such as $N_2O$) is the principal way in which nitrogen returns to the atmosphere.

A number of microorganisms including some found in symbiotic associations with higher plants can reduce $N_2$ gas to the ammonium level (**nitrogen fixation**, addition of $3\,e^-$). Major transfers from $N_2$ to $NH_3$ also occur in the production of fertilizer. The abundant atmospheric pool of $N_2$ gas could, theoretically, be oxidized to nitrate and enter biological soil systems in that form. The free energy change for dinitrogen oxidation is favorable, but the activation energy is very large and the process occurs naturally only with lightning discharges in the atmosphere, and to some extent in diesel motors, resulting in small fluxes of nitrate in rainfall (1–5 kg N ha$^{-1}$ y$^{-1}$). A Nobel prize awaits the student who discovers an efficient means for burning $N_2$ to $NO_3^-$. That would provide a source of energy, and exhaust from tractors operating on $N_2$ fuel could serve as fertilizer. A second prize might be needed, however, for the person able to evaluate the global consequences of the process.

### A generalized nitrogen cycle

The generalized nitrogen cycle presented in Fig. 8.2 includes all the major pools and transfers found in cropping systems and pastures. For simplicity, nitrification is shown as a single process because accumulation of the intermediate nitrite form is rare. Soil organic matter (SOM) is subdivided here into four pools:

F, fresh organic matter (dead and decaying material);
B, flora and fauna biomass (mainly bacteria and fungi);

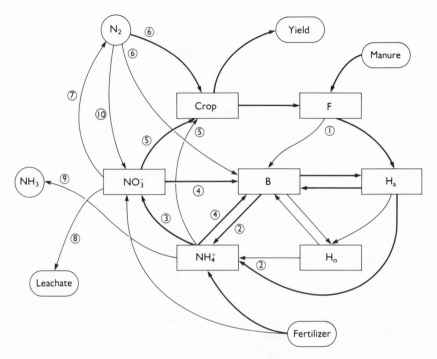

**Fig. 8.2. A generalized nitrogen cycle for agricultural systems. Fresh organic matter (F) added to soil decays (1) to microbial biomass (B), active humus (H$_a$), and eventually to old humus (H$_o$). B, H$_a$, and H$_o$ are subject to mineralization (2) to NH$_4^+$ and then by nitrification (3) to NO$_3^-$. The mineral forms are subject to immobilization (4) to B and then to H$_a$ and H$_o$. Uptake to a crop (5), fixation of N$_2$ (6) to crop (symbiotic) or to B (free-living), and denitrification (7; to various N oxides as well as N$_2$) complete the biological transfers. Also shown: loss by leaching (8), volatilization (9) and yield; and inputs from lightning (10), manure, and fertilizer. NH$_3$ is also volatilized (process 9) from Crop and F (fresh residue). The major paths are emphasized by heavy lines.**

H$_a$, 'active' organic matter (active humus); and
H$_o$, old organic matter (old humus).

The distinction between the H$_a$ and H$_o$ pools is based on observations with carbon isotopes that some SOM fractions turnover more quickly than others (Paul & van Veen 1978). Active organic matter probably consists of slowly degradable intermediate products such as ligno- and phenol–protein complexes and is not distinguished from old humus in most assays. Protection of both humus pools comes from phenolic components, by adsorption to clays, or by being sequestered within soil aggregates and not accessible to attack by microbes. The H$_a$ pool can be quite large (in the order of 1 t N ha$^{-1}$) and its turnover is fairly rapid (15–20 y). The B and H$_a$ pools are the principal sources of the nitrogen released in mineralization. By contrast, the old pool is highly resistant to further decay and its half-life is typically measured in thousands of years.

Dinitrogen gas in the atmosphere is the central reservoir in exchanges of nitrogen among terrestrial and aquatic ecosystems, including the oceans. Its entry to soils and crops occurs mainly through biological and industrial fixation to ammonia. The atmosphere also supplies nitrate in rainfall and ammonia that has volatilized from adjacent ecosystems. Inputs of nitrate and ammonia to a system from the atmosphere occurs by both wet and dry 'deposition'. Aquatic systems receive nitrogen in runoff and drainage from terrestrial systems. Sea waters are very low in nitrogen, however, and little is atomized by storms so the mineral flux from ocean to land is small; fluxes via harvest of fish by humans and birds (e.g. the guano of 'Chilean nitrate') are also small. The principal avenue by which nitrogen returns to the atmosphere (and then by fixation to land) is through denitrification to $N_2$ from wet soils and aquatic systems.

Cycling of sulfur is similar to that of nitrogen in the sense that bacteria, soil organic matter, changes in oxidation–reduction state, and gaseous phases are involved. Cycling patterns of other mineral elements are rather different since they do not have gaseous forms and many of them enter a variety of insoluble mineral combinations. Potassium, for example, is subject to leaching and to chemical and physical fixation with clay minerals. Phosphorus cycles through organic matter and is sometimes present in organic forms such as phytic acid. In addition, phosphorus is fixed by clay and forms sparingly soluble compounds with iron, aluminum, and calcium. The oceans are the major sink for most nutrient elements and only modest amounts are recycled from there through atomization and rainfall. Without gaseous forms for recycling from oceans, agricultural systems are dependent for their main supply of most minerals on weathering of parent material and on recycling via inputs of fertilizer. The principal sources for K, P, S, and Ca fertilizers, for example, are mineral deposits laid down in ancient lakes and oceans.

## Microbial populations

Four major groups of organisms are involved in nitrogen processes: bacteria, fungi, cyanobacteria (blue-green algae), and algae. Each group is highly diverse. Cyanobacteria and algae are generally surface-dwelling and autotrophic, developing their own carbon supplies through photosynthesis. Most bacteria and fungi are heterotrophic and obtain reduced carbon from organic matter. Some important exceptions are chemautotrophic and obtain energy for carbon reduction by oxidizing iron, sulfur, or nitrogen.

In soils, the abundance and activity of various microorganisms change quickly as substrates and physical conditions change. Differences in species' growth rates influence patterns of succession in microbial communities inhabiting crop residues. Fast-growing microbes have reproductive rates as great as $0.5 \, d^{-1}$ while others grow very slowly. The populations are also affected by grazers such as protozoa. Paul & Clark (1989) reported average residence times for microbial biomass ranging from 0.24 y under sugarcane in Brazil to 6.8 y with a wheat–fallow rotation in Canada. Long residence times indicate that most of the microbes exist as resting spores or are quiescent.

The amount of microbial biomass can be estimated by the 'fumigation–incubation' method. Fresh samples of soil are fumigated with an agent such as chloroform to kill the microbes and release their contents. Some organisms survive and utilize the released materials in their metabolism allowing the amount of respiratory $CO_2$ released during a subsequent incubation period to serve as a measure of the biomass that was killed. The size of the microbial pool found by such methods is surprisingly large: 1000–6000 kg dry material ha$^{-1}$ (Jenkinson 1988). The large size of this pool indicates that the supply of substrates must be a principal factor limiting microbial activity. Dry microbial biomass seems to have relatively constant proportions of C (0.45) and N (0.067); thus the C/N ratio of microbial biomass is near 6.7 (0.45/0.067) allowing quite large amounts of nitrogen (67 to 420 kg N ha$^{-1}$) to be held in the pool.

In addition to nutritional factors, soil microbiological processes are dependent upon temperature, water, and pH. Little activity occurs near 0 °C; process rates increase with a $Q_{10}$ of 2 as temperature increases to an optimal range near 40–50 °C.

## 8.3   DECAY AND IMMOBILIZATION

### Decay

Soil flora and fauna meet their energy and nitrogen requirements through attacks on the organic residues of higher plants. Bacteria are found throughout the succession of organisms that attack residues and they generally dominate in the final stages. Fungi are important in the early stages of decay and with acid residues and soils; bacteria are more prominent at higher pH.

Carbohydrates and proteins are abundant in plant biomass and thus also in fresh organic matter (Chapter 1). Proteins, lipids, and non-structural carbohydrates are excellent substrates for bacterial growth and they disappear quickly during decay while cellulose and hemicellulose decay more slowly. Other chemicals, including lignin, phenols, and higher-order aromatic and heterocyclic compounds, are metabolized slowly and thus increase in relative abundance as decay proceeds. Mineral elements such as K, Ca, Mg, P, and S are also released during decay.

The disappearance of each of the organic substrates can usually be described by first-order kinetics, i.e. the rate declines in proportion to the amount of substrate remaining:

$$dX/dt = -kX,$$   [Eq. 8.1]

where $X$ is an amount of substrate and $k$ is the rate constant for its disappearance. By integration, the amount remaining at time $t$ can be calculated from the original supply, $X_0$:

$$X_t = X_0 e^{-kt}.$$   [Eq. 8.2]

Under optimal conditions in the laboratory, $k$ is about 0.2 d$^{-1}$ for proteins, 0.08 d$^{-1}$ for cellulose and hemicellulose, and 0.01 d$^{-1}$ for lignin (Paul & Clark 1989). The half-life of a material is $0.693/k$; under optimal conditions, then, half of the lignin in a crop residue would decay in 69 d (0.693/0.01 d$^{-1}$) and three-quarters would be gone in 138 d. Most of the nitrogen and a large portion of the carbon in the various substrates is transformed into microbial biomass. When substrates are exhausted, microbes sporulate or die. Materials released from dead bacteria can be used by other bacteria or higher plants whereas resistant spores may remain in soils for many years.

Under field conditions, where moisture and temperature fluctuate and generally are nonoptimal, decay is slower and more variable than in the laboratory. Some of the variation is due to variation in the size of residues: coarse residues decay more slowly than finely divided ones.

## Immobilization

**Immobilization** refers to the incorporation of nitrogen into microbial biomass, and then more permanently to humus. Fresh residues are relatively rich in carbon compared with nitrogen (C/N = 25 to 100). Soil organisms utilize reduced carbon as a respiratory substrate while accumulating both carbon and nitrogen in the proteins and walls of their bodies. As a consequence, the C/N ratio of the residues declines as decay proceeds. In agricultural soils, the C/N ratio of older fractions usually stabilizes between 10 and 13. In addition to nitrogen from crop residues, ammonium and nitrate ions from the surrounding soil are also highly suitable substrates for microorganisms and these mineral forms are also immobilized to microbial biomass and humus.

Immobilization is particularly evident during decay of residues having a small content of nitrogen. In that case, microbial growth and decay are nitrogen-limited and the concentration of free mineral nitrogen in the soil may be reduced to a very low level. Cereal straw with 0.5% N and 45% C has a C/N ratio of 90 whereas the ratio in the microbial pool, as noted above, is near 6.7. Given rich sources of C, the increase in microbial biomass depends on use of mineral nitrogen from the soil (including fertilizer N). Not only is the mineral pool depleted, but continuing fluxes from mineralization also are usurped. The time-course of mineral pools during immobilization is characterized in Fig. 8.3. In aerated soils, some immobilization occurs with residues having C/N as low 25 (i.e., 1.8% N in dry matter) but a ratio of 45 (1% N) or more is needed for a noticeable effect. Fermentative metabolism is inefficient in the use of carbon (more is given off as $CO_2$ and $CH_4$ than under aerobic conditions) and C/N ratios as great as 80 can be incorporated into anaerobic soils without causing significant immobilization. This is an important consideration in the culture of flooded rice.

Immobilization leads usefully to humus formation but the tie-up of mineral nitrogen may interfere with its availability to subsequent crops. As much as 200 kg N ha$^{-1}$ may become temporarily unavailable through the incorporation of high-carbon residues. Anticipating the timing and amounts of mineralization and immobilization that occur with inputs of organic materials and fertilizer is very difficult. One solution is to incorporate residues during the fallow period, allowing time for decomposition, rather than just before planting. This has the advantage that carry-over mineral nitrogen is captured in the decay process and prevented

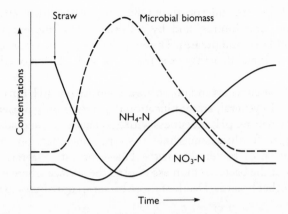

**Fig. 8.3. Immobilization illustrated with a hypothetical time course of [NH$_4^+$] and [NO$_3^-$] in a soil before and for several weeks after the incorporation of residues low in nitrogen content.**

from leaching. Another solution is to apply fertilizer nitrogen with the residues, i.e. to feed the decomposer populations. That capital investment in nitrogen carries the risk that the nitrogen may be lost and not recoverable from humus in the future. Fresh manures that have been collected on straw bedding typically cause immobilization during their decay in soil. That problem can be avoided by storing the manure and allowing it to decay to a low C/N value before applying it to the field.

Immobilization problems are among the reasons that grass and cereal stubbles are sometimes burned or left as surface mulches (no-till systems) thereby reducing the amount of carbon entering the soil. Burning is particularly common in Mediterranean climates where the wet season and thus the decay period coincides with the growth of winter crops such as wheat and barley. Cycling of mineral nutrients is accelerated by burning and the amount of nitrogen lost through burning (e.g. 0.005 kg N kg$^{-1}$ straw × 3000 kg straw = 15 kg N ha$^{-1}$) is small compared with savings in nitrogen fertilizer. Other reasons for burning include disease control, avoidance of soil acidification, and because less tillage is then needed in seed bed preparation.

## 8.4   MINERALIZATION AND NITRIFICATION

Nitrogen in soil organic matter is unavailable to higher plants. Processes that transform these materials into mineral forms (NH$_4^+$ and NO$_3^-$) that can be used by higher plants are important steps in nitrogen cycles.

**Nitrogen mineralization**

Release of NH$_4^+$ and NH$_3$ from organic forms is termed **ammonification**, or **nitrogen mineralization** (in contrast to the release of other nutrients). Ammonification is accomplished by microbial populations during their attacks on dead bacteria, residues, and humus, and by cell-free, hydrolytic enzymes including proteinases, peptidases, and ureases. The enzymes are released from decaying plant material and bacteria and they may exist free in the soil solution or adsorbed to soil colloids.

Both extracellular enzymes and microbes are sensitive to pH, ion concentration, and temperature. In general, ammonification depends mainly on aerobic bacteria and is favored by neutral pH, moistness with good aeration, and adequate carbon substrate. Nitrogen fertilizer sometimes has a priming effect on ammonification through stimulation of bacterial growth. Tillage promotes aeration and it also brings a portion of the bacterial biomass pool to the surface where it is exposed to desiccation and other hazards. Death of those bacteria contributes to the ammonification flux.

Rates of ammonification of humus are usually rather small in proportion to amounts of organic matter present. In relative terms, 0.01 to 0.03 of the total organic matter may be mineralized annually in a tilled soil. Most of the $NH_4^+$ comes from residues (and organic amendments), microbial biomass, and active organic material ($H_a$). It needs to be stressed that mineralization varies not only with weather and tillage but also with the amounts and types of residues and manures incorporated with the soil.

### Nitrification

The important process of oxidation of ammonium ions to nitrate, termed **nitrification**, is mediated by chemoautotrophic bacteria of the Nitrobacteraceae family. These bacteria gain energy from the oxidation of ammonium and use it in the fixation and reduction of bicarbonate to organic material. Nitrification takes place in two steps. In the first, bacteria of the *Nitrosolobus* and *Nitrosomonas* groups oxidize ammonium to nitrite ($NO_2^-$). In the second, nitrite ions are oxidized to nitrate, principally by *Nitrobacter*.

Ammonium oxidation to nitrite is usually the limiting step, and free nitrite seldom accumulates to high levels in soil although exceptions occur at high pH. Nitrification is rapid in most agricultural situations but is strongly suppressed in many natural systems. Acid soils are a factor under coniferous vegetation and in tropical Oxisols, but it seems that natural inhibitors of nitrification also exist. In contrast to $NH_4^+$ which is held by cation exchangers, both $NO_2^-$ and $NO_3^-$ are mobile in soil solutions. They are drawn toward plant roots along with the transpiration stream or leached gradually from the profile in drainage waters.

### 8.5  LOSS OF NITROGEN

Several processes contribute to losses of nitrogen from agricultural systems. Included here are runoff, denitrification, leaching, and volatilization.

## Source materials

The popular belief that most losses of nitrogen and pollution occur only with fertilizer and that organic sources do not contribute to losses is not correct. Significant amounts of nitrogen are in fact lost directly and indirectly from organic materials. Organic as well as mineral nitrogen is suspended and leached from surface residues (and animal wastes) and carried away in runoff or by erosion. In cases where organic materials enter surface waters, mineralization and gasification of the nitrogen are simply transferred to streams and lakes. As was illustrated in Fig. 8.2, the principal losses occur through leaching or denitrification from the pool of nitrate-nitrogen. That pool is supplied as much or more by mineralization of soil organic matter as it is by fertilizer. Applied properly, fertilizer nitrogen enters quickly into organic forms through uptake by plants and microbial immobilization. When residues of those crops and microbial biomass cycle to the older fractions of soil organic matter pool, the original source of nitrogen becomes indistinguishable from other sources including legume fixation and manure. Whereas fertilizer applications can be timed and placed for efficient use by plants, mineralization of organic matter occurs whenever conditions are favorable, whether a crop is present or not. The mineralization flux is therefore generally the principal source of nitrate losses (Jenkinson 1991). Because organic farming systems require high levels of organic inputs and high rates of mineralization to meet crop needs, they are particularly vulnerable to nitrate losses.

## Denitrification

Nitrate-nitrogen can be converted to gaseous $N_2O$ or $N_2$ under anaerobic conditions by a variety of bacteria. This process of **denitrification** is the principal route by which nitrogen returns to the atmosphere. Without it, reduced and oxidized nitrogen would accumulate in the biosphere and the nitrogen content of the atmosphere would decline. The organisms thought to be the most active in denitrification, bacteria of the *Alcaligenes* and *Pseudomonas* groups, are abundant in soil. These heterotrophic bacteria gain their energy from metabolism of carbon substrates. The key feature of their metabolism is that under anaerobic conditions they use nitrate rather than oxygen as an electron acceptor for respiratory activity. This represents 'dissimilatory' (in contrast to 'assimilatory') nitrate reduction. Given an abundant supply of nitrate, denitrification can result in significant losses of nitrogen: nitrogen that might have been used by crop plants or that might have leached from the profile.

Heavy soils with poor drainage as well as the water tables found within most soils offer favorable anaerobic environments for denitrification. Denitrification also occurs in well-drained soils during brief periods of saturation and at anaerobic microsites in the interior spaces of aggregates. In addition to anaerobic conditions, supplies of nitrate and carbon substrates are needed. Rolston *et al.* (1978) observed peak rates of loss as great as 70 kg N ha$^{-1}$ d$^{-1}$ from a wet soil heavily supplied with nitrate fertilizer (300 kg N ha$^{-1}$) and manure (34 t ha$^{-1}$). Total loss during the season was 198 kg N ha$^{-1}$. The explanation for such rapid rates seems to be that Pseudomonad populations supported by carbon from manure or residues, although lacking an effective fermentative metabolism, can switch quickly to nitrate as their respiratory acceptor when oxygen is deficient. Nitrate supplies are seldom large enough to support such rates for more than a few hours and observations of seasonal rates in crops are much smaller, in the order of 5–10% or less of the flux of mineral nitrogen. Crops compete effectively for the available nitrate; their transpiration dries the soil and thereby improves aeration. In addition, carbon supplies are less. In the experiments of Rolston *et al.* (1978), treatments with 300 kg fertilizer N ha$^{-1}$, but without manure, were applied to uncropped land and to a stand of perennial ryegrass. In contrast to the manured treatment, total denitrification for the season was only 5.7 kg N ha$^{-1}$ from wet fallow and 30 kg N ha$^{-1}$ from well-irrigated grass, demonstrating dependence of denitrification on carbon supply.

Special conditions favoring denitrification develop with flooded rice. A thin surface layer of the soil is aerated by dissolved $O_2$ and mineralization and nitrification are favored in that region. The bulk of the soil profile is anaerobic, however, and nitrate that leaches into the anaerobic zone is denitrified. The problem of supplying rice crops with nitrogen is resolved by using an ammonium fertilizer and placing it in the reducing zone where nitrification is inhibited.

## Leaching

Ammonium ions are strongly absorbed by soil colloids and thus are protected from being leached from the profile whereas the anion-exchange capacity of soils is weak and nitrate moves rather freely with drainage. Downward movement is proportional to nitrate concentration and water flux. The conditions for loss of nitrate ions, then, are rainy periods, permeable soils, and an abundant supply of nitrate. The dangers are that nitrate will be leached beyond the rooting depth or moved into an anaerobic zone and denitrified. Nitrogen is lost from the crop and may become a pollutant of surface and ground waters. In addition, nitrate leaching is an important factor in soil acidification (Section 7.5). A long fallow period and tillage set up conditions favorable for mineralization but leaching is prevented if crop residues are incorporated with the tillage and the mineral nitrogen is immobilized.

Where winters are mild and rainfall adequate, a **cover crop** (e.g. ryegrass) can be grown during the fallow period to catch the nitrification flux. That lessens the potential for nitrate pollution but adds costs (additional tillage and seed), a new problem with residue incorporation, and uncertainty about the mineral flux during the subsequent cropping period.

Less leaching occurs from natural vegetation than from pastures and cultivated fields. While the amounts are small, seasonal evapotranspiration is generally large resulting in high concentrations of $NO_3$–N (up to 100 ppm; 7 mM) in ground waters under natural vegetation in semiarid and arid regions. Pastures are similar to natural vegetation in water use. In addition, dung and urine create locally high concentrations of nitrogen that contribute to nitrate leaching. Steele & Vallis (1988) report examples of unfertilized ryegrass–clover pastures in New Zealand that lost over 100 kg N $ha^{-1}$ $y^{-1}$ through leaching from dung and urine.

It is convenient in some systems to apply ammoniacal fertilizer during the fallow when labor is generally more available than during the busy period of land preparation and planting. Fallow applications work well in temperate climates where low temperature limits microbial activity during the winter, but with mild conditions the nitrogen is exposed for a long time during which nitrification, denitrification, and leaching can occur. Problems of that sort have prompted research towards controlling the rate of nitrification of ammoniacal fertilizers. Chemicals such as nitrapyrin slow ammonia oxidation, apparently by affecting copper enzymes of bacteria. These chemicals find some use in agriculture as fertilizer amendments despite their expense. Some nitrogen fertilizers (e.g. urea–formaldehyde compounds) are themselves inhibitors of nitrification and thus act as slow-release materials. Slow release is also obtained with plastic-encapsulated fertilizer (used in the nursery industry) and with manures. Slow release is generally an undesirable trait for materials that are applied to crops during the growing season.

Nitrate pollution of ground and surface waters gives rise to two environmental concerns. One is that nitrogen can promote the growth of algae in surface waters. The second is that nitrite, which may be produced from nitrate by bacteria under anaerobic conditions in the digestive tract, can cause a toxic blood disorder (methemoglobinemia) in animals. In dry regions, livestock may encounter nitrite toxicity through drinking from surface waters with high concentrations of nitrate (500 ppm $NO_3$–N; 36 mM). In human populations, methemoglobinemia occurs mainly in infants and is very rare. The US Public Health Service has set a standard of 10 ppm $NO_3$–N (0.7 mM) as the maximum safe level for drinking water. The standard is set well below the level at which health problems have sometimes been observed and thus is conservative (Lee 1970).

## Volatilization

$NH_3$ is a volatile gas and can be lost to the atmosphere from aqueous solutions. In water:

$$NH_3 + H^+ + OH^- \rightleftharpoons NH_4^+OH^-. \qquad \text{[Eq. 8.1]}$$

The equilibrium is strongly dependent upon the buffer pH of the soil solution: at pH 5 and below, about 0.004% of the nitrogen is present as free $NH_3$ but that fraction increases approximately 10-fold with each unit increase in pH so that nearly 40% is volatile at pH 9 (Nelson 1982). As a result, gaseous losses of $NH_3$ are significant only with dry or calcareous soils and where $NH_4^+$ is abundant at the surface. In tilled soils and with dispersed $NH_4^+$, nitrification rapidly depletes the vulnerable supply of ammonium nitrogen. Volatilization losses from ammoniacal fertilizers is circum-vented by incorporation with soil.

Animal manures are neutral to slightly alkaline and lose ammonia easily through volatilization. Cattle excrete 0.1 to 0.3 kg N animal$^{-1}$ d$^{-1}$ of which about 50% is $NH_4^+$ or urea, mostly in urine. Urea is hydrolized readily to $NH_4^+$ and on drying dissipates as $NH_3$. The efflux of ammonia to the atmosphere can amount to 10 kg N ha$^{-1}$ y$^{-1}$ from ordinary pastures and up to 45 kg N ha$^{-1}$ y$^{-1}$ from fertilized pastures subject to heavy grazing (Vertregt & Rutgers 1988). Animal lots, if kept dry, lose considerable $NH_3$ by volatilization; when wet, losses of nitrogen are smaller and occur principally by denitrification. Ammonia and volatile amines are also lost directly from the leaves of some plants. Ammonia losses are linked with the process of photorespiration (Chapter 10). The magnitude of such fluxes may be significant in agriculture when plants are well supplied with nitrogen.

An important property of gaseous ammonia is that it is readily absorbed by any wet system including moist soils, the interior surfaces of leaves, and surface waters. The negative surface charge of soils and plant materials favors adsorption. The half-life of ammonia in the atmosphere thus is short and what is lost from one system is soon gained by another. Annual influxes of 5–10 kg ammonia-N ha$^{-1}$ are not uncommon (Jenkinson 1982) and in regions with intensive dairying (e.g. The Netherlands) they can be much greater.

## 8.6    ASSIMILATION OF MINERAL NITROGEN BY PLANTS

Higher plants absorb and use both ammonium and nitrate forms of nitrogen from soils. Nitrate ions are the dominant form in crop nutrition because they are both more abundant (in tilled soil) and more mobile than ammonium ions. $NH_4^+$ is assimilated directly into amino acids and other organic forms. By contrast, $NO_3^-$ ($+5$) must first be reduced to the ammonium level. That eight-electron change requires respiration of at least 0.33 mol of glucose-level substrate mol$^{-1}$ N (67 MJ kg$^{-1}$ N based on 15.6 MJ kg$^{-1}$ as $\Delta H_c$ of glucose at 20 °C). Although most plant tissues are capable of nitrate reduction, it takes place mainly in leaves where a portion of the process is done in chloroplasts through direct transfer of photosyn-thetic reductant without the intervening steps of carbohydrate synthesis and respiration. Photoreduction of nitrate does not appear to compete with the rate of $CO_2$ fixation (Bloom *et al.* 1989) bringing the real cost to considerably less than 67 MJ kg$^{-1}$ N.

Despite the large energy expenditure involved, most plants grow better with nitrate than with ammonium nitrogen. Ammonium-fed plants seem to encounter difficulty with control of their internal pH level because an $H^+$ remains when $NH_4^+ \rightarrow$ amino compounds ($R–NH_2$). Plants do not have good systems for buffering or disposing of $H^+$. In contrast, plants supplied with nitrate encounter surplus negative charges when the nitrate is reduced ($NO_3^- \rightarrow R–NH_2 + e^-$). The charge is easily transferred to organic acids (Section 7.5) which have excellent pH-buffering properties with $K^+$ and find service as osmotica in vacuoles.

## 8.7 NITROGEN FIXATION

### Fixation systems

Reductive fixation of $N_2$ to the $NH_3$ level is the principal route by which new nitrogen enters agricultural systems. This is accomplished biologically by several groups of microorganisms and industrially. The process is expensive: it requires three electrons for reduction (in terms of glucose, 0.125 mol glucose $mol^{-1}$ N; 25 MJ $kg^{-1}$ N) plus significant energy for activation of the nitrogen. The biological systems also encounter the costs of constructing and maintaining the microorganism. Legumes support the bacteria in root nodules; theoretically, their combined cost for bacteria, nodules, and nitrogen fixation is at least 0.7 mol glucose $mol^{-1}$ N (140 MJ $kg^{-1}$ N). Measured costs are significantly larger, however, ranging from 1.2 to 1.3 mol glucose $mol^{-1}$ N fixed (240–260 MJ $kg^{-1}$ N) (Ryle *et al.* 1979; Schubert 1982). That is several times the cost of nitrate reduction by non-legumes. A modern fertilizer plant employing the Haber–Bosch process for $NH_3$ production from $N_2$ also uses much less energy: about 60 MJ $kg^{-1}$ N. In that process, pure $H_2$ ('synthesis gas') is reacted with $N_2$ over a catalyst under heat and pressure (for activation) to yield $NH_3$. Hydrogen gas is generated through the partial combustion of natural gas (or other fossil fuel) to $H_2$ and CO; CO is then reacted with water to yield additional $H_2$ and byproduct $CO_2$. $H_2$ can also be produced by electrolysis of water, i.e. with nuclear or solar power.

Nitrogen-fixing microorganisms divide broadly into those found as free-living organisms and those found in symbiotic associations. Most employ the enzyme **nitrogenase** in nitrogen fixation. The enzyme is composed of two Fe–S proteins, one of which carries a Mo–Fe center. In the absence of molybdenum, some microorganisms generate an alternative protein without Mo but, for practical purposes, Mo is considered an essential micronutrient for nitrogen fixation. In addition to $N_2$, the nitrogenase system can reduce $H^+$ to $H_2$ and acetylene to ethylene. Wasteful hydrogen evolution with a minimum ratio of one $H_2$ per $N_2$ contribute to the high cost of fixation observed for legumes. Because acetylene is not common in soil and ethylene concentration is easily measured with a gas chromatograph, acetylene reduction is used sometimes as an assay of the potential rate of nitrogenase activity. Nitrogenase is inactivated by $O_2$ and fixation occurs only under anaerobic conditions, or in organisms with protective systems against oxygen. Another common property of these organisms is that their ability to fix nitrogen is repressed in the presence of nitrate or ammonium ions and they then live on mineral nitrogen rather than expending energy and reductant in fixation.

### Free-living organisms

The ability for nitrogen fixation is found in a wide range of free-living organisms including bacteria, cyanobacteria (blue-green algae) and actinomycetes. Cyanobacteria are autotrophic for carbon whereas bacteria and actinomycetes are heterotrophic. Heterotrophic forms are able to exploit environments low in N and rich in reduced C and are common in decay processes. The free-living bacteria include *Clostridium*, *Azospirillum* and *Azotobacter* among others. These are mostly slow-growing; with few exceptions, the principal one being *Azotobacter*, they require anaerobic or near-anaerobic conditions for fixation. Low-nitrogen residues of cereals would seem to be a good substrate for these organisms but their slow growth and aeration introduced by tillage disrupt performance. Estimates for annual rates of fixation by free-living organisms in agricultural soils are small, in the range of 1 to 5 kg N ha$^{-1}$ y$^{-1}$. Some grasses develop a carbohydrate-based gelatinous sheath external to their roots and there is evidence that free-living bacteria may form loose associations with grasses under such conditions ('associative fixation'). Cyanobacteria are found in a number of agricultural situations. In humid areas of Europe, for example, cyanobacteria may occur at the soil surface under cereals; rates of fixation are similar, 1–5 kg N ha$^{-1}$ y$^{-1}$, to those with free-living bacteria; in Asia, cyanobacteria sometimes contribute significantly to the nitrogen economy of flooded rice (Hamdi 1982).

Cyanobacteria enter into associations with other organisms. Lichens are fungal–cyanobacterial associations and the cyanobacterium *Anabaena azollae* occupies cavities in the water fern, *Azolla*, that is sometimes employed as a nitrogen source for rice culture in Asia.

### Symbiosis with legumes

There are many natural symbiotic systems. Of these, facultative associations involving members of the legume family and *Rhizobium* bacteria are by far the most important agriculturally. For convenience, we will use the name **rhizobia** in referring to both the fast-growing *Rhizobium* group and the slow-growing *Bradyrhizobium* group. The associations are facultative since rhizobia survive in soils as free-living bacteria and legumes flourish on mineral nitrogen. The symbiotic phase can be recognized from nodules that form on fine roots of the host plants and by the superior performance of those plants in nitrogen-poor environments. Individual species of *Rhizobium* are distinguished by their association with specific hosts as outlined in Table 8.1. Within these groups, bacterial strains can be recognized that differ widely in their effectiveness at nodulation and/or nitrogen fixation. It is important to have crop plants inoculated by effective strains of the proper group. That can be done by coating seed with inoculum produced from cultured bacteria, but the efficacy of that method is highly uncertain. Where the land has not seen legumes, inoculation can be very effective. With periodic culture of legumes in rotation, however, rhizobia strains, some of them ineffective in fixation, increase as soil populations and are highly competitive with inoculated bacteria. No practical solution to that problem has been found; inoculation is no longer practiced in many areas of Europe and North America.

Table 8.1 *Cross-inoculation groups of the legume–rhizobia symbiosis*

| Group | Host plants | *Rhizobium* spp. |
|---|---|---|
| Alfalfa | *Medicago* spp., *Melilotus* clovers | *R. meliloti* |
| Clover | *Trifolium* clovers | *R. trifolii* |
| Pea & vetch | Peas (*Pisum* and *Lathyris spp.*) and *Vicia* spp. (vetch and broad bean) and lentils (*Lens*) | *R. leguminosarum* |
| Cowpea | Cowpea (*Vigna*), *Lespedeza* spp., *Crotalaria* spp., peanut (*Arachis*), and lima bean (*Phaseolus*) | Several species |
| Bean | Common bean (*Phaseolus vulgaris*) | *R. phaseoli* |
| Lupin | *Lupinus* spp. | *R. lupini* |
| Soybean | (*Glycine max*), trefoil (*Lotus* spp.), garbanzo bean (*Cicer arietinum*) | *R. japonicum* |

*Source:* Adapted from Hamdi (1982).

### Factors affecting legume performance

The amounts of nitrogen fixed annually by legume crops are variable. Total nitrogen assimilation and thus fixation are proportional to biomass production by the host crop and therefore influenced by any factor that causes variation in host performance. In addition to weather and mineral nutrition, rates are affected by legume species, stand density, degree of nodulation by effective strains, and the supply of mineral nitrogen in the soil. Biomass production and nitrogen fixation by most legumes are severely reduced by low soil pH and by low supplies of P, Ca, and K. P fertilization is common practice for production of legume forages on many soils and lime is necessary for acid soils. Extensive areas of Australia need both Mo and P fertilizers for legume symbiosis (as well as acid-tolerant cultivars; Section 7.5); in California, P, S, and Zn deficiencies are found in the annual-legume component of annual grasslands.

The corollary of good supplies of P, Ca, and K for legumes is that their uptake and export of these nutrients is also relatively large. Examples of the nutrient content of legumes and grains are given in Tables 12.1 and 17.2. An alfalfa crop yielding 20 t hay ha$^{-1}$ each year, for example, carries with it 254 kg Ca, 308 kg K, and 56 kg P (Table 12.1). Those removals coupled with balancing organic anions contribute significantly to soil acidification (Section 7.5). By contrast, good crops of maize or wheat grain remove somewhat less P (30–40 kg) and much less Ca (3–4 kg) and K (40 kg), and their production is less sensitive to pH and P supply.

The facultative nature of rhizobial fixation in the presence of mineral nitrogen is illustrated in Fig. 8.4 with data for soybean. Fixation is repressed in the presence of mineral nitrogen. On fertile soils, less than half of the nitrogen removed with legume crops may be obtained from rhizobia. Piha & Munns (1987) found that nodules were sloughed quickly from legume roots following large additions of mineral nitrogen to sand–vermiculite cultures. Under field conditions, where supplies of mineral nitrogen are not so strong, nodules may simply become inactive. Several mechanisms may be involved. Carbon supplies of plants well supplied with mineral nitrogen may be monopolized in rapid growth, leaving less for nodule formation and fixation (see 'functional equilibrium', Section 11.3). While that seems to be a principal mechanism, there is also evidence that accumulation of ammonium ions and/or amino acids within the plant can be repressing. Most legumes seems to reach higher yields with mineral nitrogen than through symbiosis, owing, presumably, to the smaller costs of growth on nitrate. Fixation by free-living forms is also repressed by mineral nitrogen.

Flexibility of legumes in their use of mineral and rhizobial nitrogen is viewed as a vexing problem by some but it in fact allows legumes to serve an important scavenger role in agriculture. Mineralization of soil organic matter continues while the legume is growing and, if unused, that nitrogen might be lost through leaching or denitrification.

### Estimates of nitrogen fixation by legumes

There is no satisfactory method for determining amounts of nitrogen fixed by legume crops despite efforts with a range of ingenious approaches (LaRue & Patterson 1981; Herridge & Bergersen 1988). Measurements of changes in soil nitrogen content are conceptually simple but experimentally difficult because even a large addition of nitrogen is very small relative to the total nitrogen content of most soils. Changes can be detected only in long-term experiments.

Nitrogen accumulation in legume biomass is a poor index of apparent fixation because the proportion acquired from the soil is unknown. Legumes always acquire some mineral nitrogen and they are completely dependent on it during the time required for nodule formation on new seedlings. It is tempting to conclude that nearly all of the biomass nitrogen in the later years of an alfalfa sequence is fixed but alfalfa is so deeply rooted that it can scavenge mineral N from deep in a profile, or from a water table, for many years. Comparisons of nitrogen accumulation between legume and non-legume crops and between nodulated and non-nodulated legumes also encounter problems because the crops may differ in rooting habits, total nitrogen requirements, and seasonal patterns of demand.

Some methods for distinguishing a legume's source of nitrogen rely on differences in the ratios of natural isotopes of nitrogen in air and soil. Denitrifying organisms discriminate against $^{15}N$ and soils therefore are slightly enriched in that isotope relative to $^{14}N$; thus mineral nitrogen taken up by plants is also enriched in $^{15}N$. One problem with this method is that denitrification, and thus the isotopic ratio, varies with soil depth. Addition of $^{15}N$-labeled background fertilizer can be helpful in establishing the portion of legume's nitrogen that came from mineral sources providing its distribution within a profile can be matched with the distribution of mineralization and root activity. Acetylene reduction assays are also used. These are simple and rapid (harvested roots are placed in an acetylene atmosphere for a few minutes) and they say something about potential rates of fixation (independent of internal N status) but are worthless for other purposes. Actual rates are much smaller than acetylene values in part because fixation varies

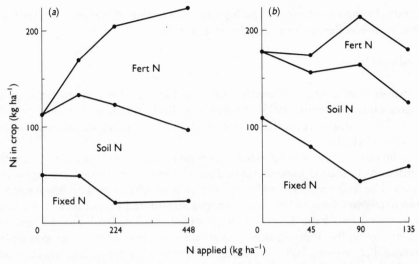

**Fig. 8.4.** Amounts of nitrogen in mature soybean grain acquired from fertilizer, soil, and fixation. (*a*) Redrawn from Johnson *et al.* (1975); (*b*) data from Diebert *et al.* (1979).

diurnally and seasonally in response to the host's status for carbon and nitrogen.

LaRue & Patterson (1981) and Herridge & Bergersen (1988) provide tables showing estimates of nitrogen fixation reported for a number of legume crops. The values range from 10 to over 300 kg N $ha^{-1}$ $y^{-1}$. From Herridge & Bergersen's review, it seems that 100–200 kg N $ha^{-1}$ $y^{-1}$ is a reasonable average for soybean under good conditions. Long-season forages subjected to repeated cutting tend to have the largest rates. Record annual yields of alfalfa (30 t dry matter $ha^{-1}$ with 2.5% N) contain as much as 750 kg N $ha^{-1}$ and it seems that fixation rates in excess of 500 kg N $ha^{-1}$ $y^{-1}$ are possible. However, LaRue & Patterson's conclusion that 'There is not a single legume crop for which we have valid estimates of the N fixed in agriculture' was reaffirmed by Herridge & Bergersen.

Estimates of nitrogen fixation for the globe as a whole are also crude. The annual input of fixed nitrogen to agricultural lands is perhaps 90 Mt with 40% provided by biological fixation and 60% by manufactured fertilizers. Additional amounts also come by atmospheric deposition. Total inputs amount to about 17 kg N $capita^{-1}$ for the present world population compared with 2.9 kg N $cap^{-1}$ $y^{-1}$ as the *minimum* dietary requirement (50 g protein $cap^{-1}$ $d^{-1}$). If we assume that foods actually supply 5 kg N $cap^{-1}$ $y^{-1}$, the apparent efficiency of agriculture is 5/17 or about 0.3. Most of the nitrogen consumed by humans is dissipated in sewage in contrast to animal manures and crop residues which recycle within farming systems.

## 8.8 EXAMPLE NITROGEN CYCLES

The magnitude of various fluxes in nitrogen cycles varies enormously among agricultural systems (Frissel 1977). To gain an appreciation of when small fluxes are important, and when they are not, and which pools are involved, we will examine agricultural systems differing in the intensity of farming. A nitrogen budget for a farm in medieval Europe provides the first example.

### A medieval farm

An English farm of the fourteenth century is the basis for construction of this nitrogen budget (Loomis 1978). Slicher van Bach (1963) and others provide historical data, drawn from the meticulous records of abbey estates, on farming methods and yields.

This imaginary farm was operated in communal fashion by peasants under the organization of a manor. Land was abundant relative to population but farming was not easy. The farm employed an 'open-field' (unfenced) system with wheat rotated in alternate years with fallow, and with pea substituted on occasion for wheat. Fallow served two basic functions: it provided weed control and it improved nitrogen supply. By cropping only in alternate years, two years of nitrogen inputs from rainfall, free-living bacteria, and leguminous weeds were accumulated for each crop of wheat. In addition, residues from previous crops were allowed time for decomposition thus avoiding complications due to immobilization. Wheat yields were low, in the neighborhood of 1000 kg ha$^{-1}$. Nitrogen was probably the most limiting nutrient.

This farm was also involved with livestock: bullocks for tillage and haulage; other cattle for meat and cheese; and sheep for wool. Meadows and woodlands were grazed by cattle and sheep, and swine were run in the woodlands. The mild climate of England allowed some grazing through winter but the supply of hay (saved grass) was small, limiting the number of cattle and sheep that could be kept. A critical feature of the system is that the animals were penned at night for protection. That resulted in accumulations of manure containing nitrogen 'refuged' (Hamilton & Watt 1970) from meadows: manure that could then be spread on arable lands. With a ratio of 4 ha meadow:1 ha arable, access was gained to a significant additional supply of nitrogen. The meadow was sustained by natural inputs of nitrogen.

This farm illustrates two different applications of the non-uniformity principle for the concentration of a scarce soil resource. The crop–fallow sequence represents non-uniform treatment of land in time, while grazing of meadows with manure transfer to arable land involves non-uniform use of space. Although not highly efficient in accumulation and retention of nitrogen, crop–fallow rotations still serve to supply nitrogen in some farming systems.

Construction of the nitrogen cycle displayed in Fig. 8.5 begins with the wheat crop. With 0.02 N in grain, a harvest index of 0.33, and 0.005 N in straw, the mature wheat crop contained 20 kg N in grain plus 10 kg N in straw for a total of 30 kg N ha$^{-1}$. If we assume that half of the residues remained with the land and half were harvested for feed and bedding, 25 kg was removed from the land and 5 kg (2.5 kg N ha$^{-1}$ y$^{-1}$) was returned to the soil. Other inputs to the soil (free-living fixation, wet and dry deposition, and a small credit for the pea crop) are estimated to total 8 kg N ha$^{-1}$ y$^{-1}$. Reproductive rates for medieval farming were very small: only four times as much grain generally was harvested as was sown so the input from seed, 2.5 kg N ha$^{-1}$ y$^{-1}$ (5 kg N ha$^{-1}$ crop$^{-1}$), was significant.

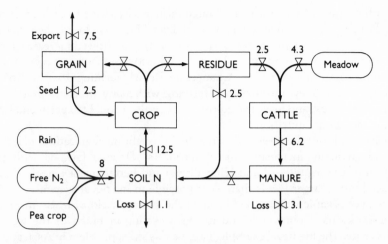

**Fig. 8.5. Nitrogen transfers in a medieval farm. Major pools are identified in rectangles; transfers (solid lines with gate valves and arrows) carry numbers indicating the annual flux in kg N ha$^{-1}$y$^{-1}$ (multiply by 2 to obtain the flux for the full crop–fallow cycle). (Data from Loomis (1978).)**

To estimate the amount of nitrogen supplied from manure, we used information from Slicher von Bath (1963) that a minimum of one bullock was needed for each 4 ha of arable land, and from Azevedo & Stout (1974) that 1000 kg dry manure with 25 kg N could be collected from each bullock in a year. If manure from sheep and cows matched that of bullocks, 12.5 kg N ha$^{-1}$ was available in manure. Only 2.5 kg of that nitrogen originated from the arable land; the balance was acquired from grazed areas. If 25% of manure nitrogen was conserved, the estimated flux to arable land was 3.1 kg N ha$^{-1}$.

Total nitrogen input (2.5 seed + 2.5 residue + 3.1 manure + 8 fixation and rain = 16.1 kg N ha$^{-1}$ y$^{-1}$) was 32.2 kg N per wheat crop compared with 30 kg N uptake by wheat. Inputs and outputs of nitrogen by dust, pollen, insects, and birds are assumed to balance, leaving 2.2 kg N to cover losses by leaching, runoff, and denitrification in the field. Leguminous weeds may have had some input; that plus the possibility of a larger supply of manure allow for the possibility of larger losses.

Several basic points about farming with limited nitrogen emerge from this example. First, very small fluxes of nitrogen are significant in poverty systems. Second, yields are very low in relation to land, labor, insolation, water, and other inputs. Third, annual fluxes of nitrogen and other nutrients from manure, rainfall, and weathering would probably have been adequate to sustain yields from this 'low-input' system indefinitely unless soil erosion or acidification were severe.

## Transitions

The present systems of agriculture found in most of Europe and America evolved from such medieval systems. Major changes were effected in the fifteenth and sixteenth centuries by Flemish and Dutch farmers. Released from feudal control, those farmers owned their own plots of land. They enclosed their fields and developed fodder systems (particularly with beet) that allowed increases in animal numbers and supplies of manure. They also rediscovered Roman practices involving legume rotations and lime. Changes in British farming 1650 to 1850 that followed brought a revolution of 'new farming' with many improved practices, new breeds of livestock, and new crop cultivars. They also brought experimental studies in plant and animal nutrition.

Further evolution between 1850 and 1940 brought mechanization, plant breeding, and gradually increasing use of fertilizers. Organic farming with proper nutrition of the legumes (P and K fertilizers) and better management of manure produced much larger yields than were possible in medieval systems. By 1940, a high state of organic farming had brought the average yield of wheat in Britain to near 2500 kg ha$^{-1}$ but yields and nitrogen cycling in much of the world still approximated the medieval example. Famine was still a problem in Asia, and in the USA the dietary protein supply per capita had declined steadily as population increased.

Much has changed since the 1940s. Isolated examples with medieval levels remain but the intensity of farming is generally much greater. Nitrogen cycling still follows the same pathways and still includes legume rotations and improved methods for recycling residues and manures. Nitrogen is now also supplied in mineral fertilizers and nitrogen deficiency no longer need be a limit to yield. The necessary external inputs of nitrogen are much greater than could be supplied by animals through manure and the amounts of nitrogen exported in harvested crops are large (100–200 kg N ha$^{-1}$ are common). British wheat yields now exceed 6000 kg ha$^{-1}$. American maize yields, which in 1940 were static near 2000 kg ha$^{-1}$ with organic methods, now exceed 7000 kg ha$^{-1}$.

Nitrogen budgets have changed significantly. Seeding rates have increased slightly but reproductive rates are much larger and contributions from seed nitrogen can generally be ignored. Free-living fixation is also a small fraction of total nitrogen supply, whereas wet and dry deposition appears to have increased significantly in some cases.

The data in Table 8.2 illustrate some of the changes in nitrogen cycling of grazed pastures and harvested forages in The Netherlands, 1800–1972. One-third of the animals on the 1800 pasture were draft animals, whereas the 1937 and 1972 budgets involve only dairy cattle. Nitrogen transfers between pastures and arable lands occurred on all of these farms via harvested hay and barnyard manure. On the 1937 farm, a leguminous forage crop was also involved in nitrogen transfers. The 1972 pasture actually received more nitrogen back in manure applications than was exported in animal products and hay. Many of the numbers are uncertain, particularly for events in the soil compartment. The authors assumed that the large surplus shown in the balance for the fertilized pasture (1972) accumulated as soil organic matter. Small rates of mineralization and immobilization are expected in untilled pasture whereas zero values are shown in 1937 and 1972. At Rothamsted, nitrate leaching (corrected for rainfall inputs) continued at rates of 30–45 kg NO$_3$–N

Table 8.2 *Nitrogen cycling in the pasture component of Dutch dairy farms 1800, 1937 and 1972*

Values in table are kg N ha$^{-1}$ y$^{-1}$

| Year: | 1800 | 1937 | 1972 |
|---|---|---|---|
| Stocking rate, animals ha$^{-1}$: | 0.5 | 0.9 | 2.5 |
| *Supplies to soil* | | | |
| Wet and dry deposition | 8 | 14 | 14 |
| Mineralization | 13 | 0 | 0 |
| Plant residues | — | 26 | 180 |
| Nitrogen fixation | 80 | 120 | 0 |
| Dung and urine | 44 | 46 | 178 |
| Application of manure | 0 | 0 | 149 |
| N fertilizer | 0 | 0 | 400 |
| Total supply | 145 | 206 | 921 |
| External input | 88 | 134 | 563 |
| *Removals from soil* | | | |
| Plant uptake | 71 | 158 | 450 |
| Immobilization | 13 | 0 | — |
| Volatilization | 34 | 7 | 26 |
| Leaching | 5 | 11 | 39 |
| Denitrification | 16 | 49 | 169 |
| Total removal | 139 | 225 | 684 |
| *Output* | | | |
| Harvest of hay | 32 | 50 | 126 |
| Animal production | 1 | 19 | 72 |
| Losses | 55 | 67 | 234 |
| Total output | 88 | 136 | 432 |
| *Input − ouput* | 0 | −2 | +181 |
| *Total grazing plus hay* | 71 | 111 | 270 |

*Source:* Interpreted from J. P. N. Damen and C. H. Henkins in Frissel (1977).

ha$^{-1}$ y$^{-1}$ for more than 40 y from bare, untilled soil, indicating continued mineralization of soil organic matter (Addiscott 1988).

The 1972 farm represents an extreme example of nitrogen supply: the pasture received fertilizer and manure nitrogen considerably in excess of plant needs. Fertilizer nitrogen was applied at regular intervals during the growing season because it promotes much greater growth of grass, with higher digestibility, than is obtained with manure and legumes. As a result, the carrying capacity of the 1972 ryegrass pasture was 2.9 times that of the 1937 ryegrass–clover pasture. Optimal rates of nitrogen application to intensively grazed ryegrass pastures in Europe range between 300 and 600 kg N ha$^{-1}$ y$^{-1}$. A recent survey of Dutch dairy farms, cited by Vertregt & Rutgers (1988), indicates an average use of 350 N ha$^{-1}$ grassland y$^{-1}$ with a stocking rate of 3.5 cows ha$^{-1}$. Use of fertilizer, however, leads to problems of manure disposal because dairying is concentrated in regions with only small amounts of arable land that can utilize manure effectively.

Our analysis identifies manure as the main source of the excess nitrogen on the 1972 farm. Dairy herds receive supplemental feed (saved grass, silage from arable portions of the farm, and purchased feed) during the winter while confined to barns. Manure in excess of what could be applied to the available arable land (149 kg N ha$^{-1}$) was applied to pastures for disposal. That is done during winter since applications during the summer cause cattle to reject the forage. Summer applications also contribute to recycling of diseases and parasites. The principal merits of the manure application were that large amounts of surplus organic material and nitrogen were disposed at low cost and the grass was supplied with essential mineral elements. As shown by the 1800 and 1937 farms, however, nitrate leaching occurs from concentrated dung and urine even in the absence of the fertilizer or manure.

Despite the excessive supply of nitrogen, the 1972 farm produced 3.8 times as much human-edible nitrogen products per hectare, and at about the same efficiency per unit nitrogen transferred, as the 1937 farm. With less manure, its nitrogen-transfer efficiency would have increased sharply. Although the 1972 pasture was a much greater polluter of ground water than the 1937 one, the ratios of leached nitrogen to product nitrogen were similar. These farms were located on wet clay soils and most of the losses occurred by denitrification; had they been located on light soils, nitrate pollution and acidification would have been significant problems. Use of both manure and fertilizer allows The Netherlands to maintain a positive food balance from a small land area but contamination of surface and groundwaters has led to intensive efforts at finding alternative uses for manure.

A study in England by Wellings & Bell (1980) supports the view that manure may have been the main source of nitrate in the 1972 farm. Those workers found tenfold greater concentrations of nitrate under a ryegrass pasture that received slurried manure than was found with an equivalent rate of fertilizer nitrogen (376 kg N ha$^{-1}$). Most farming systems employ much more conservative rates and methods of nitrogen supply than the Dutch as is evident in other examples presented by Frissel (1977) and in Chapters 16 and 17. Fertilization practices will be examined in more detail in Chapter 12.

## 8.9    FARMING WITH ORGANIC SOURCES OF NITROGEN

Comparison of the 1937 and 1972 dairy farms illustrates the enormous advance in carry capacity that is possible when farming systems are supplemented with nitrogen fertilizer. By 1940, farming with strictly organic sources of nitrogen had proven inadequate for meeting world food supplies. Since then, world population has more than doubled and most farms now meet some of their nitrogen needs with fertilizer. Some systems that do not use nitrogen fertilizer have also survived, particularly in regions where pastoral dairy farms generate surplus manure, and in poor countries where farmers do not have access to other technologies. The special management issues that arise in using legumes and manures as sources of nitrogen deserve comment.

## Legume rotations

Inclusion of legume crops in rotation with non-legume crops is a traditional practice, involving non-uniform treatment of land in time, for supplying nitrogen to cropping systems. In addition to satisfying much of their own need for nitrogen, legumes can also increase the average level of soil nitrogen. A major limitation of legume rotations is that legume roots are not high in nitrogen. Carry-over nitrogen from legume crops other than green manures is generally sufficient for only moderate production by a following crop unless a factor such as water supply or length of season is limiting. Grain legumes carry most of their nitrogen away in seed and most of that produced by forage legumes is removed in harvested hay.

When non-legumes in the rotation are supplied with supplemental nitrogen from fertilizer or manure, yields increase but their residues and the soil then contain more nitrogen. That suppresses fixation by a following legume and the legume's role as a consumer of mineral nitrogen increases. This phenomenon and the inadequacy of legumes as the sole source of nitrogen have contributed to less use of legumes in rotations as nitrogen fertilizers became available. Legumes now must depend more on the value of their production than on their contributions through nitrogen fixation.

Farming with legumes as sources of nitrogen is an uncertain business. The amounts of nitrogen carried over and their release through decay and mineralization are variable, making quantitative predictions about supply difficult. Interesting problems relative to spatial variability also arise. Fixation is greatest in nitrogen-poor portions of a field, favoring uniformity for subsequent crops, but variability in the legume stand, due for example to soil pH, drainage, or winter damage, increases spatial variability for nitrogen.

In the absence of practical means for assessing carry-over supplies of nitrogen, the experience of farmers and extension workers guides most farming practice. The general experience is that legume residues have about the same value as those of other crops. About 100 kg N ha$^{-1}$ can be expected as carry-over from a good stand of alfalfa, but that is only about twice the amount found in residues of non-legumes. The major difference is that some of it came through fixation. Iowa farmers interviewed as background for Chapter 17 made no allowance for extra nitrogen from soybean residues and were nervous about allowing as much as 30 kg N ha$^{-1}$ extra following red clover. California farm advisors find some increase in soil nitrogen after 4 y of alfalfa but that is coupled with declines in phosphorus and potassium supplies; as one noted, 'It all went with the hay'.

Major increases in soil nitrogen from legumes come only when forage is incorporated with the soil (green manure) or through recycling in animal manure produced by feeding leguminous forages. Vetch, berseem clover (both cool climate), and sweet clover (warm climate) are used as leguminous green manures. Some estimates of nitrogen production by summer green-manures exceed 200 kg N ha$^{-1}$. Leguminous green-manure residues decompose rather quickly, however, so the supply of nitrogen can be excessive relative to needs of the next crop, and beneficial effects on soil structure are slight at best (MacRae & Mehuys 1985).

Green manures are generally uneconomic simply as a source of nitrogen. They require tillage, seed, proper soil pH and fertility, and they consume significant amounts of water. In effect, 1.5 to 2 ha of land are cropped but only 1 ha is harvested for useful products. For the farming system, production per unit input of water, labor, and fuel is reduced by as much as half. That results in a very high cost for nitrogen that only farmers with specialty markets for organic foods or without access to fertilizer can afford to meet.

Grass–legume mixtures are used widely for pastures and for forage production. In addition to supplying nitrogen, legume forages add to the protein content of feed. Transfers of nitrogen from legume to grass occur by several mechanisms. The principal pathway is through the dung and urine of grazing animals. Another occurs with legume residues including dead roots and nodules. Grazing or mowing interrupts carbon supplies needed for maintenance of roots and nodules resulting in nodule sloughing and root death. Nitrogen released by decay is then available to associated non-legumes. As noted in the discussion of Dutch pastures, however, the productivity of such polycultures may be significantly less than that of a well-fertilized grass monoculture.

### Animal manures

Animal manures are the principal means by which nutrients are transferred among fields. Manures have two virtues in addition to their nutrient content: ash alkalinity removed in crop harvests is returned to the soil; and they benefit soil structure. In addition to manure, muck soil or vegetation obtained from other fields, composted sewage sludge, and various refuses also serve as organic amendments. Sewage sludge may be contaminated with heavy metals, however, and generally is to be avoided.

In the USA, over 80% of the animal manure comes from cattle; swine account for another 10%. Bouldin *et al*. (1984) estimated that nearly 8 Mt N was excreted by animals in the USA in 1975 but only half was from confined animals and thus collectible. Nearly all collectible manure was recycled to cropland but because only about 50% of it finally reached the soil, manures were estimated to supply only about 2 Mt N to crop production. Those numbers can be compared with 1.4 Mt N consumed by Americans, of which very little is recycled. Two million tonnes of nitrogen translates to about 12 kg N $ha^{-1}$ crop land $y^{-1}$, demonstrating that widespread dependence on manures as nutrient sources is not possible. In an area of 'intense' livestock production (southeastern Minnesota, USA), manures were estimated to satisfy only 40–50% of the nitrogen needs of local maize crops grown in rotation with legumes (Legg *et al*. 1989).

**Handling and composition of manures**   The efficiency of manure recycling could be improved in most cases, but the costs are high. All manures have common traits: their nutrient content is small and variable, and their behavior during storage and after application to the field is difficult to quantify. The composition of representative *fresh* manures (feces and urine combined) is presented in Table 8.3. It is difficult to make any general statement about nutrient content of *collected* manure

Table 8.3 *Approximate production and nutrient contents of fresh animal manures (dung and urine combined)*

Numbers in parentheses are coefficients of variation.

| Source | Daily manure production[1] | | Nutrient content (kg t$^{-1}$ fresh mass) | | | Dry matter (kg t$^{-1}$ fresh mass) |
|---|---|---|---|---|---|---|
| | (kg animal$^{-1}$) | (animals t$^{-1}$) | N | P | K | |
| Beef cattle | 21 (0.20) | 47.6 | 5.9 (0.21) | 1.6 (0.29) | 3.6 (0.29) | 146 (0.30) |
| Dairy cattle | 55 (0.29) | 18.2 | 5.2 (0.21) | 1.1 (0.26) | 3.4 (0.32) | 140 (0.22) |
| Swine | 5.1 (0.28) | 196 | 6.2 (0.40) | 2.1 (0.56) | 3.4 (0.55) | 130 (0.57) |
| Broilers | 0.076 (0.15) | 13 200 | 12.9 (0.26) | 3.5 (0.18) | 3.4 (0.16) | 250 (0.06) |

*Note:*
[1] Fresh mass production per animal and number of animals needed to produce 1 t d$^{-1}$.
*Source:* Adapted from ASAE (1989).

even on a single farm because decomposition and nitrogen losses during storage and handling are highly variable (Azevedo & Stout 1974). The degree of decomposition and whether bedding material (straw) is included are important factors. Caution is advised in using the values given in Table 8.4 as a point of departure. For example, the nitrogen content of the solid cattle manures in this table range from 2 to 2.7% N on a dry basis but values of 1 to 2% also are common for farm-lot manures.

About 50% of the nitrogen in urine and dung of cattle is present as ammonium ions and urea which can convert quickly to ammonia. Volatilization of ammonia is favored by warm, drying, conditions and the alkaline pH of voided materials; this apparently accounts for much of the variation reported in nitrogen content. Volatilization losses are less when dung and urine are caught on bedding material.

Dung decomposes rapidly during storage, bulk volume decreases, and nutrient concentrations increase. Storage also helps in reducing the viability of weed seed and animal parasites passed in dung. The nature of the final product depends on conditions during storage. Under traditional dry-lot conditions, manure accumulates for 3–6 months before being scrapped and distributed to fields. Decomposition in built-up manure is an aerobic process leading to a humus-like final product that retains up to 50% of the original nitrogen. Flies may be a problem during aerobic decay but few odors are produced. Nitrate accumulates if decomposition proceeds too far and may denitrify or leach if the manure is wetted. Potassium is also subject to leaching. Humification and nitrogen conservation are accomplished more efficiently when the manure is collected frequently and allowed to age in a moist condition in well-aerated piles. In addition, the high temperatures that develop within the piles help in killing weed seed and animal parasites.

Table 8.4 *Approximate nutrient contents of aged animal manures obtained with good methods of conservation*

| Animal | Form | Handling | Nutrient content ($kg\,t^{-1}$ fresh mass) | | | Dry matter | $NH_4$-N |
| | | | N | P | K | | Total N |
|---|---|---|---|---|---|---|---|
| Beef cattle | solid | air, no bedding | 10 | 6 | 19 | 520 | 0.33 |
| | solid | air, bedding | 11 | 8 | 22 | 500 | 0.38 |
| | liquid | pit[1] | 18 | 5 | 13 | 110 | 0.60 |
| Dairy cattle | solid | air, no bedding | 5 | 2 | 8 | 180 | 0.44 |
| | liquid | pit[1] | 11 | 4 | 11 | 80 | 0.50 |
| Swine | liquid | pit[1] | 16 | 5 | 8 | 180 | 0.72 |
| Poultry | solid | no bedding | 16 | 21 | 28 | 450 | 0.79 |

*Note:*
[1] 1 $m^3$ of pit slurry is assumed to weigh 1 t, i.e. 1 l = 1 kg.
*Source:* Adapted from Midwest Plan Service (1985).

When fresh manure is placed in unaerated piles or pits for storage, anaerobic conditions develop and 80% or more of the nitrogen may be conserved. Ammonium is the main form in the final product. Odors (methane, mercaptans, skatole) can be a serious problem, however, Confinement dairies and piggeries commonly handle manure as slurry. Daily scrappings are slurried with water and aged anaerobically in a pit or, after further dilution, in tanks. Because of dilution, nitrogen concentration after tank storage (3–5 kg N m$^{-3}$) is less than is shown in Table 8.4 for pit slurry. Slurries are distributed to fields in tank wagons. Odor problems, avoided during storage, arise after surface spreading but can be avoided if the slurry is injected into the soil.

Regardless of the method used for handling manure, low concentration of nutrients and costs of facilities, labor, and fuel required in collection and storage result in a high cost per unit nutrient. Slurry facilities are particularly expensive (Bouldin *et al.* 1984) and long-distance cartage is generally prohibitive for any form of manure. As a result, some farmers tend to approach manure handling as a disposal problem rather than as a nutrient source.

**Rates and timing of manure applications**   Placement and precise rates of application are not possible with solid forms of manure. Surface spreading followed quickly by incorporation with a moldboard plow seems to be the best practice. Volatilization of ammonia (particularly from anaerobic manures; see the $NH_4$–N/ total N ratio in Table 8.4) and runoff losses increase with time that the manure remains unincorporated. Because of limitations in labor, most farmers find timely incorporation of solid manure difficult to achieve. As was the case for the 1972 Dutch farm, manure is sometimes spread in the winter; the danger with arable land is that nutrients are lost to runoff and leaching before spring tillage begins. Slurries have an advantage in this regard because they can be injected with chisels well in advance of tillage.

The C/N ratio of decomposed manures is low enough that immobilization does not occur when they are applied to soil. The ammonium fraction of the nitrogen is quickly available to plants after incorporation but the humic portion mineralizes slowly. Pratt *et al.* (1973) suggested allowing a 'decay series' of 0.3, 0.1, and 0.05 for the fractions of organic material mineralized during each of the first 3 y following application. Midwest Plan Service (1985) offered a somewhat different decay series.

Given the uncertain nature and behavior of manure, it is difficult to use it in an optimum fertilizer program. Minimal rates encounter the least risk of adding to pollution through leaching or runoff but risks of reduced and more variable performance of the fertilized crop are greater. With manure as the sole source of nitrogen, large rates are needed to insure sufficient nitrogen mineralization per year. Using the decay series outlined above, manure containing 240 kg N must be applied each year to provide a mineral flux of 100 kg N $y^{-1}$. That corresponds to 11 t $ha^{-1}$ of beef manure decomposed with bedding (Table 8.4) but supplies of P (176 kg $ha^{-1}$ $y^{-1}$) and K (484 kg $ha^{-1}$ $y^{-1}$) would then greatly exceed the requirements of any crop. It is immediately obvious that these amounts could not have been obtained from the feed produced on a single hectare and that nutrients are being refuged from rather large areas. Manure continues to mineralize whether a crop is present or not. Some of the excess nutrients would accumulate as soil organic matter but serious losses and pollution of ground water by nitrate also occur (van der Meer *et al.* 1987).

Farmers who employ high rates of manure sometimes find it useful to grow a cover ('catch') crop of grass during the fallow period to capture the continuing mineral flux. In pastures, excess potassium contributes to an imbalance with magnesium, leading to 'grass tetany' disorders in grazing cows and ewes. In arid regions, the high salt content of cattle manures may contribute to salinity problems. The solution to these problems, and the nutrient imbalances, reached by most farmers is to apply modest amounts of manure only to main crops. A base fertility is established for the field, which is then fine-tuned by applying specific mineral fertilizers.

## Rule-based organic farming

All farming is organic in the sense that the produce is composed of organic material and most of the nutrients flow through a phase in soil organic matter. Some farmers, however, practice a form of 'organic' farming following special rules about external inputs of chemicals. Their produce, under labels of 'natural' or 'organic', is aimed at a market niche created by public apprehensions about biocides and other aspects of modern agriculture and food processing. The rules are established by associations of farmers but some governments have placed them into legal codes to aid organic farmers in marketing.

Methods used by these farmers can be termed 'rule-based organic farming' to differentiate them from other types of farming. Use of 'synthetic' materials is generally proscribed but that constraint is directed more at 'modern' than at synthetic or manufactured since traditional practices involving highly toxic inputs of copper salts and sulfur are permitted. The inconsistencies are apparent in the list of materials permitted in California which includes manufactured chelates, petroleum oil, and fermentation products such as gibberellic acid and antibiotics. Biocides are generally proscribed although Bordeaux mixture (copper sulfate and lime) for control of fungi and natural materials such as pyrethrum insecticides are allowed.

Management of nutrient supplies in rule-based systems is neither logical nor well based in scientific principles. Animal manures and leguminous green manures are favored as sources of nitrogen. Organic farms in Europe refuge nitrogen from an average 3 ha of pasture and legume forages in order to achieve acceptable yields on 1 ha of arable land (Boeringa 1980). Refuging also occurs when organic farms purchase manure composts from other farms. Animal manures purchased from 'chemical farms' is accepted as 'organic'. The 'organic' label generally depends only on practices during the current year and carry-over from excessive fertilizer applications in previous years is considered organic. Most rules permit the use of lime, rock phosphate, $NaNO_3$, and $K_2SO_4$ as 'organic amendments' whereas KCl and beneficiated phosphate rock are 'chemical' and not permitted. Such attempts to differentiate rule-based farms arbitrarily as special sources of food is generally wasteful of high-grade phosphate ores and an unnecessary expense for potassium. These irrationalities are small, however, compared with claims of alchemical and astrological bases for organic methods by some European groups (Boeringa 1980).

Rule-based organic farming is demanding of high levels of managerial skills. Weed control requires larger amounts of labor and fuel in cultivation than are used by most farmers. Diseases, of which seedling diseases are the most damaging, generally are not controlled well. Narrow reliance on organic sources of nitrogen, while seemingly wholesome, introduces several problems including the large nutrient requirements of legumes and the unbalanced nutrient content of animal manures. Uncertain release of mineral nitrogen from organic sources can be ameliorated to some extent by extended composting and with catch crops. It is difficult or even impossible, however, to achieve an adequate flux of mineral nitrogen from organic matrials without also creating a considerable potential for leaching of nitrate and potassium.

Rule-based organic farming fills roles in utilizing surplus manure and in providing specialty foods but the costs are high and rule-based farmers generally must depend on unique labeling of their produce to provide the higher prices they need. Greater costs are inevitable given the less efficient use of land, energy, labor, nutrients, and water inherent in strict-organic methods.

## 8.10   SUMMARY

The atmosphere offers an unlimited supply of dinitrogen gas for plant and animal nutrition, but reduced nitrogen is required in living organisms. The problem for agriculture is to manipulate the oxidation–reduction states of nitrogen so that it is available in mineral forms for plants and as protein for animals at the right times and places. Transfers of $N_2$ into agricultural systems depends on fixation to the ammonia level ($NH_3$) through biological and industrial processes. Free-living microorganisms found in soils, and symbiotic bacteria, particularly the rhizobial systems found with leguminous plants, contribute about 40% of the flux of fixed nitrogen that enters agricultural systems. The balance comes with rainfall and as fertilizer produced principally by the Haber–Bosch process employing natural gas.

The microbial populations of soils are highly active and diverse in their use of nitrogen. All require nitrogen as an essential constituent of protoplasm. Many microorganisms make their living through consumption (decay, mineralization) of plant and animal residues and soil organic matter containing nitrogen, or by manipulating the oxidation-reduction states of mineral nitrogen. Nitrification ($NH_4^+ \rightarrow NO_3^-$) and denitrification ($NO_3^- \rightarrow N_2$, $N_2O$) are central processes in nitrogen cycles because nitrate is the nutrient form preferred by higher plants while denitrification is the avenue by which nitrogen returns to the dinitrogen pool. One of the final end-products of microbial attack on residues is humus. Because humus is resistant to further breakdown, it accumulates in soils. It is a major reservoir of nitrogen and it also confers important properties on soils.

Soil microorganisms aggressively attack almost any substrate that comes their way. An interesting comparison can be made between microbial activity in soil and in the gastrointestinal tract of cattle (Chapter 1). Whereas the cow offers a highly stable system with regulated intake, temperature, water status, and pH, none of those factors is constant in soil. With normal feeding, cattle operate near the limit of their capacity for microbial activity; in contrast, soil populations generally have capacity to process considerably more organic matter and nitrogen than they normally receive. Large portions of soil microbial populations are quiescent.

As a result, agricultural management has to be concerned with the composition, timing, and placement of organic materials and fertilizers that are incorporated with soil. Regardless of how that is done, large degrees of variability and uncertainty surround the management of nitrogen cycles in agricultural fields.

## 8.11 FURTHER READING

Frissel, M. (ed.) 1977. Cycling of mineral nutrients in agricultural systems. *Agro-Ecosystems* (Special issue) 4:1–354.

Gallon, J. R. and A. E. Chaplin. 1987. *An introduction to nitrogen fixation.* Cassell Educational, London. 276 p.

Hauck, R. D. (ed.). 1984. *Nitrogen in crop production.* Am. Soc. Agron., Madison, Wisconsin. 804 p.

Haynes, R. J. (ed.). 1986. *Mineral nitrogen in the plant–soil system.* Academic Press, New York. 496 p.

Paul, E. A. and F. E. Clark. 1989. *Soil microbiology and biochemistry.* Academic Press, San Diego. 273 p.

Prosser J. I. (ed.), 1986. *Nitrification.* Spec. Pub. Soc. Gen. Microbiol. vol. 20. IRL Press, Oxford, UK. 217 p.

Stevenson, F. J. (ed.). 1982. *Nitrogen in agricultural soils.* Agronomy Monograph no. 22. Am. Soc. Agron., Madison, Wisconsin. 940 p.

Wilson, J. R. (ed.). 1988. *Advances in nitrogen cycling in agricultural ecosystems.* CAB International. Wallingford, Oxon, UK. 451 p.

# 9

## *Water relations*

## 9.1 INTRODUCTION

The leaves of most crop plants have evolved with a large surface area per unit leaf mass that lends efficiency in the interception of light and provides an extended surface and a short pathway for the diffusive exchange of atmospheric gases. The pathways for $CO_2$ and water vapor differ in length because evaporation of water takes place mainly from the capillary water in the exposed walls of the mesophyll cells while $CO_2$ exchange involves additional transport across the plasmalemma and into the cytoplasm of the cell. The stomatal pores in the epidermis can exert considerable control over diffusion of both $CO_2$ and water vapor.

The water vapor pressure in the protected interior spaces of the leaves is always near to the saturation value ($e^*$) determined by leaf temperature (see Fig. 6.11, Eq. 6.14). Even when leaf water potential ($\Psi_l$) falls to $-2$ to $-3$ MPa, the depression of water vapor pressure below saturation is small. Ambient air is generally much drier, therefore $CO_2$ uptake through open stomates during photosynthesis is inevitably coupled with a substantial loss of water in transpiration along the strong vapor pressure gradient between leaf and air.

Water is a primary reactant in photosynthesis but the proportion of water required by plants that is chemically incorporated in their structure, or is used to maintain their water content as they grow, is very small. Transpirational losses are several hundred times greater. It is apparent that plants behave as rather efficient conduits for the flow of water from soil, through roots and stems to leaves, and then to the atmosphere. That pathway is termed the **soil–plant–atmosphere continuum**.

Crops differ significantly in rooting habit and thus in ability to acquire water from the soil. Owing to differences in epidermal wax and in size, frequency and behavior of stomates, they also vary in ability to control transpiration from leaves. For crops, the continuum of water flow from soil to atmosphere through plants (**transpiration, $E_p$**), is accompanied by direct evaporation of water from the soil surface (**soil evaporation $E_s$**), particularly when the surface is wet and unprotected by foliage. Crops with incomplete foliage cover during a considerable proportion of their growth cycle, may lose up to 50% of total water use (**evapotranspiration, ET**) by $E_s$.

## 9.2 FLOW OF WATER THROUGH A CROP

Evaporation of water from wet cell walls of leaf mesophyll lowers the water content and water potential of leaves. In response, water moves to them passively in the liquid phase from other parts of the plant and ultimately from the soil along gradients of water potential ($\Delta \Psi$). Water moving across the root cortex through cell walls (apoplast, the non-living system) encounters a barrier at the endodermis surrounding the central stele. The cell walls of that tissue are rendered impermeable by the waxy deposits of the Casparian strip, so passage is across membranes and through living cells (symplast).

Once across the endodermis and into the xylem of the root, there is a continuous apoplastic route through the xylem to leaf mesophyll. The tissues of the stele, stem and leaf are in hydraulic contact with the xylem stream and exchange water with it depending upon local gradients of water potential. As a result, the water status of a crop adjusts continually to changing patterns of environmental demand and water uptake. Equilibrium between uptake and loss is rare so the simple descriptions (and models) of water flow that follow must be taken cautiously as approximations to field behavior.

A general view of the water relations of a crop is presented in Fig. 9.1. For particular purposes, this model can be extended or simplified. It considers the amounts of water (mm) in each of three crop compartments (foliage, stem and root) together with three soil layers defined as the surface soil from which soil evaporation occurs, the current root zone, and the subsoil into which roots will extend as the season progresses. The water content of the crop compartments depends upon their size and on the exchanges between them and the xylem pathway. The water contents of the soil compartments (volumetric water content $\theta \times$ depth $z$) are renewed intermittently from above by rainfall ($P$) or irrigation ($I$) as each is successively wetted above field capacity. $E_s$, runoff ($RO$), and drainage ($D$) below the root zone are included to complete the **hydrological balance**, i.e.

$$P + I + E_p + E_s + D + RO + \Delta\theta z = 0. \qquad \text{[Eq. 9.1]}$$

With the soil–plant system, the flux of water ($F$) between contiguous compartments can be written as $F = -k\Delta\Psi$ or $-\Delta\Psi/r$. $\Delta\Psi$ is the difference in water potential; $k$ and $r (= 1/k)$ are, respectively, the hydraulic conductance and resistance to flow. Here, resistance will be used where it leads to simpler equations for the catenary flow of water in crop systems. Experimenters are reminded of the distinct statistical treatments that are required of conductances and resistances. Repeated measurements of leaf conductance, for example, can be averaged to find mean conductance of the leaves that comprise a crop canopy. If recorded as resistances, the geometrical mean is the appropriate treatment.

The response of $\Psi$ in any compartment to the gain or loss of water depends upon cell wall elasticity, the degree of osmotic adjustment, and other traits, none of which are an explicit part of this model. The capability of tissue to lose or gain water can be termed capacitance ($d\theta/d\Psi$) in analogy with electrical circuits. In general, crop plants have low capacitance while in trees, the amount of water that exchanges

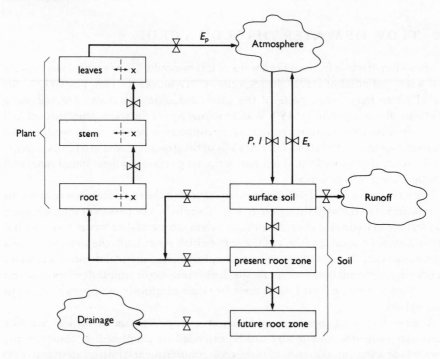

Fig. 9.1. **Compartment model of the water relations and water balance of a crop. The compartments define the distribution (mm) of water throughout the system. In the crop, tissues of leaves, stem and root are in hydraulic contact with the xylem (x) through which water flows from soil to atmosphere.**

between active xylem and older wood of the stem and root is considerable and can exceed the transpirational loss over a single day (Running 1980).

In herbaceous crops with low capacitance, it is possible to describe water relations by ignoring the stem and the internal redistribution of water. For example, a wheat crop of 9 t ha$^{-1}$ dry mass contains around 50 t water ha$^{-1}$ (5 mm). Under heavy evaporative demand its water content might fall to 0.9 of its water content at full turgor, i.e. its **relative water content** (RWC) would be 0.9. This represents a change equivalent to 0.5 mm or only 8% of total daily water use at $E_p = 6$ mm.

Changes in RWC lead to changes in $\Psi$. Fig. 9.2 presents an 'idealized' picture of changes in root zone water potential ($\Psi_s$) during six consecutive diurnal cycles of a crop growing in a fixed volume of initially wet soil ($\Psi \sim -0.02$ MPa). Over six days, transpiration lowered $\Psi_s$ to around $-1.5$ MPa and the diurnal pattern of water potential in the leaves ($\Psi_l$) responded differently even though the daily evaporative demand remained unchanged. During day 1, with freely available water in the soil, $\Psi_l$ fell to $-0.6$ MPa at midday but recovered completely, i.e. to $\Psi_s$, by dusk. Although water uptake during daylight hours was inadequate to maintain $\Psi_l$ close to $\Psi_s$, the small gradient between soil and roots ($\Psi_s$ and $\Psi_r$) ($\sim 0.1$ MPa) reflects the high conductance to flow in moist soils and accounts for the rapid recovery by dusk.

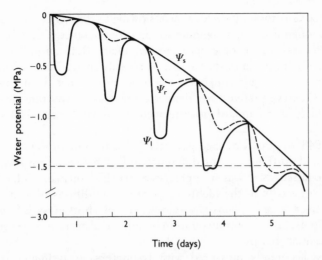

**Fig. 9.2.** Diagram illustrating idealized changes in water potential of leaf, root and soil during a drying cycle of a field crop commencing when the soil is at field capacity (after Cowan 1965; Slatyer 1967).

As the soil dried further during days 2 and 3, $\Psi$ in each part of the system fell gradually and the gradients widened. Equilibration of $\Psi_l$ and $\Psi_r$ with $\Psi_s$ was incomplete by dusk but was achieved by the subsequent dawn. On day 4, $\Psi_l$ fell below $-1.5$ MPa and stomates began to close, arresting further fall in $\Psi_l$ and the plant recovered to near $\Psi_s$ by dawn of the following day. With further drying (day 6), stomatal closure failed to maintain $\Psi_l$ above $-1.5$ MPa and recovery was incomplete even by dawn of the next day. The decreasing conductance to water flow from the drier soil to the root system, seen in the widening gradient of that part of the pathway, played an important role in the failure of the root system to maintain water supply to the crop. Without water or additional root length, or some reduction in demand through reduced leaf area, tighter closure of stomates, or change in weather, this crop would be in danger of suffering internal desiccation and injury.

The challenge in crop ecology is to measure and interpret such responses under the difficult and variable conditions of the field.

## 9.3 EVAPOTRANSPIRATION AND ITS COMPONENTS

An extensive crop of full cover, well supplied with water, exerts minimum stomatal control over transpiration and evaporates water at a rate determined by the evaporation demand of the atmosphere. That rate of water use, the maximum for those environmental conditions, is termed **potential evapotranspiration** (ET*). It defines the upper bound to actual evapotranspiration (ET$_a$) that will be smaller than ET* when cover is incomplete and the soil surface is dry or when restricted availability of water to the crop causes leaf conductance to fall. ET* at full cover varies by 10–20% between individual crops owing to differences in color, height, aerodynamic roughness, and maximum canopy conductance (Fig. 9.3).

Short green grass, or in some places mown alfalfa, 8–15 cm tall and with full foliage cover, is an important, special case. It is easily grown in most locations and has minimum aerodynamic roughness that does not change during the growing season. ET* of such vegetative cover defines a **reference evapotranspiration** ($ET_0$), a practical, widely used standard measure of environmental demand (Doorenbos & Pruitt 1977).

Penman (1948) originally defined potential ET as the rate of water loss from the short-grass standard ($ET_0$) but the difference in ET* between crops was not then generally recognized. Nor was it appreciated that ET* of many full-cover crops exceeds $ET_0$, especially in the highly evaporative conditions of arid zones. The terminology used here explains the significance of short-grass $ET_0$ and allows discussion of potential evapotranspiration of individual crops in a way comparable to that of potential growth.

ET is most accurately measured with **lysimeters**. A lysimeter is simply a container of soil arranged so that measurements of gains and losses of soil water can be made (e.g. by weighing). They should be large in order to minimize edge effects and be located within a representative crop of adequate extent (see Section 6.9 on fetch). Accurate weighing of the soil and crop combined, provides a measure of the loss of water over time since the gain in mass due to crop growth is small relative to that due to water loss. Using pivot scales or electrical transducers in the under-ground structures that support the lysimeter, mass changes as small as 1 kg can be detected in a lysimeter of 50 t total mass. As a result, well-designed lysimeters can measure hourly ET as small as 0.03 mm. Needless to say, such installations are expensive and lack mobility. They are found at few research stations.

ET can also be measured from the soil water budget that expresses the

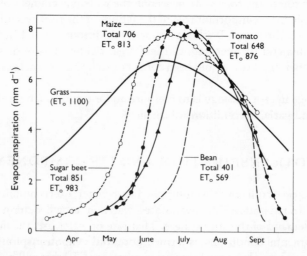

Fig. 9.3. Seasonal evapotranspiration of various well-watered crops compared with a grass reference ($ET_0$) at Davis, California. The curves are means of seven years' data (after Pruitt (1986).)

Table 9.1 *Some equations used to predict reference crop evapotranspiration (ET$_0$) of crops and pastures*

(Variables: $r_a$, aerodynamic resistance; $r_c$, canopy resistance; LAI, leaf area index; $f(u)$, function of windspeed; $\rho_a$, the density of moist air; and $C_p$, specific heat of air at constant pressure. See text and Section 6.7 for further explanation of terms.)

| Name | Equation |
|---|---|
| Penman (1948) | $ET_0 = [s(R_n + G) + \gamma\, f(u)\, (e^* - e_a)]/(s + \gamma)$. |
| Monteith (1964) | $ET_0 = [s(R_n + G) + \rho_a\, C_p\, (e^* - e_a)/r_a]/[(s + \gamma)\, (1 + r_c/r_a)]$. |
| Priestley & Taylor (1972) | $ET_0 = \alpha s(R_n + G)/(s + \gamma)$. |

hydrological balance of a crop (Eq. 9.1). ET* and ET$_0$ can be measured in this way provided the condition of free water supply can be maintained for the prolonged period (4 to 7 days) necessary to establish a measurable change in soil water content ($\Delta\theta z$); $\theta$ is measured at the beginning and end of the period by oven-drying soil cores, or indirectly using instruments such as the neutron moisture meter.

ET$_0$ has been commonly estimated by measurements of evaporation from the pans of standard shape and exposure that are a part of standard meteorological observations. Empirical pan coefficients ($k_{pan}$) must be established to estimate ET$_0 = k_{pan}E_{pan}$. Increasingly, however, ET$_0$ is calculated from a range of formulae, that have, in their development, been calibrated against data collected from lysimeters (Table 9.1). Crop radiation balance (Section 6.7) provides the energy for ET while the vapor pressure gradient ($e^*-e_a$) is maintained by the turbulence of the atmosphere. These two weather components are evident in the equations.

The Penman and Monteith equations in Table 9.1 explicitly combine energy balance and vapor pressure deficit. In contrast, the Priestley–Taylor equation relates evaporation to radiation alone. It is derived from equilibrium evaporation (Eq. 6.16), the parameter $\alpha$ (*ca.* 1.0–1.3) providing the correlated, additional effect of atmospheric turbulence. Monteith's equation is an extension of Penman's. It explicitly includes aerodynamic resistance ($r_a$) rather than the simpler windrun ($f(u)$) of the Penman equation that must be established for each location (Doorenbos & Pruitt 1977). Monteith's modification also includes canopy resistance ($r_c$) that depends upon leaf resistance ($r_l$) and LAI and so can describe ET* for different crops under the same environmental conditions (different $r_a$ or minimum values of $r_c$). The equation can also describe the difference between ET* and ET$_a$ for a single crop as water supply diminishes and $r_c$ increases. The use of Monteith's equation is restricted to research studies which can provide the detailed measurements on the crop canopy parameters that the method requires. The other two equations use standard meteorological observations and can be used routinely in crop management.

In general, the relative magnitude of the evaporation rates for particular crops and locations will be in the order ET$_a$ < ET$_0$ < ET*. ET* of individual crops can be related to ET$_0$ by crop coefficients (i.e. ET* = $c$ET$_0$). Values are established locally from measurements of the type presented in Fig. 9.3. For most short-stature crops

Table 9.2 *Monthly crop coefficients (c = ET/ET$_0$) for several well-watered crops at Davis, California*

Values established from measured crop water-use presented in Fig. 9.3.

| Month | Crop | | | |
|---|---|---|---|---|
| | Bean | Maize | Sugarbeet | Tomato |
| April | — | — | 0.22 | — |
| May | — | 0.17 | 0.41 | 0.12 |
| June | 0.08 | 0.61 | 1.08 | 0.35 |
| July | 0.45 | 1.22 | 1.15 | 1.15 |
| August | 1.13 | 1.18 | 1.13 | 1.04 |
| September | 0.40 | 0.79 | 1.06 | 0.79 |

of full cover, ET* ~ ET$_0$ (i.e. $c$ ~ 1); for some aerodynamically rough, tall crops, and forests, $c$ may rise to 1.25. Crop coefficients are also used to estimate ET$_a$ of well-watered crops from ET$_0$ when cover is incomplete and the soil surface is intermittently dry. Monthly coefficients suitable for irrigation scheduling of several crops at Davis, California, are presented in Table 9.2. Seasonal values of crop coefficients for many combinations of crops and locations are presented in irrigation management manuals such as that of Doorenbos & Kassam (1986).

The explanation of the values of $c$ during development of crop cover is seen in the changing balance between $E_p$ and $E_s$. $E_p$ approaches ET$_a$ except when cover is small (< 50%) and the soil surface is wet. This is an important point. The surface of exposed, wet soil dries quickly after 1–2 days of evaporation at the potential rate; without rewetting, ET* cannot be maintained. This is seen clearly in Fig. 9.4. As a crop leaf area develops, ET$_a$ matches $R_n$ whenever the soil surface is wetted but falls back quickly to the underlying rate of $E_p$ as it dries. $E_p$ builds up to equal $R_n$ as full cover is achieved. This is a nice example of the energy balance of a wet system; $R_n$ goes predominantly to ET.

As shown in Fig. 9.3, real crops depart from ET* for a number of reasons. Incomplete cover is one. In that case, the partitioning of ET between $E_p$ and $E_s$ depends upon the exchange of net radiation by the crop ($R_n$) and the soil surface ($R_{ns}$). This partitioning is a function of LAI and canopy geometry but is dominated by the same gap frequency that controls the penetration of radiation into canopies (Ritchie 1972). It can be written in the form of the Bouguer–Lambert Law (Eq. 2.4) as:

$$R_{ns} = R_n \, e^{(-\omega L)}, \qquad\qquad \text{[Eq. 9.2]}$$

where $\omega$ is an extinction coefficient for net radiation and $L$ is LAI. Separate (individual) estimates for $R_n$ and $R_{ns}$ allow, using one of the equations of Table 9.1, the partitioning of ET* between potential soil evaporation ($E_s$*):

$$E_s^* = ET^* \, R_{ns}/R_n, \qquad\qquad \text{[Eq. 9.3]}$$

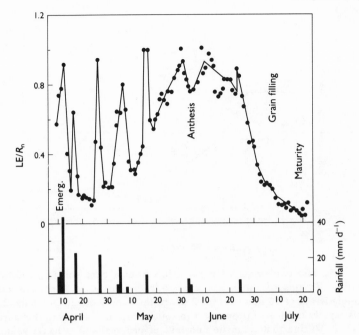

**Fig. 9.4.** Seasonal course of ET (expressed as latent heat, LE) of grain sorghum as a fraction net radiation ($R_n$) and rainfall at Temple, Texas. The early season peaks represent high rate of $E_s$ following rainfall. $E_p$ dominates late season ET (after Ritchie (1971).).

and its complement, potential transpiration ($E_p^*$):

$$E_p^* = ET^* (1 - R_{ns}/R_n).$$ [Eq. 9.4]

## 9.4   EVAPORATION FROM DRYING SOIL

After rainfall or irrigation, evaporation from bare soil proceeds in two successive stages (Fig. 9.5). In the first (**stage 1**), evaporation is determined by the energy exchange at the soil surface and proceeds at $E_s^*$, of similar magnitude to ET*. In **stage 2**, it is dependent upon the supply of water to the evaporating surface and declines rapidly as the surface soil dries. $E_s^*$ persists until an air-dry condition, characteristic of the soil type, is reached. The cumulative evaporation is small, in the range 6–10 mm for sandy and loamy soils respectively, so that stage 1 evaporation for exposed soils is short lived. The transition to stage 2 is abrupt and can be detected experimentally by measurement of surface soil temperature. As $E_s$ declines, $R_{ns}$ goes increasingly to sensible heat.

The decline in $E_s$ during stage 2 is inversely proportional to the square root of time after the transition from $E_s^*$ ($E_s = ct^{-1/2}$) (Fig. 9.5). The constant of proportionality, $c$, depends upon soil hydraulic properties and can be evaluated for individual

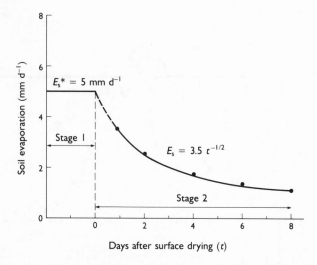

Fig. 9.5. The two stages of evaporation from a bare soil ($E_s$) following wetting. In this example, the energy-dependent stage 1 persists for a cumulative $E_s$ of 10 mm (i.e. for 2 d). In the supply-dependent stage 2, $E_s$ falls rapidly in inverse proportion to square root of days from the start of stage 2. During that time the constant of proportionality has a value of 3.5 mm d$^{-\frac{1}{2}}$.

soils from measurements of cumulative evaporation ($\Sigma E_s$) during a single drying cycle. Typical values for $c$ fall in the range 3–4 mm d$^{-1/2}$.

The cause of the rapid decline in $E_s$ during drying is the increasing depth within the soil from which water is being drawn. That distance and the low hydraulic conductivity of unsaturated soil (Section 7.6) limit the evaporation rate.

## 9.5   COLLECTION OF WATER BY ROOT SYSTEMS

In semiarid regions, crops may be subjected to maximum daily ET* of 8–10 mm whereas rates of 5–6 mm are more common in humid regions with smaller ($e^*-e_a$). If the root system supporting a canopy is 1 m deep and has a small **root length density** ($L_v$, units cm cm$^{-3}$, commonly written cm$^{-2}$) of only 0.5 cm$^{-2}$ then the 5 km of root per m$^2$ of crop area must maintain a mean daily rate of uptake of 0.02 cm$^3$ cm$^{-1}$ d$^{-1}$ for the crop to meet ET* = 8 mm d$^{-1}$. However, transpiration is essentially limited to daytime, reaching a maximum rate of 1.3 mm h$^{-1}$ near mid-day. Thus the peak performance required of the root system is actually about three times greater, i.e. 0.06 cm$^3$ cm$^{-1}$ d$^{-1}$.

The movement of that quantity of water from the soil into the root system occurs down a gradient of water potential established between the root system and the bulk soil midway between the roots, i.e. ($\Psi_s-\Psi_r$), by the transpirational loss from the crop canopy. The relationship between that flow ($Q$, mm s$^{-1}$) and the hydraulic resistances of the two consecutive segments of the pathway in the soil ($R_{soil}$) and across the root system ($R_{root}$), respectively is (Gardner 1965):

$$Q = -(\Psi_s - \Psi_r)/(R_{soil} + R_{root}).$$ [Eq. 9.5]

The resistance of water flow from cylinders of soil surrounding roots ($R_{soil}$) depends upon the hydraulic conductivity of the soil ($k_s(\theta)$) and the distance between the roots. Therefore, it depends, within each depth interval ($\Delta z$), on the surface area of active roots that in turn is a function of root length density ($L_v$) and root diameter ($d_r$), i.e. as:

$$R_{soil} = [\ln(\pi L_v) + 2\ln(d_r)]/[4\pi L_v \, \Delta z k_s(\theta)].$$ [Eq. 9.6]

$R_{soil}$ increases markedly as soil dries from saturation to wilting point (e.g. by a factor of $10^4$) because hydraulic conductivity decreases exponentially in this range. For that reason, the flow of water to a root system falls rapidly as soil dries within the available range.

The resistance of the root system ($R_{root}$) depends upon the total root surface area and the radial conductance to flow ($k_r$). It is usually expressed per unit root length rather than surface area, i.e.

$$R_{root} = 1/(L_v \, \Delta z k_r).$$ [Eq. 9.7]

The relative importance of $R_{soil}$ and $R_{root}$ (Eq. 9.5) can be estimated from measurements of $E_p$ and $\Psi_r$, (the latter approximated from $\Psi_l$). Such measurements show that $R_{soil}$ becomes more important as the soil dries from saturation. At high water contents, $R_{root} \approx 10^2 \, R_{soil}$, but as the soil dries, $R_{soil}$ increases rapidly and quickly becomes the major limitation to the collection of water.

In contrast to knowledge of water conductivity of soil and complete root systems, little is known about the physical contact between roots and soil. Roots of many species secrete mucigels which assist in maintaining good contact with soil but roots have a tendency to penetrate soil through planes of weakness and to use macropores developed by previous roots. This coupled with the fact that roots, like all parts of plants, shrink diurnally and seasonally when RWC declines results in uncertain contact between roots and soil. Larger resistances are observed for root systems in the field than is apparent from measurements in the laboratory due, perhaps, to poor contact made in drying soils subject to shrinkage.

Eqs 9.5–9.7 are the basis for the analyses of the performance of root systems presented in Fig. 9.6 (Cowan 1965). The equations were solved repeatedly at short time intervals to account for the marked diurnal pattern of $E_p$ and the strong dependence of $R_{soil}$ on $\Psi_s$. $\Psi_r$ was constrained to remain above a critical value of $-1.5$ MPa to mimic the intervention of perfect stomatal control on crop water use. The calculations relate to a full-cover crop ($E_p \rightarrow ET$) with root depth of 20 cm in a medium-textured soil.

Fig. 9.6a shows crop transpiration under three rates of ET*. At ET* $= 6$ mm d$^{-1}$ the root system can supply $E_p^*$ in wet soil ($\Psi_s > -0.2$ MPa) but as ET* decreases from 4 to 2 mm d$^{-1}$ so does $\Psi_s$ to which $E_p^*$ can be maintained. This latter point is explored further in Figure 9.6b, which displays the importance of root density under moderate ET* of 4 mm d$^{-1}$. As root density increases from 0.12 to 1.0 cm$^{-2}$ and beyond, crop transpiration is maintained at the maximum rate to increasingly lower soil water potentials.

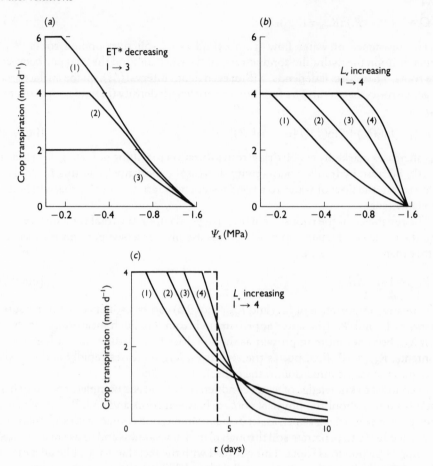

Fig. 9.6. Simulated crop transpiration ($E_p$) in response to soil water potential for (a) three levels of ET* = 6, 4 and 2 mm d$^{-1}$; (b) four levels of root length density ($L_v$ = 0.12, 0.25, 0.5 cm$^{-2}$ and very dense); and (c) the decrease in $E_p$ with time from an initially wet soil is shown for four levels of $L_v$ (0.12, 0.25, 0.5 cm$^{-2}$ and very dense) (after Cowan (1965).)

Figure 9.6c analyses sequences of daily transpiration ($E_p$) for crops with a range of $L_v$ as transpiration gradually dries the profile from an originally wet condition. Since greater $L_v$ can maintain $E_p$* to lower $\Psi_s$, $E_p$ declines first with low $L_v$ and progressively later with greater $L_v$ and capacity to extract water from the soil. However, $E_p$ is subsequently greater for crops of low $L_v$. Their more conservative use of water during early stages of drying has extended the duration of crop water use, though extraction at any $\Psi_s$ was always slower than by crops of high $L_v$. This response would be amplified if stomatal control occurred at higher values of $\Psi_l$.

Those simulations stress the dynamic nature of the uptake of water by crops. The availability of water depends not only upon $\Psi_s$ and how it changes with $\theta$, but also on ET*, $L_v$, root depth, and the pattern of $\Psi_l$ and $\Psi_r$. The results are consistent with the observations (Fig. 9.7) on maize plants growing in pots within a field crop. Those

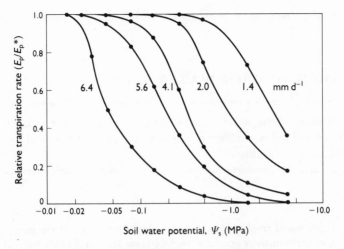

Fig. 9.7. Relative daily crop transpiration as a function of soil water potential for days of different $E_p*$ as shown on the curves (after Denmead & Shaw (1962).)

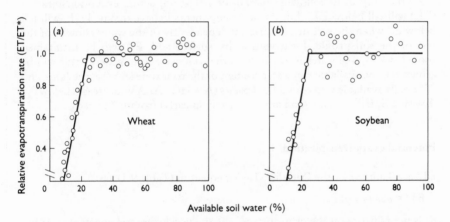

Fig. 9.8. Relative crop evapotranspiration rate ($ET_a/ET*$) as a function of available soil water content for (*a*) wheat, and (*b*) soybean (after Meyer & Green (1981).)

data also show that relative transpiration ($E/E_p*$) declined with soil water content but that the form of the response depended upon $E_p^*$. With $E_p^* = 1.4$ mm d$^{-1}$, $E_p$ was maintained almost to wilting point but when $E_p^*$ was 6.4 mm d$^{-1}$, a slight drying below field capacity was sufficient to lower $E_p$ below $E_p^*$.

The restriction of transpiration by soil water content is less evident in the field. Thus observations of the relative evapotranspiration ($ET_a/ET*$) of a number of full-cover field crops have shown (e.g. Ritchie & Burnett 1971; Meyer & Green 1981; Shouse *et al.* 1982) that rates are often maintained until the relative available soil water content falls below 0.3. This relationship (Fig. 9.8) holds across a range of soil textural classes independently of $\Psi_s$. Below that water content, the decline of $ET_a/$

ET* is essentially linear, an approximation widely used in models of crop water balance.

## 9.6  A MODEL OF CROP WATER BALANCE

Box 9.1 *A model of crop water use constructed from the separate responses of transpiration and soil evaporation to atmospheric evaporative demand, crop cover, and soil water content*

### Rationale

Under conditions of freely available water, crops use water at the potential rate (ET*). The contribution of potential transpiration ($E_p$*) and potential soil evaporation ($E_s$*) to ET* depends upon interception of radiation by the canopy and soil surface, respectively. Penetration of radiation through the canopy follows an exponential relationship with LAI.

As the crop dries following rainfall or irrigation, actual evapotranspiration (ET$_a$) will fall below ET*, but its two components behave distinctly. $E_s$ will fall below $E_s$* when the soil surface dries, independently of the water content of the rest of the soil profile. Even with a dry surface soil, $E_p$* will be maintained provided adequate water is available to the root system. In general, this will be achieved if the available soil water content of the root zone (AW) exceeds around 30% of its available water-holding capacity (AWHC). As AW decreases below 0.3 AWHC, $E_p$ falls quickly (and approximately linearly) from $E_p$* to zero.

### Potential evapotranspiration

ET* is calculated by the Priestley–Taylor equation (Table 9.1) as:

$$ET^* = a \, [s/(s+\gamma)] \, R_n.$$

$R_n$ is net radiation at the crop surface, $\gamma$ is the psychrometric constant, $s$ is the slope of the saturation vapor pressure – temperature curve at the mean crop temperature and $a$ (*ca.* 1.35) is a constant of proportionality that is established locally.

$R_n$ is partitioned between crop and soil depending upon LAI and leaf geometry. The proportion ($\tau$) that penetrates the canopy to the soil determines $E_s$*. The relationship to LAI is exponential (Eq. 9.2) as:

$$\tau = R_n \exp(-k\text{LAI}),$$

with the extinction coefficient of net radiation ($k$) taking values of the order of 0.4.

With this relationship, $E_s$* and $E_p$* can be separated as

$$E_s^* = \tau ET^*$$

and

$$E_p^* = (1-\tau) \, ET^*.$$

**Evapotranspiration at non-potential rates**

As the crop system dries, evapotranspiration ($ET_a$) falls below $ET^*$. The two components respond as follows.

**Soil evaporation**
The dryness of the soil surface is measured as cumulative $E_s$ ($\Sigma E_s$, mm) since last wetting. Soils must be calibrated individually for this value (*ca.* 6–10 mm). When $\Sigma E_s$ exceeds this value, surface evaporation moves from an 'energy-dependent' into a 'supply-dependent' stage (Section 9.4), falling rapidly according the relationship:

$$E_s = ct^{-1/2},$$

where $c$ depends on soil hydraulic properties and $t$ = days from start of the dry condition. Typical values of $c$ are in the range from 3 to 4 mm d$^{-1/2}$.

**Transpiration**
When AW falls below 0.3 AWHC, $E_p$ falls below $E_p^*$, reaching $E_p = 0$ at AW = 0, i.e.

$$E_p = E_p^* \, AW/(0.3 \, AWHC). \qquad AW < 0.3 \, AWHC$$

**Evapotranspiration**
Under the many combinations of wet and dry surface and root zone water content, $ET_a$ is given by:

$$ET_a = E_s + E_p.$$

Rosenthal *et al.* (1977) provide further details of this approach, which was pioneered by Ritchie (1972). Other versions include an improvement that accounts for the additional evaporative demand imposed on a sparse crop canopy over a dry soil surface.

---

The concepts introduced in this chapter concerning crop water use and its response to crop and environmental factors are drawn together in the form of a model of crop water use (Box 9.1). It concerns a crop initially well supplied with water. $ET^*$ of that crop can be calculated using the Priestley–Taylor equations (Table 9.1) and be partitioned, as a function of canopy geometry, between $E_s^*$ and $E_p^*$ according to Eq. 9.3 and 9.4. Then as the crop dries, $E_s$ and $E_p$ fall below $E_s^*$ and $E_p^*$, but their responses are distinct. $E_s$ responds quickly as the surface soil surface dries, moving into the 'energy-dependent' phase and decreasing rapidly below $E_s^*$ (Fig. 9.5). In contrast, $E_p^*$ is maintained as long as root zone water content exceeds 30% of its maximum available water holding capacity. Below that content, $E_p$ falls linearly from $E_p^*$, reaching zero when available soil water (AW) is exhausted (Fig. 9.8). This simplification, relative to the principles of the collection of water by root systems presented in Section 9.5, is made because alternatives require more detailed information on root length density and plant and soil water potentials than is usually available.

Those equations can reproduce the dynamics of crop water use under intermittent rainfall and/or irrigation, variable ET* and changing crop cover. They form the core of several published models of crop water balance. Ritchie (1972) pioneered this approach that has since been applied successfully to the analysis of many field problems. Rosenthal *et al.* (1977) have applied it to the analysis of the water balance of maize crops in Kansas. The same approach was able to describe observed patterns of water use by sunflower crops under two irrigation regimes at Tatura, Australia (Fig. 9.9).

## 9.7   RESPONSES OF CROPS TO WATER DEFICIT

The principles controlling water flow through the soil–plant–atmosphere continuum (Section 9.1) and the diurnal patterns of plant water potential presented in Fig. 9.2 emphasize that an imbalance between water uptake and transpirational loss is a diurnal feature of the water status of crops in all environments. Difficulties arise when the internal water deficit, which expresses this imbalance, is either great or prolonged. Under conditions of diminishing water supply or increasing evaporative demand, the maintenance of crop water status within tolerable limits depends upon the crop's ability to restrict transpiration to the uptake capacity of its root system.

Transpiration can be reduced either by reducing leaf area or the loss per unit leaf area. Adjustments to leaf area are achieved over periods of days or weeks by less expansion and/or more senescence. In contrast, stomatal closure and leaf movement operate in minutes or hours to reduce transpiration per unit leaf area. Stomatal closure reduces leaf conductance, while leaf movements reduce radiation interception and hence the temperature and saturated vapor pressure of the transpiring leaf. However achieved, reduced transpiration will generally be associated with reduced growth. The common link in the case of stomatal closure and leaf movement, is through reduced photosynthesis per unit leaf area. With less LAI, interception of solar radiation and photosynthesis are reduced. Quantitative aspects of the link between photosynthesis, growth, and water use will be discussed later in Section 9.10.

The penalty of continuing water use is severe if the crop fails to recover from the prolonged internal deficit when water becomes again available. Where economic yield depends on critical development events such as flowering (Chapter 5), the effects of transient water deficits on yield can be greatly magnified relative to effects on total growth.

## 9.8   PATTERNS OF WATER SHORTAGE

Drought is a meteorological term signifying a prolonged dry period; **drought resistance** is the ability of a crop to withstand it. The definition of drought is purposefully broad to encompass the wide range of drought conditions that exist in agriculture, depending upon rainfall–evaporation balance, weather variability, soil water holding capacity, crop type, rooting habit, and stage of development. In areas

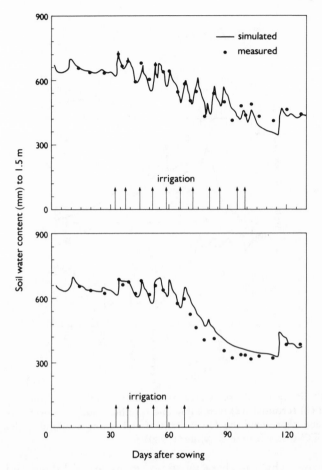

**Fig. 9.9. Measured and simulated soil water content under sunflower crops of two different irrigation regimes at Tatura, Australia (D. J. Connor, unpublished).**

of high rainfall, a week without rain may cause significant yield loss. In semiarid areas such 'droughts' are common and cropping practices are modified to account for longer-than-usual dry spells (droughts) which can extend into months or years. It is the variability and uncertainty of moisture supply that makes the design of cropping practice difficult for drought-prone regions (Chapter 13).

Three generalized patterns of water supply, depicted as relative available water contents of the root zone, emerge in relation to crop duration (Fig. 9.10). In the first, drought is terminal following the major growth period during which water supply is adequate. This is characteristic of the winter–spring rainfall areas of mid-latitudes, i.e. Mediterranean climates, in which late spring and early summer bring high evaporation rates and low rainfall. In the second, the crop suffers an initial period of drought because it is necessary to sow in anticipation of a short, reliable period of rain. This pattern is found in tropical, monsoonal areas where the break in season is sharp and reliable but the wet season is short relative to the growth cycle of the crop.

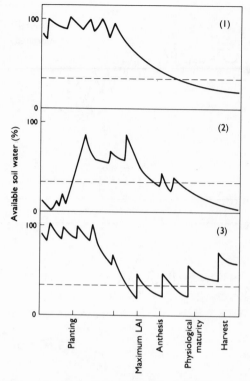

Fig. 9.10. Patterns of soil water availability identifying three types of drought: (1) terminal, (2) unreliable and terminal, and (3) unreliable. The dashed line represents the lower limit of soil water availability that will support ET* (after Jordan & Miller (1980).)

In the third case, which is characteristic of many areas (humid and semiarid), seasonal rainfall totals may be reliable but intra-seasonal variability is large. Under those conditions, significant drought can occur at any time during the season when temperature and radiation are otherwise suitable for crop growth.

The subsequent sections deal with the adaptations of crop plants to drought. The management of crop water relations is discussed in Chapters 13 and 14.

## 9.9   ADAPTATION TO DROUGHT

Evolution has found many avenues for plant growth and survival in drought-prone areas. The challenge is to understand those responses so that crop yield can be improved in drought-prone areas by better management of existing cultivars and by purposeful breeding of better cultivars.

Plants can succeed in drought-prone regions by either escaping the periods of drought or by resisting them. **Drought escape** relies upon developmental attributes that permit synchrony of the life cycle to periods when there is a high probability for satisfactory conditions for growth. **Drought resistance** is achieved by various combinations of developmental, morphological and physiological traits that allow

Table 9.3 *Characteristics that enable plants to escape or resist drought*

1. Drought escape
      Rapid phenological development
2. Drought resistance
      (a) Drought avoidance (high plant water status)
            (i)  Reduction in water loss
                        high stomatal and cuticular resistance
                        avoidance of radiation load
                        low leaf area
            (ii) Maintenance of water uptake
                        deep roots
                        high root length density
                        high hydraulic conductance
      (b) Drought tolerance (low plant water status)
            (i)  Maintenance of turgor
                        osmotic adjustment
                        high cell wall elasticity
                        small cell size
            (ii) Tolerance of dehydration or desiccation
                        protoplasmic tolerance
                        cell wall properties

plants either to balance transpiration and uptake and therefore **avoid** internal water deficits or to continue growth and water use and to **tolerate** them. There are many genes involved in the component traits of those adaptations summarized in Table 9.3.

In practice the distinctions between the classes are blurred. Drought escapers benefit from the ability to resist drought, and among drought resistors there are many beneficial combinations of avoidance and tolerance. Our attitude to the development of improved cultivar–management combinations should be to respect evolution's well-tested solutions for survival but to realize, too, that in agriculture, production rather than survival is the major objective. In drought adaptation, solutions emphasizing survival may be disadvantageous in agriculture.

### Developmental traits

**Rate of development**    Rapid development can assist a crop to complete its life cycle without serious water shortage. This is the behavior of many wild, desert ephemerals that also permits successful cropping in many water-short environments. The challenge for plant breeders is to develop cultivars that make best use of water in dry years and yet possess flexibility for good use of wetter years. This was illustrated by a genetic advance in Fig. 3.3 and will be seen again in Fig. 13.9.

Some workers have reported that water stress can hasten phenological development. Certainly crops often develop more rapidly in dry years and this can stabilize yield. However years that are drier than usual are often also warmer because $R_n \rightarrow H$ (see Chapter 6) so the more rapid phenological development may be a thermal response rather than a direct effect of water stress.

**Time of flowering**   The annual cycle of daylength is a reliable environmental signal and carefully tuned photoperiodic responses offer a precise way to time flower development. That is not easy, given the enormous range of possible planting dates at different latitudes, however, and a common thrust in modern crop breeding has been to reduce the dependence of flowering time on daylength (Chapter 5). This widens the geographic range of individual cultivars and may also be a valuable adaptation to variably hot and dry environments since photoperiodic requirement could restrain more rapid development in the warmer conditions of drier years.

**Duration of flowering**   In addition to timing of flower initiation, the duration of flowering has important implications for seed crops in drought-prone areas. Determinate crops, in which flowering occurs quickly and signals a rapid switch from vegetative growth to seed-filling, are vulnerable to transient stresses. A stress of even short duration which occurs at a critical time may cause mortality of a high percentage of ovules, pollen, or fertilized embryos. In such crops, there is little possibility to compensate for the lowered yield potential. In some cereals such as sorghum, each tiller is determinate but tillering may extend over a relatively long period. In that case, late tillers may compensate to some extent for losses by earlier tillers.

Crops with an indeterminate habit (e.g. soybean and field bean) maintain vegetative apices and flower from axillary buds over protracted periods. Transient stresses may cause the loss of a particular age class of flowers and hence yield sites, but with the return of more favorable conditions, flowering continues and yield potential can be re-established. The indeterminate habit is less efficient under favorable conditions (Chapter 5) in the production of seed yield but that inefficiency is a small price to pay for the yield stability it lends in uncertain environments.

The different responses of determinate and indeterminate crops to transient stresses are summarized in Fig. 9.11. The vulnerability of the determinate crop, wheat, is further emphasized in Fig. 9.12, which illustrates the relative effect on final yield of stresses at various stages in development. Early stress is serious if it causes poor establishment. Reproductive development is sensitive at flower initiation, during the subsequent period of spike formation and around anthesis itself.

Maize is also sensitive to water stress around flowering. In that species, water stress has been shown to delay silking, causing asynchrony between the release of pollen and the exposure of receptive silks (Hall *et al.* 1982*a*). Under stress, this leads to reductions in grain set and yield. Large differences exist among maize genotypes (Bolanos & Edmeades 1988) that can form a basis for selection of breeding material used in the development of cultivars for drought-prone areas. Fig. 9.13 compares the duration of the anthesis–silking interval in a number of elite maize lines grown under irrigation and under drought. Those lines that maintained a short anthesis–silking interval under stress also maintained grain set and yield. No other physiological or morphological parameter, from a wide range that was measured, was similarily highly correlated with yield maintenance under stress. The similar behavior of all lines under irrigation emphasizes that selection for this trait can only be made under conditions of water shortage.

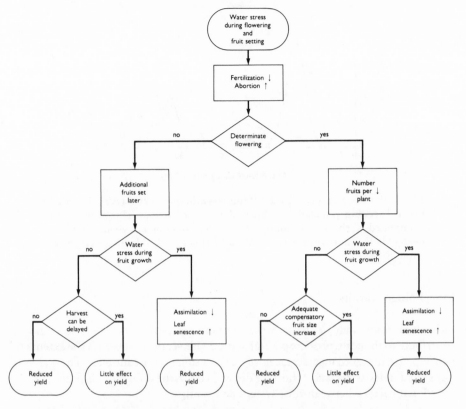

**Fig. 9.11.** The effects of water stress during reproductive development on the grain yield of crops. The flow chart differentiates responses on grain number and grain size of determinate and indeterminate crops (after Hsiao *et al* (1976).)

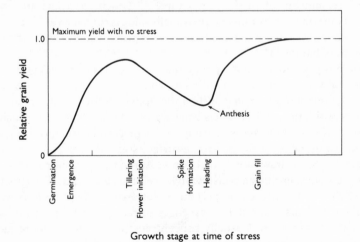

**Fig. 9.12.** Relative grain yield of wheat in response to water stress at various times during crop development (after various authors).

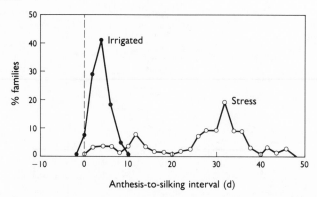

Fig. 9.13. The response of the silking-to-anthesis interval (ASI) in an elite maize breeding population subjected to water stress. Those plants that maintained a short ASI under stress also maintained yield. Yield was negligible in plants with ASI > 15 d (after Bolanos & Edmeades (1988, and unpublished).)

### Morphological traits

Individual traits may increase water uptake or reduce transpiration and so contribute to the control of crop water status. This section deals with the extent and behavior of the exchange surfaces of root systems and canopies. The value of individual traits under water shortage depends upon the total crop response, i.e. the functional balance between root system and canopy.

**Root exploration**   Crops can maintain high internal water status by exploring large soil volumes. Deep, dense root systems deliver water more readily and over a longer period (see Section 9.5). The value of those traits depends, of course, upon occasional replenishment of deep moisture. Although the traits are useful for productivity in some environments, their main value is for survival. The problem is that large amounts of assimilate are required for growth and maintenance of large root systems (Chapter 11).

Grasses possess a dual root system that enables them to adapt to variable conditions of water supply. Seminal roots with small $L_v$ provide slow access to water throughout the soil profile. When the upper profile is wet, nodal (adventitious) roots proliferate. Indeed it has been argued that the high root densities that develop ($L_v > 10 \, \text{cm}^{-2}$) are excessively high and deplete soil water more quickly than is desirable for monocultures. When the surface soil is dry, the few seminal roots that penetrate deeply draw more slowly upon stored water in the subsoil. The low density root system ensures a conservative use of stored water. Perhaps the high root density near the surface is in part an evolutionary adaptation to competition with unlike neighbors that quickly scavenges surface water following rainfall and also gains access to nutrients usually concentrated there. However, surface roots may be the only effective means to collect surface soil water that otherwise evaporates quickly to the atmosphere.

The strategy of conservative use of water has interesting ecological implications.

The chaparral communities of California and Chile comprise a diversity of shrub species that show similar morphological adaptations to drought and employ a similar conservative strategy of water use (Mooney & Dunn 1970). No species could afford to adopt such a strategy if its competitors have the same access to soil water and continue to use it at high rates.

Different rules are possible in agricultural monocultures where the question of water-use strategy is simplified but little attention has yet been given it in breeding programs. Passioura (1983) outlined an interesting proposal for the selection of root systems of large resistance that delay water use until the critical reproductive phase. A major problem is that the options for patterns of root growth and water use are too numerous for experimental evaluation. Modeling efforts that focus breeding efforts to the most favorable options (Chapter 13) will help in this difficult area for crop improvement.

**Canopy properties**   Analysis of the dynamics of leaf area under stress must consider the component responses of **leaf initiation**, **leaf expansion** and **leaf senescence** if a complete picture of the response is to be obtained.

Apical meristems are small and relatively isolated from water shortage with the result that leaf initiation is the last process affected by water stress. Under severe stress, leaf primordia may accumulate on the meristem until relief provides conditions of assimilate supply and turgor suitable for cell division and expansion. In studies of the canopy dynamics of cassava under water shortage, Connor & Cock (1981) recorded that deformed leaves appeared first after a 90-d period of rainfall exclusion, but were quickly followed by entire leaves.

Leaf expansion is particularly sensitive to slight internal water deficit so reduced expansion of leaves plays an important role in the adjustment of crop LAI to water shortage. As crops go into stress, leaf expansion rates fall rapidly and measurement of leaf elongation provides a rapid and effective means of measuring the onset and severity of water stress. Water stress reduces the rate of LAI increase; this, combined with leaf senescence, may cause LAI to decrease. Both responses reduce the effect of water shortage on crop water status but at the expense of reduced LAI.

Increased rates of senescence and loss of leaves are common responses to stress. Older leaves at the bottom of the canopy generally senesce first. Ecologically, the extreme version of this tactic is the drought-deciduous behavior of many wild species. The hazard of not reducing leaf area is that complete canopies require greater amounts of substrate in maintenance respiration (Chapter 11) during a period when assimilation is severely reduced. In contrast, reduced leaf area has a lasting effect on crop water use and, with its smaller respiratory load, can allow growth and survival for considerable periods. Provided that crop cover is incomplete, reduction in leaf area will reduce crop transpiration although the reduction is not proportional to the change in leaf area (Fig. 9.14). Crops of incomplete cover experience additional radiation by reflection (shortwave) and radiation (longwave) from the soil surface particularly when it is dry. This together with the direct loss of rainfall by soil evaporation are the major inefficiencies of this adaptation to water shortage. Despite this, low crop density can achieve long growth duration and is a basis for successful cropping in drought-prone areas (Chapter 13).

Interception of radiation can also be reduced by either increased leaf reflectivity

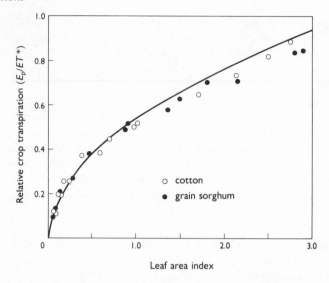

Fig. 9.14. Relative crop transpiration ($E_p/ET^*$) as a function of LAI for cotton and grain sorghum under nonlimiting conditions of soil water (after Ritchie and Burnett 1971).

or leaf movement. In some plants, water shortage increases leaf reflectivity to shortwave radiation by either increased pubescence or the thickening of epidermal wax. In contrast to adjustment of LAI, leaf movement is a valuable short-term tactic from which crops can recover quickly when water again becomes available. Some species, especially legumes, have finely tuned heliotropic leaf movement that aligns leaves relative to the solar beam. Others, such as maize, are positioned spatially and in some cases azimuthly during development into open positions in the canopy. Leaves of some crops will only move passively, i.e. wilt or roll when they lose turgor, but these movements also contribute to reduced interception of radiation and hence to improved crop water status under water shortage.

**Root–shoot balance**   The balance of expansive growth determines the value of the morphological and physiological traits of the root system and canopy to water shortage. When water is not limiting, the abundance of active meristems in the shoot portion of the crop can monopolize the available assimilates. Root growth is then restricted owing to substrate shortage. Water stress changes the activity of the sources and sinks of assimilate around the plant. Stem elongation and leaf expansion are more sensitive than photosynthesis to stress. Therefore stress tends to allow an accumulation of assimilate. Root systems experience higher and less variable water potential than do shoots (Fig. 9.2). Given adequate substrate, their growth is generally less restricted by stress. These advantageous adjustments bring root and shoot functions into a new balance more appropriate for the current environment. Brouwer (1983) studied this process and gave it the name **functional equilibrium**. Depending upon the duration of stress there may be lasting effects following recovery.

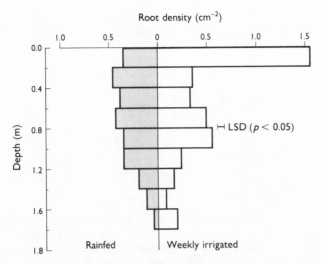

Fig. 9.15. **Comparison of the root density profile five days after flowering for sunflower crops irrigated weekly or rainfed from sowing. The total root lengths were 7.8 and 5.2 km m$^{-2}$ ground area respectively (after Connor & Jones (1985).)**

The morphological combination of reduced leaf area and high density of roots is an important means for drought avoidance. High root/shoot ratios are a feature of many crops as well as wild species under drought. Changes in root/shoot ratios can be dramatic. Fig. 9.15 illustrates profiles of $L_v$ under weekly irrigated and rainfed sunflower. The difference is marked only in the surface layer, which was persistently dry in the rainfed treatment and generally moist under irrigation. The irrigated crop had a more extensive root system than the rainfed crop (7.8 compared with 5.2 km m$^{-2}$ ground area). However, the LAIs of the two crops were vastly different so that the rainfed crop, with 5.8 km root m$^{-2}$ leaf area, had a greater capacity for balancing supply with demand (cf. 2.5 km m$^{-2}$ leaf area for irrigated control).

**Reproductive yield**   Current photosynthesis, stored assimilate, and materials mobilizable from leaves, stems, and roots serve as sources of assimilate for seed-filling. Stored and current assimilates are equally available but the distinction identifies a tactic by which plants can compensate, through mobilization of stored material, for limitations to photosynthesis during stress.

The proportion of final seed yield that is attributable to preanthesis assimilate is variable. In severely stressed wheat crops it may be as great as 70% while in unstressed crops the contribution usually accounts for less than 10% of a higher, final grain yield. Cultivars differ in the extent that preanthesis reserves are used in seed-filling. The trait, potentially important to the maintenance of yield under drought, can be purposefully selected and managed in crop cultivars.

Fig. 9.16 illustrates three alternative responses to stored assimilate when photosynthesis is reduced by drought. In case A, yield is maintained by an increased contribution from reserves. In case B the increased contribution is inadequate to

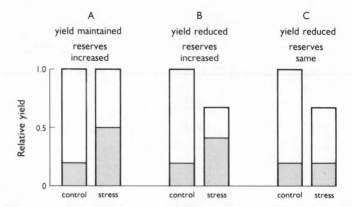

**Fig. 9.16. Three alternative responses of the contribution of preanthesis assimilate to grain yield in terminally-stressed cereals. In strategy A, yield is maintained under stress by increased transfer. In B, increased transfer does not maintain yield; in C, transfer does not increase in response to stress (Turner & Begg 1981).**

maintain yield, while in case C there is no compensatory contribution from reserves. Even in case C, however, the proportional contribution of preanthesis assimilate to yield is increased by stress. The alternatives also raise the question of the extent and value of unused assimilate that might remain in crops at maturity. Greatest grain yields will always be achieved when reserves are completely transferred to grain. If reserves remain at maturity, then the major advantage to grain yield lies in yield stability under variable growth conditions (e.g. case A).

## Physiological traits

**Leaf resistance**　The rate of leaf transpiration (g $H_2O$ m$^{-2}$ s$^{-1}$) at temperature $T_{leaf}$ (°C) can be expressed in the form:

$$\text{Transpiration} = (217/(T_{leaf} + 273))\,(e^* - e_a)/(r_b + r_l),\qquad\qquad \text{[Eq. 9.8]}$$

where $r_l$ (s m$^{-1}$) is the leaf diffusive resistance to water vapor transfer and $r_b$ (s m$^{-1}$) is the boundary layer resistance of the still layer of air associated with the leaf surface. Parameters $e_a$ and $e^*$ (mbar) are, respectively, the vapor pressure of the air and the saturated vapor pressure at $T_{leaf}$. The ratio $(217/(T_{leaf} + 273))$ converts vapor pressure (mb) to water vapor concentration (g m$^{-3}$) upon which diffusion depends.

Stomatal closure that increases $r_l$ is the major mechanism by which plants can reduce transpiration per unit leaf area. This leads to higher leaf temperature and therefore closure must be nearly complete to overcome the higher vapor pressure gradient that increased temperature causes. The basic stomatal response is a feedback to low $\Psi_l$. However, the stomates of many species that maintain high water status during drought respond directly to atmospheric humidity sensed by the water status of the guard cells independent of bulk $\Psi_l$ or to an unidentified hormonal signal generated in response to root water status (see Turner 1986). This

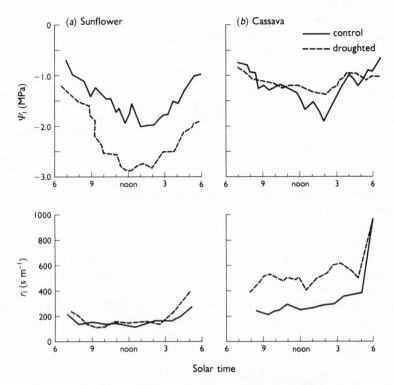

Fig. 9.17. Comparison of leaf diffusive resistance ($r_l$) of sunflower and cassava in response to water stress. In cassava, stomata close in response to humidity and maintain the leaf water potential ($\Psi_1$) of stressed crops. In sunflower, stomata remain open and $\Psi_1$ deviates markedly from the unstressed control. In neither case is there a clear relationship between $\Psi_1$ and $r_l$ (after Connor & Palta (1981) and Connor *et al.* (1985*b*).)

gives such species a feedforward response by which stomates close before the onset of plant water deficits. In that way they maintain high internal water status, explaining why leaf resistance in some species is independent of bulk $\Psi_1$.

Data for well-watered and water-stressed sunflower and cassava (Fig. 9.17) demonstrate two extreme reactions of leaf diffusive resistance ($r_l$) to water shortage. Sunflower maintains open stomates to low $\Psi_1$ but in cassava a feedforward response to atmospheric humidity closes the stomates at high $\Psi_1$. Stressed crops of cassava have comparable diurnal patterns of $\Psi_1$ to well watered crops even though their growth is severely limited by water shortage. This example demonstrates that while $\Psi_1$ does define the internal water status of a crop, it is not possible to understand the nature of the response to water shortage without associated measurements of $r_l$.

**Canopy resistance**    The Monteith equation (Table 9.1) can be used to assess the importance of stomatal closure to crop water use. In this case, $r_c$ is the diffusive resistance of the canopy composed of a number of leaf layers transpiring in parallel. If leaf resistance is $r_l$ (two surfaces also in parallel) then $r_c = r_l$ /LAI; $r_a$ is the aerodynamic resistance to water vapor transport from the bulk air to the effective crop surface ($= 1/K_{H_2O}$, Section 6.8) that depends on crop structure and windspeed. As $r_l$ increases due to stomatal closure, or LAI decreases, $E_p$ will fall below $E_p^*$ according to:

$$E_p/E_p^* = (s + \gamma)/(s + \gamma(1 + r_c/r_a)). \qquad \text{[Eq. 9.9]}$$

Results of calculations using Eq. 9.9 at $T_{air} = 20$ °C are presented in Fig. 9.18. At usual aerodynamic resistances, stomatal closure must be substantial to have much effect. In dense canopies, $r_a$ is large (*ca.* 700 s m$^{-1}$) and an increase in $r_c$ has little effect on $E_p$. Such canopies are said to be 'uncoupled' from the atmosphere. Stomatal closure has more effect in sparse canopies in which $r_a$ is small, but in those canopies $E_s$ may be an important part of ET and this simple equation is not suited to a complete analysis.

Stomatal closure is most effective when temperature and hence vapor pressure deficit are highest. Thus afternoon stomatal closure is an effective way to reduce daily crop water consumption. The extreme case of stomatal control is seen in CAM plants, of which pineapple is the notable crop species (Ekern 1965). As that crop reaches full cover, transpiration, and hence crop water use, can be essentially suspended during daylight hours. Nocturnal uptake of $CO_2$ (stored temporarily in organic acids) when vapor pressure gradients and hence transpiration are least, accounts for the high water-use efficiency of this crop.

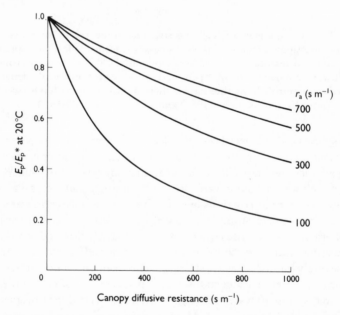

Fig. 9.18. Simulated relationships between crop relative transpiration rate ($E_p/E_p^*$) and canopy diffusive resistance ($r_c$) for various values of aerodynamic resistance ($r_a$). For full cover canopies, changes in $r_c$ are mediated by stomatal closure ($r_c = r_l/LAI$, where $r_l$ is leaf diffusive resistance, both surfaces). At normal values of $r_a$ for closed canopies, 300–700 s m$^{-1}$, stomatal closure has little effect on $E_p$. Calculations based on Eq. 9.9.

**Maintenance of turgor**    Many cellular processes respond to turgor and there-fore adjustments that maintain turgor at low plant water potential are valuable attributes for avoidance of desiccation. Osmotic adjustment, increased elasticity of the cell wall, and small cell size contribute to maintenance of turgor.

Osmotic adjustment has been extensively studied in crop plants and is a common feature of those species that maintain open stomata, active metabolism, leaf and root expansion and the continued extraction of soil water at low internal water potential. Plants adjust osmotically by accumulating organic and inorganic solutes held within limiting membranes. The adjustment requires that stress develop slowly and the response be reversible since recovery of some osmotic compounds does occur. In osmotic adjustment the cost to productivity will vary depending upon the way it is accomplished (Loomis 1985). Adjustment through the accumu-lation of mineral ions ($K^+$, $Cl^-$) and organic acids has only small cost (0.5 to 2 mol ATP per mol osmoticum). Sugars are metabolically costly but are mobile and can be used later in growth, so the actual life-cycle cost will also be low and is attributable mainly to transport. The same can be said of ordinary, highly oxidized organic acids but not of highly reduced and therefore expensive substances such as proline and betaine.

Suggestions that we attempt to enhance the abilities of crop plants to accumulate proline and betaine are misguided. That can be illustrated with reference to a modest wheat crop of 9 t ha$^{-1}$ above-ground biomass containing about 50 t of $H_2O$ when fully turgid. A portion of that water is in cell walls (the apoplast) so, as the relative water content declines with the onset of stress, perhaps 40 t (40 000 l) remain in the osmotic space. A lowering of the water potential by 0.6 MPa would require, according to the Van't Hoff relation (Eq. 7.7), about 10 000 mol of osmoticum (0.25 mol l$^{-1}$). If the osmoticum were sucrose (0.342 mol$^{-1}$), 3420 kg sugar would be required. Adjustment with proline would require 1150 kg containing 140 kg N (proline $= 0.115$ kg mol$^{-1}$ at 122 g N kg$^{-1}$). The biosynthesis of that proline would consume 12 500 mol of glucose (2250 kg) and 10 000 mol of nitrate, both of which are non-toxic osmotica in their own right (see Section 11.2 for a discussion of growth yield). The ratio of osmoticum consumed to that produced would be 2.25:1. Such adjustment from $-1.5$ to $-2.1$ MPa would make available only about 10 mm of water per meter of rooting depth in a clay soil (Fig. 7.8) which is far less than would be required in transpiration to generate the necessary glucose substrate.

Strategies to gain access to additional water may detract from productivity of monocultures. For such communities a conservative strategy, closing stomata near $-1.5$ MPa and waiting for the next rain or irrigation, is often more appropriate (de Wit 1958). As noted earlier, the situation for natural communities and mixed agricultural stands can be very different. In those cases, if one species adjusts, the rest must do likewise to survive. The result is a less efficient use of the scarce resource, water.

How plant tissues tolerate varying degrees of dehydration is not well understood. Differences between species are assumed to be related in some way to cellular composition, membrane stability and enzyme activity. Some extreme examples of tolerance to low water status exist, for example lichens and the vegetative parts of the group of higher plants known as 'resurrection plants' (Gaff 1981). Those plants, and the seeds of most plants, tolerate great desiccation. The vegetative tissues of crop plants face much less extreme water loss diurnally and during droughts, but the ability to regain function when stress is relieved is no less important.

## 9.10   WATER-USE EFFICIENCY

### Terminology

Dry matter production per unit of water used by a crop depends upon the responses of both growth and water use to environmental conditions. This important ecological and agronomic response can be expressed with various efficiency indices. **Crop water-use efficiency** can be expressed as the ratio of production of total biomass (w), yield (y), or the glucose equivalent of those masses (g) (see Section 11.2) against evapotranspiration (ET), i.e. as $WUE_w$, $WUE_y$ or $WUE_g$. $WUE_w$ and $WUE_y$ are most commonly appropriate; $WUE_g$ is of particular interest in comparisons between crops of differing chemical composition.

During the growth of an annual crop, $E_s$ dominates ET early in the season whereas $E_p$ is the major component once full cover is achieved. For the entire cycle, $E_p$ accounts for 30–70% ET. These considerations are important because the best chance for a causal relationship exists between growth and transpiration ($E_p$), i.e. within corresponding **crop transpiration efficiencies**. This derives from the functional relationship between photosynthesis and transpiration of individual leaves (Eq. 10.5) that extends collectively to entire crops. Strong correlations between crop growth and ET only develop when the surface soil is dry and $E_s$ is small, or when $E_p$ and ET are themselves highly correlated, as occurs in full-cover crops.

### The link between growth and transpiration

The transpiration rate of a crop canopy is proportional to the atmospheric evaporative demand ($ET^*$) and inversely proportional to the resistance of the entire pathway from leaf interiors to the atmosphere. In a crop, the source of transpiration is dispersed and the pathway, comprising components attributable to stomates, leaf boundary layers and turbulent transfer, is complex. The magnitude of this resistance ($r_c + r_a$, Eq. 9.9) can be estimated as $ET^*/E_p$ or, because $ET^*$ is often proportional to $(e^* - e_a)$, by $(e^* - e_a)/E_p$. In calculating $e^*$ it is commonly assumed that canopy temperature is close to that of air in contact with it.

$CO_2$ moves by turbulent transfer from the bulk air above the canopy to the intercellular spaces down a gradient of $[CO_2]$ along the same path, and hence against a comparable resistance, to which the water evaporates to the atmosphere (the similarity principle) (Section 6.8). Therefore, if canopy photosynthesis is not restricted by water supply, light, or nutrients then its rate will be proportional to $E_p/ET^*$ or $E_p/(e^* - e_a)$. Over a specified interval when growth is proportional to photosynthesis we can write $\Delta W = TE_w E_p/ET^*$ in which $TE_w$ is a specific transpiration efficiency, i.e. a transpiration efficiency ($W/T$) adjusted for environmental

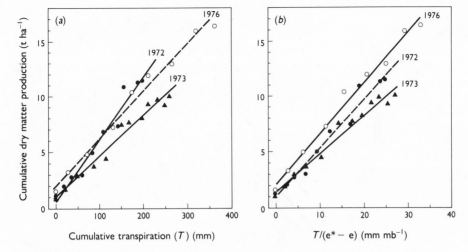

**Fig. 9.19. Relation of total dry matter production in potato crops during the period of tuber growth with (a) cumulative transpiration (*T*), and (b) *T*/*e\**–*e*). (After Tanner (1981).)**

evaporative demand. In a different form, $(e^* - e_a)$ could replace ET\*. A derivation of these intuitive relationships can be found in Tanner & Sinclair (1983).

### Relationships between crop growth and water use

There are many data to demonstrate linear relationships between growth and transpiration and they have been variously summarized (e.g. de Wit 1958, Arkley 1963, Hanks 1983). An example of a relationship between cumulative biomass (*W*) and cumulative transpiration (*T*) of individual potato crops is presented in Fig. 9.19. In those data, *W* of three crops is plotted against *T* for individual periods of 3–4 months. *W* is plotted directly against *T* in Fig. 9.19*a* and against $T/(e^* - e_a)$ in Fig. 9.19*b*. Both graphs show strong linear relationships but, for the latter, there is a smaller difference between years. That arises because inclusion of $e^* - e_a$ accounts for one important source of year-to-year variation in TE, i.e. variation in evaporative demand. The gradients of the relationships in Fig. 9.19*b* are the most generally applicable estimates of TE from these experiments. They can be applied to other potato crops at the same or comparable locations for which $(e^* - e_a)$ is available.

The functional link between *W* and *T* also dominates relationships between *W* and ET. Fig. 9.20 compares progressive *W* and ET for six sunflower crops grown simultaneously at a single site but under different irrigation regimes. Here, the gradients of the lines approximate $TE_w$ so that the intercept estimates $E_s$ for the growing season. The data show that $TE_w$ did not vary between irrigation regimes and that differences in $WUE_w$ resulted from differences in $E_s$/ET. $E_s$ was greatest in crops that were irrigated frequently (treatments 1, 2 and 3) because in those cases surface soil remained moist for a great part of the growing season. $E_s$ was smallest in the

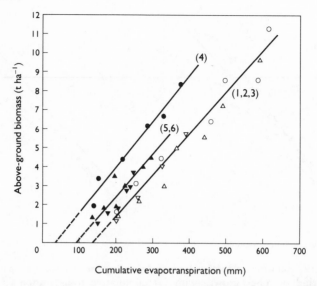

**Fig. 9.20.** Growth and progressive evapotranspiration (ET) of sunflower crops subjected to six different irrigation sequences (1–6). Three linear relationships describe the responses of the crops as shown. Transpiration efficiency ($TE_w$, gradients of the lines) were comparable for all crops but soil evaporation ($E_s$) (the intercepts of the lines with the abcissa) were different because of differences in wetting patterns and exposure of the soil surface. Differences in evapotranspiration efficiency ($\Delta W/\Delta ET$) were due to the differences in $E_s$ (after Connor *et al.* (1985a).)

crops that received no irrigation (treatment 4) because then the surface soil was mostly dry. It was intermediate in other treatments (5 and 6) that received various patterns of infrequent irrigation.

Table 9.4 presents estimates of $TE_w$ (adjusted for $e/e^*$) during the growing season for a number of species (Arkley 1982, from Shantz & Piemeisel 1927). The data illustrate that C4 species have greater $TE_w$ than C3 species and that $TE_w$ of legumes is lower than for non-legumes. The larger $TE_w$ of C4 species arises from greater photosynthesis rates (Chapter 10). One reason for the low TE of legumes is that symbiotic N fixation has a metabolic cost that reduces growth of the host plant (Chapter 8). The extensive measurements on maize included a range of cultivars of similar TE, introducing a point emphasized with additional data by Tanner & Sinclair (1983). During more than half a century of plant improvement since 1916, there is no evidence of any improvement in $TE_w$ of maize. Over that period, partitioning of biomass to grain has increased, however, and hence so has $TE_y$.

## 9.11   SUMMARY

Crops maintain an internal aqueous environment for growth and consequently lose water by transpiration when leaves absorb $CO_2$ through the stomates in photosyn-

Table 9.4 *Transpiration efficiencies (g biomass kg$^{-1}$ water) of various crop species adjusted for relative humidity (e/e\*) of the atmosphere*

| Species | n | $a\mathrm{TE_w}^1$ | Standard error |
|---|---|---|---|
| C4 grasses | | | |
|    Millet | 10 | 179 | 5.6 |
|    Sorghum | 10 | 183 | 2.2 |
|    Sudan grass | 5 | 129 | 3.1 |
|    Maize | 33 | 144 | 1.6 |
| C3 grasses | | | |
|    Barley | 12 | 93 | 1.7 |
|    Wheat | 37 | 87 | 1.6 |
|    Rye | 6 | 77 | 2.2 |
|    Oat | 18 | 84 | 1.6 |
|    Rice | 2 | 76 | 2.5 |
| C3 crops | | | |
|    Rapeseed | 1 | 78 | |
|    Potato | 6 | 96 | 5.3 |
|    Cotton | 6 | 89 | 4.5 |
| C3 legumes | | | |
|    Red clover | 1 | 74 | — |
|    Vetch | 3 | 90 | 4.1 |
|    Sweet clover | 2 | 67 | 6.5 |
|    Field pea | 2 | 70 | 5.0 |
|    Alfalfa | 13 | 60 | 3.7 |

*Note:*
[1] $a = 100(1 - e/e^*)$, range 38 to 64.
*Source:* From Arkley (1982).

thesis. This means that crops in effect exchange water vapor for $CO_2$ and are dependent upon continuing uptake of water to maintain internal conditions suitable for growth. The result is a strong link between transpiration and growth and with a wide range of mechanisms that maintain internal water status within tolerable limits.

In addition to transpiration, crops also lose water by direct evaporation from the soil surface. The separate identification of these two components of crop water use is necessary to explain the water use of crops of incomplete cover, to determine the relationship between crop water use and growth, and to understand the response of crops to water storage. When water is freely available and crops have large LAI, most water use is by transpiration. The water use under those conditions is determined by $R_n$ and the evaporative demand of the atmosphere. That potential rate of evapotranspiration (ET\*) sets the upper boundary to water use at which there is no restriction to crop growth.

There are small but significant differences in ET\* of different crops but the major determinants of total water use under the same environmental conditions are the duration of growth cycle and the rapidity that crops achieve complete foliage cover.

When water supply falls below demand, crops demonstrate a range of morphological and physiological responses that have the effect of either increasing uptake or reducing loss. Transpiration and growth rates fall together, but the consequence of internal drying is damage to structure and function and ultimately death.

It is possible to distinguish escape mechanisms mediated mostly by phenological response from resistance mechanisms dependent upon morphological and physiological characteristics. A major distinction within resistance is made between those that restrict water loss relative to water uptake and so avoid internal water deficit, and those that confer an ability to tolerate low water content and therefore to continue activity. In the field, the value of these strategies depends upon the expectancy of rainfall and the behavior of the competing species.

The effect of water shortage on reproductive yield depends upon the timing of growth restrictions and internal stresses relative to the phenological cycle of flower initiation, flowering, and growth. Prolonged flowering (indeterminate habit) allows plants to compensate for loss of flowers during a stressful period. However, if stresses can be avoided during flowering, that strategy is inferior to determinate flowering in which an optimum balance can be achieved between vegetative and reproductive growth for a given availability of water and cycle length.

In the development of agricultural cultivars, most success has been achieved by adjusting phenological responses, i.e. by selecting the growing season and growth duration to suit the period and amount of water that is available through weather or can be made available by management. Improvement of performance in the face of water shortages during the growth cycle can be achieved in many ways so that progress in plant improvement requires careful definition of the target environment for which alternative strategies can be evaluated.

## 9.12   FURTHER READING

Begg, J. E. and N. C. Turner. 1976. Crop water deficits. *Adv. Agron.* **28**:161–217.

Fischer, R. A. and N. C. Turner. 1978. Plant productivity in arid and semiarid zones. *Ann. Rev. Plant Physiol.* **29**:277–317.

Lange, O. L., P. S. Nobel, C. B. Osmond, and H. Ziegler. 1982. *Physiological plant ecology*. II. *Water relations and carbon assimilation*. Encyclopedia of plant physiology, New Series 12B. Springer-Verlag, Berlin. 747 p.

Ludlow, M. M. and R. C. Muchow. 1990. A critical evaluation of traits for improving crop yields in water-limited environments. *Adv. Agron.* **43**:107–53.

Taylor, H. M. and B. Klepper. 1978. The role of rooting characteristics in the supply of water to plants. *Adv. Agron.* **30**:99–128.

Taylor, H. M., W. R. Jordan, and T. R. Sinclair (eds). 1983. *Limitations to efficient water use in crop production*. Am. Soc. Agron., Madison, Wisconsin. 538 p.

Turner, N. C. (1986). Crop water deficits: a decade of progress. *Adv. Agron.* **39**:1–51.

# 10

*Photosynthesis*

## 10.1  OVERVIEW

Photosynthesis, the primary process in crop production, supplies the reduced carbon that serves for the construction of biomass and the chemical energy for metabolism.

Leaves are the functional units of crop photosynthesis; their efficiency of capture and utilization of solar energy determines productivity. $CO_2$ diffuses from the atmosphere to the sites of fixation in leaves down the concentration gradient that photosynthesis establishes by biochemical fixation in the chloroplast. Diffusion along the pathway is limited by the boundary layer of air surrounding the leaf, by stomatal pores in the leaf epidermis, and by the interior structure of the leaves.

The area (LAI) and arrangement of the foliage, i.e. the canopy architecture, determine the interception of solar radiation by a crop and the distribution of irradiance among individual leaves. The community geometry, established by plant spacing and morphology of the plants, determines canopy structure. Leaf area and arrangement change during the life of a crop and, by leaf movement, even during the course of a single day. Maximum crop production requires complete capture of incident solar radiation and can only be achieved with supporting levels of water and nutrients. When water or nutrients are in short supply, productivity is reduced by incomplete capture of radiation and/or less efficient utilization of it.

Crop photosynthesis varies spatially and temporally in response to environmental factors and from day to day in response to the accumulated effects of past environments on canopy size and its physiological status. This chapter commences with a discussion of photosynthesis and the photosynthetic responses of leaves progressing to analyses of the spatial and temporal variation and manipulation of photosynthesis of crop canopies.

## 10.2  PHOTOSYNTHETIC SYSTEMS

### The central processes

The fundamental feature of photosynthesis is the incorporation of inorganic substrates into organic products. The central reaction, the reduction of $CO_2$ to carbohydrate ($CH_2O$), the principal first product, can be summarized as:

$$CO_2 + 4e^- + 4H^+ \longrightarrow (CH_2O) + H_2O. \tag{Eq. 10.1}$$

The electrons and protons are liberated by solar energy in the photolysis of water:

$$2H_2O \longrightarrow 4H^+ + 4e^- + O_2. \tag{Eq. 10.2}$$

These two processes, respectively the '**dark**' and '**light**' reactions of photosynthesis, occur in the chloroplasts of green leaves. $NO_3^-$ and $SO_4^{2-}$ are also reduced in chloroplasts but they are minor substrates so the dark reactions of photosynthesis are principally concerned with the reduction of $CO_2$. Plant biomass consists of around 45% C but only 2% N and 0.2% S, and there are other sites where $NO_3^-$ and $SO_4^{2-}$ are reduced.

Equations 10.1 and 10.2 explain that photosynthesis can be measured by the uptake of $CO_2$, the evolution of $O_2$, and the production of carbohydrate. The latter can be expressed as mass or as its heat of combustion. $CO_2$ exchange offers a practical way of measuring photosynthesis of crops with infrared gas analyzers (IRGA) that allow easy and accurate measurement of $[CO_2]$ in air streams. As their name suggests, they measure $[CO_2]$ by its absorption of infrared radiation (Fig. 6.6). There is no equally convenient method to measure photosynthesis by $O_2$ exchange.

These equations also establish the maximum energetic efficiency of photosynthesis because the minimum number of photons required to generate sufficient reductant for a molecule of $CO_2$, the **quantum requirement**, is around 12–16. Its reciprocal, termed **quantum efficiency**, has a maximum value in the range 0.06 to 0.08.

## Diffusion model

Those chloroplast events provide a strong sink for $CO_2$, attracting its transport by diffusion across a series of barriers from the atmosphere to the chloroplasts. Net $CO_2$ uptake by a leaf (**net photosynthesis, $P_n$**) can be presented as a diffusion process involving $CO_2$ gradients and resistances:

$$\begin{aligned} P_n &= (C_a - C_c)/(r'_b + r'_l + r'_i) \\ &= (C_a - C_i)/(r'_b + r'_l) \\ &= (C_i - C_c)/r'_i, \end{aligned} \tag{Eq. 10.3}$$

where $C_a$, $C_i$, and $C_c$ are the $[CO_2]$ in the air, internal leaf spaces, and chloroplasts respectively. Transport across the leaf boundary layer and across the leaf surface is by gaseous diffusion; the resistances for these two steps are $r'_b$ and $r'_l$. The resistances are written $r'_b$ and $r'_l$ to distinguish them from the resistances to water vapor transport ($r_b$ and $r_l$) along the same physical pathway introduced previously in Eq. 9.8. The relationship between the two sets of resistances depends upon the relative diffusivities of the two molecules. $CO_2$ is the larger and heavier molecule so its larger resistances are given by $r' = 1.6\,r$.

$C_i$ depends upon the balance between $r'_l$ and the internal resistance to transfer ($r'_i$), also known as the mesophyll resistance, of $CO_2$ from substomatal cavities to the sites of fixation within chloroplasts. The $r_i'$ pathway is complicated because $CO_2$

Table 10.1 *Some important crops classified according to product type and photosynthetic system*

| Product | Photosynthetic System | | |
| --- | --- | --- | --- |
| | C3 | C4 | CAM |
| Beverages and drugs | Tea Coffee | Quinoa | Agave |
| Root crops | Potato Cassava | | |
| Grains | Wheat Sorghum Amaranth Barley Rice | Maize | — |
| Sugars | Sugarbeet | Sugar cane | — |
| Fibers | Flax Cotton | — | Sisal |
| Oils | Soybean Sunflower Rapeseed | | |
| Fruits | Apples Banana | | Pineapple *Opuntia* spp. |
| Forages | Ryegrass Alfalfa Clovers | Panic Rhodes grass (no legumes) | — |

does not move along it by gaseous diffusion and respiration releases $CO_2$ within the leaf tissue.

## Photosynthetic groups

Plants have evolved three different chemo-anatomical systems (termed **C3**, **C4** and **CAM**) which provide suitable internal environments for the light and dark reactions. Terrestrial plants evolved from algae with the C3 system and retain it. Some have since evolved to either the C4 or CAM variants. The floristic distribution of C3 and C4 types (Evans 1971) suggests that they have evolved separately on more than one occasion. Crop plants, like the flora generally, are dominated by C3 species. Table 10.1 records the distribution of some important crop plants according to their photosynthetic system.

**C3 photosynthesis**   In the presence of the universal photosynthetic enzyme rubisco, the 5-carbon sugar ribulose bisphosphate (RuBP) accepts $CO_2$ and the unstable product splits to form the 3-carbon phosphoglyceric acid hence the name C3. The cycle of reactions involved in C3 carboxylation was worked out in the

1940s by a group at University of California, Berkeley, led by A. Benson and M. Calvin, after whom the chemical sequence is named. While $CO_2$ fixation (carboxylation) is its major activity, rubisco also behaves as an oxygenase. In the light, $O_2$ competes with $CO_2$ for the active sites on the enzyme and subsequent metabolism, in a process called **photorespiration**, releases $CO_2$. Internal leaf tissues have high $[O_2]$ because the atmospheric concentration is high (21% $O_2$ v/v) and also because it is produced by photosynthesis. In consequence, photorespiration is an inescapable process that reduces the net $CO_2$ gain in C3 plants. Escape of gaseous ammonia ($NH_3$) from live leaves has also been associated with photorespiration.

In C3 plants, $CO_2$ from the interior spaces of the leaf is adsorbed into the cell walls of the mesophyll as dissolved $CO_2$ and as $HCO_3^-$. The enzyme carbonic anhydrase hydrates dissolved $CO_2$ to form $HCO_3^-$, thus increasing the effective concentration of $CO_2$ at the chloroplast. However, the low conductance of this part of the pathway strongly restricts the flux of $CO_2$ from the atmosphere to the chloroplasts and for this reason $C_i$ in the substomatal spaces is high, in the range 200–260 $\mu l\, l^{-1}$.

**C4 photosynthesis**   The C4 system occurs mostly in tropical members of the family Gramineae but also in a few floristically diverse dicots. It is an adaptation that enables higher photosynthetic rate than does C3 under high $[O_2]$. With modified leaf anatomy, a 'front-end' fixation of $CO_2$ occurs in the mesophyll cells by the enzyme phosphoenolpyruvate (PEP) carboxylase to form C4 acids after which the system is named. The C4 acids are transported to the specialized chloroplasts of bundle sheath cells that surround the vascular traces. There, $CO_2$ is released from the C4 acids and enters C3 photosynthesis through rubisco and the Benson–Calvin pathway. PEP carboxylase has a high affinity for $CO_2$ so this combination of chemistry and anatomy reduces $C_i$ to 100–150 $\mu l\, l^{-1}$ and concentrates $CO_2$ in the bundle-sheath chloroplasts, thereby enhancing the performance of rubisco. C4 leaves reveal no photorespiration because rubisco is isolated in interior cells and $CO_2$ released internally by photorespiration is readily recycled through PEP carboxylase in mesophyll cells. As a result, they have higher rates of photosynthesis than C3 leaves, especially at high irradiance and high temperature.

**CAM photosynthesis**   CAM, or crassulacean acid metabolism, is named after the family Crassulaceae where it prevails. It occurs only in succulent plants of which few are grown as crops (Table 10.1). CAM photosynthesis is also of recent evolutionary origin and like C4 is an adaptation of C3. The CAM system has the same additional 4-carbon sequence of C4 but not its spatial compartmentation within the leaf. In CAM, separation of the two systems is largely temporal. Under drought conditions, CAM plants maintain open stomates only during the night and $CO_2$ accumulates in C4 organic acids. These are stored in the large aqueous volume of their tissues. During the day with stomates closed, the stored $CO_2$ is released into C3 photosynthesis. Daytime stomatal closure greatly reduces transpiration so that the ratio of $CO_2$ gain to $H_2O$ loss by transpiration over 24 h is much greater than in the C4 or C3 systems. Photosynthetic capacity is limited, however, by the capacity for acid storage.

When water is freely available, many CAM plants, such as pineapple, open stomates during the day and behave chemically as C3 plants. In this way some CAM plants are capable of very high production. For pineapple, this behavior is best expressed in regions with warm days and cool nights where the nocturnal accumulation of $CO_2$ and the daytime C3 system are both active. Under the right conditions, commercial crops of pineapple approach the carbohydrate productivity of C4 sugarcane (Bartholomew 1982). In many CAM plants, such as the cultivated cactus *Opuntia ficus-indica* (Acevedo *et al.* 1983), high production is achieved by consistent rather than high daily productivity. In that case an annual production of 13 t dry matter $ha^{-1}$ was achieved with a canopy cover of 32% and daily production that ranged from only 20 to 70 kg $ha^{-1} d^{-1}$.

**Intermediate photosynthetic types**   Recent surveys have identified plants with structure, enzyme distribution, and photosynthetic behavior intermediate between C3 and C4. Cassava, for example, possesses substantial quantities of the enzyme system of the C4 pathway but without the typical leaf anatomy, and many of its gas exchange characteristics are intermediate between C3 and C4 species (Cock *et al.* 1987). The agriculturally important grass genus *Panicum* contains C3 and C4 as well as intermediate types (Holaday & Black 1981). Further studies of comparative photosynthesis may explain the evolution of C4 and rekindle interest in the possible incorporation of the pathway in C3 crops for situations in which C4 photosynthesis has the productive advantage (see Section 10.5).

## 10.3   LEAF PHOTOSYNTHESIS

The photosynthetic behavior of crops and pastures derives from the responses of individual leaves. Eq. 10.3 identifies the main environmental and physiological influences on the photosynthesis of the component leaves in crop canopies. $C_a$ and leaf resistance ($r'_1$) are explicitly identified. Solar radiation drives the photochemical reduction of $CO_2$ and reduces $C_c$ below $C_a$. Water stress operates initially by increasing $r'_1$ through stomatal closure, but if severe, it also affects carboxylation, increasing $r'_i$ also. Temperature affects $C_i$ through respiration within the normal range and reduces carboxylation (further increases $r'_i$) at extremes.

### Light

Net photosynthesis responds to increasing irradiance ($I$) as presented in Fig. 10.1. At $I=0$, the leaf evolves $CO_2$ by **dark respiration** at the rate $R_d$. At $I=I_c$, the **light compensation point**, $P_n=0$ because photosynthesis exactly balances loss by dark respiration. As $I$ increases above $I_c$, $P_n$ increases rapidly to become **light-saturated** at a maximum net photosynthesis rate of $P_n{}^*$. In this example (Fig. 10.1) $P_n$ becomes light-saturated well below full sunlight, a characteristic of most C3 species. $P_n{}^*$ varies greatly between and within C3 and C4 groups. However, the initial slope ($a$) of the response curve is relatively constant for all plants.

If $R_d$ remains constant as $I$ increases, we can define **gross photosynthesis** ($P_g$) as $P_n + R_d$. That arithmetic maneuver estimates the true photosynthetic rate because it accounts for the simultaneous respiratory efflux that is a part of leaf $CO_2$ exchange. It is, however, only an approximation because it is not certain that $R_d$ continues at the same rate in the light, or what portion of it is recycled when a leaf is illuminated. Note that photorespiration is not included. Ecologically it is simply an unavoidable process that reduces $P_n$ of C3 species in the light.

Observations of the response of $P_g$ to irradiance ($I$) can be fitted to various functional forms, e.g. the rectangular hyperbola:

$$P_g = aP_g^*I/(aI + P_g^*), \qquad\qquad\qquad \text{[Eq. 10.4]}$$

in which $P_g^*$ is the maximum rate at saturating irradiance and $a$ is the maximum radiation-use efficiency. The rectangular hyperbola is useful in describing leaf photosynthetic response to irradiance because it provides a good explanation of experimental data and identifies two important physiological components of the response ($P_g^*$ and $a$). Other equations fit some data better but require additional parameters.

**Radiation-use and quantum efficiency**    The radiation-use efficiency of leaf photosynthesis (RUE = slope $dP_n/dI$ of the response in Fig. 10.1) decreases from its maximum value $a$ with increasing irradiance. The important consequence is that greatest efficiency for foliage canopies occurs when most leaves receive low irradiance and operate near maximum radiation-use efficiency. Canopy architecture (Section 10.5) determines the distribution of irradiance over the photosynthetic surfaces and hence, relative to the leaf photosynthetic response, the possibility for high canopy radiation-use efficiency.

When $I$ is given in PAR units ($\mu mol\ m^{-2}\ s^{-1}$) and corrected for losses due to reflection and transmission, the initial slope is the quantum efficiency of photosynthesis. It provides a basis for comparing the intrinsic efficiency of photosynthetic systems.

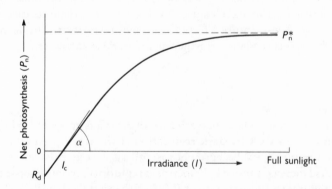

Fig. 10.1. A typical response curve of leaf net photosynthesis ($P_n$) to irradiance ($I$) at ambient $CO_2$ concentration. $R_d$ is dark respiration, $I_c$ light compensation point, $a$ radiation-use efficiency at low light, and $P_n^*$ photosynthesis rate at light saturation (see Eq. 10.4).

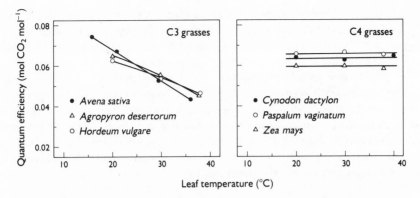

Fig. 10.2. The relationship of quantum efficiency of leaf photosynthesis to temperature for C3 and C4 grasses. Measurements made under normal atmospheric conditions (after Ehleringer & Pearcy (1983).)

In theory, C4 plants have a smaller quantum efficiency than C3 plants because of the additional carboxylation and the membrane transfers of intermediate compounds (Osmond *et al.* 1982). However, photorespiration reduces the quantum yield of C3, depending upon temperature and [$O_2$], so that in the range 20–25 °C and 21% $O_2$, both C3 and C4 have **quantum efficiencies** near 0.06 $CO_2$ per quantum in low light. At lower temperatures, C3 performs best, and at higher temperatures, C4 are generally better. Experimental observations of the quantum efficiency of a range of species (Fig. 10.2) are consistent with these predictions.

**Maximum rates**   Maximum rates of leaf photosynthesis ($P_n^*$) are achieved at high irradiance under optimum conditions of nutrition, water supply, and temperature. Under those conditions, photosynthesis is limited at ambient concentrations, by $CO_2$ diffusion in all species and by $O_2$ diffusion in C3. Maximum rates of C4 plants are generally greater than for C3 plants (Fig. 10.3a). $P_n^*$ values vary widely among species within both groups (e.g. Ludlow & Wilson 1971), however, and they also vary with differences in age and in response to environmental conditions during leaf development and later.

Extensive searches for germplasm with high $P_n^*$ that might contribute to higher yield have not been successful (e.g. Evans *et al.* (1984) for rice). It is easy to find large variations but it seems that most of that is related to development or secondary traits such as stomatal frequency rather than being due to some difference in metabolism. Apparently the basic components of chloroplast systems are highly conservative in a genetic sense. Additional difficulties arise from the remoteness of yield from photosynthesis. As a result of their similar quantum efficiencies in low light, the productivity of C3 and C4 species is generally comparable in low-radiation environments. C4s are markedly more productive at high irradiance, however, because they are less light-saturated.

**Photoinhibition**   Low temperature, salinity, water stress, and acclimation to shade can predispose primary photosynthetic sites to damage by excess light. This damage is known as photoinhibition and is best known from studies of the reaction of shade plants to high irradiance and from plants exposed experimentally to low [$CO_2$] at high light (see Evans *et al.* 1988). The damage is associated with the dissipation of excitation energy not consumed in carbon reduction and may show its effect as a decline in either quantum efficiency or $P_n{}^*$.

The importance of photoinhibition to the productivity of crop plants is unknown, although it seems unlikely that they have not evolved to resist it. The stresses that cause photoinhibition, for example low temperatures and severe water deficit, also affect photosynthesis directly. Ludlow & Powles (1988) have recorded photoinhibition induced by water stress in grain sorghum. They concluded, however, that its additional effect to the severe water stress that induced it is unlikely to have any agronomic significance.

## CO₂ supply

$P_n$ responds to [$CO_2$] over a wide range that covers present and likely future variations in atmospheric composition. Fig. 10.3*b* compares $P_n{}^*$ over a range of [$CO_2$] from 0 to 600 $\mu l\, l^{-1}$ with saturating light. Here $P_n{}^*$ responds linearly to [$CO_2$]. $P_n{}^*$ of C4 leaves is positive down to around 5 $\mu l\, l^{-1}$ $CO_2$ but C3 leaves leak $CO_2$ ($P_n$ is negative) in air with less than about 50–100 $\mu l\, l^{-1}$ $CO_2$. The [$CO_2$] at which $P_n = 0$ is called the **CO₂ compensation point**.

Equation 10.4 can be used to represent the response of $P_g$ to [$CO_2$] over the range of *I* up to saturation by setting $P_g{}^* = (C_a - C_i)/\Sigma r'$ where $\Sigma r'\, (= r'_b + r'_1 + r'_i)$ is the total resistance of the $CO_2$ pathway from the bulk air to the sites of fixation in the chloroplasts. The linear relationship will hold provided there are no other responses to [$CO_2$] but it is known that, in some species, stomata respond to [$CO_2$] with the effect of maintaining a constant value of $C_i$. That was observed with maize whereas in sunflower, $\Sigma r'$ remained constant and $C_i$ varied proportionately with $C_a$ (de Wit *et al.* 1978).

## Temperature

Leaves vary widely in their photosynthetic response to temperature. In general, C4 species perform well in warm climates and are tolerant of high temperature (Fig. 10.3*c*). Few C4 species perform well at low temperature and most suffer irreversible damage to membranes (**chilling injury**) at temperature around 10–12 °C. Many C3 plants such as cotton and sunflower perform well at high temperature (30–40 °C) and some warm-climate C3s (e.g. banana) are sensitive to chilling. Most C3 leaves, however, can withstand temperatures down to 0 °C.

The generally broad optimum of the photosynthetic response to temperature contrasts with the narrower response of growth found with most species. This emphasises the importance of other factors that control photosynthetic gain and utilization of assimilate. The relationship between photosynthesis and temperature gives C4 the productive advantage at temperatures above about 25 °C. This is consistent with the observed relationship between quantum efficiency and temperature (Fig. 10.2) and the maximum production rates of C3 and C4 crops (Table 2.2).

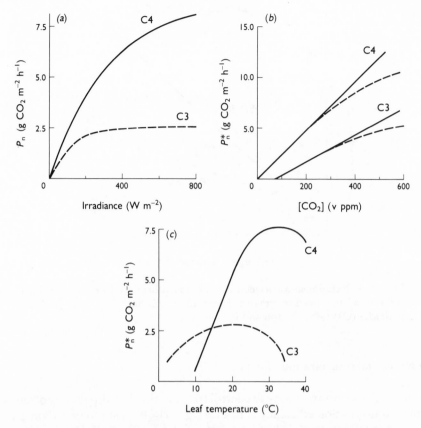

Fig. 10.3. Comparative response of leaf photosynthesis of C3 and C4 species to (*a*) irradiance at ambient [$CO_2$] and optimum temperature, (*b*) [$CO_2$] at high irradiance, and (*c*) temperature at high irradiance and ambient [$CO_2$]. Arrows in (*b*) indicate stomatal closure. (After de Wit *et al.* (1978).)

### Nitrogen

C4 leaves generally have smaller nitrogen content than C3 leaves because PEP carboxylase is a smaller molecule than rubisco and contains less nitrogen. In C3s, rubisco accounts for around 25% of leaf nitrogen. As a result, C4 plants have greater photosynthesis per unit leaf nitrogen and also develop more operational leaf area per unit nitrogen supply than C3 plants (Fig. 10.4).

Legumes characteristically have large nitrogen concentrations in reproductive and vegetative parts. For this reason their seeds are valuable food for humans, poultry and swine and their biomass is valuable fodder for grazing animals. In contrast, the low nitrogen content of C4 grasses is an important reason why they are lower-quality fodder for grazing animals than are C3 grasses. C4 grasses also have higher contents of indigestible lignin because a greater proportion of their leaf anatomy is given to vascular traces.

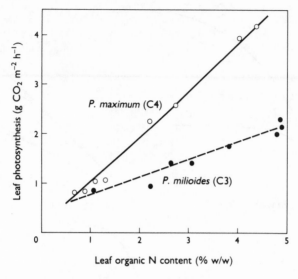

Fig. 10.4. Relationship between leaf photosynthesis and organic nitrogen content of the pasture grasses *Panicum maximum* (C4) and *Panicum milioides* (C3) (after Bolton and Brown 1980).

## Stomates and transpiration efficiency

Stomates give plants the ability to control transpiration but also the opportunity to control **transpiration efficiency** (TE, g $CO_2$ g$^{-1}$ $H_2O$), the ratio of carbon gain by photosynthesis to water loss by transpiration (Chapter 9). Combining equations for leaf transpiration (Eq. 9.6) and the complete photosynthesis pathway photosynthesis (Eq. 10.3):

$$TE = (C_a - C_c)(r_b + r_l)/[(e^* - e_a)(1.6(r_b + r_l) + r_i')].$$  [Eq. 10.5]

The equation shows that the effect of stomatal closure (increasing $r_l$) depends upon the magnitude of $r_b$ and $r_i'$. The $r_b$ is very small except in still air and in C3 species $r_i'$ is a significant proportion of the total resistance pathway for $CO_2$. An increase in $r_l$ through stomatal closure has a larger effect on the numerator (resistance to water loss) than on the denominator (resistance to $CO_2$ uptake). As a consequence, TE increases when the rates of photosynthesis and transpiration are restricted by stomatal closure.

Evaporation demand and photosynthetic potential vary diurnally and from day to day. Restricting attention to stomatal response, if a leaf is to maximize TE, then optimization theory requires that leaf resistance vary with environmental conditions such that the additional gain of $CO_2$ for each extra unit of water lost maintains a constant maximal value (Cowan 1982). To achieve this, a leaf must have feed-forward stomatal response such as is provided by the response to humidity that has been demonstrated for some species (see Schulze 1986).

The same argument can be extended from individual leaves to crop canopies to

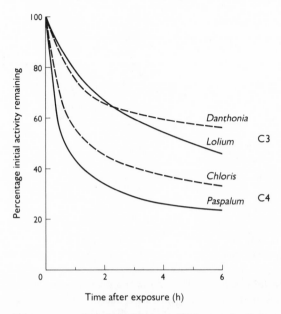

**Fig. 10.6. Time course of loss of radioactivity during the light at 25 °C from leaves of C3 and C4 grasses previously exposed to $^{14}CO_2$ (after Lush & Evans (1974).)**

than is photosynthesis. Eventually, as storage sites are filled, photosynthesis declines, and this has been interpreted as end-product (feedback) inhibition (Neales & Incoll 1968).

The observations of Evans & Dunstone (1970) on the 50% decline in $P_n^*$ of wheat along an evolutionary series towards cultivated wheats may have involved feedback inhibition. The plants were grown in pots (side lighting) and well supplied with nitrogen and water (no leaf senescence). The modern wheats, with limited tillering ability and short stature, may have been sink-limited relative to the primitive wild-type wheats having vigorous vegetative growth. Sink limitations are much less likely with closely spaced plants under field conditions.

Feedback control could occur in several ways. Though chemically isolated, chloroplast starch can slow photosynthesis by interfering with the penetration of light and $CO_2$ to the active sites and, when in large amounts, by physically distorting chloroplast membranes. Recent studies suggest that high levels of sugars in leaves sequester a large part of the inorganic phosphorus in hexose phosphates and that the unavailability of phosphorus slows photosynthesis (Foyer 1988).

Translocation of assimilates from leaves is mainly as sucrose and depends on the activity of bundle sheath cells surrounding vascular traces which serve in loading assimilates into phloem. The concentration of chloroplasts in the bundle sheaths of C4 species in close proximity to the phloem may confer an advantage by reducing the possibility of end-product inhibition. Experiments with a range of pasture species have shown that translocation rate of assimilate may be greater from C4 leaves than from C3. This is shown in Figure 10.6, which illustrates the persistence of the radioactive label $^{14}C$ introduced into leaf photosynthesis early in the

Table 10.2 *Comparison between C3 and C4 photosynthesis*

| | C3 | C4 |
|---|---|---|
| *Leaf photosynthesis* | | |
| Max. rate (g $CO_2$ m$^{-2}$ h$^{-1}$) | 1.5–4.5 | > 3.5 |
| PAR for saturation | low to mod. | v. high |
| Temperature optimum | low to high | high |
| Max. leaf conductance | similar | |
| Mesophyll conductance | low | high |
| $CO_2$ compensation point (vppm) | 50–100 | < 5 |
| $CO_2$ evolution in light | high | none |
| Transpiration efficiency | low | high |
| Nitrogen use efficiency | low | high |
| *Canopy photosynthesis* | | |
| Max. rate (g $CO_2$ m$^{-2}$ h$^{-1}$) | 3.5–9 | 5–10 |

photoperiod. The label is lost more rapidly from C4 leaves. Greater translocation is one explanation, but there are complicating factors. C3s have greater respiration than C4s in the light (photorespiration) and this could account for some of the difference. Equally it may reflect different patterns of storage and export of assimilate. To be an effective marker, a label must mix freely in the assimilate pool so that its dilution defines input–output balance. If, for example, it became embedded in the inner layers of starch granules it could no longer serve this purpose. Diurnally, the residence time of assimilate in leaves does display such 'first in' – 'last out' dynamics.

## Comparison of C3 and C4 photosynthesis

Various attributes of C3 and C4 photosynthesis are summarized in Table 10.2. Their comparison raises a number of important evolutionary and ecological questions.

One important ecological difference between the two groups is that the enzyme systems of the C4 group are poorly adapted to temperatures below 10 °C whereas C3 systems maintain function to near 0 °C. As a result, C3 species are widely distributed while C4s are in general restricted to warm climates. Further, because the dominant group of C4s are grasses, the major distribution of C4 is in tropical and semitropical grasslands. However, many C3s can also be productive at high temperatures, a fact attested to by the productivity of C3 crops such as cotton in hot climates. That arises because the adaptation to temperature among C3s is wide. It is easy to find examples of distinct temperature optima between C3 and C4 species in the literature but proper comparisons of the effect of temperature on C3 versus C4 photosynthesis will compare plants of similar temperature adaptation.

The second major difference between the two groups occurs in their response to

$O_2$. In the absence of $O_2$, they perform similarly, but with ambient (21%) $O_2$, $P_n$ of C3 plants is depressed by photorespiration. It may be that C3 photosynthesis represents an adaptation to the Carboniferous Period when terrestrial plants evolved and $[CO_2]$ was high and $[O_2]$ was low. Unless photorespiration is found to have an important beneficial function, the ecological conclusion is that the high $[O_2]$ of Earth's atmosphere is detrimental to C3 species. C4s are clearly better suited to atmospheres low in $CO_2$.

Alternatively, C4 photosynthesis may be an adaptation to low nitrogen availability (Brown 1978). The difference in leaf nitrogen content between C3s and C4s is striking as is the fact that the large and varied plant family Leguminosae, which fixes nitrogen symbiotically, has no C4 members.

The superior performance of C4 raises the important possibility that the trait could be found or introduced into the germplasm of C3 plants. If C3 and C4 plants are grown together in a confined space, $[CO_2]$ quickly falls below the $CO_2$ compensation point of C3. C4 plants then maintain positive $P_n$ at the expense of C3 plants, which gradually respire themselves away. This technique was used to screen the world collections of several C3 crop plants for the presence of C4 photosynthesis (Menz *et al.* 1969). Neither that nor hybridization of C3 and C4 species within the same genera, e.g. *Atriplex* (Björkman *et al.* 1969), have been successful. That is not surprising considering that the extensive differences in biochemistry and anatomy between C3 and C4 are the expression of many genes.

## 10.4   CANOPY PHOTOSYNTHESIS

Crop canopies have more complex photosynthetic responses than their component leaves because they interact within the canopy as interceptors of light and absorbers of $CO_2$. Despite this complexity, a useful parallel can be drawn between the photosynthesis of crop surfaces and of single leaves. Thus by analogy to Eq. 10.3:

$$P_n \text{ (crop)} = (C_a - C_l)/r'_a = (C_l - C_i)/r'_c, \qquad \text{[Eq. 10.6]}$$

where $P_n$ (crop) is the flux of $CO_2$ into the canopy (net photosynthesis). $C_a$ and $C_l$ are $[CO_2]$ of the bulk air and at the effective crop surface, respectively; $r'_a$ is the aerodynamic resistance to $CO_2$ transfer from the bulk air to that surface ($= 1.6r_a$, the aerodynamic resistance to $H_2O$ transfer; see Eq. 9.9). $C_i$ is $[CO_2]$ in the substomatal cavities of the leaves, and $r'_c$ is the canopy resistance comprising all leaves acting in parallel. It can be related to the diffusive resistance of the canopy water vapor $(r_c)$ as $r'_c = 1.6 \, r_c$.

In dense crops of high photosynthetic rate, $C_l$ can fall to $250 \, \mu l \, l^{-1}$, or nearly $100 \, \mu l \, l^{-1}$ below $C_a$ on windless days with little atmospheric mixing (Fig. 6.12). Under those conditions, $[CO_2]$ in the crop canopy strongly restricts leaf photosynthesis. In contrast, for sparse canopies and windy conditions, depletion of $CO_2$ is much less.

Techniques are available to study the role of more detailed characteristics of canopy architecture in crop photosynthetic responses. These are discussed in Section 10.5.

## Measurement

Crop photosynthesis is most easily measured in transparent **field chambers**, but **aerodynamic techniques** (Chapter 6) are also available to measure uptake from the $[CO_2]$ gradients that photosynthesis establishes over crops. Such measurements are useful in linking crop productivity with the photosynthetic responses of individual leaves. Short-term measurements can be used in the analyses of community architecture and in studies of the effect of changes in leaf photosynthetic characteristics and environmental factors on canopy performance. Longer-term measurements maintained for hours or days assist in the interpretation of crop growth by estimating the total assimilation from which new biomass is constructed.

**Field assimilation chambers**    Three types of portable, transparent field assimilation chambers that enclose segments of crops, commonly 1–3 $m^2$ in area, are used in measurements of crop photosynthesis. In **closed systems**, crop photosynthesis is determined from the rate of depletion of $CO_2$ in the known volume of the chamber. To provide continuous measurements, such chambers are sequentially opened and closed. In **open systems**, air flows continuously through the chamber fast enough to maintain $[CO_2]$ close to ambient but slowly enough to provide a measurable $[CO_2]$ depletion between inlet and outlet air. The rate of $CO_2$ exchange is the product of air flow through the chamber and the drop in $[CO_2]$ across it. In **closed-compensating systems**, chamber $[CO_2]$ is maintained at the ambient level by injecting $CO_2$, or $CO_2$-enriched air, to balance uptake by photosynthesis. The rate of injection measures crop photosynthesis rate.

It is possible to offset the inevitable heating in open and closed-compensating systems and to operate all chambers with $[CO_2]$ and humidity close to ambient levels. All versions of the chamber technique require forced mixing of the air inside the chamber so that uptake can be measured accurately. The mixing decreases the aerodynamic resistance ($r_c'$) of the canopy (Eq. 10.6) and so may increase canopy photosynthesis above that occurring in open fields.

## Seasonal photosynthesis of wheat crops

The data in Fig. 10.7 record the daily (24 h) net $CO_2$ gain of three wheat crops made with field chambers on many individual days beginning 110 days after sowing (DAS) when the crops were tillering. The three crops had different patterns of water supply. R was rainfed, W1 was irrigated weekly, and W2, biweekly. The upper curve defines the seasonal assimilation pattern of W1. In this crop, daily assimilation rose to around 75 g $CO_2$ $m^{-2}$ $d^{-1}$ at flowering and then declined to zero at maturity (185 DAS) as crop leaf area senesced. This crop showed no evidence of transient water shortage between irrigations. The measurements for W2 define the effect of drying cycles between irrigation. From 140 DAS, photosynthesis of W2 decreased with the establishment of water shortage during the second week after

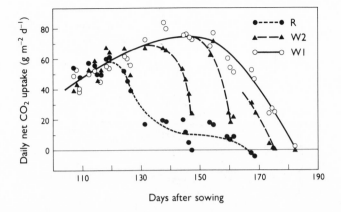

Fig. 10.7. Daily (24 h) net $CO_2$ uptake of wheat crops in response to three conditions of water supply: R, rainfed; W2, irrigated at 2-weekly intervals; and W1, irrigated weekly (D. M. Whitfield, in press.)

each irrigation. Comparison of those crops with W1, however, show that they recovered fully after irrigation. The rainfed crop had significantly depleted soil moisture by 120 DAS and thereafter assimilation fell rapidly until photosynthesis ceased at 170 DAS.

## Comparative photosynthesis of C3 and C4 crops

The photosynthetic responses to irradiance for a range of full-cover crops are presented in Fig. 10.8. The data were assembled from field-chamber measurements by a small group of workers. Each is a diurnal response to ambient irradiance under optimum conditions of water and nutrients. The temperature regimes varied from crop to crop but were within the optimal range for each species. Comparison of these data with many other responses available in the literature indicates that the maximum rates are medium to high responses for each of the crops considered.

The responses cover a range from strongly asymptotic to quasi-linear. In the case of crops, as opposed to individual leaves, linear responses of photosynthesis to full sunlight are not restricted to C4 species. In these data, wheat, sunflower, and alfalfa crops also display strongly linear responses. Such responses are achieved when there is little light saturation of individual leaves in the canopies. Maize, and to a lesser extent sunflower, can achieve this independently of canopy structure by virtue of leaf responses that do not saturate to full sunlight (cf. Fig. 10.3 for C3 versus C4 comparison). In contrast, wheat and alfalfa rely upon high leaf angles, and in the case of alfalfa, small leaves also, to distribute light evenly at low irradiance over the leaf surfaces. Strongly asymptotic responses are typical of C3 species with leaves that saturate at low irradiance and are displayed in canopies of low leaf angle (here tobacco, bean, and potato). In those cases, a significant proportion of the upper canopy is light saturated.

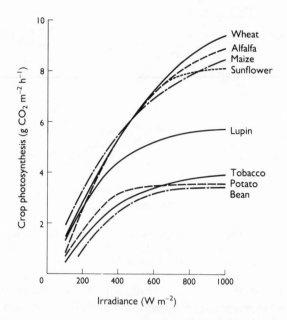

**Fig. 10.8.  Response of crop photosynthesis to irradiance in full-cover C3 and C4 crops well supplied with water and nutrients. All measurements made with field assimilation chambers. (Data from Connor *et al.* (1985b), Sale (1974, 1975, 1977), Whitfield *et al.* (1980, 1986) and D. M. Whitfield, unpublished.)**

### Radiation-use efficiency

The photosynthetic rates of crops depend on the quantity of radiation they intercept and on the efficiency achieved in utilization. Thus radiation-use efficiency (RUE) can be defined relative to incident or intercepted radiation, two values that converge as crops achieve full cover. To provide a general analysis, crop cover can be approximated across all LAI ($L$) by the expression:

$$\text{Cover} = 1 - \text{gap} = 1 - e^{-kL},\qquad\qquad\text{[Eq. 10.7]}$$

derived from the Bouguer–Lambert analysis (Eq. 2.4) of radiation interception by canopies with randomly oriented and randomly dispersed foliage. Variable $k$ is the extinction coefficient relating leaf angle to the ability of unit leaf area to intercept radiation.

The equation is readily extended to describe canopy photosynthesis in terms of RUE ($\epsilon$) of intercepted radiation as:

$$P_g = \epsilon I_o\,(1 - e^{-kL})\qquad\qquad\text{[Eq. 10.8]}$$

in which $I_o$ is incident irradiance so that $I_o\,(1 - e^{-kL})$ is interception. If radiation were distributed over the canopy at low intensity, $\epsilon$ would approximate the maximum RUE established from leaf photosynthesis–irradiance response as presented in Fig. 10.1 and Eq. 10.4.

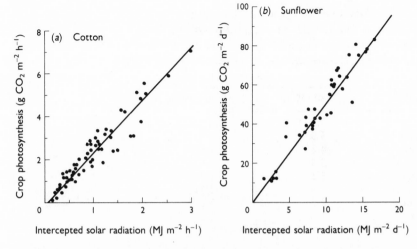

**Fig. 10.9. Relationships between crop net photosynthesis and canopy inter-ception in (*a*) cotton (after Baker & Meyer (1966)), and (*b*) sunflower crops (after Connor *et al.* (1985*b*).)**

Observation has shown that canopy photosynthesis is often closely related to intercepted radiation in this way. Fig. 10.9 illustrates this for cotton and sunflower crops of a range of canopy cover. In these data, RUE from instantaneous photosynthesis measurements on cotton is $2.3\,g\,CO_2\,MJ^{-1}$. For sunflower, it is $5.3\,g$ $CO_2\,MJ^{-1}$ for daily totals. The two values are not strictly comparable because they were made by different techniques over different timescales. However, the larger value for sunflower does reflects the unusually large leaf photosynthetic rate of that C3 species.

Comparisons of RUE for eight crop species are presented in Table 10.3. They were derived from the crop photosynthetic responses of full cover crops presented in Fig. 10.8. Values range from 1.2 to $4.2\,g\,CO_2\,MJ^{-1}$ with generally higher values at low ($330\,W\,m^{-2}$) than at high ($800\,W\,m^{-2}$) irradiance, reflecting progressive light saturation of component leaves at high irradiance. This effect is greatest in crops that have horizontal leaves and leaf photosynthetic responses that saturate at low irradiance, e.g. tobacco and potato.

## 10.5 MODELING CANOPY PHOTOSYNTHESIS

Much of the variation in radiation-use efficiency measured for entire crops can be laid to complex canopy geometry. At first inspection, canopies of leaves may seem hopelessly complex, but their geometry can be described in relatively simple ways and the consequent photosynthetic behavior can be explained through mathematical analyses. This section introduces two approaches that explain the nature and use of models of canopy photosynthesis.

Table 10.3 *Radiation-use efficiencies of canopy photosynthesis (g $CO_2$ $MJ^{-1}$ intercepted shortwave radiation) for the crop responses presented in Fig. 10.9*

| Crop | Efficiency at | |
|---|---|---|
| | 300 W $m^{-2}$ | 800 W $m^{-2}$ |
| Wheat | 3.2 | 3.1 |
| Alfalfa | 3.3 | 2.8 |
| Maize | 4.2 | 2.8 |
| Sunflower | 3.3 | 2.7 |
| Lupin | 3.2 | 1.9 |
| Tobacco | 1.9 | 1.3 |
| Potato | 2.7 | 1.2 |
| Bean | 1.9 | 1.2 |

## Exponential extinction model

Davidson & Phillip (1958) pioneered this approach by combining the exponential extinction profile (Monsi & Saeki 1953) for the penetration of radiation into canopies (Eq. 2.4) with the photosynthesis response of individual leaves to irradiance (Eq. 10.4). Thornley (1976) and Johnson & Thornley (1984) provide more recent discussion on this approach and its utility. The combination of those leaf and light profile characteristics allows calculation of the gross photosynthesis of component leaf layers and of entire canopies. Calculation of net photosynthesis requires additional information on respiration. The simplest case occurs when all leaves have the same dark respiration ($R_d$) regardless of depth in the canopy. This is included in the detail of the method presented in Box 10.1.

The model can be used to investigate the vertical profile of photosynthesis within the canopy in response to incident irradiance, canopy structure and leaf photosynthetic response. It shows that the productive structure of canopies of large LAI can be divided conceptually into two parts, the upper layers where $P_g > R_d$, and the lower layers where $P_g \leq R_d$ (Fig. 10.10). The point of division is the leaf layer in the canopy that is at light compensation point. Davidson & Phillip (1958) made such a division and described a 'productive' upper canopy in which photosynthesis exceeds respiration and a 'parasitic' lower canopy in which respiration exceeds photosynthesis. They were attracted to this proposal by observations of D. J. Watson with kale at the Rothamsted Experiment Station (see Watson 1952) showing that CGR decreased at high LAI to give an optimum response, and they sought an explanation for that behavior in their model.

Measurements of crop photosynthesis have also shown that respiration determines the shape of the response between $P_n$ (crop) and LAI, but not as Davidson & Phillip expected. Ludwig & Saeki (unpublished; see Loomis *et al.* 1967) constructed cotton communities in controlled environments by packing individual plants grown in widely spaced pots into a range of densities to produce 'crops' of varying LAI. Hourly measurements of photosynthesis (Fig. 10.11) showed that the crop

Box 10.1 A *model of crop photosynthesis constructed by combining the exponential extinction profile of light penetration into a canopy with a leaf photosynthesis–light response function*

## PHOTOSYNTHESIS OF INDIVIDUAL LAYERS

At depth $L$ in the canopy (LAI units from top), the mean irradiance of the downward flux on a horizontal sensor is $I_o e^{-kL}$ falling at depth $(L + \Delta L)$ to $I_o e^{-k(L + \Delta L)}$. The difference is the mean irradiance absorbed by the layer $\Delta L$ and is $kI_o e^{-kL}$, so the irradiance incident on the leaves is $kI_o e^{-kL}/(1 - m)$, where $m$ is the leaf transmission coefficient (Saeki 1963). There is also an upward flux, which can be reasonably related to the downward flux by the leaf reflection coefficient ($\phi$) (Thornley 1976) to estimate the mean irradiance additively incident on both surfaces of leaves in the layer as $(1 + \phi) kI_o e^{-kL}/(1 - m)$. The mean net photosynthesis per unit leaf area ($P_n(l)$) of this increment of leaf area at depth $L$ can be obtained by substitution in Eq. 10.4 to give:

$$P_n(l) = (P_g{}^* a k \beta I_o e^{-kL})/(a k \beta I_o e^{-kL} + P_g{}^*) - R_d, \qquad \text{[Eq. 10.9]}$$

where $\beta = (1 + \phi)/(1 - m)$ will typically have a value of 1.2 since $m = \phi = 0.1$ for radiation incident on most leaves. The omission of this term will not have a serious effect on the performance of the model since its effect can be taken up in $k$.

## PHOTOSYNTHESIS OF A CANOPY

The photosynthesis of the entire canopy per unit ground area ($P_n(crop)$) is the sum of component layers. In this model, summation can be made by analytical integration of Eq. 10.9 over all leaf area $L$ to give:

$$P_n(crop) = P_g{}^* \ln[\{akI_o + \beta P_g{}^*)/(akI_o e^{-kL} + \beta P_g{}^*)]/k - LR_d. \qquad \text{[Eq. 10.10]}$$

This equation describes crop photosynthesis in response to environment ($I_o$), canopy structure (LAI, $k$, $m$, $\phi$), and leaf $CO_2$ exchange ($P_g^*$, $a$, $R_d$). Even simple models like this that combine few essential non-linear functions can describe the major responses of complex systems.

Further detail and examples of application can be obtained from Davidson & Phillip (1958) and Johnson & Thornley (1984).

response adjusted rapidly after packing. Initially it had an optimum response as predicted by Watson because $R_d$ was proportional to LAI, but in less than 3 d the response was asymptotic with LAI. Measurements showed that this was due to a rapid decline in crop respiration per unit LAI as lower, shaded leaves adjusted to their smaller supply of photosynthate with smaller rates of respiration.

It seems that the optimal responses of crop photosynthesis to LAI that have been recorded are either experimental artifacts or are short-term responses that would

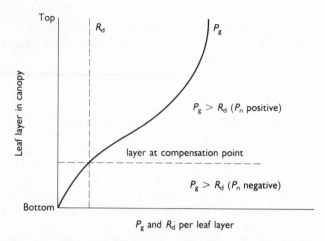

Fig. 10.10. **Vertical distribution of gross photosynthesis ($P_g$) and dark respiration ($R_d$) in a canopy according to the model of Davidson & Philip (1958).**

not persist in the field. Plant physiological observations support this conclusion. One cause of respiration, the biosynthesis of new organic compounds, for example, depends on substrate supply (Chapter 11). There is no evidence that mature leaves import assimilate and that those low in the canopy could continue in biosynthesis as parasitic organs in the sense introduced by Davidson & Phillip (1958).

The model explains the importance of canopy architecture and leaf response to canopy photosynthesis. Canopies with horizontal leaves (large $k$) receive high irradiance on the top leaves, which, with small $P_g{}^*$ (because $a$ is relatively constant), are increasingly light-saturated. Canopies with erectly displayed leaves (small $k$) have more even distribution of low irradiance over their leaf surfaces (Cosine Law) and hence have less light saturation and higher photosynthesis per unit of intercepted radiation at any value of $P_g{}^*$.

If the light response of the component leaves were linear, there would be no light saturation within the canopy and so at full cover, canopy structure would have no significance to $P_n$ (crop). That condition was assumed in the simple model of potential productivity presented in Table 2.1. Crops of C4 grasses approach this condition more closely than the best C3 crops (Connor & Cartledge 1970).

### Geometrical models

The analytical expression for crop net photosynthesis (Eq. 10.10) cannot be formed when structure, photosynthesis and respiration are not the same for each component layer in the canopy. For those conditions, layer-by-layer numerical solutions can be made to investigate biologically more complex situations. Even so, such simple exponential extinction models of light distribution have three limitations. First, they apply easily only to crops that are horizontally homogeneous and so are

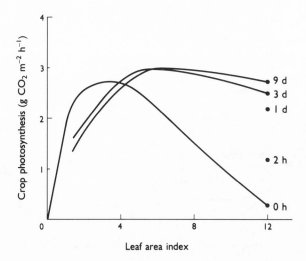

**Fig. 10.11. Acclimation of space-grown cotton plants to crowding in a phytotron experiment. The 0 h curve was measured when the plants were first packed together as a 'crop'. The other curves present successive measurements at the specified times after packing (from L. J. Ludwig & T. Saeki, unpublished.)**

inappropriate for many row crops, orchards, or intercrops. Second, proper calculation of radiation distribution within the canopy requires a different value of $k$ at least hourly as the sun tracks across the sky. Third, the model predicts only mean irradiance that leaves receive and not the distribution of sunflecks and diffuse light. Since the photosynthesis of many leaves saturates at relatively low irradiance, the use of mean irradiance overestimates their photosynthesis in canopies.

The nature of the more complex geometrical models is depicted in Fig. 10.12. This shows two aspects of the interaction between leaf angle and solar altitude on the penetration and irradiation of foliage by the direct solar beam. Fig. 10.12a shows the relationship between $k$ and solar altitude for horizontally continuous canopies in which leaves are inclined at a range of angles to the horizontal and are randomly dispersed and oriented. Fig. 10.12b shows how the incident radiation can be spread over larger leaf area, to a maximum sunlit LAI of near four, as leaf angle and solar altitude increase. With leaves arranged obliquely to the sun's rays, the sunlit leaf area index increases and their mean irradiance declines.

The relationships in Fig. 10.12a deal with the direct solar beam but can be extended to diffuse radiation, which originates from many point sources over the sky. Using the underlying equations (Hanau in Duncan *et al.* 1967), photosynthesis of crops irradiated in complex patterns of light and shade by direct and diffuse radiation can be calculated as the sun tracks across the sky (Eq. 6.6). The calculations can be made for classes of foliage, profile layers, or for entire canopies. The multitude of calculations is readily made by fast computers, but in practice, it is also possible to calculate a set of general solutions from which the behavior of

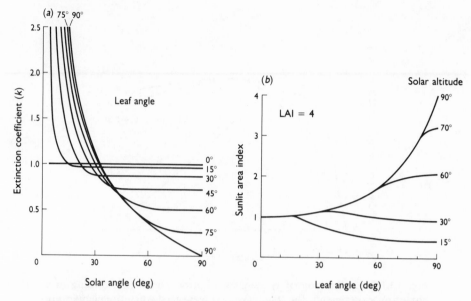

**Fig. 10.12. Components of geometrical models of canopy photosynthesis.**
(*a*) The relation of extinction coefficient (*k*) to solar altitude and leaf angle;
(*b*) sunlit area index of a canopy of LAI = 4 in relation to leaf angle and solar
altitude. (After Warren Wilson (1967).)

particular structure–irradiance–leaf response combinations can be estimated by
interpolation.

Fig. 10.13 presents examples of simulations of canopy photosynthesis of maize.
As leaf angle increases, more foliage can be irradiated and the lower irradiance over
the foliage leads to higher radiation-use efficiency. At low leaf angle, increases in LAI
do not lead to more photosynthesis because most radiation is intercepted by the
upper leaves, which are generally light-saturated.

## 10.6   CANOPY STRUCTURE FOR PRODUCTIVITY AND COMPETITIVENESS

The display of leaves in crop canopies is determined by planting density, planting
pattern, and morphological characteristics of the component species. Two aspects
of canopy display dominate the productivity and persistence of a species. The first is
the rapid attainment of optimum cover for the environment. The second is the
advantage that height confers on competitive ability in mixed communities.

### Canopy dynamics

The development of foliage canopies involves a number of overlapping stages
related to crop phenology (Chapter 5). The first is the initiation of new leaf

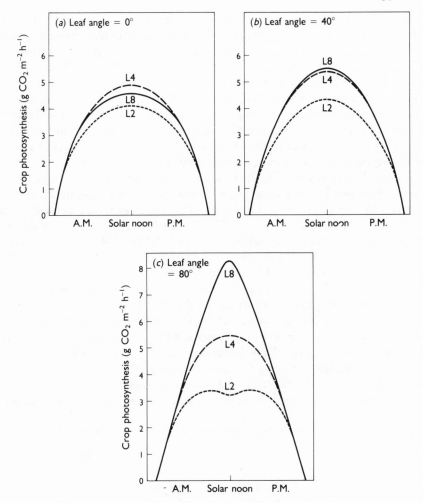

**Fig. 10.13.** Computed hourly net photosynthesis of crop canopies of LAI equal to 2, 4, or 8 in response to leaf angle: (*a*) all leaves horizontal; (*b*) all leaves at 40° (*c*) all leaves at 80° (near vertical. (After Duncan *et al.* (1967).)

primordia at vegetative apices. The second is the expansion of leaves to take their place as the youngest, generally best located, and most productive in the canopy. The third and last stage is senescence, which is characterized by a gradual loss in assimilatory activity and mobilization of cell contents to other sites. That process sometimes ends with leaf abcission.

Full cover is achieved most rapidly when population density is high, when the seedlings partition a significant proportion of new assimilate to leaf development, specific leaf mass is small, and leaf angle is low. The interception of radiation and early productivity are then maximum and the crop is also able to shade out shorter weed competitors.

Highly productive canopies have the characteristics of full cover and erect leaves, at least at the top of the canopy. The best design, however, depends upon the radiation environment and aspects of the photosynthesis and respiratory responses of the leaves. In a simple case with all leaves with the same photosynthesis and respiration-response functions, maximum crop photosynthesis will be achieved when all leaves receive the same low light flux at the level where radiation-use efficiency is greatest. This would require an extinction coefficient ($k$) that changes continuously with depth in the canopy. If the response functions vary with depth, or if plant morphology restricts leaf display, then the best achievable design will be different. Simulations of crop photosynthesis have shown themselves to be an effective way to investigate questions of canopy design.

The examples presented in Fig. 10.14 summarize several important points about canopy architecture by comparing the photosynthesis of maize (C4) and clover (C3) canopies over a range of LAI and leaf angle. The responses were generated by the simulation model of Duncan *et al.* (1967). With LAI < 2, canopies of horizontal leaves are the most productive. With intermediate LAI of 2–4, leaf angle has little influence on productivity, but increases in LAI beyond 4, given erect leaves so that the available radiation is spread over more leaf area, lead to progressively greater assimilation. The high productivity of maize arises from its C4 traits: high unit leaf rate and limited saturation at high irradiance (Fig. 10.2).

Leaves that have become acclimated to low irradiance, but have not yet begun to senesce, may be able to respond to management that places them once again in a high-irradiance environment. Thus the productivity of a canopy following removal of some of its leaf area (pruning, harvesting, grazing, or insect or disease attack) depends upon which leaf area is removed because that determines what productive structure remains. The design of improved management strategies for canopies

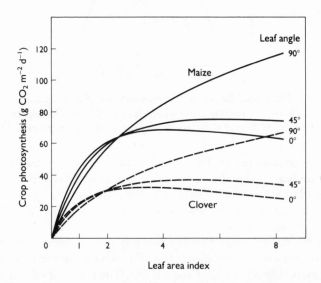

Fig. 10.14. Simulations of daily crop photosynthesis for maize and clover communities of various LAI and leaf angle combinations. Solar and skylight data are for lat. 38° N on July 1 (after Loomis & Williams (1969).)

requires an understanding of the dynamics of leaf formation, expansion and longevity.

## Nitrogen distribution for maximum canopy photosynthesis

Large amounts of nitrogen are required in the construction of dense canopies, especially of C3 species (Chapter 2). Canopies receive diminishing photosynthetic gains for each increment of leaf area above full cover and, without internal redistribution, the additional nitrogen required is considerable. C3s such as sugarbeet and wheat contain about 12 kg N ha$^{-1}$ leaf (SLM = 40 g m$^{-2}$ with 30 g N kg$^{-1}$). Legume leaves generally have greater [N], ranging from 30 to 50 g kg$^{-1}$ DM. Even in the C4 maize, where much less nitrogen is needed for maximum photosynthesis rate, there is around 10 kg N ha$^{-1}$ per unit LAI (SLM = 50 g m$^{-2}$ with 20 g N kg$^{-1}$).

When nitrogen is in short supply, crop photosynthesis may be limited by both leaf area and leaf capacity for photosynthesis. Given leaf photosynthetic response functions to irradiance and [N] of the form presented in Figs. 10.2 and 10.4, the question arises how, given some amount of leaf area and nitrogen, an additional unit of nitrogen should be distributed between growing new leaves or increasing the nitrogen content of existing leaves? The optimum solution, that will maximize photosynthesis per unit nitrogen in the total canopy (one definition of nitrogen-use efficiency, NUE), depends upon N supply, canopy architecture, solar track, leaf longevity and other factors.

Hirose & Werger (1987) compared the distribution of leaf [N] through a canopy of *Solidago* sp. with the optimum distribution simulated with a canopy photosynthesis model comparable to that presented in Section 10.5. They concluded that the observed distribution of leaf [N] provided a 20% greater canopy photosynthesis than would occur with a uniform distribution, but that it was 4.7% less efficient than the optimal distribution in which leaf [N] decreased exponentially with depth in the canopy.

## Maximum yield at less than maximum assimilation

In many crops, maximum yield or quality are obtained with less than maximum canopy photosynthesis. In the case of total biomass, this occurs because the last unit of photosynthetic gain does not return the investment in leaf area and associated stem. However, there are issues in crop production other than maximum biomass. For example, high irradiance is frequently required low in the canopy for growth or color development of particular organs for harvest. Canopies that allow this usually have incomplete capture of radiation and hence assimilation is less than maximum. In the production of Virginia tobacco, for example, the leaves contributing most to high yield and quality are those below the midpoint of the stem. Yield is determined by leaf size and quality by a high carbohydrate content. Maturing tobacco leaves are disposed to accumulate carbohydrate because the important 'sinks' are removed, flowers by 'topping' and adventitious 'suckers' by hand or chemical suppressants. Leaves low in the canopy cannot accumulate carbohydrates, however, if their photosynthetic activity is low, so the crop is grown in widely spaced rows to allow penetration of light to the lower leaves. Canopy interception is incomplete and biomass production is less than maximum, but economic yield is maximized.

The same principle can be seen in the culture of many crops grown for their reproductive yield. High insolation is required within the canopy to fill fruit distributed through it. Stone and pome fruits often require high light flux to develop the color that determines quality. In addition, next year's reproductive capacity of many perennial fruit trees depends upon the assimilate supply to meristems distributed through the canopy.

Control of canopy shape to improve yield and quality is well known in horticultural crops in which pruning and systems of trellising are common. Espalier, for example, is an ancient horticultural practice. An interesting modern example is the Tatura Trellis, used initially for stone fruit but now increasingly employed with other tree-fruits. In its simplest form (Fig. 10.15a), this trellis arranges the foliage in sloping planes formed from N–S lines of trees, each pruned to two E–W branches. The trees are planted at high density to encourage rapid development of cover and early fruit-bearing. The structure of the trellis is determined by the spacing between rows and the angle to which the E–W branches of each tree are trained along the trellis wires. The depth of foliage in each arm is controlled by mechanical pruning. In the earlier designs, the arms of adjacent rows were allowed to meet; present versions leave a gap along the ridge lines to increase penetration of light into the canopy.

It has not been possible to use grower experience to settle questions about optimum geometrical design of the Tatura trellis, i.e. row direction, row spacing,

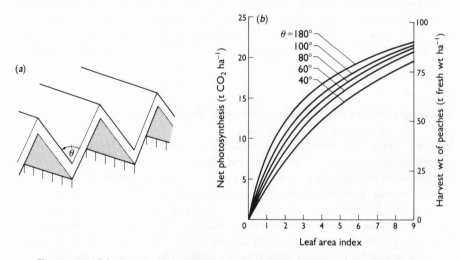

Fig. 10.15. (a) Design of the Tatura Trellis. (b) Simulated seasonal photosynthesis as a function of LAI in Tatura trellis canopies of various fork angles ($\theta$) in response to direct sunlight plus diffuse irradiance. (After Denholm & Connor (1982).)

fork angle and foliage depth, but Denholm & Connor (1982) have constructed a simulation model to analyze the potential productivity of these trellises during fruit-filling. Diffuse radiation from skylight and from scattering within the canopy played an important part in the photosynthetic response of these trellises. The analysis showed that depth of canopy was critical to the performance of the trellises and that optimum canopy thickness differed with trellis angle. One surprising result (Fig. 10.15*b*) was that photosynthetic productivity of angled trellises was inferior to continuous horizontal canopies of appropriate thickness. The original hypothesis of the trellis designers, that radiation-use efficiency would be improved by increasing the upper surface area of the orchard, proved wrong.

If angled trellises are more productive of fruit than horizontal canopies then it is apparently due to reasons other than total photosynthetic productivity, perhaps with the relationship between the distribution of fruit and photosynthesis within the canopy, or with the role of light flux in fruit initiation. The model could be extended to include these issues.

Trellises are rarely practical for field crops and optimum canopy design must be achieved by genetic means. There are, however, examples to which the principles of trellising apply. Climbing beans are a case in point. Their small investment in stem means that they cannot display their canopy without mechanical support. Given this by canes, strings or wires, yield is advantaged by the small diversion of assimilate to stem. Climbing beans are commonly grown as an overlap crop in the tropics supported by stalks of maturing maize. In that culture, the issues of canopy display and productivity are further complicated by the presence of the additional species.

## Polycultures

The principles of competition for light and the role of canopy structure in polyculture were developed from studies of light relations and productivity in pastures, particularly by Donald and co-workers at Adelaide, South Australia, who concentrated on simple mixtures of annual ryegrass and subterranean clover. This combination of tall grass and short legume exemplifies the structure of most grass–clover mixtures. Important exceptions occur, however, in improved tropical pastures, which often combine climbing legumes with grasses.

The stability of ryegrass–subterranean clover mixtures depends upon mutual shading by the two species. Under low nitrogen supply or heavy grazing, there is little shading of the clover by grass, but as fertility increases over the life of the pasture, or if pastures are fertilized with nitrogen or 'closed' from grazing in preparation for fodder conservation, clover growth suffers while grass flourishes. The suppression and gradual loss of clover from pastures of high nitrogen is caused by shading from the taller grass. This was shown in the studies of Stern & Donald (1962) who investigated above- and below-ground components of competition between annual ryegrass and subterranean clover. Clover production fell sharply as nitrogen supply increased and the effect could be explained entirely by light relationships in the canopy (Fig. 10.16). A close correlation was established between

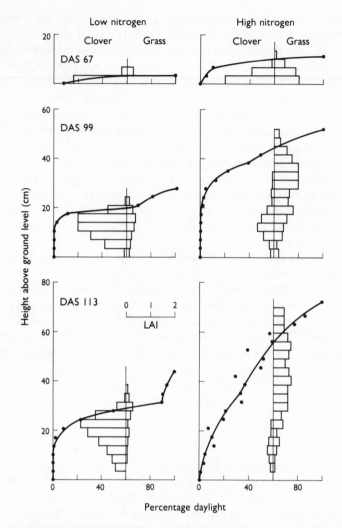

**Fig. 10.16.** Vertical distribution of light flux and leaf area within grass–clover mixtures grown at two levels of available nitrogen on three occasions (days after sowing) during the season (after Stern & Donald (1962).)

the growth of clover and the radiation that penetrated the upper grass canopy to the clover. The studies also demonstrated an important feature of interspecific competition that was introduced in Chapter 2. At high nitrogen, growth of clover is suppressed sufficiently to lead to mortality. Over time, the low-growing species may be excluded from the mixture. On the farm, grass (and pasture) productivity subsequently decline as nitrogen is depleted by grazing and reseeding may be necessary to reestablish clover in the pasture.

Arable crops may also be grown in combination on the same land. Such polycultures aim to achieve LER > 1 (Chapter 2) and are usually successful only where niche differentiation occurs for limiting soil resources or because the duration of green cover is extended, leading to better use of the growing season. Careful evaluation of intercrops is essential. To establish the real LER, the polyculture must be compared with pure crops that are also optimally managed with regard to density, planting pattern, and duration.

The classical mixed crops of the tropics are legume–non-legume combinations of annual and perennial crops grown with limiting nitrogen. Maize and beans as annuals and coffee or cocoa under leguminous trees as perennials are the main examples. The leguminous shrub *Leucaena* fixes nitrogen that improves maize yield, and its leaves are harvested frequently to provide animal fodder. The trees themselves are coppiced occasionally for firewood. These manipulations of the leucaena canopy serve to limit its potential dominance of the site and hence its suppression of maize yield by shading. Optimum management will seek to meet yield and stability objectives which will vary from farmer to farmer.

The range of possibilities in mixed cropping, herb–herb, shrub–herb, tree–herb, legume–non-legume, deciduous–non-deciduous, is enormous. Even where water and/or nutrients are limiting, attention is needed to light relationships in these mixtures. Planting pattern is one part of such management but manipulating canopy shape and extent is another. A feature of species mixtures, especially mixtures of trees and herbs, is the great morphological and physiological differences that exist between components. Difference in stature plays a dominant role in the competition for light between component species (Connor 1983).

In productive agroforestry systems there will always be competition for light. Models of canopy photosynthesis, such as those discussed above, can play a major role in making preliminary assessments of the likely outcome of species combinations, planting patterns and management practices. Even given this start, the amount of experimental work that is required for the development and management of these complex systems is enormous.

## 10.7 SUMMARY

The basic chemistry of photosynthesis is embedded in chloroplasts but the area of leaves that contain them is the critical factor in light interception and the diffusion of limiting gases. Leaf photosynthetic performance depends upon the microclimate they experience in the canopy and upon their physiological status. Light relations in crop canopies play a major role in the competition between individuals and in the productivity of the community. Under conditions of adequate water and nutrients, light capture and utilization are the ultimate factors limiting survival and productivity. When water or nutrients limit growth, optimum canopy design must balance canopy productivity with the water and nutrients required to produce the canopy and to maintain physiological activity.

The structure of canopies is influenced by the pattern of individuals, and species, at planting or establishment but also by the size, angles, and distribution of leaves. Because leaves are generally short-lived relative to the lifespan of crops, the dynamics of initiation, expansion, and senescence determine the age structure of the canopy which plays a major role in the physiological status of the canopy.

Computer models are well suited to handle the interaction between leaf display, leaf photosynthesis response and canopy performance. Detailed geometrical models are available to study this interaction in continuous and discontinuous canopies and in monocultures and polycultures. Such models have already had an impact on the design and management of crop canopies and offer an efficient way to screen many future possibilities, particularly those complex arrangements involved in polycultures.

## 10.8   FURTHER READING

Black, C. C. 1971. Ecological significance of dividing plants into groups with distinct photosynthetic production capacities. *Adv. Ecol. Res.* **7**:87–114.

de Wit, C. T. *et al.* 1978. *Simulation of assimilation, respiration and transpiration of crops.* Pudoc, Wageningen, 141 p.

Evans, J. R., S. von Caemmerer, and W. W. Adams (eds). 1988. *Ecology of photosynthesis in sun and shade.* CSIRO, Canberra.

Hatch, M. D., C. B. Osmond, and R. O. Slatyer (eds). 1971. *Photosynthesis and photorespiration.* Wiley–Interscience, New York. 565 p.

Ludlow, M. M. 1985. Photosynthesis and dry matter production in C3 and C4 pasture plants, with special emphasis on tropical C3 legumes and C4 grasses. *Aust. J. Plant Physiol.* **12**:557–72.

Schulze, E.-D. 1986, Carbon dioxide and water vapor exchanges in response to drought in the atmosphere and in the soil. *Ann. Rev. Plant Physiol.* **37**:247–74.

Ting, I. P. 1985. Crassulacean acid metabolism. *Ann. Rev. Plant Physiol.* **36**:595–622.

# 11

*Respiration and partitioning*

## 11.1 INTRODUCTION

The use of new carbon in growth and respiration are critical processes in crop productivity. The term **partitioning** is used to describe patterns of carbon use. 'Allocation' is used in this sense by some authors but it can imply control by a central authority that does not exist in plants. The main features of partitioning are seen in the changing morphology of the plants during a season: in the changing distribution of number, size, and growth of various organs.

Assimilates are also consumed in respiration and that process must also be considered as a component of carbon partitioning. Respiration furnishes energy and reductant for new construction and for the maintenance of existing structures. The portion linked with growth is termed growth respiration, $R_g$. The magnitude of $R_g$ varies with the chemical nature of the new construction. Maintenance respiration, $R_m$, also depends on tissue composition and has precedence over growth for assimilate; together $R_m$ and $R_g$ ordinarily consume 0.3 to 0.5 of gross photosynthesis. Respiration and the chemical composition of new biomass, then, are important aspects of carbon partitioning.

The new assimilates from photosynthesis that serve as substrates for growth and respiration are mainly carbohydrates. Sucrose is the principal transport form in crop plants and sucrose and starch are the main storage forms. For simplicity, we will sometimes represent these by glucose. 'Old' assimilates, including materials such as starch that accumulated during earlier periods as well as materials mobilized during the senescence of old leaves and other organs, also serve as substrates for respiration and growth. 'Mobilization' is used here to describe salvage from earlier constructions in preference to 'remobilization', since we do not know if the materials were mobilized previously. We begin the discussion of partitioning with assimilate use in respiration and biosynthesis.

## 11.2 CARBON USE IN RESPIRATION AND SYNTHESIS

**The respiratory process**

Respiration occurs in mitochondria of all living cells and is termed 'mitochondrial' or 'dark' respiration, thus avoiding confusion with photorespiration (Chapter 9).

The tricarboxylic acid (TCA) cycle and electron transport chain accomplish the major portions of the work. Respiration involves oxidation of carbon substrates through removal of $H^+$ and $e^-$ and the release of $CO_2$. The electrons are transported to $O_2$, forming water, while released chemical bond energy is retained in reducing agents (nucleotides such as NADH and NADPH) and in energy carriers such as ATP (adenosine triphosphate). Carbon enters mitochondria in the form of organic acids (pyruvate and malate) derived in the cytosol from protein, carbohydrate, or lipid. The glycolytic and pentose pathways are involved in the production of organic acids from carbohydrate and some reductant is generated in those processes.

Reduced nucleotides and ATP act as energy carriers within cells, supporting biosyntheses and maintenance processes. Reduced nucleotides can serve also as intermediates in ATP production. This permits variation in the proportions of reductant and ATP produced. Carbon substrates are transported between cells but the energy carriers are not. A total of 24 $e^-$ is released from the complete oxidation of a glucose molecule (taken here as the standard substrate). That is sufficient for production of 12 reduced nucleotides or 36 molecules of ATP. Respiration of glucose can be summarized as follows:

$$C_6H_{12}O_6 + 6O_2 \rightarrow 6CO_2 + H_2O, \text{ and} \qquad\qquad \text{[Eq. 11.1]}$$

$$36(ADP + P_i) \rightarrow 36ATP, \text{ or}$$

$$12(NAD^+ + \text{reductant}) \rightarrow 12(NADH + H^+),$$

where ADP is adenosine diphosphate, $P_i$ is inorganic phosphate, and $NAD^+$ and $NADH + H^+$ (or $NADH_2$) are the oxidized and reduced forms of nicotinamide adenine dinucleotide, respectively. ATP and $NADH_2$ are the main carriers in plants. In this equation with glucose, the **respiratory quotient** (RQ; $CO_2$ released/$O_2$ consumed) is 1.0 but when lipid serves as the substrate as in the germination of oil-seeds, the RQ is only about 0.7.

Respiration normally is **closely coupled** with the availability of ADP and oxidized nucleotide ($NAD^+$). If those carriers are scarce, i.e. if ATP and reduced nucleotides accumulate, respiration ceases. Debate exists over possibilities for uncoupled respiration and for respiration by an alternative, 'cyanide-resistant', and less efficient, pathway (Laties 1982; Amthor 1989) but those do not seem to be major factors with crops.

The free energy released by the complete oxidation of glucose is near 2.80 MJ $mol^{-1}$ (15.6 kJ $g^{-1}$ at 20 °C). Bond energy associated with reduction of nucleotides and formation of ATP varies with the concentrations of their reactants and products in the cells. Approximate values are 0.22 MJ $mol^{-1}$ nucleotide and 0.053 MJ $mol^{-1}$ ATP; approximate efficiency for the formation of reducing power $[(12 \times 0.22)/2.80 = 0.94]$ is greater than for ATP formation $[(36 \times 0.053)/2.80 = 0.68]$. The remaining energy is lost as heat.

## Respiration related to growth and maintenance distinguished

The close coupling of respiration allows us to proceed directly to questions about use of reductants and ATP. Bacteriologists and animal scientists routinely distinguish between biosynthesis and maintenance activities as causes of total respiration (R) but plant scientists came to that view only after pioneering work by McCree (1970). The partition can be written:

$$R = R_g + R_m. \tag{Eq. 11.2}$$

The terms can be expressed as mass of C, $CO_2$, $O_2$, or glucose, per unit time. As with photosynthesis, R is most easily measured as a $CO_2$ flux in closed or open systems because measurements of the disappearance of substrate and $O_2$ are difficult.

Respiration by mature seed is presumably all $R_m$, because they are not engaged in biosynthesis, but growth and maintenance activities occur simultaneously in most vegetative tissues. Mature leaves, for example, import nitrate ions and synthesize amino acids that are then exported and used in growth. Therefore, $R_g$ related to new construction actually occurred throughout the plant. Special accounting is required for mobilized materials. The first synthesis of a protein, for example, embodies the large cost of nitrogen assimilation from nitrate or $N_2$ gas (Chapter 8). When protein is mobilized, costs of hydrolysis, transport as amino compounds, and synthesis into a new protein at another site are also properly assigned to $R_g$. Those costs are less, however, than are needed to acquire additional nitrogen and synthesize a new amino acid, and the plant has conserved both carbon and nitrogen resources. The protein content of the plant remains unchanged while $R_g$ has increased.

Two principal methods, neither entirely satisfactory, are used to distinguish $R_g$ and $R_m$ in growing plants. In one, the plants are held in a controlled environment at their light compensation point where gross photosynthesis equals dark respiration (i.e. $P_n = 0$; Fig. 10.1). Total R is measured during brief periods of darkness. With photosynthesis balanced exactly by respiration, we can assume that no assimilate is being used in forming new biomass, that $R_g$ is therefore zero, and $R = R_m$. In the second, 'starvation', method, plants are placed in the dark so that free assimilates are consumed and growth ceases. Total R declines to a minimum value (after about 48 h in some experiments) that serves as an estimate of $R_m$. In both methods, the difference between normal respiration and $R_m$ then provides an estimate of $R_g$. The problems with these methods are that maintenance activity may be greater in rapidly growing plants than in non-growing ones, and that $R_m$ may be substrate-dependent, proceeding faster in unstarved plants. Neither method serves to identify the particular sources of $R_m$ and $R_g$.

## Maintenance activities

Maintenance activities in higher plants include turnover of proteins and lipids and maintenance of electrochemical gradients across membranes (Penning de Vries 1975). Proteins and lipids are subject to slow rates of breakdown or hydrolysis and ATP is then consumed in resynthesis at the same site. Because net increases in protein or lipid content do not occur and, unlike senescence-mobilization phenomena, growth does not take place, turnover is classified as maintenance. Some enzymes turn over rapidly but rates for structural proteins and lipids are small and it seems that an equal or larger portion of $R_m$ is due to maintenance of electrochemical gradients. Cells concentrate solutes such as $K^+$ and sugar within the plasmalemma and tonoplast compartments, but these materials may leak to the apoplast or to the soil solution. ATP is then expended to transport solutes back across the membranes.

Specific $R_m$ increases with temperature and declines with plant age as is illustrated in Fig. 11.1. These effects are important ecologically. The exponential increase in $R_m$ with temperature up to an injury point at 40–50 °C (depending on species) has a $Q_{10}$ near 2 (rates double with each 10 °C increase) as is characteristic of chemical reactions. Leakage and turnover presumably increase as molecular activity increases with temperature. Age effects correlate in most species with an increase in the proportion of mature tissues and thus with increases in plant size. Mature tissues have large proportions of materials such as cellulose, lignin, and starch that do not require maintenance. $R_m$ rates increase linearly with nitrogen content. Nitrogen content reflects not only the amount of protein subject to turnover but also the total amount of protoplasm, and thus surface area of membranes and solute content, as opposed to wall material and starch.

In general, larger portions of new assimilates are required for maintenance in warm climates, or with nitrogen-rich plants, than in small plants, cool environments, or with nitrogen-poor plants. As plants increase in size, specific $R_m$ ($R_m$ per g dry mass, sometimes termed the maintenance coefficient) declines but that is offset by an increase in the proportion of non-photosynthetic tissues requiring maintenance. As a result, a greater portion of new assimilates goes to maintenance. This is particularly evident in crops after they achieve full cover: photosynthesis continues at a constant rate while biomass and $R_m$ continue to increase.

Specific maintenance rates observed with different crop plants vary considerably depending on the way the plants are grown and how $R_m$ is measured (Amthor 1989). Values obtained by the starvation method seem the least variable. Typical rates at 20–25 °C for vegetative tissues measured by that method range between 15 and 50 mg $CO_2$ $g^{-1}$ DM $d^{-1}$. Expressed as a ratio of the masses of glucose and dry matter, specific rates vary between 0.01 and 0.035 $d^{-1}$. Values reported for root systems (up to 0.15 $d^{-1}$) are much larger than expected from their nitrogen content. Those observations are mainly from nutrient cultures, however, where ion leakage may be greater than occurs in soil. Extended to field conditions, they would cause much greater $CO_2$ fluxes from soil than are observed.

Reduction of maintenance costs remains as one of the under-explored possibilities for improvements in biological efficiency. In one example, ryegrass selections having small $R_m$ rates for mature leaf tissue produced greater forage yields under field conditions than the parent population (Wilson & Jones 1982). The lines had similar nitrogen content but whether they differed in rates of turnover and gradient maintenance was not determined. Related work by Robson (1982) indicated that the yield advantage of the selection was due in part to greater leaf longevity and thus greater leaf area in the selections than in the parent.

## Growth respiration, $R_g$, and growth yield

Growth requires substrate carbon both to form new chemical structures and as a source of reducing power and energy for synthesis. Denoting substrate that enters

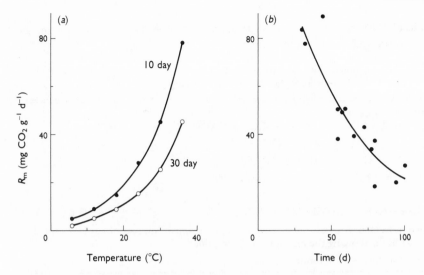

Fig. 11.1. (*a*) Variation in specific maintenance respiration of whole radish plants with temperature. The 10-day-old plants had a significantly greater specific maintenance expenditure than 30-day-old plants. (Redrawn from Lopes (1979).) (*b*) Variation of specific maintenance of whole sorghum plants with age at 30 °C. (Redrawn from Stahl & McCree (1988).)

into the structure of new product by $S$, the mass ratio of product formed ($W$) to total substrate used during the same interval of time ($S + R_g + R_m$) is termed the **apparent growth yield** ($Y$):

$$Y = W/(S + R_g + R_m). \hspace{2cm} [\text{Eq. 11.3}]$$

$S$, $R_m$, and $R_g$ are amounts of glucose substrate and the usual units for $Y$ are g product $g^{-1}$ glucose. Consideration of just the substrate used in growth ($S + R_g$) allows calculation of the **true growth yield** ($Y_g$):

$$Y_g = W/(S + R_g). \hspace{2cm} [\text{Eq. 11.4}]$$

Bacteriologists handle the problem of distinguishing between $R_g$ and $R_m$ neatly in chemostats (Pirt 1965) and animal scientists have found ways to calculate the net energy contributions of feeds for gain or maintenance (Chapter 1). An independent means for measuring or calculating $Y_g$, $S$, and $R_g$ was needed for plants, and two approaches have emerged. One approach depends upon analysis of proximate biochemical composition and calculation of $S$ and $R_g$ from biochemical pathways. (Proximate analysis was introduced in Chapter 1.) The other method begins with the elemental composition of the biomass. The methods are presented here in some detail because the principles are important in crop productivity.

## $Y_g$ and $R_g$ from proximate analyses

Starting from basic materials such as glucose and nitrate, it is possible to trace the metabolic pathways by which plants synthesize various organic materials and thus

Table 11.1 *The component and overall reactions for the biosynthesis of glutamic acid from glucose and nitrate via the glutamine synthetase process*

$\alpha$-KG is $\alpha$-ketoglutaric acid; Gln is glutamine; $P_i$ is inorganic phosphate; ATP, ADP, NADH, and $NAD^+$ represent the energy and reducing-power carriers as before.

---

*Component processes*[1]:

$\text{Glucose} + 4\,NAD^+ + ADP + P_i \rightarrow \alpha\text{-KG} + 4\,NADH + H^+ + CO_2 + ATP;$

$NO_3^- + 4\,NADH + H^+ \rightarrow NH_3 + OH^- + 4\,NAD^+;$

$\text{Glutamic} + NH_3 + ATP \rightarrow \text{Gln} + P_i + ADP;$

$\alpha\text{-KG} + \text{Gln} + NADH + H^+ \rightarrow 2\,\text{Glutamic} + NAD^+.$

*Overall reaction*:

$\text{Glucose} + NO_3^- + NADH + H^+ \rightarrow \text{Glutamic} + CO_2 + NAD^+ + OH^- + 2\,H_2O.$

The requirement for reduced NADH is met by respiring an additional 1/12 mol glucose (0.0833 mol), allowing the reaction to be simplified to:

$1.0833\;\text{Glucose} \rightarrow 1\;\text{Glutamic.}$

---

*Summary*:

The mass of 1.0833 mol glucose is 195 g, and 1 mol glutamic acid weighs 147 g; therefore the estimated $Y_g$ (termed production value, PV) is:

   $PV = 147/195 = 0.75$ g glutamic acid $g^{-1}$ glucose;

and the glucose requirement (GR) is:

   $GR = 195/147 = 1.33$ g glucose $g^{-1}$ glutamic acid.

---

*Note*:

[1] $\alpha$-KG is an intermediate in the TCA cycle and it is drawn from there for amino acid formation. The first reaction shown here is the net of many individual steps.

calculate $Y_g$ and $R_g$. The method is illustrated in Table 11.1 for the biosynthesis of glutamic acid. An overall reaction for the synthesis is constructed first. The inputs are then expressed in terms of glucose for the calculation $Y_g$. In this method, the estimate of true growth yield is termed the **production value** (PV) and its inverse (1/PV; the amount of glucose consumed to form the product) is the **glucose requirement** (GR) (Penning de Vries *et al.* 1974). In glutamic acid synthesis, one $CO_2$ molecule is released in the formation of $\alpha$-KG and 0.5 $CO_2$ arises from the respiration of additional glucose to supply reducing power. Thus specific $R_g$ equals 0.25 mol glucose per mole glutamic acid (1.5/6) or 0.306 g glucose $g^{-1}$ product.

Penning de Vries *et al.* (1974) carried out such calculations for a large number of organic materials including organic acids, lignin, lipids, proteins, and carbohydrates. Their key assumption was that plants use the least costly of any alternative pathways for biosynthesis. Penning de Vries and his associates sometimes included additional respiratory costs covering turnover of enzymes ('tool maintenance'), ion uptake, and membrane transport between cells as a part of the glucose requirement for growth.

Estimates of PV obtained for various compounds within a given biochemical class such as lipid are generally very similar to each other. Therefore, each class of

Table 11.2 *Glucose use in the biosynthesis of 1 g of product of the major classes of organic compounds from glucose obtained from calculations for type compounds in each class*

The units are: production value (PV), g product g$^{-1}$ glucose; glucose requirement (GR, the inverse of PV), g glucose g$^{-1}$ product; and $R_g$, g $CO_2$ g$^{-1}$ product.

| Class of compound | PV | GR | $R_g$ |
|---|---|---|---|
| Carbohydrate | 0.83 | 1.21 | 0.12 |
| Protein (with reduced N) | 0.62 | 1.62 | 1.67 |
| Protein (with nitrate N) | 0.40 | 2.48 | 0.42 |
| Lipid | 0.37 | 2.71 | 1.61 |
| Lignin | 0.52 | 1.92 | 0.58 |
| Organic acids | 1.10 | 0.91 | $-0.04^1$ |

*Note:*
[1] A net uptake of $CO_2$ occurs.
*Sources:* Adapted from Penning de Vries *et al.* (1983); Vertregt & Penning de Vries (1987).

compounds can be represented by a single GR value (Table 11.2) which can be used with proximate analyses to estimate GR and $R_g$ for complex biomasses.

## $Y_g$ and $R_g$ from elemental analyses

The cost of synthesizing organic compounds can also be estimated from elemental analyses, without knowledge of biochemical composition or pathways (McDermitt & Loomis 1981). The calculations depend on the conservation of mass and electric charge and are demonstrated here with synthesis of glutamic acid using glucose and nitrate as substrates. The molecular formulae and relative molecular masses ($M_r$) of glucose and glutamic acid are:

| Glucose | $C_6H_{12}O_6$ | $M_r = 180$ |
|---|---|---|
| Glutamic acid | $C_5H_9O_4N$ | $M_r = 147$ |

Evidently, 5/6 moles of glucose are needed to provide the C skeleton of glutamic acid. In addition, carbon in glutamic acid may be more oxidized or reduced than in glucose. The oxidation numbers (valences) of H and O are fixed at $+1$ and $-2$, respectively. Organic N (R–NH$_2$) is at the $-3$ level while $NO_3^-$ is $+5$. By contrast, C may vary between $-4$ and $+4$. The oxidation–reduction state of a compound is assumed to balance to 0, allowing the reduction level ($r$) of carbon to be predicted from:

$$r + h - 2x - kn - ms = 0, \qquad [\text{Eq. 11.5}]$$

where $h$, $x$, $n$, and $s$ are the moles H, O, N, and S in the compound ($C_cH_hO_xN_nS_s$); $k$ is the oxidation number for nitrogen taken to standard state ($k = 5$ for nitrate); $m$, the oxidation number for sulfur, is normally $+6$; r is 0 for glucose. For formation of glutamic acid from nitrate:

$$r_{glutamic} = 9 - 8 - 5 \times 1 - 0 = -4 \text{ mol e}^- \text{ mol}^{-1} \text{ glutamic acid,}$$

indicating that the carbon in 1 mol of glutamic acid has 4 mol electrons more than the carbon in glucose, i.e. it is more reduced. Oxidation of a mole of glucose yields 24 mol e$^-$, therefore an additional 4/24 mol glucose must be respired to supply reducing power for the synthesis. A summary of these steps defines the amount of glucose required (glucose equivalent, GE):

$$GE = c/6 - r/24 \quad \text{(mol glucose mol}^{-1} \text{ product)} \quad \text{[Eq. 11.6]}$$

and

$$GE_{glutamic} = 5/6 - (-4/24) = 1.083 \quad \text{mol glucose mol}^{-1} \text{ glutamic acid.}$$

That is the same result as was obtained in Table 11.1 from pathway analysis. The estimate of true growth yield on a mass basis obtained by this method is called the **glucose value** (GV).

GV (equivalent of PV)

$$= 147 \text{ g product}/(1.083 \text{ mol} \times 180 \text{ g mol}^{-1} \text{ glucose})$$

$$= 0.75 \text{ g product g}^{-1} \text{ glucose.}$$

This value of GV also is the same as was obtained in Table 11.1 for PV. Formation of some compounds involves additional production or consumption of ATP, however, and GV does not always equal PV. For complex biomass with an unknown biochemical composition, an empirical relationship exists:

$$PV_{biomass} = E_g GV, \quad \text{[Eq. 11.7]}$$

where $E_g$ is the fraction of total substrate electrons retained in the product. $E_g$ for biomasses appears to be reasonably constant in the range 0.84 to 0.89, indicating that nearly 90% of the free energy of glucose is retained in the products of biosyntheses (Lafitte & Loomis 1988*a*). (Biochemistry is reduced to a constant!) It seems, then, that there is little promise in genetic selection aimed at improving the efficiency of biosyntheses in crop plants. Respiration associated with growth and the heat of combustion of the product biomass can also be predicted from GE (Lafitte & Loomis 1988*a*).

The elemental method, like the proximate approach, offers an important tool for understanding growth yield and biomass composition. Calculations usually proceed from glucose and nitrate but other substrates such as amides may be employed. Analyses for C, H, N, and S are easily and accurately obtained by the Dumas pyrolysis method. That provides direct measures of net photosynthesis ($P_n$) in carbon terms as well as of the amounts of N removed with the biomass. Unfortunately, a satisfactory direct method for measuring organic O does not exist. O can be obtained by difference after measuring C, H, N, S, and all of the mineral elements (a laborious procedure). That method was used to obtain the empirical formulae for grain sorghum biomass presented in Table 11.3. Alternatively, mineral content can be estimated as equal to 0.6 of the ash content.

Table 11.3 *Growth yields and* $R_g$ *values derived from empirical formulae for biomass of young grain sorghum plants grown with and without an adequate supply of nitrogen*[1]

| Elemental formula for the organic materials in 100 g biomass[2] | | | | |
| --- | --- | --- | --- | --- |

| | $r$(mol e$^-$ per 100 g) | | GE (mol glucose per 100 g) | |
| --- | --- | --- | --- | --- |
| −N | $C_{3.55}H_{5.71}O_{2.83}N_{0.068}S_{0.002}$ | | | |
| +N | $C_{3.59}H_{5.74}O_{2.68}N_{0.126}S_{0.002}$ | | | |

| | $r$(mol e$^-$ per 100 g) | | | GE (mol glucose per 100 g) |
| --- | --- | --- | --- | --- |
| −N | $2(2.83) - 5.71 - 5(0.068) - 6(0.002) = -0.40$ | | | $3.55/6 - (-0.402/24) = 0.61$ |
| +N | $2(2.68) - 5.74 - 5(0.126) - 6(0.002) = -1.02$ | | | $3.59/6 - (-1.022/24) = 0.64$ |

| | GV (g g$^{-1}$ glucose) | PV (g g$^{-1}$ glucose) | GR (g glucose g$^{-1}$) | $R_g$ (g $CO_2$ g$^{-1}$) |
| --- | --- | --- | --- | --- |
| −N | 0.91 | 0.77 | 1.30 | 0.35 |
| +N | 0.87 | 0.73 | 1.37 | 0.43 |

*Notes:*
[1] Data are from Lafitte & Loomis (1988a) for samples collected 61 d after planting. Here, fewer significant figures were carried in the calculations causing slight differences in results.
[2] 100 g is the conventional 'molecular mass' for unknown materials. −N samples contained 5.39 g minerals including nitrate, sulfate and silica; 6.45 g minerals were found in the +N samples.

**Variations in $R_g$**

In contrast to $R_m$, specific $R_g$ depends entirely on the biochemical composition of the new biomass and thus is independent of any direct effect of temperature. The actual rate of $R_g$ varies indirectly with temperature, however, depending on the effects of temperature on growth rate and the balance of photosynthesis and $R_m$.

The effects of biochemical composition on $R_g$ are dramatic. Of the vegetative structures, leaves have the largest contents of both protein and lipid and their construction costs are significantly larger than those for stems or roots. The effects of differences in composition are illustrated in Table 11.4 with calculations of growth yields for maize and soybean grains. It is obvious, given equal quantities of photosynthate for grain production, that the weight yield of soybean with its high contents of lipid and protein can never be as great as for maize. Because the two crops grow in the same climate zone and have similar growth duration, the price received by farmers for soybean grain must be at least 1.5 times that of maize if they are to choose it as a crop in place of maize. In practice, the yield difference is widened by the fact that C4 maize is more productive of photosynthate than C3 soybean. In the American maize–soybean region, the usual ratio of grain yields (soybean/maize) is near 0.33. Maize production is somewhat more costly, however, and the price ratio is usually near 2.5.

Table 11.5 illustrates the effects of composition and nitrogen source on growth

Table 11.4 *Construction costs of maize and soybean grains compared using glucose requirements from Table 11.2*

The calculation is done as the sum of products of composition × the individual GR values.

| Source | Composition in g per 100 g grain × GR | | | | | GR per 100g | PV |
|--------|--------------------|------------|------------|------------|---|------|------|
| | Crude fiber[1] | Carbo-hydrate | Lipid | Protein | | | |
| Maize | 2.2(1.32) + | 82.2(1.21) + | 4.4(2.71) + | 10(2.48) | = | 136.4 | 0.73 |
| Soybean | 5.6(1.32) + | 27.2(1.21) + | 20(2.71) + | 42.1(2.48) | = | 198.9 | 0.50 |

*Notes:*
[1] Crude fiber is assumed to be 85% cellulosic material and 15% lignin; 1.32 is the weighted average of their individual GR values.
*Source:* Proximate composition was obtained from National Research Council (1982).

yields and glucose requirements for a range of crop seeds and fruits. Costs were calculated beginning with nitrate, ammonium, or $N_2$ gas. A conservative value of the cost of nitrogen fixation was used in these calculations (see Section 8.7). The ammonium basis isolates costs of nitrate reduction (or nitrogen fixation) from other aspects of fruit growth and assigns them to the vegetative tissues where they generally take place. In this table, average glucose requirements were 11% more with nitrate and 32% more with nitrogen fixation than with ammonium. The implications are seen clearly with soybean: that crop has the potential for producing 1.3 times as much yield without the nitrogen fixation system. Greater yields of legumes are sometimes obtained on mineral nitrogen than with nitrogen fixation (Silsbury 1977; Piha and Munns 1987) but more definitive experiments need to be done.

The small growth yields of expensive compounds explain observations by plant breeders of inverse relationships between yield and protein or lipid content of grains and grain legumes. The effect is apparent even in attempts to alter the amino acid composition of grain protein; lysine is an expensive compound and high-lysine grains have smaller yields than normal grains (Bhatia & Rabson 1976).

## Seasonal patterns of respiration in crops

Few measurements exist of the seasonal course of respiration in crops: the experimental difficulties are simply too great. Among the problems: daytime respiration cannot be estimated accurately and $R_g$ and $R_m$ are not distinguished easily. Work by Thomas & Hill (1949) and Biscoe *et al.* (1975) define the general pattern of total respiration, R. Thomas & Hill found that about 40% of the gross photosynthesis of vigorous alfalfa crops was expended in respiration during the season. Respiration was about equally distributed between roots and shoots. Root respiration dropped dramatically when shoots were harvested and then increased

Table 11.5 *Glucose requirements (GR) calculated for several seeds from their principal constituents beginning with ammonium or nitrate ions or dinitrogen*

A value of 3.43 was used for GR for protein by nitrogen fixation based on the minimum theoretical costs of nitrate reduction and nitrogen fixation (67 and 200 MJ kg$^{-1}$ N, respectively).

| Species | Composition (% dry matter) | | | GR (g glucose g$^{-1}$ biomass) with N from | | |
|---|---|---|---|---|---|---|
| | $(CH_2O)$ | Protein | Lipid | $NH_4^+$ | $NO_3^-$ | $N_2$ |
| Rice | 88 | 8 | 2 | 1.26 | 1.32 | 1.46 |
| Corn | 84 | 10 | 5 | 1.33 | 1.42 | 1.58 |
| Wheat | 82 | 14 | 2 | 1.28 | 1.40 | 1.63 |
| Chickpea | 68 | 23 | 5 | 1.35 | 1.54 | 1.92 |
| Safflower | 50 | 14 | 33 | 1.83 | 1.95 | 2.18 |
| Soybean | 38 | 38 | 20 | 1.68 | 2.01 | 2.64 |
| Rape | 25 | 23 | 48 | 2.13 | 2.33 | 2.71 |
| Peanut | 25 | 27 | 45 | 2.10 | 2.33 | 2.78 |
| Sesame | 19 | 20 | 54 | 2.19 | 2.36 | 2.69 |
| Mean | | | | 1.68 | 1.85 | 2.18 |

during the regrowth cycle reflecting the dependence of growth and nitrogen fixation on carbohydrate supply. Thomas & Hill (1949) enclosed their crops in assimilation chambers whereas Biscoe *et al.* (1975) left their barley crop open to the air and estimated $CO_2$ fluxes by the Bowen ratio (daytime) and aerodynamic (nighttime) methods (Chapter 6). Soil $CO_2$ flux (sum of root and microbial activity) was measured in small enclosures while daytime respiration was calculated, with adjustments for temperature, from the nighttime value. Estimated crop respiration ranged from 33 to 87% of gross photosynthesis, increasing during the season as biomass accumulated. Their results are illustrated in Fig. 11.2.

Loomis and Lafitte (1987) used the elemental method to calculate $R_g$ and $P_n$ of maize crops during flowering and grain-filling. $R_m$ was estimated using a published maintenance coefficient with corrections for diurnal temperature and nitrogen content. $P_g$ of maize was found as the sum of $P_n$ and the calculated values of $R_g$ and $R_m$. In that study, 14% of $P_g$ went to $R_g$ and 34% to $R_m$. Those proportions were unaffected by moisture stress or by a doubling of the ambient $CO_2$ level.

Another approach for exploring crop respiration is to incorporate knowledge of maintenance and growth respiration coefficients and their dependence on tissue composition and temperature into a crop simulation model where photosynthesis and respiration can be simulated independently. Ng & Loomis (1984) did that for potato (Fig. 11.3). Simulated dry matter production by this crop agreed closely with field observations. Simulated $R_g$ exceeded $R_m$ for small plants early in the season while the reverse was true later. Daily $R$ fluctuated widely depending upon current weather. For the season as a whole, close to 40% of the simulated gross photosynthesis was expended in respiration. That was about equally distributed between maintenance and growth.

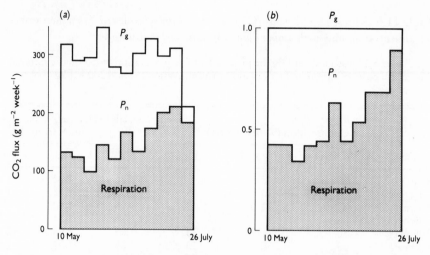

Fig. 11.2. (*a*) Weekly $CO_2$ fluxes relating to gross photosynthesis ($P_g$), net production ($P_n$), and respiration for a barley crop grown in the field at Nottingham, England. The crop was sown 18 March and harvested 21 August. (*b*) Data from (*a*) presented on a relative basis. (Data from Biscoe *et al.* (1975).)

It appears from sketchy available evidence, then, that respiration may account for 40–50% of the carbon assimilated by crops under good conditions. With low radiation and/or high temperature, that fraction may be much greater. Respiration clearly represents a major drain from the carbon supply that can be partitioned in plant growth.

## 11.3   MORPHOLOGICAL ASPECTS OF PARTITIONING

### Coordination of morphological plasticity

Multicellular organisms face special problems in the coordination of growth and development of their various parts. Development in mammals, for example, is highly constrained to a usual form and size, in part because embryonic development continues for an extended period of time under controlled conditions. Throughout development, powerful control also is exercised by hormones produced in a central place. Embryo development in higher plants, by contrast, is minimal. A central hormone center for coordination does not exist, and subsequent growth is highly plastic. Plasticity is possible because plants have numerous meristematic centers that continue activity throughout most of the life of the plant. Each is capable of expanding some dimension of the organism. The collective potential use of substrates by those meristems can easily exceed supplies and it is important how resources are partitioned among the competing meristems. Without coordination of what grows when and how rapidly, growth could be chaotic and inefficient, if not fatal. Such coordination does occur, however, and usually leads to a plant form well

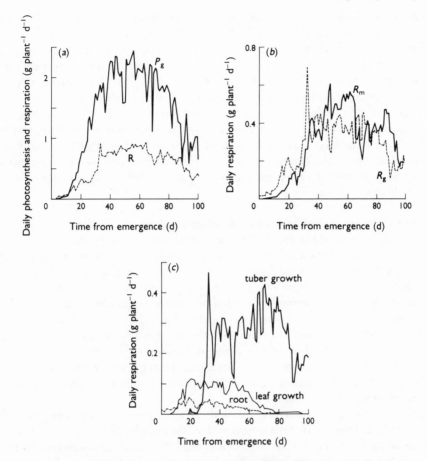

Fig. 11.3. (*a*) Simulated course of gross photosynthesis ($P_g$) and total respiration ($R$) for a potato crop at Aberdeen, Idaho, beginning with emergence on 9 June. (*b*) Total respiration partitioned between $R_m$ and $R_g$. (*c*) $R_g$ partitioned among the costs of growing fine roots, leaves, and tubers. (After Ng and Loomis (1984).)

suited to its environment (Trewavas 1986). Understanding qualitatively and quantitatively how such activity is coordinated remains as perhaps the most significant problem facing plant scientists.

## Controls of partitioning

The principal control over partitioning rests in the capacity of meristems to grow through cell division and enlargement. Intrinsic, maximum rates of division and maximum extent of enlargement determine whether a meristem can play a vigorous role in partitioning. When it plays and to what extent depend on the internal and external milieu. Internally, growth substances and substrate supplies act as coordinating agents with growth substances serving as on–off switches of activity and substrate supply controlling rate and extent. (The term hormone implies long-distance transport; growth substances of plants, in contrast, may act at a distance or where they are produced.) Temperature, radiation, and status of nutrients and water are the major environmental factors that affect growth. Temperature and water, for example, exert control through effects on metabolic rates.

There are two bodies of knowledge about the controls of partitioning, one focused in a reductionist way on growth substances and nuclear control, and the other in an integrative way on control by substrate and environment. Unfortunately, there are few linkages between those approaches. Some single-gene controls of partitioning are known but most aspects appear to behave as quantitative traits under the control of many genes.

**Control by growth substances**  A general theory of coordination based on growth substances alone has yet to be constructed. One problem is that the principal growth substances, auxins, cytokinins, gibberellins, and abscisic acid, are produced by most tissues (no central point) and their effects in controlling growth and development differ from one tissue to another in bewildering ways.

Control by growth substances is seen most clearly in **apical dominance**. In that, development of axillary meristems is suppressed by a flux of auxin from the apical meristem. Removal of the apex removes that control and the axillary meristems can then develop as branches and a different pattern of assimilate utilization is established. Apical dominance is very strong in plants poorly supplied with carbon substrates, because of crowding or other factors, but it has much less influence when substrates are adequate.

Growth substances are involved in wide array of phenomena ranging from the control of cell differentiation to the control of flowering by photoperiod and by low temperature. Evidence for their involvement in flowering comes from transmission of induced states through grafts. The easiest way to relate control by growth substances to crop behavior is to establish, by experiment, a set of operational ('genetic') rules about what a plant can or cannot do under particular circumstances. Apical dominance, for example, can be reduced to rules and carbohydrate response functions (Denison & Loomis 1989). We used that approach in Chapter 5 as a practical way to describe the complexity of flowering. In the operational approach, growth substances can be viewed as switches: on, an organ may grow dependent on temperature, water status, and substrate level; off, the organ cannot grow.

**Nutritional control**  The nutritional theory of control is based on the fact that finite amounts of substrate are required for cell division and enlargement and other processes involving chemical syntheses. The amounts used are predicted by growth yield calculations. A key point to understand is that the Conservation Law imposes absolute limits on partitioning because substrate used in respiration or embodied into new construction cannot be used elsewhere. In addition, rates of synthesis and growth vary with substrate level. These principles couple operationally to carbon balances from photosynthesis and respiration and provide a powerful basis for interpreting ecological phenomena.

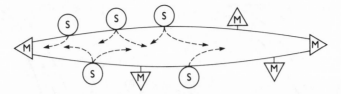

Fig. 11.4. Arrangement of source leaves (S) and meristematic sinks (M) along a common channel. Unloading by sinks is a driving force in transport and a major factor in competition among sinks for transported substrates. The channel offers some resistance to transport with the result that remote sinks can be disadvantaged in the competition.

Organs capable of meristematic activity, additional differentiation, or storage serve as importers (**sinks**) for substrates transported from other organs (**sources**). Assimilate sources and sinks can be identified by supplying individual photosynthesizing leaves with $^{14}CO_2$ and tracing the movement of labeled sugars. Such experiments reveal the existence of 'normal' patterns of transport (this leaf to that sink), but they also show, after excision of various sources and sinks, that the patterns are very flexible. In the absence of other sources, any leaf can supply labeled assimilate to any sink. Young leaves are generally sinks for carbohydrate and older leaves are sources, while stem tissues may be either sinks in which growth occurs and starch accumulates, or sources of mobilized starch. An organ that is currently a source of one substance can at the same time serve as a sink for another. Leaves, for example, are sinks for nitrate absorbed from the soil and sources of newly formed amino acids.

A 'channel' analogy (Fig. 11.4) accounts, operationally, for a 'distance effect' in assimilate use seen among competing sinks. In this, a number of growing organs are distributed along a common channel of substrate (phloem tissue) fed by source leaves. If the flow of substrate along the channel is restricted (by phloem conductance) or depleted (by phloem unloading to intervening sinks), supplies to remote sinks will be less than for nearby ones. Such effects are seen in experiments where roots cease growing when leaves are shaded or removed because source activity or phloem conductance are less than the capacity of the intervening sink tissues to use assimilates.

In crop simulation models, distance effects can be modeled by introducing transport resistances between assimilate sources and sinks. Proper simulation of phloem resistance, however, is difficult. Alternatively, sinks can be assigned different 'priorities' over a common pool, as illustrated in Fig. 11.5a. Both approaches recreate observed patterns of partitioning. The order of the curves in Fig. 11.5a is the central part of the partitioning theory used in some crop models structured to simulate accumulation and partitioning of dry matter. In those models, the order leaves > stems > fine roots simulates the behavior of real plants whereas any other order fails (Fick *et al.* 1973). Priorities are expressed in the figure as diminishing-returns relationships to substrate supply (Hunt & Loomis 1976), but simple linear (Liebig's law) designs work as well.

Some priority rules such as those related to flowering are genotype-specific, while

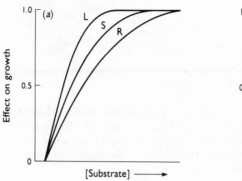 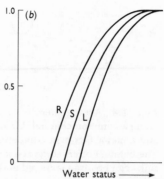

**Fig. 11.5.** Priority schemes useful for understanding the partitioning of a common pool of substrate among several sink tissues. The schemes are based on patterns observed with varying supplies of substrate and water. The order of the lines accounts, in most cases, for nearness to source and other mechanisms that influence partitioning. (*a*) Dependence of growth of leaves (L), stems (S), and roots (R) on carbon substrate level. (*b*) Dependence on plant water status.

others can be stated as general rules for all crops. Maintenance respiration, for example, appears always to have priority over growth and storage, which take place only when adequate substrate is available.

## Sink capacity and activity

**Sink capacity** of an organ is defined by the maximum rate at which it can use substrates. That depends upon its size ($W$), the fraction capable of growing ($F_c$), and the maximum specific growth rate of that fraction ($\mu$):

$$\text{Capacity} = \mu F_c W \text{ (g organ}^{-1} \text{ day}^{-1}\text{).} \qquad \text{[Eq. 11.8]}$$

Capacity can be expressed in glucose equivalents by replacing $\mu$ with $\mu/Y_g$, where $Y_g$ is the true growth yield (or an estimate of it such as PV). Actual growth rates approach capacity when temperature is optimal and supplies of substrates and nutrients are not limiting. Those conditions sometimes can be achieved experimentally by pruning competing sinks from the plant. **Sink activity** refers to the growth or storage rate actually achieved. Operationally:

$$\text{Activity} = \text{Capacity} \times \text{Limit}, \qquad \text{[Eq. 11.9]}$$

where Limit is a function that describes effects of limiting factors such as unfavorable temperature or substrate supply. Examples of functions that assign different priorities over leaves, stems and roots for the effect of water stress are illustrated in Fig. 11.5*b*.

The diurnal course of restrictions on sink capacity shown in Fig. 11.6 were produced by a substrate-dependent model of the potato crop constructed with Eq. 11.9, using priority rules of the type illustrated in Fig. 11.5. Young simulated potato

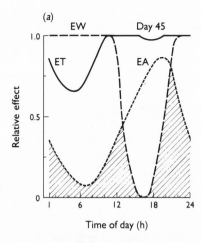 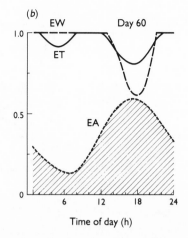

Fig. 11.6. Simulated diurnal patterns of the effects of temperature (EW), substrate (EA), and water status (EW) limitations on tuber growth of potato. The shaded area represents the net effect (Liebig's Law) on tuber growth. (From Ng & Loomis (1984).) (*a*) Day 45 after emergence; young tubers are limited by carbon substrate during the dark period and by water status during the day. The tubers are insulated by the soil and escape the effects of low night temperatures. (*b*) Day 60. Fine roots have increased and are now better able to meet the evaporative demand. Photosynthate production has also increased but intense competition among several active tubers results in a limitation by carbon substrate at all hours of the day.

plants began with abundant substrate supplies from seed pieces, and leaf and root growth was limited for a time only by temperature. By day 45 (Fig. 11.6*a*), the plants were dependent on their own photosynthesis but the supply of substrate was small and growth of newly initiated tubers was limited more at night by substrate than by temperature. As is the case for most competitively grown crops, these plants became 'sink-dominated' and 'source-limited'. Transpiration exceeded the capacity of fine roots for water uptake on this day and tuber growth was strongly limited at midday by a low plant water status. By day 60 (Fig. 11.6*b*), leaf area and photosynthesis had increased further but the root system was also larger and water stress was much less. Tuber growth then was limited throughout the day by substrate level. Hourly integration with this model provides a realistic simulation of interactive effects of temperature, water, and substrate supply on partitioning between leaves, roots, and tubers over the daily period.

## Growth correlations

**Growth–differentiation balance** When growth of vegetative organs and fruiting bodies is less than the current rate of assimilate production, carbohydrates accumulate in temporary pools in leaves and stems, or find use in differentiation. Differentiation, including increases in secondary products (oils, alkaloids, etc.) and

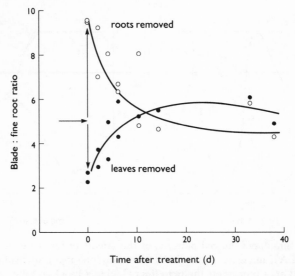

Fig. 11.7. **Time course of a functional equilibrium between leaf and root growth in sugarbeet plants. When the plants were 30 d old, 0.5 of the leaf blades were removed from one group of plants and 0.5 of the fine roots were removed from another. Control plants (omitted for clarity) maintained a ratio of leaf blade mass to root mass near 5. Blade/root ratio of the treated plants returned over time to that of untreated controls. (Redrawn from Fick *et al.* (1971).)**

wall materials (lignin, hemicellulose), is favored by conditions such as nitrogen deficiency and moisture stress that restrict growth. Trade-offs between growth and differentiation are an important feature of partitioning (Loomis 1932). Lorio (1986), for example, employs growth-differentiation balances to explain interannual variations in beetle attacks on southern pine.

**Functional equilibrium between roots and shoots**   Important examples of control of partitioning are found in the interactions between roots and shoots. Leaves are dependent upon roots for water and nutrients and roots in turn require photosynthate from leaves. When plants well supplied with nutrients and water are stressed for carbohydrates, by shading for example, carbon partitioning follows the priority noted above (leaves > fine roots). Given adequate carbohydrate but only limited water or nutrient, the priority in carbon use is reversed, with root growth being favored. One reason is that root tips extending into moist soil do not experience the same severity of stress as shoots. Xylem differentiation begins some distance behind the root apex and the apex is isolated somewhat from water deficits generated by transpiration. Brouwer (1983) referred to such phenomena as examples of functional equilibria between plant organs.

Results from an experiment with root and leaf pruning of sugarbeet plants grown in a constant environment are illustrated in Fig. 11.7. Root removal caused shoot growth to slow relative to root growth as proportions of root and shoot returned

Table 11.6 *Variation in yield components of 'Insignia' wheat with planting density at Glen Osmond, South Australia*

| | Planted density (plants m$^{-2}$) | | | | |
|---|---|---|---|---|---|
| | 1.4 | 7 | 35 | 184 | 1078 |
| Density at maturity | 1.4 | 7 | 35 | 154 | 447 |
| Tillers per plant | 41 | 30 | 14 | 7 | 3 |
| Spikes per tiller | 0.71 | 0.63 | 0.50 | 0.28 | 0.23 |
| Grain per spike | 33 | 38 | 30 | 22 | 19 |
| Mass per grain (mg) | 34 | 35 | 33 | 33 | 33 |
| Grain per plant (g) | 33 | 25 | 7 | 1.5 | 0.4 |
| Grain yield (kg ha$^{-1}$) | 460 | 1730 | 2470 | 2340 | 1850 |

*Source:* Adapted from Puckridge & Donald (1967).

towards control values (near 5). Similarly, leaf removal resulted in a temporary reduction in root growth. Nutritional theory adequately explains this example of internal homeostasis. The plants were grown in nutrient culture and uptake of water and/or nutrients became limiting to leaf growth after roots were removed. Note that while mass of organs serves as the morphological basis here, leaf area × evaporative demand and root surface × uptake capacity are the mechanistic basis.

A similar explanation applies to partitioning between roots and shoots with limiting supplies of nitrogen. Roots acquire new supplies of nitrate nitrogen but leaves are the principal sites of nitrate reduction. As a result, shoots generally enjoy a priority over roots in use of nitrogen. That priority is reversed in nitrogen-deficient plants, however, and the ratio leaves/roots is smaller for such plants. Roots of nitrogen-deficient plants are well supplied with carbohydrate; Radin (1977, 1983) proposed that the small capacity of roots for nitrate reduction serves to insure that root apices then capture adequate nitrogen despite the limited supply.

### Environment-dependent variations in yield components

Morphological plasticity also is seen from examination of variations in yield components with density. We considered changes in numbers of branches or tillers as a response to changes in density in Chapter 2 (Fig. 2.7). Numbers of inflorescences per tiller (0–1), grains per inflorescence, and grain mass also vary in turn, as is illustrated for wheat in Table 11.6. Individual grain mass varied over only a small range. Examples of the responses of determinate and indeterminate field bean to variations in density are presented in Table 11.7. Of the yield components, numbers of branches and pods plant$^{-1}$ were strongly affected by density whereas seeds pod$^{-1}$ were affected less and mass per seed was unchanged.

A sequential response to environment is the basis of partitioning patterns in both bean and wheat. Branching (and tillering) occur early in the vegetative phase and take place only if nutrients and substrates are adequate and apical dominance is

Table 11.7 *Variations in yield components of field bean with variations in spacing*

Determinate 'Taishō-kintoki' (T) and semideterminate 'Gin-tebō' (G) are commercial cultivars in Japan.

| Attribute | Cultivar | Density (plants m$^{-2}$) | | |
|---|---|---|---|---|
| | | 64 | 16 | 4 |
| Nodes per main stem | T | 5.4 | 5.8 | 5.8 |
| | G | 14.3 | 19.9 | 24.6 |
| Branches per plant | T | 1.6 | 3.9 | 4.1 |
| | G | 0.2 | 1.8 | 9.0 |
| Pods per plant | T | 4.4 | 10.1 | 17.2 |
| | G | 8.0 | 28.1 | 70.4 |
| Seed per pod | T | 3.0 | 3.3 | 3.6 |
| | G | 3.7 | 4.3 | 5.4 |
| Mass per seed (mg) | T | 376 | 345 | 334 |
| | G | 364 | 336 | 348 |
| Seed yield (g plant$^{-1}$) | T | 4.8 | 11.5 | 20.7 |
| | G | 10.8 | 40.6 | 132.3 |

*Source:* Data from Tanaka & Fujita (1979).

overcome. As growth continues in bean plants, numbers of axillary flower sites, flowers, seed per pod, and finally mass per seed are determined in sequence. Considerable plasticity exists at each stage: an unfavorable stress during the branching phase of bean, for example, usually can be compensated later in number of pods or seed per pod if conditions improve. Determination of inflorescence size during the preanthesis period is the critical step in small grains. Thereafter, plasticity is limited mainly to reductions of grain number. In most plants, seeds and grains are subject to only small variations in mass.

Some species, including bean, are notorious for the numbers of flowers they abort, even under good conditions, as they balance reproductive effort to resources. The temptation is to wonder what the yields might be if the flowers were retained and more seed were produced. The answer is that seed number generally balances rather well with photosynthate supply. Abortion serves to bring retained flowers into balance with photosynthate supply. Plants lose little through abortion and pollination failures since flowers generally represent a relatively small cost in carbon and nitrogen resources. More serious drains result from commitment of carbon and nitrogen to the additional stem growth that provided the flowering sites.

Other species adjust numbers of flowers and seeds in less obvious ways. Distributive timing of anthesis in wheat (from the middle of the ear towards basal and acropetal regions) and sunflower (centripetally from the outer flowers towards the center of an indeterminate head) offers opportunities for adjusting numbers of grains within the inflorescences. A series of decision stages is evident in maize. The

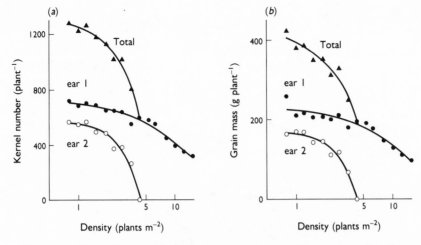

Fig. 11.8. **Reproductive plasticity in maize in response to crowding for space. (Data from Tetio-Kagho & Gardner (1988).) (*a*) Number of grains per ear for the first and second ears produced on each plant. (*b*) Mass of grain for the two ears.**

results depicted in Fig. 11.8 were obtained by varying plant density to cause variations in substrate supply per plant. Ears (female inflorescences) are indeterminate with progressive apical development of additional female spikelets. Silks (stigma) of distal spikelets emerge later than those of basal ones. When substrates are limiting, silks grow slowly, many of the distal ones fail to emerge and be pollinated, and grain number is less. When plants are well endowed with substrates, those silks emerge and are pollinated; in addition, the ears then develop with more columns of spikelets than occurs with limited substrate. As a result, more kernels develop per ear on widely spaced plants than on densely spaced ones. A hierarchy is also evident among successive ears. The upper ear is strongly dominant and development of axillary buds at lower positions into additional ears is very dependent upon resources.

Conservatism in seed size is not a matter that seed cannot be small (some orchid seed are as small as 2 $\mu$g) or large (a coconut may weigh > 1 kg). It seems that each population has found a compromise between embryo size, amounts of seed reserves, and seed number that provide adequate reproductive fitness, and that those traits become fixed genetically. Final seed size for a particular species is usually set by limitations on the duration of cell division early in seed development. Early, in the sense of an overlap with development of other seed in the same or different fruit so that substrate supply or growth substance signals can influence seed set. Differences in timing of ovule growth also occur within multi-seeded fruit and seem to be the basis of variation of seed number per fruit. In alfalfa, as may be the case for most legumes, the ovaries generate as many as 20 ovules but only a few develop as seed. Those few are usually near the stigma end of the ovary and presumably were the first to be reached by pollen tubes.

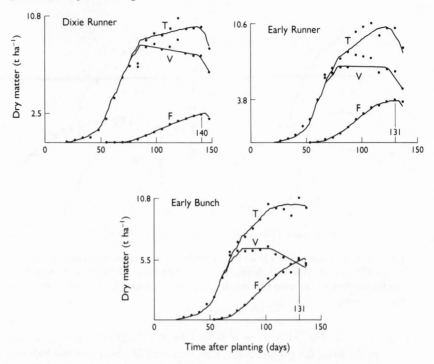

Fig. 11.9. Simulated (—) and observed (●) partitioning patterns of three peanut cultivars grown at Gainesville, Florida. Cumulative masses of leaves and stems (V), fruit (F), and total biomass (T = V + F) are shown. (Redrawn from Duncan *et al.* (1978).)

## Phenotypic variations in partitioning

Differences in patterns of partitioning are readily apparent among genotypes. Whether the phenotype of a bean cultivar has prostrate or erect growth, whether a maize line is 'prolific' (more than one ear) or not, and whether a wheat is tall or short in stature are important attributes. Alteration of the pattern of dry matter partitioning towards a larger harvest index has been an underlying principle in the domestication and continuing improvement of crops (Donald & Hamblin 1976, 1983; Chapter 4).

Such phenotypic differences are illustrated in Fig. 11.9 in the time-course of dry matter accumulation by several peanut cultivars. This series of cultivars represents a genetic advance in which seasonal dry matter production changed little while the proportion that accumulated as economic yield increased. The increase apparently resulted from restrictions on stem growth coupled with advances in fruit size and fruit growth rate since similar changes in the simulation model designed by Duncan *et al.* (1978) allowed it to match the patterns of real plants. We can hypothesize that competitiveness of fruit increased compared to that of stem apices. In other words,

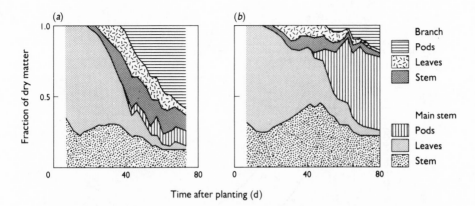

Fig. 11.10. Relative dry matter distribution during the season for two types of dry beans grown at Cali, Colombia. (Redrawn from White (1981).) (*a*) Plant type with a determinate pattern of mainstem growth. Most of the pods are produced on branch stems. (*b*) With an indeterminate mainstem, only a few pods appear on branch stems.

nutritional limitations led to a semideterminate habit of stem growth. Less stem mass also means less $R_m$, perhaps compensating for the smaller growth yield ($Y_g$) of fruit relative to stems.

White (1981) examined partitioning in a wide range of field bean cultivars. Dramatic differences were evident between 'Type I' cultivars (Fig. 11.10*a*), where the mainstem is determinate and the bulk of the yield occurs on branches, and 'Type II' cultivars (Fig. 11.10*b*) where flowers occur mainly on an indeterminate mainstem. These bean cultivars also demonstrate strong compensatory relations among yield components. A negative association between seed number and mass is apparent in Fig. 11.11. Seed size was relatively constant within a genotype but differed widely among genotypes. Given the same seasonal supply of photosynthate, the Conservation Law makes such negative correlations inevitable. As a result, improvements in yield are seldom achieved through selection for an increase in only one yield component. The yield isoquants drawn in Fig. 11.11 demonstrate a wide range in yields among cultivars, independent of seed size, however, indicating opportunities for progress in selection for yield.

Some interesting examples of phenotypic plasticity are found with root crops. The species *Beta vulgaris*, for example, includes chard (silver beet) grown for its large edible leaves. Chard has a small storage axis in contrast to root-crop forms (sugarbeet and fodder beet) that have much larger roots and smaller leaves. Those differences result from chard having a much smaller cell size (but not fewer cells) in the storage roots, and a smaller leaf initiation rate (Rapoport & Loomis 1986). That combination of a small root-sink capacity coupled with fewer leaves results in chard having a much greater substrate supply per growing leaf and ultimately larger leaves than sugarbeet.

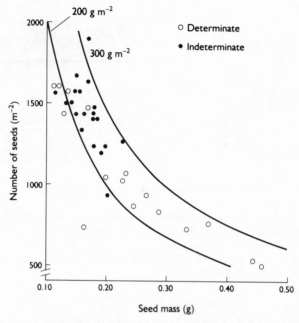

Fig. 11.11. Relation between number of seeds produced m$^{-2}$ land and individual seed mass for a large number of determinate and indeterminate dry-bean cultivars grown at Cali, Colombia. The yield isoquants reveal that similar yields were achieved over wide ranges in seed number and size. (Redrawn from White (1981).)

## Ideotype concepts

Plant breeders generally must choose their breeding objectives from among a wide array of alternative opportunities and problems. Unless objectives are chosen carefully, the specialized, time-consuming efforts that follow may go for naught. Traits such as resistance to insects, disease, or lodging are usually self-evident and may demand priority. They are also easier to approach than more complex traits such as yield and efficiencies in use of nutrients, water, and light. As adequate crop nutrition became a reality during the past 50 y, plant breeders have given more attention to biological efficiency of crops, crop photosynthesis, and optimum partitioning patterns.

Colin Donald (1968) provided an approach to the problem of optimum partitioning with his concept of an **ideotype**, a model of an ideal phenotype. 'Ideal' embraces both morphological and physiological features of the phenotype that would suit it to a particular cropping system. Donald's ideotype for wheat (Fig. 11.12) was designed for an intensive monoculture system with nutrients and water supplied in adequate amounts and weeds controlled. Key features of his ideotype included strongly restricted plasticity and competitive ability to achieve a large harvest index. Elimination of tillering, for example, would require precision spacing in dense

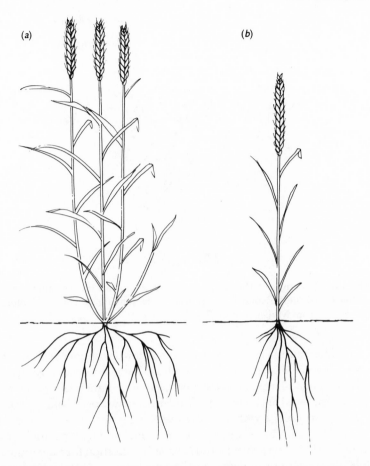

Fig. 11.12. A comparison between standard wheat (*a*) and C. M. Donald's (1968) ideotype of wheat (*b*) for high-density monocultures with soil resources not limiting. The ideotype is characterized by short stiff straw, minimum number of erect leaves, and large spike. These traits aim for non-competitive behavior, large harvest index, and maximum community performance.

stands but would save the waste of carbon and nitrogen associated with excess tillers and leaf area (Table 11.6 reveals that many tillers may fail to produce grain). Minimum stem growth and early flowering followed by a long grain-filling period also would help to maximize harvest index. Donald & Hamblin (1983) elaborated further on this theme, arguing that all annual plants will have similar ideotype rules. Although Donald's wheat might fit with intensive production schemes in Europe and Japan, practices in America, Australia, and elsewhere are still geared to extensive cultivation by low-cost methods. There, economic optimization is the target and tillering is still a desirable trait. Ideotype concepts for wheat and other crops continue to be advanced (Bingham 1972; Loomis 1979; Smith & Banta 1983; Rasmusson 1987).

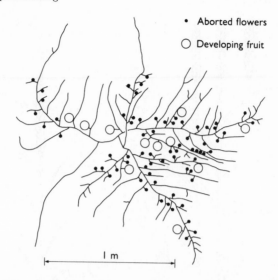

**Fig. 11.13. Stem growth and fruiting patterns of an indeterminate netted melon (muskmelon) plant grown with wide spacing at Davis, California. (Redrawn from McGlasson & Pratt (1963).)**

Fig. 11.13, illustrating a map of netted melon grown without competition, serves to illustrate ideotype design. The indeterminate habit is useful in gardens but the need for several hand-harvests create a problem in commercial production. Even with repeated harvests, only a few ripe fruit are obtained per plant. As was the case for peanut, a morphology with a greatly restricted potential for stem growth and flowering sites would be advantageous in a melon ideotype for commercial production. The breeding project is thus defined as selection for a determinate plant type while maintaining or improving two easily measured integrative traits, yield and harvest index.

Ideotype questions are usually more complex than the melon example, and considerable empirical testing may be required to match each new phenotype to its optimum environment before legitimate yield comparisons can be made. The optimum space relations for bush- and vine-type plants, for example, may be quite different. As a result, most breeders seek ideotypes for existing systems (standard spacings and so forth) rather than seeking new systems for alternative phenotypes. The point made here is that optimum systems can be defined for each system.

Ideotype questions extend beyond morphology to embrace optimal physiological traits (e.g. capabilities of roots for nutrient uptake) and optimal use of scarce resources. As an example, leaves are expensive to construct because of their high contents of protein and lipid. An optimal canopy of leaves, then, should have no more photosynthetic apparatus in each leaf than is needed in its light environment.

Ideotypes are useful in focusing attention on critical traits, integrative approaches, and optimization. Progress in designing and testing ideotypes remains slow, however, in part because it requires the integration of many traits. Single genes may control the main features of development, but alteration of partitioning, including relations between growth and differentiation, results in changes in the carbon balance with immediate, quantitative feedback to many phenotypic traits. The sugarbeet–chard example cited above, where the 'gene' for large leaves is effective through changes in root morphology, serves as an example. Put simply, conservation of mass in partitioning confounds genetic expressions. Plant breeders continue to receive too little training in physiology, morphology, and ecology to approach such problems effectively, and the interest and skill of physiologists in dynamic integration are still poor.

Integrative simulation models offer a means for dealing with such complexity. Through repeated simulations under various climates, promising ideotype concepts can be compared in a quantitative way before commitments are made to large breeding programs. The peanut example presented in Fig. 11.9 illustrates the approach; additional examples with applications to water-limited agriculture are given in Chapter 13. Optimization is an implicit goal in selection of partitioning patterns but plant scientists have done little in this area with crop simulation models and they lack training in optimization theory and in alternative techniques such as linear programming. Givnish's (1986) monograph and a review by Bloom *et al.* (1985) provide helpful introductions into biological cost–benefit analyses of adaptive traits in terms of C, N, and water. The example of optimal distribution of nitrogen within a foliage canopy (Chapter 10), and analyses by Cowan (1986) and Gutschick (1987) of optimal strategies for dealing with limited water, offer insights into some very sophisticated ideotype concepts.

## 11.4  SUMMARY

The patterns of carbon use in growth and respiration are critical aspects of production ecology. Even in vigorous crops, 40–50% of gross photosynthesis is expended in respiration related to maintenance ($R_m$) and growth ($R_g$). Both aspects of respiration are dependent on tissue composition. Proteins and lipids, for example, are costly to synthesize and maintain in comparison with cellulosic material and nonstructural carbohydrates. The negative correlation between specific $R_m$ and age, the increases in $R_m$ with nitrogen content and temperature, and the independence of growth yield and specific $R_g$ from temperature are useful principles in ecological analyses. Unknown at this time are whether $R_m$ varies with substrate supply and whether selection for low maintenance might enhance production.

Carbon not expended in respiration becomes a part of the structural biomass of the plant or accumulates in storage materials. The capacity for growth is distributed throughout the plant in meristematic tissues. Meristems are relatively independent of each other with the result that partitioning is dynamic and highly plastic in response to environment. For practical purposes, our limited understanding of how partitioning is controlled can sometimes be formalized in operational rules. The rules can then be incorporated into simulation models to integrate cellular- and molecular-level information for predictions of whole-plant behavior. Several feedback systems operating at whole-plant and crop levels exert homeostatic control over the underlaying biochemical processes. Those controls come in part from the Conservation Law and therefore impart quantitative characteristics and a highly polygenic inheritance to many aspects of partitioning. Included here are functional equilibria between roots and shoots, growth–differentiation balances, and compensation among yield components.

Only a few features of partitioning have been altered during domestication of crop species: gigantism of useful organs and harvest index are the main ones. Natural selection operates through the reproductive success of *individuals*, and it remains to be seen how far we can go in identifying and selecting for rules that will optimize *community* performance. Exciting questions emerge about the fine details of partitioning and whether we can define new ideotypes possessing ideal physiological and morphological traits for particular cropping systems. Thus far, progress has been mainly with simple aspects of form and dry matter partitioning. Critical questions about the optimal patterns of carbon and nitrogen use remain to be explored.

## 11.5    FURTHER READING

Amthor, J. S. 1989. *Respiration and crop productivity*. Springer-Verlag, New York. 215 p.

Bloom, A. J., F. S. Chapin and H. A. Mooney. 1985. Resource limitation in plants – an economic analogy. *Ann. Rev. Ecol. Syst.* **16**:363–92.

Givnish, T. J. (ed.). 1986. *On the economy of plant form and function*. Cambridge University Press. 717 p.

Hay, R. K. M. and A. J. Walker. 1989. *An introduction to the physiology of crop yield*. Longmans Scientific & Technical, Burnt Mill, Harlow, Essex, UK. 292 p.

Jennings, D. H. and A. J. Trewavas (eds). 1986. *Plasticity in plants*. Symp. Soc. Exp. Biol. no. 40. Cambridge University Press. 372 p.

Donald, C. M. and J. Hamblin. 1983. The convergent evolution of annual seed crops in agriculture. *Adv. Agron.* **36**:97–143.

Smith, W. H. and S. J. Banta (eds). 1983. *Potential productivity of field crops under different environments*. International Rice Research Institute, Los Banos, Philippines. 526 p.

Wardlaw, I. F. 1990. Tansley review no. 27. The control of carbon partitioning in plants. *New Phytol.* **116**:341–81.

# FOUR

# Resource management

Knowledge of the biology of crops, their production processes, and relations with environment is a central issue in crop ecology. Placing this knowledge into practical farming systems is another. At this point we give attention to how farm management joins ecological principles and technology in the design of cropping practices. Given the possibility to select a portion of the annual cycle for production, to choose appropriate cultivars and spacings, and to modify environment by tillage, drainage, fertilization, weed control, correction of soil pH, and other means, the range of management options is extremely broad. Ecological factors determine what may be grown and where, but human decisions about labor supply, economics, and available technology are equally important in management.

We attempt to bridge this gap by considering technologies for soil management in Chapter 12, how cropping practices may be adapted to supplies of water in Chapter 13, and how water supply may be enhanced through irrigation in Chapter 14. Dependence of farming on external energy and whether energy supplies may be adequate in the future are addressed in Chapter 15. One's picture of farming remains fuzzy, however, until the operation of representative farms is considered in detail. Two imaginary farms, one Australian and one American, are constructed in Chapters 16 and 17 as models to assist readers in further analyses of farming systems of importance to them.

How modern agriculture may evolve in an uncertain future is considered in Chapter 18. Many in society, because of disillusionment with technology, concerns about environment, or political reasons, now attack the premises and methods of modern agriculture. Whether such concerns are justified, whether proposed alternatives will be sufficient for the future, and what issues particularly need attention, are addressed.

# 12

## Soil management

## 12.1  INTRODUCTION

Proper management of soil resources is the key to sustaining agriculture because soil properties constrain, sometimes to a major degree, the type of farming that may be practiced and because soils are altered by farming practices in ways beneficial or deleterious to their long-term value for agriculture. The complex and variable nature of soil processes make accurate predictions about below-ground conditions difficult, however, and farming usually must proceed with only general knowledge of fertility levels, drainage, water-holding capacity, and tillage responses.

Soil characteristics important for sustainability include the ability to supply essential plant nutrients and water and the ease of tillage. Fertility management employs crop rotation, return of residues and animal wastes, and application of fertilizers to maintain adequate supplies of essential nutrients in the face of losses by removal in crops, by leaching below the root zone, and by erosion. Maintenance and improvement of profile depth suitable for rooting requires control of erosion and proper drainage and tillage. Tillage is the primary tool for soil management and has important effects on fertility, erosion, and weed control. Ease of tillage depends upon several factors including water content and the distribution and types of clays and organic matter in the profile.

**Spatial variability**

Soil management practices aim at creating reasonably uniform, favorable, conditions for plant growth in all parts of a field. Spatial variability of landscapes limits attainments of those goals. Profiles are seldom uniform across a field. For optimum management, places with different textures, profile depths, gradients, drainage, and native fertility would be farmed differently. Fields usually must be small, however, if each is to have reasonable uniform properties over its entire area. Because small fields introduce another set of problems related to access roads, fencing, unused headlands, and excessive turning, efficient farming requires compromises between field size and the degree of heterogeneity. Width of machinery and best directions and patterns for tillage and planting must also be considered.

Farmers are aware of the larger variations in their fields, such as spots of low fertility or wetness and sandy areas that may be droughty. Uniform tillage and cropping help reduce fertility and structural heterogeneity over time. Other practices including drainage to control wet areas, and amendments of manure, fertilizer, and lime can be varied to some extent for different portions of a field. Leveling and terracing reduce variations in gradient but by subtracting and adding from topsoil, other variations may be introduced. Some of these practices are also employed with pastures. Grazing commonly contributes to another source of variability through non-uniform distribution of dung and urine.

If we could identify microscale variations in fertility and pH, and presence or absence of weeds, pests, or disease, it might be possible to prescribe and apply specific microscale (e.g. plant-by-plant) solutions. One approach, now in research and development stages, involves video cameras coupled to image analyzers and microprocessor-controlled tools. Cultivation then could be aimed at individual weeds, and crop plants might be supplied individually with nutrients.

## 12.2  PLANT NUTRITION

### Essential nutrients

A small number of chemical elements are known to be **essential nutrients** for the growth of crop plants. Plant mass is composed mainly of C, acquired from atmospheric $CO_2$, and O, from $CO_2$ and $H_2O$. As is shown in Table 12.1, these two elements normally make up more than 85% of plant mass; H is usually near 6%. The remainder is composed of N and mineral elements acquired from soil, and is the basis of widespread occurrence of nutrient deficiencies in agriculture.

The presence of an element in plant tissues does not mean that it is essential for plant growth. It may be a surface contaminant or it may be a passive companion of water uptake. Appreciable silicon (as silica, $SiO_2$) is found in the biomass of sorghum (Table 12.1) and rice but Si is not known to be an essential nutrient for any crop. Essentiality is established by showing that a plant grows poorly or not at all in the absence of an element and that it cannot be replaced by another element. The essentiality of C, H, O, N, S and several metallic elements is further confirmed by their participation in specific organic compounds.

Essential nutrients can be divided roughly into two groups, macronutrients and micronutrients, depending upon amounts required for plant growth. Requirements for some micronutrients are so small that it was exceedingly difficult to establish whether or not they are essential for growth, and the role of other trace elements remains uncertain. A small requirement also means, however, that the chance of the nutrient being deficient in agricultural soils is also small. Among the micronutrients, Zn deficiencies seem to be the most widely occurring but Fe, Cu, Mn, and B deficiencies are also known. A classic case occurs in Australia where legumes respond over large areas to very small additions of Mo. Mo is essential for nitrogen fixation by rhizobia. In agriculture, deficiencies of the macronutrients N, P and K are the most common.

Global stocks of most nutrients are essentially infinite relative to the needs of

Table 12.1 *Elemental composition (% dry matter) of above-ground biomass of several crops and forages and maize and soybean grains*

All of the elements shown, except Si, are essential for growth of these species. Essential micronutrients (Fe, Zn, Cu, Mn, Bo, and Cl) and other elements appear in the category 'Other'.

| Material | C | O | H | N | S | P | K | Mg | Ca | Si | Other |
|---|---|---|---|---|---|---|---|---|---|---|---|
| Sorghum biomass[1] | 43.0 | 44.0 | 5.7 | 2.0 | 0.62 | 0.14 | 1.80 | 0.32 | 0.26 | 1.2 | 0.15 |
| Maize biomass[2] | 43.6 | 44.5 | 6.2 | 1.5 | 0.17 | 0.20 | 0.92 | 0.18 | 0.23 | 1.2 | 0.37 |
| Maize grain[2] | 44.7 | 45.3 | 7.0 | 1.7 | 0.12 | 0.29 | 0.37 | 0.14 | 0.03 | na | |
| Alfalfa[3] | 47 | 40 | 6 | 2.7 | 0.26 | 0.22 | 1.54 | 0.28 | 1.27 | na | |
| Bluegrass[3] | 46 | 41 | 6 | 2.7 | 0.29 | 0.34 | 1.98 | 0.17 | 0.33 | na | |
| Soybean grain[3] | 54 | 29 | 7 | 6.8 | 0.24 | 0.65 | 1.82 | 0.29 | 0.27 | na | |
| Wheat grain[4] | 46 | 45 | 6 | 2.3 | 0.15 | 0.43 | 0.49 | 0.13 | 0.05 | na | |

*Notes:*

na: Not available.

[1] At anthesis; data from Lafitte & Loomis (1988a).

[2] At maturity; all data from Latshaw & Miller (1924) except the nutrient contents of grain are from Tables 1 and 2 of National Research Council (1982).

[3] Approximate data developed from Tables 1 and 2 of National Research Council (1982). N from Table 1; C, O, and H from proportions of proximate and NDF fractions of Table 1 using elemental compositions for those fractions from McDermitt & Loomis (1981); and minerals from Table 2. Alfalfa and bluegrass biomasses both at early stages of flowering.

[4] Hard red winter wheat; N content varies from near 1.8% for soft wheats to over 2.6% for hard wheats (National Research Council 1982); data developed as per footnote 3.

agriculture. $N_2$ gas, for example, makes up 78% (v/v) of the atmosphere, and nearly 50 times that much is present in igneous rock of Earth's mantle. By contrast, the amount in soils and crops is only 0.006% of the amount in the atmosphere. K is abundant in oceans and salt deposits. Concern exists about the relative scarcity of high-grade P ores suitable for mining. Low-grade sources of P are abundant but they require considerably more treatment for use in agriculture. In addition, it may become practical to recycle P from sewage or from the ocean floor where it accumulates. The problem for agriculture is not limiting supplies of nutrient elements but that work must be expended to concentrate those sources into forms suitable for use as fertilizer.

Elements are sometimes present in amounts too great for healthy growth. The most widespread toxicities arise from $Al^{3+}$ and $Mn^{2+}$ in acid soils and from $BO_3^{3-}$ and $Na^+$ in saline and alkaline soils. In arid regions, Se levels in forages and drainage waters are sometimes toxic to animals. Special problems occur with soils derived from serpentine minerals high in Mg and low in Ca. Not only do plants grow poorly in the face of the unfavorable Ca/Mg ratios, but they also encounter toxic levels of heavy metals such as Ni and Cr.

## Crop responses to nutrient level

Crop response to variations in nutrient supply is seen most clearly in fertilizer trials. The diminishing-return relationship between maize grain yield and increasing supplies of fertilizer nitrogen illustrated in Fig. 12.1a is the general pattern for all nutrients. Responses of this sort are usually clear evidence that the supply or availability of that nutrient was inadequate. The yield obtained without added nitrogen reveals the amount of nutrient supplied by soil. As was the case in medieval farming (Chapter 8), this soil was extremely poor in nitrogen and supplied enough nitrogen (31 kg N ha$^{-1}$) for only 900 kg grain in the absence of fertilizer. The slope of the yield response to added nitrogen provides a measure of apparent fertilizer-use efficiency. Efficiency is large when the nutrient is strongly deficient (rising portion of the curve). In this example, 58 kg of grain yield was obtained per kg N applied over the range of 0–112 kg N ha$^{-1}$. The $^{15}$N-depleted fertilizer used in this experiment allowed the researchers to measure the proportions of the crop's uptake of nitrogen that came from fertilizer and soil sources. Applied nitrogen stimulated mineralization and increased the supply of native nitrogen to between 50 and 80 kg N ha$^{-1}$; 61% of the fertilizer nitrogen was captured by above-ground portions of the crop with 112 kg N ha$^{-1}$ applied and 67% with 224 kg N ha$^{-1}$. With less than 224 kg N ha$^{-1}$ applied, little inorganic N remained in the soil after harvest but that increased sharply with larger applications. The field was kept moist and between 15 and 22% of the applied N seemed to have been denitrified; the balance of the applied N accumulated in soil organic matter.

The transition between deficiency and adequate supply (the breaking portion of the curve in Fig. 12.1a) is rather sharp with nitrogen, and particularly so with maize. Nitrogen is not a costly input and the economic optimum for adding nitrogen as fertilizer (and maximum efficiency in the use of external energy; Fig. 15.1)

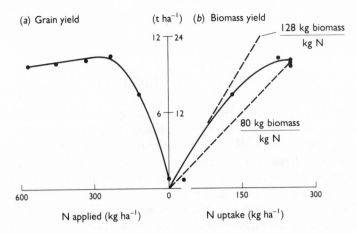

Fig. 12.1. Maize response to nitrogen fertilizer. The experiment was conducted in California with $^{15}$N-depleted ammonium sulfate by Broadbent & Carlson (1978). The graphical method used here and in Figs. 12.4 and 12.5 follows van Keulen (1982). (*a*) Grain yield as a function of increasing applications of the limiting nutrient, nitrogen. (*b*) Biomass yields as a function of nitrogen actually taken up by the crop. The dashed lines indicate the maximum and minimum amounts of biomass produced per kg N.

corresponds closely with the maximum yield point. In Fig. 12.1*a*, the optimum is near 224 kg fertilizer N ha$^{-1}$. Where the transition zone is broad, i.e. a strongly diminishing return, or the nutrient source is expensive, the economic optimum is found on the deficient side of maximum yield. The plateau region of the nitrogen response curve is quite broad for most species indicating a wide tolerance of excess supply. In Fig. 12.1*a*, yield declines slightly beyond 224 kg N ha$^{-1}$ owing to a salt effect in this irrigated field rather than to nitrogen toxicity. An excess supply of nitrogen can lead to waste because of the possibilities for loss (Chapter 8).

In Fig. 12.1*b*, biomass yields (calculated from grain yield assuming a harvest index of 0.5) are plotted as a function of nitrogen uptake. This curve also follows a diminishing return but stops short of a plateau. The slope of the curve with units of kg dry matter kg$^{-1}$ N defines nutrient-use efficiency (NUE), i.e. how well the crop translated an additional kg of absorbed N into biomass.

Two important concepts relating to the range of nutrient content in plant tissues are revealed Fig. 12.1*b*. The first is seen in the slopes of the dashed straight lines. These define the maximum (128 kg) and minimum (80 kg) amounts of above-ground biomass that maize can produce per kg N taken up. The reciprocals of these numbers correspond, respectively, to the minimum (8 g N kg$^{-1}$ biomass) and maximum (12 g N kg$^{-1}$ biomass) possible nitrogen contents of maize. The range is rather small because of the stoichiometric relationship between wall material and protein content (Section 1.4). The second arises from the fact that the crop ceased taking up nitrogen when it reached a maximum possible nitrogen content. In contrast to ideas about 'luxury consumption' as a general phenomenon, over-fertilized maize crops in this example (e.g., 560 kg N applied ha$^{-1}$) contained only 12% more nitrogen than the crop with an optimal amount of fertilizer (224 kg N ha$^{-1}$). Some of that increase would be found in the crop as nitrate serving a useful role as osmoticum.

## 12.3  MANAGEMENT OF SOIL FERTILITY

Soil fertility is defined by the ability of a soil to supply essential nutrients to crops through the soil solution and from ion-exchange complexes. Nutrient supplies are depleted by leaching and plant uptake and are restored through natural inputs, decay and mineralization of recycled organic materials, and solubilization of soil minerals. Plant uptake plays an important role in maintenance of fertility. Nutrients that might otherwise be lost by leaching are recycled from lower portions of the soil profile through crop residues to surface horizons. Supplies of nutrients are depleted over time because removals through leaching and harvest of crops generally exceed natural inputs. As a result, steps must be taken to maintain fertility if production is to be sustained.

**Nutrient depletion**

An example of the yield decline that occurs over years with exhaustion farming is illustrated in Fig. 12.2. Yields of rye grain did not decline to zero in this case but appear to have stabilized near 900 kg ha$^{-1}$. Rye is not highly extractive of nutrients.

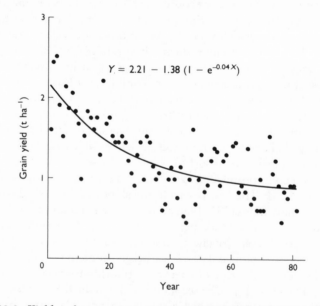

$$Y = 2.21 - 1.38 \left(1 - e^{-0.04 X}\right)$$

**Fig. 12.2.** Yields of rye grain over the period 1880–1960 in a German experiment without fertilizer inputs. Yields declined in a negative exponential fashion to an equilibrium level near 900 kg ha$^{-1}$. (Adapted from Schouten (1986).)

:imated average annual removals in 900 kg grain ha$^{-1}$ are 20 kg N, 4 kg K, 3 kg P, d 1 kg or less of each Ca and Mg. Similar patterns are evident in long-term periments with maize on the Morrow Plots in Illinois (Fig. 7.5) and with wheat in ld-field' experiments at Rothamsted in England. Like the rye experiment, those periments recreate situations found in low-input agriculture with yields near 800– .00 kg ha$^{-1}$. Such yields were characteristic of European agriculture through the edieval period (Section 8.8) and, until recently, of many areas of the world. Since 1en, increased use of fertilizer has raised yields significantly.

The reason that agricultural fields come to an equilibrium under exhaustion irming that sustains production at a low level indefinitely is that the soils receive a eady flux of natural inputs of nutrients from several sources. In Section 8.8, we entified sources for significant inputs of nitrogen. Weathering of parent material, infall and irrigation water, and dust are the principal sources of mineral nutrients. or cereals, the limiting nutrient is usually nitrogen since they extract less of the her elements; legumes, on the other hand, supply their own N but deplete P, Ca, κ, and Mg strongly and those elements come to determine production.

### Diagnosing nutrient needs

Nutrient deficiencies can be diagnosed from visual symptoms, from soil or plant analyses, and from responses to added nutrients. Marginal deficiencies, not evident from any symptoms other than reduced growth, can sometimes be detected through chemical analyses of plant material, or predicted from soil analyses. The most practical evidence is an observation of increased plant growth when nutrient supply is increased. A combination of methods is needed in some cases. Crops grown on a soil deficient in both N and S may respond well to $(NH_4)_2SO_4$ but poorly or not at all to nitrogen fertilizer without sulfur. Similarly, improved growth with an application of sulfate ($SO_4^{2-}$) may actually be a response to phosphorus displaced from fixation complexes by sulfate.

**Visible symptoms**  When the rate at which nutrients can be acquired by plants is less than the current demand for growth, plants develop characteristic symptoms that vary according to the mineral element and plant species involved. In some cases, new growth is affected most, in others, older tissues show symptoms. Shortage of N, for example, generally leads to yellowing and senescence of older leaves as N is mobilized from those tissues and utilized in new growth. New leaves may have normal green color but they are generally smaller and fewer in number. In addition to a smaller leaf area, photosynthetic ability also is less in N-deficient crops. In combination, these two effects can lead to sharply smaller growth rates and yields. Recognition of such symptoms is an important tool and is aided for most crops by picture atlases.

**Soil analyses**  Chemical analyses of soil samples are used in attempts to predict the supply of nutrients that is or may become available to plants. Soil analysis requires support by chemical laboratories and establishment of **critical nutrient**

**concentrations for the soil** (CNC$_s$) above which nutrient supply will be adequate for the crop and below which it will be deficient. Analyses on a single sample can include a range of nutrients as well as measures of salinity and pH (and thus the need for lime).

Locally established CNC$_s$ values are needed because soils differ and because a supply that is adequate for one species or level of production may not suffice for others. Difficulties arise in defining 'plant-available' supply and because there is no way of knowing whether a crop will actually access the nutrients. Plant-available P, for example, has been defined variously as the water-soluble, acid-soluble, or biocarbonate-soluble fraction. Use of these solvents represent attempts to mimic effects of $CO_2$ production by living roots on the availability of P.

Assessment of plant-available N is especially complex. The mineral pool ($NH_4^+$ and $NO_3^-$) is dynamic, reflecting variable rates of mineralization and immobilization. In some methods, soil samples are assayed twice for mineral N, immediately after sampling and again after moist incubation for several weeks to learn the amount of organic N that may be mineralized during a growing season. Blackmer *et al.* (1989) have simplified that to a single analysis for nitrate in soil samples collected in late spring after crop emergence. [$NO_3 - N$] at that time reflects the net of fallow-season mineralization, immobilization due to residues incorporated during primary tillage, and fertilizer additions. With their system, the same critical nitrate level for maize production was found for a large number of soils within a climatic region.

**Plant analysis**   Concentrations of nutrients in plant tissues reflect the balance between continued dilution by growth and actual uptake. Uptake integrates all factors influencing soil supply, plant availability, root distribution and activity, and plant assimilation. The nutrient content of a plant therefore reflects its past success in acquiring nutrients.

Plant nutrient status is assessed from the concentration of a nutrient in total biomass or just in selected organs. The actual concentration in plant biomass relative to the two lines in Fig. 12.1*b*, for example, can be related to degree of deficiency. Individual organs are easier to sample than biomass, however, and nutrient levels in recently formed ones correlate best with recent nutrition of the crop. For most elements, analyses are done for total content but with nitrogen, greater sensitivity to uptake-assimilation balances is obtained by analyzing for unassimilated [$NO_3 - N$] rather than [total N]. Similarly, [$SO_4 - S$] is a more sensitive indicator of crop status than [total S]. By selecting a sensitive form of nutrient and a sensitive tissue to sample, a rather sharp **critical nutrient concentration for the plant** (CNC$_p$) can be defined as is illustrated in Fig. 12.3*a*.

With sugarbeet, [$NO_3 - N$] is the most sensitive measure of nitrogen and petioles of recently matured leaves the most sensitive tissue. An application of periodic 'petiole analysis' to nutrient management in sugarbeet production is presented in Fig. 12.3*b*. CNC$_p$ established in the experiment shown in 12.3*a* is drawn as a horizontal line in Fig. 12.3*b*, where levels and trends of [$NO_3 - N$] define the nitrogen status of the crops. [$NO_3 - N$] increased following fertilization and declined when the crop's assimilation of nitrate exceeded its ability to acquire additional nitrogen.

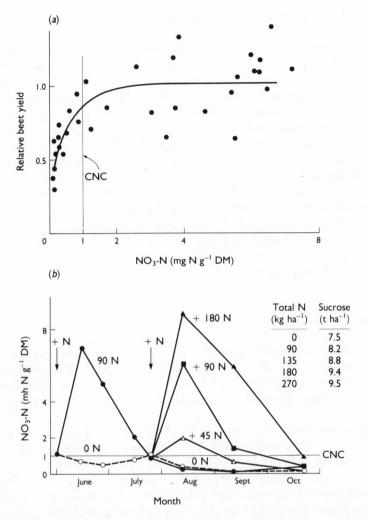

Fig. 12.3. (*a*) CNC$_p$ for nitrogen status of sugarbeet, defined near 1 mg NO$_3$-N g$^{-1}$ dry tissue from petioles of recently matured leaves. The relationship was established with plants grown in a field experiment with different supplies of nitrogen. (*b*) Time course of petiole NO$_3$-N levels for sugarbeet crops supplied with different amounts of nitrogen split into two applications. Also shown are the CNC$_p$ levels established in (*a*). Yields ranged from 7.5 t sucrose ha$^{-1}$ with 0 N to 9.4 t with optimum nitrogen supply (90 + 90 kg). (Redrawn from Ulrich *et al.* (1959).)

Unlike soil analysis, plant analysis cannot carry a prescription for amounts of nutrients that need to be added. Values less than CNC$_p$ indicate that the crop is deficient, but not why that occurred or how deficient. A decline in plant nutrient content may be due to soil exhaustion, or it may be that disease or soil dryness has sharply reduced uptake. Conversely, deficiency of one nutrient slows the rates at which other nutrients are diluted by growth, and their concentrations tend to increase.

Local field experience with a crop is needed to define the amount of nutrient to add. Another type of $CNC_p$, the continuously declining '**safe-level**', attempts to combine such local knowledge with plant analysis. The idea is that if crops are at or above this line early in the season, they will not become deficient before a proper time. This approach must be calibrated for each soil–crop–climate system and depends on the assumption that the system will behave in the same way each year. Because sampling is reduced to a single time, the safe-level method is favored with short-season vegetable crops where, unlike sugarbeet, there is not sufficient time to establish trends.

A more general method for the application of plant analysis is found in the 'Diagnosis and Recommendation Integrated System' (DRIS) (Walworth & Sumner 1987). In this, a large number of observations of yield and nutrient concentrations from production fields within a region are compared to arrive at 'normal' nutrient concentrations and 'normal' ratios of selected nutrients that discriminate between high- and low-yielding fields.

### Fertilizer practices

Given a diagnosis that the supply of a particular nutrient is inadequate to support best growth of a crop, decisions are required regarding the form, amount, timing, and method of applying fertilizer. Use of organic amendments was examined in Section 8.9. Here we consider mineral fertilizers.

**Uptake efficiency**   The response to added nitrogen illustrated in Fig. 12.1 can be extended with the relationship between nitrogen uptake and nitrogen applied as fertilizer shown in Fig. 12.4c. Uptake is almost invariably a straight line function of fertilizer supply (van Keulen 1982, van Keulen & van Heemst 1982). The slope of the line defines fertilizer-uptake efficiency and it seems generally to be constant over ranges as great as 0 to 400 kg N ha$^{-1}$ under high-yielding conditions. Constancy over the entire range is not surprising when one considers the enormous dilution of fertilizer in soils: 400 kg N ha$^{-1}$ is a very small amount when added to upwards of $1.5 \times 10^6$ kg soil and water. It is also not surprising to find that this slope varies from experiment to experiment due to variations in chemical form of the nutrient, method of application, root distribution, soil properties, and other factors. Indeed, control of those differences is among the reasons why mineral fertilizers can be managed more precisely and with less environmental concerns than is the case for manure.

**Mineral fertilizers**   The importance of chemical form is especially clear with phosphorus fertilizers. Apatite ores ('rock phosphate', $Ca_{10}Z_2(PO_4)_6.CaCO_3$, where Z is generally F or Cl, and Ca and P are variously substituted) are the principal source of phosphorus. Even when finely divided, these are only slowly soluble and fertilizer-uptake efficiency is small compared with soluble ('beneficiated') materials

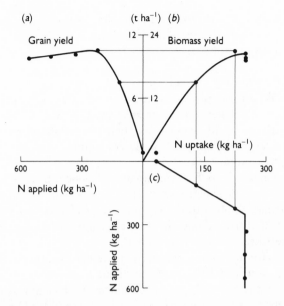

Fig. 12.4. Maize response to nitrogen fertilizer: (*a*) grain yield and (*b*) biomass yield as in Fig. 12.1. (*c*) Relation between nitrogen applied to the soil and nitrogen uptake by the crop. The slope of the rising portion of the curve defines fertilizer-uptake efficiency.

such as 'superphosphate' and 'concentrated superphosphate' fertilizers. Superphosphate [$Ca(H_2PO_4)_2.H_2O + CaSO_4$] is obtained by treating rock phosphate with sulfuric acid; treatment with phosphoric acid yields concentrated superphosphate [$Ca(H_2PO_4)_2.H_2O$]. Distillation of apatite ore concentrates phosphorus even more to polyphosphoric acid, $(H_3PO_4)_n$. A wide array of ammonium and potassium substituted materials are now made from phosphoric acid. Experience in a large number of field trials in Western Australia (Bolland & Gilkes 1990) illustrated the general principle that fertilizer-use efficiency of finely divided rock phosphate sources was only 5–20% that of superphosphate. In those experiments, rock sources were unable to support as great a yield as superphosphate and their residual effectiveness in subsequent years was only 15–50% as great as that of superphosphate.

The behavior of nitrogen compounds depends upon their solubility and whether nitrate or ammonium ions are released in the soil. Ammonium ions tend to be adsorbed quickly by the cation exchange complex whereas nitrate ions move more freely. Exchanged ions are available only to nearby roots or, in the case of ammonium ions, after they are nitrified by bacteria and move to roots. Ammonia gas and aqueous solutions of ammonia should be injected into the soil; applied in bands, these materials sterilize a small zone of soil, causing a slight delay in nitrification while bacteria invade the area. Ammonium sulfate and urea are soluble. They are dispersed by water through a larger soil volume than ammonia and consequently nitrify more rapidly. Ammonium nitrate is highly soluble and is almost as quickly available to plants as is calcium nitrate. The order of response times is nitrate sources > urea > ammonium sulfate > ammonia (Loomis *et al.* 1960). Urea and ammonia (gas or aqueous solutions) are currently the cheapest and most widely used nitrogen fertilizers.

**Placement of fertilizers**   Broadcasting of dry materials onto the soil surface is the simplest method for applying fertilizers and it is the only suitable method for pastures. Surface applications are not efficient, however, unless the material is incorporated with soil by tillage or carried there by rainfall or irrigation. Ammoniacal materials, for example, are particularly vulnerable to losses through volatilization when they remain on the surface.

Placement strongly affects fertilizer uptake efficiency. In Chapter 8, denitrification loss from flooded rice fields were described; rice yields obtained in response to ammonium nitrogen applied to the soil surface or placed into the reducing zone, where it is protected from denitrification, are compared in Fig. 12.5*a*. With row crops, knifing fertilizer in bands parallel to the row allows plants to reach it quickly. Banding provides for more interception by crop roots than broadcasting (Fig. 12.5*b*) and restricts the supply of nutrients to competing weeds.

Another reason that banded applications are more efficient is that less nutrient is exposed to fixation and immobilization. As much as 300–500 kg P ha$^{-1}$ may be needed with a broadcast application to saturate phosphorus-fixing abilities of soils high in iron and aluminum oxides (Section 7.5). Bands containing much smaller amounts of soluble phosphorus are able to saturate fixation in a local zone and a large portion of the application remains available to plants. Phosphorus dissolving slowly from rock phosphate, by contrast, may be captured mainly by soil fixation processes.

Soil dilution and fixation are also avoided with foliar applications of nutrients. Application from airplanes is useful when the ground is too wet for traffic or when travel would damage the canopy. Only small rates of fertilizer can be tolerated by foliage, however. Where irrigation is practiced, nutrients are sometimes run with the irrigation water. This avoids the need for trafficking the field, and the cost of application is small, but fertilizer distribution is no better than the distribution of water (Chapter 14).

**Time of application**   Plants have their greatest need for nutrients during the vegetative phase to support leaf growth. To make full use of the growing season, some nutrients must be available early so that full cover and maximum growth rate are reached quickly. The easiest procedure is to apply all of the needed material at or before planting although some loss may occur during the lag phase of seedling growth when nutrient uptake is small. Losses can be reduced for row crops by splitting the application between a 'starter', applied in bands near the seed and a later band application ('side-dressing') made just before canopy closure. The amount of the second application can be adjusted according to intervening weather and crop growth.

Applications of nitrogen late in the vegetative period or after flowering favor nutrient accumulation in reproductive organs. Responses are species specific. Wheat, for example, can absorb considerable nitrogen after flowering and responds

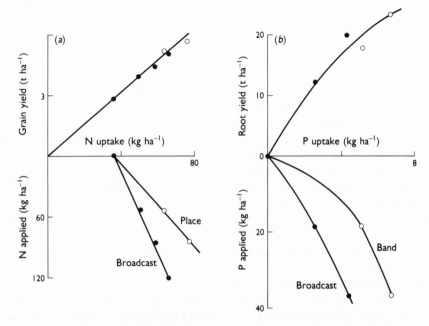

Fig. 12.5. Economic yields for flooded rice and rutabaga (*Brassica napobras-sica*) as a function of nutrient uptake (redrawn from van Keulen and van Heemst (1982).) (*a*) Rice grain yield responses in Indonesia to urea fertilizer broadcast to the surface (0.27 recovered) or placed 0.1 m deep in the reducing zone (0.56 recovered). (*b*) Fresh root yields of rutabaga obtained in England in response to phosphorus fertilizer broadcast and incorporated or placed in a band near the seed.

with an increased protein content in grain. Late application of nitrogen has an unfavorable effect on sugarbeet since it stimulates vegetative growth rather than sucrose accumulation and leads to a higher content of non-sucrose materials in the beet. Sucrose yield then is less and extraction more difficult. In general, late applications of nitrogen increase the risk of greater carry-over of mineral nitrogen and thus of greater losses during the fallow period.

The solubility of phosphate minerals is strongly dependent on temperature as was illustrated in Fig. 7.10. Plantings in cool soils sometimes reveal deficiency through very large responses from starter bands of soluble phosphorus on soils where warm-season crops show no response to added phosphorus.

**Managing nutrient supply**  Regardless of the method or material used, the objective of fertilization is to satisfy crop needs, not the soil's. Efficient use of fertilizers and organic amendments is important. The best approach usually is to treat the need for each nutrient (relative to an expected yield level) as an independent question. Accurate diagnosis of the amount of nutrient needed is the first step, and the most difficult. Once that assessment is made, fertilization can be done in an efficient way with appropriate pure or mixed sources. Problems of doing that with organic sources were considered in Section 8.9.

There is no way of predicting accurately the amount of nutrients that must be supplied to a crop so that its growth rate is not limited during a growing season, yet at the same time not being in surplus. Mineralization–immobilization balances are always uncertain; additional variation arises from effects of weather variations, insects, and disease on nutrient use. Uncertainties about availability and plant access to applied nutrients are controlled to some extent with proper decisions about the form, timing, and placement of mineral fertilizers, but farmers must rely heavily on field histories and past experience for expectations about yields and nutrient requirements. Good record keeping is a must. Soil and plant analyses and simple experiments are also useful. Experiments with zero, normal, and double-normal amounts of fertilizer as treatments, created by skipping a strip of land on one pass of the applicator and doubling on the next, are helpful.

Most surplus nutrients remain in the soil and can be taken as a credit towards future crops. The cost is one year's interest on the investment and most farmers accept that in preference to risks of serious nutrient deficiencies. Immobilization, fixation, leaching, and denitrification (of nitrogen) intervene in the calculation of the carryover supply.

**Replacement fertilization**, in which as much N, P, and K are applied as are removed by crops, was advocated in the past by some agriculturalists as a way to educate farmers about the extractive nature of farming and the importance of land stewardship. It is the wrong approach to crop nutrition, however, because a soil may be able to supply one nutrient indefinitely while being only marginally deficient in another, and woefully deficient in a third. Replacement fertilization emerged recently among environmentalists in an amended form: farmers should not be allowed to apply more nutrients than they remove. That concept ignores inevitable losses of some nutrients and fixation of others. The approach would result, in most instances, in a downward spiral of yields and fertilization, with accompanying inefficiencies in use of energy, labor, capital, radiation, and water.

## 12.4  TILLAGE

Movement and mixing of soil through tillage accomplishes several important functions. The most important are control of residues and competing vegetation. Tillage also is used to control flow of water, distribute fertilizers, pesticides, and amendments, and to create favorable environments for stand establishment and root development. Each soil and each farming system present unique tillage problems and solutions. Clayey-textured soils, for example, behave very differently from sandy-textured ones, and freeze–thaw and wet–dry cycles modify the amount of tillage required. Given the wide array of tillage implements and continuing innovation, knowledge of local conditions and terminology for machinery is required in evaluating various approaches. Understanding the consequences of tillage is almost as complex as understanding plant growth and it is not surprising that decisions regarding types of tillage and when and how to use them are not made easily.

**Primary tillage**

**Residue control**  Some form of plowing to dispose of residues and to crumble soil for planting is the major tillage activity in most cropping systems. Incorporation of residues promotes decay and efficient cycling of nutrients. Incorporation also is effective in control of some weeds, foliar diseases, and insects. Coarse residues (e.g. maize) and heavy yields of fine straws (e.g. wheat) may have to be cut with a shredder or disk prior to plowing. Without that, seedbeds may be too loose for control of planting depth and good moisture contact with seed.

The nitrogen content of residues influences methods of disposal. Residues with C/N ratios greater than about 45 (N content < 1% of dry matter) decompose slowly while immobilizing available nitrogen from soil. When surface residues are burned prior to tillage, nitrogen and carbon are lost to the atmosphere but foliar diseases are controlled, subsequent tillage is simplified, and complications from nitrogen immobilization are avoided. Burning of rice stubbles has an additional benefit in greatly reducing production of methane (a greenhouse gas) during decay under flooded conditions. Where livestock are included in the farming system, stubbles can be grazed or straw can be harvested, used as bedding, and then returned to the field as composted manure. Complete incorporation or removal of residues is not always the best solution since surface residues are very useful in erosion control.

**Tillage implements**  The moldboard, turning, plow has been the basic tool for tillage in western cultures since its invention in the 1700s. Its great contribution is to provide a way of cutting and turning meadow residues, facilitating crop rotations involving leguminous forage crops as a source of nitrogen and animal feed. Usual depths of tillage are 20–25 cm; with a standard moldboard, only about 10% of the residues remain on the surface. Fields are left in a rough state resistant to water erosion. Moldboards are the preferred plow for heavy soils, heavy stands of weeds, and/or heavy residues.

A turning action is also achieved with disk plows and heavy disk harrows but with less coverage of residues (*ca.* 50%). Disk plows employ a gang of several large (up to 1 m dia.), angled disks that till soil to a depth of 12–15 cm. Heavy disk harrows use a larger number of smaller disks (up to 0.6 m), usually mounted in 'tandem' fashion on two axles. These are set to a smaller angle of attack and less depth (8–13 cm). Disks are useful for primary tillage with moderate residues; scalloped disks are sometimes used to aid in cutting residues.

Chisel plows consist of a gang of rigidly mounted chisels fitted with small sweep points. Set to 15–20 cm depth, they create a churning action and leave the soil in a rough condition with more than 50% of the residues on the surface. Infiltration rates are high and the resistance of the plowed surface to wind and water erosion is generally excellent. Chisel plows with twisted shanks and/or larger points produce greater churning action and residue incorporation. Field cultivators, essentially light chisel plows equipped with wide (30 cm or more) sweep points, also create a churning action. Run at about 15 cm depth, field cultivators are more effective against perennial weeds than are chisels and they leave as much as 90% of the residues on the surface. They are used for primary tillage with light residues.

Chisel plows require only about 0.6 as much drawbar power per meter width as conventional moldboards and, given a large tractor, they can be pulled in wide spans at higher speed than moldboards resulting in twice the labor productivity of conventional moldboards. Risk avoidance through timely operations is one important consequence. Those benefits and erosion control have increased their popularity in recent years. New, high-speed moldboards having wider spacing of the bottoms and flatter boards than conventional moldboards also achieve those goals.

**Primary tillage systems**  Use of a moldboard plow, usually preceded and followed by a disk, is termed **conventional tillage** in contrast to various **reduced-tillage** and **no-till** systems. Many variations of these concept names exist. **Conservation tillage**, usually with chisels, disks, or field cultivators, describes reduced tillage systems that leave significant amounts of surface residues. Conservation tillage with chisel plows is now the most common method for maize and soybean production in America. **Stubble-mulching**, a subsurface tillage method used with wheat production in the American Great Plains to control wind erosion, served as an antecedent of conservation tillage. In typical stubble-mulch systems, field cultivators are used at the beginning of the fallow period to loosen the soil. Weeds that emerge during the fallow are destroyed with 'rod weeders' (a rotating square rod is pulled under the loosened stubble). In no-till systems, the crop is planted directly into the residue of the previous crop. Erosion control is excellent but the soil dries and warms slowly in the spring (a disadvantage in temperate zones) and mechanical cultivation is impeded by residues.

Several trade-offs are involved in the choice of tillage systems. Conventional tillage deals most effectively with heavy stubbles. It also provides the most uniform seed beds, the best assurance of a crop stand, and the best weed control. Yields tend to be greater with conventional tillage than by other methods but risk of erosion during the crop period is also greater. Dependence on herbicides for weed control increases with each reduction in tillage and no-till systems are entirely dependent upon pre- and post-emergence herbicides, rotation, and competitive effects for control. Herbicides cannot be incorporated into the soil in that system and the surface residues intercept herbicide sprays resulting in less effective control.

Nutrient cycling and fine root development vary with the degree of residue incorporation accomplished in tillage. In untilled fields, nutrients tend to be leached from residues by rainfall and losses to runoff are generally greater than when residues are incorporated. In comparison with soils under conventional and reduced tillage, the surface layer of no-till soils has much more organic content, more nutrients, and dramatically lower pH whereas lower horizons generally have less organic matter and less nutrients. With nutrients and root growth concentrated near the surface, no-till crops are vulnerable to nutrient deficiency as the soil dries. Deep placement of fertilizer is an effective solution to that problem.

## Secondary tillage

The looseness of freshly plowed ground makes a poor seed bed since planting depth and seed contact with soil moisture are not assured. Several tools find use in smoothing and firming the ground. Field cultivators (set to a shallow depth), light disks, and spring- and spike-toothed harrows are the most common tools. Toothed harrows present arrays of curved springs or short, rigid spikes. In semiarid regions where low-organic soils often are tilled dry, ring rollers (closely spaced, toothed rings that rotate loosely on a common axle) are useful for breaking clods and firming soils.

Incorporation of fertilizer, herbicides, and amendments such as lime are sometimes integrated with secondary tillage operations. Broadcast fertilizer, for example, can be incorporated with a field cultivator. In some systems, planting is done on ridges or beds for control of erosion, drainage, or soil temperature, or to facilitate irrigation. Ridges and beds are formed with a wide variety of furrowing and bed-shaping devices. Fertilizer and herbicides broadcast prior to furrowing end in a band through the middle of the bed or ridge.

## Planting and cultivation

Most planting operations also involve some tillage of the soil. Lister planters used for sorghum production in the American Great Plains represent an extreme example: a small plow clears a symmetrical furrow ahead of the planter so that seed are placed into moist soil at the bottom of the furrow. The furrow is closed during later cultivations. Furrow closure provides weed control and promotes adventitious rooting from stem bases. Knife openers are common on planters where the surface is free of residues, whereas various types of coulters or single- and double-disk openers are needed in systems with surface residues. The last elements of most planters are a covering device and packing wheels to firm the soil-seed contact.

Weed control can be accomplished with several types of cultivation. Wide spans of tine weeders (a dense array of small spring tines) and rotary hoes (closely spaced spiked wheels) that can be pulled at high speed ($ca.$ 18 km h$^{-1}$) are useful for eliminating small weeds and crusts during early stages of a crop. Light ring rollers are also popular as crust breakers. The basic tool for inter-row cultivation is a tractor-mounted array of spear- or sweep-pointed shanks arranged to till the spaces between the rows. These operate slowly (6 km h$^{-1}$) in narrow spans so labor and fuel costs are high. Control of weeds within rows can be achieved with sweeps arranged to move soil from the middle to form a slight ridge within the row.

## Modification of soil temperature

Tillage can be directed towards avoiding or modifying unfavorable soil temperatures. In extreme cases, fields can be converted into hot beds by shaping the soil to

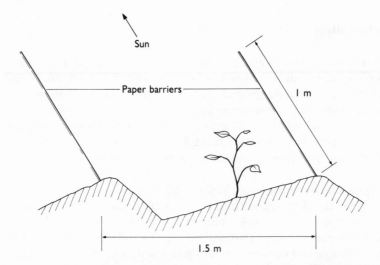

**Fig. 12.6. Sloped seed bed with protective paper shelters used for forcing vegetable production in a cool climate. The arrangement creates non-uniform soil temperatures (cold behind the barrier, warm towards the sun) while protecting plants from wind and, at night, from radiation frost.**

create a non-uniform distribution of the limiting resource, short-wave radiation. The sloping beds illustrated in Fig. 12.6 represent a sophisticated way of forcing vegetables. Such practices are obviously labor-intensive and expensive, and thus suited only to high-value crops. They are less expensive, however, than glasshouse production or transplanting seedlings from hotbeds. As long-distance aerial transport has increased, forcing of fruits and vegetables in local areas has been replaced by conventional production in warmer regions and in the opposite hemisphere.

The strongly competitive markets faced by field crops have never justified horticultural forcing. Nevertheless, attention to land form, residues, and timing of cultivations and irrigation can be rewarding. Considerable benefit from more rapid warming is achieved by ridging the soil in fall and planting into the tops of the ridges in spring. Where soil temperatures too high for plant survival are encountered, planting in furrows (lister planting), under stubbles or residue mulches, or cooling the soil by irrigation are effective practices.

Surface residues affect soil temperature by elevating the plane of $R_n$ exchange and by protecting soil from turbulent transfer. In temperate regions, retention of stubble through the winter traps a layer of snow, insulating crops such as winter wheat, and extending their range into colder climates. Moldboard plowing in the fall protects fallow ground against deep freezing because the increase in pore space reduces soil thermal conductivity. In spring, the dark, absorbing, surface of tilled soil warms and dries sooner and spring operations of seed-bed preparation and planting can be accomplished earlier than with surface mulches. Conversely, the slower warming of soils under surface mulches has limited adoption of no-till farming in some areas.

## 12.5 DRAINAGE

Drainage practices aim at relieving soil profiles of excess water and at preventing flooding or seepage of water onto farmlands. Annual evapotranspiration is less for cultivated fields and heavily grazed pastures than for natural vegetation because the duration and/or degree of green cover are less. As a result, runoff and drainage terms are also larger (see Eq. 9.1, the hydrologic balance). Consequently, levees and channels are essential to divert water and to drain the root zone in areas subject to seepage or flooding.

Few crops, the outstanding exception being rice, can withstand the anaerobic conditions of waterlogged soil for more than a few hours or days. Benefits of drainage extend well beyond just improved survival of crops, however. In temperate climates, wet soils are slow to warm in spring. That and/or a high water table limits the diversity of species that can be grown and their depth and extent of rooting. Decay and mineralization are slowed in wet soil while denitrification is accelerated and problems with metal toxicities and root diseases are more severe. Wet soils will not support machines or animals and the timeliness of operations can be sharply restricted. Tillage of a wet soil degrades its structure, and wet areas of pastures are easily destroyed through 'poaching' by animals. The principal effect of drainage is a marked increase in yield level. Stability is also improved because a major source of spatial and temporal variability is eliminated.

Many seasonally flooded or boggy upland areas, both regional and on individual farms, have been converted to productive land by drainage. In addition, significant areas of floodplains and wetlands receive drainage. The earliest known examples of drainage were made by Roman and Chinese farmers over 2000 y ago. Between AD 1100 and 1300, a significant expansion of farmland and colonization in eastern Europe was based on drainage. Today, nearly 70% of the farm lands in Britain and The Netherlands are under drainage compared with about 25% in the USA.

The first requisite for drainage is an outfall sufficiently low in altitude, or provided with pumps, to rapidly convey excess water from a region. Individual farmers then connect their own drains to these channels. Outfalls are usually provided by a regional authority through construction of principal drainage canals or by straightening the course of meandering rivers. Channel straightening steepens a river's gradient increasing its flow rate for channel scouring. Slow-moving streams tend to fill with sediment causing seasonal flooding from the overflow as well as the cutting of new channels.

The simplest systems of field drainage engage only excess surface water through channels constructed between topographical depressions and an outfall, or along the base of hills to prevent flooding of the footplain by runoff or seepage. The problem of saturated profiles requires more elaborate works. The oldest approach, still used in many parts of the world, depended on construction of mounds or raised beds of land separated by drainage channels. A cambered surface to the beds provides runoff and height above the channel provides subsurface drainage. Scottish farmers revolutionized drainage practice through experiments in the 1820s with permanent subsurface drains. In their first designs, a trench was dug, partly filled with gravel, then back-filled. Spectacular benefits and the high cost of gravel led quickly to development of clay tile, first as simple inverted U-channels and later as cylinders, and of tile-making machines. Scotsman John Johnston of Geneva, New York, introduced stone and then tile drains to his farm, beginning in 1835. His experience and writings spread the practice in the USA. In the present century, mechanized trenchers greatly eased the work of laying drainage lines.

Modern subsurface drains are constructed with corrugated plastic pipe that is perforated at intervals to admit water. These are laid with a trencher or pulled in with a 'mole' plow while maintaining a constant gradient towards the outfall. The depth and separation of parallel drain lines are established with engineering formulae depending upon groundwater conditions and soil texture. Lines must be spaced more closely in clayey soils having low hydraulic conductivity than in light-textured soils.

## 12.6   EROSION

### An active landscape

Earth's surface is highly active with uplift and formation of new land mass countered through continual erosion by wind and water. Erosion over geologic time by glaciers, water, and wind is given perspective by examining the 5000 m of sediments laid open in a transect of America's Grand Canyon, Vermilion Cliffs, Zion Canyon, and Cedar Breaks. Natural erosion has slowed since the evolution of gymnosperms and flowering plants began to provide protective cover to the land during the past 100 million years yet regions such as California and New Zealand, with highly active landscapes due to tectonic plate movement and volcanic activity, continue to have very high natural rates of erosion. Rapid erosion can also occur with agriculture.

There is more to erosion than just the carrying away of solid particles by water. All of the primary and secondary minerals found in soils are soluble to some degree, indeed that is the basis of soil formation, and downwearing of a landscape is also driven by solubilization.

### Loss and replacement of soil

Erosion reduces the potential productivity of a soil through removal of nutrient-rich surface layers, reduction in profile depth capable of holding moisture, and by altering landforms. Off-site damage through air and water pollution and silting of river channels and reservoirs may accompany erosion. That humans have long recognized this problem is evidenced by ancient terracing and river works and windbreaks in many parts of the world. Serious mistakes continue to be made, however. In this century, the 'Dust Bowl' crisis of the American Great Plains in the 1930s, failures in the Soviet New Lands projects in the 1960s, and continuing high rates of erosion in many areas point to the need for greater understanding and effort directed at erosion problems.

Some erosion during cropping cycles is inescapable but all sites also have some **tolerance to erosion**. Evaluations of tolerance require judgments about rates of soil formation (an uncertain proposition) and the time horizon over which land use is to be sustained. Older views of soil quality emphasized topsoil and its content of nutrients. Because humus levels can be restored quickly and nutrients can be replenished from external sources, depth of profile and its water-holding capacity have assumed greater importance as criteria of soil quality.

A strict tolerance with the soil loss rate equal or less than the soil formation rate would allow production to continue indefinitely. Estimates of formation rates at undisturbed sites are generally near 0.1 to 0.2 mm depth $y^{-1}$ (i.e., about 1.3 to 2.6 t $ha^{-1} y^{-1}$). Rates increase with rainfall. These values are found by dividing the depth of profile by time since the last great disturbance, for example, the last glaciation, but tenfold greater rates (1–2 mm $y^{-1}$, 13–26 t $ha^{-1} y^{-1}$) are observed during the first century or two following such disturbances. Formation rates for eroding agricultural soils probably fall into that category of greater rates because subsoils are less insulated from tillage, percolation, leaching, and weathering as top soil is removed through erosion (Morgan & Davidson 1986).

In the absence of good data on formation rates, soil conservation workers view tolerance in terms of the time span for a measurable yield decline of, say, 10%, or in relation to depth of profile available for formation. 'Acceptable' rates of erosion generally have time spans of 25 to 50 y for a yield decline. That is a short period relative to our views of sustainability. In practice, yield declines are measurable only with extreme erosion; in most cases, they have been masked by technological advances in yield. In addition, yield level can usually be restored quickly by some alternative treatment of the land, for example, by fertilization or by conversion to pasture for a period of time. Tolerances assigned to deep loess soils are generally large: 10 t $ha^{-1} y^{-1}$ or more corresponding to a depth of about 0.8 mm $y^{-1}$. In China, some loess soils have sustained even greater rates for thousands of years but China also has numerous examples of extensive areas ruined by gullying. In contrast to loess, shallow soils with underlaying agglomerations or bedrock may have little or no tolerance to erosion.

In the future, it is likely that tolerable soil loss will be judged not just on sustainability but also on more demanding criteria relating to levels of atmospheric pollution, sediment and chemical fluxes, and turbidity of surface waters. In other words, the public may take an increasingly strong position about off-site effects of erosion.

## Water erosion

**Erosion processes**  Water from rainfall and snowmelt causes several types of erosion. Uniform erosion over an area is termed overland (or 'sheet') erosion. A film of water, agitated in some cases by rainfall, can detach and move soil particles along a slope. With a long slope, transport accelerates and small rill channels form. A continuing stream of snowmelt can cause considerable rill erosion in soils loosened by freeze–thaw cycles. Erosive action within rills can be rather powerful. Long-term, down-slope, movement by overland and rill erosion causes gradual

Table 12.2 *Factors influencing soil movement by water*

Letter codes (R, K, LS, C, and P) are those used in the Universal Soil Loss Equation.

| Factor | Influence on soil movement |
|---|---|
| R, rainfall | Erosion increases with intensity (mm h$^{-1}$) as well as amount of rain (mm). |
| K, soil erodibility | Fine sands and silts are moved more easily than coarse sand and clay. Soil particles are detached more easily from poor structure with poorly aggregated clays due to low Ca or humus, or high Na content. |
| LS, gradient and length of slope | Erosion rates increase rapidly as the gradient increases above 4% and as length of slope increases. |
| C, surface protection | Erosion is greatest with bare ground not covered by plants or residues. Standing crops break the force of raindrops. Stony surfaces and residue mulches absorb the impact and prevent movement. |
| P, management | Erosion is greater with up and down rows than with contour plantings. Terracing and drainage lessen erosion. |

downwearing of hilltops, backwearing of slopes, and accumulation of alluvial footplains at the base of hills.

Gullies develop when larger torrents repeatedly follow the same untended tracks. Whereas small rills are easily disrupted by tillage, gullies destroy the landform for cultivation. Gully formation is rather complex. It can start with rills, from subsurface tunneling by drainage water, or, most commonly, by a scouring action of water passing over the upper face of small depressions on a hillside. The scouring action creates a retreating headland that eventually becomes a gully. Gullying is often spectacular but it can be addressed easily if caught early, or avoided completely with simple engineering works and management practices that divert down-slope movement of water.

An impressive body of physics and engineering knowledge exists relating to explanation, prediction, and prevention of water erosion. A summary of the main factors affecting water erosion is presented in Table 12.2. Overland and rill erosion are greatest when surface soils are saturated by snowmelt or intense rainstorms. Impacts of raindrops loosen and suspend particles from saturated soils. The ability of a rainfall to dislodge soil depends upon its intensity (mm rainfall h$^{-1}$) and the kinetic energy of the raindrops (J m$^{-2}$ land mm$^{-1}$ rainfall). The relationship varies with drop size and thus with the type of rainfall. The example in Fig. 12.7 illustrates that maximum energy was achieved at that site with any rainfall intensity greater than 25 mm h$^{-1}$. Only a fraction of the storms that occur have sufficient intensity and duration to cause significant erosion. A single storm per year, or just one in 5 y, may account for nearly all of the long-term average erosion from a system.

Sand is easily detached by raindrops, whereas clay particles tend to bind together and are not easily detached. Coarse sand and soil aggregates are large enough to

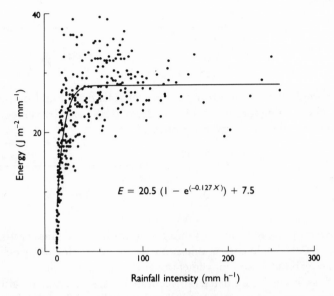

$$E = 20.5 \, (1 - e^{(-0.127 X)}) + 7.5$$

**Fig. 12.7. Kinetic energy of rainfalls at Holly Springs, Mississippi, as a function of rainfall intensity. (Redrawn from McGregor & Mutchler (1977).)**

resist movement by water leaving very fine sand and silt as the most susceptible to runoff when rainfall exceeds infiltration capacity. Loess soils, lacking a sand component that might protect the surface and small rills, are particularly susceptible to erosion. Infiltration to clay can be as little as 2–5 mm h$^{-1}$ compared with the common occurrence of rainfall > 20 mm h$^{-1}$. In contrast, infiltration into a drained sand will accommodate almost any rainfall.

**The Universal Soil Loss Equation**  A number of quantitative tools have been developed to predict erosion (Morgan & Davidson 1986). The **Universal Soil Loss Equation** (USLE), for example, was developed by the USDA Soil Conservation Service (Wischmeier & Smith 1978) from statistical analyses of more than 10 000 experimental plot-years covering diverse soils, crops, and weather in humid areas of the USA. The equation attempts to predict the average annual soil 'loss', $A$, in ton acre$^{-1}$ or t ha$^{-1}$:

$$A = R_i K_i LSCP. \hspace{3cm} \text{[Eq. 12.1]}$$

$R_i$ is a rainfall–runoff index relating to the power of storms in the region; $K_i$ is the erodibility index of the local soil; $LS$ combines length and gradient of slope; $C$ represents crop and residue cover; and $P$ is the beneficial effect of preventive management practices such as terracing. $LS$, $C$, and $P$ parameters express erosion relative to rates that would occur with bare soil, of specific slope and length, and cultivated up and down the slope. Length ($L$) and steepness ($S$) of the hills generally dominate the equation as is illustrated with $LS$ values drawn from tables in Wischmeier & Smith (1978):

*Slope:*

| Length | 2% | 8% | 16% |
|--------|------|------|------|
| 30 m | 0.20 | 0.99 | 2.84 |
| 90 m | 0.28 | 1.72 | 4.92 |

Cover provided by crops and residues protect soils from raindrop impact and slow runoff. The C value for bare soil is 1.0; dramatically smaller values are found when soils are provided cover by crops or residues:

*Percent cover:*

| Type of cover | 0% | 50% | 100% |
|---------------|------|------|------|
| 1 m tall crop | 1.0 | 0.65 | 0.30 |
| Residues | 1.0 | 0.30 | 0.03 |

Good meadow crops (grasses and legumes grown for hay) and grass pasture have C values less than 0.01. Inclusion of a meadow phase in rotation sequences sharply reduces the probability of soil movement over the rotation cycle.

The term 'loss' in the USLE name is inaccurate because movement within a field rather than export from the region is predicted. The annual flux of sediment in the Mississippi River, for example, comes more from gullying and bank cutting than from field erosion. Total movement of sediments and dissolved minerals in that river is only about 0.1 of the amount of soil movement predicted in its watershed by the USLE indicating either that the equation over-predicts or that most eroded material is deposited on lowlands or is captured in reservoirs.

Empirical equations such as the USLE require an enormous amount of experimental work to establish appropriate parameter values for local soils and practices and to adjust the equation to changing technology. In practice, the rarity of erosive storms creates uncertainties in $R_i$, and $K_i$ sometimes must be arrived at by guesswork. Use of USLE is supported by detailed soil maps, extensive tables and nomographs providing quantitative values for terms in the equation, and by local experience. It is a poor predictor of actual erosion, however, and research continues to upgrade or replace it. Process-based models are less site-specific and seem to offer more promise (Rose 1985). Despite the equation's limitations, USLE parameter values reflect the relative effect of different farming practices on erosion sufficiently well to be used in USA as a basis for national and local conservation programs.

**Terraces and contours**    Farming along elevation contours reduces erosion to about half that observed with up and down cultivation. Strip contouring and terracing give further benefit by interrupting the length of slopes. These techniques form beautiful (to an agriculturalist's eye) and highly effective patterns on large hills with gently changing gradients (Fig. 12.8). With short, rapidly changing gradients, however, contours can only approximate the general trend of the land.

The remarkable effectiveness of terraces is seen in level benches with stone retaining walls that have continued in use for centuries in Asia, South America, and Mediterranean regions. Unfortunately, the great cost of such terraces in capital and human effort now limits their maintenance (and expansion) even for high-value

**Fig. 12.8. Aerial view of contour strip-cropping in Jasper County, Iowa. Soils are derived from loess and slopes range from 2 to 18%. Dark strips are maize; light-colored ones are ripening oat. Water courses are grassed, and the most erodible lands are assigned to permanent pasture (right center). (Photograph courtesy of USDA Soil Conservation Service.)**

crops. Simpler terraces with 'narrow' (grassed) or 'broad' (farmed over) bases shaped with earth-moving equipment are widely used for field crops (Fig. 12.9). These are designed to slow the rate of runoff and to either convey it off the land (humid climates) or to conserve it through infiltration (semiarid climates).

**Seasonal watercourses** Seasonal watercourses formed by the intersection of two slopes present special problems to farming. Such courses collect seepage from adjacent hills and may be too wet to support traffic. In addition, heavy flows of water can turn the course into a gully. Two solutions to these problems are illustrated in Fig. 12.9. One involves shaping the course with a wide bottom vegetated with grass and providing subsurface drains along the bases of the intercepting slopes. This leaves the grassed area sufficiently dry for crossing traffic. The second involves construction of narrow-base dams across the water course to transfer surface flows through perforated standpipes to subsurface drain lines. Sediments settle within the basins; over time, a level terrace is formed.

**Farm boundaries and erosion** Erosion and drainage are watershed problems whereas farm boundaries typically are based on different principles and rarely follow contours. Small farms generally control only a portion of a problem hill or water course and, for them, allocation of land to permanently grassed headlands and water courses has a greater relative effect on annual income than it does for large farms. Large farms tend to do a better job of setting aside or correcting problem

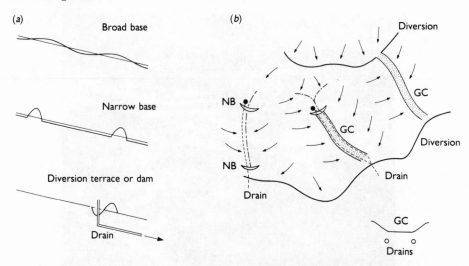

Fig. 12.9. (a) Diagrams of broad-base, narrow-base, and diversion terraces. In each case, tillage and planting follow the contour; broad-base terraces are farmed across, while the others are permanently grassed. Installation of a drain line with perforated riser is illustrated with the diversion terrace. (b) Map of a landscape headed and footed by diversion terraces. Water courses ($\cdot - \cdot -$) are treated variously with: (left) narrow-base dams (NB) and drain lines (– – –); (middle) NB dam and a shaped and grassed channel (GC) supplied with drain lines; and (right) grassed channel. The cross-section of a shaped water course with drain lines is illustrated below.

areas in part because they more easily afford the capital costs of conservation and changes in tillage practice. The present worth of future benefits from projects such as terracing, however, is invariably less than the cost of conservation. As a consequence, most western nations have programs in which costs of projects such as terracing are shared by government.

## Wind erosion

Wind erosion is a hazard mainly in semiarid and arid regions of the world because dry soil will detach with wind whereas wet soil does not. In addition, strong winds are more common where sensible heat flux dominates the energy balance. The processes of wind erosion are rather different than those with water. Aggregated silt and clay are not easily detached by wind; coarse sand has too great a ratio of mass to cross-sectional area to move. Erosion begins with the movement of easily detached, fine sand (0.1 to 0.25 mm). Blown sand bounds along the surface ('saltates') with a highly abrasive action. Seedling plants are particularly vulnerable to abrasion because they offer little drag (Section 6.8) to slow the air and sand. On striking dry soil, the sand detaches aggregated clay resulting in further erosion and dust storms. Saltation increases with length of fetch and wind erosion is therefore most severe from broad, flat areas.

Prediction equations have also been developed for wind erosion (e.g. Woodruff & Siddoway 1965). These are generally more complex, but also better based on mechanical principles, than those for water erosion.

Maintenance of vegetative cover is the basic measure for control of wind erosion. Vegetation displaces the zero plane of wind profiles so that wind velocity near the ground is too small to be erosive. Residue mulches on fallow ground are helpful, particularly if they remain anchored to the soil, a key feature of stubble-mulch systems with subsurface tillage. Fallow lands can be protected to some extent by ridge tillage or by rough, cloddy surfaces created by plowing moist soil. Tillage operations such as plowing or furrowing are used in emergency situations to control ongoing wind erosion. Where wind erosion is a common hazard, maintenance of the land in grassland is the best means for preventing erosion.

Windbreaks ('shelterbelts') of trees and shrubs planted in rows at right angles to prevailing winds are an ancient solution to wind erosion that is still employed in many regions. Hedgerows, with about 50% porosity to the wind, control erosion by creating a layer of slow-moving air near the ground. Tallness is important; as a general rule, a permeable windbreak will reduce the relative wind velocity near the ground by 50% for a distance downwind of 10 times its height. A 10 m tall break thus protects about 100 m of cropland but the break itself will occupy perhaps a 10 m wide strip.

Faced with strong onshore winds, early farmers along the California coast planted rows of tall-growing eucalypts in shelterbelts. These trees usurp moisture and light from a wide band of land, however, and a current trend is to replace them with rows of maize distributed at intervals across the field. A special problem of wind erosion of peaty soils in the California Delta region was solved in a similar way. Culture of white asparagus required continued tillage to keep the asparagus covered as it elongated, but that led to storms of black peat dust. Control was achieved with sprinkler irrigation on windy days and by interplanting with rows of barley.

## 12.7  LAND CAPABILITY

The value of land for farming is reflected in its current market price, an index that integrates economic factors such as commodity prices, distance to market, and discount rates as well as traits such as water supply and production potential. We also need means for assessing the merit of land independently of current economics. Two methods have emerged. It is useful, for example, to evaluate land from its potential for cultivation, giving weight to the ease with which it can be farmed and to hazards that may accompany farming, rather than to production potential. Factors such as wetness, erosion hazards, ease of tillage, spatial variability, and depth of profile can be included in the evaluation. The Land Capability classification system of the USDA Soil Conservation Service is the pioneering example of this approach. Alternatively, we can consider production potential expressed in terms of expected yields of principal crops. Regional and local planners make considerable use of both approaches.

Table 12.3 USDA *Land capability classes*

| |
|---|
| *Class I.* Few limitations to cultivation. Soils are level, with deep, well-drained profiles, never subject to flooding; inherently productive or responsive to fertilization. |
| *Class II.* Moderate limitations restrict the range of crops that may be grown or require some special management or conservation practice. Subclasses e (erosion), w (wetness), s (soil morphology problem), and c (climate) indicate the nature of the limitation. |
| *Class III–IV.* Severe and very severe limitations, respectively. Subclasses are the same as for Class II. |
| *Class V.* Lands without an erosion hazard but unsuited to cultivation owing to wetness, shallow soil, or other factor. |
| *Class VI–VIII.* Severe and very severe limitations make these lands unsuited for agriculture except, in some cases, grazing. |

*Source:* Klingebiel & Montgomery (1961).

## USDA Land Capability classes

The USDA Land Capability system (Klingebiel & Montgomery 1961) places each unit of land into one of seven classes as summarized in Table 12.3. This scheme provides a basis for map overlays characterizing possible agricultural uses. By emphasizing erosion and drainage problems, the approach relates well to sustainability. Within regions, classes are further divided into subclasses and 'units' denoted by a numeral. The Muscatine silty clay loam in Fig. 12.10 (soil 119 in the figure) has the highest Capability, I; Tama silt loam has Capabilities IIe (soil 120B) and IIIe (soils 120C2 and 120D2) based on increasing slope (2–5% for B, 5–9% for C, and 9–14% for D) and degree of water erosion; and Colo (soil 5B), which is subject to seepage and flooding, is classified IIw (Nestrud & Worster 1979).

Similar land capability systems are now used in other countries. Portugal's new system will follow the same general pattern as USDA's. In England and Wales, Class V is omitted and land gradients are weighted more to their suitability for machines than to erosion. Canada also omits Class V while retaining an emphasis on erosion.

## Production indices

Land capability classes provide a qualitative statement about the ease of farming whereas production indices make a quantitative statement about success in farming and are more easily interpreted by farmers. Expected-yield tables form the basis of land capability evaluations in many European countries. These can be constructed in several ways. USDA soil survey reports, for example, include local knowledge of yields attainable with good management. In 1979, the expected yields of dry maize grain on the Tama soils described above ranged from 7000 down to 5800 kg ha$^{-1}$ with increasing slope (Nestrud & Worster 1979). Current yields now exceed that

Fig. 12.10. Portion of the soil map for Jasper County, Iowa. Two 'sections', each one square mile (640 acres, 259 ha), are shown. Subclasses of each soil series relate to slope and drainage as described in the text. Light streaks in the unmapped section at the right are grassed water courses. (From Nestrud & Worster (1979).)

range, however, demonstrating the possibility for technological obsolescence. Dutch scientists make considerable use of potential yield models dependent upon radiation. As is discussed in Chapter 18, Buringh & van Heemst (1979) used de Wit's model of potential production at various latitudes along with local data on soils, rainfall, and length of growing season to construct estimates of agricultural production for each region of the globe. The estimates were expressed in wheat equivalents as a standard unit.

The Storie Index (Storie 1933), used in California and parts of Latin America, offers a quantitative index of a soil's potential in production that ranges from 0 for non-agricultural land to 100 for the best sites. The index is derived by multiplying tabulated factors for parent material and profile development, surface texture, slope, and limitations imposed by salinity, drainage, and nutrient supply. The Storie index ignores climate factors and the indices compare relative merits of soils only within a given climate zone.

## 12.8  SUMMARY

Soil quality is central to the sustainability of agriculture. Cropping depletes soils of their stock of nutrients and exposes them to increased erosion. Soil management must also take into account the significant spatial variability that occurs in most fields. Management is facilitated by adjustments in the size and shape of the fields. In addition, tillage, rotations, and soil amendments can be varied to some extent according to spatial patterns in individual fields. Adequate drainage is also an important aid for reduction of variability and for improving production.

Nutrients are recycled in residues and manure but those sources are inadequate to replace losses that occur through animal feeding and in the human food chain. Diagnosis of nutrient deficiencies and proper attention to fertilization are important elements of farm management. Deficiencies of nitrogen, phosphorus, and potassium are the most common because their supply in soils is small and crop requirements are relatively large. Management of nitrogen supply is the most difficult and was accorded special attention in Chapter 8. Fertilizer-use efficiency is dependent upon the degree that a nutrient is deficient (response functions are typically plateau in nature), on the timing and placement of the fertilizer, on the form of the nutrient, and on events such as immobilization and fixation within the soil.

A wide range of primary tillage systems is in use today. Conventional moldboard plowing provides the best incorporation and recycling of residues and the best seed beds. It is also the most costly and, under some circumstances, the most subject to erosion. No-till systems are less costly and much more effective in erosion control but they are more dependent upon herbicides and appear to lead to stronger gradients of nutrients and pH in soils. In temperate climates, slow warming of soil under no-till is an important consideration.

Sustainability of agriculture depends upon controlling erosion to less than the rate of soil formation. Formation is more rapid in tilled than in untilled soils but we lack good information about both formation and erosion. Experiments have revealed large differences in erosion with different farming practices and their relative effect can be embodied in erosion-prediction equations. Cover provided by residues and growing crops is especially effective in minimizing erosion by both water and wind. Rotation with sod crops and strip cropping (on the contour for water or normal to the prevailing wind) are helpful practices.

## 12.9  FURTHER READING

Cornish, P. S. and J. E. Pratley. 1987. *Tillage: New directions in Australian agriculture*. Inkata Press, Melbourne, Australia. 448 p.

Marschner, H. 1986. *Mineral nutrition of higher plants*. Academic Press, Orlando, Florida. 674 p.

Morgan, R. P. C. and D. A. Davidson. 1986. *Soil erosion and conservation*. Longman Scientific & Technical, Harlow, Essex, UK. 298 p.

Singer, M. J. and D. J. Munns. 1987. *Soils: an introduction*. Macmillan, New York. 492 p.

Tisdale, S. L., W. L. Nelson and J. D. Beaton. 1985. *Soil fertility and fertilizers*. 4th edn. Macmillan, New York. 754 p.

Troeh, F. R., J. A. Hobbs, and R. L. Donahue. 1980. *Soil and water conservation for productivity and environmental protection*. Prentice-Hall, Englewood Cliffs, New Jersey. 718 p.

Unger, P. W. 1984. *Tillage systems for soil and water conservation*. FAO Soils Bulletin No. 54. FAOUN, Rome. 278 p.

# 13

## Strategies and tactics for rainfed agriculture

### 13.1 INTRODUCTION

Most agriculture is practised under rainfed conditions with varying supplies of water, in some cases including local additions by surface flow and seepage. Farming strategies and tactics divide roughly into those aimed towards coping with too much water and those for coping with too little. This chapter concentrates on the management of water for rainfed agriculture in dry regions because a greater diversity of methods have been developed for those conditions and because the relations between production and water supply are seen there most clearly. Chapter 14 examines the principles of irrigation as a separate topic. We begin first, however, with brief comments on management of farming in wet regions where the hazards and the methods employed to counter them are rather different from those in dry regions.

### 13.2 AGRICULTURE OF WET REGIONS

Rainfed agriculture in humid regions would seem to have a blessing of a free good in its water supply. That supply is seldom ideal, however, varying from excess to transient deficiency. Excess supply leading to surface flooding and saturated soils is a major problem that generally requires drainage works (Section 12.5). Water erosion (Section 12.6) and nutrient loss are also greater concerns with abundant rainfall than in drier regions. Leaching of nitrogen was considered in Chapter 8. The importance of vegetative cover in controlling erosion and nutrient losses dictates that many sloping sites be maintained in pasture. Many low-lying sites also remain in pasture because cold, wet soil and poor drainage combine to make them unsuited to cropping. Special techniques such as ridge culture are sometimes employed to overcome cold and wet conditions.

The most persistent problem of frequent rainfall is its disruptive effect on farming operations. Delays in tillage and planting due to wet soil tend to have a cascading effect, exposing the crop to greater attack by insects and disease or to early frosts. The time-windows for critical operations are sometimes very small because tillage of wet soils can seriously damage soil structure. Farmers can counter that problem with over-sized machinery so that critical tasks can be completed through round-the-clock efforts whenever the soil dries. They can also be prepared, when operations are delayed, to substitute a different cultivar (or even crop) having a shorter growing season. Where short seasons are common, there is greater use of grain driers to insure the quality of the harvest from long-season cultivars. Another common tactic is to harvest a crop such as maize for ensilage rather than grain. Because rain also disrupts hay production and damages the product, ensilage is also a solution with forage crops in humid areas.

Weeds are a general problem in humid areas, and opportunities for mechanical cultivation can disappear quickly. That problem is not easily solved with herbicides. Topical dressings may encounter the same problem as cultivation; pre-emergence weedicides incorporated into the soil must be chosen with the correct balance between solubility and persistence.

Drought is an occasional hazard in all types of rainfed agriculture. In wet regions, crops are seldom prepared with an appropriate root:leaf ratio for a sudden dry spell and the effects of drought can be more severe than in a dry region. Yield variation is less in humid areas than in dry ones (Chapter 3); however, the capital costs of standby irrigation equipment and water supplies are seldom justified except for high-value horticultural crops. Conversely, farmers can rarely avoid capital investments in shelters for animals and farm equipment in wet regions.

Finally, it bears emphasis that the climates of humid and dry regions differ in more than just rainfall. Cloudiness and a humid atmosphere result in significantly less solar radiation and a smaller diurnal amplitude in temperature than is found in dry regions. The major effect is that production potential is less. Despite this, comparisons between regions find smaller differences in economic performance of farms. Low yields due to less radiation are offset by greater water supply and the absence of costs for irrigation are offset by capital investments in drainage and shelter.

## 13.3   PRINCIPLES OF THE EFFICIENT USE OF WATER

The water supply available to a crop consists of stored soil moisture plus rainfall during the growing season. The efficient use of that limited water relies upon the application of relatively few principles (Loomis 1983). The most basic is that evapotranspiration (ET) must be restricted to match supply. However, given the many possible interactions between water supply, water use, and crop growth there is a wide range of management options that can be employed to achieve it. To increase crop yield under water-limited conditions, management must be directed first toward maximizing the total water available to the crop (ET), second toward maximizing transpiration ($E_p$) by minimizing soil evaporation ($E_s$), and third toward selecting and managing crops with high transpiration efficiency (TE) in the production of their economic yield.

Options aimed at maximizing ET include control of water supply by varying the fallow, promoting deep root systems, reducing runoff, increasing infiltration, weed control, selecting soils with a high capacity for water storage, and planting long-season cultivars. Those that seek to maximize $E_p$ (minimize $E_s$) include surface mulching, increasing plant populations, encouraging active surface roots, sowing early, planting short-season cultivars, and cultivars with rapid early growth. Finally those that seek to maximize TE include avoiding periods of high evaporative demand by selecting cultivars of suitable length of growing season and sowing them at the optimal time, by controlling pests and diseases, and by the use of fertilizers (e.g. Cooper *et al.* 1987).

For farmers, optimal production strategies comprise cropping patterns (sequences of genotype-management combinations) that will meet their long-term objectives. That goal is commonly maximal net return, but it may be the minimization of risk to ensure cash flow and to protect the viability of the enterprise. In this context, tactics are opportunistic variations in the optimal strategy to accommodate the variability of the environment (including the economic climate that will not be discussed here) and hence to improve the performance of individual crops or minimize losses in poor years. These concepts of variability of environment and of long-term and short-term objectives are critical to understanding cropping strategies and the nature and role of tactical decision making.

A general principle of the effective use of a scarce resource is to concentrate it to exceed the threshold level for its activity. This concentration requires the establishment of a non-uniform distribution of the resource in space and/or time. In the case of water and plant growth, the existence and importance of this can be seen in the ecological relationships that enable wild plants to prosper in arid regions. There, locations where water concentrates by runoff or seepage are favorable sites for growth. Elsewhere, plants can survive only at low density with root systems that command the rainfall over areas significantly larger than their canopies. In those cases, canopy structures may channel water down stems to sites of high infiltration close to the plant and hence to storage deep in the soil profile. Deep root systems ensure that little water infiltrates below the root zone. The application of the non-uniformity principle is seen repeatedly in the management of crops and pastures in water-short environments.

## 13.4 PATTERNS OF WATER SHORTAGE AND CROP TYPES

Success in rainfed farming depends upon the selection of appropriate crops and their cultivars. The general principle is that crops will be most successful when their developmental cycle avoids or tolerates periods of water shortage and makes the best use of the pattern of water supply in the formation of yield. An important characteristic of semiarid and arid zones, is the high year-to-year variability of rainfall. It is the variability, not the low rainfall itself, that presents the major challenge to the development of productive agricultural systems.

Forage species including annual and perennial grasslands, and crops sown specifically for grazing, are the successful production systems in regions with little or highly unpredictable water supplies. In those regions, intermittent or short periods of water supply can be managed to produce fodder, but the low probability of sustaining the reproduction cycle of crops generally precludes successful seed yield as a viable option. While self-regenerating pastures do rely upon seed production for continuity, the quantity of seed required is less than for successful cropping enterprises. Additionally, pastures accumulate seed banks in the soil that serve to overcome years of low seed production (Chapter 5).

Root and tuber crops provide an interesting option in drought-prone areas because yield accumulation is indeterminate and pulses of growth can be added to the yield organs with each rainfall. Cassava is an excellent example of a drought-resistant root crop. This plant can survive extended drought periods (> 3 months) while maintaining a high internal water status by stomatal closure, restricted leaf expansion, establishment of a favorable LAI/fibrous root-length ratio, and ultimately by leaf fall (Connor *et al.* 1981). Recovery of leaf area following rain is rapid, probably involving some mobilization of starch from the storage roots. Over one or more seasonal cycles cassava can amass considerable yields (> 20 t ha$^{-1}$), as in Africa, where cassava is preserved as the disaster food for the deepest droughts.

Indeterminate flowering seed crops are best suited to regions where the length of the growing season (total water supply) is highly variable so that growing seasons are punctuated by unpredictable periods of drought. In crops with total life cycles of 100–150 days, an extended flowering period of (say) 50 days allows the chance of replacement of yield organs after a short drought to which a determinate-flowering crop might lose a substantial part of its yield potential.

Determinate-flowering crops may be particularly sensitive to even short stresses near anthesis that can substantially reduce yield potential. In addition, because yield is accumulated during the final phase of crop growth, yield reduction may be severe under terminal drought. Individual cultivars have relatively constant growth patterns (Chapter 5) so that stress periods can be avoided by timely sowing of appropriate cultivars. The most effective way to avoid terminal stress, and maintain yield stability, is to use short-season cultivars. The pitfall of this approach is that such cultivars make poor use of the better years and may over the long term yield more poorly than less conservative, longer-season cultivars. The best choice depends upon the weather variability at the site and the grower's objective: long-term gain, yearly cash flow, or whatever.

Determinate crops are best suited to regions where the length of the growing season is relatively constant from year to year. In practice, determinate crops, particularly cereals, are the dominant food crops of semiarid agriculture. The key to success is the optimal use of the available water in the development of the maximum yield sink (seeds ha$^{-1}$) that can be filled using the water remaining for seed filling.

## 13.5  OPTIMUM PATTERN OF WATER USE

There are two components to the determination of the water-use efficiency of crops. The first is the relationship between biomass production and ET (WUE$_w$ = W/ET) that varies with environmental conditions affecting both growth and transpiration during the crop growth cycle. The second concerns the relationship between the seasonal pattern of growth and the formation of economic yield. At that level, the overall performance of crops is expressed as WUE$_y$ (= Y/ET). With forage plants for which yield is the same as the seasonal aggregation of growth, no distinction need be made between $WUE_w$ and $WUE_y$.

The details of the relationship between crop water use and growth were introduced in Chapter 9, where it was emphasized that transpiration $(E_p)$ is the part of ET that is related to growth. $E_p$ is proportional to the saturation vapor pressure deficit $(e^* - e_a)$ and therefore $W/E_p = k/(e^* - e_a)$, where $k$ is a crop-specific efficiency factor (Tanner & Sinclair 1983). As a result, the efficiency of water use by any crop:

$$WUE_w = W/ET = [k/(e^* - e_a)][1 - E_s/ET] \qquad [Eq. 13.1]$$

is greatest when $E_p$ is maximized (i.e. soil evaporation $(E_s)$ is minimized) and when the crop is grown while $(e^* - e_a)$ is small and while radiation and temperature are suitable for growth.

The importance of seasonal conditions on WUE is shown in Table 13.1 for sunflower sown at two times, December and March, at Cordoba, Spain (lat. 38° N). The December sowing is very early by local standards; crops sown at that time establish slowly and are less competitive with weeds than are crops sown in March. Early-sown crops develop more slowly but despite a longer total crop cycle they are exposed less to the highly evaporative conditions of summer. In consequence, they have higher maximum growth rates, maintain them for longer, and have higher $WUE_w$. For these crops there was no additional effect of treatment on HI ($= 0.25$) and therefore $WUE_y$ responded proportionately to growth. This is not always the case.

### Pre- and post-anthesis water use

How to optimize growth duration in relation to water supply, and how to optimize the allocation of that supply between pre- and post-anthesis periods of growth are important questions with annual crops. If water supply is small it must be carefully divided between the two periods. On the one hand, the development of excess numbers of floral primordia by anthesis (yield potential) uses water that would have been better saved for post-anthesis growth. On the other hand, any crop that fills its grain and has water remaining at maturity would have been better served by the development of more grains.

Fischer (1979) analyzed the problem of the efficient use of water in wheat production using data from southern Australia (Fig. 13.1). Increasing pre-anthesis growth (abscissa) leaves progressively less water for source activity during grain filling and sets a 'water-limited' boundary to grain yield. The other boundary in the diagram is the 'potential sink capacity', the estimate of potential crop yield calculated from the product of grain number at anthesis and potential grain size. The analysis shows that source activity in the post-anthesis period becomes water limited at high biomass. If 10% of the biomass at anthesis is stored assimilates that can be mobilized to the grain, then the optimal allocation of water to pre-anthesis growth is achieved in this example at a biomass at anthesis of 6.2 t ha$^{-1}$, for which the resultant grain yield is 4.2 t ha$^{-1}$. The resulting HI is 0.43. This flowering

Table 13.1 *Growth and water-use efficiencies of winter- and spring-sown sunflower at Cordoba, Spain*

| | Performance at $CGR_{max}$ | | | | | Seasonal performance | | |
| Sowing date | CGR (kg ha$^{-1}$ d$^{-1}$) | Duration (d) | ET (mm d$^{-1}$) | WUE (kg ha$^{-1}$ mm$^{-1}$) | | Biomass[1] (t ha$^{-1}$) | ET (mm) | WUE$_w$ (kg ha$^{-1}$ mm$^{-1}$) |
|---|---|---|---|---|---|---|---|---|
| Dec. 15 | 300 | 27 | 5.0 | 60 | | 12.2 | 481 | 25 |
| March 15 | 244 | 16 | 6.4 | 38 | | 5.3 | 372 | 14 |

*Note:*
[1] The harvest index of 0.25 was unaffected by sowing date.
*Source:* From Gimeno et al. (1989).

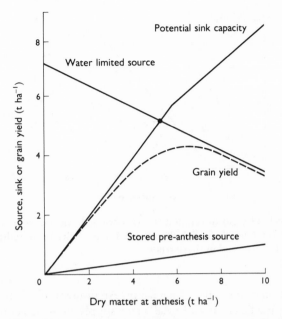

**Fig. 13.1. The relationship between growth, water use, and grain filling in wheat under post-anthesis drought. Development of increased sink capacity during the pre-anthesis period leaves less water remaining to support source activity after anthesis (after Fischer (1979).)**

and growth strategy would maximize yield under average conditions in this environment.

## Water-use efficiency of rainfed wheat

The results of many field experiments performed in the semiarid wheatbelt of South Australia to investigate the relationship between yield and water use in wheat are summarized in Fig. 13.2. In these experiments rainfall during the growing seasons varied between 186 and 566 mm and pan evaporation from 560 to 850 mm. The results show that yield increased with ET in the range 150–500 mm. The maximum yield achieved at each level of ET depends upon a seasonal distribution of rainfall that optimizes water-use behavior, i.e. minimizes $E_s$ and optimally supports the development and expression of grain yield in the pre- and post-anthesis phases. In the data of Fig. 13.2, this establishes a maximum transpiration efficiency in grain production ($TE_y$) of around 20 kg ha$^{-1}$ mm$^{-1}$ as a working approximation for the sites and seasons included in this study. $TE_y$ would be smaller at sites of higher evaporative demand.

The position of individual crops relative to the line of maximum efficiency in Fig. 13.2 is of some interest. While the lowest yielding crops at each level of water use probably reflect limitations to yield caused by factors other than water supply, such as diseases, high or low nitrogen supply, weeds, frost, or poor management, non-

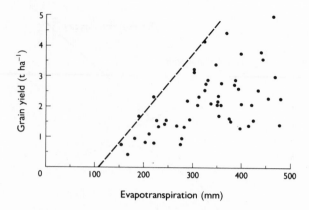

**Fig. 13.2. Wheat yield in relation to evapotranspiration in semiarid South Australia (after French & Schultz (1984).) The dashed line indicates the maximum TE$_y$ observed in these trials.**

optimal distribution of rainfall is also a factor. An unfavorable distribution would contribute to the inefficient use of total water supply by its effect on the balance between $E_p$ and $E_s$ and the seasonal pattern of $E_p$ and hence on the distribution of growth between vegetative and reproductive phases.

## 13.6   CULTIVARS AND SOWING TIME

The selection and timely sowing of adapted cultivars are basic steps for the efficient use of water in rainfed agriculture. The most appropriate cultivars are those that use most efficiently (high $k$, Eq. 13.1) all the water that management can make available. In the absence of other factors limiting growth, efficiency depends upon avoiding or tolerating transient water shortages during the growth cycle and distributing seasonal water use in an optimum way between vegetative and reproductive phases.

Crop development depends upon thermal, photothermal, and vernalization responses (Chapter 5). A characteristic of all crop species is the great variability in developmental patterns that can be manipulated in breeding programs to provide suitable cultivars for many environments. One thrust of crop improvement is to achieve optimum developmental patterns in the variable seasonal conditions of rainfed environments. One example occurs with wheat cultivars grown in Mediterranean regions. These commonly are spring types that flower without vernalization. The introduction of some 'winterness' controls flowering time so that crops sown early in autumn, that otherwise might develop too quickly, will flower in the spring after the danger of frost is past. This offers growers a valuable tactical alternative in years when the rains begin early in autumn. They can sow part of their crop early, or all of it if they anticipate that soil conditions will hamper cultural operations through to winter. Early-sown winter cultivars have a longer vegetative phase than do spring wheats that are sown later.

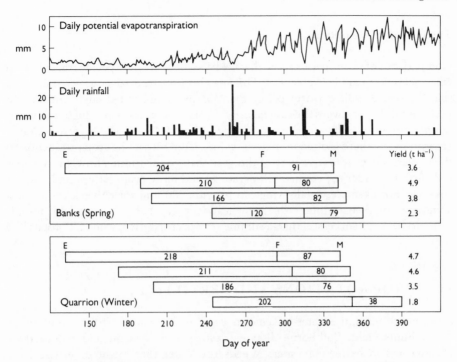

**Fig. 13.3. Development and yield of spring (Banks) and winter (Quarrion) wheat cultivars at four times of sowing (May, June, July and September 1984) at Werribee, Victoria, Australia (38° S). The numbers within the phenology histograms record mm ET during the respective phenophases (S. Theiveya-nathan & D. J. Connor, unpublished).**

The question then arises whether winter cultivars use additional water for vegetative growth that would be better used for grain filling, i.e. do not show optimal behavior. An experimental program has analyzed the growth and water use of spring and winter wheat (cvs Banks and Quarrion) of otherwise comparable genetic background sown on four occasions in each of two successive years at Werribee, near Melbourne, in southern Australia. The patterns of phenological development and water use showed that total ET decreased as sowing was delayed from fall to spring (Fig. 13.3). Although the crops sown late matured under more evaporative conditions, their total crop cycle was significantly shortened. The winter cultivar had a longer crop cycle and used more water (higher total ET) than the spring cultivar, particularly at the latest sowing. The winter cultivar performed better at the May sowing and worse at the September sowing, but the two cultivars behaved comparably in development, water use, and yield at the intermediate sowings in June and July. A major imbalance of water use between vegetative and reproductive phases occurred with the winter cultivar sown in September. Of a total ET of 240 mm, only 38 mm (16%) was used during grain filling with the result that grain yield was restricted to 1.8 t ha$^{-1}$ compared with the highest yield of 4.9 t ha$^{-1}$ achieved in the same year from the spring cultivar sown in June.

**The C3 versus C4 option**

Comparisons of crop species show that C4 types have greater specific transpiration efficiencies ($k$) than C3 (Table 9.4). This may lead to the erroneous generalization that C4 species will perform better than C3 in water-limited environments. In practice this is not always the case because C3 species are more productive at lower temperatures and therefore at lower ET* than C4 species. In water-limited environments, there is often more to be gained from restricting crop production to the cooler, less evaporative part of the year than concentrating on C4 crops that only flourish under the warmer temperatures and more evaporative conditions of summer. For example, if fallowing can provide 300 mm for either a winter or a summer crop, then a winter crop, say wheat with seasonal ET* around 450 mm, is likely to be more successful than a summer maize crop grown when ET* totals 900 mm.

## 13.7   CROP ROTATIONS AND FERTILIZER

Strategies to maximize water-use efficiency will be most successful when no other factor limits yield. Soil-borne diseases destroy root systems and reduce their effectiveness in extracting water. Weeds use water that might otherwise have remained available to the crop. Low fertility, acidity, or the development of hard pans adversely affect the capacity of roots to recover water. Hardpans, formed by accumulations of minerals in the B horizon or through compaction by implements, physically restrain the depth of penetration of the root system and restrict the infiltration of water into the profile. Farmers can avoid or reduce some of those problems through rotations. They also use rotations to manage water availability by sequencing crops that have different patterns and amounts of water use. In that way the system can be fine-tuned to rainfall variations over years.

### Weeds

Weeds use water that might have otherwise been available to support crop growth and yield. Without weed control, it is not possible to establish the optimum patterns of water use required to maximize yield under water-short conditions. Weeds can be controlled by cultural operations and by the competitive situations that are established and managed in rotational farming. In addition, there is an increasing range of general and specific weedicides that can be used at sowing or during the crop phase to deal with individual problems. Within rotations, fallows must be maintained weed free if they are to serve in the conservation of water and mobilization of nitrate for the subsequent crop (Section 13.9).

There is a need for compromise when the weeds of crops are also desirable components of pasture phases of the rotation. This is the case in the wheat–sheep zone of southern Australia, where annual ryegrass is a productive component of the pasture phase but a competitive weed in wheat crops as well as an alternative host for certain root-borne diseases of cereals. This is considered further in Chapter 16.

## Diseases

Diseases divert assimilate from crop growth and yield, thereby lowering the water-use efficiency of crops. Any disease can reduce yield in this way, but soil-borne diseases exert an additional effect. They damage root systems and so restrict the water-absorbing capacity of crops and their ability for thorough exploitation of the soil water reserve. If diseases are not controlled, there is little chance that other management tactics aimed at improving crop water-use efficiency will have a chance to work.

Table 13.2 provides an example of the importance of disease and pest control in the yield of wheat in southern Australia. There, rhizoctonia root rot and a soil-living parasite, cereal cyst nematode, combine to curtail the application of strategies developed to manage water and nitrogen supply. The table records wheat yields, water use and $WUE_y$ for a range of rotations. The lowest yield (0.87 t ha$^{-1}$) was achieved in continuous wheat and the highest (2.13 t ha$^{-1}$) immediately following a 9 month fallow period. In the other four rotations there was no fallow period and wheat followed a leguminous crop or pasture. All crops used the same amount of water (mean 255 mm) so it is concluded that the major advantage of fallow here is in the control of grassy weeds and associated wheat diseases rather than the supply of additional water or nitrogen.

## Soil fertility

Over a short period, crops that are not limited by the availability of nutrients will grow best and will have the highest short-term water-use efficiency. Over the course of a growing season, however, growth and water use at certain times can lead to water shortages at others. That occurs because early growth depletes soil water reserves and the effect on yield is exacerbated when increased early growth has the effect, with greater leaf area, of increasing subsequent demand for water. The result is that the optimum nutrient supply for yield is less than for biomass production.

The response applies to any nutrient but in practice adjustments to nitrogen nutrition are the most important in controlling the degree of crop cover and water use. Low-nitrogen crops develop cover slowly so $E_p$ is small, although at the expense of greater proportional loss by $E_s$ when the frequency of rains is high. By maintaining low fertility it is possible to match water supply to the demand per plant. When water is strongly limiting, nitrogen deficiency reduces growth and distributes water use more favorably between vegetative and reproductive periods, and grain yield is maximized relative to water supply, i.e. nitrogen is not limiting to grain yield. Low nitrogen availability leads, however, to stable but unnecessarily low yields, and, as is the case with short season cultivars, to low water-use efficiency.

Under the variable conditions of rainfed agriculture, management of nitrogen is

Table 13.2 *Crop water use, yield and WUE$_y$ of wheat under several rotations at Walpeup in the Victorian Mallee, Australia, under a Mediterranean pattern of rainfall*

| Annual rotation | Crop water use (mm) | Yield (t ha$^{-1}$) | WUE$_y$ (kg ha$^{-1}$ mm$^{-1}$) |
|---|---|---|---|
| W–M–F–W[1] | 262 | 2.13 | 8.1 |
| W–W–W–W | 247 | 0.87 | 3.5 |
| L–W–P–W | 272 | 1.74 | 6.4 |
| R–B–L–W | 257 | 1.79 | 7.0 |
| W–M–L–W | 256 | 1.84 | 7.2 |
| M–W–M–W | 234 | 1.62 | 6.9 |
| LSD (p < 0.05) | ns | 0.31 | |

*Note:*
[1] W = wheat; B = barley; M = medic; F = fallow; L = lupin; P = pea; R = rape.
*Source:* After Griffiths & Walsgott (1987).

most easily accomplished with fertilizer because it is possible to control availability in relation to crop requirements and weather. The alternative, the reliance on legumes in crop sequences, provides uncertain additions related to the variability of their growth in response to weather. That introduces additional difficulty in matching crop requirements to seasonal yield potential.

One of the great challenges in semiarid regions is to develop cropping strategies that operate at the highest appropriate level of nitrogen for long-term yield and allow for tactical responses to weather (and price) based on manipulations of nitrogen level with fertilizers. In favorable seasons, nitrogen supply can be increased by topical applications in midseason. Examples are provided in Section 13.10 and in Chapter 16.

## Grazing management

In zones where rainfall is too low or too erratic for crop production, grazing animals are often the only way to harvest the fodder that is produced from grasslands. Proper management depends on choosing the timing, distribution, and intensity of grazing that will maintain pasture condition for continuing productivity. Given the erratic nature of plant production this is a difficult task except in extensive systems where stocking rates are kept deliberately low. Excessive grazing first displaces the palatable species but ultimately removes plant cover, permitting increased erosion. In practice, the effective utilization of many low-rainfall pastoral areas is limited more by the provision of drinking water for stock than by the low or erratic nature of rainfall for plant production. Without well-distributed watering points, stock are not able to graze extensively during dry periods but instead concentrate near water, with resultant overgrazing and damage.

## 13.8   DENSITY AND PLANTING ARRANGEMENT

### Density

In water-short environments, crops are planted at low densities, at the expense of increasing the fraction of ET lost as $E_s$, to maximize the water available to each plant in the crop. The principle here is to provide as much soil volume (stored water) and catchment area (later rains) as possible per plant or per unit LAI and thus extend the duration of growth.

Plants at low density experience greater radiation per LAI than do high-density plants and the aerodynamic roughness of the crop is greater. In consequence, the photosynthesis per unit leaf area and the evaporative demand per LAI are greater. This is known as the 'clothesline effect' and is responsible in part for the non-linear relations between radiation absorption and $E_p$ and LAI (Fig. 9.14). Despite this disadvantage, low density is the only feasible strategy other than fallow that allows plants of a long-season cultivar sufficient water supply to complete their life cycle in a low rainfall environment in which $E_p \ll ET^*$. In practice, low density is usually the first option employed and fallow is added in the progression to areas of lower rainfall.

### Planting pattern

Crop density can be manipulated by varying row width or row density. Densities can be maintained but the development of cover and the pattern of crop water use are altered by sowing plants more densely in wider rows. These effects operate mostly through interaction between root systems within the soil volume available for rooting.

Use of stored moisture by annual crops depends in part on the rate at which roots expand into the available soil volume. The possibility exists, through variations in planting pattern, for control of the time when the crop reaches moisture. A uniform spacing (e.g. in a hexagonal pattern) allows for the shortest time for roots to reach the perimeter of the space. In contrast, crowding plants within wide rows, a further example of the non-uniformity principle, leads to early and intense competition for water within the row, thus restricting water use and early growth. In this way, water use is distributed over longer periods before the perimeters are reached later.

Under some circumstances, planting patterns can serve the purposes of both crop production and fallow because bare areas can accumulate and store moisture from rains early in the crop cycle. In general, the choice of uniform or non-uniform arrangements depends upon soil depth and water-holding capacity as well as the relative amount and distribution of rainfall during the crop cycle and the preceding fallow. If the crop relies upon stored water, then non-uniform arrangements such as wide rows are appropriate because $E_s$ will be small and the stored water can be metered out slowly. Under these conditions, density would be adjusted to storage (soil type) and growth duration. On the other hand, if the crop relies upon rainfall during the growth cycle then a uniform arrangement with appropriate spacing will enable each plant to extract the water as it becomes available while minimizing the unproductive loss by $E_s$ and perhaps by drainage.

Myers & Foale (1981) have analyzed the results of a number of experiments performed to test the importance of row spacing in sorghum under dryland conditions. They compared yields obtained at row spacings between 0.25 and 1.00 m. At sites of low rainfall where yield at the high density was less than 2 t ha$^{-1}$, the widest spacing gave the highest yield. At sites where the yield of the narrow spacing exceeded 3.7 t ha$^{-1}$, the narrow spacing was the most productive. In the range from 2 to 3.7 t ha$^{-1}$, the differences in performance were small with the advantage gradually shifting from wide to narrow spacing. The analysis was extended to weed control. In a comparison between yields of crops in rows 0.30 and 1.00 m apart they showed, not surprisingly, that weeds exerted their greatest effect at the wide spacing and at low rainfall sites where the yield at 0.30 m spacing was low. Only at yield < 0.4 t ha$^{-1}$ was it better to use widely spaced (1 m) rows for weedy crops.

Spacing arrangements serve as a practical means for managing the performance of root systems. An alternative, proposed by some workers (e.g. Passioura 1983), is to select cultivars with differing rooting patterns or resistance to water uptake. Selection for factors that determine the resistance of root systems – root length density, root conductance and the timing of root growth during the crop cycle – could complement techniques to collect and conserve water in the soil during a period before cropping.

## 13.9  FALLOW

In rainfed agriculture, extended weed-free fallows are commonly included in rotations to accumulate the annual and sometimes the biennial rainfall for the growth of a single crop. They also allow time for mineralization of soil nitrogen and the reduction of soil-borne diseases so careful analysis is required in assessing the response of crops to fallow. The temporal non-uniformity that fallows introduce into cropping sequences concentrates limiting resources above the thresholds for crop response.

In environments in which water supply is relatively assured in some part of the year (Types 1 and 2 of Fig. 9.10), storage of moisture in fallow is an effective way to extend the period of crop growth. In others (Type 3, Fig. 9.10), fallows may be essential to success but their value requires careful analysis of rainfall probabilities and soil water-storage capacity.

### Fallow management

The principles of fallow management derive directly from the water-holding characteristics of the soil and evaporation ($E_s$) from the exposed soil surface. Before rainfall can penetrate the surface layer and become less vulnerable to loss by evaporation, it must rewet the surface layer to field capacity, usually from an air-dry state. For sand, loam and clay soils this requires up to the first 6, 10, or 12 mm of each rainfall event. As a result, the proportion of rainfall lost by evaporation increases with the frequency of showers and is greatest on clay soils into which penetration is least. Although rainfall penetrates deeply into sandy soils, their total water-storage capacity is low, e.g. 50 mm m$^{-1}$ of profile depth compared with 150 for loam and 250 for clay. Therefore, loss by drainage below the potential root zone of the ensuing crop is most likely to occur on sandy soils.

Management of fallows is aimed at maximizing the penetration of rainfall and minimizing losses by evaporation and drainage. Farmers can improve the efficiency of fallows by careful management of surface water. Even in semiarid areas, rainfall can be sufficiently intense to exceed the rate of infiltration. Where rainfall intensity is high, the construction of terraces, contour banks, ridges, and other surface irregularities increases surface storage, thereby prolonging the opportunity for infiltration. Terraces and ridging can also be used to concentrate water spatially (non-uniformity principle) so that infiltration occurs where plants will be grown. In some cases, ridging is even useful on relatively flat land. Where runoff is a problem, farmers must direct efforts toward maintaining the infiltration capacity of the soil. Infiltration is such an important component of the management of surface water that minimum tillage, deep ripping, organic matter incorporation, or application of amendments, such as gypsum, may be justified to improve the water storage capacity of poorly structured soils.

## Minimum tillage

Previously, the only way to maintain weed-free fallows was by tillage after each significant rainfall. At some locations, during early days of cereal cultivation in Australia and North America, fallow ground was tilled as many as 14 times with horse-drawn implements at great expense to soil organic matter and soil structure as well as the risk of erosion. Farmers and researchers developed the theory that tillage was essentially to break the soil capillaries through which they believed water was lost by evaporation to the atmosphere. In reality, the main value of tillage lay in the control of weeds that otherwise dry not only the surface but also the deeper soil. Understanding the dynamics of fallows allows us to manage them without tillage. Evidence is that fallows maintained with herbicides ('chemical' fallows) are more efficient than cultivated ones, although clearly they have many different properties. A comparison of fallow techniques in the Great Plains, USA, showed that stubble-mulched fallows (partial incorporation of residues) without herbicides conserved 32% of rainfall whereas those maintained by herbicides conserved 42% (Smika 1970). Australian experience is similar and is reviewed in Cornish & Pratley (1987).

The surface residues found with chemical fallows intercept rain and thereby restrict the penetration of water into the soil. This loss is proportionally greater with light showers. The mulch does, however, protect the wet surface from direct evaporation, especially during the initial energy-dependent stage of evaporation

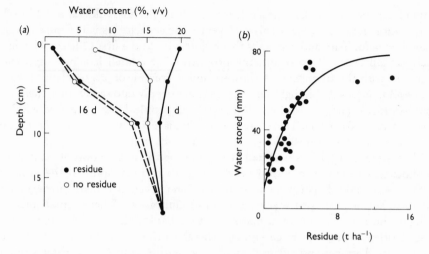

Fig. 13.4. **Effect of presence or absence of crop residue on soil water content of fallow. (*a*) Surface soil water content 1 and 16 d after rain. (*b*) Effect of residue level on soil water content after a short fallow (after Cornish (1987)).**

from wet soils. Because the surface stays wet longer (Fig. 13.4*a*), the probability that subsequent showers will penetrate below the vulnerable surface layer is increased. This helps explain why fallows with surface residues conserve more water than those where residues are removed or incorporated (Fig. 13.4*b*). Also, because the surface soil remains moist longer after each rainfall, the farmer has greater opportunity to sow and establish crops at the optimal time: a critical component of efficient management of limited water.

## Fallow efficiency

Because fallows are open to inevitable losses by evaporation from the surface, transpiration by weeds, and drainage below the root zone, their efficiency, i.e. the proportion of total rainfall that contributes to production during subsequent cropping, is low and variable from year to year. Fallow efficiency depends upon soil type, rainfall amount and distribution, and ET*.

Fig. 13.5 compares the performance of spring–summer fallow on two contrasting soil types (sand and clay) over three successive seasons in South Australia. In this area of winter rainfall, the major effect of weed-free fallow was to prevent transpiration of soil water accumulated before commencement of the fallow. Storage did not increase significantly during the fallow, except in the second year when heavy spring rains occurred. The difference in storage of water between the two soil types was marked, reflecting their different water-holding characteristics.

A comparison of the performance of fallows at nine sites in the Great Plains of USA was made by USDA (1974) (Table 13.3). In that climate, continuous cropping to wheat permits short (6 month) fallows during summer and early fall. There, 65

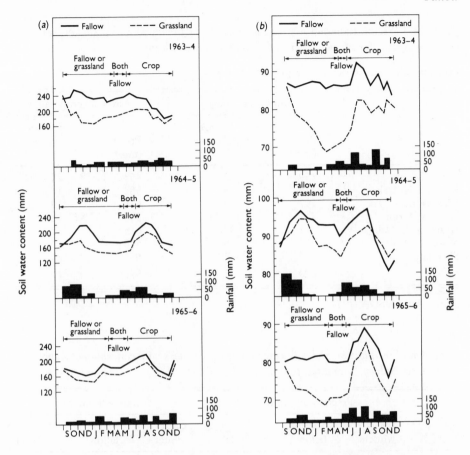

Fig. 13.5. Soil water contents and rainfall between recording dates on two soils over three successive seasons (1963–4 to 1965–6) in South Australia: (*a*) Clay at Northfield; (*b*) sand at pinery (adapted from Schultz (1971)).

mm of the 200 mm rainfall were conserved, an average efficiency of 32%. Cropped only in alternate years (the fallow-crop system), the longer (18-month) fallows received greater rainfall, 577 mm, and stored more, 107 mm, but the fraction conserved was only 19%. In those long fallows, 50–70% of the water was stored by the end of the first winter and 84% in 12 months to midsummer. Only small additional gains were made in the second winter.

In regions of summer rainfall, the efficiency of summer fallow in conserving rainfall may also be low because it is commonly associated with high ET*. This is shown with data from Sidney, Montana (Table 13.4). For 14 successive winter and summer periods, the storage efficiency of 216 mm summer rainfall was 6% compared with 71% for the average winter rainfall of 124 mm. In 5 of the 14 years, summer fallows lost water and storage efficiencies were as low as −11%. In this area, as in the winter rainfall area of southern Australia, summer fallows have low efficiency for concurrent rainfall and weed control is critical to the preservation of water previously stored in the soil profile.

Table 13.3 *Precipitation and storage efficiency during the uncropped period of two cropping systems for spring wheat in the northern Great Plains*

Data for individual stations cover periods of 20–47 y.

| Station | Annual cropping | | Alternate crop–fallow | |
|---|---|---|---|---|
| | Precip. (mm) | Storage efficiency (%) | Precip. (mm) | Storage efficiency (%) |
| Havre, Mont. | 159 | 30 | 454 | 24 |
| Mandan, N. Dak. | 178 | 35 | 582 | 17 |
| Dickinson, N. Dak. | 197 | 29 | 618 | 19 |
| Huntley, Mont. | 211 | 30 | 546 | 18 |
| Ardmore, S. Dak. | 211 | 37 | 615 | 18 |
| Newell, S. Dak | 214 | 28 | 618 | 17 |
| Sheridan, Wyo. | 250 | 40 | 637 | 25 |
| Mean | 200 | 32 | 577 | 19 |

*Source:* After USDA (1974).

Table 13.4 *Precipitation and soil water storage efficiencies with conventional stubble mulching at Sidney, Montana, for the period 1957–70*

| Year | Precipitation (mm) | | | Storage efficiency (%) | | |
|---|---|---|---|---|---|---|
| | Over-winter | Summer fallow | Total | Over-winter | Summer fallow | Total |
| 1957 | 155 | 165 | 320 | 66 | 9 | 37 |
| 1958 | 206 | 97 | 302 | 49 | −8 | 31 |
| 1959 | 127 | 193 | 320 | 56 | 11 | 29 |
| 1960 | 71 | 175 | 246 | 154 | 0 | 44 |
| 1961 | 61 | 183 | 244 | 54 | 25 | 32 |
| 1962 | 109 | 343 | 452 | 77 | 20 | 34 |
| 1963 | 142 | 241 | 384 | 70 | −3 | 24 |
| 1964 | 170 | 206 | 376 | 52 | −11 | 18 |
| 1965 | 76 | 305 | 381 | 123 | −5 | 21 |
| 1966 | 71 | 127 | 198 | 89 | 12 | 40 |
| 1967 | 99 | 211 | 310 | 62 | 10 | 26 |
| 1968 | 86 | 302 | 387 | 56 | 21 | 29 |
| 1969 | 122 | 206 | 328 | 56 | 5 | 24 |
| 1970 | 244 | 267 | 511 | 35 | −2 | 16 |
| Mean | 124 | 216 | 340 | 71 | 6 | 28 |

*Source:* Adapted from USDA (1974).

## Yield stability

Fallow not only increases yield but also makes yield more reliable. In the Great Plains, a 30-year comparison of continuous wheat with fallow–wheat showed that the long-term mean yields per crop were 0.7 and 2.5 t ha$^{-1}$ respectively (Smika 1970; USDA 1974). 37% of continuous-wheat crops were economic failures, with yields below 0.4 t ha$^{-1}$, whereas the lowest yield in the fallow–wheat system was 1.2 t ha$^{-1}$ (Fig. 13.6). Yield per year in the fallow–wheat system was 2.5/2 = 1.25 t ha$^{-1}$, still significantly greater than 0.7 t ha$^{-1}$ for continuous wheat. The fallow–wheat system is more efficient of seed, fertilizer, labor, and support energy.

In a recent Australian analysis (Ridge 1986), the performance of wheat following year-long fallow was compared with that in short fallow, in which land preparation commenced in February, three to four months before sowing. The study took place in two distinct parts of the wheatbelt of northwest Victoria. The Mallee, the more northern region, is drier (*ca.* 330 mm y$^{-1}$) with lighter-textured soils (loamy sands) than the Wimmera (*ca.* 440 mm y$^{-1}$, deep friable clay soils). The economic analysis (Table 13.5) showed that the annual median profits from the two management systems were similar at an average wheat price of A\$130 t$^{-1}$, but the range,

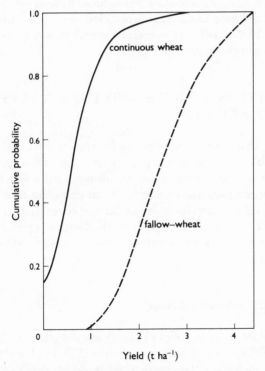

**Fig. 13.6. Cumulative yield distribution for fallow–wheat (broken line) and continuous wheat (solid line) during 1940–70 at North Platte, Nebraska (adapted from USDA (1974).)**

Table 13.5 *Seasonal variation in the yield and profitability of wheat sown on short fallow and the equivalent effects on the profitability of wheat sown on long fallow in two areas of northwest Victoria, Australia*

The distribution of crop performance is expressed by the median and the lower and upper quartiles.

| | Wimmera | | | Mallee | | |
|---|---|---|---|---|---|---|
| | Lower | Median | Upper | Lower | Median | Upper |
| *Short fallow* | | | | | | |
| Yield (t ha$^{-1}$) | 0.68 | 1.60 | 2.48 | 0.74 | 1.13 | 1.50 |
| Profit (A\$ ha$^{-1}$ y$^{-1}$) | −50 | 70 | 184 | 4 | 55 | 103 |
| *Long fallow* | | | | | | |
| Yield | 1.82 | 2.62 | 3.38 | 1.44 | 1.76 | 2.06 |
| Profit (A\$ ha$^{-1}$) | 42 | 145 | 244 | 65 | 107 | 146 |
| Profit (A\$ ha$^{-1}$ y$^{-1}$) | 21 | 73 | 122 | 33 | 54 | 73 |

*Source:* After Ridge (1986).

represented by the difference between the upper and lower quartiles of performance (for both yield and return), was considerably reduced by long fallow. At both sites, the range in economic return under the long-fallow system was only 40% of that under short fallow. In the Mallee, growers can expect losses of the order of one year in four from crops grown without long fallow.

## 13.10   SIMULATION MODELS AND THE ANALYSIS OF CROPPING STRATEGIES

Simulation models that portray the response of crops to environmental, site, and management variables offer the best opportunity, other than seemingly endless experimentation, to investigate the genotype–management interactions that combine to produce optimal patterns of water use by crops under variable environmental conditions. A range of examples is presented here covering the use of models to assist in the analysis of cultivar characteristics, the design of cropping systems, and in tactical management. A recurring feature is the analysis of yield variability over long runs of seasons.

### A simulation model of the wheat crop

The wheat crop model developed by O'Leary *et al.* (1985) for southern Australian conditions was developed upon the ideas presented by Fischer (1979), discussed earlier in Fig. 13.1. It displays the nature of most models that seek to explain the interaction of genotype with water supply. The model comprises three submodels that deal on a daily basis with phenological development, water balance, and the

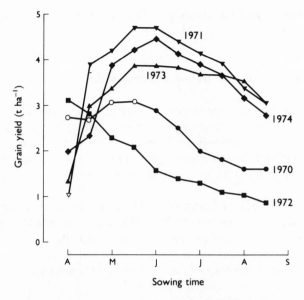

**Fig. 13.7.** Simulated response of wheat yield to time of sowing over five years at Horsham, Victoria (from O'Leary *et al.* (1985).)

accumulation and partitioning of biomass. This is a relatively simple model using just seven state variables to define the condition of the crop.

The submodel of phenology predicts the occurrence of five phenostages by combinations of thermal and photothermal responses. The water-balance sub-model follows the water content of the current root zone and of the subsoil layer into which roots may extend during the growing season. ET is separated into the components $E_p$ and $E_s$ so that crop water use can be estimated accurately and growth can be calculated from transpiration efficiency and saturation deficit. Grain number $ha^{-1}$ is calculated from biomass at anthesis, so the model does not respond to critical periods of stress that may affect reproductive development more than they affect growth (Section 9.9). The water remaining for grain filling, the efficiency of its use, and the numbers of grains set determine yield. In the model, 10% of biomass at anthesis is assumed to be nonstructural assimilate that can be translocated to the grain depending upon post-anthesis assimilate supply.

These few simple equations are able to simulate growth and yield of wheat in regions where water supply is the major factor limiting yield and can be used to investigate various management issues. For example, one major option is to delay sowing because this will shorten the duration of the pre-anthesis period and save water for grain filling. If anthesis is delayed slightly by late sowing, then the slightly longer exposure to the higher evaporation rates of late spring will not seriously reduce the potential saving in water. However, a long delay will push grain filling too far into the summer under high evaporative demand. The resulting stress during grain filling and decline in WUE lead to low yields. An analysis of the optimal sowing time (Fig. 13.7) can thus combine the seasonal dynamics of water supply, growth, and yield in individual years. In this case, the responses for the five years emphasize the year-to-year variability but show that sowings made in midwinter commonly result in the greatest yield.

## Rainfall distribution, soil evaporation and crop yield

It is important to assess what natural variation can occur in the yield–ET relationship (Fig. 13.2) at any site owing to rainfall distribution, because this sets the yield framework within which manipulations to improve crop water-use efficiency must function. Without this information, deviations from maximum transpiration efficiency might be unreasonably interpreted to be a result of factors other than water supply.

Rimmington *et al.* (1987) used a model similar in most respects to that of O'Leary *et al.* (1985) to analyze crop response to 100 y of rainfall data at Walpeup in the dry northern Mallee (330 m y$^{-1}$) of the Victorian wheatbelt (Fig. 13.8). Crop performance was simulated on a sandy soil and on clay. Both soils were assumed to be fully recharged with water at the start of each season. Yields were greater on the clay because of additional water stored during the fallow.

Even with the same soil water content at sowing, the model showed considerable variation in yield from year to year at each level of ET. These differences reflect variable losses to $E_s$, which depend upon the pattern of rainfall relative to crop cover and the pattern of $E_p$ relative to ET*, and the developmental cycle of the crop.

## Tactical variations in fallow management

The performance of fallows varies from year to year depending upon weather and weed growth, as well as from nutrient and disease status. In regions where fallowing is a valuable part of the long-term strategy, there will be years when the cost of it does not pay for the benefit. For example, tillage experiments during periods of continuous wheat production in southern New South Wales, Australia, have revealed that in some years a few cultivations (VF, a variable length fallow) commencing when weeds first appear after harvest (November–December) conserves more water up to sowing than does an unmanaged fallow (NoF). The question is whether VF is a good long-term strategy and what the value might be of certain tactical adjustments to it. Fischer & Armstrong (1987) have used the SIMTAG wheat simulation model (Stapper 1984) to analyze fallow management tactics over the 41-year period 1943–83 for which climatic data were available. The analyses (Table 13.6) showed that NoF carried a substantial penalty in terms of available water at sowing. Under the VF strategy, the available soil water for a fall planting (on 1 May) was increased on average by 28 mm, the probability of a successful fall sowing was increased from 56% to 75%, and the best sowing date advanced by one week.

The model was also used to assess various alternative tactics by which fallowing could be initiated if soil moisture and/or weed conditions appeared favorable. After subtracting realistic costs for tillage, they expressed the accumulated benefits of the

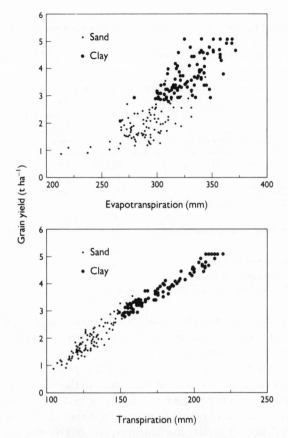

**Fig. 13.8. Simulated relationship between wheat yield and ET and Ep on two soils (sand and clay) at Walpeup in northwest Victoria. Both soils were assumed to be at field capacity at sowing in each year.**

additional stored water as wheat grain. The tactics based on the presence of 50 mm soil moisture at harvest and the appearance of weeds during summer were better than VF because they avoided or delayed fallowing in many years when the yield advantage did not cover the cost of additional tillage.

### Crop duration, root depth, osmotic adjustment and yield in sorghum

Plant breeding programs seek to combine traits that are advantageous to crop yield. Many traits, for example those that concern disease resistance and product quality, perform consistently so the assessment of their value to improved cultivars is relatively straightforward. However, the assessment of traits concerned with drought resistance and identification of appropriate ideotypes (Section 11.3) is complex. First, many traits that have the potential to improve yield under drought have been identified but it is difficult to predict their performance in the various

Table 13.6 *Simulated advantages of several fallow management tactics over no fallow*

The analysis relates to wheat after wheat over the period 1943–83 at Wagga, NSW, Australia.

| Condition for initiation of cultivation | Years with fallow | Average extra AW[1] May 1 (mm) | Accumulated net yield benefit (kg ha$^{-1}$) |
|---|---|---|---|
| First appearance of weeds after harvest (VF) | 39(33)[2] | 28 | 6010 |
| On Feb. 15 if weeds present | 22 | 29 | 5480 |
| After harvest if AW > 50 mm | 25(13)[2] | 35 | 6420 |
| After harvest if AW > 50 mm and on Feb. 15 if weeds present | 29(13)[2] | 33 | 7120 |

*Notes:*
[1] AW, available soil water content.
[2] Years when fallow began before Feb. 15.
*Source:* After Fischer & Armstrong (1987).

possible combinations. Second, the variability of water supply in drought-prone regions means that the value of traits varies from season to season so their optimum combinations must be evaluated over a number of years.

Jordan *et al.* (1983) have used a model of sorghum growth to evaluate drought resistance attributes of grain sorghum at three sites in the American Great Plains. Cultivar characteristics of phenological development, root exploration, and osmotic adjustment were varied. Earliness to flower, at either the 15- or 17-leaf stage, controlled the balance of water use during pre- and post-anthesis. Osmotic adjustment allowed the crop to extract a greater amount of soil water from the root zone, and increased root depth (2.8 versus 2.0 m) allowed the crop access to additional stored water whenever rainfall was sufficient to recharge the profile to depth. The analysis of crop performance over 30 y of weather allowed the assessment of cropping options in a variable climate. In this, the soil water balance was carried forward each year.

The advantage of the long-season cultivar (Fig. 13.9) was substantial at Manhattan, Kansas, the wettest site, but it was also superior at the driest site, Lubbock, Texas, although the advantage there was slight. Crop performance at Temple, Texas, demonstrated that the performance of the best cultivar varies from year to year. Over the 30-year period, the long-season cultivar outyielded the short-season cultivar, but when yields were less than the long term average (33% of years), the short-season cultivar performed better. If it were possible to predict weather patterns, one could select the best cultivar for each year; however given the variability in weather, growers must choose between maximizing long-term return and minimizing short-term risk. This is always the case when maximum use of a variable, limiting resource is attempted.

Osmotic regulation offered no advantage through increasing soil-water availability at any site either alone or in combination with deep rooting (Table 13.7). Since the model did not make allowance for the metabolic cost of osmoregulation

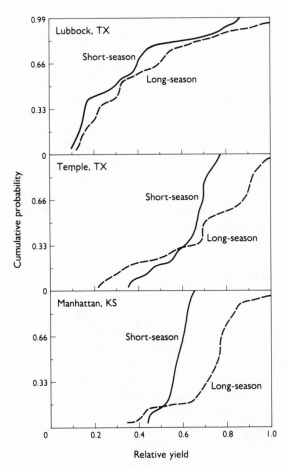

**Fig. 13.9.** Cumulative probability of a given yield of grain sorghum at Lubbock and Temple, Texas, and Manhattan, Kansas, for an early and late maturity genotype (from Jordan *et al.* (1983).)

(Section 9.9), that strategy may actually decrease productivity. Deep rooting increased yield by 50% in 20% of years at Temple and Lubbock. The benefit of deep rooting depends upon the continuing replenishment of subsoil moisture and was least at the driest site. It would also depend upon the carbon costs of growing and maintaining the additional roots (Section 11.3). As was the case for osmotic adjustment, Jordan *et al.* (1983) did not consider these costs, so the real benefits will be less.

**Choosing opportunistic combinations of winter and summer crops**

Berndt & White (1976) used a simulation model to make risk-benefit analyses of alternative cropping systems for three sites on the Darling Downs, Australia. The Darling Downs is a semiarid, subtropical region 300 m above sea level and about 150 km inland from the coastal city of Brisbane, Queensland (lat. 27° S). The annual rainfall of 500–700 mm is highly erratic and small compared with annual ET* (*ca.* 1500 mm). Despite a dominance of summer rainfall, the most appropriate cropping strategy is not clear. Both the minimization of risk and the danger of erosion on fallow during high-intensity, summer storms must be balanced against overall crop performance. Berndt & White (1976) used a simulation model comprising sub-models of phenology, water balance, growth, and soil erosion, to analyze cropping options over a 30-year historical weather sequence. The options were summer (sorghum) and winter (wheat) crops and preceding fallow in any combination. Cropping sequences could be varied depending upon the available soil water content (AW) at the proposed sowing time. If the available soil water at sowing exceeded 0.2 of the available water-holding capacity of the soil, the continuous crop sequence was maintained. If the soil was drier, the land was kept fallow until the next cropping season (Table 13.8).

Strategies were tested to find those that would

maximize long-term yield, or
minimize the probability of low income, or
minimize the erosion risk to fallow land.

At the Cambooya site, double cropping was the optimum choice for each of the three objectives. At the remaining sites, growers faced conflicts. At the Dalby and Roma sites, as at Cambooya, erosion was minimized by maintaining year-around crop cover, although the summer crop was the more important requirement. Double cropping (provided AW > 0.2) maximized yield at Dalby but a single annual crop of wheat minimized the probability of low income. At Roma, the most inland and driest site, a yearly winter crop of wheat provided the best financial return against either criterion, but at the expense of soil erosion.

**Response farming**

In regions of variable rainfall, farmers sometimes adjust their overall cropping strategy to suit current weather conditions. In Mediterranean climates, for example, where cereals are the primary crop, they adjust first by changing to short-season cultivars of the intended crop as the opening rains are progressively delayed, later by changing to a shorter-season crop, such as from wheat to barley, and finally by deciding not to sow at all when the seasonal break is delayed so late that the chance of success is unacceptably low.

These are examples of tactical responses to the year-to-year variability of weather in which the crop is changed in an attempt to improve a long-term 'fixed' strategy. A further possibility is to vary the management of already-established crops once the likely outcome of the season can be identified. These possibilities widen in situations where seasonal outcomes can be identified early.

An example of 'in-season' tactics can be found in the 'response farming' proposed by Stewart & Hash (1982) (see also Stewart 1988) following analyses of rainfall patterns in semiarid Kenya. There, annual rainfall is bimodally distributed provid-

Table 13.7 *Benefits from specific genetic modifications of sorghum and wheat cultivars grown at Temple, Texas (TEM), Manhattan, Kansas (MAN) and Lubbock, Texas (LUB) as predicted by the crop models SORGF and TAMW*

| | | Percentage of years that yield of modified crop exceeded normal crop by at least | | | | | |
| | | 20% | | | 50% | | |
| Crop | Trait | TEM | MAN | LUB | TEM | MAN | LUB |
|---|---|---|---|---|---|---|---|
| Sorghum | Osmoregulation | 3 | 0 | 10 | 0 | 0 | 0 |
| | Deep rooting | 38 | 29 | 20 | 21 | 20 | 7 |
| | Osmoregulation plus deep rooting | 38 | 29 | 27 | 24 | 20 | 10 |
| Wheat | Deep rooting | 21 | 30 | 28 | 14 | 20 | 17 |

*Source:* From Jordan *et al.* (1983).

Table 13.8 *Location details and optimum cropping strategies at three Queensland sites*

| | Site | | |
| | Cambooya | Dalby | Roma |
|---|---|---|---|
| *Site factors* | | | |
| Altitude (m) | 464 | 345 | 308 |
| Rainfall (mm) | 672 | 637 | 519 |
| ET* (mm) | 1540 | 1560 | 1740 |
| Water extraction zone (cm) | 0–75 | 0–90 | 0–90 |
| Max. available water (mm) | 60 | 230 | 160 |
| *Cropping strategy to:* | | | |
| Maximize income | wheat and sorghum[1] | wheat and sorghum[1] | wheat only |
| Minimize probability of low income | wheat and sorghum[1] | wheat only | wheat only |
| Minimize erosion | wheat and sorghum[1] | wheat and sorghum[1] | wheat and sorghum[1] |

*Note:*
[1] Crop is planted provided available water content (AW) at sowing exceeds 0.2 of available water-holding capacity (AWHC).
*Source:* After Berndt & White (1976).

ing two distinct but variable growing seasons each year. Analyses identified workable correlations between total seasonal rainfall and the timing and nature of the opening rains. Response farming proposes that maize should be established with the opening rains and then managed according to early-season rainfall to which follow-up rains are correlated. It is recommended that nitrogen fertilizer be applied to crops 40–50 days after sowing when the probability of a higher-than-normal rainfall and hence the likelihood of a yield response is high. When the outlook is for

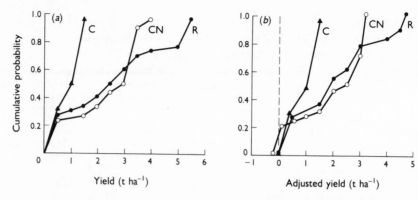

Fig. 13.10. **Cumulative probability of a given yield of maize under alternative management systems during the 'long' rains (March–June) at Katumani, Kenya. Conventional: C = 20 000 ha$^{-1}$ with no fertilizer; CN = 30 000 ha$^{-1}$ and 30 kg N ha$^{-1}$ at sowing. Response farming tactics: (R) = plant population thinned from 50 000 to 20 000 ha$^{-1}$ and N applied at 20–60 kg ha$^{-1}$ depending upon seasonal conditions. (*a*) Grain yield. (*b*) Grain yield adjusted for grain value of N fertilizer using a price ratio of 10:1 for N:grain. (Unpublished data of B. Wafula.)**

less than normal rainfall, crop thinning is recommended at the same stage of growth to maximize yield.

B. M. Wafula (pers. comm.) used the CERES–maize model (Jones and Kiniry 1986) to assess response farming tactics. As a preliminary step, the model was tuned to Kenyan cultivars and soil characteristics and shown to handle the response farming manipulations of fertilization and thinning. The analysis (Fig. 13.10) compares yield distributions for various management strategies and tactics simulated over a 29 y historical sequence of rainfall for the long rains (March to June) at Katumani, Kenya. Conventional management (C) uses a plant population of 20 000 ha$^{-1}$ and no nitrogen fertilizer. Response farming (R) includes a number of options depending upon sowing time and early-season rains. It covers a final plant population of 20 000 to 50 000 ha$^{-1}$ and nitrogen application of 20–60 kg ha$^{-1}$. CN is a variant of C. It uses a fixed population of 30 000 ha$^{-1}$ and 30 kg N ha$^{-1}$ at sowing.

Fig. 13.10*a* compares the yield distributions of the three management systems. Response farming provided consistently higher yields than conventional management, but the performance of CN suggests that a large part of the advantage related to the use of nitrogen fertilizer. This simpler system actually performed better than response farming except during seasons that produce the highest yields. With the response treatment, greater populations and more nitrogen make better use of the wetter seasons.

Nitrogen fertilizer is not generally applied by Kenyan subsistence farmers because it requires a substantial cash outlay. To investigate the return from nitrogen fertilizer, a set of distributions of adjusted yield are presented in Fig. 13.10*b*. These are derived directly from Fig. 13.10a by discounting yield for nitrogen applied at the cash value rate of 10:1 for N:grain. In the yield range 0–1 t ha$^{-1}$, there is little advantage to the outlay on fertilizer, although response farming does perform better than CN which has smaller populations and lower nitrogen. Response farming also performs better than conventional management, but the advantage lies in nitrogen application and other simpler systems may perform equally.

## 13.11   SUMMARY

Few principles are involved in the efficient use of water in crop production. It requires correction of other limiting factors, concentration of the available water in space or time to exceed the threshold for response (the non-uniformity principle), restricting crop water use to the available supply, maximizing transpiration by water-efficient species, and optimally distributing $E_p$ between vegetative and reproductive periods. However to achieve those objectives, essentially all aspects of a crop management, cultivation, selection of crop, and cultivar, sowing time, sowing density, fertilizer practice, weed and pest control are open to manipulation.

From the wide range of options, individual farmers generally seek optimum cropping strategies that are rotational sequences that best meet their objectives for particular combinations of climate, soil, and markets. Farmers can also introduce tactical variations to the overall strategy to take advantage of favorable weather, or reduce inputs, even skipping component crops entirely, when unfavorable weather conditions mean that the marginal benefits of individual activities will not meet the costs incurred. Recognizing those opportunities requires a closer analysis of the variability of environment and crop performance than is needed to establish the overall cropping strategy itself.

Because the environment and hence crop performance may be highly variable, such strategies and tactical variations can only be established by analysis of their performance over a substantial number of seasons. Crop simulation models offer the best opportunity yet to explore and explain crop performance in environments and under different management and hence to design strategies and tactics (including new ideotypes) for water-limited agriculture in low rainfall climates. There is a clear need to continue to improve crop simulation models for these analyses of complex decision structures. The powerful predictions that are possible with these techniques are not easily established by farmer experience.

## 13.12   FURTHER READING

Cornish, P. S. and Pratley, J. E. (eds) 1987. *Tillage: new directions in Australian agriculture.* Inkata Press, Melbourne. 448 p.

Loomis, R. S. 1983. Crop manipulations for efficient use of water: an overview. In *Limitations to efficient water use in crop production* (ed. H. M. Taylor, W. R. Jordan and T. R. Sinclair), pp. 345–74. Am. Soc. Agron., Madison, Wisconsin.

Tanner, C. B. and Sinclair, T. R. 1983. Efficient water use in crop production: research or re-search? In *Limitations to efficient water use in crop production* (ed. H. M. Taylor, W. R. Jordan and T. R. Sinclair) pp. 1–27. Am. Soc. Agron., Madison, Wisconsin.

# 14

## Water management in irrigated agriculture

### 14.1 INTRODUCTION

Irrigation provides the opportunity to avoid the constraints that low availability of water places on crop production by matching supply to environmental demand. The most spectacular irrigation schemes are those in arid regions of mid-latitudes where fully irrigated crops can achieve the high yields made possible by high insolation. However, irrigation practice covers the wide range from full to strategic irrigation designed to remove the most serious limitations of water shortage during the crop cycle. There is insufficient water to irrigate all land completely and over-irrigation, which is the easiest, practical approximation to full irrigation, may depress productivity and have deleterious effects on the environment. Consequently, the efficient use of water in irrigation is a key issue in crop ecology.

Rainfall carries considerable quantities of salts added by dust and by spray during ocean storms. Irrigation water has the potential to add much more. All surface- and groundwaters contain dissolved salts. In arid regions $Na^+$ and $Cl^-$ are common together with $Ca^{2+}$, $Mg^{2+}$, $K^+$, $HCO_3^-$, $CO_3^{2-}$, $NO_3^-$, $SO_4^{2-}$ and $BO_3^{3-}$. The chemical composition of water reflects its origin and determines its quality for irrigation. Direct surface runoff is usually 'cleaner' than water from rivers because they also contain water that has percolated through soil and underlying parent material. Groundwater accumulates by deep percolation, so it usually has the highest concentration of dissolved salts. The quality of runoff, stream flow and ground water varies substantially from place to place depending upon geology, leaching history, and the present hydrological balance.

Thus the practice of irrigation requires the management of both water and salt. The global hydrological balance has already concentrated much of the global salt in the oceans and the process is continuing. Large scale irrigation changes the hydrological and salt balances of entire regions by diverting water from drainage systems that mostly lead to the sea. The design of irrigation systems must allow for the dispersal of large amounts of salt that are fractionated by ET. The best solution is to reroute them to the ocean but this is not always economically feasible.

Water and salt management in irrigation usually requires action at the regional level as well as on individual farms. At the regional level there are two considerations:

(i) the selection of areas for irrigation schemes; and

(ii) the management of the overall water supply and associated drainage.

On farm, there are four components to proper irrigation practice:

(iii) irrigation scheduling for individual crops;

(iv) optimal strategy for allocation of the available water between alternative cropping activities;

(v) accurate application and uniform distribution of water to the crops; and

(vi) provision and management of drainage.

When water comes from surface runoff, management includes its collection, storage, and distribution to individual farms. When water is pumped by individual irrigators from aquifers, regional management may be needed to match withdrawal and replenishment. In both cases, management of groundwaters into which excess water drains is critical because of the dangers that rising water tables pose to cropping and groundwater pollution pose to livestock and humans when water supply is drawn from them.

## 14.2 SALINITY AND ALKALINITY

### Salt accumulation

Soluble and insoluble salts accumulate in the profiles of soils formed under semiarid and arid conditions. That occurs because salts released by weathering of parent material and those added by rainfall are not leached away through the profile. With shallow leaching, the salts tend to accumulate in the B horizons. Concretion nodules and 'hardpan' layers of $CaCO_3$ and cemented clay at the leaching depth are common.

Soluble salts such as NaCl are more mobile. Where hardpans and low rainfall prevent deep leaching, such soluble salts may be carried by internal, lateral drainage and by surface runoff to the oceans or to topographically lower areas where they become concentrated by evaporation. There, the sodium-saturated clays remain dispersed, effectively sealing the low-lying areas from further drainage. In Chapter 16, a problem with that type of saline seepage is examined in relation to dryland farming.

A soil with a high content of neutral salt (e.g. $Na^+$ with $Cl^-$ or $SO_4^{2-}$) is said to be **saline**. Sodium is generally an important constituent of the salt, and terms such as sodic and natric are used in soil descriptions. $Na^+$ plus weak anions ($HCO_3^-$, $CO_3^{2-}$) gives rise to **alkaline soil** with pH > 8.5. Alkalinity coupled with a high salt content results in a **saline–alkaline** condition.

### Water quality

The quality of water for irrigation is primarily determined by the total salt content, summarized as total dissolved solids (TDS) in mg $l^{-1}$ but better described by its

Table 14.1 *Guidelines for the interpretation of water quality for irrigation*

| Irrigation problem | Degree of problem | | |
|---|---|---|---|
| | nil | increasing | severe |
| Salinity (affects water availability) | | | |
| EC (dS m$^{-1}$) | <0.75 | 0.75–3.0 | >3.0 |
| Permeability (affects infiltration rate) | | | |
| EC (dS m$^{-1}$) | >0.5 | 0.5–0.2 | <0.2 |
| SAR | | | |
| montmorillonite | <6 | 6–9 | >9 |
| illite–vermiculite | <8 | 8–16 | >16 |
| koalinite–sesquioxides | <16 | 16–24 | >24 |
| Specific ion toxicity | | | |
| sodium (SAR) | <3 | 3–9 | >9 |
| chloride (meq l$^{-1}$) | <4 | 4–10 | >10 |
| boron (mg l$^{-1}$) | <0.75 | 0.75–2.0 | >2.0 |
| Miscellaneous effects (susceptible crops) | | | |
| NO$_3$-N or NH$_4$-N (mg l$^{-1}$) | <5 | 5–30 | >30 |
| HCO$_3$ (meq l$^{-1}$)[1] | <1.5 | 1.5–8.5 | >8.5 |
| pH (normal range) | | [6.5–8.4] | |

*Note:*
[1] By overhead sprinkling.
*Source:* After Ayers and Westcot (1985).

particular chemical composition. Concentration measured indirectly as electrical conductivity (EC in dS m$^{-1}$) does take some account of the range and proportion of ions present. In soils the ratio Na$^+$:Ca$^{2+}$ is in the range 2:1 to 5:1 (cf. 40:1 for sea water). Given an average ionic composition found in arid regions, it is possible to make the following practical correspondences: EC = 1 dS m$^{-1}$; TDS = 640 mg l$^{-1}$; and molar concentration = 11 mm. For comparison, the EC of sea water is in the range 50–60 dS m$^{-1}$.

Salt content and the sodium adsorption ratio (SAR; see Section 7.5) determine the suitability of water for irrigation. SAR is of particular importance in the irrigation of clay soils because they have high exchange capacity and form structures that are susceptible to destruction by dispersion when irrigated with water of high SAR. Table 14.1 provides guidelines for the safe use of irrigation water according to salt and sodium content.

The amount of salt added by irrigation depends upon the quantity of irrigation water as well as its salt content. Even with high quality water, irrigation adds large quantities of salt to crops. For example a 500 mm irrigation season with good quality water (EC = 0.5 dS m$^{-1}$, TDS = 320 mg l$^{-1}$) will add 1.6 t ha$^{-1}$. Without leaching, this salt must accumulate within the root zone and will ultimately reach levels detrimental to the productivity of crops.

Table 14.2 summarizes the electrical conductivity of samples of irrigation water from various locations around the world. The list separates river and well waters because they form distinct classes of quality with respect to suitability for irrigation.

Table 14.2 *Electrical conductivities (EC, dS m$^{-1}$) of irrigation water from rivers and wells around the world*

| Country | River | EC | Well | EC |
|---------|-------|-----|------|-----|
| Afghanistan | Kunduz at Seh Dorak | 0.60 | Kunduz (D-92) | 4.50 |
| Australia | Goulburn at Nagambie | 0.10 | Shepparton | 3.40 |
| Colombia | Cauca | 0.87 | Hda. Marsella | 0.38 |
| Egypt | Nile at Cairo | 0.40 | Nakel | 2.20 |
| India | Ganges at Patna | 0.31 | Rohtak | 1.98 |
| Mexico | Colorado in Mexico | 1.35 | Mexicali Valley | 1.27 |
| Malawi | Tangazi | 0.15 | Tambordera | 0.37 |
| Philippines | Jalaur at Iloilo | 0.31 | Laguna (P-18) | 0.48 |
| Spain | Guadalquivir at E. de Mengibar | 0.89 | Bardenas Alto | 2.70 |
| USA | Feather at Nicolaus | 0.09 | Denver | 0.63 |
| USA | Rio Grande at El Paso | 1.32 | Riverdale | 0.97 |

*Source:* From Ayers and Westcot (1985).

Comparison cannot be strict, however, because the locations are few and individual measurements do not capture the temporal variation that can occur at individual sites. The data illustrate that river waters are generally less saline than ground waters and that the two classes overlap. The overall range is great and shows that some waters have the potential to cause moderate to severe salinity problems. Ayers & Westcot (1985) have compiled an extensive analysis of salinity and chemical composition of irrigation waters.

## Salinity tolerance

The sensitivity of crops to salinity can be summarized by linear relationships between relative (%) yield ($Y/Y_0$) and EC of the soil saturation extract of the form:

$$Y/Y_0 = 100 - b(EC - t),$$ [Eq. 14.1]

which holds for EC $> t$ (Fig. 14.1); $t$ is the threshold EC (dS m$^{-1}$) below which there is no effect of salinity on productivity, and $b$ is the salt sensitivity, expressed as the relative yield reduction to salinity (% per dS m$^{-1}$) for EC $> t$. Table 14.3 records the effect of salinity on a range of crop species. Sensitive crops are affected by EC $< 2$ dS m$^{-1}$. Some field crops such as barley and sugarbeet perform reasonably well up to 8–10 dS m$^{-1}$, but little production can be achieved beyond 15–20 dS m$^{-1}$ with any crop. Sodium-ion toxicity and reduced availability of soil water are the main reasons. As a group, grasses are significantly more tolerant than legumes.

## Leaching requirement

Continued farming in the face of rising salinity depends on removing the excess salt through drainage. The annual hydrological balance (Eq. 9.1) for the cropping

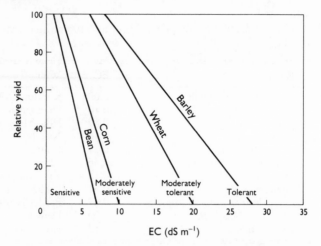

**Fig. 14.1. Sensitivity of some agricultural species to soil salinity. EC is the electrical conductivity of the saturation extract (after Maas & Hoffman (1977).)**

system must allow for drainage ($D$). Because storage and runoff are small relative to the other terms, drainage will occur when $(P + I) > ET$. That is accomplished by reducing ET (e.g. shortening the duration of cropping) or increasing $I$. The additional amount of $I$, termed the **leaching requirement**, can be calculated by assuming a steady state salt balance (salt$_{in}$ = salt$_{out}$). Most of the input salt comes from the irrigation water with a conductivity of EC$_i$, so the necessary salt balance is:

$$EC_i I - EC_d D = 0. \qquad\qquad \text{[Eq. 14.2]}$$

With EC$_d$ of the drainage set to the tolerance of the crop and $I$ equal to $ET - P + D$, then after rearrangement:

$$D = EC_i(ET - P)/(EC_d - EC_i). \qquad\qquad \text{[Eq. 14.3]}$$

In this equation EC$_i$ and $P$ are known. ET is also known or can be estimated from relationships of the type presented in Table 9.1; EC$_d$ is set according to the sensitivity of the crop. Thus if EC$_i$ = 0.5 dS m$^{-1}$ and $ET - P$ = 500 mm, then for EC$_d$ = 2 dS m$^{-1}$, $D$ = 167 mm. If EC$_d$ can be relaxed to 4 dS m$^{-1}$, then $D$ falls to 71 mm.

The salinity profiles that are established in soils depend upon the leaching fraction and the pattern of plant uptake from the root zone. Fig. 14.2 shows the salinity profiles expected to develop after long-term use of water of 1.0 dS m$^{-1}$ at three leaching fractions, 0.1, 0.2 and 0.4. In this case, forty percent of the transpiration requirement is met by root uptake from the upper layer, declining to 10% in the lowest of four layers of the root zone.

In practical applications where farmers are restricted by the salinity of their irrigation water, EC$_d$ is often set to the value corresponding to a 50% reduction in yield of the species in question. If the increase in EC is linear from the soil surface to the drainage depth (cf. LF = 0.4 in Fig. 14.2), the average salinity in the root zone

Table 14.3 *Salt tolerance of agricultural crops*

| Crop | Threshold $(t)^1$ (dS m$^{-1}$) | Sensitivity $(b)^1$ (% reduction per dS m$^{-1}$) |
| --- | --- | --- |
| *Sensitive* | | |
| Bean | 1.0 | 17 |
| Carrot | 1.0 | 14 |
| Strawberry | 1.0 | 33 |
| Onion | 1.2 | 16 |
| Orange | 1.7 | 16 |
| Peach | 1.7 | 21 |
| *Moderately sensitive* | | |
| Radish | 1.2 | 13 |
| Lettuce | 1.3 | 13 |
| Clover, white | 1.5 | 12 |
| Broadbean | 1.6 | 10 |
| Maize | 1.7 | 12 |
| Potato | 1.7 | 12 |
| Sugarcane | 1.7 | 6 |
| Alfalfa | 2.0 | 7 |
| Tomato | 2.5 | 10 |
| Vetch | 3.0 | 11 |
| Rice | 3.0 | 12 |
| *Moderately tolerant* | | |
| Sudangrass | 2.8 | 4 |
| Wheatgrass | 3.5 | 4 |
| Zucchini | 4.7 | 9 |
| Soybean | 5.0 | 20 |
| Ryegrass | 5.6 | 8 |
| Wheat | 6.0 | 7 |
| Sorghum | 6.8 | 16 |
| *Tolerant* | | |
| Date palm | 4.0 | 4 |
| Sugarbeet | 7.0 | 6 |
| Wheatgrass | 7.5 | 4 |
| Cotton | 7.7 | 5 |
| Barley | 8.0 | 5 |

*Note:*
[1] See Eq. 14.1.
*Source:* After Maas (1984).

under this strategy will cause a yield reduction of 5 to 10% for many crops (Reeve & Fireman 1967).

There must also be a place for the drainage water to go. In the early years of an irrigation project, it is common to simply move the salt down below the root zone. This carries the danger of adding salt to ground waters which may be an irrigation source, or of filling the profile. 'Perched' water tables due to impervious zones in the soil represent another problem. With the water table near the surface, **capillary rise**

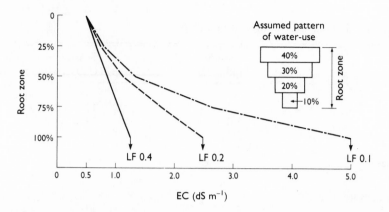

Fig. 14.2. Salinity profiles expected to develop after long-term use of water of EC = 1.0 dS m$^{-1}$ at leaching fractions (LF) = 0.1, 0.2, and 0.4 (after Ayers & Westcot (1985).)

tends to return the salt to the root zone and may form a crystalline deposit on the surface. The most practical, permanent solution is to install subsurface drains. These are usually perforated plastic tubes laid 1 to 1.5 m deep and emptying to an outlet drain. Finding an appropriate outlet for the drain is an increasingly worrisome problem in irrigated areas. Disposal of drainage water, and methods for reclamation are discussed further in Section 14.7.

It might seem that the use of salt-tolerant plants (e.g. barley) would provide a solution to the continuation of agriculture under conditions of increasing salinity. Even if the production of those crops offers an economically viable option to the farmer, the gain is likely to be transitory. In the absence of adequate drainage, most irrigated agricultural systems eventually succumb to salt accumulation. Since precipitation ($P$) and irrigation ($I$) generally remain < ET*, salt accumulates wherever water is applied. Without management to prevent continuing salinization, change to a tolerant crop only forestalls the inevitable endpoint at a higher EC at which agricultural production becomes impossible.

## 14.3   WATER USE AND PRODUCTIVITY

The principle has been developed (Section 9.10) that maximum efficiency of water use in the production of biomass will be achieved when direct loss by soil evaporation is minimized and when the crop season occurs during the period of lowest ET* consistent with the temperature and radiation requirements of the crop. Crop reproductive yield will be maximized when the pattern of water availability, water use and hence growth least restricts the development and expression of crop yield.

These ideas of the response of crop yield ($Y$) to the seasonal pattern of water supply can be condensed (J. W. Jones 1983) as:

Table 14.4 *Susceptibilities of various irrigated crops to water shortage during various stages of growth*

The sensitivity parameter $\lambda$ is defined in Eq. 14.4.

| Crop | Growth stage | Sensitivity ($\lambda$) |
|------|------|------|
| Maize | | |
| | vegetative | 0.25 |
| | silking | 0.50 |
| | tasselling to soft dough | 0.50 |
| | after soft dough | 0.21 |
| Cotton | | |
| | prior to flowering | 0.00 |
| | early flowering | 0.21 |
| | peak flowering | 0.32 |
| | late flowering | 0.20 |
| Rice | | |
| | vegetative | 0.17 |
| | reproductive and ripening | 0.30 |
| Pea | | |
| | vegetative | 0.13 |
| | flowering to early pod | 0.46 |
| | pod growth to maturity | 0.43 |
| Soybean | | |
| | vegetative | 0.12 |
| | early to peak flowering | 0.24 |
| | late flowering to early pod | 0.35 |
| | pod growth to maturity | 0.13 |

*Source:* After Hiler *et al.* (1974).

$$\max(Y/Y_o) = \prod_{i=1}^{i=n} (ET_a/ET^*)^{\lambda_i}. \qquad \text{[Eq. 14.4]}$$

Growth during each of the n successive phenophases of the crop cycle is actually proportional to relative transpiration $E_p/ET^*$, but for these purposes can be approximated by $ET_a/ET^*$. The effect of growth restrictions on final yield (Y) relative to potential yield ($Y_o$) depends upon timing. The variable $\lambda_i$ ($i=1$ to $n$) describes the sensitivity of final yield to stress in each phenophase. In this model, the cumulative effect of stress during successive phenophases is multiplicative, as indicated by the symbol $\Pi$ (cf. $\Sigma$ for summation). Examples of such effects on a range of crops are presented in Table 14.4.

Eq. 14.4 provides a practical basis for management of water supply in irrigated agriculture. When there is insufficient water to meet total seasonal demand, crop yield is greatest when water is supplied in a pattern that avoids the most serious

Table 14.5 *Irrigation techniques arranged according to the degree of control they offer over application rate and distribution*

Capital costs increase in the same order.

| *Surface* | basin<br>border check<br>furrow | |
| *Sprinklers* | hand move<br>wheel line<br>center pivot<br>linear move<br>permanent set | increasing<br>control<br>over<br>quantity and<br>placement |
| *Micro-irrigation* | drip emitters<br>micro sprays | |

effects of stress on yield, i.e. when Eq. 14.4 is maximized. This requires that water be managed to ensure that crops suffer water shortage least during sensitive stages (large $\lambda$ in Table 14.4).

## 14.4    IRRIGATION METHODS

A range of techniques by which water can be applied to crops is summarized in Table 14.5 according to the control they afford over the amount and placement of the water to be applied. The cost of installation and maintenance of the systems generally increases with their degree of control. The choice depends upon the economics of producing the crops, topography, soils, salinity and the need for frost protection.

**Surface irrigation**

In surface irrigation, water flows onto and over land down slopes managed to control infiltration into the soil. Soil physical properties determine infiltration rate and the slope determines the period of time that water remains on the surface for infiltration. The most primitive form is **wild flooding (water spreading)** but most forms (**basin, border-check, furrow**) require land grading to control the evenness and rate of flow of water and hence of infiltration. Flat land is most suitable for surface irrigation because the cost of its preparation is least. It is, however, possible to reform almost any land surface into a series of irrigable areas as is witnessed by the ambitious terracing projects of ancient peoples, e.g. Incas of South America and those that still operate in Asia, e.g. in the Philippines.

Surface irrigation is not suitable for soils of high infiltration (sands and sandy loams) because it is not possible to run water down suitable slopes rapidly enough to avoid excessive drainage through the profile without causing serious erosion. On impermeable soils it is possible to maintain standing water at low and spatially even rates of infiltration. This is the technique used in paddy rice (basin irrigation) where already impermeable soils are further 'puddled' to lower infiltration. On other soils, the size and slope of the individual managed units and the rate of water supply are matched to the infiltration behavior of the soil. The objective is even wetting of each bay or furrow although in practice this is difficult to achieve. Surface irrigation requires the addition of excess water and its subsequent recovery as tail-water flowing off each bay or furrow. Depending upon the irrigation layout on a farm, this tail-water may be cycled back to irrigation supply channels or used for lower-lying fields.

Surface irrigation subjects a crop to a sequence of conditions of water supply from one irrigation to the next. During irrigation and shortly afterwards, at least the upper root zone of the crop may be waterlogged. Then there is a period of optimum supply of water and oxygen as the upper profile drains. Towards the end of the irrigation cycle, extraction by the crop may reduce soil water content below the level which will sustain maximum growth. Despite these limitations, heavy soils perform best under irrigation because they store the largest amounts of water and because the transitions in $\Psi_{soil}$ during extraction near WP are more gradual (Fig. 7.8$a$). An exception occurs on soils with a slowly permeable subsoil. In that case, the subsoil can only be recharged by prolonged irrigation and hence waterlogging of the surface soil. When such a soil is watered on a cycle of 70 mm of ($ET^* - P$), corresponding to say 10 days at a daily rate of 7 mm, the period of optimum water supply may persist for only 4–5 days, i.e. for less than 50% of the total growing period. This is the problem that irrigators face on the Duplex soils of northern Victoria, Australia (Cockroft & Mason 1987).

In **basin** and **border-check** irrigation, the penetration of irrigation water into the profile is even. Consequently when saline water is applied, salt moves evenly down the profile except for minor concentration by evaporation in the check banks. In the case of furrow irrigation, however, salt is concentrated by evaporation in each of the rows in use, especially when crop cover is incomplete and $E_s$ is high. This can be especially hazardous to seedlings, which are often more sensitive to salt than mature plants and also have shallow root systems with little access to the cleaner water below. One solution is to irrigate alternate furrows and so move the salt past the rows into the unirrigated furrows. In severe cases, a change of irrigation practice may be necessary to bring a field back into production (Section 14.7).

Although flood irrigation is the most primitive form of irrigation because of its limited control over placement and infiltration of water, the technique has been recently vastly improved by the precise land forming that is possible with laser-controlled equipment. It is now possible to set the desired grades, often as small as 1:1000, with precision and to do that over bigger bays and longer furrows. The outcome has been improved productivity, more efficient use of water, reduced drainage, and less expense to labor. The removal of low 'wet' spots reduces accessions to the water table and more even watering has improved overall yield. The reduction of the total area given over to control levees and the change from

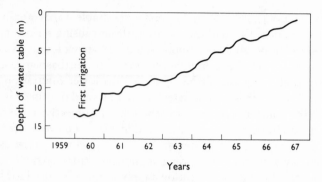

**Fig. 14.3. Rising water tables under irrigation in Solano County, California (after Houston (1967).)**

irregular-shaped contour basins has lifted productivity on well-managed irrigation farms of the Central Valley of California by an estimated 7 to 10%.

The measurement of the water applied by surface irrigation requires attention to input and to loss. Weirs and wheels (e.g. Dethridge Wheel) can measure flow in ditches but it is unlikely that many irrigators can know within 20% what water has entered the soil. The usual reaction to this uncertainty, especially to satisfy the minimum leaching requirement, is to over-irrigate. Over an irrigation season of 500 mm this may add an additional 100 mm to ground water or drainage. If the watertable were originally at 20 m it would take 80 years to bring a dry clay profile to saturation (400 mm m$^{-1}$, wilting point to saturation; Section 7.6). If the soil were initially wet, the soil water holding capacity less, or if annual accessions were augmented by rainfall on recently irrigated land, then the watertable would rise more quickly. This has been a relatively common occurrence in irrigation schemes around the world (e.g. Fig. 14.3).

### Sprinkler irrigation

A range of **high-pressure** systems is used to spray water onto crops. They are especially suited to light soils and rolling land. Application rates can be adjusted to suit topography and the infiltration characteristics of the soil. With care, an even wetting pattern can be achieved. Many systems use equipment which is moved periodically by hand (**simple lines, side roll, water cannons**) but in others, movement is automatic and is mostly slowly continuous (**wheel line, hose drag**). Automation is most highly developed in the **linear move** systems. With a width of up to 400 m and supplied by a channel of 1000 m length, they command an area of 40 ha. A more widely used mobile sprinkler system is the **center pivot**, which rotates around its central point of supply. With an arm of up to 500 m in length and one complete revolution in one day or so, such systems can irrigate an area of 80 ha. During a period of 20 years up to 1975, center pivot systems were used to develop 4 Mha of irrigated crop land in the Great Plains of USA.

Permanent irrigation systems are used mainly with high value horticultural crops.

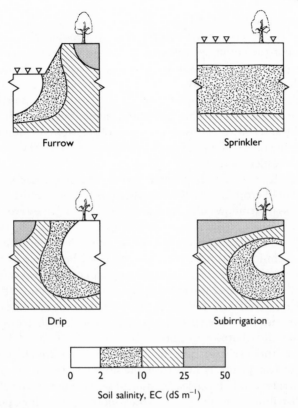

Fig. 14.4. Patterns of salt accumulation under irrigation by a range of techniques in an orchard (after Oster *et al.* (1984).)

They are usually **set sprinklers** fed by a network of underground pipes with a riser to each outlet nozzle.

In sprinkler irrigation the supply water is confined to pipes, and since there need be no runoff, the measurement of the water applied is straightforward and accurate. It is possible to account for losses by evaporation from the foliage and soil surface and to estimate the water that enters the soil with an accuracy of around 5%. Unlike surface irrigation, these systems do, however, require moderately clean water so that the sprinkler nozzles are neither blocked nor damaged by suspended sediment.

Sprinkler irrigation can provide even wetting and hence even movement of salt vertically through the profile (Fig. 14.4). If, as is common in horticultural crops, sprinklers are used to wet rows or the root zones of individual plants (trees), then salt will migrate horizontally to the margins of the wetting front.

### Micro-irrigation

The various forms of micro-irrigation are the most recent development in irrigation technology. Pioneered in Israel, the technique has spread rapidly around the world.

It offers the most precise control of the amount and placement of irrigation water and opens new horizons for the control of crop productivity. There are many arrangements but the common feature is that water is delivered at **low pressure** through tubing to many emitters, often arranged to service individual plants. The emitters may be **drippers** or **sprays** of low output arranged to control the shape and volume of the root zone that is wetted. In orchards it is possible to irrigate individual trees and at the same time restrict $E_s$, maintaining the inter-row space dry, weed-free and trafficable. It is possible to control the wetted volume to match the size of the growing root system and to control the availability of water to the crop to meet agronomic objectives.

Although ideally suited to high-value perennial crops, these systems are now extending into field crops in which removal or replacement of the supply lines and emitters is necessary to allow cultivation and sowing as each new crop is planted. An interesting development is subsurface drip irrigation. In this case, the supply lines and emitters are below the cultivation layer but otherwise operate in a comparable manner. This technique has high water-use efficiency because it avoids the significant losses that result from $E_s$ in crops of incomplete cover. However, if saline water is used, salt will concentrate by evaporation in the root zone and at the surface (Fig. 14.4) unless there is sufficient rainfall to leach it below the root zone.

The complex patterns of wetting that are characteristic of drip irrigation produce equally complex distributions of salt in the soil profile (Fig. 14.4). Salt becomes concentrated at the periphery of the wetted volume which, with drips and microsprays between plants, is away from the sites of watering, cf. salt distribution under furrow irrigation. This can lead to difficulties during a crop cycle if infrequent heavy rain redistributes the salt back into the root zone of seedling plants. With the completion of the crop, especially a perennial one, attention must be paid to eliminating pockets of high salt concentration to enable success of the subsequent planting pattern.

As with sprinkler irrigation, the water supply is confined to pipes so that accurate measurement of flow is possible. The arrangement of the surface emitters limits the area of wet surface and hence of the losses by evaporation. Control of the volume of water entering the soil is possible within 1%. The systems do, however, require clean water that is usually achieved by filtration. Unless due care is taken, evaporation can block the emitters with either sediment or salt.

## Comparative cost of irrigation methods

A comparison of the annual cost, investment plus maintenance, of various irrigation methods is presented in Table 14.6. Flood irrigation is the cheapest being about two-thirds the cost of permanent-set sprinklers (Fereres *et al.* 1981). Large increases in productivity are required to justify the cost of irrigation, but considering the differences in the degree of control that the systems afford, the differential between the various techniques is not as large as might at first be expected.

Surface irrigation requires much less energy for operation and maintenance than do sprinkler systems, but automation is less and consequently labor costs are

Table 14.6 *Comparative annual costs of various irrigation methods, all applying around 900 mm to field crops*

| Method | Overhead[1] | Operating | Total |
|---|---|---|---|
| Flood | 21 | 42 | 63 |
| Furrow | 25 | 46 | 71 |
| Sprinkler | | | |
|    Center pivot | 43 | 44 | 87 |
|    Wheel line | 37 | 45 | 82 |
|    Hand move | 32 | 60 | 92 |
|    Permanent set | 58 | 42 | 100 |
| Drip | | | |
|    Field crop | 137 | 44 | 181 |
|    Orchard | 56 | 44 | 100 |

*Note:*
[1] Annual cost of investment in land preparation, supply and drainage, equipment. In 1981 the cost of permanent set irrigation in this study (100 units in table) was US$205 ha$^{-1}$.
*Source:* After Fereres *et al.* (1981).

greater. The energetics of irrigation have some interesting interrelationships. The comparison of the energy cost of surface and sprinkler irrigation in three zones of California (Fig. 14.5) illustrates that when the cost of delivery of the water is low there is considerable energy saving with surface irrigation. However, when the water is pumped to fields at great cost, e.g. 5.9 GJ Ml$^{-1}$ in the San Diego River area, the additional cost of pressurization, 0.6 GJ Ml$^{-1}$, is more than offset by the 20% saving in water. That explains why the energy cost of sprinkler irrigation is less than surface irrigation at that site. The relative costs of various irrigation techniques will vary as the components of the cost change. It is unlikely, though, that there will be major reversals because a law of economics, if not of ecology also, is that the cost of biological effort (here, labor) and its replacement (here, electricity) are functionally related (Chapter 15).

## 14.5   IRRIGATION SCHEDULING

The decisions of how much water to apply and when next to irrigate a crop depend upon many factors. It requires an estimate of ET*, knowledge of the water holding capacity of the soil, an understanding of the consequence of a current deficit on the ultimate yield, an estimate of the amount of irrigation water available to complete the crop cycle, and an estimate of the probability of rainfall throughout the remainder of the growing season. It also requires information on the salt content of the irrigation water and the sensitivity of the crop to salinity.

Scheduling can be accomplished with crop water budgets calculated with models of the type presented in Box 9.1 and this is done successfully in many parts of the world. On some farms the technique is assisted by measurements of soil water

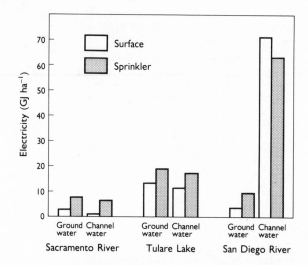

**Fig. 14.5. The seasonal energy cost of irrigating alfalfa (950 mm) in three hydrologic basins in California. For each basin, a comparison is made between surface and sprinkler irrigation with water obtained from channels or from ground water. The calculations assume that sprinklers use 20% less water than surface methods (after Knutson *et al.* (1977).)**

content now made routinely possible using equipment such as the neutron moisture meter. Observation of crop water status can also be used. Direct measurements of leaf water potential or leaf conductance are possible but require specialized equipment and skill and for that reason are rarely used in practice. Indirect measurements are more easily applied. For example, visual detection of wilting and leaf movement can indicate when irrigation is required. If such observations are made on parts of the crop (lighter soil) that are known to experience water stress first, a form of local calibration, this technique is highly successful. A technique that is showing great promise uses the measurement of canopy temperature to detect the onset of water shortage. This can be accomplished by infrared thermometry (see Section 6.6) that is easily applied in practice.

The adoption of water scheduling has been most rapid where the cost of water and/or the consequences of over-irrigation are most expensive to the producer. In areas of low rainfall, scheduling irrigation is relatively easy because the low probability of rainfall least complicates the decision of how much of the immediate water requirement should be added as irrigation. In such areas, irrigation may even be effectively scheduled chronologically and, in community schemes, water is often delivered to farms on this basis. Fixed irrigation intervals are, however, an infrequent component of good irrigation practice.

Emphasis can too easily be placed on frequent irrigation to maintain high soil water, low soil salt, and high productivity. However, irrigation practice should also allow for the maximum utilization of rainfall and hence for the minimization of runoff and the control of drainage. Fully charged profiles cannot accept additional rainfall so that its fate must be as either runoff or drainage. Runoff can be spectacular and may cause erosion, sedimentation and eutrophication of streams and lakes. Excessive drainage, in contrast, is unseen but is often insidiously more dangerous.

Yield is, generally maximized when $ET_a \to ET^*$ during all growth stages (Eq. 14.4) but there are some crops in which limited (deficit) irrigation actually improves yield. Cotton is an excellent example of a field crop in which favorable conditions for growth promote vegetative growth at the expense of reproductive yield. Grimes & El-Zik (1982) recommend scheduling irrigation when $\Psi_l$ falls to $-1.6$, $-2.0$ and $-1.8$ MPa during vegetative growth, at 'squaring', and at peak bloom respectively. Growth is certainly reduced by this watering regime but yield is not. In the San Joaquin Valley of California maximum yields of cotton are achieved with irrigation totalling 400–500 mm during a growing season in which $ET^*$ approaches 800 mm.

Perennial horticultural crops also have reproductive relationships that can be favorably manipulated to improve yield. In stone fruits such as peach, fruit growth proceeds in double sigmoidal fashion in which the pause coincides with the development of seed and associated tissues. If water is withheld at this stage, vegetative growth of the crop is reduced and on rewatering the growth of the fruit is enhanced. This technique is referred to as **regulated deficit irrigation** (Chalmers *et al.* 1981).

## 14.6 ALLOCATION OF WATER ON FARMS

The decision of how to distribute the water on individual farms is complex and mostly uncertain. The irrigator's objective is not to maximize the yield from individual crops but to maximize net return (gross return less fixed and variable costs) from the entire operation. The variables include choices between crop types, summer versus winter, irrigated versus rainfed, and the level of irrigation. It is possible to formulate the objective function for $k$ crops each occupying a proportion $p_i$ of the farm as an extension of Eq. 14.4 as follows:

$$\max (P) = \sum_{i=1}^{i=k} p_i \left[ V_i Y_{0_i} \prod_{j=1}^{j=n} (ET_{ij}/ET_{ij}^*)^{\lambda_i} - \sum (C_{ij} I_{ij}) \right]. \qquad \text{[Eq. 14.5]}$$

Here, $P$ is the net return (US\$ ha$^{-1}$), $V_i$ is the value of one unit of yield of crop $i$ (US\$ kg$^{-1}$), and $C_{ij}$ cost of water applied ($I_{ij}$ mm) to crop $i$ during growth stage $j$ (J. W. Jones 1983). Research to support these approaches is developing rapidly but at present irrigators must rely on much less specific bases for management. Allocation of labor and capital is more easily managed in irrigation schemes located in arid zones. In humid zones, management is made difficult by the less predictable rainfall and evaporation but techniques of irrigation scheduling are being extended to such regions (e.g. Villalobos & Fereres 1989).

The fixed cost of investment in land preparation and general infrastructure for irrigation and drainage is high and the variable cost of water is often low. Under these conditions the likely optimum strategy is to irrigate for maximum yield. However, many irrigators do not have sufficient water (irrigation plus rainfall) to achieve maximum yield over their entire area of land. In addition, suboptimal irrigation may be an economically efficient means of controlling accessions to the water table. For these reasons, rainfed crops have an important place in irrigation regions especially because their sowing and their productivity can be assured by limited, strategic irrigation. This is a part of the production strategy of the Central Valley of California, where winter cereals are produced with about 100–200 mm of strategic irrigation in the spring compared with 600–800 mm for summer-irrigated crops of tomato, corn, or beans, and 1000 mm for alfalfa.

In the Goulburn Valley irrigation area of Victoria, Australia, where the dominant irrigated crop is summer pasture of perennial ryegrass, paspalum, and white clover, irrigators divert some of their water to strategic irrigation of annual pasture (wimmera ryegrass and subterranean clover). One watering can assure a timely start to pasture growth in the autumn (March) and if necessary one or two waterings in the spring (September–October) will ensure continuing growth until the summer irrigated pastures are productive. In this area, too, wheat can be grown with similar management to annual pasture using around 300 mm of water compared with 700 mm needed to water a summer crop of pasture, alfalfa, tomato, soybean, or sunflower.

## 14.7   MANAGEMENT OF WATER SUPPLY AND DRAINAGE

Good irrigation practice depends upon water being available when it is needed. In each irrigation region the pattern of crop production and hence the demand for water are similar from farm to farm. This presents great difficulties in the provision of water, depending upon the size of the major storage and the delivery characteristics of the distribution network. In practice the performance of irrigators is improved when they have their own supply, e.g. they pump individually from rivers, lakes, or ground water, or when they have on-farm storage for water delivered to them. On-farm storage can accept water when it is available even if the rate of delivery is less than that required for efficient, direct irrigation. On-farm storage also assists the cycling of tail-water from surface irrigation and introduces the possibility of incorporating drainage water into the irrigation reserves of the farm.

At the regional level, the need to maintain separate drainage and supply systems depends upon water quality. Drainage water can be added to the supply system provided the chemical composition of both is known and, if necessary, the greater leaching requirement for irrigation with saline water is provided. Fig. 14.6 illustrates an on-farm scheme for the utilization of drainage water. Crops can be chosen (Table 14.3) to accommodate the quality of the water that is available. This scheme also applies to entire irrigation schemes because many need additional water to supply all farms completely and few have completely separate supply and drainage systems. For this reason it is characteristic of irrigation areas that the quality of irrigation water gradually decreases as it moves through the system. This is seen dramatically in Fig. 14.7, which records the salinity levels along the course of the Murray River of southern Australia. As the river passes through irrigation areas it

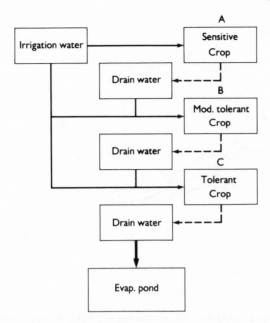

**Fig. 14.6. A scheme for use of drainage water in irrigated agriculture. At each step, drainage water is mixed with water from the irrigation source. Crop types A, B, C have increasing salinity tolerance.**

picks up additional drainage so that its quality for agriculture, industry, and stock and human consumption gradually declines.

Fig. 14.8 presents a long term analysis (1942–73) of the salinity of the lower Colorado River as it enters the Imperial Valley Irrigation District of southern California. The steady increase over this period from 1 to 1.5 dS m$^{-1}$ reflects the gradual development of other irrigation activities upstream in the states of Colorado and Utah. For completeness, the graph also shows the salinity of the drainage from the area as it enters the inland Salton Sea. The increased salinity of the effluent reflects the reclamation of the saline soils of this arid region after problems of salinization during its early development.

Reservoirs usually also serve purposes other than the provision of irrigation water and so their management is governed by other motives also. One common activity is the generation of electricity, another is flood mitigation, and a third, is recreation. These various objectives lead to some conflicts. For example, secure irrigation requires maximum storage at the start of irrigation seasons whereas flood mitigation requires that reservoirs should be maintained sufficiently empty to handle sudden runoff. Recreation in reservoirs is usually best when they are full, but electricity generation and downstream recreation require continuous release of water. Sensible coordination and rational use of water can be developed by charging fairly for its use. Irrigators pay fees but the basis of charging is often uncertain. Some would have irrigators pay for the entire cost of amortizing and maintaining irrigation systems even though the benefits are spread widely through society.

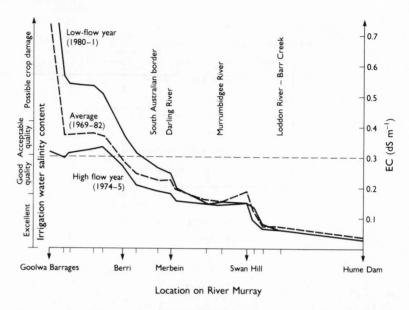

**Fig. 14.7. Increasing salinity down the length of the Murray River, southern Australia. Salinity is recorded as it passes from the Hume dam on its upper reaches through the irrigation regions of New South Wales, Victoria and South Australia. The locations of three tributaries that enter from the irrigation areas are also shown (after Anon. (1988).)**

## Reclamation of alkaline and saline soils

Saline soils ($EC > 3$ dS m$^{-1}$, $TDS = 2000$ mg l$^{-1}$) will reduce the growth of moderately tolerant crops and if EC exceeds 10 dS m$^{-1}$ reclamation will improve the productivity of any crop (Fig. 14.1). The reclamation of salt-affected land requires that farmers coordinate their irrigation and drainage.

With neutral salinity, medium and light-textured soils can be improved quickly by leaching. Theoretical analyses (Gardner & Brooks 1957) have shown that from 1.5 to 2 pore volume changes are needed to reduce salinity to below 30% of its initial value. In practice this can be achieved by leaching the profile with an equivalent depth of water (1 m water to leach the top 1 m of the profile). Heavy-textured, saline soils are difficult to reclaim by irrigation because sodium-saturated clays disperse, sealing them against further leaching. Ca$^{2+}$ must be supplied to replace excess Na$^+$ on the exchange complex. Cation exchange proceeds slowly when the common ameliorant, gypsum (CaSO$_4$), is used because its solubility is low. In practice it is possible to dissolve 1 t of gypsum in 1 Ml of water with mechanical mixing. Repeated treatments over several years are usually required to reclaim the soil to 1 m depth. Direct application to the soil and physical incorporation by ploughing may improve its effectiveness, but this requires more gypsum. Intermittent flooding and sprinkler irrigation are more effective than continuous flooding because they cause more water flow through the smaller pores leading to more efficient leaching.

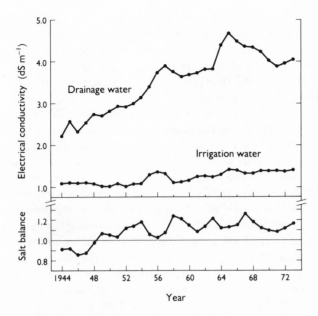

**Fig. 14.8. Salinity of irrigation water, drainage water, and the annual salt balance (output/input) of the Imperial Valley irrigation area of southern California, USA, over the period from 1944 to 1973 (after Kaddah & Rhoades (1976).)**

Alkaline and saline–alkaline soils present a different problem. Perhaps the best way to lower pH is to incorporate sulfur. This is readily oxidized biologically in most soils to $SO_4^{2-}$, releasing $H^+$ from water for $Na^+$ displacement.

It has been proposed from time to time that crops could be used to reclaim saline land by harvesting time to remove their salt content. This has been shown to be an unrealistic proposition for eight agricultural species. For these, Lyerly & Longeneker (1957) measured average salt removal of 200 kg ha$^{-1}$, of which 60% was NaCl. To grow the crops, 900 mm of irrigation with a salt content of 6000 kg ha$^{-1}$ was applied. Thus the crops actually removed less than 5% of the extra salt that was added. Even halophytes, which may accumulate 50% of their small biomass as salt, are unlikely to remove more than 200 kg ha$^{-1}$, and that production would also require irrigation.

## 14.8  SELECTION OF AREAS FOR IRRIGATION SCHEMES

Most irrigation schemes are located in arid and semiarid regions. The impact of irrigation is greatest there despite the difficulties and the disadvantage of low water-use efficiency. As was explained earlier, soils and subsoils of arid and semiarid regions often have high salt concentrations because they have experienced little leaching. The high salt content is mobilized by irrigation and augmented by the salt accessions from irrigation itself. Ideally one would choose non-saline areas and best-quality water to minimize difficulties and costs of amelioration. Whereas all irrigation areas require drainage systems, those in saline areas require them bigger, better, and sooner! There are many cases where realization of the scope of adequate drainage has come too late. If there are no natural drainage lines to the ocean or to inland sinks that can be used, then continuation of irrigation requires the provision of an independent drainage system.

In the Goulburn Valley of Victoria, southern Australia, 500 000 ha are irrigated in a semiarid region. The natural drainage is the Murray River that provides water for irrigation, industry, and for human consumption down the length of its course (Fig. 14.7). It is not generally acceptable to use the river as a drain. The alternatives are to divert the drainage water to inland depressions or to pipe it south to the ocean with a lift of 500 m over the coastal range. An inland drain is not acceptable because its consequences are unknown, and the cost of a pipeline to the ocean is prohibitive. The remarkable social issue is that the necessity of managing the salt balance for the continuing productivity of irrigation should come as such a surprise to so many.

In arid and semiarid regions, $ET^*$ is highest and so the efficiency of water use in irrigation is least. Under comparable temperature and radiation regimes more production can be achieved from the same quantity of water in more humid areas. Tanner & Sinclair (1983) have used the concept of the water-use efficiency (Section 9.10) to explain how the efficiency of utilization of irrigation water in the USA would be improved if more attention were paid to water management and irrigation in humid areas. There, rainfall would provide the major proportion of the water required and, with smaller transpiration, greater efficiency would be achieved from irrigation. From the previous discussion it will be clear that irrigation management in more humid areas would also suffer less problems of salinity but the more variable climate would render it technically more complex.

## 14.9  SUMMARY

The relationships between crop water use and productivity and the consequences of stresses at various stages during development are well understood. There remains, however, much local work to apply these principles to individual situations. Progress can be measured by the ability of the models used for irrigation scheduling to account for the interaction on individual crops or farms between evaporative demand, irrigation technique, soil water holding capacity, crop response to stress, and the expectancy of rainfall. Control of irrigation cannot be perfect when rainfall is uncertain because rainfall on recently irrigated land causes damage by waterlogging and runoff. Optimal management is most easily established in arid and semiarid areas where infrequent rainfall least interferes with irrigation practice but is achieved at the expense of low water-use efficiency induced by high evaporative demand.

Water is diverted from rivers and drawn from underground aquifers for irrigation. The quality of water reflects its origin and is a critical issue in irrigation practice. Surface runoff, and hence the major component of river flow, is low in dissolved salts whereas underground water often contains considerable salt dissolved during passage through soils and rocks. However, regardless of origin, all irrigation waters contain appreciable quantities of salt that can accumulate in surface soils through distillation by evapotranspiration.

Irrigation management should prevent the accumulation of salt to levels that depress productivity of irrigated land. That is achieved by irrigating beyond the requirement of potential evapotranspiration to maintain a flow of water through the root zone. That additional leaching requirement is determined by the quality of water used. Without drainage from the site, the watertable may rise close enough to the surface for salt to move into the root zone by capillary flow. The major cause of rising watertables is excessive irrigation arising from inappropriate or poorly applied techniques rather than by careful attention to the leaching requirement. Because water and salt are intimately associated in irrigation, drainage is an essential component of irrigation practice but has often been neglected, particularly in the early years of irrigation schemes, with subsequently disastrous results.

Most crop plants are sensitive to low levels of salinity. There is some capacity for farmers to change to more tolerant cultivars or crops as salinity increases but success in irrigated agriculture lies in management to prevent it. Breeding more salt-tolerant cultivars or alternative crops can only offer temporary advantage without attention to salt management. The consequence of attending to salt tolerance rather than to drainage is that salinity will continue to rise, exacerbating the difficulties of 'living with salt'.

## 14.10   FURTHER READING

Ayers, R. S. and D. W. Westcot. 1985. *Water quality for agriculture*. Irrigation and Drainage Paper 29 (rev. 1). FAO, Rome. 174 p.

Doneen, L. D. 1975. Water quality for irrigated agriculture. In *Plants in saline environments* (ed. A. Poljakoff-Mayber and J. Gale), pp. 56–76. Springer–Verlag, Berlin.

Grieve, A. M., E. Dunford, D. Marston, R. E. Martin, and P. Slavich. 1986. Effects of waterlogging and soil salinity in the Murray Valley: a review. *Aust. J. Exp. Agric.* **26**:761–77.

Hagan, R. M., H. R. Haise, and T. W. Edminster (eds.). 1967. *Irrigation of agricultural lands.* ASA, Madison, Wisconsin. 1180 p.

Houston, C. E. 1967. *Drainage of irrigated land*. Calif. Agric. Exp. Sta., University of California, Berkeley, CA. 40 p.

Poljakoff-Mayber, A. and J. Gale (eds). 1975. *Plants in saline environments*. Ecological Studies Series no. 15. Springer–Verlag, Berlin. 213 p.

Staples, R. C. and G. H. Toenniessen (eds). 1984. *Salinity tolerance in plants. Strategies for crop improvement*. Wiley Interscience, New York. 443 p.

Stewart, B. A. and D. R. Nielsen (eds). 1990. *Irrigation of agricultural crops*. Am. Soc. Agron., Madison, Wisconsin. 1218 p.

Taylor, H. M., W. R. Jordan, and T. R. Sinclair (eds). 1983. *Limitations to efficient water use in crop production*. ASA, CSSA, SSSA, Madison, Wisconsin. 538 p.

# 15

*Energy and labor*

## 15.1   INTRODUCTION

All human activity requires energy. The inescapable minimum is the dietary energy to maintain the population. In earlier times, if one hunter-gatherer could be sure to collect around 33 MJ each day of the year for the family unit (man, woman and two children), then survival of the population was possible. In practice, more organic materials, some with a dietary value, were needed for clothing and shelter. In some cases, there were additional, compulsory contributions to support chiefs, priests, and warriors.

Agriculture provided a way to secure that supply of food and other biological raw materials with less environmental hazard and less competition from other organisms. By its success in raising and stabilizing yields, agriculture has supported an increasing population and released an increasing proportion of it from the persistent chore of food production. With a productive agriculture, societies are more able to participate in the leisure, recreational, cultural, and scientific activities that improve wellbeing. Agricultural productivity has increased per worker and per hectare because the declining number who remain laboring in the field are supported by machines and because inputs of information, improved cultivars, fertilizer, water, and agrochemicals amplify the performance of crop systems.

The development and maintenance of industrialized cultures is based upon the substitution of energy for labor in the non-optional activity of food provision. At the same time, everyone in such cultures, including those who work in agriculture, has developed even greater energy demands for other activities. The purpose of this chapter is to explain the extent, pattern, and significance of energy use in agriculture so that we might understand how agricultures at various stages of development can respond to changes in the supply and cost of energy.

## 15.2   ENERGY AND FOOD PRODUCTION

### The work of farming

Farming requires the expenditure of considerable effort, typically during relatively short periods distributed unevenly through the growing season. Without the

Table 15.1 *Field operation schedules for paddy rice production in Taiwan using hand tools, 1963*

| Operation | No. in team | Days | h ha$^{-1}$ | % Sample using practice |
|---|---|---|---|---|
| First plowing | 1 | 4.4 | 44 | 100 |
| Application of manure | 2 | 2.2 | 44 | 20 |
| Harrowing and puddling | 1 | 14 | 140 | 100 |
| Transplanting | 7 | 1.7 | 119 | 100 |
| First additional fertilizer | 1 | 1.3 | 13 | |
| & cultivation | 5 | 1.7 | 85 | 52 |
| Second additional fertilizer | 1 | 1.3 | 13 | |
| & cultivation | 4 | 2 | 80 | 63 |
| First disease control | 1 | 1.2 | 12 | 91 |
| Third additional fertilizer | 1 | 1.3 | 13 | |
| & cultivation | 4 | 2.1 | 84 | 54 |
| Removing barnyard grass | 2 | 1.5 | 30 | 91 |
| Second disease control | 1 | 1.3 | 13 | 83 |
| Harvesting | 8 | 2.9 | 232 | 100 |
| Cleaning, drying, transport | 2 | 5 | 100 | 100 |
| Average for farm | | | 855 | |

*Source:* Adapted from Chang (1963).

assistance of draft animals or powered machines, the operations of tillage, sowing, fertilizing, irrigating, removing weeds, controlling pests, harvesting, and storage of products, involve much human muscular effort: digging, hoeing, lifting, and carrying.

The data in Table 15.1 emphasize these aspects of the extent and irregular seasonal distribution of effort in work schedules for paddy rice production in Taiwan. There, the seasonal average of around 850 h ha$^{-1}$ in 1963 was performed by teams of up to seven over a total of 40 d with a large part (14 d) taken up in preparing the paddy for transplanting.

Human work is slow because the body has poor energetic performance. The human body can convert around 25% of dietary energy to mechanical energy as physical work and most humans can continuously sustain a maximum power output of 75 W. Many laboring tasks in agriculture, such as digging, lifting, and carrying, require consumption of dietary energy at rates of 300–600 W (Stout *et al.* 1979) and so such work must be interspersed with substantial rest periods.

In most tasks, the rate of effective work is considerably less than 75 W. In harvesting, for example, 75% of muscular effort is expended in lifting body, tools, and containers, and just 25% in getting the harvest into storage. Expended over a 10 h working day that rate of net effective work (6.25% of 12.5 MJ dietary energy) is only 22 W. Animals are superior to man because they are bigger and stronger, not because they are intrinsically more efficient. A horse, for example, can sustain 750 W (1 HP) and over a 10 h day deliver 27 MJ, but once again only around 6% of that is converted to useful work. In contrast, moderate-sized tractors can continuously

Table 15.2 *Task times (h ha⁻¹) in cereal production under various systems*

| Operation | Production system | | |
|---|---|---|---|
| | Manual | Draught animal | Power equipment |
| *Land preparation* | | | |
| Spade | 500–1000 | | |
| Plow | | 16–27 | 2 |
| Harrow | | 3–5 | 0.5 |
| *Sowing* | | | |
| Broadcast | 2–4 | | |
| Machine | 10 | 1–6 | 0.5 |
| *Fertilization* | 2 | 1–2 | 0.3 |
| *Weed control* | | | |
| Hoeing | 65 | 3–5 | 1 |
| Spraying | 4–5 | 2 | 0.5 |
| *Harvesting*[1] | | | |
| Scythe | >1000 | | |
| Machine steps | | 500 | |
| Combine | | | 2 |

*Note:*
[1] Based on a yield of 6 t ha⁻¹.
*Source:* Adapted from Unger (1984) and van Heemst *et al.* (1981).

deliver 50 kW at the power take-off and 35 kW at the drawbar, converting (non-dietary) fuel to useful work at efficiencies around 35% at the crankshaft, and 25% at the drawbar under average soil conditions.

Farming operations can be performed more expeditiously and with less human effort by the use of draft animals and powered machinery. For example, the inclusion of one draft animal per worker reduces the time needed in paddy rice production from 850 to around 500 h ha⁻¹. In mechanized systems all work can be completed in 25 h ha⁻¹. A comparison of the duration of operations using human, animal, and mechanical power in cereal production has been compiled in Table 15.2. Again, without machines and fuel, many participants are required to complete the tasks in the timely manner that successful crop production demands. When a large proportion of a society toils in the fields to provide staple foods, it is not possible for that society to develop a high standard of living. The price of human labor has to be very low to compete with the internal combustion engine.

The human body and mind are more suited to control independently powered machinery than to perform strenuous physical tasks. Machines can perform tasks better, more quickly and more efficiently than can the human body. Furthermore, human ingenuity has devised efficient ways to replace some physical activities in non-mechanical ways. Examples in crop production are biocides that supplement the physical effort (human or machine) of hoeing weeds or squashing insects, and nitrogen fertilizers that replace the effort of growing green manure (legume) crops in rotation with grain crops for food.

## On the farm

Energy is expended directly and indirectly in food production. Direct consumption on the farm is by food for human and animal labor and by fuel for machines. Indirect expenditure includes the energy cost in the manufacture of machines, structures, tools, and agrochemicals used on farms to support crop and animal production. The energy cost of these goods and services is the sum of the human effort and (usually) fossil energy that was expended in their production. That sum is termed **embodied energy**. A tractor, for example, has embodied energy reflecting the human labor and fossil energy used in its manufacture, namely mining, smelting, fabrication, distribution, sales, and maintenance. Table 15.3*a* presents energy contents and energy costs of a range of materials and inputs relevant to crop production; Table 15.3*b* compares energy use by a variety of field machinery. In that case strict comparisons are difficult. For example in the case of tillage, energy expenditure depends strongly upon soil type, as shown, but also upon soil water content and the condition and setting of the implements.

For proper comparison between the energetics of human endeavors and that of machines, the details of human energy, fuel, and the appropriate lifetime share of the embodied energy of all inputs to humans, are needed. The real (i.e. embodied) energy cost of human labor is determined more by lifestyle and standard of living of society than by the dietary energy for survival. The major components are the provision and heating of homes, clothing, meal preparation, medical services, transport, the care and education of replacement workers, and the care of retired workers. An analogy to a dairy herd may be helpful here. In addition to the dietary needs of the lactating cows, the dairy farmer must also budget feed for dry cows, replacement heifers, and bulls, as well as the energy expended in the provision of shelters, feed storage, and milking facilities. In the USA, about 40% of on-farm consumption of fossil fuel is in the maintenance of the farm household. Compared with a dietary cost of 12.5 MJ d$^{-1}$, the embodied energy of the average American and Dutch farm worker, i.e. the employment-generated energy requirement, is around 600 MJ d$^{-1}$ (Fluck 1981), comparable with that of his urban counterparts. Explained in these terms, human labor is seen to be very costly of energy.

**A crop energy budget**   The analysis of energy use in maize production in Indiana in 1975 presented in Table 15.4 (p. 411) is adapted from Doering (1977). In this example, the total energy used to produce 8.8 t ha$^{-1}$ of maize grain (14% moisture) was 23.5 GJ. The major component of that support energy was nitrogen fertilizer (55%), followed by tractor fuel (14%), drying (11%), P and K fertilizers (9%), herbicides (6%), seed (1.6%), machinery (1.6%), and human labor (1.2%) in that order. In this energy intensive system, the proper accounting of the embodied energy of human labor makes little difference to the total energy use of 23.5 GJ ha$^{-1}$.

Table 15.3. (a) *Energy values for analysis of the energetics of cropping systems*

| Material | Energy content | |
|---|---|---|
| *Heats of combustion* | | |
| Plant material | | |
|   Carbohydrate | 14–16 | MJ kg$^{-1}$ |
|   Protein and lignin | 25 | |
|   Fatty oils and fats | 38–40 | |
|   Waxes | 45 | |
|   Terpene hydrocarbons | 45 | |
|   Typical biomass | 17 | |
| Liquid fuels | | |
|   Gasoline | 44 | MJ kg$^{-1}$ |
|   Diesel | 43 | |
|   Ethanol | 28 | |
|   LPG | 46 | |
| Solid fuels | | |
|   Coal | 17–30 | MJ kg$^{-1}$ |
|   Wood | 18–23 | |
|   Bagasse (30% moisture) | 15 | |
| Gaseous fuels | | |
|   Natural gas | 35 | MJ m$^{-3}$ |
|   Propane | 86 | |
|   Coal gas | 18 | |
|   Producer gas | 6 | |
| *Energy costs of production* | | |
| Machinery | | |
|   Tractors | 87 | MJ kg$^{-1}$ |
|   Implements | 70 | MJ kg$^{-1}$ |
| Fertilizers | | |
|   Nitrogen (via NH$_3$) | 60 | MJ kg$^{-1}$ |
|   Phosphorus } (mine and | 14 | |
|   Potassium } refine) | 10 | |
| Biocides | 100–500 | MJ kg$^{-1}$ |
|   Paraquat | 460 | MJ kg$^{-1}$ |
|   MCPA | 130 | |
|   Glyphosate | 450 | |
| Pesticides | 100 | MJ kg$^{-1}$ |

(b) *Fuel requirements of field machinery*

(Data adapted from power requirements (Hunt 1983) by applying a 25% fuel efficiency.)

| Operation | Fuel requirement (MJ ha$^{-1}$) |
|---|---|
| *Tillage* | |
| Moldboard plow (18 cm deep) | |
|    light soil | 125–250 |
|    medium soil | 210–370 |
|    heavy soil | 320–665 |
| Disk (8–13 cm deep) | 105–235 |
| Chisel plow (18–23 cm deep) | 115–530 |
| Harrow | |
|    light tandem | 55–110 |
|    heavy tandem | 110–185 |
|    spike tooth | 10–35 |
| Rotary tiller (8–10 cm deep) | 370–745 |
| *Seeding* | |
| Grain drill | 15–55 |
| *Chemical applicators* | |
| NH$_3$ applicator | 65–95 |
| Sprayer | 0.3–0.6 |
| Broadcaster | 3–6 |
| *Grain harvesting* | |
| Combine | |
|    maize | 260–390 |
|    small grain | 105–320 |
| *Fodder conservation* | |
| Mowing (pasture) | |
|    cutter bar | 15–25 |
|    rotary | 130–350 |
| Raking | |
|    side-delivery | 10 |
| | (MJ t$^{-1}$) |
| Baling | |
|    rectangular bales | 15–22 |
|    round bales | 25–30 |
| Forage harvesting | |
|    green forage | 10–30 |
|    corn ensilage | 20–50 |

It becomes an increasingly important issue, however, as the labor intensity of the farming system increases. Low-input farms and subsistence agriculture serve as examples where the energy cost of labor is a major component.

The gain of the system, in this case 147 GJ ha$^{-1}$, is the contribution that the crop makes to dietary energy from the solar flux. That maize crop actually fixed about twice as much solar energy into chemical bonds but the rest, in the stover, has little dietary value except to soil organisms or cattle and is not included in this analysis. Solar radiation is not included either because it is a free good that is lost to food production if not captured by agriculture (see also Jones 1989). Analysis of the potential productivity of biological systems (Chapter 2), showed that the potential efficiency of solar energy capture is 4–5%, while 2% is a reasonable average under favorable conditions of nutrient and water supply.

## From farm to table

Farms produce only the ingredients of most food and additional labor and energy are required to provide and prepare the finished products for the consumer. For individual products, this requires varying amounts of transport, storage, processing, refrigeration, merchandizing, and cooking. In developed countries, the energy used in this second part of the food production system far exceeds that used to produce the ingredients at the farm gate.

This pattern of energy expenditure in the provision of food is evident even in staple foods like wheaten bread which is produced and delivered comparatively efficiently to the point of consumption. In a Californian study, Avlani & Chancellor (1977) estimated that of the embodied energy of bread at the table, only 40% was used up to the farm gate. More than half of the total energy was expended after the bread left the bakery or, for less efficient home baking, after flour left the mill. That more energy is consumed in toasting a slice of bread than in growing the wheat it contains is perhaps the most startling point of the analysis.

Foods other than staples generally have much higher embodied energy per unit dietary energy. Frozen, canned, and prepared foods, and fruits and vegetables, particularly those grown out of season or in controlled environments or transported by airplane from the opposite hemisphere, substantially increase the energy cost of the food production system. For the USA, the energy expended after the farm gate is five times that expended up to the farm gate. Comparable values apply to other developed countries; in Australia the ratio is 3:1 (Gifford & Millington 1975).

## National energy use

If farming and its inputs of machinery, fuel, and fertilizer are the smaller part of energy expended in the food production system, then how does it compare with total national energy use? This becomes an important issue in any search for increased energy-use efficiency. Industrialized societies use 10–15% of total energy on their food production systems and 3–5% on the farming component. Given the magnitude of national energy use, it is surprising how little, not how much, energy is used in the essential activity of farming. It shows that most opportunities to adjust to changing costs of energy exist not just outside farming, but also outside the entire food production system.

## 15.3  SOURCES AND UTILIZATION OF ENERGY

### From Earth and beyond

There are two sources of energy which originate on Earth. They are the small geothermal heat flux and the essentially 'limitless' nuclear energy of matter. These sources, especially the latter, remain virtually untapped. In addition, there is energy captured by Earth systems from outside. The planetary motion of the moon transfers kinetic energy to currents and tides in oceans, but the dominant external source is the flux of radiant energy from the Sun (Chapter 6). Solar energy is collected on Earth by physical and biological systems. Temperature, wind, rain, and flowing water are all maintained by solar energy. In addition, the chemical bond energy of organic matter originates in the solar energy collected by green plants in photosynthesis (Chapter 10). The solar flux is the sole energy source upon which the natural biological environment has evolved.

### Renewable and non-renewable

A further distinction is useful. The solar flux is permanently available and, together with the recent solar energy contained in wind, water, and the standing biomass of vegetation, is a **renewable** form of energy. Much use is now made of such energy forms, and research is improving the efficiency of their capture. In contrast to those fluxes of renewable energy, there is an accumulation of earlier photosynthetic products in oil, coal, natural gas, shales, and tar sands. Those together with the nuclear energy, form the **non-renewable** energy resource.

Fossil energy was first tapped 800 y ago and has been consumed in significant quantities only during the past 100 y. At present, a known reserve of 10 000 Gt (40% recoverable) is being consumed at 5 Gt y$^{-1}$ and increasing at 4–5% y$^{-1}$ as the world population grows and an increasing proportion of it develops from subsistence agriculture to industrialized societies. It is concern over the inevitable depletion of fossil energy that has 'fueled' public concern about energy use and energy-use efficiency.

There are two technologies for the extraction of nuclear energy. The existing technology extracts the heat of **nuclear fission** of uranium-235 to generate electricity. Large amounts of energy are available; for example 3 kg d$^{-1}$ U-235 will maintain a 1000 MW power plant (33% thermal efficiency) equivalent to 8.1 kt coal (81 railroad cars of 100 t capacity). The supply of high-quality U-235 is limited and would supply energy for only a few decades. However, breeder reactors can greatly extend the supply of fissionable materials, so that the energy available from this non-renewable source is hundreds to thousands of times that of the original supply of fossil fuel. The serious restriction to this technology is the public concern over production of radioactive waste, essentially equivalent in mass to that which is consumed in the reaction.

An alternative, but yet undeveloped technology, is **nuclear fusion**. In that process, energy is released during the fusion of isotopes of hydrogen to form helium. Nuclear fusion is a clean process, known as the source of solar radiation, but has so far been achieved only in the uncontrolled explosion of the hydrogen bomb. The fusion material is present in enormous quantities in the sea, so the potential is for essentially continuous energy. For example, the energy contained in 1% of the deuterium in the ocean would provide 500 000 times the energy of the initial fossil fuel resource.

New technologies can only be assessed within the scope of present knowledge. The most promising emerging technologies are improvements to photovoltaic cells, the development of nuclear fusion, also for the generation of electricity, and the use of $H_2$ gas as a cleanly combustible fuel. Direct conversion of solar energy to electricity by using photovoltaic cells is improving rapidly. Presently available cells have efficiencies of 15–20%, but new multilayer designs promise increases up to 37%. Either value substantially exceeds the conversion efficiency of solar energy to biomass (Section 15.7). Designs are also improving for electricity generators driven by wind and tidal power.

### Energy, transformations and patterns of use

The twin foci of energy use are **heating** and **motive power**. Heat is required in large amounts for many industrial processes and in a more distributed form for cooking and comfort in the home. Internal combustion and jet engines provide the motive power for transport and, with electrical motors, the motive power for a myriad of industrial and domestic applications.

Agriculture has a distinctive pattern of energy use. The dominant form used in crop production is liquid fuel for internal combustion engines (mostly diesel) of tractors and self-propelled combines. Heat is used in limited amounts, particularly for crop drying in some environments. Electricity finds a major use in pumping water for irrigation but is also important for crop drying, domestic water, and in dairies and grain elevators. Off-farm, a significant amount of natural gas is used in the production of nitrogen fertilizer. Farm homes are increasingly connected to electricity networks, and are provided with bottled gas, to provide the same services as urban dwellings.

All forms of fossil carbon can be combusted for direct heat or their energy can be concentrated into other forms, typically into liquid and gaseous fuels and electricity. Those transformations are achieved with varying convenience and efficiency so there are preferred pathways.

Petroleum is the most efficient source of the liquid fuels, gasoline, diesel, kerosene, and liquid petroleum gas (LPG). The limited reserves of petroleum and the demand and convenience of liquid fuels for mobile engines has placed much emphasis on the various possibilities for the production of liquid fuels from other fossil forms and from biomass. In addition, LPG is highly suited to the production of ammonia.

Coal is bulky and difficult to distribute and so is most effectively used to generate heat or electricity close to the site of its excavation. Also, burning coal causes significant atmospheric pollution (e.g. $SO_2$) and is best done away from urban areas. Natural gas is readily distributed by pipe networks and so, like electricity, is well suited to the dispersed requirements of industry and urban homes.

Electricity is valued for ease of distribution and versatility of application. Non-fossil sources fit well with electrical technology. Electricity can be added to the grid by hydro, geothermal, solar, tidal, wind, biomass, and nuclear sources. Those sources will grow in importance as the availability of fossil fuel declines. Electricity is not readily stored, however, so the key to its efficient application is the synchronization of generation with utilization. This is least possible with solar energy, so strategies such as pump storage of water for subsequent hydroelectric generation are required.

## 15.4 ENERGY ANALYSES

### On the nature of energy ratios

Energy ratios (output/input) calculated for any human activity from individual summations of output and input express its energetic efficiency. They are directly useful when one form of energy is expended to harvest more of the same, e.g. in mining coal when some of the production is used to power the excavation, or in subsistence agriculture using only human labor to gather a survival diet. However, life and agriculture are generally more complex. The forms of energy expended in all but the most primitive agriculture are varied, comprising some or all of: human and animal labor, solar, agrochemicals, machines, biomass, and liquid fuel (see Table 15.4).

The purpose of agriculture is the management of biological systems to optimize the flow of solar energy into the growth of valuable products. Most agriculture is directed towards food production and the energy used to support it has no direct food value. Therefore to use energy ratios as a sole basis for the comparison of agricultural systems can be seen to assume (Edwards 1976) that:

(1) the energy content of food is an adequate measure of its value to consumers;
(2) equal inputs of energy from different sources can be treated as identical regardless of scarcity, convenience, and pollution generated; and
(3) inputs other than energy used in food production can be treated as though they have no value.

Despite the implausibility of these assumptions, comparisons are frequently made between the energy ratios of different farming systems and between modern agriculture and the systems from which it evolved. In previous primitive systems, only human energy is expended in the production and processing of food, and energy ratios of 16 (e.g. Rappaport 1971) calculated there have been used (e.g. Odum 1967) to demonstrate to what depths of energetic inefficiency modern agriculture has sunk. Even those primitive systems are often more complex than many people realize. Their energetic efficiency is actually much lower, approaching unity, when account is taken of the embodied energy cost of labor. In those systems, workers have also to be provided with shelter, fuel for cooking, and the dietary costs of dependants. But that aside, the real issue is that energy ratios of subsistence and modern agriculture have such different construction that direct comparison is impossible.

From the viewpoint of energetics, the important feature of agriculture is that it collects extraterrestrial, solar energy and transforms it into human dietary energy. No other human activity fills this essential role. Energy is expended (currently fossil energy) to reduce the human physical labor (Table 15.2) and to make the transformation of solar energy more productive and predictable. The energy ratio that is observed is no more than the rational result of the managerial responses of farmers to the relative prices of inputs and products. As with other human activities, agriculture must pay attention to its energetic efficiency, but this is properly done by careful interpretation of the components of energy expenditure (Table 15.4) rather than by simplistic use of overall energy ratios.

### Energy and economics

Farmers, as do other consumers, respond to price signals and not to energy ratios. For them, this is rational behavior, but it will only lead to rational energy use if the price of energy is consistently related to the price of products and inputs, including human labor. Energy will not be applied rationally if prices are controlled artificially high or low, or if consistent pricing is not allowed to develop between alternative forms of energy.

Costanza (1980) made an analysis of the value of energy in the 92 sectors of the USA economy. This was achieved by comparing a complete inventory of energy use with the output value of production in goods and services. The sectors have distinct patterns of energy consumption. Some, such as government, are high in human labor; others, such as transportation, rely dominantly upon fossil fuel. Yet others, including the primary sectors of agriculture and forestry, have a broad mix of energy types. The analysis established that energy is valued consistently in all sectors of the American economy despite the range of alternatives and combinations of use. Under such conditions, response to price signals leads to changes in allocation of energy and labor between sectoral activities. Political or monopolistic intervention distorts those allocations, as was revealed for the use of natural gas (price controlled) in Costanza's study.

It has been proposed that society will soon not be able to afford food because of the rising price of energy. Given the small proportion of energy allocated to food production, consumers will have plenty of other adjustments to make before they have to return to the fields to grow their daily bread. A bigger problem exists in those societies where the price of food is kept so low that farmers are not able to

Table 15.4 *Energy budget for maize production in Indiana, 1975*

| Input | Quantity per ha | | MJ ha$^{-1}$ |
|---|---|---|---|
| Labor[1] | | 3.8 h | 280 |
| Machinery | prop. for farm (150 ha) | | 366 |
| Fuel | diesel | (55 l) | 2104 |
| | gasoline | (29 l) | 1136 |
| Fertilizer | | | |
| | nitrogen | (167 kg) | 13 000 |
| | phosphorus | (78 kg) | 1097 |
| | potassium | (110 kg) | 1076 |
| Seeds | | (26 kg) | 384 |
| Herbicides | | (4 l) | 1314 |
| Drying | | | |
| Fuel | | | 2607 |
| Electricity | | | 86 |
| Total | | | 23 500 |
| Maize yield (8.8 t ha$^{-1}$) | | | 146 800 |
| Output/input ratio | 6.2 | | |

*Note:*
[1] Daily proportion of embodied energy of labor of 600 MJ d$^{-1}$.
*Source:* Adapted from Doering (1977).

purchase the necessary inputs of fertilizers, fuel and agrochemicals that would sustain their productivity and profitability.

## 15.5 IMPROVING THE EFFICIENCY OF ENERGY USE

Energy accounts such as those of Table 15.4 identify the component energy costs of agriculture. Their real value is their capacity to identify where energy savings can have the biggest impact as agriculture adjusts to changing values of energy. Agriculture, as other community activities also, will continue such adjustment to changes in the price of energy.

### Mechanization

Mechanization of crop production substitutes for human and animal muscular effort and removes the drudgery of heavy physical work. It improves the effectiveness and competitiveness of human labor which, with machines, can perform tasks better, more quickly, and hence more timely to the requirements of crop production. Much of the understanding that has been developed about how to improve crop production cannot be applied in practice without mechanization. Thus crop cultivars with well-adapted phenological response must be sown quickly so that the entire crop may realize that advantage. Tillage, or the application of biocides to control weeds, pests, and diseases, must be accomplished expeditiously. At the end of the crop cycle, farmers rely on machines to harvest the crop with minimum loss. Looked at another way, mechanization enables crops to be grown successfully in areas where hand labor would have insufficient time for critical operations.

Farms and farm machinery are gradually increasing in size in response to the rising cost of human labor. To perform operations in the same time over larger areas cannot simply be achieved by driving implements faster. In operations involving tillage, for example, increased ground speed requires specially designed implements. Without attention to that, soil structure will be damaged. Big tractors cover ground faster by drawing wide implements at appropriate speeds. In addition they are more economical of fuel and labor (Hunt 1983) and offer security that operations can be carried out quickly while conditions remain favorable. This contribution to risk avoidance is an important aspect in the selection of machines of appropriate work capacity (e.g. Whitson *et al.* 1981).

Mechanization is a major contributor to the strongly bimodal distribution of farm size and production that is occurring in developed countries. Here, proper comparisons are relative within enterprise types to account for the differences that exist between the field crop and horticultural extremes (interestingly the differences in capitalization are much less). The efficiencies of scale that mechanization offers leads to amalgamation of medium-sized operations or, in areas close to urban centres, their division into smaller units. Thus in the USA, 85% of the 2.4 million farms produce less than 30% of the total farm output. Small operations cannot sustain the ownership of machines but depend instead on contracts with larger neighbors for 'custom' work such as tillage and harvest. In reality, most small farms in the western nations are not dedicated production units; rather they offer rural living to people dependent on off-farm income.

The age of electronics is introducing new possibilities to mechanization and thereby improving the energetic efficiency of crop production operations. For example, seed drills can be programmed to vary seed and fertilizer rate depending upon location in a single field. Such decisions can be based upon prior surveys of microtopography and soil chemical and physical properties. In the future, when tillage, sowing pattern, fertilizer level, and weed control can be adjusted according to currently sensed conditions, perhaps cross-checked against spatially referenced data collected during previous operations, e.g. yield recorded during the harvest of the previous crop, then farmers really will have 'smart' machines in their service. Under those conditions, human labor that does supplement its low biological efficiency with short cuts evaluated on the spot (e.g. rows or parts of rows that have no weeds are not hoed) will face more severe competition from machinery of greatly improved efficiency.

## Tillage

Previously, tillage was the only effective way to control vegetation for the establishment of new crops and pastures. Fire and grazing were valuable adjuncts, but tillage

Table 15.5 *Diesel fuel requirements (l ha⁻¹) for various tillage systems*

| Operation | Tillage system | | | | |
|---|---|---|---|---|---|
| | Moldboard plow | Chisel plow | Disk plow | Till & plant | No tillage |
| Chop stalks | — | — | — | 5.1 | — |
| Plow | 21.0 | 9.8 | — | — | — |
| Fertilize | 5.6 | 5.6 | 5.6 | 5.6 | 5.6 |
| Disk | 6.9 | 6.9 | 6.9 | | — |
| Disk | 6.9 | 6.9 | 6.9 | — | — |
| Harrows | 4.0 | 4.0 | 4.0 | 4.0 | — |
| Plant | 4.9 | 4.9 | 4.9 | 6.4 | 5.6 |
| Spray (2) | — | — | — | — | 4.3 |
| Total | 49.3 | 38.1 | 28.3 | 21.1 | 15.5 |

*Source:* Adapted from Dickey & Rider (1981).

was the key to success. Under those conditions, tillage, not fertilizer (Table 15.4), was the major component of energy use. Now herbicides offer possibilities to control vegetation at significantly less cost (and energy). The characteristics of alternative tillage systems are discussed in Chapter 12.

Given the rapid increases in the price of oil in the early 1970s, farmers adapted to change by replacing tillage with herbicides. The chemicals and technology for minimum tillage had been available for many years but there had been no incentive to adopt them. Herbicides are now replacing tillage in many cropping systems throughout the world. Once commenced, this trend is being supported by the development of additional chemicals, better application equipment, and an improved understanding of their use.

Reduced tillage provides a significant reduction in on-farm energy use (Table 15.5). The benefits in energy use, however, are only significant in rainfed systems, particularly those without or with low inputs of nitrogen (e.g. Chapter 16). Under intense, irrigated production, energy saved by reducing tillage has little effect on total energy expenditure of crop production (Table 15.6).

## Crop nutrition

**Fertilizers**  In the Middle Ages, cereals in Europe yielded up to 1 t ha⁻¹, compared with present average yields of around 7 t ha⁻¹. That increase results from higher fertility, achieved mainly by the use of fertilizers. Without that, the improved cultivars and husbandry could not exhibit their potential. Fertilizers have raised the productivity of agricultural systems, lifting the efficiency of utilization of solar radiation in photosynthesis from around 0.25 to 2%. In this way, fertilizers can be interpreted as a substitution of energy for land because without higher productivity, more land would be required to achieve the same production.

The energy cost of this is substantial, accounting for 15.2 GJ ha⁻¹ (64% of energy

Table 15.6 *Diesel fuel requirements (l ha$^{-1}$) to produce irrigated maize with conventional and no-tillage*

| Operation | Conventional tillage | No-tillage |
|---|---|---|
| Tillage and planting | 38 | 9 |
| Fertilizers | 283 | 283 |
| Herbicide and insecticide | 10 | 13 |
| Irrigation | 289 | 289 |
| Harvest | 10 | 10 |
| Total | 630 | 604 |

*Source:* Adapted from Howard (1981).

used) in the example of maize production in Table 15.4. This is a common pattern in the production of high yielding crops and yet fertilizers still account for only 2% of world-wide energy use.

Nitrogen is the most expensive nutrient because it is required in large amounts as a constituent of biomass (1.5–3%) and because considerable energy (60 MJ kg$^{-1}$) is required to produce it (Chapter 8). It is for this reason that much of the emphasis on the energetics of fertilizer use concentrates on nitrogen. It is an ironic feature of plant evolution that the abundant $N_2$ in the atmosphere is unavailable to all except leguminous plants. Most crops must be supplied directly with nitrogen fertilizer or indirectly by rotation with legumes in cropping systems. Compared with the energy cost of nitrogen, that required to mine and refine the other macronutrients (14 MJ kg$^{-1}$ P; 10 MJ kg$^{-1}$ K) is small (Table 15.3).

**Leguminous rotations**    As the price of nitrogen fertilizer increases relative to the price of products, farmers reassess their mix of legume and fertilizer nitrogen within the economics of entire alternative production strategies. Nitrogen fertilizer is most likely to remain profitable in those systems well supplied with water and other nutrients because leguminous rotations are unable to supply the nitrogen demand of the potential yield (Chapter 8). For example, a cereal yield of 12 t ha$^{-1}$ requires a seasonal nitrogen supply of 340 kg N ha$^{-1}$, of which 240 kg N ha$^{-1}$ is removed in the harvested grain. Leguminous rotations cannot supply this quantity of nitrogen to the ensuing crop.

Heichel (1978) has analyzed the savings of energy achieved by growing maize within leguminous rotations (Table 15.7). Yields of individual maize crops were maintained in all systems with supplementary nitrogen fertilizer. In the rotations including legumes, the energy savings relative to continuous maize (25–50%) relate mostly to less nitrogen fertilizer and to less tillage in those rotations with alfalfa. Since much of the nitrogen content (60–70%) of leguminous seed crops is removed by harvest, soybean contributes little nitrogen to the ensuing maize crop. In contrast, leguminous forages may contribute significantly. In this case, the residual contribution of fixed nitrogen by alfalfa after three years of hay production was estimated to be 150 kg N ha$^{-1}$.

Table 15.7 *Intensity and efficiency of energy use in rotations of maize and legumes*

M, maize; S, soybean; O, oat; A, alfalfa; W, wheat.

| | Rotation | | | |
| --- | --- | --- | --- | --- |
| | M–M | 2M–S | 2M–O–2A | 3M–3S–W–3A |
| Mean annual biomass (t ha$^{-1}$ y$^{-1}$) | 7.8 | 6.2 | 6.7 | 5.2 |
| Fossil energy flux (MJ ha$^{-1}$ d$^{-1}$) | 182 | 135 | 116 | 93 |
| Energy efficiency (J J$^{-1}$) | 6.1 | 6.7 | 8.1 | 8.2 |

*Source:* Adapted from Heichel (1978).

Such analyses show how agronomic practices can reduce energy use but the market for the products will determine if the options are adopted. In general, economically viable rotations will be found where markets are available for products from all crops within them (see Chapters 16 and 17).

**Improving nitrogen-use efficiency** The high energy cost of nitrogen and its mobility in agricultural systems mean that good opportunities exist to improve profitability by controlling losses and improving the efficiency of use. Single large doses of nitrogen fertilizer are more likely to suffer losses by volatilization, denitrification, and leaching than are applications more closely metered to the uptake dynamics of the crop. Improvements to the formulation and application of nitrogen fertilizer offer significant savings. The benefit from such practices is most likely to be achieved under conditions of intensive crop production.

High crop yields require high levels of available nitrogen. The question arises as to the effect of nitrogen fertilization on the energetics of crop production. Fig. 15.1 adds the output–input energy ratio to the response of maize yield to nitrogen fertilizer previously presented in Fig. 12.1. Without nitrogen fertilizer, yield is extremely low and the energy ratio for the entire operation is about unity. Yield and energy ratio increase with nitrogen application up to the maximum yield of 11 t ha$^{-1}$ achieved with around 200 kg N ha$^{-1}$. There is no suggestion in these data that high energy-use efficiency is achieved at sub-optimal levels of nitrogen supply, a widely promulgated conclusion of an early analysis of the energetics of nitrogen fertilization (Pimentel *et al.* 1973).

Because nitrogen fixation is suppressed by mineral nitrogen, legume rotations function best on soils of low N fertility and long rotations to legumes do not continue to accumulate nitrogen. For this reason, importance has been placed on the need to improve the fixation capacity of legumes, particularly on fertile soils. On a world-wide scale, however, the more serious problem is to find legumes that will grow with less acidifying effect (Section 7.5) on soils of low pH and high Al, and to establish the phosphorus, trace element, and symbiotic requirements that are needed for effective growth and nitrogen fixation. In practice, much research is

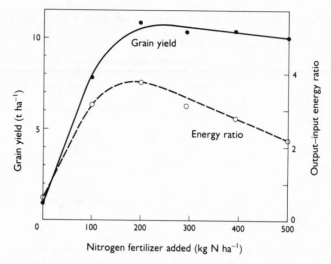

**Fig. 15.1. Response of maize grain yield to fertilizer nitrogen and of the overall output–input energy ratio for each system of production. (from unpublished data of P. R. Stout, U. C., Davis).**

needed to improve the efficiency of fertilization and the fixation and management of nitrogen in leguminous rotations.

It has also been proposed that 'leguminous' versions of cereal crops might be developed by genetic engineering so that the problems of nitrogen supply, acidification, and pollution of ground water might be avoided. Such crops would suffer a yield disadvantage due to the biological energy cost of nitrogen fixation (Chapter 11) and would still be grown in rotations to minimize the effects of pests and diseases and would not avoid the problems of soil acidification (Chapter 7). Even so, the value of such plants would seem large but their early development seems unlikely. Ecologically, the ability of legumes to gain access to the large supply of nitrogen in the atmosphere has given them an important adaptive advantage that has not been widely repeated during natural selection in other groups. Even if the proposal for nodulated wheat becomes a reality, agronomists will still need to continue their work of improving the use of legumes in rotations.

## Biocides

Management of water and nutrients frequently come to nothing in the face of competition from weeds, disease, or attack by insects. It is in those situations that small amounts of energy, judiciously applied as biocides, provide highly leveraged improvements in efficiency of production.

**Herbicides** The use of non-selective herbicides in minimum and zero tillage was introduced earlier (Section 15.5). In addition, selective herbicides find application in the control of weeds in crops and in the management of species composition in pastures. In all cases their low energy cost (including application) replaces substantial quantities of mechanical and human labor. In the case of maize production, for example, a single well-timed spray that eliminates or reduces weed competition might easily prevent a yield loss in excess of 20% (2 t ha$^{-1}$ containing 34 GJ of combustible energy). Including around 1.3 GJ ha$^{-1}$ in chemicals and application costs in a total energy expenditure of 23.5 GJ ha$^{-1}$ (Table 15.4) is a small energy cost that provides a significant marginal economic benefit.

The efficiency of herbicide use is improved by biological studies on the target weeds that identify the nature and timing of the competitive effects they exert on the crop, their modes of dispersion, and the vulnerable points in their lifecycles. Such information increases the options of management, not only leading to less herbicide use but also to biological alternatives of weed control.

**Pesticides** Pesticides (fungicides, insecticides) are not a major component of energy use in the broad-acre production of field crops. Many crops, including cereals, are often grown without them, although others, such as sunflower and soybean in temperate latitudes and many crops of the tropics, are often protected with one or more sprays of insecticide during the growing season. The situation is different in fruit and vegetable production and in crops such as cotton. Those crops incur more problems with insects, and concern about physical appearance and quality leads to more intensive use of pesticides.

The development of resistant cultivars is a means of reducing the need for biocides but the occasional loss of resistance means that biocides will often be needed to stabilize yield. In practice, the development and management of resistant cultivars and better biocides should proceed together to ensure a clean, safe environment and a slow breakdown of resistance. Ideal biocides are selective of their target species and are nonresidual. Research on the development of such chemicals should have high priority because of the efficiencies that biocides afford crop production.

## Role of animals

Animals play a dual role in human nutrition and in the management of agricultural systems. The view that they compete directly with man for food and therefore could have only a luxury role in an energy-short society ignores the capabilities of their digestive systems and the nature of their diets (Chapter 1). The most important domestic animals, the ruminants, rely heavily upon cellulose that is almost indigestible by man. Not only do they convert this to protein, but as grazers they harvest their own food supply, an activity that demands much energy in regions of low productivity. The importance of forages in crop rotations to control soil erosion, renew fertility (nitrogen fixation), and improve structure, underscores the continuing importance of grazing animals for their management and economic viability.

While animals add biological and economic value to crop and pasture production systems, they do so at a potential ecological cost. Animals play a major role in the mobilization of nitrogen in agricultural systems, thereby contributing to losses to the atmosphere by volatilization and to leaching of mineral nitrogen (Chapter 8). In turn, the leaching of mineral nitrogen is a central component of the processes of soil acidification that are inevitable with time (Chapter 7). Examples of the role of animals in agricultural systems are presented in Chapters 16 and 17.

Despite these disadvantages, our conclusion is that ruminants, rather than being excluded by crop production, would play an increasingly important role in low-energy systems. Under conditions of severe (energy) food shortage, chickens and swine, which can compete with man for food, will probably be less important sources of protein than is presently the case in some industrialized societies. They will, however, retain their role as scavengers of waste material from the production and consumption of human food and remain an important buffer supply of protein in peasant cultures.

## 15.6   LOW-INPUT FARMING

Farmers have been criticized (Odum 1967) for 'subverting nature' and creating systems that 'convert oil rather than sunlight into food'. The charge is untrue; the reality is that it is sunlight energy that appears in food and that the support energy has enormously increased the efficiency and amount of solar radiation fixed in farming. Odum's energy fundamentalism has become a tenet of proponents of some 'alternative agricultures' who consider that it is somehow wrong to use fossil energy on food growing, and others see a return to low-input farming as the answer to an 'inevitable' energy shortage.

Underlying these views is the assumption that the energetic efficiency of farming will be improved by reducing expensive inputs of machines and fertilizers. This assumption seems to arise from several misinterpretations: the high efficiency ratios reported for subsistence agriculture that ignore the embodied energy of labor; a failure to properly construct and understand the energy budget for modern agriculture; and particularly, the failure to recognize the sources and magnitude of the nutrient requirements for crop production. In addition, those views have ignored the relationship between population and productivity. Production systems that are adequate for small populations by selecting the best land and leaving it idle as necessary to refurbish its fertility are not sufficient as population and the demand for food increase. Low-input systems are not efficient convertors of sunlight, nor are they efficient in the use of scarce resources of water and nutrients.

Johnson *et al.* (1977) made a detailed analysis of one type of low-input agriculture by comparing the productivity and energy use of conventional farmers with those skilled practitioners of the art of organic agriculture, the Amish farmers of Pennsylvania, Illinois, and Wisconsin. In each comparison, the two groups produced the same crops and animals under identical climatic conditions within the same market constraints as the wider community, so the analyses show how withdrawal of energy from conventional farms might affect productivity and energy use.

The Amish used considerably less energy in production and lifestyle than their conventional neighbors. The percentages were 48% (Pennsylvania, dairy), 49% (Illinois, maize and swine) and 13% and 20% for two groups of the strictest Amish, both dairying without fertilizer and using only stationary engines, in Wisconsin and Pennsylvania respectively. The effect on yields varied from place to place. In Pennsylvania, yields were comparable despite the 50% reduction in energy use. In Illinois, on flat land and better soils, the higher energy use of the conventional farmers was rewarded by a corresponding increase in yield so the input–output relationships were similar. For the strictest adherents in Pennsylvania and Wisconsin, yields were less, but not in proportion to the substantial reductions in energy use.

The most striking difference between the Amish and their conventional neighbors lies outside farm energy use and productivity but is relevant to the issue of energy and lifestyle. In Pennsylvania, the conventional farm families used energy outside farming at a rate of 1800 MJ $d^{-1}$, comparable to that in the wider community, and in stark contrast to the Amish families, who consumed a mere 175 MJ $d^{-1}$. The Amish achieve that by their preference for horse transport, their rejection of networked electricity, and their limited use of fossil fuel (bottled gas) for cooking and lighting. It is their frugal lifestyle, not agricultural productivity, that enables them to purchase more land so that their children may achieve what is to them the most fulfilling of occupations: farming.

Some of those who propose that the assured future of agriculture is in small, labor-intensive, low-input farms have attempted to farm in that way. Not surprisingly, the increasing number of these 'small farmers' generally compete poorly with large-scale mechanized agriculture. The many social issues involved are beyond the scope of this book but the comparative energetics of small and large farms are not. Quite apart from the demonstrable economies of scale in farming, the support of small farms in terms of personal transport, roads, homesteads, and power networks greatly increase the energy cost per unit farm product. On energetic grounds, it would be preferable to have fewer large farms for the production of food or fuel. In the case of small farms, it might be preferable to concentrate farm families in villages where services can be supplied more efficiently. This is how the manorial system operated in the Middle Ages and how small scale farming is still practiced in many parts of Europe and Asia.

In practice, the possibilities for low-input farming are greatly improved when, as now, it is carried out on a limited scale within a region that is dominated by conventional farmers. Under these conditions, low-input farmers are, like the Amish, able to buy supplementary feed for their animals and accumulate its nutrient content on their farms. For others, the use of pesticides and herbicides by conventional neighbors reduces invasion by weeds and pests. Organic farmers often rely for financial success on the premium price they receive from some consumers for their products. This is a subsidy that society pays them for the form of their stewardship of the land. Of course that premium price for organic products is only possible when conventional farmers produce a cheaper product. Ironically, the biological subsidy, the transfer of nutrients in feed and manure from conventional to 'organic' farms or fields, does not infringe the legal requirements that secure this premium. Scientists argue that nutrients are the same from any source, but legislators require one cycle through plants to cleanse some 'artificial' plant nutrients.

The major problem facing humanity is the provision of adequate food for all. To achieve this while permanently sustaining our agricultural potential will require care of soils and landscapes. The safe solution is more likely to involve the more intensive management of crops for high yields on the least vulnerable soils and the protection of more vulnerable soils in extensive agriculture, forestry, and conservation zones. Without adequate nutrients, crop yields will not meet the food requirements of the population. Fertilizers enable greater production from the same area of land. Under the pressure for food from a large world population, they provide an opportunity to manage the natural resources in a safe and productive way.

## 15.7   ENERGY FROM BIOMASS

Before the present era of fossil fuel, mankind relied largely upon biomass for energy for heating, cooking and later for transport. Three-quarters of the world's population of 5 billion remain reliant on biomass for their constrained energy needs. It is not surprising, therefore, that industrialized societies now look to the possibilities of using biomass for energy, not only in traditional form for combustion, but also as a source for more concentrated liquid fuels for engines and to extend the generation of electricity.

The use of biomass for energy is one of the rare cases where energy ratios are useful in assessing the viability of crop production. The primary output is now combustible energy and the major inputs are readily converted to it. When the objective is the production of liquid fuels, the correspondence between the product and the principal inputs is very close indeed. Consequently, in the analysis of biomass for energy, unless the energy ratio is substantially greater than unity, the project is unlikely to be economically viable.

The energy content of biomass and the possible forms in which it can be extracted depend upon the chemical composition (Table 15.3). The energy contents of the constituents range from 14 to 45 MJ kg$^{-1}$, the higher values being obtained at lower biomass yield because of the energy costs of metabolism from primary photosynthetic products (Chapter 11). Because cellulose is the major constituent, the typical value for herbaceous biomass is about 17 MJ kg$^{-1}$ and, for woody materials, 18 MJ kg$^{-1}$.

In addition to its low energy content (cf. gasoline and coal), biomass has a low specific gravity, which causes substantial handling problems. In addition it is distributed at low yield over wide areas. In practice, this means that unless biomass is used *in situ*, energy must be expended to gather and compress it into a transportable form. The particular advantage of wood as combustible fuel relative to other biomass sources lies in its high bulk density and relative transportability rather than in its calorific content, which is comparable to most other cellulose-based biomass.

Table 15.8 *Conversion of plant biomass into useful forms of energy*

| Process | Energy form | Applicability |
|---|---|---|
| Combustion | steam<br>electricity | general for dry biomass<br>wood, stubbles, prunings |
| Gasification<br>then | methane<br>methanol | dry biomass |
| Anaerobic digestion | methane | organic wastes |
| Fermentation | ethanol | carbohydrates<br>cellulose after acid digestion |
| Pressing or solvent<br>extraction | oil | oil crops |

There are a number of ways in which energy can be extracted from biomass. They are summarized in Table 15.8. Combustion is generally applicable and can be used directly for heat or to produce steam for engines. The conversion to electricity by turbine driven generators involves further inefficiency but electrical power is then readily distributed in power grids and finds use in a wide range of applications. Combustion in controlled atmospheres (**gasification**) can be used to form a range of combustible gases, including methane ($CH_4$) and producer gas (CO and $H_2$) from most forms of biomass. The liquid fuel methanol (wood alcohol) can be synthesized from methane.

Two biological processes, **fermentation** to ethanol and anaerobic **digestion** to methane, are well understood and can be implemented with biomass substrate. Fermentation is suited to starch and sugars and thus to grains, sugarbeet, and sugarcane. Efficiency of fermentation to ethanol is high (0.44 kg ethanol $kg^{-1}$ glucose) but drying by distillation consumes considerable energy. Cellulose can enter this process following digestion. At present, biomass is more efficiently used to produce methanol after gasification to methane. Digestion is particularly suited to biological wastes such as sewage but the process is slow.

Vegetable oils offer the simplest method for the production of usable energy because it involves only the extraction (by pressing or with a solvent) of oil from plant material, usually seed. Edible oil from crops such as sunflower, rapeseed, and peanut, and oil from non-edible crops such as linseed, can be used directly in diesel engines. Heat is required to redistil the solvent if extraction is by that method.

## Organic by-products

The major by-products on farms are residues of field crops, prunings from tree crops, and animal wastes from intensive animal production. Energy can be extracted from these materials for use on the farm, or on a larger scale, to be added to the energy grid. As well as the costs of collection and processing of biomass, there are competing values to the farm in terms of nutrient and organic matter contents, animal feed value, and soil protection that must be assessed.

Cereal straw is the major residue and offers the largest potential. In quantity it compares with the mass of grain harvested (since $HI \approx 0.5$) but it is considerably more bulky. The heavy stubbles of high-yielding crops (say $> 8$ t ha$^{-1}$) offer considerable physical inconvenience to subsequent cropping operations (Chapter 12). Incorporated in soil, their decay can immobilize large amounts of nutrients, particularly nitrogen, in the soil microflora and fauna (Chapter 8). On the positive side, stubbles contain significant amounts of nutrients (typical values 5 g N kg$^{-1}$, 2 g P kg$^{-1}$, 20 g K kg$^{-1}$) and in addition the incorporation of organic matter in the soil play important roles in the maintenance of soil structure and control of erosion.

The question then arises, under what conditions and in what amounts can straw be removed for use in fuel production and at what cost to soil fertility and stability? Jenkins & Knutson (1984) have assessed the potential for the generation of electricity by combustion of straw from the concentrated plantings of high-yielding rice crops (grain = stubble = 6 t ha$^{-1}$) in the Central Valley of California. Their energy accounts show a total use of 3.8 GJ of fossil fuel in production operations and straw processing for each 4 GJ of electricity produced. They argue that the analysis would be appropriate to other regions of similarly concentrated crop production and that the outcome is effectively a gain of 4:1 because it takes 4 J of fossil fuel to produce 1 J of electrical energy by combustion. The analysis accounted for replacement of the P and K content of the straw but not for N. Because rice stubbles are usually burnt in California, nitrogen is gasified and lost to the atmosphere rather than retained in the cropping system.

The analysis emphasized the importance of high cropping intensity so that much biomass is available without the energy expense of long-distance cartage (e.g. 5 MJ t$^{-1}$ km$^{-1}$). This analysis cannot easily be extrapolated to other areas because the economics and agronomic applicability of straw removal vary considerably from place to place. Widely distributed crops of high yield are generally not suitable because of the cost of transport, and in regions of low yield, the straw is more likely to have greater value for its nutrient and organic content, and the protection it affords the soil surface, than for energy.

The production of liquid fuels (ethanol and methanol) from crop residues is summarized in Table 15.9 (OTA 1980). When used as straight fuels, the gain from the system is small, 10–60% (v/v) of the premium fuel used in production from residues gathered in the field. The performance of the processes are doubled when they are used as additives to unleaded gasoline but the gain is still only 2:1, affording little margin for error or seasonal variation.

Animal wastes have important nutrient value and are usually more economically returned to the land than used for their energy content. Crops often respond better to animal manures than to the equivalent amounts of the major nutrients as chemical fertilizer due to the beneficial effects of organic matter on soil structure. However, when nearby land cannot hold the quantities available and cartage to more distant areas is uneconomic, anaerobic digestion to methane is an option that will reduce the bulk and the disposal problem. The nutrient values are conserved in the spent liquors that can be economically returned to distant fields.

Organic by-products are also produced by food-processing plants and by food preparation in the home. In industry, the need for heat and the dominance of

Table 15.9 *Premium liquid fuels obtained from various sources relative to equivalent fuel (v/v) used in production*

Individual comparisons are made for fuels used as gasoline additives and as straight fuel.

| | | Ratio as | |
|---|---|---|---|
| Feedstock | Product | Additive | Fuel |
| *Residues* | | | |
| wood | methanol | 1.9 | 1.4 |
| wood | ethanol | 2.1 | 1.6 |
| stubble | methanol | 1.8 | 1.3 |
| stubble | ethanol | 2.0 | 1.5 |
| *Crops* | | | |
| corn | ethanol | 1.9 | 1.4 |
| sorghum | ethanol | 1.7 | 1.1 |
| wheat | ethanol | 2.0 | 1.5 |
| oats | ethanol | 2.0 | 1.5 |
| barley | ethanol | 2.0 | 1.4 |
| sugarcane | ethanol | 1.9 | 1.3 |

*Source:* Adapted from OTA (1980).

stationary engines offer possibilities for the conversion of by-products to energy not found on farms. A classical example occurs with extraction of sucrose from sugarcane. In that process, the byproduct from the crushing (bagasse; 30% water, 15 MJ $kg^{-1}$ dry mass) is combusted to provide the energy supply for the entire extraction operation and usually additional energy (electricity) for sale. Sawmills also produce more energy than they consume. Similar opportunities exist to operate food-processing plants on energy derived from biomass by combustion and anaerobic digestion. Urban wastes are commonly combusted or pyrolized for disposal and energy extraction, and methane is increasingly harvested from landfill waste disposal sites. In these processes of combustion the nutrient content is not returned to the sites of production.

## Crops for energy

Use of complete crops for energy adds three new issues to the discussion of the potential for production of fuels from biomass. First, there are further possibilities arising from the compactness and distinct chemical forms of seeds. Second, there is the possibility of developing new crops specifically for energy. Third, it exposes the important issue of the competition for land between crops for energy and crops for food.

In contrast to energy budgets developed using by-products and farm wastes, the entire (energy) cost of crop production must now be added to the costs of collection, processing to fuel, and nutrient return. Yields of complete crops are greater, as is often the energy content also, but the higher costs of production mean that the cost of fuel production is little different from that produced from by-products.

The energetic gain in using crops for energy is very small. Stewart *et al.* (1981) have shown an energy gain of 3:1 in the production of diesel fuel from sunflower. For maize grain grown with an energetic efficiency of 6.2 (Table 15.4), the conversion to ethanol is of the order of 1.4:1 (liquid fuel basis) or 1.9:1 when used as an additive to gasoline (Table 15.9). These figures are consistent with estimates for other grain crops (sorghum and winter cereals) also presented in Table 15.9. Sugarcane in that analysis has liquid fuel gain of 1.3:1 or 1.9:1 as an additive. Hudson (1975) provided an interesting view of the energetics of energy production from sugarcane in the West Indies. In a mechanized system of cutting and transporting to the mill, the energy ratio of sugar production was just 2.7:1 but with hand labor by poorly paid workers (little embodied energy) it rose to 5.4:1.

The land required for any significant contribution to the supply of energy is enormous. Australia, for example, currently utilizes around 50 Mha in its cropping systems. The major crop is wheat, producing around 15 Mt grain annually at an average yield of 1 t ha$^{-1}$, typically in rotation with leguminous pasture (see Chapter 16). There is a further 26 Mha, mostly in northern Australia, that could be developed for other crops, such as sorghum, maize, and cassava. Australia exports around 80% of its crop production so the agricultural production per citizen is high. It has been estimated, however (Stewart *et al.* 1979), that all currently available residues from agriculture and forestry, together with new crops and their residues from the additional 26 Mha would provide only 50% of the liquid fuel requirement (1979) of the small population of 16 million.

For the immediate future, there is no economic justification to produce energy from crops because it can be done more cheaply from coal. Although biomass can supply energy other than dietary energy, the demand for food and other organic raw materials will prevent it being a major source of energy for the present population or for the level of activity to which mankind has become accustomed.

## 15.8   FUTURE PROSPECTS FOR ENERGY

Total fossil carbon reserves are estimated at 10 000 Gt with 4000 Gt considered to be recoverable with present technology. Given the current consumption rate of 5 Gt y$^{-1}$, and projecting increasing use and new discoveries, the reserves of petroleum are expected to last until the middle of the twenty-first century, and the solid fuels for a further 200–300 y. Even with more conservative use, the Age of Fossil Fuel will appear as a very short interlude (Fig. 15.2) of a few centuries in the long history of mankind. The population and lifestyle that Earth will then support will depend upon what supply of energy can be harnessed to replace fossil fuel. There are a number of possibilities, including hydroelectric, wind, solar, geothermal and tidal energy, that could provide a mix of sources during the transition from fossil fuel to a more permanent supply. Only two of the alternatives, solar energy

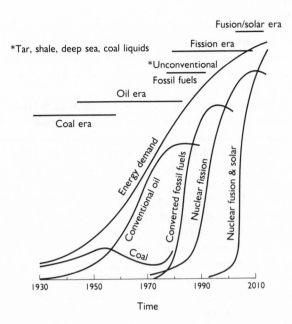

Fusion/solar era

Fission era

*Tar, shale, deep sea, coal liquids

*Unconventional
Fossil fuels

Oil era

Coal era

Energy demand

Conventional oil

Converted fossil fuels

Nuclear fission

Nuclear fusion & solar

Coal

1930    1950    1970    1990    2010

Time

**Fig. 15.2. Schematic representations of world energy demand and sources of supply (adapted from Newland & Price (1975).)**

and nuclear fusion, appear to offer real potential for large-scale, sustainable power generation. Neither are practical options at present.

If energy becomes scarce, farmers will assess the option to produce their own energy needs. The allocation of resources to that activity would not, however, be inconsiderable. The energy required to maintain farm living and production would require that up to 16% of farm area be allocated to energy crops provided that allocation were combined with the use of passive solar energy for heating and drying. The problem, of course, is that if energy becomes sufficiently scarce (and expensive), then food production will assume priority over increasing areas of land. Under those conditions, more of the population will be forced back to food production and the entire community will have to accept a lower standard of living. If agriculture is to provide food, fibre, and energy for a technological society, then the population that it could support would be very small indeed.

The longer it takes to develop alternative, large-scale power production from solar energy or nuclear fusion, the longer will be the period during which energy becomes increasingly scarce or is generated by nuclear fission. If those options for large-scale energy generation never eventuate then it is hard to envisage large world population let alone an energy-rich society.

## 15.9   SUMMARY

The brief period of exploitation of fossil energy has emancipated mankind from the restricting energy supply of current photosynthesis, and the human population has increased dramatically in response. From a population of 500 million 300 y ago, it is now (1992) over 5 billion and is expected to reach 10–12 billion by the end of the twenty-first century. Only about 25% of the world's population now have access to substantial amounts of fossil energy, so as the population grows and the distribution of energy becomes more equitable, the demands on energy supplies, agriculture, and the environment will increase rapidly.

The end of the fossil fuel era is approaching and so there is much concern for the future. Given the enormity of the solar flux and of the nuclear energy of matter, there is no shortage of energy but there is uncertainty of how and when it might be made available. Solar technology is not yet well developed and nuclear fusion hardly at all. In the meantime, there is public concern over the safe storage of radioactive wastes from nuclear fission. Concerns over climatic change may cause us to slow the use of fossil fuel in an attempt to control atmospheric $CO_2$ and thereby hasten the conversion to alternative sources of energy.

Energy in the form of motive power, fertilizers, improved cultivars, agrochemicals, and knowledge amplify and stabilize the productivity of agricultural systems. In this way, the productivity per hectare and per worker increases and so a small proportion of the community working in agriculture can support a majority engaged in alternative pursuits. The system is also efficient in the use of solar radiation, water and nutrients.

In energy-rich societies, there are many opportunities to use energy more efficiently and this also applies to food production and agriculture although they, and particularly agriculture, account for a small part of national energy use. However, given the greatly improved efficiency that has already resulted from the widespread adoption of reduced systems of tillage, it is problematical if there are other areas for similarly major economies in crop production. In particular, use of fertilizer cannot be reduced significantly without a concomitant loss in yield. As far as nitrogen is concerned, we could return to a greater dependence on legumes grown in rotations with major crops. Even if the yields of crops grown in such rotations could be maintained, the production of the region as a whole would fall in proportion to amount of land resting to recover fertility.

In the concern for the future of energy supplies, there are some startling conflicts. On the one hand, there are those who believe that the end of the fossil fuel era signals a return to the past with a greater proportion of the population once again in an energy-frugal agrarian society. On the other hand, there are those who look to agriculture to supply not only food, fibre and other organic products, but also the combustible and derived fuels for an intensely technological society. In the middle are others with concern for the fate of those natural ecosystems that have not yet been converted to agriculture, and yet others, ourselves included, concerned to establish a rational view of the productivity of agricultural lands and their balance with natural systems.

The future depends upon the availability of energy and regardless of the level of that supply, agriculture will remain a supplier of food and organic products and not become a major supplier of energy. If energy is available for a technological society, then agriculture could become concentrated on the best land where all inputs are used most efficiently so that fragile lands can be preserved for their other values. The major factor limiting population will be the capacity of the environment to support the impact of the population and the inevitable conflicts that will arise. On the other hand, if energy is scarce, land will be less productive and able to support a much smaller population. Without successful adjustment to it, including the transition from previous levels, it will be difficult to maintain productivity and to divert food production away from fragile environments.

## 15.10 FURTHER READING

Fluck, R. C. and C. D. Baird. 1980. *Agricultural energetics*. AVI Publishing, Westport, CT.

Hubbert, M. K. 1969. Energy resources. In *Resources and man*, ch. 8, pp. 187–242. National Academy of Sciences, W. H. Freeman & Co., New York. 259 p.

Knorr, D. (ed.). 1983. *Sustainable food systems*. AVI Publishing Co., Westport, CT. 416 p.

Lockeretz, W. (ed.). 1977. *Agriculture and energy*. Academic Press, New York. 750 p.

Loomis, R. S. 1984. Traditional agriculture in America. *Ann. Rev. Ecol. Syst.* **15**:449–78.

Pimentel, D. (ed.). 1980. *Handbook of energy utilization in agriculture*. CRC Press, Boca Raton. 475 p.

Stanhill, G. (ed.) 1984. *Energy and agriculture*. Springer-Verlag, Berlin. 192 p.

Stout, B. A., C. A. Myers, A. Hurrand and L. W. Faidley. 1979. *Energy for world agriculture*. FAO, Rome. 286 p.

# 16

*Analysis of wheat–sheep farming in southern Australia*

## 16.1 INTRODUCTION

In southern Australia most wheat is grown on farms that also produce sheep for wool and for meat (prime lambs). Successful farming began in this region in the 1800s with wheat grown in an alternating sequence with bare fallow while sheep grazed on separate grass pastures. The legume content of those pastures was low because the soils were deficient in phosphorus and often in molybdenum also. Under that early system, yields of wheat, originally near 1 t ha$^{-1}$, had fallen to around 0.5 t ha$^{-1}$ by 1900 owing to the loss of soil N and the build-up of soil-borne diseases. Carrying capacity of those pastures was around 2 sheep ha$^{-1}$, relatively low for the rainfall.

The advantages of introducing legumes into pasture and growing them in sequences (rotations) with cereal crops to increase the productivity of both crop and pasture was recognized by the 1930s. Suitable pasture legumes had been available since the turn of the century but it was not until the 1950s, when wool prices increased, that the widespread use of phosphorus fertilizer became profitable.

The present legume–wheat system continues to evolve in response to changing ecological and economic conditions. A traditional cropping sequence was two to four crops of wheat following several years of leguminous pasture. In recent years, developing markets and acceptable prices for grain legumes (pea, lupin, faba bean) and rapeseed have made it possible to include them in more complex pasture–crop rotations. However, it is rarely possible to replace pasture completely with grain legumes because much of the nitrogen they fix is removed by harvest and also because few soils of the region will tolerate continuous cropping without unacceptable loss of structure, even with minimum tillage. Other benefits to be had from diversification of activities include reduction of risk and more efficient utilization of labor (Chapter 15).

The wheat–sheep system occupies about 50 Mha (Fig. 16.1) in a semiarid region where variable, winter–spring rainfall supports variable plant growth, and where summer is a season of high temperature and predictably low rainfall (Puckridge & French 1983). It has a 'Mediterranean' climate; the dominant agricultural plants were introduced from that zone of ancient agriculture. This Australian farming environment has close parallels in the Mediterranean region (Middle East, North Africa, Spain and Portugal), in California and Oregon, and parts of South America (Chile and Argentina).

428

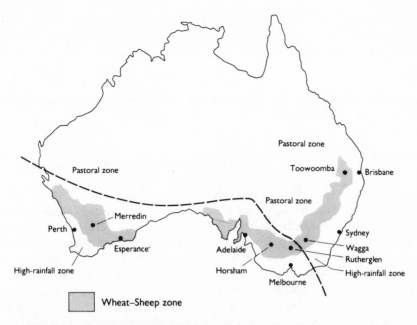

**Fig. 16.1. The location of the wheat-sheep zone in southern Australia in relation to annual rainfall. The zone of winter-dominant rainfall is to the south of the dotted line (after Puckridge & French (1983).)**

While crop and pasture compete for land, management, and investment, their combination here is mutually beneficial to profitability. Crop productivity is limited by the low and variable rainfall and by the infertility of the soils. Legumes provide a major benefit to the rotation through nitrogen fixation. Other benefits from the rotation include a break for pests, diseases, and weeds that build up during the crop cycle. The wheat crop provides similar benefits for the pastures as well as opportunities for their periodic renewal. In ecological terms, the crop sequence exploits the fertility that has accumulated under the pasture.

The optimum balance between wheat and sheep depends on the complementary production gains from pasture and crop, and on the relative prices for the two commodities which, like the weather, change unpredictably. For this reason, farmers do not follow fixed rotations. Rather, the proportions of crops and pasture are varied tactically according to changing prices of limiting resources such as land, labor, capital, and nitrogen fertilizer to maximize long-term profitability and other objectives.

Management of the system follows the critical principle of concentration of limiting resources of water and nitrogen to maximize plant productivity. The sequence of leguminous pasture accumulates soil organic and mineral nitrogen to a concentration that increases the yield and profitability of subsequent wheat crops. Summer fallows retain rainfall while organic nitrogen mineralizes for autumn-sown wheat, further concentrating the yearly supply of moisture and nitrogen for plant growth during later parts of the year. Crop and pasture species adapted to grow in winter-spring use that water at a time when ET* is low and water-use efficiency is high (Chapter 13).

This chapter outlines the management and performance of a representative farm in northeast Victoria. The analysis starts with the climate, moves to the objectives of the farmer, and then provides an ecological explanation of how the system operates, how it responds to management, and how it might be modified. The principles are appropriate to the wheat–sheep zone generally, although the detail varies across it. But first, a brief explanation of how the wheat–sheep system relates to adjacent agricultural zones.

## 16.2   RELATIONSHIP TO ADJACENT AREAS

The wheat–sheep zone produces mostly for overseas markets but has economic relationships with adjacent agricultural zones. There is an extensive pastoral zone in the drier regions towards the interior of the continent (Fig. 16.1) that concentrates on fine-wool, 'Merino' sheep. Parts of the drier interior and the drier margins of the wheat–sheep zone produce first-cross ewes (typically Merino × 'Border Leicester') that are used in the higher rainfall parts of the wheat–sheep zone, where they are bred to sires such as 'Southdown' or 'Poll Dorset' to produce prime lambs. The interior zone also provides the Merino wethers (castrated males) that are grazed instead of ewes in the drier extremes of the wheat–sheep zone, and in combination with ewes in wetter parts. Such mixed flocks are able to cope better than ewe flocks with variable feed supply. There is also exchange of feed supplies between zones, in particular hay from the coastal zone for grain from the wheat–sheep zone. In addition, flocks can be transferred from dry areas to pastures rented from farmers ('agistment') in higher-rainfall areas.

## 16.3   SOILS

Soils of the Australian wheat–sheep zone range from heavy clays to deep sands, but the most extensive, the Red Duplex Soils (Northcote *et al.* 1975), also known as Red Brown Earths (Stace *et al.* 1968), are also the dominant profile type in northeast Victoria. They have a shallow, acidic, loam surface (pH = 4.5 to 5.0) overlying massive clay beginning at about 15–20 cm depth. The subsoil restricts the penetration of water and roots and the surface soil is vulnerable to sealing when it becomes low in organic matter following repeated cropping or loses structure owing to excessive tillage.

## 16.4   CLIMATE

Sufficient rainfall for plant growth becomes available each year in autumn and ceases in spring (Fig. 16.2). A simple climatological analysis of mean monthly climatic data identifies the months during which rainfall exceeds one-third of potential evapotranspiration (i.e. when $P > ET^*/3$) as those with **effective rainfall** (Trumble 1939). Across the wheat–sheep zone, the months of effective rainfall, are

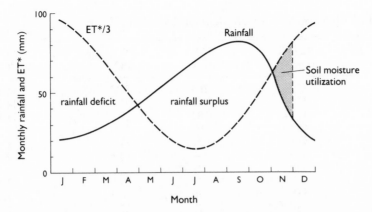

**Fig. 16.2 Seasonal relationship of rainfall and potential evapotranspiration (ET\*) in the wheat–sheep zone of southern Australia.**

generally consecutive and range, with average annual rainfall, from about four to nine but with considerable variation from year to year. The timing of the first heavy rains ('autumn break') and the end of effective rains in the spring (the 'finish') can each vary by up to 2 months, leading to great year-to-year variation in length of growing season and hence in plant productivity.

The climatic conditions relevant to our farm are those for Rutherglen, summarized in Table 16.1. Even though average summer rainfall is not much less than that of winter, its effectiveness for plant growth is negated by the great summer evaporation. The mean period of effective rainfall ($P > ET^*/3$) is 7 months, from April to October. Plant production is restricted by low temperature in June and July.

Low temperatures during winter depress but do not prevent plant growth. Stock are able to graze throughout the year but usually require supplementary feeding with hay during periods of low pasture availability in winter (hay for roughage value) and with grain (for greater energy and nitrogen for digestibility) in summer–autumn as the dry pastures deteriorate.

## 16.5   FARMING OPERATIONS

Our farm comprises 700 ha of gently undulating land (maximum slope 5%) of which 500 are well drained and arable and 50 are unused or devoted to road reserves, woodlots, stockyards, and buildings. The farm is subdivided into paddocks (fenced fields), mostly according to topography and soil type, ranging in area from 20 to 50 ha. Water is piped to troughs in each paddock, supplied by dams distributed around the property to collect runoff.

The arable land is sown to wheat, oat, and lupin in rotation with pasture containing subterranean clover and annual ryegrass. On average across the farm, the pasture and cropping phases both last around 5 y, and at present there are equal areas (250 ha) of both activities on the arable land. Of the 250 ha crop, there are currently 150 ha wheat and 50 ha each of oat and lupin.

Table 16.1 *Monthly mean climatic data for Rutherglen, Victoria*

| Month | Rainfall (mm) | ET* (mm) | Max. temp (°C) | Min. temp (°C) |
|---|---|---|---|---|
| Jan. | 37 | 265 | 31.0 | 14.3 |
| Feb. | 37 | 223 | 31.0 | 14.2 |
| March | 41 | 182 | 27.7 | 11.5 |
| April | 45[1] | 99 | 22.8 | 8.1 |
| May | 52[1] | 51 | 17.7 | 4.9 |
| June | 58[1] | 34 | 13.5 | 3.2 |
| July | 60[1] | 29 | 13.1 | 3.1 |
| Aug. | 62[1] | 51 | 14.7 | 3.6 |
| Sept. | 53[1] | 76 | 18.3 | 5.2 |
| Oct. | 58[1] | 127 | 22.3 | 7.3 |
| Nov. | 42 | 173 | 27.4 | 9.7 |
| Dec. | 43 | 259 | 30.8 | 12.7 |
| Total | 588 | 1569 | | |

*Note:*
[1] Months of effective rainfall (mean rainfall > ET*/3).

The remaining 150 ha are unsuitable for cropping because of shallow soil on the higher ground or, in the case of lower areas, susceptibility to waterlogging in winter. That land carries permanent pasture improved by broadcasting subterranean clover seed and by biennial application of phosphate fertilizer. Two perennial grasses, phalaris (*Phalaris aquatica*) and cocksfoot (*Dactylis glomerata*), were also introduced by sod-seeding into suitable areas. These grasses are important components of improved pastures in higher-rainfall areas of southern Australia. In the Rutherglen area, they produce valuable green feed in the wetter summers and yet are sufficiently drought-resistant to survive the drier ones. Productivity of the permanent pasture on shallow soil is restricted because it dries out early in spring owing to its low water-holding capacity. By contrast, the pastures of the lower areas are usually more productive because the soils are deeper and retain the additional moisture needed to sustain growth longer into the spring. However, growth is restricted there in winter by waterlogging in wet years.

Sheep are the only grazing animals. The flock comprises 750 wethers, 1000 ewes and 30 rams giving an average stocking rate of 6.9 DSE ha$^{-1}$. The DSE, dry sheep equivalent, is a unit of stocking. An adult wether is 1 DSE; a value of 2 DSE for each ewe covers lambs, rams and non-breeding ewes. On this farm, all replacement ewes, wethers and rams are purchased off the farm.

The workforce comprises an owner–operator and one permanent employee supplemented by contract labor for specialized tasks such as shearing and fencing, and for periods of peak demand during fodder conservation and harvesting.

The present (1990) value of the land, equipment and stock is around A\$1 400 000. Income varies unpredictably from year to year, particularly in response to variable yields but also to prices for products. With average yields, annual operating profit, i.e. the return to capital after allowing for owner's labor and management, would be around A$60 000. With above-average yields, operating profit increases dispropor-tionately because the variable costs of production and overheads tend to remain fairly constant per unit of output. In good years, operating profit may rise to A$100 000 or it may fall sharply in poor years to less than A$30 000.

These financial returns are low relative to the size of the investment. Farmers generally accept low return to labor and management and rely upon a few good years and capital gain to cover return on investment. If in the long term, the returns (including capital gain) to labor, managerial skill, and capital do not match those from alternative enterprises (agricultural or non-agricultural), then farmers tend to reinvest elsewhere.

## 16.6   WHEAT PRODUCTION

### Conversion from pasture to crop

The change from pasture to a new sequence of crops requires substantial reduction in the seed bank of pasture and weed species that has built up during the pasture phase. The reduction of that seed bank is accomplished traditionally by tillage that kills establishing seedlings and brings other seed into microenvironments that stimulate germination (Chapter 5). The best control is achieved when tillage begins in spring before the annual pasture species and weeds set seed and is repeated when sufficient seed germinate in response to rainfall, but that usually involves a considerable loss of spring–summer grazing (Fig. 16.6). Other disadvantages of this form of weed control include the high cost of tillage (Chapter 15) and the potential for soil erosion from unvegetated ground (Chapter 12). Cutting hay to prevent seed production and delaying tillage until autumn offers a reasonable compromise even though weed control is less thorough.

Herbicides are increasingly used to convert pasture to crop. In that case, the procedure commences after the autumn break when pasture and weed seedlings germinate. Heavy grazing of the pasture just prior to herbicide applications exposes the germinating seedlings and improves the effectiveness of the operation. Herbi-cides provide a number of advantages over full and prolonged seed bed preparation. Soil organic matter is retained better, giving benefits in soil structure and additional grazing that increases animal production. Use of herbicides also allows the farmer to delay decisions about conversion until the last moment and respond to the latest climatic and economic signals.

On the other hand, there are also some disadvantages. Delaying land preparation from pasture until after the autumn break may reduce yield of the first crop because neither water nor nitrate were conserved during the period of preparation. In addition, sowing may be later than optimal. In a wet year it may become impossible to sow wheat as the season progresses, although that is less likely on ground that was sprayed rather than cultivated. In practice, a combination of minimum tillage and chemical methods usually provides the cheapest method of weed control and seed-bed preparation.

In many ways, farming with herbicides is environmentally safer than farming exclusively with tillage. There is less damage to soil structure, and the retention of vegetation and surface residues protects the surface soil from the danger of erosion. The use of chemicals does, however, require safe-handling procedures and attention to residual effects within the crop rotation.

### Selection of cultivars

Cultivars of spring wheat (long-day plants, no vernalization response) are used in the wheat–sheep system. They have been selected for flowering in October following sowing over a relatively broad period in autumn. October flowering is preferred because it avoids late spring frosts that would seriously damage flowering crops. Late flowering pushes grain filling into the usual conditions of terminal drought, but this pattern of water use maximizes water-use efficiency for the system (see Chapter 13).

Wheat crops are grazed only in emergencies, either in winter during the vegetative phase or towards the end of very dry seasons when crop failure is certain. In this way, wheat may sometimes provide a buffer to feed supply. Sheep can graze cereal crops with least damage in the vegetative phase provided it is done before stem elongation exposes the reproductive apices to consumption.

Additional winter fodder is obtained more efficiently from oat, a crop with excellent winter growth that can be managed flexibly for grazing, grain, or both. Oat fits well into the cropping sequence, being commonly used as a companion crop for undersown subterranean clover in preparation for the return to pasture. Table 16.2 records winter fodder production and spring hay yield for a range of available oat cultivars. The data show that it is possible to make selections for winter vigor and spring regrowth.

### Weed control

Weeds can be controlled in wheat crops by pre- and post-emergence herbicides. The advantage of pre-emergence control is that competition is avoided in the seedling stands; the disadvantage is that the need for it may be uncertain. Post-emergence weed control is possible with selective herbicides but decisions have to be taken quickly because effective control requires application of individual herbicides at specified stages, usually during early seedling growth. By the time a weed problem is evident, interspecific competition (Chapter 2) may already have reduced yield potential although weed control is still necessary to prevent further losses.

In this system of mixed farming, annual ryegrass, the valued species of the pasture phase, becomes a serious weed in wheat crops. Ryegrass is a particular problem because, as a grass, it is physiologically similar to wheat and provides strong competition while being difficult to remove from the crop with selective herbicides. Fig. 16.3 illustrates yield reduction in wheat due to a range of ryegrass densities. Crops sown in early May grow rapidly under warmer temperatures of autumn and

Table 16.2 *Herbage production (t ha$^{-1}$) of oat cultivars*

| Cultivar | Winter herbage production | | | Spring hay yield |
|---|---|---|---|---|
| | Mid-June | Early August | Total | |
| Esk | 1.1 | 2.2 | 3.3 | 11.5 |
| Carbeen | 0.8 | 2.2 | 3.2 | 9.4 |
| Nile | 1.2 | 1.9 | 3.1 | 11.0 |
| Blackbutt | 0.8 | 1.9 | 2.7 | 10.9 |
| Cooba | 0.9 | 2.4 | 3.3 | 6.0 |
| Coolabah | 1.2 | 1.7 | 2.9 | 7.3 |
| Algeribee | 1.1 | 1.8 | 2.9 | 5.5 |
| Lampton | 1.0 | 1.3 | 2.3 | 6.7 |
| Saia | 1.1 | 1.0 | 2.1 | 6.8 |
| Swan | 1.2 | 0.8 | 2.0 | 4.5 |

*Source:* After Reeves *et al.* (1987).

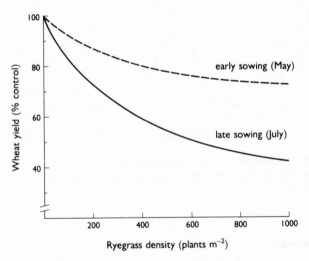

Fig. 16.3. **Effect of ryegrass density on the yield of wheat at two times of sowing (after Reeves (1976).)**

compete more strongly with ryegrass than do crops sown in July and establishing cover under the cooler temperatures of winter. The effectiveness of control thus varies from year to year depending upon time of sowing and other factors, principally nitrogen fertility which advantages wheat at the expense of ryegrass (Smith & Levick 1974). Ryegrass also serves as an alternative host for certain soil-borne diseases of wheat (Section 16.8). A further problem arises when the pasture legume (subterranean clover) is reseeded under the last cereal crop (usually oat) of a sequence because this restricts the possibilities for chemical control of broad-leaved weeds.

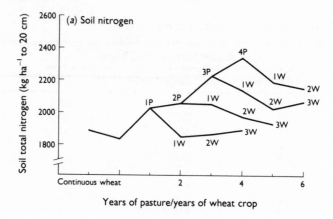

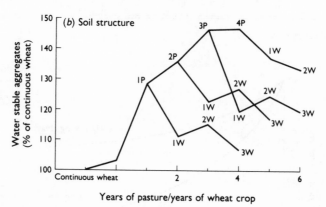

Fig. 16.4. Changes in (*a*) total soil nitrogen content to 20 cm, and (*b*) soil structure, within various crop sequences at Rutherglen (A. Ellington, unpublished).

### Length of crop sequence

In individual paddocks, the number of wheat crops grown before returning to pasture depends on how quickly the nitrogen content of the soil is depleted, and on the build-up of soil-borne diseases. It also depends on non-agronomic aspects of the entire farming enterprise, including the returns from wool and lambs relative to wheat. Fig. 16.4 illustrates the changes in soil structure and soil nitrogen content that occur under wheat–pasture sequences using tillage. An important part of the management of these sequences must be directed to preserve the fragile structure of these soils and to maintain adequate nitrogen for crop growth and yield.

More recently, the length of the cropping sequence has been extended by inclusion of crops other than cereals. In northeast Victoria, the grain legume, narrow-leafed lupin, is the most important alternative crop to wheat, but rapeseed is also used. Both crops provide a disease break, and lupin fixes nitrogen some of which remains for an ensuing wheat crop.

On our farm, each ha of pasture on arable land can be expected to add about 40 kg N y$^{-1}$ to the soil reserve, about enough to meet that removed in one average wheat crop (48 kg N in 2.4 t grain ha$^{-1}$ at 20 g N kg$^{-1}$). Because the nitrogen cycle is 'leaky' (Chapter 8) and the nitrogen harvest index of wheat is near 0.7, more nitrogen than that, about 75 kg N ha$^{-1}$, must be made available for each crop. Consequently the length of the pasture or grain legume phase needs to exceed that of the crop. In general, pasture should be maintained at least twice as long as the cropping phase.

## Stubble management

After harvest, wheat stubbles can provide useful summer feed for sheep because the massive cellulose content of the straw is supplemented by small amounts of grain and volunteer weeds. Sheep are an important element in stubble management because they consume and trample residues so that less tillage is required for the next crop. Without such reduction of stubble, chemical control of weeds is difficult, subsequent sowing of the crop may be delayed, and establishment retarded. One factor that leads to poor establishment of wheat is low soil temperature under surface mulch (see Chapter 7) but there is also the possibility of nitrate depletion, disease, and toxicity from the decomposing stubble.

Stubbles are often burnt after reduction by grazing. Depending upon weather conditions, fire restrictions are lifted in March to April. Despite the loss of nitrogen contained in the stubble (approx. 4 g N kg$^{-1}$, i.e. 16 kg N in 4 t ha$^{-1}$), the combustion decreases the C/N ratio in the surface soil, so that microbial growth is restricted and less nitrogen is immobilized in microbial biomass (Chapter 8). Burning also destroys seed in the litter and surface soil and is an effective means of controlling annual weeds, particularly annual ryegrass which is persistent in the crop phase. Burnt stubbles may also conserve more water if the better weed control they afford offsets the higher rate of soil evaporation that occurs in the absence of surface covering (Chapter 9). Farmers in this region are adopting cropping systems involving stubble retention because, on balance, benefits outweigh disadvantages.

## Yield

The yield of wheat is related to seasonal water supply and analyses of the relationship are available for Rutherglen (Connor 1975) and related areas (French & Schultz 1984; O'Leary *et al.* 1985; see Section 9.10). The yield distribution function for wheat at Rutherglen presented in Fig. 16.5 is based upon measured water-use efficiencies and the long-term (50 y) distribution of growing-season rainfall.

Wheat yields show substantial variability from year to year. Median yield of wheat is 2.4 t ha$^{-1}$. One year in ten, yields will exceed 4.0 t ha$^{-1}$ or fall below about 1 t ha$^{-1}$. Yields less than about 0.8 t ha$^{-1}$ will rarely cover the costs of crop establishment.

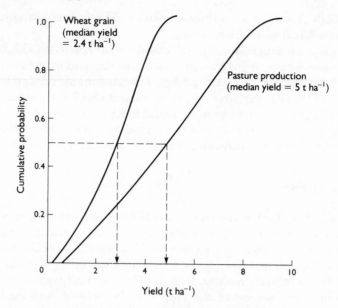

**Fig. 16.5. Probability distributions of wheat yield and pasture production at Rutherglen, Victoria.**

## 16.7   ANIMAL PRODUCTION

The health and nutrition of a large flock of sheep is an important concern for a farmer trying to achieve high production by manipulating uncertain feed supplies. The proportion of breeding ewes in the flock and the lambing time determine the seasonal variation in feed requirement through the additional feed for gestation, lactation, and growing lambs. Despite those changes, feed requirements of the flock remain considerably more constant during the year than does pasture production which peaks sharply in spring (Fig. 16.6).

The impact of a shortfall in feed depends upon the timing. Wethers are more robust than ewes and can be managed with less risk. Ewes are most sensitive to low feed supply during gestation and lactation. The penalties for providing insufficient feed for ewes are less production of lambs as well as quantity of wool.

Given this, two of the most important decisions relating to the sheep enterprise that the farmer must make are the **stocking rate** (sheep ha$^{-1}$) and the **time of lambing**. Others concern the flock replacement strategy because that has implications for seasonal feed demand, genetic improvement, disease control, and cash flow.

### Stocking rate

Pasture production varies seasonally and from year to year depending upon climatic factors, principally rainfall. Stocking rate cannot be set to the level of the most

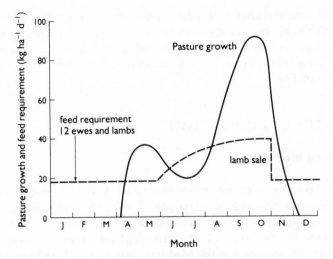

**Fig. 16.6. Seasonal pattern of pasture production and flock fodder requirement in the wheat–sheep zone of southern Australia.**

productive year nor to the most productive season. A balance must be struck, based on long-term rainfall expectancies and the state of development and level of management of the farm, that will allow fodder reserves (standing fodder, hay and grain) or funds to meet seasonal and annual feed deficits (Fig. 16.6) at acceptable risk. As stocking rate is increased, the danger and onset of a feed deficit is greater and earlier, so more seasonal and drought reserves are needed but there is then less surplus fodder to conserve.

It is possible to make a general calculation about the annual feed requirements of a sheep flock as a basis for understanding stocking rate. An annual allowance of 400 kg of medium-quality dry forage per adult wether (1 DSE) and 800 kg for each ewe plus lamb and associated stock (rams and replacement ewes) (2 DSE) allows for the mismatch between times of production and consumption. If the efficiency of grazing utilization is 60%, then the 400 ha of pasture on our farm must produce around 1800 t dry forage annually or an average of 4.6 t ha$^{-1}$ over permanent and rotational pasture for the flock of 750 wethers and 1000 breeding ewes. This forage requirement is just below the median annual pasture production at Rutherglen (5 t ha$^{-1}$; see next section). In the mixed farming system, sheep gain additional feed each year from grazing stubbles and from forage and grain crops (e.g. oat and lupin) sown for that purpose.

## Time of lambing

The time of lambing strongly influences the seasonal feed requirements of the flock. In this region, lambing in autumn provides the best match with the availability of green herbage in winter and the 'flush' of spring growth (Fig. 16.6). The alternative is to lamb in early spring. This fits better with the reproductive cycle of the sheep, and lambing percentage is greater. In addition those lambs come to market when prices are usually higher. However, supplementary feed, fodder crops, or special pastures (e.g. alfalfa) must be provided to 'finish' spring-born lambs. Spring lambing is possible on these mixed farms but the decision to implement it requires careful economic evaluation.

## 16.8  PASTURE PRODUCTION

### Pasture composition

The improved pastures of the wheat–sheep zone are dominantly mixtures of annual grasses and legumes, although perennial grasses are important in some areas as for example on the uncultivated areas of this farm. The preferred grass is annual ryegrass and the legumes are various cultivars of subterranean clover or medics (*Medicago* spp). All are native to the Mediterranean region, have long-day requirements for flowering (Section 5.3) and are well adapted to the Australian wheat–sheep zone. The cultivars are chosen by individual photothermal requirements to match the length of growing season. The medics are better suited to a short growing season and alkaline soils than subterranean clover. At Rutherglen, ryegrass and subterranean clover (cvs. Woogenellup and Trikkala) are the preferred pasture species.

Several other species are voluntary invaders of pasture. The most important are also introduced species, barley grass (*Hordeum leporinum*) and storksbill (*Erodium botrys*) from the Mediterranean region and capeweed (*Arctotheca calendula*) from South Africa. All are undesirable because they have shorter growing seasons than ryegrass and subterranean clover and are consequently less productive. In addition, the burrowing seeds of barley grass and storksbill damage the eyes and hides of sheep. Capeweed is common on high fertility sites, invading the pastures when the nitrogen level has been raised. Both barley grass and capeweed are stronger winter growers than ryegrass and subterranean clover, and either can come to dominate pasture.

The 150 ha of pasture on this farm that cannot be cropped were improved by broadcasting subterranean clover seed and by biennial applications of superphosphate. The species content is comparable to that of pastures that are managed through the cropping sequence but with valuable perennial grasses (phalaris and cocksfoot) and overall a greater proportion of less desirable, weedy species. In this case, carrying capacity is 50% of the rotational pastures on the farm.

### Managing pasture composition

Pasture management requires attention to interspecific competition during the growing season, especially as it affects seed production because the composition of the soil seed bank and the germination responses of the component species determine what mixture emerges at the next break of season. The timing of the autumn break is important and can have overriding effects on pasture composition, causing the grass, clover, and weed composition to vary considerably from year to year. Clover tends to be dominant when the break comes early, grass when it is late, and capeweed after a long dry summer. During the growing season, grazing, mowing, and applications of fertilizer and herbicides control species composition and ultimately the annual seed set.

The success of legumes depends upon the application of phosphorus. It is in limiting supply and is readily fixed into sparingly soluble forms in these soils by aluminum and iron. Annual applications of about 10 kg P ha$^{-1}$ to the pastures are most common, but practice varies. Some farmers rely on applications made to the wheat crops during short rotations to carry over to pasture, others apply phosphorus during the pasture phase for greater benefit to fodder production. In pastures established for over 20 y, the application of 10 kg P ha$^{-1}$ may be made in alternate years. Phosphorus fertilizer is an important tool in pasture management because it can be applied to increase clover content and hence the nitrogen fixation rate and overall productivity of the pasture.

Successful management of pasture composition by grazing requires flocks of a size that can quickly reduce pasture biomass in individual paddocks when required. In this way, timely defoliation can be effected, for example to limit seed set in capeweed or barley grass. Pastures are grazed lightly in the first year to ensure establishment of plants at a satisfactory density. Once established, heavy grazing favors short-stature clovers, medics, and capeweed over grasses. Light grazing favors the taller grasses. Time of grazing is also important. Spring grazing, as with mowing for hay, can be used to control seed production of all species. Ultimately, grazing determines the composition of the pasture.

Some of the surplus spring forage (Fig. 16.6) is commonly mown and conserved as hay. The traditional storage is in small, rectangular bales in sheds but increasingly, for reasons of quality and economy, large (round) bales are made and usually stored without cover. The ideal time to cut pasture for hay is when the grains of the grasses are still immature and the biomass and nutritive quality are high. Consequently, mowing reduces grass seed production and causes significant shifts in pasture composition. For that reason, mowing is restricted to older-established pastures while young pastures are allowed to seed freely without hay production or heavy grazing. The last pasture in a sequence is commonly used for hay production in order to reduce the seed load and hence competition during the subsequent crop sequence. Mowing is a particularly effective means of restricting dominance of barley grass because little of its seed persists over more than one summer.

Herbicides can also be used to manipulate species composition but they are expensive compared with management by grazing or hay making. However, some cheap options are available. For example, control of capeweed can be achieved by a subtoxic dose of a herbicide that slows growth causing sugar content to increase. In this condition capeweed becomes especially palatable and sheep will selectively graze it. A new and valuable use of herbicides is in 'pasture topping'. The pasture is sprayed while still green in late spring, causing rapid senescence. There is no residual effect of the herbicide on rumen activity, animal metabolism, or meat quality. Labile carbohydrate and nitrogen contents of the dry forage remain high during the summer and as a secondary effect, seed set is prevented. This effectively enhances the nutritive value of dry standing feed during the summer and also controls grass weeds, e.g. barley grass. It is especially useful in the last year of a pasture sequence as a weed control treatment prior to cropping.

### Soil seed bank

The stability of annual pastures depends upon the ability of the component species to reestablish each autumn from the seed bank in competition with invading species. With uncertain rainfall, each species must set seed in most years and in sufficient quantity to maintain a place of dominance in the seed bank in the topsoil. That bank must be large enough to tolerate depletion by ill-fated germination after early rains ('false breaks') that occur prior to the main wet season.

For subterranean clover and annual ryegrass, seed dormancy, including hard-seededness (Section 5.6), ensures that a substantial seed supply remains in the topsoil following false breaks, and even after seasons with low seed-set due to drought or heavy grazing. Most cultivars of subterranean clover produce hard seed that will persist in the soil for many years. Subterranean clover germinates in wheat crops; although it does not compete strongly, sufficient seed remains for re-establishment after the cropping phase. When pastures fail to re-establish after cropping, the cause is usually failure of inoculation due to decline in rhizobia population. Undersowing inoculated seed with the last wheat crop of a sequence ensures rapid re-establishment of a productive pasture. In drier areas of the wheat–sheep zone with shorter and more opportunistic crop sequences, the persistence of pasture legume seed through the crop phase lowers the cost of pasture re-establishment, contributing to the profitability of cropping at lower yield levels than are achieved in northeast Victoria.

Over the summer, seed, especially of subterranean clover, form an important part of the sheep diet. Their high content of nitrogen (32% crude protein) aids sheep in digesting the low quality roughage that is usually on offer at that time. Annual production of subterranean clover seed can reach 500 kg ha$^{-1}$.

### Disease control

The pasture phase provides an important break in the reproductive cycle of soil-borne pests and diseases that build up under continuous cropping. In northeast Victoria, on acid soils, the important fungal diseases of wheat are take-all (*Gaeuman-nomyces graminis* var. *tritici*), eyespot lodging (*Pseudocercosporella herpotrichoides*) and speckled leaf blotch (*Septoria tritici*). In other parts of the wheat–sheep zone, on neutral and alkaline soils, rhizoctonia root rot (*Rhizoctonia solani*) and the cereal cyst nematode (*Heterodera avenae*) cause serious losses in wheat yield, often in combination. Table 16.3 presents observations made on yield, grain nitrogen content, and disease incidence in wheat grown in various sequences with lupin at Rutherglen. The responses reveal that lupin provides an important disease break in addition to greater available nitrogen.

Table 16.3 *Yield, grain nitrogen content, and disease incidence of wheat in the third year of various wheat–lupin sequences at Rutherglen*

The diseases of wheat were *Gaeumannomyces graminis*, *Fusarium* spp. and *Pseudocercosporella herpotrichoides*.

| Rotation | Grain yield (t ha$^{-1}$) | Nitrogen content (%) | Disease incidence (%) |
|---|---|---|---|
| W–W–W | 2.58a | 2.31a | 36a |
| L–W–W | 3.00b | 2.51b | 2b |
| W–L–W | 3.34b | 2.65c | 1b |
| L–L–W | 3.41b | 2.73c | 1b |

*Note:*
Within columns, values followed by different letters are significantly ($p < 0.05$) different.
*Source:* Adapted from Reeves *et al.* (1984).

The effectiveness of pasture as a disease break is reduced by the presence of grasses that provide inferior but alternative hosts to diseases and pests of wheat. Pure legume pastures offer disease control comparable with that of grain legumes, such as lupin and pea, or the oilseed crop, rapeseed, and are now a practical option with the use of herbicides. They are recommended in some areas of the wheat–sheep zone, but not currently in north-east Victoria.

Cropping and pasture rotations also provide the basis for controlling internal parasites of sheep, particularly worms. The crop sequence provides a longer break in disease cycles than is possible by rotational grazing of pastures themselves. Rotational grazing is usually not sufficient to control internal parasites at the stocking rates concerned and is supplemented by drenching with anthelmintics.

**Pasture productivity**

Pasture productivity depends upon the establishment and maintenance of LAI over the season. A pasture of low LAI will never 'grow away' from sheep, so the advantage to pasture production that accrues from closing some paddocks after an early autumn break ('deferred grazing') can be considerable. The penalty is a temporary but significant decline in animal production because after a dry summer the stock are in condition to respond to green pasture, even a small amount, to supplement the dry standing feed that remains. Until the rainy season is established, however, it is probably better to graze what grows in response to early rains, given that feed is scarce and if not eaten may desiccate and blow away.

Because grazing can reduce green cover below that needed for maximum growth rate, rotational grazing of paddocks plays an important role in allowing LAI to increase towards the level needed for high production. In practice, however, farmers stock at rates that result in overgrazing of some paddocks in most years.

Pasture production is closely related to growing-season rainfall. We can again use a yield versus ET relationship (Section 9.10) to analyze the variability of annual pasture production. The distribution of annual pasture production presented in Figure 16.5 was estimated from growing-season rainfall and water-use efficiency determined for vegetative growth of wheat (Connor 1975; O'Leary *et al.* 1985) but appropriate to the growth of C3 pastures. The distribution function emphasizes that pasture production, like wheat yield, varies considerably from year to year. Median annual production is 5 t DM ha$^{-1}$ but the range is wide. One year in ten will have pasture production above 8 or below 1.5 t ha$^{-1}$. Fodder reserves of grain (oat and lupin) and pasture hay provide for feed transfer from years of high to years of low production.

### Nitrogen fixation and cycling

Pastures that accumulate 5 t ha$^{-1}$ dry forage at a nitrogen content of 25–30 g N kg$^{-1}$ contain about 140 kg N ha$^{-1}$. That translates to 875 kg crude protein ha$^{-1}$. Not all of that nitrogen will be obtained from symbiotic fixation because the pastures are not pure legume, and because legumes utilize inorganic nitrogen when it is available. Uptake of mineral nitrogen by legumes would occur particularly in the seedling phase when soil nitrate levels are high following the summer drought.

The cycling of nitrogen through the soil–plant–animal system is complex (Chapter 8). When pastures are grazed, the major portion of the nitrogen consumed is excreted by the animals and returned to the pasture in urine and feces. Perhaps 50% is lost by volatilization with the remainder returning to the soil. That means that nitrogen is rapidly recycled through the pasture during the rainy season and more slowly in the dry season when pasture growth is small.

Estimation of the contribution of legume nitrogen to the rotation is difficult. The available data for these pastures suggest a mean net nitrogen fixation of about 40 kg ha$^{-1}$ y$^{-1}$ with a range of 20–80 kg ha$^{-1}$ y$^{-1}$. The amount varies with growing conditions and pasture productivity and declines as mineral nitrogen and organic matter accumulate under the pasture. Natural additions by lightning, rainfall, dust, and free-living organisms are about 2 kg ha$^{-1}$ y$^{-1}$ and therefore minor. Symbiotic fixation is the major source for the entire system since nitrogen fertilizer is rarely used.

The 250 ha of rotational pasture on our farm have the capacity to bring 10 t N ha$^{-1}$ y$^{-1}$ into the system. The portion of this nitrogen that has accumulated at the end of a pasture sequence influences the performance and determines the possible length of the ensuing cropping phase.

## 16.9   NUTRIENT BALANCE OF THE SYSTEM

Table 16.4 summarizes some components of the macronutrient balance of the farm. Fertilizer practice aims to correct phosphorus deficiency which limits plant growth, especially of subterranean clover. Using superphosphate, that also adds substantial amounts of calcium and sulfur but much of the added phosphorus becomes fixed in relatively unavailable forms so that annual additions are necessary even though they

Table 16.4 *Annual nutrient balance (kg) of a 700 ha wheat–sheep farm, Rutherglen, Victoria*

50 ha are unused.

|  | N | P | K | Ca | S |
|---|---|---|---|---|---|
| *Inputs* | | | | | |
| Pasture (250 ha rotational pasture)[1] | 10 000 | 2500 | — | 5250 | 3050 |
| Pasture (150 ha on non-arable land)[2] | 3000 | 750 | | 1570 | 920 |
| Wheat (150 ha) | — | 1500 | — | 3150 | 1840 |
| Oat (50 ha) | — | 500 | — | 1050 | 610 |
| Lupin (50 ha)[1] | 2000 | 500 | — | 1050 | 610 |
| *Products* | | | | | |
| Lambs (1000 @ 35 body wt = 35 t) | 980 | 240 | 60 | 440 | 135 |
| Wool (1750 @ 5.0 kg cap$^{-1}$ = 8.8 t) | 865 | 1 | 1 | — | 230 |
| Wheat (150 ha @ 4 t ha$^{-1}$ = 600 t) | 7200 | 1080 | 1510 | 720 | 900 |
| Oat (50 ha @ 3 t ha$^{-1}$ = 150 t) | 2000 | 300 | 420 | 200 | 250 |
| Lupin (50 ha @ 1.5 t ha$^{-1}$ = 75 t) | 3300 | 390 | 1080 | 160 | 145 |
| *Balance* | | | | | |
| Oat and lupin sold | + 665 | + 3740 | − 3070 | + 10 550 | + 5370 |
| Oat and lupin consumed | + 5955 | + 4430 | − 1570 | + 10 910 | + 5765 |

*Notes:*
[1] All N inputs are net gains from legume–rhizobia symbiosis.
[2] Pasture on non-arable land is fertilized in alternate years.

exceed annual removal. Potassium is not commonly added but removal in wheat grain (0.42%) is high, totalling 1.5 t. It can be expected that potassium deficiency will eventually become widespread on land that is consistently cropped. The system uses no nitrogen fertilizer but relies on nitrogen fixation by subterranean clover during the pasture phase. The budget shows that the system is closely balanced. The estimated annual addition on the rotational system of 12 t (based on 40 kg ha$^{-1}$ for lupin and pasture) would be exceeded by removals if the fodder grains (oat and lupin) were sold. The wheat harvest removes the major proportion, 7.2 t. Stock transfer some proportion of the nitrogen fixed on the non-arable pasture to the cropping system but the real difficulty in constructing the budget is that the actual rate of nitrogen fixation is uncertain. Despite the uncertainties, the estimates illustrate, however, the critical role that nitrogen plays in continuing productivity. The complexity of the nitrogen cycle and the difficulties of measurement were discussed in Chapter 8.

Most of the nitrogen fixed by the lupin crop is harvested in the grain. This is characteristic of the nitrogen balance of grain legume crops and contrasts strongly with the accumulation of nitrogen under leguminous pasture.

The balance provides the overall summary for the farm. For individual paddocks there is a build-up of nitrogen fertility during the pasture phase that is then used during cropping. In ecological terms, stability involves cyclic rather than static nutrient levels.

## 16.10   ECOLOGICAL STABILITY

A key feature of agricultural systems that affects their long-term stability is the removal of nutrients in harvested products (Chapter 12). Phosphorus and nitrogen are critical elements in the wheat–sheep system; their levels are attended to by phosphorus fertilizer and symbiotic nitrogen fixation. In the future it may be necessary to add other nutrients, particularly macronutrients such as potassium, that are removed in large quantities in wheat grain and lambs. At the present time, however, it is becoming apparent that, for continued productivity, the wheat–sheep system must solve or adapt to two additional changes that it is imposing on the land. The first is dryland salinity, which affects low-lying parts of some topographical sequences, and the second is increasing soil acidity. Both reduce productivity, but do so in different ways. Salinity operates at a scale that is larger than the individual farm so its solution will require cooperative action. Acidity operates at the level of individual paddock and is under the control of the farmer.

These two processes are important ecological issues affecting the long-term stability of agricultural ecosystems. Agricultural fields are maintained for high productivity as disclimax communities that are prevented from successional return to natural vegetation. They are maintained by management, but can management always prevent undesirable change?

### Dryland salinity

The original woodlands and shrublands of the wheat–sheep zone were dominated by evergreen perennials, mostly of the genus *Eucalyptus*. Those communities were as active in summer as the water supply would allow. The result was maximum use of all water by drought-resistant communities tuned by evolution to erratic, winter rains. Their characteristic was substantial drying of the soil by a deep root system over summer and autumn. The change to annuals that use less water has had a major effect on the hydrology of the landscapes.

Subsoil moisture has increased under annual crops and pastures because the root systems are shallow and are inactive during the summer. Over a number of years there has been a significant rise of the watertable in some parts of the wheat–sheep zone from that established under natural woodland. The subsoils contain large quantities of salt leached from the surface layers in earlier times. Because $P < ET^*$ in this region, salt has not leached to the ocean. With rising watertables, it is brought to the surface in seeps, or to within the capillary zone, at low points of the topography. Some catchments are connected by regional watertables so that a change in land use in one area may lead to saline seepage many kilometers away.

Salinity initially reduces the productivity of crops and pastures, then causes their replacement by salt-tolerant species, and, if sufficiently severe, by bare, erodible ground. Because salts have been brought to the surface, a larger fraction can enter surface waters and streams with deleterious effects on wildlife and water supply. This problem is widespread in the wheat–sheep zone, particularly outside northeast Victoria, and is estimated to affect to varying degreees 3–4 Mha in the Australian wheat–sheep zone and to be expanding. Similar scenarios are evident in other youthful, dryland farming systems around the world, e.g. in Montana (USA). On the other hand, in very old systems of the Near East, the uplands are now salt-free but the lowlands are completely salinized unless drained.

The solution is conceptually simple. To prevent seepage reaching the lowland, and to redress the problem that already exists, it is necessary to remove the salt from the seepage areas in the low-lying land. This could be achieved by drainage, which would also export salt from the region to the ocean or to salt sinks, or alternatively by increasing evapotranspiration on the uplands that would reduce the quantity of salt mobilized towards the seepage zones.

Saline water can be drained to the sea or to inland evaporation pans. Both processes occur naturally in this zone but the issue here is if they should be expanded by engineering. Such projects are expensive and with complex socioeconomic consequences. It should, however, be possible to regain and thereafter preserve the agricultural productivity of the entire landscape. Desalinization of the Imperial Valley (USA) was achieved in 20 y. Despite the cost and complexity it should be considered as the principal planning option for the maintenance of long-term agricultural productivity.

The alternative of living with salt will also involve considerable, but continuing, cost to lower the saline watertable below the root zone. Perennial plants might be used to achieve this as they did in the native vegetation. There are some candidates among herbaceous agricultural species such as alfalfa and the grasses, phalaris and cocksfoot. These could maintain summer transpiration but would provide little grazing because of the need to maintain high LAI to be effective. Another avenue involves the introduction of native or exotic trees into the landscape. The problems to be resolved are: What species? Where in the landscape? What density? Would it work indefinitely? The evaluation of alternative pasture species and agroforestry systems for hydrologic control of salinization is now under way in southern Australia.

Whatever combination of techniques is adopted to manage salinity, the selection and breeding of salt-tolerant cultivars of present and alternative agricultural species may be a useful associated objective but will not in itself provide a solution. Salt-tolerant plants have inherently low productivity and reliance on them would inevitably worsen the problem to greater salt concentration levels from which land may be irrecoverable. Many are attracted to plant breeding as the way to solve the problem; ecological analysis teaches us otherwise.

### Soil acidification

There is now considerable evidence (see Fig. 16.7) that the soils have continued to become more acid (up to 1 pH unit) under the wheat–sheep system and that the change has already reduced productivity. It was once thought that phosphate fertilizer, despite its high calcium content, was the cause of increasing acidity. It is now apparent that it is increased production, particularly by legume pasture, and associated grazing that accelerate the change (Chapter 7).

Increased soil acidity reduces plant growth, in part, through changes to chemical

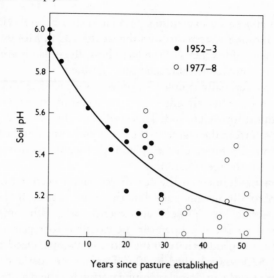

Fig. 16.7. The relationship between age of subterranean clover pasture and pH (1:5 in water), 0–10 cm. Measurements made in two periods, 1952–3 and 1977–8 (after Williams (1980).)

balances leading to aluminum and manganese toxicity and often a deficiency of molybdenum. In addition, the symbiosis between rhizobia and clover, which is the cornerstone of the system, is independently affected. The persistence of the bacterium in the soil and its capacity to form effective nodules with clover are both reduced.

As with the salinity problem, solution to soil acidity cannot rely upon the development of tolerance. More acid-tolerant cultivars and species are an interim objective. Some progress has been achieved in the development of acid-tolerant grasses (e.g. phalaris), but legumes remain a major difficulty. The limiting factor at present lays with the symbiosis because nodulation fails at higher pH than that at which the growth of the clover is affected. Soil acidification is an inevitable process under vegetation with leaching, particularly with agriculture (Chapter 7). On susceptible soils, the long-term management strategy must be to slow down and/or correct acidification of the soil profile. Concentration on the development of tolerant species may allow conditions to worsen to a point from which recovery is not economically feasible.

Acidity can be corrected by the ancient practice of adding lime, a technically feasible but expensive option. Treatment can be sustained when the expected yield increases of wheat and pasture promise sufficient return relative to the cost of lime. This is now the case in some fields in the Rutherglen area (Coventry 1985).

## 16.11   SUMMARY

Wheat is the principal cash crop in this mixed farming system. Inclusion of leguminous pasture in rotation with wheat provides the nitrogen needed for wheat production. It also provides weed, pest, and disease control so that wheat production can be managed in relation to the limiting resource, variable rainfall. It also provides diversification of income and distribution of labor requirement over the year.

The close interaction between crops and animals in this system shows how production depends upon an appreciation of both scientific and economic principles. Present farmers cope well through acquired experience but the range of interactions is great suggesting that thorough analyses, to assist in explanation and in the development of more sophisticated management, are needed. The development of comprehensive simulation models based on both agronomic and economic principles could be especially beneficial.

Although the present system was developed for a high degree of stability, particularly in terms of nutrient balance and water use, environmental problems require attention. No agricultural system, even the most primitive, can be easily managed to remain unchanged over time. As a human activity, agriculture needs attention to maintenance to adapt to internal change as well as to changes imposed upon it from outside.

## 16.12   FURTHER READING

Alexander, G. and O. B. Williams (eds.). 1973. *The pastoral industries of Australia: practices and technology of sheep and cattle production.* Sydney University Press. 567 p.

Callaghan, A. R. and A. J. Millington. 1956. *The wheat industry in Australia.* Angus & Robertson, Sydney. 486 p.

Connor, D. J. and D. F. Smith (eds). 1987. *Agriculture in Victoria.* Australian Institute of Agricultural Science, Melbourne. 231 p.

Duckham, A. N. and G. B. Masefield. 1970. *Farming systems of the world.* Praeger. 542 p.

Lazenby, A. and E. M. Matheson (eds). 1975. *Australian field crops. Wheat and other temperate cereals.* Angus & Robertson, Sydney. 570 p.

Moore, R. M. (ed.) 1970. *Australian grasslands.* Australian National University Press. 455 p.

# 17

## Mixed farming in the North American Corn Belt

### 17.1 INTRODUCTION

Farming systems of the North American Corn Belt contrast sharply with Victorian wheat–sheep farms. Cropping in an extensive area centered on the states of Iowa, Illinois, and Indiana (Fig. 17.1) is dominated by maize and soybean. Leguminous forages, oat, wheat, and pasture are also found within the region. The abundance of superior feed grains and forages leads to a strong emphasis on production of swine, beef cattle, and dairy products. The climate is too cold and the growing season too short for subtropical crops such as rice, cotton, sugarcane, and citrus. A number of fruits and vegetables can be grown but competing regions such as California generally produce those with higher quality and with less risk and less cost.

Much of the original vegetation in this region was tall-grass prairie and oak savannah on level to gently undulating glacial till, loess, and alluvium. When farming began in 1830, tall-grass prairies presented a rather hostile environment. Traditional wooden plows were inadequate for breaking sod and shortages of wood for fencing and fuel were a concern. John Deere's steel plow (1840) pulled by heavy oxen opened the land; invention of a practical barbed wire (1870) allowed development of mixed farming with livestock; and invention of elevator grain storage buildings facilitated handling and shipping of grains by rail and barge. Technological change has continued to be a fundamental feature of Corn-Belt farming. Hybrid maize resistant to stalk rot (1930), soybean as a new crop (1935), low-cost ammonium fertilizer (1950), herbicides (1950), and chisel plows (adopted in the 1970s) are recent innovations that have brought dramatic change to crop production.

Diffusion of new technology was sometimes very rapid and sometimes slow. Transition to hybrid maize was 99% complete in 10 years but the combine harvester, invented in Michigan in 1840 and widely used in California and Washington since 1870, was not scaled to the Iowa farm until the 1930s. Innovation came from within the system as well as from outside. The Parson trencher, developed in Grinnell, Iowa, for installation of subsurface drainage, came to worldwide use, and immigrant Dutch and German farmers introduced legume rotations.

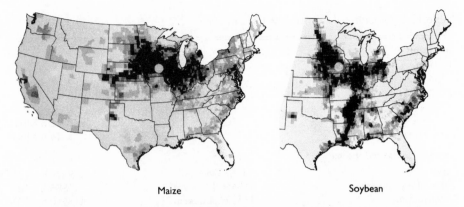

Maize                                    Soybean

Fig. 17.1. Maps of continental USA illustrating the concentration of maize production (left) in a 'Corn Belt' across various counties in upper midwest states. Soybean (right) has a similar distribution except that it is also found in the lower Mississippi Valley (bottom center of map) and along the Atlantic coastal plain. A total of 32 Mha is given to maize and 26 Mha to soybean. Maize and soybean production also extend into Ontario, Canada. Location of the example farm is indicated by a white circle. (From Bureau of the Census (1984).)

## Farming in Iowa

An analysis of farming in Iowa provides insights into the character of the Corn Belt. Evolution of the Iowa systems was as strongly influenced by the knowledge, energy, and culture of the pioneer settlers (English, German, Dutch and Scandinavian) as it was by the great fertility of prairie soils. The land was settled in homestead grants of 65 ha and is privately owned as family farms. In the American survey system of sections, a square-mile section (640 acres, 259 ha) was subdivided into 40-acre (16.2 ha) units; four of these, a 'quarter-section' (160 acres, 64.8 ha), constituted a homestead grant. The change from animal power to tractor power significantly increased the productivity of labor and thus the possible size of a family farm. Combined with greater incomes from urban jobs, that has caused farm population to decline since 1940 while farm size has increased (Loomis 1984). Farms are now fewer and farm families smaller, in part because mechanization reduced the advantage from child labor.

Most farms were once involved in raising both cattle and swine for market. Swine production is still a major activity in Iowa but it is restricted now to a small number of intensively managed operations. Beef production and with it areas of land given to pasture and forages have declined sharply in recent years. High prices for grain during the 1970s, consumer concerns about dietary cholesterol, and increased competition from the Great Plains contributed to making small-scale beef operations less profitable in Iowa. Since 1960, new pump-irrigation systems have been introduced in the Plains states. These produce low cost grains close to cattle ranches and have led to the development of large, highly efficient, feedlots. With the loss of that traditional source of feeder cattle, beef production in Iowa is now mostly in

Table 17.1 *Agricultural statistics for Iowa in 1987*

| *Iowa farms* Size class | Number | Area |
|---|---|---|
| 0–20 ha | 18 960 | |
| 20–72 ha | 66 630 | |
| > 72 ha | 19 600 | |
| All farms | 105 200 | |
| Total area of state | | 12.8 Mha |
| | | 14.6 Mha |

| *Estimated value and income* | Mean | Total value |
|---|---|---|
| Land | US$2340 ha$^{-1}$ | US$29.9 × 10$^9$ |
| Value of equipment | US$58 400 farm$^{-1}$ | US$6.1 × 10$^9$ |
| Gross income | US$99 000 farm$^{-1}$ | US$10.8 × 10$^9$ |
| Expenses | US$77 500 farm$^{-1}$ | US$8.5 × 10$^9$ |
| Net income | US$21 400 farm$^{-1}$ | US$2.3 × 10$^9$ |

| *Livestock products marketed* | Total amount | Total value |
|---|---|---|
| Swine | 21.3 × 10$^6$ head | US$2.7 × 10$^9$ |
| Beef cattle | 2.9 × 10$^6$ head | US$1.4 × 10$^9$ |
| Dairy | 1.6 × 10$^9$ l | US$0.4 × 10$^9$ |
| Poultry | | US$0.1 × 10$^9$ |

| *Harvested crops* | Area | Production Mean | Production Total | Total value |
|---|---|---|---|---|
| Maize (grain) | 4.0 Mha | 7050 kg | 28.2 Mt | US$1.8 × 10$^9$ |
| Soybean | 3.2 Mha | 2620 kg | 8.4 Mt | US$1.6 × 10$^9$ |
| Oat | 0.3 Mha | 1540 kg | 0.4 Mt | US$42.0 × 10$^6$ |
| Hay | 0.8 Mha | 7500 kg | 6.3 Mt | US$0.3 × 10$^9$ |
| Other crops[1] | 0.3 Mha | | | |
| Not harvested[1] | 1.5 Mha | | | |
| Other land[1] | 3.3 Mha | | | |

| *Fertilizer use* | N | P | K |
|---|---|---|---|
| Total state (t) | 840 700 | 68 200 | 420 100 |
| Per ha cropland (kg) | 98 | 8 | 49 |

Note:
[1] 'Other crops' are mainly wheat and rye; 'not harvested' includes approximately 32 kha of crop failure and 1.4 Mha of new seedings in set-aside and CRP programs; 'other land' includes established CRP, woodland, farmsteads, farm roads, and pasture.
*Sources:* From Iowa Agricultural Statistics (1988); Bureau of the Census (1984).

areas having permanent pastures on soils marginal for farming. Elsewhere, cash sales of grain for export have replaced cattle feeding. Engaged as they are in bulk production of low-value commodities (maize and soybean), net income per ha for most Iowa farms is small. In addition, commodity prices and land values have been unstable in recent years.

Data presented in Table 17.1 illustrate the present character of agriculture in Iowa. Maize and soybean acreage now seeded to grass in government-sponsored conservation reserves accounts for much of the 'not-harvested' area shown in the table. In Iowa, the numbers of large and small farms are both increasing gradually while the total number of farms is declining. The smallest farms (18% of total farms) average about 8 ha in size and occupy only 1.1% of the arable land. Most small farms consist of surplus homesteads and marginal farm land sold from large farms. They can be viewed as an urban extension because the principal employment and income of these 'weekend farmers' comes from urban jobs. In contrast, more than half of the arable land is held by farms larger than 200 ha.

### An example farm

We will analyze an imaginary farm located along the North Skunk River in Jasper County, Iowa (70 km east of Des Moines at 41° N, 93° W). The analysis is based in part on information about yields and crop and livestock management obtained from local farmers. The farm consists of 400 ha extending from flatlands in the river floodplain, over hill lands of the river breaks (5–18% slopes), to undulating uplands (Fig. 17.2). Extensive, low-cost methods of production are used and yields are average for the region (i.e., about 0.6 of local record yields). The distribution of cropland and pasture is dictated by spatial patterns of soils and topography. All of the principal crops of the region (maize, soybean, oat, and legume forages) are grown on the cropland. The farm does not have swine or dairy cattle. Swine production is found on one-third of farms in this county but dairying, for local markets, is a specialized activity on only 2% of farms. Whereas most of northern and western Iowa are given to grain production, farms on hilly loess soils in southern portions of the state are still involved in beef production. This farm possesses elements of both systems.

## 17.2 CLIMATE

The Corn Belt climate is midcontinental and temperate with cold winters and a limited frost-free season (140–170 days). Summers are warm (July mean near 24 °C with diurnal amplitude of 4 °C) and humid; 70% of the moderate annual rainfall (700–1000 mm) is received during the growing season from May through September. Our farm averages 160 days of frost-free weather and $840 \pm 150$ (SD) mm of precipitation. Humidity limits daily total radiation to 20–23 MJ $m^{-2}$ $d^{-1}$ in midsummer. Crop ET during summer averages 5 mm $d^{-1}$ whereas rainfall is only about 3.5 mm $d^{-1}$. Therefore, most crops also depend upon soil moisture that accumulates from spring rains and snowmelt. Severe drought, hail from strong storms, early frost in fall, and difficult conditions in spring (too dry, cold, or wet) are the principal environmental risks. Drought is not uncommon and crops would sometimes benefit from supplemental irrigations but supplies of surface and ground waters are limited and capital costs of standby sprinkling equipment are large. Maize (determinate development) is most susceptible to drought at anthesis while soybean (indeterminate), given the absence of an early frost, can compensate for loss of early flowers.

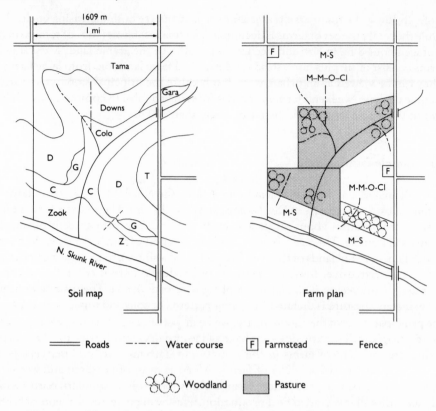

Fig. 17.2. Map of soil types, field boundaries, and land use for the
example Iowa farm. M–S, maize–soybean rotation on level land;
M–M–O–Cl, maize–maize–oat–clover rotation on sloping land. Pasture and
woodland areas are shaded. The distribution of area is given in Table 17.2.
The soils are described by Nestrud & Worster (1979).

## 17.3   SOILS

Glaciation during the Recent Quaternary Period was a dominant factor in landscape
and soil formation in this region. Compared to Australian soils, Corn Belt soils are
all young and relatively unleached of their original nutrients. Early extensions of the
Canadian glaciers ('Nebraskan' and 'Kansan' periods) deposited 5–10 m of till over
most of the region. During the most recent, 'Wisconsin', glaciation (14 000 BP), ice
lobes extended into central Iowa (the 'Des Moines lobe') and northern Illinois, and
soils in those areas formed on gently undulating till. Surface drainage is poor and
marshes and lakes are common. South of those lobes, paleosoils of the Kansan till
(29 000–14 000 BP) were covered by as much as 15 m of silty loess blown from glacial
outwash during the Wisconsin Period. In both regions, fire served to maintain
grasses in the prairie and oak-savannah while protected areas supported mixed
hardwood forest. In places, river valleys have cut through the over-mantles of loess
and till, exposing earlier tills and paleosoils, and creating alluvial plains. Mollisols

Table 17.2 *Land utilization and production on the example Iowa farm*

Production figures are given as dry mass. Normal moisture levels are: maize, 0.15; soybean, 0.13; oat, 0.11; hay, 0.12. Nutrient contents of the crops are adapted from National Research Council (1982).

| Crop | Area (ha) | Yield (kg ha$^{-1}$) | Production (t) | Nutrient content (kg kg$^{-1}$) | | |
|---|---|---|---|---|---|---|
| | | | | N | P | K |
| Maize: grain | 130 | 7000 | 910 | 0.016 | 0.0029 | 0.004 |
| stover | | 6000 | 780 | 0.009 | 0.0010 | 0.015 |
| Soybean | 50 | 2350 | 118 | 0.068 | 0.0065 | 0.018 |
| Oat | 40 | 2100 | 84 | 0.021 | 0.0038 | 0.004 |
| Forage | 40 | 6000 | 240 | 0.025 | 0.0025 | 0.016 |
| Pasture | 100 | 4000 | 400 | 0.020 | 0.0034 | 0.020 |
| Set-aside | 13 | — | — | — | — | — |
| Uncropped | 27 | — | — | — | — | — |
| Total | 400 | | 2532 | | | |

(FAO, Chernozems) dominate grassland sites, while Alfisols are found with woodland influence.

Our imaginary farm lies southeast of the Des Moines lobe and its soils were formed mostly on loess (Nestrud & Worster 1979; Fig. 17.2). Well-drained, Tama silty clay loam (Mollisol on loess with grassland) and Downs silt loam (Alfisol on loess with oak–savannah) are found on uplands. Patches of Gara loam (Alfisol on Kansan till paleosoil with woodland) occur on lower slopes. Colo silt loam occurs on alluvial fans, and Zook silty clay loam in alluvial river plains. Colo and Zook soils are both Mollisols, formed under poorly drained grassland. Tama, Downs, and Gara soils are all subject to erosion. Water courses on the slopes are provided with subsurface drains (perforated plastic pipe) and are permanently grassed. Farming is done in approximate contour strips with permanently grassed headlands for turning. Conservation rotations with a sod–crop phase are practiced on the steeper (6–14%) slopes. Colo soils receive runoff and seepage from the uplands and are mostly left in permanent pasture. The level Zook soil is also wet and subject to occasional flooding; it is provided with subsurface drainage and cropped continuously.

## 17.4 FARMING OPERATIONS

Of the 400 ha (1000 acres) on the example farm, 270 are arable, 100 are permanent pasture, and 30 are given to farmsteads, grassed headlands and watercourses, and woodland. An additional 300 ha are farmed for a retired neighbor under a share-cropping arrangement. That operation is not included in the present analysis. Permanent streams supply water for cattle in the pastures; deep wells service the house and cattle lots. The present cropping plan and normal production levels are given in Table 17.2.

The arable land is subject to two different rotations based on low-cost methods of production. Level lands are in a maize–soybean rotation (MS) while a maize–maize–oat–forage (MMOCl) sequence is used on sloping land. The basic forage crop is a mixture of red clover (a short-lived perennial) and smooth bromegrass. Alfalfa and birdsfoot trefoil (both perennials) are incuded when the sod is to be maintained beyond the second year. Forages are seeded in spring with oat as a companion crop. The unimproved permanent pastures evolved under grazing and are dominated by common perennial bluegrass with an understory of trefoil.

The cattle herd consists of 120 cows and 5 bulls. On average, 114 calves (95% yield) are reared each year.

The work force consists of father and son as owner–operators. Present value (1990) of land, farmsteads, equipment, and stock is near US$1 700 000. Investments in machinery are significant. The main tractor (225 kW (300 HP), four-wheel drive, diesel) is supported by two 100 kW (133 HP) machines. These tractors are about 30% more powerful than are needed for the annual work of the farm and share-cropped land. Smaller machines would suffice if tillage were done in fall but this farm needs crop aftermaths for grazing during winter and sloping lands need a protective cover of residue. Most of the tillage is done during a short period in spring when the land is sufficiently dry on less than 50% of the days. Timeliness is important and a powerful tractor pulling wide tools at moderate speed represents an efficient means for risk reduction. The main tractor is matched with 8 m chisel plow and tandem disk and an 8 m field cultivator. It can cover 5 ha $h^{-1}$ with the chisel plow on medium soils, and 3 ha $h^{-1}$ on heavy soils. Other major implements include a self-propelled combine harvester (with a row-crop head for maize and cutter-bar head for oat and soybean), baler, cultivators, mowers, grain trucks, hammer mill (for grinding grain), and feed mixer.

Income varies widely from year to year depending on yields and prices (which tend to be negatively correlated) and success in marketing. Gross sales from the 400 ha with average yields range from US$190 000 to US$230 000 per year with about 50% of that from sale of stock. Annual profit (after allowance for owner's labor and management and all costs, including maintenance, depreciation, and land tax), as was the case in Australia, is only 1–2% on capital. That small rate of return explains why almost all American farmland is and will continue to be held in family farms rather than by investors.

Farm operations and income are affected strongly by several government programs. Current programs are responses to world-wide commodity surpluses that have undercut the Corn Belt's traditional role in export trade of maize and soybean. If a farmer agrees to certain acreage limitations on maize production (crop land is 'set aside' and planted to grass) and certain conservation practices, government will accept harvested maize as collateral for short-term loans and provide 'deficiency' payments for the difference between the loan price and a 'fair' price based on costs of production. In addition, erodible crop land may be leased to the government for 10 y periods in a 'conservation reserve program' (CRP). CRP lands must be maintained in grass or planted to trees and, like the set-aside, may not be grazed or harvested for forage.

Set-aside and CRP programs have brought commodity surpluses to manageable levels and have elevated and stabilized farm incomes but not without some negative effects. Rotations are disturbed because farmers feel pressured to maintain large areas in row crops (maize and soybean) in order to meet set-aside requirements. One result is that soybean, which leaves little protective residue, is sometimes planted on erodible land. In addition, the floor under grain prices has made livestock production less profitable.

## 17.5　MAIZE AND SOYBEAN PRODUCTION

### Tillage systems

This farm employs conservation tillage using a chisel plow (Chapter 12). Sloping lands that need protection against erosion with surface residues are plowed in spring. That allows grazing of maize residues ('stover') by cattle during winter but it is difficult to achieve timeliness in spring operations of seedbed preparation. Early planting of maize is important in this region to minimize damage by the European corn borer (*Pyrausta nubilalis*) and corn rootworm (*Diabrotica longicornis*) which begin activity in early summer, and to reduce the risk of injury from drought or high temperatures at anthesis. Soils warm too slowly with no-till for timely planting of maize and that method is used by only a few farmers and only for soybean. To ease the burden of spring operations, our farmers chisel the flatlands in fall.

During land preparation, residues of sod crops (forages) and maize sometimes need to be cut with the heavy disk before chiseling. Soybean offers only light residues and preparation for the following crop of maize is accomplished with disk or field cultivator. Fertilizers impregnated with pre-emergence herbicides are spread by contractors and incorporated with disk or field cultivator during spring tillage.

### Maize crop

Maize is the principal crop in this system. Commercial, single-cross cultivars of a '120-day' maturity class are planted, beginning in late April when temperatures can be expected to remain above 13 °C (maize is a C4 species and subject to chilling injury). The crop is drilled with 5.7 grains $m^{-1}$ in 0.76 m rows for a final population of 75 000 $ha^{-1}$ (30 000 $acre^{-1}$). If cold, wet weather delays planting into May, an earlier-maturing cultivar may be used, or, in emergencies, the land may be diverted to soybean. That substitution is not possible, however, where fertilizer and pre-emergence herbicides are already in place.

The normal phenological advance for maize in Iowa is illustrated in Fig. 17.3. Progress is slow during cool weather in spring but in summer, high average temperature and small diurnal amplitude cause a relatively rapid rate of development. As a result, the effective grain-filling period is generally only 38–40 calendar days. In contrast, at Davis, California, in a semiarid environment with nearly the same mean temperature but twice the diurnal amplitude of Iowa, effective grain-filling periods for the same cultivars are 44–48 days. The growth and partitioning

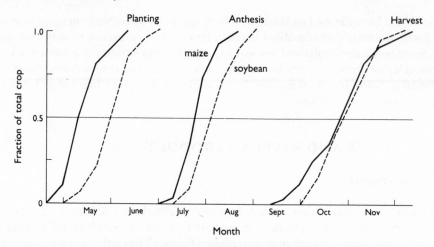

Fig. 17.3. Average seasonal phenology of maize and soybean crops in the western Corn Belt. The graphs depict cumulative occurrence of planting, flowering, and harvest. Distortion in the maize harvest curve occurs when it is interrupted to harvest soybean. Individual years vary from these patterns by as much as several weeks. At the example farm, timing of events falls at about the 50-percentile level. (Redrawn from Iowa Agricultural Statistics (1989).)

patterns for maize presented earlier in Fig. 2.1 are representative of those seen on this farm. The canopy closes about 40 days after emergence and thereafter crop growth rate is nearly constant for 70 d at 150–170 kg ha$^{-1}$ d$^{-1}$. Peak leaf area index is near 4; assuming 80% interception, radiation-use efficiency is about 1 g biomass MJ$^{-1}$.

Maize grain contains 0.013 to 0.016 N. With expected yields of 7 ± 1.5 t ha$^{-1}$, 120 kg N ha$^{-1}$ as granular urea are used on this farm for maize after maize and maize after bean. After forage, 90 kg N ha$^{-1}$ are applied. Our farmers also apply 25 kg P and 75 kg K ha$^{-1}$ for each crop of maize.

Diseases are not a major problem for maize production in Iowa and fungicide treatment of seed is the only general practice. Conservation tillage with surface residues results in a greater frequency of foliar diseases and *Diplodia* and *Gibberella* stalk rots than occurs with moldboard plowing. Resistant cultivars, rotation, and adequate nutrition are the main elements in control. Rootworms and stalk borers are the principal insect pests. Present cultivars offer adequate resistance to borers and insecticides are employed only with severe infestations. Rootworm is controlled mainly by rotation. In maize–maize (MM) sequences, evidence of root lodging in the first year of maize is the basis for banded application of insecticide at planting of the second crop, or for altering the rotation. A population of the northern corn rootworm with an extended, 2 y diapause is an increasing problem in the maize–soybean (MS) rotation. This farm occasionally has problems with other soil insects, particularly after the sod phase in the MMOCl rotation, but no controls are employed.

Weeds offer a serious challenge to maize production, particularly after sod. Intense competition and repeated mowing provide general weed control in the oat–

forage sequence, and herbicides are employed in maize portions of the rotation. Control by those means is significantly less effective, however, than the alternating sequence of maize and soybean herbicides plus tillage found in the MS rotation. The preplant herbicides employed with maize (EPTC or cyanazine and alachlor) usually provide effective suppression of the principal annual grass (foxtail, *Setaria* spp.) and broadleaf species (lambsquarters, *Chenopodium album*; ragweed, *Ambrosia artemisii-folia*). Post-emergence herbicides (2,4–D and dicambia or tridiphane and atrazine) are directed at other dicots including cocklebur (*Xanthium canadense*), pigweed (*Amaranthus* spp.) and perennial bindweed (*Convolvulus arvensis*). Cocklebur has an interesting two-seeded fruit. One seed germinates after one winter, the second has extended dormancy and tends to germinate in the following year. Control of other perennials such as hemp dogbane (*Apocynum cannabinum*), Canada thistle (*Cirsium arvense*), on the other hand, is poor because they tend to escape damage by the chisel plow. The wide sweeps of the field cultivator are effective on perennials but our farmers find it useful to also mechanically cultivate maize with sweeps once after emergence and to spot spray thistle and other persistent weeds with specific herbicides.

Maize grain maturity, indicated by formation of a black layer at the base of the grain, occurs at a rather high moisture content (*ca.* 0.23). The crop can be left standing to dry naturally to a safe storage level (0.15) but that involves exposure to weather and lodging damage, particularly when harvest is delayed by rain. Yields are less and risks are reduced only a small amount with early maturing cultivars. The general practice in the Corn Belt is to combine-harvest the grain wet (0.18 to 0.22 moisture) and dry it artificially. Elevator companies provide that service. Our farmers are able to do it more cheaply, however, with a 500 t storage building equipped with a propane-fired drier plus two 500 t storage units for dry grain. This practice also allows more flexibility in marketing. Part of the crop is sold and part is fed to the growing cattle.

## Soybean crop

The soybean cultivars grown in this system have shorter life cycles than maize (Fig. 17.3). That distributes spring field work more evenly because beans are planted in early May after maize operations are completed.

Soybean is grown only in the MS rotation and tillage consists of heavy disk (if needed) followed by chisel plow and field cultivator. This tillage system leaves insufficient residues for erosion protection on sloping land, however, and the MS rotation is limited to level soils. Locally grown seed of commercial cultivars is drilled in 0.76 m rows with a final stand near 325 000 ha$^{-1}$ (130 000 acre$^{-1}$). Use of the same row spacing for both maize and soybean simplifies planter adjustments to change of plates and depth control and eliminates the need to adjust wheel spacings of tractors during post-emergence cultivations.

Farmers in this region do not apply rhizobia inoculum to soybean because the soils are populated with rhizobia and there is no measurable benefit from specific inoculum. Small 'starter' applications of nitrogen (*ca.* 40 kg N ha$^{-1}$) are employed by some farmers but are omitted from our budgets. Soybean establishes full cover in about 45 days and eventually reaches LAI 4 or more. During the period of full cover, crop growth rates are nearly constant (Hanway & Weber 1971) and, for our crop, would average 14 g m$^{-2}$ d$^{-1}$ for about 45 d. Radiation utilization with 80% interception is near 0.9 g biomass MJ$^{-1}$. As was the case for maize, our farmers' yields are about average for the Corn Belt (2400 ± 500 kg ha$^{-1}$ at 0.12 moisture). Attainable yields at the best locations exceed 4000 kg ha$^{-1}$.

No serious insect or disease problems interfere with soybean production in this part of Iowa. No seed treatment is used and insect control is limited to suppression of spider mite in dry years.

Weed problems with soybean are similar but generally less severe than those encountered with maize. If the maize program is successful, then the bean ground will be relatively clean. Preplant applications of alachlor or metolachlor herbicides are incorporated with the field cultivator and followed by a post-emergence herbicide (usually chlorimuron), if needed, and cultivation. Tall weeds and volunteer maize that emerge from the canopy are sometimes attacked with glyphosate herbicide from an overhead 'wick' boom. The height of the boom is set to contact foliage of plants that emerge above the crop.

Soybean is also combine-harvested. In this case, grain is delivered directly to the elevator since none is consumed on the farm. Marketing can be delayed if storage fees at the elevator are met. Because soybean is more subject to lodging and shattering losses than maize, the crop is harvested when mature in early October; maize harvest is worked around that of soybean (see Fig. 17.3).

## 17.6   OAT AND FORAGE PRODUCTION

The forage needs of this farm are significant. With a base of 120 cows, the minimum annual feed requirement is more than 700 t dry matter of which nearly 200 t is legume–grass hay (Table 17.3). This is produced in the sod phase of the MMOCl rotation. After 2 y of maize, erodible lands are disked and broadcast seeded in early spring to legume and grass forages with oat as a companion crop. Improved cultivars of each are used. Farmers sometimes save their own oat seed, one of few such examples remaining in the Corn Belt. The seed are incorporated with the field cultivator or light disk harrow. These simple methods generally provide good stands of both oat and forage providing care is given to achieving an even distribution of a high rate of forage seed. Variations in legume stands, in addition to lowering forage yield and increasing opportunities for weeds, cause spatial variability in the supply of nitrogen to subsequent crops. No herbicides are used for weed control during the two years of the oat–forage sequence.

The companion oat crop is combine-harvested in midsummer (yields average 2100 kg ha$^{-1}$). The straw is normally baled and saved as bedding for livestock. Developing stands of forages are left alone during the remainder of the first year unless mowing for weed control seems desirable. Some grazing is done in dry years when bluegrass pastures are unproductive. In the second year, the forage is cut three times, sun-cured, and put up in round, 600 kg bales. The bales are stored on high

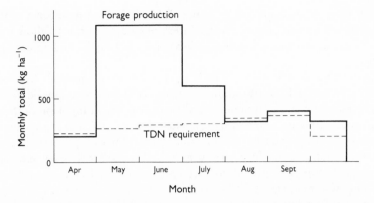

**Fig. 17.4. Monthly patterns of dry matter production in bluegrass pastures, and TDN requirements of 1.25 cow–calf units per hectare. The factor 1.25 adjusts for stocking rate. Because the TDN value of the forage is only 0.7, hay must sometimes be fed in late summer and fall. (Data from Littlefield (1980).)**

ground in field margins where they can be accessed in winter. Storage losses of 5–10% can be reduced by wrapping the bales in polyethylene but that practice is not common. In the third year, the sod is normally returned to maize.

Forage mixtures vary. Red clover and smooth brome are the principal components on this farm but alfalfa and birdsfoot trefoil are also included. Digestibility of the hay by cattle is low (about 0.55) but palatability and intake are good. The market value of such hay is low and while surplus supplies can be sold locally, intensive dairies in adjacent states (Wisconsin, Minnesota) turn in emergencies to high quality alfalfa produced in the Great Plains. Our farmers prefer clover to alfalfa because of a smaller risk of winter injury but that problem is less with new cultivars and pure stands of alfalfa (with or without the oat companion) are now used on some farms in this area.

## 17.7 PASTURE PRODUCTION

The 100 ha perennial-bluegrass pasture is the least intensively managed portion of the farm and, in some years, is its weakest link. These pastures evolved from prairie communities dominated by big bluestem grass with native bluegrass as only a minor component. The pastures are now dominated by Kentucky bluegrass, which seems to be of Eurasian origin and to have migrated through North America with settlers and wild animals.

Growth resumes in spring as temperatures rise in late April. The seasonal pattern of production is illustrated in Fig. 17.4 along with the forage requirements of the herd. Calculations in Table 17.3 reveal that the herd will need only 246 t of the 400 t dry forage produced in average years and forage is surplus in late spring but frequently in short supply in late summer. Such mismatches plague most grazing systems. The size of the cow herd is balanced optimistically to normal years. Palatability and digestibility (0.7) of the young forage are excellent but quality declines if the grass is undergrazed. Some rest is desirable for rhizome growth in bluegrass to insure stand vigor. The pastures are fenced in units to allow rotation during the season but most rhizome growth occurs during the undergrazed period in spring.

Nitrogen dressings (40–80 kg N $ha^{-1}$ $y^{-1}$) increase the yield of bluegrass and extend its production later into summer but generally are not economic. Birdsfoot trefoil produces well in late summer and also is a desirable component of the sward for its nitrogen contribution and its tolerance of wet soil (Colo in this example). Pastures can be improved by seeding trefoil into narrow, tilled strips but the expense is generally not justified by returns. Cropping to maize or oat as a basis for reseeding with superior grasses and legumes is impractical because of slope, wetness, and water courses.

Bluegrass and trefoil are intolerant of acid soil. The pastures are amended occasionally with lime because the soils tend to acidify under grazing due to base metal extraction and leaching. The pastures are usually mown once in summer for weed and brush control. The original savannah was maintained by fire. With elimination of fire, the tendency for succession to brush and trees is very strong. Canadian thistle is a special problem requiring spot sprays of herbicides.

## 17.8   CATTLE OPERATIONS

### Annual plan

The beef herd consists of 120 head of cross-bred English cows (Angus × Hereford breeds, black with white face) and five European bulls (Limousin, Charolais, and Simmental breeds). The cows and bulls are purchased from other farmers who engage in purebred programs with the various breeds. The farm employed a local strain of large, purebred, English Shorthorn cattle during its first 100 y, and this new herd represents a sharp change in animal husbandry. The principles underlying the crossbred cows are to have small (500 kg, 1100 lb) animals for minimum feed requirement yet hardy of severe winters. In addition, the Angus strain carries with it a trait for small-headed calves (fewer calving problems). The bull breeds also favor small head size. More important, they throw 36 kg calves of high growth rate with a good size at weaning (190 kg at 5 months), a slightly greater dressing percentage to red meat, and a smaller fat content than traditional English breeds.

The general plan of cattle operations is as follows. The cows are turned to pasture for calving when grass growth begins in April. Calving extends over an 8–10 week period during which bulls are segregated from the herd. The animals have access to mineral supplements while on pasture. Calves are weaned in November (after crop harvest) and put in the feeding lot on hay with supplements of grain and minerals. Feeding is done on a concrete platform where the growing calves have ready access to feed, shelter, and water. The cattle are vaccinated and wormed at various times in the year. The male calves are castrated by pinching when young. All animals are de-liced in the fall, and calves are given hormone implants when they enter the feedlot.

At weaning, the cows are culled, based on pregnancy tests, condition, and age, and turned into stalk fields with access to shelter from severe winter storms (sheds and woodlands serve as windbreaks). Between 10 and 15% of the cows are replaced each year. The supply of maize stover, including a small amount of lost grain, averages 6000 kg ha$^{-1}$ with digestibility near 0.6. Grazing in stalk fields is limited by snow cover, wetness, and by the need to retain about 4000 kg residue ha$^{-1}$ until the beginning of spring tillage.

Feeding of the calves begins in earnest in January when the hay ration is reduced and concentrate (ground corn mixed with soybean meal, antibiotics to optimize rumen flora, and mineral supplements) is supplied *ad libitum*. The TDN factor for the ration is near 0.85. The calves remain on full feed until their sale in September at 500 kg live mass (1100 lb).

**Feed requirements**

The annual pattern of TDN and dry matter use by the cattle operation is summarized in Table 17.3. For simplicity, rations were calculated on a TDN basis (total digestible nutrients; the mass equivalent of DE in Table 1.3), rather than net energy (NE); TDN values tend to underestimate the merit of hay and overestimate that of concentrate. Given the seasonal movement of animals and diets common in this area, Table 17.3 was constructed by using TDN requirements assembled by Littlefield (1980). At the bottom of the table, the amounts of hay and concentrate are increased by 10% to 194 t and 211 t, respectively, to accommodate waste in feeding. The critical role of forages in ruminant diets is apparent. The annual requirement of 468 t TDN is met 70% from roughage and 30% from concentrate. Only 10.5 t or 1.5% of the 711 t is purchased oil-seed meal. For simplicity, stover consumption from stalk fields is shown only during late fall (October–December). In practice, cows and bulls are left there as long as a supply of feed remains in order to minimize their maintenance cost. The 60 t of stover consumed translates to 462 kg ha$^{-1}$ of the 6000 kg supply.

This budget uses 194 t of the normal annual supply of 240 t hay. That seems like a generous margin but, with losses in storage and the need to supplement pastures in drought years, hay is sometimes in short supply. The option of additional use of stover adds a margin of safety, however. The animal-carrying capacity of this farm could be increased significantly through pasture improvement (e.g. by fertilizer) and through expansion of acreage given to forages. That route is likely with a further decline in grain prices because cattle would then provide greater added value to the maize. The grain base would also support a return to swine production; our farmers have avoided that because of the large capital and labor requirements. Instead, they buy additional feeder cattle (weaned calves) at local markets when prices are favorable.

The average gain per animal in the feedlot is 310 kg (500 kg finish − 190 kg at weaning) providing a total gain of 35.3 t for the 114 animals on feed. A total of 247 t of feed (36 t hay + 211 t concentrate) is used to achieve that. That ratio, 247/35.3 = 7

Table 17.3 (a) *Feed requirements for a 120-cow beef herd and for feeding the 114 calves produced each year*

Data are for the example Iowa farm. TDN requirements are from Littlefield (1980); TDN factors are from the National Research Council (1982). The patterns of feed sources employed are typical for central Iowa; H, hay; P, pasture; and S, maize stover.

| Month:<br>Cows on: | Jan<br>H | Feb<br>H | Mar<br>H | Apr<br>H–P | May<br>P | June<br>P | July<br>P | Aug<br>P | Sept<br>P | Oct<br>P–S | Nov<br>S | Dec<br>S–H |
|---|---|---|---|---|---|---|---|---|---|---|---|---|
| *TDN requirements, kg animal$^{-1}$ day$^{-1}$* | | | | | | | | | | | | |
| Cow | 3.68 | 3.81 | 4.13 | 6.08 | 6.67 | 6.67 | 6.67 | 6.08 | 5.40 | 4.80 | 3.54 | 3.59 |
| Calf | — | — | — | 0.18 | 0.50 | 1.00 | 1.50 | 2.00 | 2.81 | 3.68 | — | — |
| Lot-fed | 4.45 | 4.68 | 4.95 | 5.18 | 5.40 | 5.63 | 5.86 | 6.08 | 6.31 | — | 3.95 | 4.19 |
| Bull | 4.31 | 4.31 | 4.31 | 4.31 | 4.31 | 4.31 | 4.31 | 4.31 | 4.31 | 4.31 | 4.31 | 4.31 |
| *Number of animals* | | | | | | | | | | | | |
| Cows | 120 | 120 | 120 | 120 | 120 | 120 | 120 | 120 | 120 | 120 | 120 | 120 |
| Calves | 0 | 0 | 0 | 60 | 116 | 115 | 114 | 114 | 114 | 114 | — | — |
| Lot-fed | 114 | 114 | 114 | 114 | 114 | 114 | 114 | 114 | 114 | — | 114 | 114 |
| Bulls | 5 | 5 | 5 | 5 | 5 | 5 | 5 | 5 | 5 | 5 | 5 | 5 |
| Total TDN/d | 970 | 1012 | 1081 | 1353 | 1496 | 1579 | 1661 | 1673 | 1710 | 1017 | 897 | 930 |
| Days | 31 | 28 | 31 | 30 | 31 | 30 | 31 | 31 | 30 | 31 | 30 | 31 |
| TDN/month | 30070 | 28340 | 33530 | 40580 | 46380 | 47370 | 51490 | 51860 | 51300 | 31520 | 26900 | 28840 |
| *TDN sources* | | | | | | | | | | | | |
| Hay | 16120 | 15010 | 17800 | 13310 | 2440 | 2360 | 1770 | 1770 | 1710 | | 8378 | 16529 |
| Stover | | | | | | | | | | 15760 | 13400 | 7000 |
| Pasture | | | | 11280 | 26620 | 27470 | 30790 | 30360 | 29710 | 15760 | 5130 | 5300 |
| Feed | 13960 | 13330 | 15720 | 15990 | 17330 | 17540 | 18930 | 19730 | 19870 | | | |

(b) *Totals* $(t\ y^{-1})$

| Source | TDN | TDN factor | Dry matter | Waste allowance | Total feed |
|---|---|---|---|---|---|
| Hay | 97 | 0.55 | 176 | 18 | 194 |
| Stover | 36 | 0.60 | 60 | — | 60 |
| Pasture | 172 | 0.70 | 246 | — | 246 |
| Grain | 154 | 0.85 | 182 | 19 | 200 |
| Soybean meal | 9 | 0.85 | 11 | — | 11 |
| Total | 468 | 0.69 | 674 | 37 | 711 |

kg feed $kg^{-1}$ gain, is better than the Iowa average $(8 \pm 1kg\ kg^{-1})$ reflecting the small (190 kg) entry mass and the high proportion of concentrate in the ration. The average daily gain, 0.93 kg (2.04 lb), is also within the range found in an Iowa survey. In southern Iowa, greater returns are obtained by moving calving to March and April, placing calves on full feed in fall, and marketing in late spring. At our location, however, the Colo soil is too cold in early spring for the grass growth needed in that practice.

## 17.9   HYDROLOGY

ET* of maize crops in this environment, provided with adequate water supply, is near 610 mm and that of soybean about 560 mm. Annual precipitation (840 mm) exceeds those levels but summer rainfall is only about 450 mm and the balance of crop requirements must be met from soil moisture that accumulates during the fallow period. Drought is a principal factor limiting yields of crops and pastures to moderate levels; brief periods of drought occur in most summers and severe drought is experienced one year in 10.

The soil freezes in winter, and fall tends to be dry, therefore most profile replenishment occurs in spring. In addition to some sublimation of snow during winter, rapid snow melt coupled with spring rains result in significant runoff; runoff also occurs with heavy summer rains. The cropland averages 130 mm annual runoff. Runoff from pasture is less but its complete cover tends to be offset by steepness and 50–60 mm loss is common. With an undulating landscape, runoff–runon patterns occur and lower lands tends to receive too much moisture and generally must be protected by diversion channels constructed along the base of hills. Subsurface drainage is also needed for successful crop production.

Approximate hydrologic budgets for the various crops are presented in Table 17.4. The risk of drought is apparent: consumptive use by good crops of maize and soybean amounts to 70% or more of annual precipitation and the standard deviation for precipitation is 150 mm. The marked increase in drainage under cropping is a general phenomenon in agriculture since the duration of green cover is less than with natural vegetation. This contributes to the need for subsurface drain lines.

Table 17.4 *Approximate annual hydrologic terms for various crops in central Iowa*

| Crop | Precipitation (mm) | Runoff (mm) | Winter ET (mm) | Summer ET (mm) | Drainage (mm) |
|---|---|---|---|---|---|
| Maize | 840 | 125 | 30 | 610 | 75 |
| Soybean | 840 | 125 | 30 | 560 | 125 |
| Pasture & other | 840 | 85 | 30 | 700 | 25 |

*Source:* Personal communication of R. Kanwar & E. Taylor, Iowa State University.

## 17.10   NUTRIENT DYNAMICS

As was the case with the Australian farm, operations on this farm reveal the importance of considering nutrient dynamics on a farm basis. Our focus on nitrogen cycling begins with calculation of amounts of nitrogen consumed by the animals and amounts that can be recycled in manure.

   To estimate amounts of nitrogen in dung and urine, feed intakes from Table 17.3 were converted to N by using factors for the N content of the feeds (Table 17.2). The annual intake of the herd is 14.3 t N (Table 17.5). Calculations of amounts of nitrogen entering the feedlot and exiting to market were done by using a gut-fill regression from the Agricultural Research Council (1980) and nitrogen-content coefficients for empty-body and carcass masses from Garrett & Hinman (1969). Nitrogen in gut fill was estimated from data on digesta in cattle and sheep (Table 9–1 in Church (1976)). Export per marketed animal was:

| | | |
|---|---|---|
| Live mass | 500 kg | |
| Gut fill | 66 kg | |
| Empty-body mass (EBW) | 434 kg | |
| N in EBW (0.027 × EBW) | 11.7 kg | |
| N in gut fill | 0.2 kg | |
| N per animal | 11.9 kg | |
| N per dressed carcass | 7.4 kg | (0.017 of EBW; 0.025 of carcass) |

Total export then is 114 animals × 0.0119 t N animal$^{-1}$ = 1.36 t N of which 0.84 t is in red meat. Similar calculations indicate that 0.11 t of that nitrogen was accumulated during gestation, 0.39 t during grazing on pasture, and 0.86 t in the feed lot. It is assumed that the nitrogen content of cows sold is matched by that of replacement cows. Therefore, 4.91 t N intake from pasture (Table 17.5) − 0.39 t N exported with cattle = 4.52 t N deposited in dung and urine in pastures; for the lot, 5.55 t N in feed (Table 17.5) − 0.86 t N exported = 4.69 t N deposited in manure. For field and shelter areas, 3.62 to N were consumed, 0.11 t N exported, and 3.51 t N excreted.

   Nitrogen in dung and urine deposited by animals grazing pasture and stover recycle (or is lost) in the same fields. It is assumed that 30% of the nitrogen deposited during grazing is lost through volatilization of ammonia. Manure gathered from winter shelters where hay is fed, and the feedlot, is collected and

Table 17.5 *Annual intake (t) of feed and its content (t) of N, P, and K by the beef herd on the example Iowa farm arranged by sources of feed and place of feeding*

The example follows from Table 17.3 for a 120-cow herd producing 114 calves a year. The nutrient content factors came from Table 17.2.

| | Source of feed | | | | | |
| | Hay | Pasture | Stover | Maize | Meal | Total |
|---|---|---|---|---|---|---|
| Total feed: | 194 | 246 | 60 | 200 | 10.5 | 711 |
| *Place of feeding and total nutrient content* | | | | | | |
| N pasture | — | 4.91 | — | — | — | 4.91 |
| N field | — | — | 0.54 | — | — | 0.54 |
| N shelter | 3.19 | — | — | — | — | 3.19 |
| N lot | 1.67 | — | — | 3.20 | 0.67 | 5.55 |
| Total N | 4.86 | 4.91 | 0.54 | 3.20 | 0.67 | 14.19 |
| P pasture | — | 0.83 | — | — | — | 0.83 |
| P field | — | — | 0.19 | — | — | 0.19 |
| P shelter | 0.40 | — | — | — | — | 0.40 |
| P lot | 0.08 | — | — | 0.58 | 0.07 | 0.73 |
| Total P | 0.48 | 0.83 | 0.19 | 0.58 | 0.07 | 2.15 |
| K pasture | — | 4.85 | — | — | — | 4.85 |
| K field | — | — | 0.92 | — | — | 0.92 |
| K shelter | 2.58 | — | — | — | — | 2.58 |
| K lot | 0.57 | — | — | 0.74 | 0.23 | 1.54 |
| Total K | 3.15 | 4.85 | 0.92 | 0.74 | 0.23 | 9.89 |

applied as an external input to cultivated fields. Some composting occurs with the lot manure. We assume, optimistically, that about 36% of the nitrogen deposited in shelter areas ($0.365 \times 3.51 = 1.28$ t N), and 50% of that deposited in the lot ($0.5 \times 4.69 = 2.35$ t N), a total of 3.63 t N, can be recycled and added to soils in cultivated fields. The balance of the nitrogen deposited in shelter areas and lot (4.25 t N) seems to be lost mainly to the atmosphere. Runoff losses (mostly as suspended organic matter) have been increased slightly for the grazed areas and manured fields. Support for the assumption that runoff of mineral nitrogen is small comes from estimated total runoff (area in Table 17.2 × runoff per ha in Table 17.4) and observations that nitrate concentrations in the Skunk River decline sharply when runoff dominates stream flow (Baker & Johnson 1976). Because only 1 t of $NO_3$-N would bring its concentration in total runoff from this farm (*ca.* 200 000 $m^3$) to 0.36 mM, it seems that any significant loss through runoff would have to be in organic forms.

Phosphorus and potassium are not subject to gaseous losses and therefore survive better in manure than does N. Loss of P by leaching and runoff after spreading is less than for N while that of K is greater. About 1 t P and 4 t K are deposited in collectable manure on this farm.

Construction of nitrogen budgets for various fields (presented in Table 17.6) is

Table 17.6 *Estimated average annual nitrogen fluxes in the Iowa crop rotations* $(kg\ ha^{-1}\ y^{-1})$

| System: | MS | | MMOCl | | | | |
|---|---|---|---|---|---|---|---|
| Crop: | Maize | Soybean | Maize-1 | Maize-2 | Oat-Cl. | Grass–clover | Pasture grass–clover |
| Area (ha) | 50 | 50 | 40 | 40 | 40 | 40 | 100 |
| *Supplies to soil* | | | | | | | |
| Deposition[1] | 15 | 15 | 15 | 15 | 15 | 15 | 15 |
| Mineralization | 80 | 80 | 90 | 80 | 45 | 25 | 20 |
| Residue, previous crop[2] | 44 | 48 | 80 | 48 | 48 | 40 | 50 |
| Symbiotic fixation | 0 | 120 | 0 | 0 | 30 | 130 | 12 |
| Manure[3] | 27 | 13 | 5 | 20 | 10 | 5 | 32[4] |
| N fertilizer | 120 | 0 | 90 | 120 | 0 | 0 | 0 |
| Total supply | 286 | 276 | 280 | 283 | 148 | 215 | 129 |
| *Removals from soil* | | | | | | | |
| Plant uptake | 160 | 204 | 160 | 160 | 106 | 170 | 100 |
| Immobilization | 80 | 80 | 80 | 80 | 50 | 30 | 20 |
| Volatilization | 2 | 0 | 2 | 2 | 0 | 0 | 14[4] |
| Runoff | 6 | 4 | 6 | 5 | 4 | 2 | 2 |
| Leaching | 5 | 5 | 5 | 5 | 3 | 2 | 1 |
| Denitrification | 9 | 7 | 4 | 5 | 3 | 2 | 4 |
| Total removal | 270 | 300 | 257 | 257 | 166 | 206 | 145 |
| *Balances* | | | | | | | |
| Crop removal[5] | −112 | −160 | −112 | −112 | −44 | −150 | −4 |
| Losses[6] | −22 | −16 | −17 | −17 | −10 | −6 | −21 |
| Total output | −134 | −176 | −129 | −129 | −54 | −156 | −25 |
| External input[7] | 162 | 148 | 108 | 155 | 55 | 150 | 25 |
| Annual balance[8] | 28 | −28 | −21 | 26 | 1 | −6 | 0 |
| Cycle balance | | 0 | | | | 0 | 0 |

*Notes:*
[1] 8 kg N ha$^{-1}$ in rain and 7 kg as dry deposition and free fixation.
[2] Residue N is the net of residue and manure from stover grazing.
[3] Manure supplies 3.63 t N net to soil distributed equally to maize after soybean and maize after maize for an average of 40 kg ha$^{-1}$ y$^{-1}$. Availability of this nitrogen is distributed with the decay series 0.5, 0.25, 0.125, and 0.125 over successive years (Midwest Plan 1985).
[4] 70% of manure N deposited during grazing is cycled to the soil; 30% is shown as volatilization.
[5] Harvested crop × N content given in Table 17.2; meat export from pasture is explained in text.
[6] Sum of volatilization, runoff, leaching, and denitrification.
[7] Sum of deposition, fixation, manure from external sources, and fertilizer.
[8] Imbalances within and between years include undecomposed manure and residues plus some mineral N.

rather subjective because only a few of the fluxes can be estimated closely. Average crop yields and fertilizer applications are known but rainfall (and thus runoff and drainage), yields, nitrogen contents of produce and residues, nitrogen fixation, and nitrogen processes in soils are all subject to considerable spatial and temporal variation. No allowances have been made for differences in the yield potential of various soils and only slight differences in their nitrogen dynamics are shown. For simplicity, the set-aside is not included in the rotations.

Observations of nitrogen deposition through precipitation in this part of Iowa range from 4 kg ha$^{-1}$ N y$^{-1}$ (in 1985–7; personal communication, National Atmospheric Deposition Program) to 12.5 kg N ha$^{-1}$ y$^{-1}$ (in 1971–3; Tabatabai & Laflen 1976). Dry deposition is not known. The difference in these observations may reflect nearness of the collection stations to sources of cattle (more than 5 kg ammonia-N ha$^{-1}$ y$^{-1}$ is lost from manures on this farm), or changes in cattle numbers between the 1970s (12 × 10$^6$ cattle in Iowa) and the late 1980s (4 × 10$^6$). To be conservative, we have been generous in estimating inputs; the present analysis uses 8 kg ha$^{-1}$ for wet deposition and takes 7 kg as an additional allowance for dry deposition and fixation by free-living bacteria.

Mineralization of nitrogen in tilled soils was assumed to equal 0.012 y$^{-1}$ of total organic nitrogen content typically found in the surface layer (0.3 m) of these soils under cropping; that corresponds to about 0.03 y$^{-1}$ of an active stabilized fraction of the organic matter (Chapter 8). Smaller values were assigned to sod crop and pastures. In the real farms that served as models, yields and fertility practices have changed little in 15 y so we assumed that organic matter formation equals mineralization. Carry-over N in residues was set to the N content of residues at harvest. The fixation flux for soybean was set at 58% of plant uptake, in line with observations on moderately fertile land (Fig. 8.5) (Diebert *et al.* 1979), while that for clover was set to balance plant uptake within years and over the cycle. Fixation inputs, like those for rainfall, residue, and manure, are generous yet within the range of common observations.

Variables considered in the analysis to this point involve relatively large fluxes. The magnitudes of volatilization, leaching, and runoff fluxes are smaller and are not estimated easily. The total of such losses was obtained by difference from the other numbers; the distribution was made with help from observations reported by Kanwar *et al.* (1988*a*, *b*), with adjustments for soil type and position in rotation. Those estimates can be compared with observed concentrations of NO$_3$-N in drainage waters by placing the leaching estimate into the expected depth of drainage given in Table 17.4. The 5 kg N ha$^{-1}$ (357 mol) for soybean would be diluted into 1250 m$^3$ of drainage yielding a 0.3 mM effluent (i.e. 4 ppm NO$_3$-N); with maize, 5 kg would be diluted into 750 m$^3$ and the effluent would be 0.5 mM (7 ppm NO$_3$-N). Waters from wells, tile drains, streams, and lakes in Iowa range from 0.2 to over 1.0 mM NO$_3$-N; the approximate annual average observed for the Skunk River in 1972 was 0.7 mM (Baker & Johnson 1976).

Complex models of this sort deserve analysis of their sensitivity to important underlaying assumptions. To illustrate the frailty of this model, a decline in the nitrogen content of maize grain from 0.016 to 0.015 reduces nitrogen export in grain by 7 kg ha$^{-1}$; those 7 kg would allow for large increases in the estimates of nitrogen losses in Table 17.6. One obviously must be careful about placing confidence in small numbers estimated from differences between large, uncertain variables. Confidence in the present analysis is reinforced by the general agreement between calculated and observed concentrations of nitrogen in drainage waters. In contrast to the fields, the nitrogen fluxes calculated for the cattle herd from feed requirements agree remarkably well with farmer and research experience. Farm management would be a much easier task if crops and soils behaved as predictably!

## 17.11   ASSESSMENTS

### Production efficiency

This farm has only a small efficiency in the conversion of short-wave radiation to chemical energy in plant material. The maize crop converts 0.9% of the radiation received during its growing season to above-ground biomass but only 0.5% to grain. The pasture is the least efficient component with an efficiency of only 0.2% conversion to forage. Water-use efficiency, by contrast, is reasonably good: 21.4 kg biomass ha$^{-1}$ mm$^{-1}$ ET and 11.5 kg grain ha$^{-1}$ mm$^{-1}$ ET for maize. The pasture produced only 5.7 kg forage ha$^{-1}$ mm$^{-1}$. Total above-ground production on cultivated land and pasture is 2870 t y$^{-1}$ or 7970 kg ha$^{-1}$ y$^{-1}$. Average ET is 648 mm y$^{-1}$; therefore production is 7970/648 = 12.3 kg ha$^{-1}$ mm$^{-1}$. That production corresponds to about 1400 t of human-edible grain equivalents or enough for 2800 people. Because of rotations and manure transfers, nitrogen-use efficiency is most meaningful on a whole-farm basis. The farm exported 22.6 t N or 66% of the 34.1 t that it received; 5.9% of the 14.2 t N consumed by all cattle and 9.4% of that fed in the lot were exported in meat (Table 17.7).

Interesting measures of efficiency could also be constructed for other nutrients, for the use of fuel, and for amounts of total external energy embodied in fuel, machines, land improvements, and labor.

### Erosion

Control of erosion is an important goal of the cropping plans on this farm. With conservation tillage, the MMOCl rotation is capable of limiting erosive movement to less than 1 t soil ha$^{-1}$ y$^{-1}$ on 6–8% slopes of the Downs soil (calculated with USLE; see Chapter 12). Cropping on contours with alternate strips of forage and maize and retention of at least 35% cover by residues after planting are necessary features of the system. The slopes form a confused pattern, however, and contour cropping is only approximate. In addition, considerable care is needed to retain 35% cover after tillage. Maize stover provides more than 70% cover in fall but a single pass in spring with disk or chisel can reduce that below 35% in some cases. Slopes steeper than 6–8% need as much as 50% cover by mulch after planting for erosion protection. That can be achieved in no-till systems if one accepts their disadvantages. Alternatives for steep slopes include a longer sod phase, terracing, or conversion to grass.

Table 17.7 *Import–export nitrogen balance for the Iowa farm*

Input in seed is ignored. The total for volatilization assumes
that most of the loss from manure occurs in that manner rather
than by denitrification.

| Inputs to the farm | | Outputs from the farm | |
|---|---|---|---|
| Deposition | 5.4 | Maize sold | 11.4 |
| Symbiotic fixation | 13.6 | Soybean sold | 8.0 |
| Fertilizer | 14.4 | Oat sold | 1.8 |
| Soybean meal | 0.7 | Cattle sold | 1.4 |
| Total input | 34.1 | Sales | 22.6 |
| | | Volatilization | 5.4 |
| | | Denitrification | 2.3 |
| | | Runoff | 1.3 |
| | | Drainage | 1.3 |
| | | Losses | 10.3 |
| | | Hay reserve | 1.2 |
| | | Total output | 34.1 |

## Nitrogen

Large losses of nitrogen occur on this farm despite reasonable care of manure and
minimum use of fertilizer (Table 17.7). A surprising finding is that annual losses of
nitrogen from manure (4.3 t from feeding stations + 1.4 t from grazing = 5.7 t) are
greater than those from cropland (3.9 t). In addition, it seems that most of the total
loss of 10.3 t is to the atmosphere through volatilization of ammonia and
denitrification in manure and soil. One benefit of those processes is that they served
to limit the nitrate flux to drainage. Only 40% of the nitrogen input is from fertilizer
while 60% is supplied by deposition and fixation; losses are distributed among all of
those sources, not just from fertilizer.

One message in Table 17.6 is that fluxes of more than 160 kg mineral N ha$^{-1}$ are in
fact required to produce even average crops. Estimates of leaching losses amount to
only a few percent of supply, and lowering them significantly may prove difficult.
Possibilities for side effects from this farm are apparent in the average concentration
of nitrate in drainage, 0.5 mM, which is only slightly less than the standard set by the
US Public Health as the maximum safe level for drinking water (0.7 mM; 10 ppm
$NO_3$-N). That 10 ppm standard is set at about 0.1 of the level at which health
problems are sometimes observed and thus is conservative (Lee 1970). A level of 0.5
mM is sufficient for eutrophication of surface waters, however, promoting growth of
green algae in lakes and streams; with green algae, streams and lakes in this region are
clear in contrast to the cyanobacterial blooms that occur here in low-nitrogen
waters.

Our farmers practice a conservative program of fertilization but excessive use of nitrogen fertilizer occurs elsewhere in the Corn Belt. Surveys of maize fields in northeastern Iowa using soil and plant analyses (El-Hout & Blackmer 1990) demonstrated large excesses of mineral nitrogen. Reasons for the excess are not clear. The low cost of nitrogen fertilizer, concerns of farmers about risks of under-fertilization, and their reliance on fertilizer dealers and applicators for advice are cited as factors. Part of the problem also is that farmers have no good means for estimating legume and manure contributions to soil nitrogen and no means for predicting weather and thus crop needs.

Nitrogen fertilizer that is broadcast and incorporated is protected from loss through runoff and volatilization but it is more vulnerable than banded applications to immobilization and denitrification. Blackmer *et al.* (1989) have established 20 ppm $NO_3$-N in surface soil after emergence in late spring as the $CNC_s$ (Chapter 12) for maize in Iowa. Analyses at that time catch both mineralization that occurred during the fallow and preplant fertilizer. This test would support an alternative practice involving a conservative initial application banded at planting. A second, banded application, adjusted according to the soil test, could be applied later if needed. That approach would provide insurance against both over- and under-fertilization and would be more efficient than the broadcast-incorporation method used on this farm. Side-dressing is more costly than broadcasting, however, in addition it causes traffic damage and surface residues can interfere with the equipment. The alternative of simply using less fertilizer would result in a significant loss of income in favorable years and, with less cover, an increased risk of erosion. Short-season cultivars would allow more drainage, diluting the leachate, but that also would reduce yield and, with a longer fallow, total loss of N and erosion might actually increase.

### Herbicides

Contamination of ground and surface waters with herbicides is also a concern. Herbicides have had a dramatic impact on farming, not only through reduced weed competition, but also in reduced tillage. Before herbicides were available, spring tillage on this farm generally involved a sequence of disk, moldboard plow, disk harrow, and tooth harrow. That was followed by two post-emergence cultivations. Conversion of the Corn Belt to conservation tillage was made possible by the appearance of atrazine in the 1970s. Mulch cover is now greater and erosion less than before.

Herbicide systems are not without problems. Atrazine, for example, was too successful. Repeated year after year, tolerant populations of weeds were selected and its effectiveness declined. One reason for atrazine's original success was its resistance to degradation but that and its solubility result in contamination of drainage waters. Similar problems can occur with cyanazine. The solution employed on this farm is to emphasize less persistent materials and to rotate herbicide systems as well as crops. Fortunately, most of the herbicides used here have very low toxicity to mammals although toxicity to fish can be a problem.

Weeds have a strong impact on production in this environment and few practical alternatives exist to our farmers' heavy reliance on high planting densities, rotation, tillage, and incorporated preplant herbicides for weed control. Performance of preplant materials varies with rainfall, temperature, and soil pH but, at present, they represent the most effective and cheapest solution. The heavy residue mulches needed on the steeper slopes for erosion control interfere with both cultivation and topically applied herbicides. Clearly, there is a need for better herbicides that are effective under a wider range of moisture conditions with less risk to the environment.

### Farms in transition

Some insights into the difficulty of optimizing farm management emerge in our analysis. A degree of inefficiency is inevitable when farming with uncertain weather and uncertain markets. Not so obvious is the fact that some part of the system is always obsolete or lacking balance with other parts. As the productivity of labor and animals continues to increase, Iowa farms continue in transitions begun 160 y ago. They are seldom optimally structured, in the sense that field areas and types, and species and numbers of livestock, match well with labor supply, equipment, managerial skills, and current markets. Furthermore, skilled farmers are not born but emerge after years of experience: years during which mistakes and inefficiencies occur. Changes in technology and markets call for new skills and adjustments throughout the system and that requires time and capital. A change in the tillage system or a return to swine production, for example, would involve heavy capital expenses for this farm. With present prices and labor productivity, the most practical change may be to increase the scale rather than the intensity of farming. Local experience demonstrates that two active workers can manage crop and beef operations efficiently on 1000 ha farms.

## 17.11   OUTLOOK

This farm characterizes the extensive nature of most agriculture in North America. Farms throughout the Corn Belt, Great Plains, and the Gulf and Atlantic coastal regions, while emphasizing different crops, are similar in ownership, capital structure, and emphasis on labor efficiency. Matching of crops and methods of production with soil capability and rainfall enables these farmers to maintain extremely low costs in the production of bulk commodities and livestock. The Iowa system appears relatively simple, yet it is quite complex and sophisticated in detail and surprisingly demanding of managerial skills.

Productivity levels are modest. Significant enhancement seems possible through labor intensification in both management and operations. Pasture production, for example, could be significantly enhanced by drainage, renovation, fertilizer, and additional lime. Irrigation, and management of crop nutrition through greater use of soil and plant analyses would increase yield levels and improve yield stability. None of those directions appear to offer benefits in excess of costs and risks, however. Home computers, now coming into use for records of field, herd, and financial affairs, could help in identifying aspects of the enterprise most deserving attention. These farmers present a seeming contradiction with conservatism and caution on one hand and rapid evolution and change on the other. With so many elements in the system, the philosophy is to leave the working parts 'well enough alone'. Not so with weeds, however, which are the most intractable problem to these farms. No present method of control is sufficient or economical and the farmers continue to experiment with new approaches.

Despite its limitations, the nitrogen-cycling model was rewarding of insights to the operation of the system and roles of legumes, livestock, fertilizer, and deposition were brought into perspective. Cattle were revealed to be the major avenue for nitrogen loss. By contrast, the small loss by leaching is a greater off-site issue. A better model, in particular, one that properly predicts temporal variations in microbial activity, is needed for a truly accurate picture of nitrogen cycling. Even without that, the farmers do surprisingly well in nitrogen management through continual observation and adjustment of practices. It would be a useful exercise to see what emerged from a similar analysis for potassium and phosphorus.

## 17.12   FURTHER READING

Bywater, A. C., and R. L. Baldwin. 1980. Alternative strategies in food-animal production. In *Animals, feed, food and people: an analysis of the role of animals in food production.* (AAAS Symposium) (ed. R. L. Baldwin), pp. 1–29. Westview Press, Boulder, Colorado.

Frissel, M. J. (ed.). 1977. Cycling of mineral nutrients in agricultural systems. *Agro-Ecosystems* (special issue) **4**:1–354.

Lee, D. H. K. 1970. Nitrates, nitrites and methemoglobinemia. *Environ. Res.* **3**:484–511.

Nestrud, L. M. and J. R. Worster. 1979. *Soil survey of Jasper County, Iowa.* US Government Printing Office, Washington, D.C. 136 p., 96 maps.

# 18

*Towards an uncertain furture*

## 18.1 INTRODUCTION

The future is uncertain in terms of population, energy supply, weather, and our ability to solve problems. Important issues now are whether agricultural production can be expanded, not just sustained, for the needs of an expanding population and whether that can be done safely. How well we succeed in achieving a sufficient agriculture will depend heavily on the magnitude of population growth and on decisions made about acceptable levels of use of natural resources and energy in food production. Preceding chapters provide some of the basis for possible advances. This chapter reviews trends in population growth and food supply and considers how the challenges of an uncertain future might be met.

## 18.2 POPULATION AND FOOD SUPPLY

### Population growth and stabilization

Concepts of carrying capacity have long been evident in the organization of human societies. The English economist Thomas Malthus (1798), however, was perhaps the first to attempt a scholarly analysis of the links between population size and demands on food resources. He concluded that the potential for food production is limited and, if human populations were not controlled by 'prudence', they would inevitably be controlled by starvation, war, or pestilence. Malthus was not optimistic about preventive restraints and he and many since have been led to dire views of the fate of mankind.

The intrinsic reproductive capacity of humans, near 40 births per 1000 population per year, is small compared to other animals but, unchecked, it is large enough to allow rapid increases in population size. Before the industrial revolution, birth rates were countered by large death rates due to disease and the low and variable productivity of farming systems. In 16th century Europe, only 30% of the people survived to age 20. As a result, human populations increased slowly. Malthus was stimulated in his studies by the rising population of Europe where industrialization provided new jobs and new farming systems (private farms with legume rotations and recycled manure) provided adequate food. The population of Ireland was surging towards the potato famine with a growth rate of 1.2% y$^{-1}$, however, while European and world populations increased at 0.3% y$^{-1}$. Malthus concluded that food production could not keep pace with population growth.

In 1798, Malthus was not able to anticipate the extent and nature of technological advances that industrialization would provide and he thus misjudged the potential carrying capacity of Earth. Energy applied directly and indirectly to agricultural land has increased its productivity allowing more, better-nourished, people to live longer. At the same time, science and technology have provided medical solutions to many diseases and death rates have declined dramatically. In developed countries, 90% of the people now can expect to live beyond 50 y. As death rates declined, an imbalance between births and deaths gave a rapid increase in world population (Table 18.1). The electronic age and ease of travel serve as symbols of change in the second half of the twentieth century but the most significant changes have been the increase in world population and attendant food supplies.

In the 1950s, the optimistic view was that world population might be stabilized, after doubling to 5 billion, through 'demographic transitions', in which birthrates decline to near 10 per 1000 per year in synchrony with death rates, as was happening in developed nations. Demographic transitions have continued in developed countries but not in the developing world. World population now exceeds 5.2 billion with a specific growth rate of 0.017 y$^{-1}$. At that rate, population will double again in 40 y (from Eq. 2.3, $t_d = \ln 2/\mu = 0.69/0.017$ y$^{-1} = 40.6$ y). The future is complicated by the fact that most of the present population is young and has yet to reproduce. In the most-optimistic view, with human reproduction henceforth limited to replacement, world population is certain to double during the next 50–100 y before reaching a stable level near 10–12 billion people. Wars have proven inefficient as controls on population and the doubling picture could change only with drastic declines in birthrates or devastation of the population through starvation or pestilence. Medical science has been perhaps too quick with solutions, however, and even the current epidemic of AIDS may have little impact on population. It would be nice if we were to share the world with fewer people but that seems not to be. Perhaps what is needed is a top carnivore to control human population!

The literature on these subjects is vast – population growth and its links with agriculture and technological change are in fact far more complex than might be inferred by this brief introduction. One important question is the extent that innovation and technological change are agents permitting population growth in contrast to being 'demand-driven' responses to growth. Boserup (1981), taking an historical perspective, argues cogently for the latter view. The danger in her analysis, unlinked as it is to the ecology of food production, is that it may lead one to conclude that technology can always supply sufficient food regardless of population size. We see little promise for major quantum jumps in biology that would allow crops to provide vastly more food than they can with present technology. That would require genetic engineering of photosynthetic systems, an area that at present holds little promise. Our conclusion is that no one now can argue rationally that ultimate limits to human population size due to food supply do not exist or that continued population growth should not be balanced with nature conservation.

Table 18.1 *Growth in world population,*
*1650 to present*

| Year | Estimated population (millions) | Specific growth rate $(y^{-1})$ |
|------|------|------|
| 1650 | 500 | |
| | | 0.0034 |
| 1750 | 700 | |
| | | 0.0045 |
| 1850 | 1100 | |
| | | 0.0082 |
| 1950 | 2500 | |
| | | 0.0183 |
| 1990 | 5200 | |

## The need for food

The production goal for agriculture is defined by the size of the human population and by its need for energy, protein, and other dietary factors. The Standard Nutritional Unit (SNU, 8.4 GJ cap$^{-1}$ y$^{-1}$) (Section 1.7) provides a simple measure of the amount of food production needed per capita. This corresponds to 500 kg grain cap$^{-1}$ y$^{-1}$ (23 MJ cap$^{-1}$ d$^{-1}$) at the farm gate or its equivalent in energy and protein from other sources. After deducting allowances for planting stock, waste, storage losses, reserves, and alternative foods (animal products, fruits, and vegetables), this amount assures a food supply at the table similar to present supplies in developed countries (14 MJ cap$^{-1}$ d$^{-1}$). World grain production now amounts to 340 kg cap$^{-1}$ y$^{-1}$. When production of other foods (sugar, potato, cassava, animal products, fish, fruits, and vegetables) is expressed in grain equivalents, the average approaches the 500 kg standard.

The next doubling of population will require more than an overall doubling of food production because many people presently are undernourished. Where and how agriculture can meet that challenge are not clear. The principal options are simple: increased yields and/or areas in production. A more vegetarian diet may assist but the contribution would be small because animal production is largely non-competitive with food crops (see Table 1.4) and is offset to some extent by the high digestibility of animal products relative to plant products. Many of the present foods of western societies may disappear or become more expensive: cold beer, alfalfa sprouts, and out-of-season fruits and vegetables, for example, embody high energy costs and/or inefficient use of land.

Increasing food supplies may be complicated by limited availability of energy supplies and by climatic change. Our problems relate to carrying capacity: areas of land that might be farmed, production levels that might be achieved, and choices about suitable technologies.

It is worthwhile referring again to Fig. 1.7 and the inverse relationship between yield and area required for a given amount of production. Relative land areas and resources needed to supply food are reduced sharply as yields are brought to higher levels through the relief of a constraint such as nitrogen deficiency. Given a yield of 1 t grain ha$^{-1}$ without added nitrogen, a hectare of land could supply adequate food for just two people (at 500 kg cap$^{-1}$ y$^{-1}$). At that level, a nation of 100 million people need 50 Mha to support its population. With improved fertility producing a modest yield of 5 t grain ha$^{-1}$, 10 people can be supported per hectare and only 10 Mha are required for the nation's food. Total nutrient extraction in harvested grain is the same and, by definition, water- and light-use efficiencies on cultivated land are increased fivefold. Labor and energy requirements for field operations are reduced by nearly as much (Chapter 15). On the other hand, energy is then required for production of nitrogen fertilizer. Assuming 2% N in grain plus an allowance for losses, 4 t ha$^{-1}$ additional yield would require 6 GJ energy ha$^{-1}$ for synthesis of 100 kg fertilizer N ha$^{-1}$. That subsidy amounts to only 2 MJ d$^{-1}$ for each of the eight additional people supported per hectare and is offset more than 20-fold by not tilling the additional land. Other nutrients, particularly P and K, would then be depleted more rapidly, albeit from a smaller area, and would require additional energy subsidies but other benefits are also significant. For example, only 20% as much biocides need be employed and soil erosion would be reduced to an even greater extent because agriculture then can be restricted to the safest lands. Also important is the fact that 40 Mha can be left to nature reserves and other uses. The inescapable conclusion is that intensive farming systems are in fact lower-input and more sustainable per unit food supply than extensive ones.

## 18.3   FOOD PRODUCTION SINCE 1940

A review of changes that have occurred in agriculture in recent times helps in identifying options for the future. In retrospect, it is rather amazing that agriculture was able to respond with improved human nutrition during the last doubling of world population. Prior to 1940, when the population was near 2.2 billion, farming was conducted throughout the world with organic methods and grain yields were only slightly greater than during medieval times. Food supplies were marginal, even for developed countries, and famine and undernourishment were common elsewhere. Remarkable increases in crop yields have been achieved in developed countries since then, followed by the much-publicized 'green revolution' in developing countries. The yield of wheat quadrupled in India, for example, and rice yields tripled in Indonesia. World grain production increased from 640 Mt in 1934–8 to 1740 Mt in 1988 (Table 18.2) through increases in the area under cultivation, improvements in cultivars and management practices (including irrigation, more effective pest and weed control, and mechanization), and, most important, improved plant nutrition.

Large differences in industrialization, energy use, and standards of living exist between developed and developing countries. At both ends of the spectrum, there are concerns for the future of agriculture because production is either insufficient or

Table 18.2 *Grain production in 1934–8 and 1988*

| Region | Area sown (Mha) | | Grain yield (kg ha⁻¹) | | Production (Mt) | |
|---|---|---|---|---|---|---|
| | 1938 | 1988 | 1938 | 1988 | 1938 | 1988 |
| World | 551 | 702 | 1210 | 2480 | 640 | 1740 |
| Africa | 38 | 76 | 640 | 1170 | 24 | 89 |
| Asia | 196 | 307 | 1280 | 2600 | 251 | 797 |
| Europe | 80 | 68 | 1480 | 4340 | 118 | 297 |
| N & C America | 104 | 89 | 1070 | 3030 | 112 | 269 |
| S America | 22 | 39 | 1230 | 2060 | 27 | 80 |
| Oceania | 6 | 14 | 820 | 1600 | 5 | 23 |
| USSR | 105 | 108 | 970 | 1720 | 102 | 187 |

*Sources:* FAO Production Yearbooks.

is perceived to be unsustainable. In developing countries, the concern is for nutrients and other inputs and for new lands to develop for agriculture to meet increasing demands for food and for income from export. In developed countries, particularly those with exportable supplies of agricultural commodities, attention is turning to the cost of that 'excess' production to the environment. There, efforts are being made to retain as much land as possible in nature reserves so that their genetic resources can be protected and the land can be enjoyed for its other values.

## Food increases in developed countries

Developed nations of Europe, North America, and Asia met the challenge of population growth through intensification. Fertilizer was the principal component of the new technology with important contributions from mechanization and from biocides, particularly fungicides for seed treatment and herbicides. The impacts of technology are illustrated in Fig. 18.1 with the time-course of maize yields in USA. Before 1935, yields were stagnant there; in fact, they had been declining since 1880 by 13 kg ha⁻¹ y⁻¹ despite expanding use of legume rotations and manure. Declines in the quantity and quality of food per capita were also evident; exports and meat consumption per capita, for example, reached historic minima in the 1930s. The 1930s saw the introduction of hybrid maize resistant to stalk rot, and mechanization, leading to a steady, 45 kg ha⁻¹ y⁻¹, rise in yields through 1955. Since 1955, yields have advanced at 115 kg ha⁻¹ y⁻¹ owing to further improvements in cultivars and mechanization combined with beneficial effects of fertilizers, herbicides, increased irrigation, and improved cultural practices (see Table 4.5). Examples of similar trends in yields can be found throughout the world.

Despite doubling their population and a decline in the area of cultivated land, people in developed nations are now well supplied with food (Table 18.3) and some

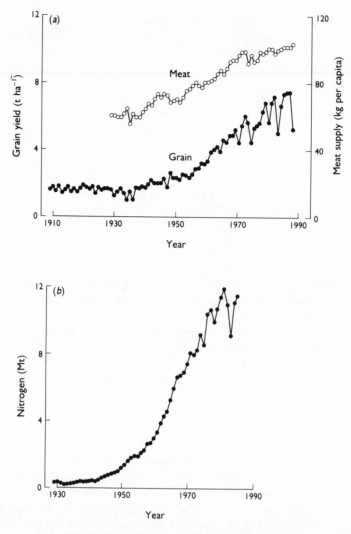

Fig. 18.1. (*a*) Trends for mean national yield of maize production and meat supply per capita in USA, 1910–89. (*b*) Trends in use of nitrogen fertilizer in USA, 1928–85. (Data from USDA Agricultural Statistics.)

nations including USA and members of the European Community are plagued with surplus production. A continuing redistribution of population between rural and urban communities has also occurred in these countries as expanding populations moved off the farm to more profitable employment in the industrial and service sectors. Mechanization associated with the agricultural revolution substituted for labor that moved and less than 10% of the work force is now directly engaged in agricultural production (Table 18.3). Because agricultural yields have been brought closer to limits imposed by climate and biology, the potential for further increases in food production in these countries is now less than before. In most areas,

Table 18.3 *Recent status of agriculture in developing and developed countries*

Data are for 1988 except as indicated in footnotes.

| Attribute | Units | Developing | Developed |
|---|---|---|---|
| Total population | M | 3879 | 1235 |
| Specific growth rate[1] | $y^{-1}$ | 0.021 | 0.007 |
| Workers in agriculture | % | 60.8 | 9.1 |
| Agricultural land[2] | ha cap$^{-1}$ | 0.21 | 0.55 |
| Grain yield | t ha$^{-1}$ | 2.26 | 3.90 |
| Grazing land[2] | ha cap$^{-1}$ | 0.51 | 1.02 |
| Grain production | MJ d$^{-1}$ cap$^{-1}$ | 11.45 | 28.74 |
| Grain import–export[3] | MJ d$^{-1}$ cap$^{-1}$ | 0.74 | −2.51 |
| Food supply[4] | MJ d$^{-1}$ cap$^{-1}$ | 10.3 | 14.1 |
| Animal products[4] | % diet energy | 8.8 | 30.2 |

*Notes:*
[1] 1975–88.
[2] 1987.
[3] 1986; positive for imports, negative for exports.
[4] 1984–5; available to the dinner table.
*Sources:* FAO Production Yearbook; FAO Trade Yearbook.

however, actual yields are still less than what is attainable with more intensive methods indicating that significant reserve capacity for production remains.

**The dilemma of food surpluses**

Developed countries have encountered difficulties in balancing supply and demand for agricultural commodities during the period of intensification since 1950. Rapid increases in production potential outstripped increases in demand. In the 1950s, surpluses of traditional exporters were absorbed by developing countries but that market diminished with the green revolution. In the 1970s, demand surged again due to population growth, change in oil prices, and droughts in Asia. That brief period of high prices stimulated fertilizer use around the world and exporters again faced declining markets during the 1980s as Europe, India, China, and other importers became self-sufficient and, in some cases, have turned to exporting.

Supplies of farm commodities in excess of demand have caused real prices for agricultural produce to lag far behind the returns achieved in other economic sectors. This continues a trend that began in the 1870s when produce of Argentina, Australia, and North America came onto world markets. Farmers in developed nations such as Britain, Canada, USA, and Australia have maintained their incomes, in spite of declining prices, through dramatic increases in labor productivity achieved with larger machines and larger farms. Others, in Japan and France, for example, have been protected with subsidies and by restrictions against cheaper imports. Both solutions may have run their course, however.

## Food increases in developing nations

In contrast to events in developed nations, birth rates remain high in many developing countries. Most people remain in rural sectors and 50–90% of the workers are employed in agriculture (e.g. 92% in Burundi and Nepal and 67% in India) but dramatic increases in urbanization also are taking place as surplus people leave the land. Two-thirds of the world's cities with more than 5 million people are now found in developing countries. The high proportion of people on the land indicates the importance of subsistence, rather than market economies, in many of these countries. Subsistence systems place a greater burden on the land since they must supply housing and fuel as well as food. Access to technological inputs is very limited in countries lacking exportable products and market economies.

During the past 40 y, the only option for increasing food supply in developing nations without access to fertilizer technology was to bring new areas into production. Significant expansion onto new lands has occurred during the past 50 y in Africa, South America, and Asia (Table 18.2). As a result, the portion of the world's ice-free land area given to permanent and arable crops increased from 9% in the 1940s to more than 11% today. Because the most productive areas were farmed first, potential yields from new lands are generally less and disproportionately larger additional areas are required to satisfy food needs. Despite improved yields and greater areas under cultivation, food supply remains precarious in many developing nations because their populations continue to expand rapidly; even single years of low yield can cause suffering in countries that have few reserves of food or currency.

Demographic transitions to stable, sustainable populations seem even more remote now than 40 y ago for some countries. It is now apparent that control of population is more complex, more deeply enmeshed with cultural values and traditions, and perhaps more intractable than once thought (Lee *et al.* 1988). In Malawi, for example, communal lands are allocated by a tribal chief to each extended family in proportion to their ability to cultivate it. This method yields special benefits in food production and social security to families with a large supply of child labor. It also leads to continued subdivision of land into smaller, less efficient, and less productive, units. Farming in many parts of the world has been plagued by subdivision at various times. Irish farms, for example, had diminished to 1 ha in size by 1840. Such trends were reversed by special land consolidation efforts in The Netherlands and elsewhere, and avoided completely by the primogeniture system used in England: there, farms were passed intact to only one child, or neighbor, who then assumed an obligation for continued support of the ageing parents.

## 18.4  THE IMPORTANCE OF A TECHNOLOGICAL AGRICULTURE

### 'Modern' agriculture

The present technological level of farming systems in developed countries is variously characterized as 'conventional' or 'modern'. Developments important in modern agriculture are increased scientific and technological knowledge, replacement of human and animal power, principally by internal combustion engines, and widespread use of fertilizers and biocides that respectively promote productivity and protect it. Replacement of human labor and animal power by machines changed the scale, speed, and timeliness of operations as well as providing sharp increases in productivity and releasing large areas of land from production of feed for work animals. Enormous increases in productivity and food supplies are the important benefits of modern agriculture.

Advances in scientific understanding, in particular of the chemistry and biology of soils, of the nutrition, metabolism, and reproduction of plants and animals, and of pests and disease, have allowed significant refinements of many long-standing practices. Our understanding of weather and microclimate also has advanced although we still are not able to predict future weather. In contrast to earlier times, agricultural practice has become more chemically based, not just in the agrichemicals that it uses, but also in the entire approach to management of biological processes central to productivity.

It is a serious mistake to assume that modern agriculture can be identified as a single concept involving uniform application of knowledge, machines, and agrichemicals. Diversity of farming practices occurs because soils, climates, access to markets and technology, and cultural influences differ greatly between regions. Farmers are numerous and independent and seek the best practices for their land and resources. Similar diversity exists within the research and extension professions. This diversity has been a priming force for continuous streams of innovation and change.

## Global carrying capacity

The large differences in yield that occur with different levels of external inputs raise important questions about the potential carrying capacity of the world's agriculture with and without such inputs. Among the most detailed studies of world carrying capacity were those done by P. Buringh and associates at the Centre for World Food Studies in Wageningen, The Netherlands (1977, 1979). Beginning with generalized climate and soil maps of the world, they calculated the production potential for each region, employing a canopy-photosynthesis model as limited by water supply, temperature, and radiation. Estimated primary production was converted to grain by using a standard harvest index. These studies, and a similar one by FAO (summarized by Srinivasan in Lee *et al.* (1988)), were relatively crude but, for the moment, they are the best we have.

With adequate energy for drainage, irrigation, fertilizer, and tillage (modern agriculture), Buringh's group estimated the absolute maximum area that might be farmed at 3420 Mha or twice that now being farmed (1740 Mha). With present technology and adequate energy, 50 Gt grain equivalents might be produced, enough for 100 billion people. Most of the additional land would come from conversion of grazing lands with attendant problems of low productivity. Possibilities for additional irrigation through desalinization and interbasin transfers of rivers were not considered and the area of irrigated land was only doubled from the present total of 230 Mha, mostly in Asia.

The authors were careful to note that their maximum estimate is unrealistic in several respects and that it is not to be viewed as a desirable goal. The estimate included land now occupied by transportation, urban centers, and natural areas. Further, it called for intensive relay cropping with grain yields near the present records in each region. The impacts of urbanization are significant. A regional center such as the adjacent Kansas Cities of Kansas and Missouri together with their suburbs, for example, occupies 200 kha of farm land. Controversy also exists regarding the practicality of farming, as they assume, up to one-half of the old soils of the Amazon basin. If agriculture does not intrude into the lowland tropics, estimated global food supply is reduced by 10%.

That scenario of intensive agriculture was compared with 'traditional agriculture' representing a high state of organic farming without external inputs of fertilizer or fuel (Buringh & van Heemst 1979). Without energy for irrigation and drainage, the maximum extent of land that might be farmed was 2460 Mha or 1.7 times the present amount. Estimates of grain production proved difficult because yields with limiting nutrients vary with the lengths of fallow periods and with amounts of land assigned in rotation to forage legumes. Their conclusion was that even good methods of organic farming (all wastes and manures recycled plus legume rotations) applied to all possible land could supply only 3.2 Gt grain (6.4 billion people). Applied to present farmlands, traditional agriculture would not support the present population. The important conclusion from this study is that fertilizer and other external inputs are essential now and in the future. The FAO study mentioned above reached a somewhat different result. They estimated that 6.5 billion people could be supported on present lands without fertilizer or machines and that the maximum carrying capacity of the globe is 33 billion. It seems, then, that a practical upper limit to carrying capacity, with present technology, is something like two doublings of our present population to 20 billion people. Applied to land now being farmed, modern agriculture can probably support a single doubling.

Two satellite points emerge from these studies. One is that the present agriculture of most developed nations operates at less than its potential. Only a few countries, including perhaps Japan and several European nations, are truly intensive in their agriculture. The second point is that more than 60% of the best farmland in terms of soils and water supply is found in Asia and North America. Australia's proportion (3.4%) is small but quite large in relation to its population. By contrast, Africa, where a population more than 40 times that of Australia is increasing at 0.028 $y^{-1}$ ($t_d = 25$ y), has only 6% of the world's good land but a large supply of lands with poor soil and/or limited water supply. The distribution of good land will change if climate changes, but the present situation suggests that Argentina, Australia, and North America will continue to have a role during the next century in meeting the world's food needs through exports. The magnitude of that role was indicated in Table 18.3 by the grain import-export balances. To continue as suppliers of food for poor nations, exporters must remain highly efficient in production and thus low in cost.

## Problems with modern agriculture

Increased productivity has not been achieved without social or ecological costs. Change was essential for increased levels and efficiencies of food production and some disruptions followed as a natural consequence of change; others occurred through poor choices and mistakes. The range of concerns raised in the minds of both the public and agriculturalists is justifiably wide:

Pollution of surface and subsurface waters by agrichemicals, their residues and contaminants, rendering them unsafe or unsuitable for other uses, and disturbing natural systems.

Contamination of products with residues of agrichemicals rendering them unsafe or uncertain for consumption.

Necessitating farms to be larger and less labor intensive in order to produce at competitive prices.

Making agrichemicals a significant part of the cost of production and thereby an economic strain in seasons of low yield or low returns and a drain on energy resources.

Providing inputs that allow farming to extend to fragile land, increasing the competition with nature conservation and, when poorly maintained, leading to problems of soil erosion and siltation.

Salinization through failure of provision for drainage.

The question now is how to address these concerns while proceeding towards an uncertain future. Regardless of directions taken, the basic strategy must be to supply sufficient food for humans through manipulation of environments and plant communities in ways that provide for efficient use of scarce resources. As we noted in Chapter 1, that requires protection from losses during production and afterwards during storage, processing, and distribution. Our view is that current problems can be reduced or eliminated through continued evolution of the existing systems supported by research and education. The view of some, however, is that modern agriculture is inappropriate to the tasks ahead and must be redirected, perhaps radically, towards 'alternative' methods.

## Views of technology in agriculture

**Alternative movements**   The range of technical, ecological, and social concerns over modern agriculture can be seen in the many groups that espouse changes. Membership of such groups is wide, including farmers and consumers, scientists and non-scientists, conservationists and industrialists. Their motives are equally diverse, ranging from reverence of nature, nostalgia for old ways, dislike of science and technology (particularly of chemistry), and survivalist goals, to political change. Agriculture has always been blessed with theorists of new ways. Cato and Jethro Tull were each important in their time. What seems different now is that more of the criticism and advice directed at agriculture in developed countries is based in political movements and lacking of practical experience in farming. In part, this reflects our encouragement of activism as a positive force in society and the dominance of urban politics over rural affairs. A plethora of concepts for farming has emerged as a result under labels such as 'organic', 'biodynamic', 'alternative', 'appropriate', and 'sustainable'. As is the case with 'organic farming' (Chapter 8), these concepts are only vaguely defined but less use of agrichemicals is usually involved.

Assignment of carcinogenic labels to many biocides is a principal basis for widespread public concerns about the use of agrichemicals. That procedures for testing carcinogenicity are open to serious question, and that natural biochemicals which could carry the same label are vastly more abundant in food (Section 3.5), are yet to be addressed, or understood, by the public. Concerns over biocides have led some consumers to seek produce grown without them ('organic' food), and some farmers to provide those products, either for similar concerns or to take advantage of the higher prices to be obtained. Alternative movements sometimes argue that farming should be free of external inputs which, they consider, represent an unsustainable drain on energy resources while destroying the natural biological order of agriculture. Some Amish religious groups never adopted agrichemicals following a philosophy that farming should rely as much as possible upon human and animal labor. In their view, the natural order provides plants as fixers of energy for the biological system within which human activity ought also to be constrained.

**Our perspective**    We see external inputs and sophisticated technology as essential in agriculture. Without them, productivity will spiral downward leading to poverty and starvation for many of the present world population. The real issue for the future is the provision and management of energy, nutrients, and agrichemicals in farming so that needs of society can be met with an acceptable balance between use of land in agriculture and conservation of natural resources. Improvement of agricultural practice, of which one critical part is the improvement of agrichemicals and their use, is a central challenge.

Agriculturalists are servants of the larger society and it is not among our privileges to shirk in providing food for people. We have no problem with alternative agriculturalists pursuing their own goals and methods. We see real dangers, however, in attempts to impose poorly researched theories on the larger society through fear or government regulation without regard to consequences.

From our perspective it is only groups that reject the use of energy or chemical inputs in agriculture that can realistically be distinguished as 'alternative' agriculturalists. It is curious that a recent, and otherwise useful, study (National Research Council 1989a) takes a different view. The NRC panel argued that 'alternative agriculture' is the province of those who care about and promote the biological integrity of agricultural systems. Whether they use agrichemicals, which remains unquestionably the most important issue, was considered less important. Most of NRC's 'alternative practices' are simply conservative methods employed to some degree by almost all farmers we know. Perhaps NRC decided to dilute extremists under a new flag and is prepared to group mistakes of theory and implementation that society, science, and farmers have made in farming practice under the title of 'conventional' agriculture. That is not a fair thing to do, however, to most farmers and agriculturalists, to whom what NRC espouses is simply conventional wisdom and common practice.

To be sufficient, agricultural systems will need to be increasingly intensive and thus increasingly dependant on external sources of nutrients. Barring a collapse in the size of human populations, we see no alternative to that course. Our vision of farming is by no means a bleak industrial landscape saturated with agrichemicals, however. Rather, it is of a healthy landscape, well managed both ecologically and economically. Modern farming systems are sustainable as long as there is energy and inputs for their maintenance. Their weakness is not low sustainability but dependance on inputs (low autonomy). The same is true for most alternatives. High-yield organic agriculture, for example, generally requires large additions of organic material collected from outside the system. In this form, it also possesses low autonomy. Production from organic farms without external inputs is inevitably low either because all fields have low yields, determined by weathering rates of soil minerals and by other natural inputs, or because large portions of land must be assigned to legumes for nitrogen production. In those forms, organic farming can be sustainable but its productivity is insufficient as was indicated by the Buringh studies and clearly demonstrated by the inadequacy of food supplies in 1940 for a world population only half the present size.

## 18.5  IMPROVING TECHNOLOGY

### Pivotal issues

Our discussion has identified three important tasks for the future: increase production; improve efficiency in the use of scarce resources; and resolve problems related to use of agrichemicals. Accomplishing these tasks involves an increasing information content of agriculture, in particular, improved understanding and management of energy, land, genetic resources, and weeds, pests, and disease. Each of these topics deserves brief attention before closing.

### Information

Our brief survey makes the point that agricultural technology, far from going away, must become increasingly sophisticated. Information is the basic element in future changes whether in the form of better understanding of the biology of a pathogen, genetic traits for insect resistance or for stability with variable weather, soil analyses, an IPM system, or smart machines; de Wit (1975) made the point rather elegantly in noting how information can be translated to technical 'know-how' that improves a system's performance. Better performance may be obtained in many ways including improved yield, lessened inputs, and lessened impact on surrounding environments. It is in this arena that molecular biology can make its greatest contribution. Imagine, for example, spraying a field with a non-reproducing (and thus limited-life) pathogen to which the crop has been engineered for resistance. Progress in that direction has already been achieved with some herbicides. It would be nice if we could also capitalize more on subtle interrelationships among soil microorganisms (e.g. suppressive soils, Section 3.4), or among predatory and phytophagous insects, but experience to date indicates that understanding and establishing reliable systems of that sort are difficult.

### Energy use

Shortage of energy for agriculture is not really an issue in the foreseeable future because agriculture uses only a small portion (3–5%) of the energy consumed in developed countries, and in the world as a whole. Other aspects of current lifestyles such as home heating, lighting, refrigeration, and travel account for much larger fractions of energy use and offer far greater opportunities for conservation. Rising prices for energy will bring conservation in all of these sectors as well as in agriculture. Agriculture's use of energy is embodied in three external inputs: labor, machines, and agrichemicals. These are linked reciprocally in the sense that energy expended in one form can substitute for either of the others (de Wit 1979).

Elimination of machines would require a return of human and animal labor to agriculture in disproportion to the savings in liquid fuels. This arises because of high maintenance energy requirements for animal and human workers and their slowness in doing work. Analyses of manual work (Table 15.1) emphasize that peak labor demands during critical procedures such as sowing and harvesting greatly restrict the overall efficiency of human work. Further restrictions arise from the large embodied energy cost of human labor with current Western standards of living (*ca.* 600 MJ day$^{-1}$). On the other hand, 'smart labor', in the sense of time spent in sophisticated management, can bring savings in total energy use. We do not expect that reduced supplies of petroleum will bring a return to horses and mules. Petroleum can be replaced by more expensive shale oil, or by $H_2$ from nuclear reactors; even biomass-fed steam engines would win in competition with animal power. Horses convert only about 7% of the combustible energy in feed to work (Section 1.5) whereas the efficiency of steam engines with similar biomass can exceed 30%.

Significant gains in energy economy were made following the surge in energy prices in the 1970s. Greater use of diesel motors, larger tractors, reductions in tillage, and increased use of fertilizer were the main elements. Larger tractors allowed improvements in yield through timeliness and uniformity as well as a significant reduction in the embodied energy of labor (per unit production) through greater labor productivity. Avenues for additional improvements include further reductions in tillage and improvements in fertilizer practices. Minimum and no-till systems, for example, can be expanded further dependent, to some extent, on further improvements in herbicides. 'Smart' machines that sense needs for tillage or fertilizer on a microscale and apply them only to selected areas offer another avenue. Irrigation and drainage systems that depend upon pumping are particularly vulnerable to diminished supplies of energy. Farming below sea level in Dutch polders and with pump irrigation in the American Great Plains are examples of activities that will encounter problems.

## Managing soil resources

Our improved understanding of soil chemistry and nutrient availability enables more critical management of fertility. Previously, management was based solely upon enhancement of mineralization and weathering by tillage, return of crop residues and animal manures, and rotation with legumes. Manipulation of organic matter remains a central theme in crop nutrition but maintenance and improvement of fertility have been sharpened with fertilizers. The major part of fertilizer practice concerns provision of the macronutrients N, P, and K. Use of fertilizers allows all fields, rather than just a few to be relieved of nutrient deficiencies. Deficiencies can be treated individually in relation to need, a practice not possible with organic materials such as manure, whereas fertilizers can be placed for ready access by crop roots and in synchrony with need.

Difficulties remain, however, because yields and nutrient use vary with weather, diseases, and pests, and because root systems may be inefficient in uptake. We are unable to make accurate predictions about those matters or about mineralization and losses by runoff, leaching, and volatilization, and fixation into unavailable forms. Those processes all vary spatially and temporally within and among fields, causing seemingly unavoidable inefficiencies in nutrient cycling and fertilizer practices. Inefficiencies resulting from poor placement and timing of fertilizer applications can be reduced. Better (and cheaper) methods for soil and plant analyses and greater attention to rooting traits also will help but, as we noted in Chapters 8 and 17, leaching of just 1 or 2% of the annual nitrogen flux in a farming system sometimes can bring drainage to unacceptable levels of nitrate. That problem occurs with any source of nitrogen from residues and manure to fertilizer and may be unavoidable. We can, however, hold farm effluents to a safe level below 10 ppm by a variety of means. Dispersal of animal production, for example would help through a more uniform distribution of manure supplies.

A popular concept for solutions to current dilemmas about surplus production is to reduce the intensity and thus the yield from farming through lower inputs of fertilizer ('low-input sustainable agriculture'; LISA). Proponents of LISA fail to realize that intensive systems have better energy efficiency per unit production than extensive ones and that agriculture in exporting nations such as USA and Australia is already more extensive than intensive, i.e. that fertilizer practices for basic commodities are conservative (see Chapters 16 and 17). From an ecological perspective, it seems better to place arable land into reserve programs than to adjust to demand through even lower levels of production. Among the reasons noted earlier: less land is then subject to erosion, water, biocide, and energy use per unit production are less, and production per unit capital and labor remain high.

Manufacture of nitrogen fertilizer has a high energy cost (60 MJ $kg^{-1}$ N). With limited energy, legumes will receive renewed emphasis because they can supply nitrogen with the expenditure of only about 10% as much fossil fuel. The extent that they may substitute for non-legumes, however, will continue to be limited by their requirement for fertile soil and by the problem of how we might use more forage. If energy really becomes scarce, it may be worthwhile by-passing forage legumes completely, provided non-legumes can be engineered to accept rhizobial symbiosis. That would, however, reduce their yields significantly and increase pressures for expansion of land under cultivation.

Perhaps now is the time, while energy remains cheap, to posture our agricultural base for significant energy savings in the future. Consider, for example, restructuring landscapes into level terraces during this period of farm surpluses. Returns for massive capital investments of that sort would come in the form of reduced costs of tillage and reduced erosion but would be delayed until the next century when food is again short.

## Management of genetic resources

Considerable emphasis has been given in recent years to conservation of genetic resources and to molecular biology as important foundations for agriculture in the future. This emphasis on molecular biology is open to criticism, however. The easy gains in genetic advance have been made and we seem now to be saying that specific improvements made with new molecular techniques is the most we can expect for the future. Those improvements will be mainly in simple, single-gene, traits relating to matters such as disease and insect resistance. While important, continued emphasis on 'defect elimination' overlooks greater opportunities for progress through understanding and advancing integrative attributes such as rooting and nitrogen-use efficiency. We know of no crop for which we have clear ideotypes to direct such breeding efforts and efforts of crop physiologists who might contribute to progress has been diverted to problems of 'stress' in extreme environments. Our groping inability at defining better objectives for plant breeders arises in part because our understanding of normal integrative controls of plants under field conditions is still primitive.

## Management of weeds, diseases, and pests

Problems arising from weeds, diseases, and pests have a number of elements in common. The species diversity of each class is very large requiring that we limit our attention to only a few key species that give the most difficulty. Infestations with any of these organisms can cause large losses in yield but such events are highly variable. In some years or locations, untended problems can cause the loss of the entire crop, in others, the effects are absent or too small to be of concern. Estimates of average losses are large; even with significant efforts at control, yield losses due to weeds, diseases, and pests runs to 10% or more.

Ecological methods are the principal means for controlling each of these groups of organisms. All are susceptible to their own arrays of diseases and predators and all generally do less damage to well-managed, rapidly growing crops than, for example, to those deficient in nutrients. Sanitation efforts (cultivation of weeds, disposal of infested residues, crop rotation) are important aspects of management. Weeds can sometimes be overcome through competition by crops and insects are subject to predation by beneficial insects. Pest organisms differ in that genetic resistance to insects, nematodes, and diseases has long been an important tool but genetic solutions to weed control are only now being explored. We might, for example, sacrifice some feature of an optimal canopy for crop photosynthesis to achieve a canopy that is more competitive with weeds.

Biocides are now also widely employed to control each of these groups. Control cannot and should not be directed at every organism in sight. Control action generally is justified only when an infestation reaches an 'economic threshold' level that may eventually cause significant economic loss. In some cases, control can be achieved by biological methods relying upon predator–prey relationships; in others, understanding of the biology of the host–pest relationship enables more efficient and effective use of biocides.

**Weed control** Weeds have only modest mobility and weed problems therefore have a residential character through soil seed banks to particular fields and to particular climates and farming systems. Movement from field to field is facilitated by machinery, grazing animals, and manure as well as by wind and other natural means. Weed management centers on limiting the size of the seed bank through control of reproduction. Sanitation is important because small untended weed populations in one year can cause crop losses over a number of subsequent years. The economic threshold for weed control is therefore generally less than a density that would cause losses in the current year. Tillage is the principal means for managing weed populations although herbicides have reduced or replaced it in many systems. Herbicides enable the work to be done more quickly, more timely, and more cheaply with significantly less energy use than with tillage or hand labor.

**Control of insects and disease** Biocides are perhaps the most controversial management tools available to farmers. Much of the objection to modern farming methods stems from indiscriminate use of a few compounds. Synthesis and application of biocides require comparatively little energy, their major component is intellectual. Like fertilizer, biocides substitute chemical expertise for land and labor. An ideal biocide would be specific for the target species and have no residual effect. Few have achieved that objective and some have been very wide of the mark. It is important that unsafe biocides be withdrawn from use and that registration procedures encourage improvement in the quality of new compounds and direct the search for ideal biocides. Problems arise in defining 'unsafe', however, and it is important to counter unreasonable criticism of their use. Investigation can establish if the chances of deleterious effects are negligible, but never better than that. To reject that analysis will place a large burden of inefficiency on farmers, consumers, and ultimately, the landscape.

Major progress has been made in developing integrated pest management programs (IPM) that base controls on careful monitoring of pest populations. This allows biocides to be used only at critical times and in optimal ways. IPM offers the opportunity to optimize ecological controls and thus reduce biocide use, and also to slow development of resistance in target species. Critics of biocides sometimes challenge their use by citing evidence of pest adaptation. Given that biocide success depends on exploitation of slight differences in response between species, it is unlikely that this situation will ever change. Pests pay a price, however. Those that adapt to biocides generally are then less effective as pests.

## 18.6   CONCLUSIONS

The twenty-first century presents the need for vastly greater food supplies while offering uncertain physical and social climates and uncertain resouces for the pursuit of agriculture. Today's surpluses will disappear and strong pressures for expanded land use and intensification of production will emerge. Fertilizers and biocides will be essential. Our posture must be one that advances production through wise use of resources: efficiency, stability, and sustainability will continue as essential attributes. Meeting these challenges calls for a myriad of specific advances in our knowledge of biological, chemical, and physical aspects of environment and in our abilities in farm management. That can be done wisely, however, only when one has a clear view of how the parts fit together: of agricultural systems and the underlying principles of production ecology.

## 18.7   FURTHER READING

Marten, G. 1988. Productivity, stability and sustainability, equitability and autonomy as properties for agroecosystem assessment. *Agric. Sys.* **26**:291–316.
de Wit, C. T., H. Huisman and R. Rabbinge. 1987. Agriculture and its environment: are there other ways? *Agric. Sys.* **23**:211–36.
Knorr, D. (ed.) 1983. *Sustainable food systems.* AVI Publishing Co., Westport, Conn. 416 p.
Lee, R. D., W. B. Arthur, A. C. Kelley, G. Rodgers, and T. N. Srinivasan (eds). 1988. *Population, food and rural development.* International Studies in Demography. Clarendon Press, Oxford.
National Research Council 1989. *Alternative agriculture.* National Academy Press, Washington, DC. 448 p.

# References

Acevedo, V., I. Badilla, and P. S. Nobel. 1983. Water relations, diurnal acidity changes, and productivity of cultivated cactus, *Opuntia ficus-indica*. *Plant Physiol.* **72**:775–80.

Adams, F. (ed.). 1984. *Soil acidity and liming*. Agronomy Monograph No. 12, 2nd ed. Am. Soc. Agron., Madison, Wisconsin. 380 p.

Addiscott, T. M. 1988. Long-term leakage from bare unmanured land. *Soil Use Manage.* **4**:91–5.

Agricultural Research Council Working Party. 1980. *The nutrient requirements of ruminant livestock*. Commonwealth Agricultural Bureaux, Farnham Royal, Slough, UK. 351 p.

Aitken, Y. 1974. *Flowering time, climate and genotype*. Melbourne University Press, Melbourne. 193 p.

Alexander, G. and O. B. Williams. 1973. *The pastoral industries of Australia: practices and technology of sheep and cattle production*. Sydney University Press. 567 p.

Allard, R. W. 1988. Genetic changes associated with the evolution of adaptedness in cultivated plants and their wild progenitors. *J. Heredity* **79**:225–38.

Ames, B. N. and L. S. Gold. 1990. Too many rodent carcinogens: mitogenesis increases mutagenesis. *Science* **249**:970–1.

Amthor, J. S. 1989. *Respiration and crop productivity*. Springer-Verlag, New York. 215 p.

Anderson, J. R. and P. B. R. Hazell (eds). 1989. *Variability in grain yields*. Johns Hopkins University Press, Baltimore, Maryland. 395 p.

Anderson, J. R., C. J. Finlay, and G. H. Wan. 1989. Are modern cultivars more risky? A question of stochastic efficiency. In J. R. Anderson and P. B. R. Hazell (eds), *Variability in grain yields*, pp. 301–8. Johns Hopkins University Press, Baltimore. 395 p.

Angus, J. F., M. W. Cunningham, M. W. Moncur, and D. J. Mackenzie. 1981. Phasic development in field crops. I. Thermal response in the seedling phase. *Field Crops Res.* **3**:365–78.

Anon. 1988. *Draft: Salinity and drainage strategy*. Discussion Paper No. 1. Murray–Darling Basin Ministerial Council, Canberra. 12 p.

Archibald, S. O. and C. K. Winter. 1989. Pesticide residues and cancer risks. *Calif. Agric.* **43**(6):6–9.

Arkley, R. J. 1963. Relationships between plant growth and transpiration. *Hilgardia* **34**:559–84.

Arkley, R. J. 1982. Transpiration and productivity. In M. Rechcigl Jr. (ed.), *Handbook of agricultural productivity*, pp. 209–11. CRC Press, Boca Raton, Florida. 468 p.

Atherton, J. G. (ed.). 1987. *Manipulation of flowering*. Proceedings of the 45th Easter School in Agricultural Science, University of Nottingham. Butterworth, London. 438 p.

Austin, R. B. and M. H. Arnold. 1989. Variability in wheat yields in England: analysis and future prospects. In J. R. Anderson and P. B. R. Hazell (eds), *Variability in grain yields*, pp. 100–6. Johns Hopkins University Press, Baltimore. 395 p.

Austin, R. B., J. Bingham, R. D. Blackwell, L. T. Evans, and M. A. Ford. 1980. Genetic improvements in winter wheat yields since 1900 and associated physiological changes. *J. Agric. Sci. (Camb.)* **94**:675–89.

493

Avlani, P. K. and W. J. Chancellor. 1977. Energy requirements for wheat production and use in California. *Trans. ASAE* **20**:429–37.

Ayers, R. S. and D. W. Westcot. 1985. *Water quality for agriculture*. Irrig. Drain. Paper No. 29(rev. 1). FAOUN, Rome, Italy. 97 p.

Azevedo, J. and P. R. Stout. 1974. *Farm animal manures: An overview of their role in the agricultural environment*. Manual 44. Calif. Agric. Exp. Stn., University of California, Berkeley. 109 p.

Bair, R. A. 1942. Growth rates of maize under field conditions. *Plant Physiol.* **17**:619–31.

Baker, D. N. and R. E. Meyer. 1966. Influence of stand geometry on light interception and net photosynthesis in cotton. *Crop Sci.* **6**:15–19.

Baker, J. L. and H. P. Johnson. 1976. Impact of subsurface drainage on water quality. In *Proceedings of the Third National Drainage Symposium*, pp. 91–8. ASAE, St. Joseph, Michigan.

Barry, R. G. and R. J. Chorley. 1987. *Atmosphere, weather and climate*. Methuen, London. 460 p.

Bartholomew, D. 1982. Environmental control of dry-matter production in pineapple. I. In I. Ting and M. Gibbs (eds), *Crassulacean acid metabolism*, pp. 278–94. Am. Soc. Plant Physiol., Rockville, Maryland. 316 p.

Beale, P. E. 1974. Regeneration of *Trifolium subterraneum* cv Yarloop from seed reserves on Kangaroo Island. *J. Aust. Inst. Agric. Sci.* **40**:78–80.

Begg, J. E. and N. C. Turner. 1976. Crop water deficits. *Adv. Agron.* **28**:161–217.

Berndt, R. D. and B. J. White. 1976. A simulation-based evaluation of three cropping systems on cracking-clay soils in a summer-rainfall environment. *Agric. Meteorol.* **16**:211–29.

Bhatia, C. R. and R. Rabson. 1976. Bioenergetic considerations in cereal breeding for protein improvement. *Science* **194**:1418–21.

Bingham, J. 1972. Physiological objectives in breeding for grain yield in wheat. In F. G. H. Lupton, G. Jenkins and R. Johnson (eds), *The way ahead in plant breeding* (Proc. 6th Eucarpia Congr.), pp. 15–29. Plant Breeding Institute, Cambridge, UK. 269 p.

Biscoe, P. V., R. K. Scott, and J. L. Monteith. 1975. Barley and its environment. III. Carbon budget of the stand. *J. Appl. Ecol.* **12**: 269–91.

Björkman, O. (1981). Responses to different quantum flux densities. In O. L. Lange, P. S. Nobel, C. B. Osmond and H. Zeigler (eds), *Physiological plant ecology. I. Responses to the physical environment* (Encycl. Plant Physiol., new ser., vol. 12A), pp. 57–107. Springer-Verlag, Berlin.

Björkman, O., M. Nobs, R. Pearcy, J. Boynton, and J. Berry. 1969. Characteristics of hybrids between C3 and C4 species of *Atriplex*. In M. D. Hatch, C. B. Osmond, and R. O. Slayter (eds), *Photosynthesis and photorespiration*, pp. 105–19. Wiley-Interscience, New York. 565 p.

Black, C. C. 1971. Ecological implications of dividing plants into groups with distinct photosynthetic production capacities. *Adv. Ecol. Res.* **7**:87–115.

Blackmer, A. M., D. Pottker, M. E. Cerrato, and J. Webb. 1989. Correlations between soil nitrate concentrations in late spring and corn yields in Iowa. *J. Prod. Agric.* **2**:103–9.

Bloom, A. J., F. S. Chapin, and H. A. Mooney. 1985. Resource limitation in plants – an economic analogy. *Ann. Rev. Ecol. Syst.* **16**:363–92.

Bloom, A. J., R. M. Caldwell, J. Finazzo, R. L. Warner, and J. Weisshart. 1989. Oxygen and carbon dioxide fluxes from barley shoots depend on nitrate assimilation. *Plant Physiol.* **91**:352–6.

Boeringa, R. (ed.). 1980. *Alternative methods of agriculture*. Elsevier Scientific, Amsterdam. 199 p.

Bohn, H., B. L. McNeal, and G. A. O'Connor. 1985. *Soil chemistry*. 2nd ed. John Wiley, New York. 341 p.

Bolanos, J. and G. O. Edmeades. 1988. The importance of the anthesis–silking interval in breeding for drought tolerance in tropical maize. *Agron. Abst.* **1988**:74. Am. Soc. Agron., Madison, Wisconsin.

Bolland, M. and B. Gilkes. 1990. The poor performance of rock phosphate fertilizers in Western Australia: part 1. The crop and pasture responses. *J. Aust. Inst. Agric. Sci. N.S.* **3**:43–8.

Bolton, J. K. and R. H. Brown. 1980. Photosynthesis of grass species differing in carbon dioxide fixation pathways. V. Response of *Panicum maximum, Panicum milioides* and tall fescue (*Festuca arundinacea*) to nitrogen nutrition. *Plant Physiol.* **66**:97–100.

Bonnett, O. T. 1966. Infloresences of maize, wheat, rye, barley and oats: their initiation and development. *Agric. Res. Bull.* No. 721. University of Illinois, Urbana. 105 p.

Boserup, E. (1981). *Population and technological change.* University of Chicago Press, Chicago. 255 p.

Bouldin, D. R., S. D. Klausner, and W. S. Reid. 1984. Use of nitrogen from manure. In R. D. Hauck (ed.), *Nitrogen in crop production*, pp. 221–45. Am. Soc. Agron., Madison, Wisconsin. 804 p.

Briggs, D. and F. Courtney. 1985. *Agriculture and environment: the physical geography of temperate agricultural systems.* Longman Group, Harlow, Essex, UK. 442 p.

Broadbent, F. E. and A. B. Carlton. 1978. Field trials with isotopically labelled nitrogen fertilizer. In D. R. Nielsen and J. G. MacDonald (eds.), *Nitrogen in the environment*, vol. 1 pp. 1–41. Academic Press, New York. 526 p.

Brody, S. 1945. *Bioenergetics and growth.* Reinhold, New York. 1023 p.

Brouwer, R. 1983. Functional equilibrium: sense or nonsense? *Neth. J. Agric. Sci.* **31**:335–48.

Brown, D. L., J. T. Scott, E. J. de Peters, and R. L. Baldwin. 1989. Influence of sometribove, USAN (recombinant methionyl bovine somatotropin) on the body composition of lactating cattle. *Am. Inst. Nutr.* **1989**:633–8.

Brown, R. H. 1978. A difference in N use efficiency in C3 and C4 plants and its implications in adaptation and evolution. *Crop Sci.* **18**:93–8.

Browning, J. A. and K. J. Frey. 1969. Multiline cultivars as a means of disease control. *Ann. Rev. Phytopath.* **7**:355–82.

Bryson, R. A. and T. J. Murray. 1977. *Climates of hunger: mankind and the world's changing weather.* University of Wisconsin Press, Madison. 171 p.

Buol, S. W., F. D. Hole, and R. J. McCracken. 1989. *Soil genesis and classification.* 3rd edn. Iowa State University Press, Ames. 446 p.

Bureau of the Census. 1984. *Census of agriculture.* Vol. 2, Part 1. *Graphic summary.* U.S. Government Printing Office, Washington, DC. 188 p.

Buringh, I. P. 1977. *An estimation of world food production based on labour-oriented agriculture.* Centre for World Food Market Research, Wageningen, The Netherlands. 46 p.

Buringh, P. and van Heemst. H. D. 1979. Potential world food production. In H. Linnemann, J. de Hoogh, M. A. Keyzer, and H. D. van Heemst (eds), *MOIRA: Model of international relations in agriculture* (*Contr. Econ. Anal.* No. 124.), pp. 19–72. Elsevier North-Holland, Amsterdam, The Netherlands. 379 p.

Bywater, A. C. and R. L. Baldwin. 1980. Alternative strategies in food-animal production. In R. J. Baldwin (ed.), *Animals, feed, food and people: an analysis of the role of animals in food production*, pp. 1–29. (AAAS Sel. Symp. No. 42.) Westview Press, Boulder, Colorado. 149 p.

Callaghan, A. R. and A. J. Millington. 1956. *The wheat industry in Australia.* Angus and Robertson, Sydney. 486 p.

Campbell, G. S. 1977. *An introduction to environmental biophysics.* Springer-Verlag, New York. 159 p.

Cardwell, V. B. 1982. Fifty years of Minnesota corn production: sources of yield increase. *Agron. J.* **74**:984–90.

Cerrato, M. E. and A. M. Blackmer. 1990. Comparison of models for describing corn yield response to nitrogen. *Agron. J.* **82**:138–43.

Chalmers, D. J., P. D. Mitchell, and L. van Heek. 1981. Control of peach tree growth and productivity by regulated water supply, tree density and summer pruning. *J. Am. Soc. Hort. Sci.* **106**:307–12.

Chang, C. C. 1963. *An agricultural engineering analysis of rice farming methods in Taiwan.* Conf. Paper No. 20. IRRI, Los Banos, Philippines.

Chapman, H. W., L. S. Gleason, and W. E. Loomis. 1954. The carbon dioxide content of field air. *Plant Physiol.* **29**:500–3.

Church, D. C. 1976. *Digestive physiology and nutrition of ruminants.* Vol. I. *Digestive physiology.* O & B books, Corvallis, Oregon. 250 p.

Cock, J. H. 1987. Stability of performance of cassava genotypes. In E. C. Hershey (ed.), *Cassava breeding: a multidisciplinary review*, pp. 177–206. CIAT, Cali, Colombia.

Cock, J. H., N. M. Riano, M. A. El-Sharkawy, Y. Lopez, and G. Bastidas. 1987. C3–C4 intermediate photosynthetic characteristics of cassava (*Manihot esculenta* Crantz). II. Initial products of $^{14}CO_2$ fixation. *Photosyn. Res.* **12**:237–41.

Cockroft, B. and W. Mason. 1987. Irrigated agriculture. In D. J. Connor and D. F. Smith (eds), *Agriculture in Victoria*, pp. 159–77. Australian Institute of Agricultural Science, Melbourne. 231 p.

Coehlo, D. T. and R. F. Dale. 1980. An energy-crop growth variable and temperature function for predicting corn growth and development: Planting to silking. *Agron. J.* **72**:503–10.

Colvin, T. S., J. M. Laflen, and D. C. Erbach. 1981. A review of residue reduction by individual tillage implements. In *Crop production with conservation in the 80's*, pp. 102–10. ASAE, St. Joseph, Michigan.

Connor, D. J. 1975. Growth, water relations and yield of wheat. *Aust. J. Pl. Physiol.* **2**:353–66.

Connor, D. J. 1983. Plant stress factors and their influence on production of agroforestry plant associations. In P. A. Huxley (ed.). *Plant research and agroforestry*, pp. 401–26. ICRAF, Nairobi, Kenya. 617 p.

Connor, D. J. and O. Cartledge. 1970. Observed and calculated photosynthetic rates in *Chloris gayana* communities. *J. Appl. Ecol.* **7**:353–6.

Connor, D. J. and J. H. Cock. 1981. The response of cassava to water shortage. II. Canopy dynamics. *Field Crops Res.* **4**: 285–96.

Connor, D. J. and T. R. Jones. 1985. Response of sunflower to strategies of irrigation. II. Morphological and physiological responses to water shortage. *Field Crops Res.* **12**:91–103.

Connor, D. J. and J. A. Palta. 1981. The response of cassava to water shortage. III. Stomatal control of plant water status. *Field Crops Res.* **4**:297–311.

Connor, D. J. and D. F. Smith (eds). 1987. *Agriculture in Victoria.* Australian Institute of Agricultural Science, Melbourne. 231 p.

Connor, D. J., J. H. Cock, and G. H. Parra. 1981. The response of cassava to water shortage. I. Growth and yield. *Field Crops Res.* **4**:181–200.

Connor, D. J., T. J. Jones, and J. A. Palta. 1985a. Response of sunflower to strategies of irrigation. I. Growth, yield and the efficiency of water use. *Field Crops Res.* **10**:15–26.

Connor, D. J., J. A. Palta, and T. R. Jones. 1985b. Response of sunflower to strategies of irrigation. III. Crop photosynthesis and transpiration. *Field Crops Res.* **12**:281–93.

Cook, R. J. and K. F. Baker. 1983. *The nature and practice of biological control of plant pathogens.* Am. Phytopath. Soc., St. Paul, Minnesota. 539 p.

Cooper, J. P. 1970. Potential production and energy conservation in temperate and tropical grasses. *Herbage Abst.* **40**:1–13.

Cooper, P. J. M., P. J. Gregory, D. Tully, and H. C. Harris. 1987. Improving water use efficiency of annual crops in the rainfed farming systems of west Asia and North Africa. *Exp. Agric.* **23**:113–58.

Cornish, P. S. 1987. Effects of residues and tillage on the water balance of a red earth soil. In T. G. Reeves (ed.), *Proceedings of the Fourth Australian Agronomy Conference*, p. 294. Aust. Soc. Agron., Melbourne. 383 p.

Cornish, P. S. and J. E. Pratley. 1987. *Tillage: new directions in Australian agriculture.* Inkata Press, Melbourne. 448 p.

Costanza, R. 1980. Embodied energy and economic valuation. *Science* **210**:1219–24.

Coventry, D. R. 1985. Changes in agricultural systems on acid soils in southern Australia. In J. J. Yates (ed.), *Proceedings of the Third Australian Agronomy Conference*, pp. 126–45. Aust. Soc. Agron., Melbourne. 425 p.

Cowan, I. R. 1965. Transport of water in the soil–plant–atmosphere system. *J. Appl. Ecol.* **2**:221–39.

Cowan, I. R. 1982. Regulation of water use in relation to carbon gain in higher plants. In O. L. Lange, P. S. Nobel, C. B. Osmond, and H. Ziegler (eds), *Physiological plant ecology II. Water relations and carbon assimilation* (*Encycl. Plant Physiol.*, new ser. vol. 12B), pp. 589–613. Springer-Verlag, Berlin.

Cowan, I. R. 1986. Economics of carbon fixation in higher plants. In T. J. Givnish (ed.), *On the economy of plant form and function*, pp. 133–70. Cambridge University Press.

Cox, G. W. and M. D. Atkins. 1979. *Agricultural ecology*. W. H. Freeman, San Francisco. 721 p.

Curtis, J. T. 1959. *The vegetation of Wisconsin: an ordination of plant communities*. University of Wisconsin Press, Madison. 657 p.

Davidson, J. L. and J. R. Phillip. 1958. Light and pasture growth. *Arid Zone Res.* 11:181–7.

Denholm, J. V. and D. J. Connor. 1982. Potential photosynthesis in trellis-type orchard canopies. *Aust. J. Plant Physiol.* 9:629–40.

Denison, R. F. and R. S. Loomis. 1989. *An integrative physiological model of alfalfa growth and development.* Publ. No. 1926. Div. Agric. Nat. Res., University of California, Oakland, California. 73 p.

Denmead, O. T. and R. J. Shaw. 1962. Availability of soil water to plants as affected by soil moisture content and meteorological conditions. *Agron. J.* 54:385–90.

de Vries, C. A., J. D. Ferwerda, and M. Flach. 1967. Choice of food crops in relation to actual and potential production in the tropics. *Neth. J. Agric. Sci.* 15:241–8.

de Wit, C. T. 1953. A physical theory of fertilizer placement. *Versl. Landbouwk. Onderz.* 59.4. 77 p.

de Wit, C. T. 1958. Transpiration and crop yields. *Versl. Landbouwk. Onderz.* 64.6. 87 p.

de Wit, C. T. 1960. On competition. *Versl. Landbouwk. Onderz.* 66.8. 82 p.

de Wit, C. T. 1965. *Photosynthesis of leaf canopies.* Agric. Res. Rep. 663: 57.

de Wit, C. T. 1975. Substitution of labour and energy in agriculture with options for growth. *Math. J. Agric. Sci.* 23:145–62.

de Wit, C. T. 1979. The efficient use of labour, land and energy in agriculture. *Agric. Syst.* 4:279–87.

de Wit, C. T. and J. P. van den Bergh. 1965. Competition between herbage plants. *Neth. J. Agric. Sci.* 13:212–21.

de Wit, C. T. *et al.* 1978. *Simulation of assimilation, respiration and transpiration of crops.* Simulation Monographs. Pudoc, Wageningen, The Netherlands. 141 p.

Dickey, E. C. and A. R. Rider. 1981. Eastern Nebraska row crop tillage systems. In *Crop production with conservation in the 80's*, pp. 85–93. ASAE, St. Joseph, Michigan. 281 p.

Diebert, E. J., M. Bijeriego, and R. A. Olson. 1979. Utilization of $^{15}N$ fertilizer by nodulating and non-nodulating soybean isolines. *Agron. J.* 71:717–22.

Doering, O. C. III 1977. *An energy based analysis of alternative production methods and cropping systems in the Corn Belt.* Purdue University, Agricultural Experiment Station, West Lafayette, Indiana. 43 p.

Donald, C. M. 1958. The interaction of competition for light and for nutrients. *Aust. J. Agric. Res.* 9 (4):421–35.

Donald, C. M. 1963. Competition among crop and pasture plants. *Adv. Agron.* 15:1–118.

Donald, C. M. 1968. The breeding of crop ideotypes. *Euphytica* 17:385–403.

Donald, C. M. and J. Hamblin. 1976. The biological yield and harvest index of cereals as agronomic and plant breeding criteria. *Adv. Agron.* 28:361–405.

Donald, C. M. and J. Hamblin. 1983. The convergent evolution of annual seed crops in agriculture. *Adv. Agron.* 36:97–143.

Doneen, L. D. 1975. Water quality for irrigated agriculture. In A. Poljakoff-Mayber and J. Gale (eds), *Plants in saline environments.* (Ecol. Studies Ser. No. 15), pp. 56–76. Springer-Verlag, Berlin. 213 p.

Doorenbos, J. and A. H. Kassam 1986. *Yield response to water.* (Irrigation and Drainage Paper no. 33.) FAO, Rome. 193 p.

Doorenbos, J. and W. O. Pruitt. 1977. *Crop water requirements.* Irrig. Drain. Paper. No. 24. FAOUN, Rome. 179 p.

Duckham, A. N. and G. B. Masefield. 1970. *Farming systems of the world.* Praeger, New York. 542 p.

Duncan, W. G. 1971. Leaf angles, leaf area and canopy photosynthesis. *Crop Sci.* 11:482–5.

Duncan, W. G., R. S. Loomis, W. A. Williams, and R. Hanau. 1967. A model for simulating photosynthesis in plant communities. *Hilgardia* **38**:181–205.

Duncan, W. G., D. E. McCloud, R. L. McGraw, and K. J. Boote. 1978. Physiological aspects of peanut yield improvement. *Crop Sci.* **18**:1015–20.

Duvick, D. N. 1989. Possible genetic causes of increased variability in U.S. maize yields. In J. R. Anderson and P. B. R. Hazell (eds), *Variability in grain yields*, pp. 147–56. Johns Hopkins University Press, Baltimore. 395 p.

Eberhardt, S. A. and W. A. Russell. 1966. Stability parameters for comparing varieties. *Crop Sci.* **6**:36–40.

Edwards, G. W. 1976. Energy budgeting. Joules or dollars? *Aust. J. Agric. Econ.* **20**:179–91.

Ehleringer, J. and R. W. Pearcy. 1983. Variation in quantum yield for $CO_2$ uptake among C3 and C4 plants. *Plant Physiol.* **73**:555–9.

Ekern, P. C. 1965. Evapotranspiration of pineapple in Hawaii. *Plant Physiol.* **40**:736–9.

El-Hout, N. M. and A. M. Blackmer. 1990. Nitrogen status of corn after alfalfa in 29 Iowa fields. *J. Soil Water Conserv.* **45**:115–17.

Elton, C. S. 1958. *The ecology of invasions by plants and animals.* Methuen, London. 181 p.

Evans, J. R., S. von Caemmerer, and W. W. Adams III (eds). 1988. *Ecology of photosynthesis in sun and shade.* CSIRO, Australia. 358 p.

Evans, L. T. 1971. Evolutionary, adaptive, and environmental aspects of the photosynthetic pathway: assessment. In M. D. Hatch, C. B. Osmond, and R. O. Slatyer (eds), *Photosynthesis and photorespiration*, pp. 130–6. Wiley-Interscience, New York. 565 p.

Evans, L. T. and R. L. Dunstone. 1970. Some physiological aspects of evolution in wheat. *Aust. J. Biol. Sci.* **23**:725–41.

Evans, L. T., R. M. Visperas, and B. S. Vergara. 1984. Morphological and physiological changes among rice varieties used in the Philippines over the last seventy years. *Field Crops Res.* **8**:105–24.

FAO/WHO. 1973. *Energy and protein requirements. Report of Joint Expert Committee.* FAOUN, Rome. 118 p.

FAO/WHO/UNU. 1985. *Energy and protein requirements. Joint Expert Consultation.* Tech. Rep. No. 724. World Health Organization, Geneva. 206 p.

Farquhar, G. D. and R. A. Richards. 1984. Istopic composition of plant carbon correlates with water-use efficiency of wheat genotypes. *Aust. J. Plant Physiol.* **11**:539–52.

Farquhar, G. G., M. H. O'Leary, and J. A. Berry. 1982. On the relationship between carbon isotope discrimination and the intercellular carbon dioxide concentration in leaves. *Aust. J. Plant Physiol.* **9**:121–37.

Fehr, W. R. (ed.). 1984. *Genetic contributions to yield gains of five major crop plants.* CSSA Spec. Publ. No. 7. Am. Soc. Agron., Madison, Wisconsin. 101 p.

Fereres, E., J. L. Meyer, F. K. Alijibury, H. Schulbach, and A. W. Marsh. 1981. *Irrigation costs.* Div. Agric. Sci., University of California, Berkeley, California. 14 p.

Fick, G. W., W. A. Williams, and R. S. Loomis. 1971. Recovery from partial defoliation and root pruning in sugar beet. *Crop Sci.* **11**:718–21.

Fick, G. W., W. A. Williams, and R. S. Loomis. 1973. Computer simulation of dry matter distribution during sugar beet growth. *Crop Sci.* **13**:413–17.

Finlay, K. W. and G. N. Wilkinson. 1963. The analysis of adaptation in a plant breeding programme. *Aust. J. Agric. Res.* **14**:742–54.

Fischer, R. A. 1979. Growth and water limitation to dryland wheat yield in Australia: A physiological framework. *J. Aust. Inst. Agric. Sci.* **45**:83–94.

Fischer, R. A. and J. S. Armstrong. 1987. Strategies and tactics with short fallows. In T. G. Reeves (ed.), *Proceedings of the Fourth Australian Agronomy Conference*, p. 300. Aust. Soc. Agron., Melbourne. 383 p.

Fischer, R. A. and R. Maurer. 1978. Drought resistance in spring wheat cultivars. I. Grain yield responses. *Aust. J. Agric. Res.* **29**:897–912.

Fischer, R. A. and N. C. Turner. 1978. Plant productivity in arid and semiarid zones. *Ann. Rev. Plant Physiol.* **29**:277–317.

Fitzpatrick, E. A. and H. A. Nix. 1970. The climatic factor in Australian grassland ecology. In

R. M. Moore (ed.), *Australian grasslands*, pp. 3–26. Australian National University Press, Canberra. 455 p.

Fleagle, R. G. and J. A. Businger. 1980. *An introduction to atmospheric physics.* 2nd ed. Academic Press, New York. 432 p.

Flint, M. L. and R. van den Bosch. 1981. *Introduction to integrated pest management.* Plenum Press, New York. 240 p.

Fluck, R. C. 1981. Net energy sequestered in agricultural labor. *Trans. ASAE* **24**:1449–55.

Fluck, R. C. and C. D. Baird. 1980. *Agricultural energetics.* AVI Publishing, Westport, Connecticut. 192 p.

Forrester, J. W. 1961. *Industrial dynamics.* Massachusetts Institute of Technology Press, Cambridge, Massachusetts. 464 p.

Foyer, C. H. 1988. Feedback inhibition of photosynthesis through source-sink regulation in leaves. *Plant Physiol. Biochem.* **26**:483–92.

Francis, C. A. 1989. Biological efficiencies in multiple cropping systems. *Adv. Agron.* **42**:1–42.

French, R. J. and J. E. Schultz. 1984. Water use efficiency of wheat in a Mediterranean environment. I. The relation between yield, water use and climate. *Aust. J. Agric. Res.* **35**:743–64.

Frey, K. J., J. A. Browning, and M. D. Simons. 1977. Management systems for host genes to control disease. *Ann. New York Acad. Sci.* **287**:255–74.

Frissel, M. (ed.). 1977. Cycling of mineral nutrients in agricultural systems. *Agro-Ecosys.* (special issue) **4**:1–354.

Fröhlich, C. and J. London. 1985. *Radiation manual.* World Meteorological Organization, Geneva.

Gaff, D. F. 1981. The biology of resurrection plants. In J. S. Pate and A. J. McComb (eds), *The biology of Australian plants*, pp. 114–46. University of Western Australia Press, Nedlands. 412 p.

Gallon, J. R. and A. E. Chaplin. 1987. *An introduction to nitrogen fixation.* Cassell Educational, London. 276 p.

Gardner, W. R. 1965. Dynamic aspects of soil-water availability to plants. *Ann. Rev. Plant Physiol.* **16**:323–42.

Gardner, W. R. and R. H. Brooks. 1957. A descriptive theory of leaching. *Soil  Sci.* **83**:295–304.

Garner, W. W. and H. A. Allard. 1920. Effect of length of day and night and other factors of the environment on growth and reproduction in plants. *J. Agric. Res.* **18**:553–606.

Garrett, W. N. and N. Hinman. 1969. Re-evaluation of the relationship between carcass density and body composition of beef steers. *J. Anim. Sci.* **28**:1–5.

Gates, D. M. 1980. *Biophysical ecology.* Springer-Verlag, New York. 611 p.

Gifford, R. M. and R. J. Millington. 1975. *Energetics of agriculture and food production.* Aust. Bull. No. 288. CSIRO, Melbourne, Australia. 29 p.

Gilmore, E. C. and J. S. Rogers. 1958. Heat units as a method of measuring maturity in corn. *Agron. J.* **50**:611–15.

Gimeno, V., J. M. Fernandez-Martinez, and E. Fereres. 1989. Winter planting as a means of drought escape in sunflower. *Field Crops Res.* **22**:307–16.

Givnish, T. J. (ed.). 1986. *On the economy of plant form and function.* Cambridge University Press. 717 p.

Gladstones, J. S. 1967. Naturalized subterranean clover strains in Western Australia: a preliminary agronomic examination. *Aust. J. Agric. Res.* **18**:713–32.

Gleason, H. A. 1926. The individualistic concept of plant association. *Bull. Torrey Bot. Club* **53**:1–20.

Goodman, D. 1975. The theory of diversity-stability relationships in ecology. *Quart. Rev. Biol.* **50**:237–61.

Goyne, P. J. and A. A. Schneiter. 1987. Photoperiod influence on development in sunflower genotypes. *Agron. J.* **79**:704–9.

Grieve, A. M., E. Dunford, D. Marston, R. E. Martin, and P. Slavich. 1986. Effects of waterlogging and soil salinity in the Murray Valley: a review. *Aust. J. Exp. Agric.* **26**:761–77.

Griffiths, J. B. and D. N. Walsgott. 1987. Water use of wheat in the Victorian Mallee. In T. G. Reeves (ed.), *Proceedings of the Fourth Australian Agronomy Conference*, p. 296. Aust. Soc. Agron., Melbourne. 383 p.

Grimes, D. W. and K. M. El-Zik. 1982. *Water management for cotton*. Div. Agric. Sci., University of California, Berkeley, California.

Gutschick, V. P. 1987. *A functional biology of crop plants*. Croom Helm, London. 230 p.

Guyol, N. D. 1977. *Energy interrelationships. A handbook of tables and conversion factors for combining and comparing international energy data*. Publ. No. FEB/B-77/166. Federal Energy Administration, Washington, D.C. 60 p.

Hagan, R. M., H. R. Haise, and T. W. Edminster (eds). 1967. *Irrigation of agricultural lands*. Am. Soc. Agron., Madison, Wisconsin. 1179 p.

Haggett, P. 1979. *Geography: a modern synthesis*. Harper & Row, New York. 627 p.

Hahn, R. E. and E. E. Rosentreter (eds). 1989. *ASAE standards 1989*. 36th edition. ASAE, St. Joseph, Michigan.

Hall, A. J., A. Vilella, N. Trapani, and C. Chimenti. 1982a. The effects of water stress and genotype on the dynamics of pollen-shedding and silking in maize. *Field Crops Res.* **5**:349–63.

Hall, G. F., R. B. Daniels, and J. E. Foss. 1982b. Rate of soil formation and renewal in the USA. In *Determinants of soil loss tolerance* (Special Publication No. 45), pp. 23–39. Am. Soc. Agron., Madison, Wisconsin. 153 p.

Hamdi, Y. A. 1982. *Application of nitrogen-fixing systems in soil improvement and management*. FAO Soils Bull. No. 49. FAOUN, Rome. 188 p.

Hamilton, W. H. III and K. E. F. Watt. 1970. Refuging. *Ann. Rev. Ecol. Syst.* **1**:263–86.

Hammer, G. L., P. J. Goyne, and D. R. Woodruff. 1982. Phenology of sunflower cultivars. III. Models for prediction in field environments. *Aust. J. Agric. Res.* **33**:263–74.

Hanks, R. J. 1983. Yield and water use relationships. In H. M. Taylor, W. R. Jordan, and T. R. Sinclair (eds), *Limitations to efficient use of water in crop production*, pp. 393–412. Am. Soc. Agron., Madison, Wisconsin. 538 p.

Hanway, J. J. and C. R. Weber. 1971. Dry matter accumulation in eight soybean (*Glycine max* (L.) Merrill) varieties. *Agron. J.* **63**:227–30.

Hardin, G. J. 1977. *Managing the commons*. W. H. Freeman, San Francisco. 294 p.

Harlan, H. V. and M. L. Martini. 1929. A composite hybrid mixture. *J. Am. Soc. Agron.* **21**:487–90.

Harlan, H. V. and M. L. Martini. 1938. The effect of natural selection in a mixture of barley varieties. *J. Agric. Res.* **57**:189–99.

Harper, J. L. 1960. *The biology of weeds*. Blackwell Scientific, Oxford, UK. 256 p.

Harper, J. L. 1977. *Population biology of plants*. Academic Press, New York. 892 p.

Hatch, M. D., C. B. Osmond, and R. O. Slatyer (eds). 1971. *Photosynthesis and photorespiration*. Wiley-Interscience, New York. 565 p.

Hauck, R. D. (ed.). 1984. *Nitrogen in crop production*. Am. Soc. Agron., Madison, Wisconsin. 804 p.

Hay, R. K. M. and A. J. Walker. 1989. *An introduction to the physiology of crop yield*. Longman Scientific & Technical, Harlow, Essex, UK. 292 p.

Haynes, R. J. 1986. *Mineral nitrogen in the plant–soil system*. Academic Press, Orlando, Florida. 496 p.

Hazell, P. B. R. 1989. Changing patterns of variability in world cereal production. In J. R. Anderson and P. B. R. Hazell (eds), *Variability in grain yield*, pp. 13–34. Johns Hopkins University Press, Baltimore. 395 p.

Heichel, G. H. 1978. Stabilizing agricultural energy needs: role of forages, rotations, and nitrogen fixation. *J. Soil Water Conserv.* **33**:279–82.

Helyar, K. R. and W. M. Porter. 1989. Soil acidification, its measurement and the processes involved. In A. D. Robson (ed.), *Soil acidity and plant growth*, pp. 61–101. Academic Press Australia, Merrickville, New South Wales. 306 p.

Herridge, D. F. and F. J. Bergersen. 1988. Symbiotic nitrogen fixation. In J. R. Wilson (ed.), *Advances in nitrogen cycling in agricultural ecosystems*, pp. 45–65. CAB International, Wallingford, Oxon, UK. 451 p.

Heydecker, W. 1973. *Seed ecology*. Butterworth, London. 578 p.

Hiler, E. A., A. T. Howell, R. B. Lewis, and R. P. Boos. 1974. Irrigation timing by the stress day index method. *Trans. ASAE* **17**:393–8.

Hirose, T. and M. J. A. Werger. 1987. Maximizing daily canopy photosynthesis with respect to the leaf nitrogen allocation pattern in the canopy. *Oecologia* **72**:520–6.

Holaday, A. S. and C. C. Black. 1981. Comparative characterization of phosphoenolpyruvate carboxylase in C3, C3 and C3–C4 intermediate *Panicum* species. *Plant Physiol.* **67**:330–4.

Hoskinson, P. E. and C. O. Qualset. 1967. Geographic variation in Balboa rye. *Tennessee Farm & Home Progress Report* **62**(2):8–9.

Houston, C. E. 1967. *Drainage of irrigated land*. Calif. Agric. Exp. Sta., University of California, Berkeley, California. 40 p.

Howard, P. M. 1981. The water erosion problem in the US. In *Crop production with conservation in the 80's*, pp. 25–34. ASAE, St. Joseph, Michigan.

Hsiao, T. C., E. Fereres, E. Acevedo, and D. W. Henderson. 1976. Water stress and dynamics of growth and yield of crop plants. In O. L. Lange, L. Kappen, and E.-D. Schulze (eds), *Water and plant life*, pp. 281–305. Ecological Studies Vol. 19. Springer-Verlag, Berlin. 536 p.

Huang, P. 1989. Feldspars, olivines, pyroxenes, and amphiboles. In J. B Dixon and S. B. Weed (eds), *Minerals in the soil environment*, pp. 975–1050. Soil. Sci. Soc. Am., Madison, Wisconsin. 1244 p.

Hubbert, M. K. 1969. Energy resources. In National Research Council. Committee on Resources and Man, *Resources and man*, pp. 187–242. W. H. Freeman, San Francisco. 259 p.

Hudson, J. C. 1975. Sugarcane: its energy relationships with fossil fuel. *Span* **18**:12–14.

Hunt, D. 1983. *Farm power and machinery management*. Iowa State University Press, Ames, Iowa. 352 p.

Hunt, R. 1978. *Plant growth analysis*. Studies in Biology no. 96. Edward Arnold, London. 67 p.

Hunt, W. F. and R. S. Loomis. 1976. Carbohydrate-limited growth kinetics of tobacco (*Nicotiana rustica* L.) callus. *Plant Physiol.* **57**:802–5.

Huxley, P. A. (ed.). 1983. *Plant research and agroforestry*. ICRAF, Nairobi, Kenya. 617 p.

Iowa Agricultural Statistics. 1989. *1989 Agricultural statistics*. Iowa Department of Agriculture and Land Stewardship. Des Moines. 107 p.

Jacobs, M. R. 1955. *Growth habits of Australian eucalypts*. Australian Government Printer, Canberra. 261 p.

Jenkins, B. M. and G. Knutson. 1984. Energy balances in biomass handling systems: net energy analysis of electricity from straw. *Proc. Am. Soc. Agric. Eng. Conf.*, New Orleans Paper **84**–3593:16.

Jenkinson, D. S. 1982. The nitrogen cycle in long term field experiments. *Phil. Trans. R. Soc. Lond.* B**296**:563–71.

Jenkinson, D. S. 1988. Determination of microbial biomass carbon and nitrogen in soil. In J. R. Wilson (ed.), *Advances in nitrogen cycling in agricultural ecosystems*, pp. 368–86. CAB International, Wallingford, Oxon, UK. 451 p.

Jenkinson, D. S. 1991. The Rothamsted long-term experiments: are they still of use? *Agron. J.* **83**:2–10.

Jennings, D. H. and A. J. Trewavas (eds). 1986. *Plasticity in plants*. (*Symp. Soc. Exp. Biol.* no. 40.) Cambridge University Press. 372 p.

Jenny, H. 1930. *A study on the influence of climate upon the nitrogen and organic matter content of the soil*. University of Missouri Agric. Exp. Sta. Res. Bull. No. 152. 66 p.

Jenny, H. 1941. *Factors of soil formation*. McGraw-Hill Book Co., New York. 281 p.

Jenny, H. 1980. *The soil resource*. Ecological Studies Vol. 37. Springer-Verlag, New York. 377 p.

Jensen, M. E. 1974. *Consumptive use of water and irrigation water requirements.* Am Soc. Civil Eng., New York. 215 p.

Johnson, I. R. and J. H. M. Thornley. 1984. A model of instantaneous and daily canopy photosynthesis. *J. Theor. Biol.* **107**:531–45.

Johnson, J. W., L. F. Welch, and L. T. Kurtz. 1975. Environmental implications of N fixation by soybeans. *J. Environ. Qual.* **4**:303–6.

Johnson, W. A., V. Stoltzfus, and P. Craumer. 1977. Energy conservation in Amish agriculture. *Science* **198**:373–8.

Jones, C. A. and J. R. Kiniry (eds). 1986. *CERES-MAIZE. A simulation model of maize growth and development.* Texas A&M University Press, College Station. 194 p.

Jones, H. G. 1983. *Plants and microclimates – a quantitative approach to environmental plant physiology.* Cambridge University Press. 323 p.

Jones, J. W. 1983. Irrigation options to avoid critical stresses: Optimization of on-farm water allocation to crops. In H. M. Taylor, W. R. Jordan, and T. R. Sinclair (eds). *Limitations to efficient water use in crop production,* pp. 507–616. Am. Soc. Agron., Madison. Wisconsin. 538 p.

Jones, M. R. 1989. Analysis of the use of energy in agriculture. *Agric. Syst.* **29**:339–55.

Jones, P. D., T. M. L. Wigley, and P. B. Wright. 1990. *Global and hemispheric annual temperature variations between 1861 and 1988.* Carbon Dioxide Information Center, Oak Ridge National Laboratory, Oak Ridge, Tennessee.

Jordan, W. R. and F. R. Miller. 1980. Genetic variability in sorghum root systems: implications for drought tolerance. In N. C. Turner and P. J. Kramer (eds), *Adaptation of plants to water and high temperature stress,* pp. 383–99. John Wiley, New York. 482 p.

Jordan, W. R., W. A. Dugas, and P. J. Shouse. 1983. Strategies for crop improvement for drought-prone regions. *Agric. Water Manage.* **7**:281–99.

Kaddah, M. T. and J. D. Rhoades. 1976. Salt and water balance in Imperial Valley, California. *Soil Sci. Soc. Am. J.* **40**:93–100.

Kampmeijer, P. and J. C. Zadoks. 1977. *EPIMUL, a simulator of foci and epidemics in mixtures of resistant and susceptible plants, mosaics and multilines.* Simulation Monographs. Pudoc, Wageningen, The Netherlands. 50 p.

Kanwar, R. S., J. L. Baker, and D. G. Baker. 1988a. Tillage and split N-fertilization effects on subsurface drainage water quality and crop yields. *Trans. ASAE* **31**:453–60.

Kanwar, R. S., Z. Shahvar, and J. L. Baker. 1988b. Use of models to simulate the effects of agricultural practices on nitrate loss with drainage water. *Math. Comput. Model.* **10**:183–91.

Kiniry, J. R., J. T. Ritchie, and R. L. Musser. 1983. Dynamic nature of the photoperiod response of maize. *Agron. J.* **75**:700–3.

Kira, T., H. Ogawa, and K. Shinozaki. 1953. Intraspecific competition among higher plants. 1. Competition-density-yield inter-relationships in regularly dispersed populations. *J. Inst. Polytech. Osaka City Univ.* **4**:1–16.

Kirby, E. J. M. and M. Appleyard. 1984. *Cereal development guide.* 2nd edn. National Agricultural Centre, Stoneleigh, UK. 95 p.

Kittrick, J. A. 1986. *Soil mineral weathering.* Van Nostrand-Reinhold, New York. 271 p.

Klingebiel, A. A. and P. H. Montgomery. 1961. *Land-use capability classification.* Agric. Handbook No. 210. U.S. Government Printing Office, Washington, D.C. 210 p.

Knorr, D. (ed.). 1983. *Sustainable food systems.* AVI Publ., Westport, Connecticut. 416 p.

Knutson, J. D., R. G. Curley, E. B. Roberts, R. M. Hagan, and V. Cervinka. 1977. Energy for irrigation. *Calif. Agric.* **31**(5):46–7.

Kølster, P., L. Munk, and O. Stølen. 1989. Disease severity and grain yield in barley multilines with resistance to powdery mildew. *Crop Sci.* **29**:1459–63.

Lafitte, H. R. and R. S. Loomis. 1988a. Calculation of growth yield, growth respiration and heat content of grain sorghum from elemental and proximal analyses. *Ann. Bot.* **62**:353–61.

Lafitte, H. R. and R. S. Loomis. 1988b. The growth and composition of grain sorghum with limited nitrogen. *Agron J.* **80**:492–8.

Laing, D. R., P. J. Kretchmer, S. Zuluaga, and P. G. Jones. 1983. Field bean. In W. H. Smith and S. J. Banta (eds), *Potential productivity of field crops under different environments*, pp. 227–48. IRRI, Los Banos, Philippines. 526 p.

Lamb, H. H. 1977. *Climate: past, present and future*. Vol. 2. *Climatic history and the future.* Metheun, London. 835 p.

Lange, O. L., P. S. Nobel, C. B. Osmond, and H. Zeigler (eds). 1982. *Physiological plant ecology. II. Water relations and carbon assimilation.* Vol. 12B. *Encyc. Plant Physiol.*, New Ser. Springer-Verlag, Heidelberg. 747 p.

Large, E. C. 1954. Growth stages in cereals. Illustrations of the Feekes' scale. *Plant Path.* **3**:128–9.

LaRue, T. A. and T. G. Patterson. 1981. How much nitrogen do legumes fix? *Adv. Agron.* **34**:15–38.

Laties, G. G. 1982. The cyanide-resistant, alternative path in higher plant respiration. *Ann. Rev. Plant Physiol.* **33**:519–55.

Latshaw, W. L. and E. C. Miller. 1924. Elemental composition of the corn plant. *J. Agric. Res.* **27**:845–60.

Laude, H. M. and E. H. Stanford. 1960. Environmentally induced changes in gene frequency in a synthetic forage variety grown outside the region of adaptation. *Proc. Int. Grassl. Congr.* **8**:180–4.

Lazenby, A. and E. M. Matheson. 1975. *Australian field crops. Wheat and other temperate cereals.* Angus and Robertson, Sydney. 570 p.

Leck, M. A., V. T. Parker, and R. L. Simpson. 1989. *Ecology of soil seed banks.* Academic Press, San Diego, California. 462 p.

Lee, D. H. K. 1970. Nitrates, nitrites and methemoglobinemia. *Environ. Res.* **3**:484–511.

Lee, R. D., W. B. Arthur, A. C. Kelley, G. Rodgers, and T. N. Srinivasan (eds). 1988. *Population, food and rural development.* International Studies in Demography. Clarendon Press, Oxford. 215 p.

Legg, T. D., J. J. Fletcher, and K. W. Easter. 1989. Nitrogen budgets and economic efficiency: a case study of southeastern Minnesota. *J. Prod. Agric.* **2**:110–16.

Leitch, I. and W. Godden. 1953. *The efficiency of farm animals in the conversion of feedingstuffs to food for man.* (Anim. Nut. Tech. Commun. no. 14.) Commonwealth Agricultural Bureaux, Farnham Royal, Slough, UK. 73 p.

Levi, J. and M. L. Petterson. 1972. Responses of spring wheats to vernalization and photoperiod. *Crop Sci.* **12**:487–90.

Lindsay, W. L., P. L. G. Vlek, and S. H. Chien. 1989. Phosphate minerals. In J. B. Dixon and S. B. Weed (eds), *Minerals in soil environments*, pp. 1089–130. Soil Sci. Soc. Am., Madison, Wisconsin. 1244 p.

Littlefield, R. R. 1980. *Alternatives which maximize the use of pasture and forage in beef production systems.* M. S. Thesis, Iowa State University, Ames. 60 p.

Lockeretz, W. (ed.). 1977. *Agriculture and energy.* Academic Press, New York. 750 p.

Loomis, R. S. 1978. Ecological dimensions of medieval agrarian systems: an ecologist responds. *Agric. Hist.* **52**:478–83.

Loomis, R. S. 1979. Ideotype concepts for sugarbeet improvement. *J. Am. Soc. Sugar Beet Technol.* **20**:323–41.

Loomis, R. S. 1983. Crop manipulations for efficient use of water: an overview. In H. M. Taylor, W. R. Jordan, and T. R. Sinclair (eds), *Limitations to efficient use of water in crop production*, pp. 345–74. Am. Soc. Agron., Madison, Wisconsin. 538 p.

Loomis, R. S. 1984. Traditional agriculture in America. *Ann. Rev. Ecol. Syst.* **15**:449–78.

Loomis, R. S. 1985. Systems approaches for crop and pasture research. In J. J. Yates (ed.), *Proceedings of the Third Australian Agronomy Conference*, pp. 1–8. Aust. Soc. Agron., Melbourne. 425 p.

Loomis, R. S. and C. W. Bennett. 1966. Competitive relationships in virus-infested sugar beet fields. *J. Am. Soc. Sugar Beet Technol.* **14**:218–31.

Loomis, R. S. and P. A. Gerakis. 1975. Productivity of agricultural systems. In J. P. Cooper (ed.), *Photosynthesis and productivity in different environments*, pp. 145–72. Cambridge University Press, Cambridge. 715 p.

Loomis, R. S. and H. R. Lafitte. 1987. The carbon economy of a maize crop exposed to elevated $CO_2$ concentrations and water stress determined from elemental analysis. *Field Crops Res.* **17**:63–74.

Loomis, R. S. and W. A. Williams. 1963. Maximum crop productivity: an estimate. *Crop Sci.* **3**:67–72.

Loomis, R. S., W. A. Williams and W. G. Duncan. 1967. Community architecture and the productivity of terrestrial plant communities. In A. San Pietro, F. A. Greer and T. J. Army (eds), *Harvesting the sun: photosynthesis and plant life*, pp. 291–308. Academic Press, New York.

Loomis, R. S. and W. A. Williams. 1969. Productivity and the morphology of crop stands. In J. D. Eastin, F. A. Haskin, C. Y. Sullivan, and C. H. M. Van Bavel (eds), *Physiological aspects of crop yield*, pp. 27–47. Am. Soc. Agron., Madison, Wisconsin. 396 p.

Loomis, R. S., J. H. Brickey, F. E. Broadbent, and G. F. Worker Jr. 1960. Comparison of nitrogen source materials for midseason fertilization of sugar beets. *Agron. J.* **52**:97–101.

Loomis, R. S., Y. Luo, and P. Kooman. 1990. Integration of activity in the higher plant. In R. Rabbinge, J. Goudriaan, H. van Keulen, F. W. T. Penning de Vries, and H. H. van Laar (eds), *Theoretical production ecology: reflections and prospects*, pp. 105–24. Pudoc, Wageningen, The Netherlands. 318 p.

Loomis, W. E. 1932. Growth–differentiation balance vs. carbohydrate–nitrogen balance. *Proc. Am. Soc. Hort. Sci.* **29**:240–5.

Lopes, N. F. 1979. *Respiration related to growth and maintenance in radish (Raphanus sativus L.)*. PhD dissertation. University of California, Davis. 151 p.

Lorio., P. L. Jr. 1986. Growth–differentiation balance: a basis for understanding Southern Pine Beetle–tree interactions. *Forest Ecol. Manage.* **145**:259.–73.

Ludlow, M. M. 1976. Ecophysiology of C4 grasses. In O. L. Lange, L. Kappen, and E.-D. Schulze (eds), *Water and plant life (Ecological Studies* Vol. 19), pp. 364–86. Springer-Verlag, Berlin. 536 p.

Ludlow, M. M. 1985. Photosynthesis and dry matter production in C3 and C4 pasture plants, with special emphasis on tropical C3 legumes and C4 grasses. *Aust. J. Plant Physiol.* **12**:557–72.

Ludlow, M. M. and D. A. Charles-Edwards. 1980. Analysis of the regrowth of a tropical grass/legume sward subjected to different frequencies and intensities of defoliation. *Aust. J. Agric. Res.* **31**:673–92.

Ludlow, M. M. and R. C. Muchow. 1990. A critical evaluation of traits for improving crop yields in water-limited environments. *Adv. Agron.* **43**:107–53.

Ludlow, M. M. and S. B. Powles. 1988. Effects of photoinhibition induced by water stress on growth and yield of grain sorghum. In J. R. Evans, S. von Caemmerer, and W. W. Adams III (eds), *Ecology of photosynthesis in sun and shade*, pp. 179–94. CSIRO, Canberra, Australia. 358 p.

Ludlow, M. M. and G. L. Wilson. 1971. Photosynthesis of tropical pasture plants. I. Illuminance, carbon dioxide concentration, leaf temperature, and leaf-air vapour pressure difference. *Aust. J. Biol. Sci.* **24**:449–70.

Lush, W. M. and L. T. Evans. 1974. Translocation of photosynthetic assimilate from grass leaves, as influenced by environment and species. *Aust. J. Plant Physiol.* **1**:417–31.

Lyerly, P. J. and D. E. Longeneker. 1957. *Salinity control in irrigated agriculture.* Texas Agric. Exp. Sta. Bull. No. 876. 19 p.

Maas, E. V. 1984. Crop tolerance. *Calif. Agric.* **38**(10):20–1.

Maas, E. V. and G. J. Hoffman. 1977. Crop salt tolerance – current assessment. *J. Irrig. Drain.* **103**:115–34.

MacRae, R. J. and G. R. Mehuys. 1985. The effect of green manuring on the physical properties of temperate-area soils. *Adv. Soil Sci.* **3**:71–94.

Major, D. J. 1980. Photoperiod response characteristics controlling flowering of nine crop species. *Can. J. Plant Sci.* **60**:777–84.

Margalef, R. 1969. Diversity and stability, a practical proposal and a model of interdependence. *Brookhaven Symp. Biol.* **22**:13–37.

Marschner, H. 1986. *Mineral nutrition of higher plants*. Academic Press, London. 674 p.

Marshall, D. R. 1977. The advantages and hazards of genetic homogeneity. *Ann. New York Acad. Sci.* **287**:1–20.

Marshall, D. R. and R. W. Allard. 1974. Performance and stability of mixtures of grain sorghum. I. Relationship between level of genetic diversity and performance. *Theor. Appl. Gen.* **44**:145–152.

Marten, G. G. 1988. Productivity, stability, sustainability, equitability and autonomy as properties for agroecosystem assessment. *Agric. Systems* **26**:291–316.

Mayer, A. M. and A. Poljakoff-Mayber. 1982. *The germination of seeds*. Pergamon Press, Oxford. 211 p.

McCauley, G. N., J. F. Stone, and E. W. Chin Choy. 1978. Evapotranspiration reduction by field geometry effects in peanuts and grain sorghum. *Agric. Meteorol.* **19**:295–304.

McCree, K. J. 1970. An equation for the rate of respiration of white clover plants grown under controlled conditions. In I. Setlik (ed.), *Prediction and measurement of photosynthetic productivity*, pp. 221–9. Proc. IBP/PP Tech. Mtg., Trebon. Pudoc, Wageningen. 632 p.

McCree, K. J. 1988. Sensitivity of sorghum grain yield to ontogenetic changes in respiration coefficients. *Crop Sci.* **28**:114–20.

McDermitt, D. K. and R. S. Loomis. 1981. Elemental composition of biomass and its relation to energy content, growth efficiency, and growth yield. *Ann. Bot.* **48**:275–90.

McGlasson, W. B. and H. K. Pratt. 1963. Fruit-set patterns and fruit growth in cantaloupe (*Cucumis melo* L., var. *reticulatis* Naud.). *Proc. Am. Soc. Hort. Sci.* **83**:495–505.

McGregor, K. C. and C. K. Mutchler. 1977. Status of the R factor in northern Mississippi. In G. R. Foster (ed.), *Soil erosion: prediction and control*, pp.135–42. Soil Conservation Society, Ankeny, Iowa. 393 p.

McIlroy, I. C. 1971. An instrument for continuous recording of natural evaporation. *Agric. Meteorol.* **9**:93–100.

Mearns, L. O., P. H. Gleick, and S. H. Schneider. 1990. Climate forcasting. In P. E. Waggoner (ed.), *Climate change and U.S. water resources*, pp. 87–137. John Wiley, New York. 496 p.

Mengel, K. 1985. Dynamics and availability of major soil nutrients. *Adv. Soil Sci.* **2**:65–131.

Menz, K. M., D. N. Moss, R. Q. Cannell, and W. A. Brun. 1969. Screening for photosynthetic efficiency. *Crop Sci.* **9**:692–4.

Meyer, W. S. and G. C. Green. 1981. Plant indicators of wheat and soybean crop water stress. *Irrig. Sci.* **2**:167–76.

Midwest Plan Service. Livestock Wastes Subcommittee. 1985. *Livestock waste facilities handbook*. Midwest Plan Service. Iowa State University Press, Ames. 110 p.

Miller, E. E. and A. Klute. 1967. The dynamics of soil water. Part I. Mechanical forces. In R. M. Hagan, H. R. Haise, and T. W. Edminster (eds), *Irrigation of agricultural lands*, pp. 209–44. Agronomy Monograph No. 11. Am. Soc. Agron., Madison, Wisconsin. 1180 p.

Moncur, M. W. 1981. *Floral initiation in field crops. An atlas of scanning electron micrographs*. CSIRO, Australia. 20 p.

Monsi, M. and T. Saeki. 1953. Uber den Lichtfaktor in den Pflanzengesellschaften und seine Bedeutung für die Stoffproduktion. *Jap. J. Bot.* **14**:22–52.

Monteith, J. L. 1964. Evaporation and environment. *Symp. Soc. Exp. Biol.* **19**:205–34.

Monteith, J. L. 1977. Climate and the efficiency of crop production in Britain. *Phil. Trans. R. Soc. Lond.* B**281**:277–94.

Monteith, J. L. 1978. Reassessment of maximum growth rates for C3 and C4 crops. *Exp. Agric.* **14**:1–5.

Monteith, J. L. and M. H. Unsworth. 1990. *Principles of environmental physics*. Second ed. Edward Arnold, London. 291 p.

Mooney, H. A. and E. L. Dunn. 1970. Convergent evolution of Mediterranean climate evergreen sclerophyll shrubs. *Evolution* **24**:292–303.

Moore, R. M. (ed.). 1970. *Australian grasslands*. Australian National University Press, Canberra. 455 p.

Morgan, J. 1983. Osmoregulation as a selection criterion for drought tolerance in wheat. *Aust. J. Agric. Res.* **34**:607–14.

Morgan, R. P. C. and D. A. Davidson. 1986. *Soil erosion and conservation*. Longman Scientific & Technical, Harlow, Essex, UK. 298 p.

Myers, R. J. K. and M. A. Foale. 1981. Row spacing and population density in grain sorghum – a simple analysis. *Field Crops Res.* **4**:147–54.

National Research Council. Committee on Genetic Vulnerability of Major Crops. 1972. *Genetic vulnerability of major crops*. National Academy of Sciences, Washington, DC. 307 p.

National Research Council. Committee on Animal Nutrition. 1981. *Nutritional energetics of domestic animals*. National Academy Press, Washington, DC. 54 p.

National Research Council. Committee on Animal Nutrition. 1982. *United States-Canadian tables of feed composition* (third revision). National Academy of Sciences, Washington, DC. 148 p.

National Research Council. Committee on Animal Nutrition. 1984. *Nutrient requirements of beef cattle*. National Academy Press, Washington, DC. 90 p.

National Research Council. Committee on Animal Nutrition. 1985. *Ruminant nitrogen usage*. National Academy Press, Washington, DC. 138 p.

National Research Council. Committee on Scientific and Regulatory Issues underlying Pesticide Use Patterns and Agricultural Innovation. 1987. *Regulating pesticides in food: the Delaney paradox*. National Academy of Sciences, Washington, DC. 272 p.

National Research Council. Committee on the Role of Alternative Farming methods in Modern, and Production Agriculture. 1989a. *Alternative agriculture*. National Academy Press, Washington, DC. 448 p.

National Research Council. Subcommittee on the Tenth Edition of the RDAs. 1989b. *Recommended dietary allowances*. National Academy Press, Washington, DC. 283 p.

Neales, T. F. and L. D. Incoll. 1968. The control of leaf photosynthesis rate by level of assimilate concentration in the leaf: a review of the hypothesis. *Bot. Rev.* **34**:107–25.

Neiburger, M., T. G. Edinger, and W. D. Bonner. 1982. *Understanding our atmospheric environment*. W. H. Freeman, San Francisco.

Nelson, D. W. 1982. Gaseous losses of nitrogen other than through denitrification. In F. J. Stevenson (ed.), *Nitrogen in agricultural soils*. (Agronomy Monograph no. 22), pp. 327–63. Am. Soc. Agron., Madison, Wisconsin. 940 p.

Nestrud, L. M. and J. R. Worster. 1979. *Soil survey of Jasper County, Iowa*. U.S. Government Printing Office, Washington, DC. 136 p.

Newland, E. V. and G. G. Price. 1975. The peaking of the oil age. *Span* **18**:4–6.

Northcote, K. H., G. D. Hubble, R. F. Isbell, C. H. Thompson, and E. Bettany. 1975. *A description of Australian soils*. CSIRO, Melbourne. 170 p.

Noy-Meir, I. 1981. Spatial effects in modelling of arid ecosystems. In D. Goodall and R. H. Perry (ed.), *Arid land ecosystems: structure, functioning and management*. (IBP 17.2), pp. 411–32. Cambridge University Press.

Ng, E. and R. S. Loomis. 1984. *Simulation of growth and yield of the potato crop*. Simulation Monographs. Pudoc, Wageningen, Netherlands. 147 p.

Nuttonson, M. Y. 1955. *Wheat climate relationships and the use of phenology in ascertaining the thermal and photothermal requirements of wheat*. American Institute of Crop Ecology, Washington, DC. 388 p.

Odum, H. T. 1967. Energetics of world food production. In The President's Scientific Advisory Committee, *Report of problems of world food supply 3*, pp. 55–94. The White House, Washington, DC.

Office of Technological Assessment. 1980. *Energy from biological processes. II. Technical and environmental analyses*. Rep. E-128. U.S. Government Printing Office, Washington, DC. 234 p.

Ofori, F. and W. R. Stern. 1987. Cereal–Legume intercropping systems. *Adv. Agron.* **41**:41–90.

O'Leary, G. J., D. J. Connor, and D. H. White. 1981. A simulation model of the development, growth and yield of the wheat crop. *Agric. Syst.* **17**:1–26.

O'Leary, G. J., D. J. Connor, and D. H. White. 1985. Effect of sowing time on growth, yield, and water-use of rain-fed wheat in the Wimmera, Vic. *Aust. J. Agric. Res.* **36**:187–96.

Osmond, C. B., V. Oja, and A. Laisk. 1988. Regulation of carboxylation and photosynthetic oscillations during sun-shade acclimation in *Helianthus annuus* measured with a rapid-response gas exchange system. In J. R. Evans, S. von Caemmerer, and W. W. Adams III (eds), *Ecology of photosynthesis in sun and shade*, pp. 237–51. CSIRO, Canberra, Australia. 358 p.

Osmond, C. B., K. Winter, and H. Ziegler. 1982. Functional significance of different pathways of $CO_2$ fixation in photosynthesis. In O. L. Lange, P. S. Nobel, C. B. Osmond, and H. Zeigler (eds), *Physiological plant ecology. II. Water relations and carbon assimilation (Encyl. Plant Physiol.*, new ser. vol. 12B), pp. 479–547. Springer-Verlag, Heidelberg. 747 p.

Oster, J. D., G. J. Hoffman, and F. E. Robinson. 1984. Dealing with salinity. Management alternatives: crop, water and soil. *Calif. Agric.* 38(10):29–32.

Paltridge, G. W. and J. V. Denholm. 1974. Plant yield and the switch from vegetative to reproductive growth. *J. Theor. Biol.* 44:23–34.

Paltridge, G. W., J. V. Denholm, and D. J. Connor. 1984. Determinism, senescence and the yield of plants. *J. Theor. Biol.* 10:383–98.

Paltridge, G. W. and C. M. R. Platt. 1976. *Radiative processes in meteorology and climatology.* (Developments in Atmospheric Science no. 5.) Elsevier Scientific, Amsterdam. 318 p.

Passioura, J. B. 1983. Roots and drought resistance. *Agric. Water Manage.* 7:265–80.

Paul, E. A. and F. E. Clark. 1989. *Soil microbiology and biochemistry.* Academic Press, San Diego, California. 273 p.

Paul, E. A. & J. A. van Veen. 1978. The use of tracers to determine the dynamic nature of organic matter. *Trans. 11th Int. Congr. Soil Sci.* 3:61–102.

Payne, P. R. 1978. Human protein requirements. In G. Norton (ed.), *Plant proteins*, pp. 247–63. Butterworth, London. 352 p.

Pearce, R. B., G. E. Carlson, D. K. Barnes, R. H. Hart, and C. H. Hanson. 1969. Specific leaf weight and photosynthesis in alfalfa. *Crop Sci.* 9:423–6.

Pearcy, R. W., J. R. Ehleringer, H. A. Mooney, and P. W. Rundel (eds). 1989. *Plant physiological ecology: field methods and instrumentation.* Chapman and Hall, New York. 457 p.

Pearson, C. J. and R. L. Ison. 1987. *Agronomy of grassland systems.* Cambridge University Press. 169 p.

Penman, H. L. 1948. Natural evaporation from open water, bare soil, and grass. *Proc. R. Soc. Lond.* A193:120–45.

Penman, H. L., D. E. Angus, and C. H. M. Van Bavel. 1967. Microclimate factors affecting evaporation and transpiration. In R. M. Hagen, H. R. Haise, and T. W. Edminister (eds), *Irrigation of agricultural lands.* (Agronomy Monograph no. 11), pp. 483–505. Am. Soc. Agron., Madison, Wisconsin. 1180 p.

Penning de Vries, F. W. T. 1975. The cost of maintenance processes in plant cells. *Ann. Bot.* 39:77–92.

Penning de Vries, F. W. T., A. H. M. Brunsting, and H. H. van Laar. 1974. Products, requirements and efficiency of biosynthesis: a quantitative approach. *J. Theor. Biol.* 45:339–77.

Penning de Vries, F. W. T., H. H. van Laar, and M. C. M. Chardon. 1983. Bioenergetics and growth of fruits, seeds, and storage organs. In W. H. Smith and S. J. Banta (eds), *Potential productivity of field crops under different environments*, pp. 37–59. IRRI, Los Banos, Philippines. 526 p.

Piha, M. I. and D. N. Munns. 1987. Nitrogen fixation potential of bean (*Phaseolus vulgaris* L.) compared with other grain legumes under controlled conditions. *Plant Soil* 98:169–82.

Pimentel, D. (ed.). 1980. *Handbook of energy utilization in agriculture.* CRC Press, Boca Raton, Florida. 475 p.

Pimentel, D., L. E. Hurd, A. C. Belloti, M. J. Forster, I. N. Oha, O. D. Scholes, and R. J. Whitman. 1973. Food production and the energy crisis. *Science* 206:1277–80.

Pirt, S. J. 1965. The maintenance energy of bacteria in growing cultures. *Proc. R. Soc. Lond.* B163:224–31.

Poljakoff-Mayber, A. and J. Gale (eds). 1975. *Plants in saline environments*. (Ecol. Studies Ser. no. 15.) Springer-Verlag, Berlin. 213 p.

Pratt, P. F., F. E. Broadbent, and J. P. Martin. 1973. Using organic waste as nitrogen fertilizer. *Calif. Agric.* **27** (6): 10–13.

Priestley, C.H.B. and R.J. Taylor. 1972. On the assessment of surface heat flux and evaporation using large scale parameters. *Mon. Weather Rev.* **100**:81–92.

Prosser, J. I. (ed.). 1986. *Nitrification.* (*Spec. Pub. Soc. Gen. Microb.* vol. 20.) IRL Press, Oxford, UK. 217 p.

Pruitt, W. O. 1964. Cyclic relations between evapotranspiration and radiation. *Trans. ASAE* **7**:271–75; 280.

Pruitt, W. O. 1986. *Prediction and measurement of crop water requirements: the basis of irrigation scheduling.* Faculty of Agriculture, University of Sydney, Sydney. 58 p.

Puckridge, D. W. and C. M. Donald. 1967. Competition among wheat plants sown at a wide range of densities. *Aust. J. Agric. Res.* **18**:193–211.

Puckridge, D. W. and R. J. French. 1983. The annual legume pasture in cereal-ley farming systems of southern Australia: a review. *Agric. Ecosyst. Environ.* **9**:229–67.

Pugsley, A. T. 1971. A genetic analysis of the spring–winter habit of growth in wheat. *Aust. J. Agric. Res.* **22**:21–31.

Pugsley, A. T. 1982. Additional genes inhibiting winter habit in wheat. *Euphytica* 21:547–52.

Putman, A. and C.-S. Tang (eds). 1986. *The science of allelopathy.* John Wiley, New York. 317 p.

Quisenberry, K. S. and L. P. Reitz. 1974. Turkey wheat: the cornerstone of an empire. *Agric. Hist.* **48**:98–114.

Radford, P. J. 1967. Growth analysis formulae – their use and abuse. *Crop Sci.* **7**:171–5.

Radin, J. W. 1977. Contribution of the root system to nitrate assimilation in whole cotton plants. *Aust. J. Plant Physiol.* **4**:811–19.

Radin, J. W. 1983. Control of plant growth by nitrogen: differences between cereals and broadleaf species. *Plant Cell Environ.* **6**:65–8.

Rapoport, H. F. and R. S. Loomis. 1986. Structural aspects of root thickening in *Beta vulgaris* L.: comparative thickening in sugarbeet and chard. *Bot. Gaz.* **147**:270–7.

Rappaport, R. A. 1971. The flow of energy in an agricultural society. *Sci. Am.* **224**(3):117–32.

Rasmusson, D. C. 1987. An evaluation of ideotype breeding. *Crop. Sci.* **27**:1140–6.

Rathcke, B. and E. P. Lacey. 1985. Phenological patterns of terrestrial plants. *Ann. Rev. Ecol. Syst.* **16**:179–214.

Reeve, R. C. and M. Fireman. 1967. Salt problems in relation to irrigation. In R. M. Hagan, H. R. Haise and T. W. Edminister (eds), *Irrigation of agricultural lands*, pp. 988–1008. Agronomy Monographs. Am. Soc. Agron., Madison, Wisconsin. 1180 p.

Reeves, T. G. 1976. Effect of annual ryegrass (*Lolium rigidum* Gaud.) on yield of wheat. *Weed Res.* **16**:57–63.

Reeves, T. G., A. Ellington, and H. D. Brooke. 1984. Effects of lupin–wheat rotations on soil fertility. *Aust. J. Agric. Anim. Husb.* **24**:595–600.

Reeves, T. G., G. Smith, and D. H. White. 1987. Integrated crop-livestock production. In D. J. Connor and D. Smith (eds), *Agriculture in Victoria*, pp. 145–58. Australian Institute of Agricultural Science, Melbourne. 231 p.

Richards, L. A. 1954. *Diagnosis and improvement of saline and alkali soils*. USDA Handbook no. 60. U.S. Government Printing Office, Washington, D.C. 160 p.

Richey, C. B., D. R. Griffith, and S. D. Parsons. 1977. Yields and cultural energy requirements for corn and soybeans with various tillage-planting systems. *Adv. Agron.* **29**:141–82.

Ridge, P. E. 1986. A review of long fallow for dryland wheat production in southern Australia. *J. Aust. Inst. Agric. Sci.* **52**:37–44.

Rimmington, G. M., D. J. Connor, and T. A. McMahon. 1987. *Agric. Eng. Rep.* 82/87. University of Melbourne.

Ritchie, J. T. 1971. Dryland evaporative flux in a subhumid climate: I. Micrometeorological influences. *Agron. J.* **63**:51–5.

Ritchie, J. T. 1972. Model for predicting evaporation from a row crop with incomplete cover. *Water Resour. Res.* **8**:1204–13.

Ritchie, J. T. and E. Burnett. 1971. Dryland evaporative flux in a subhumid climate: II. Plant influences. *Agron. J.* **63**:56–62.

Ritchie, J. T., E. Burnett, and R. C. Henderson. 1972. Dryland evaporative flux in a subhumid climate. III. Soil water influence. *Agron. J.* **64**:168–76.

Roberts, E. H. and R. J. Summerfield. 1987. Measurement and prediction of flowering in annual crops. In J. G. Atherton (ed.), *Manipulation of flowering* (Proc. 45th Easter School Agricultural Science, Nottingham University), pp. 17–50. Butterworth, London. 438 p.

Roberts, H.A. 1981. Seed banks in the soil. *Adv. Appl. Biol.* **6**:1–55.

Robertson, G. W. 1973. Development of simplified agroclimatic procedures for assessing temperature effects on crop development. In R. O. Slayter (ed.), *Plant responses to climatic factors.* (Proc. Uppsala Symp. 1970), pp. 327–43 UNESCO, Paris. 574 p.

Robson, A. D. (ed.). 1989. *Soil acidity and plant growth.* Academic Press Australia, Marrickville, New South Wales. 306 p.

Robson, M. J. 1982. The growth and carbon economy of selection lines of *Lolium perenne* cv. S23 with 'differing' rates of dark respiration. I. Grown as simulated swards during a regrowth period. *Ann. Bot.* **49**:321–9.

Rolston, D. E., D. L. Hoffman, and D. W. Toy. 1978. Field measurement of denitrification: I. Flux of $N_2$ and $N_2O$. *Soil Sci. Soc. Am. J.* **42**:863–9.

Rood, S. B. and D. J. Major. 1980. Responses of early corn inbreds to photoperiod. *Crop Sci.* **20**:679–82.

Rose, C. W. 1985. Developments in soil erosion and deposition models. *Adv. Soil Sci.* **2**:1–63.

Rosenberg, N. J., B. L. Blad, and S. B. Verma. 1983. *Microclimate, the biological environment.* Second edition. John Wiley, New York. 495 p.

Rosenthal, W. D., E. T. Kanemasu, R. J. Raney, and L. R. Stone. 1977. Evaluation of an evapotranspiration model for corn. *Agron. J.* **69**:461–4.

Ross, J. P. 1983. Effect of soybean mosaic on component yields from blends of mosaic resistant and susceptible soybeans. *Crop Sci.* **23**:343–6.

Rossiter, R. C. and W. T. Collins. 1988. Genetic diversity in old subterranean clover (*Trifolium subterranean* L.) populations in Western Australia. II. Pastures sown initially to the Mt. Barker strain. *Aust. J. Agric. Res.* **39**:1063–74.

Running, S. W. 1980. Relating plant capacitance to water relations of *Pinus contorta. Forest Ecol. Manage.* **2**:237–52.

Ruthenberg, H. 1980. *Farming systems in the tropics.* Clarendon Press, Oxford. 424 p.

Ruttan, V. W. 1982. *Agricultural research policy.* University of Minnesota Press, Minneapolis. 369 p.

Ryle, G. J. A., C. E. Powell, and A. J. Gordon. 1979. The respiratory costs of nitrogen fixation in soyabean, cowpea, and white clover. I. Nitrogen fixation and the respiration of the nodulated root. *J. Exp. Bot.* **30**:135–44.

Saeki, T. 1963. Light relations in plant communities. In L. T. Evans (ed.), *Environmental control of plant growth,* pp. 79–94. Academic Press, New York. 449 p.

Sale, P. J. M. 1974. Productivity of vegetable crops in a region of high solar input. III. Carbon balance of potato crops. *Aust. J. Plant Physiol.* **1**:283–96.

Sale, P. J. M. 1975. Productivity of vegetable crops in a region of high solar input. IV. Field chamber measurements of french beans (*Phaseolus vulgaris* L.) and cabbages (*Brassica oleracea* L.). *Aust. J. Plant Physiol.* **2**:461–70.

Sale, P. J. M. 1977. Net carbon exchange rates of field grown crops in relation to irradiance and dry weight accumulation. *Aust. J. Plant Physiol.* **4**:555–69.

Salisbury, F. B. 1963. *The flowering process.* Pergamon Press, New York. 234 p.

Salisbury, F. B. 1981. Response to photoperiod. In O. L. Lange, P. S. Nobel, C. B. Osmond, and H. Zeigler (eds), *Physiological plant ecology. I. Responses to the physical environment.* (Encyl. Plant Physiol., New Ser. Vol. 12A), pp. 135–67. Springer-Verlag, Heidelberg. 625 p.

Salisbury, F. B. and C. W. Ross. 1985. *Plant physiology*. Wadsworth, Belmont, California. 540 p.

Sanchez, P. A. 1976. *Properties and management of soils in the tropics*. John Wiley, New York. 618 p.

Schneider, S. H., P. H. Gleick, and L. O. Mearns. 1990. Prospects for climate change. In P. E. Waggoner (ed.), *Climate change and U.S. water resources*, pp. 41–73. John Wiley, New York. 496 p.

Scheiter, A. A. and J. F. Miller. 1981. Description of sunflower growth stages. *Crop Sci.* **21**: 901–3.

Schouten, H. 1986. Low-input farming. In H. van Keulen and J. Wolf (eds), *Modelling of agricultural production: weather, soils and crops*, pp. 263–76. Simulation Monographs. Pudoc, Wageningen, The Netherlands. 478 p.

Schubert, K. R. (ed.). 1982. *The energetics of biological nitrogen fixation*. Am. Soc. Plant Physiol., Rockville, Maryland. 30 p.

Schultz, J. E. 1971. Soil water changes under fallow crop treatments in relation to soil type, rainfall, and yield. *Aust. J. Exp. Agric. Anim. Husb.* **11**:236–42.

Schulze, E.-D. 1986. Carbon dioxide and water vapor exchanges in response to drought in the atmosphere and in the soil. *Ann. Rev. Plant Physiol.* **37**:247–74.

Schulze, E.-D. and A. E. Hall. 1982. Stomatal responses, water loss and $CO_2$ assimilation rates of plants in contrasting environments. In O. L. Lange, P. S. Nobel, C. B. Osmond, and H. Zeigler (eds), *Physiological plant ecology*. II. *Water relations and carbon assimilation*. (*Encycl. Plant Physiol.*, new ser. Vol. 12B), pp. 181–230. Springer-Verlag, Heidelberg. 747 p.

Shannon, M. C. 1984. Breeding, selection and the genetics of salt tolerance. In R. C. Staples and G. H. Toenniessen (eds), *Salinity tolerance in plants: strategies for crop improvement*, pp. 231–54. Wiley-Interscience, New York. 443 p.

Shantz, H. L. and L. N. Piemeisel. 1927. Water requirement of plants at Akron, Colorado. *J. Agric. Res.* **34**:1093–190.

Shibles, R. M. and C. R. Weber. 1965. Leaf area, solar radiation interception and dry matter production by soybeans. *Crop Sci.* **5**:575–7.

Shouse, P., W. A. Jury, L. H. Stolzy, and S. Dasburg. 1982. Field measurement and modelling of cowpea water use and yield under stressed and well-watered conditions. *Hilgardia* **50**:1–25.

Silsbury, J. H. 1977. Energy requirements of symbiotic nitrogen fixation. *Nature* **267**:1149–50.

Simmonds, N. W. (ed.). 1976. *Evolution of crop plants*. Longman Scientific & Technical, Burnt Mill, Harlow, UK. 339 p.

Simmonds, N. W. 1979. *Principles of crop improvement*. Longman, London. 408 p.

Sinclair, T. R. and C. T. de Wit. 1975. Photosynthate and nitrogen requirements for seed production by various crops. *Science* **189**:565–7.

Singer, M. J. and D. J. Munns. 1987. *Soils: an introduction*. Macmillan, New York. 492 p.

Slatyer, R. O. 1967. *Plant-water relations*. Academic Press, New York. 366 p.

Slicher van Bath, B. H. 1963. *The agrarian history of western Europe: A.D. 500–1500*. Edward Arnold, London. 364 p.

Smika, D. E. 1970. Summer fallow for dryland winter wheat in the semiarid Great Plains. *Agron J.* **62**:15–17.

Smith, B. D. 1990. Origins of agriculture in eastern North America. *Science* **246**:1566–71.

Smith, D. F. and G. R. T. Levick. 1974. The effect of infestation by *Lolium rigidum* Gaud. (annual ryegrass) on the yield of wheat. *Aust. J. Agric. Res.* **25**:381–93.

Smith, W. H. and S. J. Banta (eds). 1983. *Potential productivity of field crops under different environments*. IRRI, Los Banos, Philippines. 526 p.

Soil Survey Staff. 1988. *Keys to soil taxonomy*. Soil Management Support Services, AID, USDA, Cornell University, Ithaca, New York. 280 p.

Spencer, J. W. 1971. Fourier series representation of the position of the sun. *Search* **2**:172.

Spitters, C. J. T. 1979. *Competition and its consequences for selection in barley breeding*. Pudoc, Wageningen, The Netherlands. 268 p.

Spitters, C. J. T. 1980. Competition effects within mixed stands. In R. G. Hurd, P. V. Biscoe, and C. Dennis (eds), *Opportunities for increasing crop yields*, pp. 219–31. Pitman, London. 410 p.

Sprague, G. F. and S. A. Eberhart. 1977. Corn breeding. In G. F. Sprague (ed.), *Corn and corn improvement*. (Agronomy Monograph no. 18), pp. 305–62. Am. Soc. Agron., Madison, Wisconsin. 774 p.

Stace, H. C. T., G. D. Hubble, R. Brewer, K. H. Northcote, J. R. Sleeman, M. J. Mulcahy, and E. G. Hallsworth. 1968. *A handbook of Australian soils*. CSIRO, Adelaide, Australia. 435 p.

Staff of the L. H. Bailey Hortorium. 1976. *Hortus third*. Macmillan, New York. 1290 p.

Stahl, R. S. and K. J. McCree. 1988. Ontogenetic changes in the respiration coefficients of grain sorghum. *Crop Sci.* **28**:111–113.

Stanhill, G. 1976. Trends and deviations in the yield of English wheat during the last 750 years. *Agro-Ecosyst.* **3**:1–10.

Stanhill, G. (ed.). 1984. *Energy and agriculture*. Springer-Verlag, Berlin. 192 p.

Stanhill, G. 1986. Water use efficiency. *Adv. Agron.* **39**:53–85.

Staples, R. C. and G. H. Toenniessen (eds). 1984. *Salinity tolerance in plants: Strategies for crop improvement*. Wiley Interscience, New York. 443 p.

Stapper, M. 1984. *SIMTAG: A simulation model of wheat genotypes*. University of New England and ICARDA, Armidale, Australia, and Aleppo, Syria. 108 p.

Steele, K. W. and I. Vallis. 1988. The nitrogen cycle in pastures. In J. R. Wilson (ed.), *Advances in nitrogen cycling in agricultural ecosystems*, pp. 274–91. CAB International, Wallingford, Oxon, UK. 451 p.

Steeves, T. A. and I. M. Sussex. 1972. *Patterns in plant development*. Prentice-Hall, Englewood Cliffs, New Jersey. 302 p.

Stern, W. R. and C. M. Donald. 1962. Light relations in grass–clover swards. *Aust. J. Agric Res.* **13**:599–614.

Stevenson, F. J. (ed.). 1982. *Nitrogen in agricultural soils*. (Agronomy Monograph no. 22.) Am. Soc. Agron., Madison, Wisconsin. 940 p.

Stewart, G. A., G. Gartside, R. M. Gifford, H. A. Nix, W. H. M. Rawlins, and J. R. Siemon. 1979. Liquid fuel production from agriculture and forestry in Australia. *Search* **10**:382–7.

Stewart, G. A., W. H. M. Rawlins, G. R. Quick, J. E. Begg, and W. J. Peacock. 1981. Oilseeds as a renewable source of diesel fuel. *Search* **12**:107–15.

Stewart, J. I. 1988. *Response farming in rainfed agriculture*. WHARF Foundation Press, Davis, California. 103 p.

Stewart, J. I. and C. T. Hash. 1982. Impact of weather analysis on agricultural production and planning decisions for semiarid areas of Kenya. *J. Appl. Meteorol.* **21**:477–94.

Storie, R. E. 1933. *An index for rating the agricultural value of soils*. (Calif. Agric. Exp. Sta. Bull. no. 556.) University of California, Berkeley. 44 p.

Stout, B. A., C. A. Myers, A. Hurrand, and L. W. Faidley. 1979. *Energy for world agriculture*. FAOUN, Rome. 286 p.

Tabatabai, M. A. and J. M. Laflen. 1976. Nitrogen and sulfur content and pH of precipitation in Iowa. *J. Environ. Qual.* **5**:108–12.

Tanaka, A. and K. Fujita. 1979. Growth, photosynthesis and yield components in relation to grain yield of the field bean. *J. Fac. Agric. Hokkaido Univ.* **59**(2):146–238.

Tanner, C. B. 1981. Transpiration efficiency of potato. *Agron. J.* **73**:59–64.

Tanner, C. B. and W. A. Jury. 1976. Estimating evaporation and transpiration from a row crop during incomplete cover. *Agron. J.* **68**:239–43.

Tanner, C. B. and T. R. Sinclair. 1983. Efficient water use in crop production: Research or re-search? In H. M. Taylor, W. R. Jordan, and T. R. Sinclair (eds), *Limitations to efficient water use in crop production*, pp. 1–27. Am. Soc. Agron., Madison. Wisconsin. 538 p.

Taylor, H. M. and B. Klepper. 1978. The role of rooting characteristics in the supply of water to plants. *Adv. Agron.* **30**:99–128.

Taylor, H. M., W. R. Jordan, and T. R. Sinclair (eds). 1983. *Limitations to efficient water use in crop production*. Am. Soc. Agron., Madison, Wisconsin. 538 p.

Tetio-Kagho, F. and F. P. Gardner. 1988. Responses of maize to plant population density. II.

Reproductive development, yield and yield adjustments. *Agron. J.* **80**:935–40.

Thomas, M. D. and G. R. Hill. 1949. Photosynthesis under field conditions. In J. Franck and W. E. Loomis (eds), *Photosynthesis in plants*, pp. 19–51. Iowa State College Press, Ames. 500 p.

Thornley, J. H. M. (1976). *Mathematical models in plant physiology: a quantitative approach to problems in plant and crop physiology*. Academic Press, London. 318 p.

Thornley, J. H. M. and I. R. Johnson. 1990. *Plant and crop modelling*. Clarendon Press, Oxford. 669 p.

Ting, I. P. 1985. Crassulacean acid metabolism. *Ann. Rev. Plant Physiol.* **36**:595–622.

Tisdale, S. L., W. L. Nelson, and J. D. Beaton. 1985. *Soil fertility and fertilizers*. 4th edn. Macmillan, New York. 754 p.

Tollenaar, M. 1989. Genetic improvement in grain yield of commercial maize hybrids grown in Ontario from 1959 to 1988. *Crop Sci.* **29**:1365–71.

Tottmann, D. R., R. J. Makepeace, and H. Broad. 1979. An explanation of the decimal code for the growth stages of cereals, with illustrations. *Ann. Appl. Biol.* **93**:221–34.

Trabalka, J. R. and D. E. Reichle (eds). 1986. *The changing carbon cycle*. Springer-Verlag, New York. 592 p.

Trenbath, B. R. 1974. Biomass productivity of mixtures. *Adv. Agron.* **26**:177–210.

Trenbath, B. R. 1984. Gene introduction strategies for the control of crop diseases. In G. R. Conway (ed.), *Pest and pathogen control: strategic, tactical, and policy models*, pp. 142–68. John Wiley, Chichester, UK. 488 p.

Trewartha, G. T. and L. H. Horn. 1980. *An introduction to climate*. McGraw-Hill, New York. 416 p.

Trewavas, A. 1986. Resource allocation under poor growth conditions. A major role for growth substances in developmental plasticity. In D. H. Jennings and A. J. Trewavas (eds), *Plasticity in plants* (Symp. Soc Exp. Biol. no. 40), pp. 31–76. Company of Biologists, Cambridge University, Cambridge, UK. 372 p.

Troeh, F. R., J. A. Hobbs, and R. L. Donahue. 1980. *Soil and water conservation for productivity and environmental protection*. Prentice-Hall, Englewood Cliffs, New Jersey. 718 p.

Trumble, H. C. 1939. Climatic factors in relation to agricultural regions of southern Australia. *Trans. Roy. Soc. S. Aust.* **63**:36–43.

Turner, N. C. 1986. Crop water deficits: a decade of progress. *Adv. Agron.* **39**:1–51.

Turner, N. C. and J. E. Begg. 1981. Plant-water relations and adaptation to drought. *Plant Soil* **58**:97–113.

Ulrich, A. 1961. Variety climate interactions of sugar beet varieties in simulated climates. *J. Am. Soc. Sugar Beet Technol.* **11**:376–87.

Ulrich, A. and F. J. Hills. 1969. *Sugar beet nutrient deficiency symptoms. A color atlas and chemical guide*. Div. Agric. Sci., University of California, Berkeley. 36 p.

Ulrich, A., D. Ririe, F. J. Hills, A. George, and M. D. Morse. 1959. *Plant analysis. A guide for sugar beet fertilization*. (Bull. no. 766, part 1.) Calif. Agric. Exp. Sta., University of California, Berkeley, California. 24 p.

Unger, P. W. 1984. *Tillage systems for soil and water conservation*. (FAO Soils Bulletin no. 54.) FAOUN, Rome. 278 p.

USDA. 1974. *Summer fallow in the western United States*. Conservation Research Report. Agric. Res. Ser., USDA, US. Government Printing Office, Washington, DC. 160 p.

van der Meer, H. G., R. J. Unwin, T. A. van Dijk, G. C. Ennik (eds). 1987. *Animal manure on grassland and fodder crops. Fertilizer or waste?* (Proc. Intl. Symp. European Grassland Fed.) Martinus Nijhoff, Dordrecht, The Netherlands. 388 p.

Vandermeer, J. 1989. *The ecology of intercropping*. Cambridge University Press. 237 p.

Van Der Plank, J. E. 1963. *Plant disease: epidemics and control*. Academic Press, New York. 349 p.

van Heemst, H. D., J. J. Nerkelijn, and H. van Keulen. 1981. Labour requirements in various agricultural systems. *Quart. J. Int. Agric.* **120**:178–201.

van Keulen, H. 1982. Graphical analysis of annual crop response to fertilizer application. *Agric. Syst.* **9**:113–26.

van Keulen, H. and H. D. J. van Heemst. 1982. Crop supply of macronutrients. *Agric. Res. Rep.* **916**:46.

Van Soest, P. J. 1982. *Nutritional ecology of the ruminant.* O. & B. Books, Corvallis, Oregon. 373 p.

van Veen, J. A., J. N. Ladd, and M. J. Frissel. 1984. Modelling C and N turnover through the microbial biomass in soil. *Plant Soil* **76**:257–74.

van Wijk, W. R. and D. A. de Vries. 1963. Periodic temperature variations in a homogeneous soil. In W. R. van Wijk (ed.), *Physics of the plant environment*, pp. 102–43. North-Holland, Amsterdam. 382 p.

Vertregt, N. and F. W. T. Penning de Vries. 1987. A rapid method for determining the efficiency of biosynthesis of plant biomass. *J. Theor. Biol.* **128**:109–19.

Vertregt, N. and B. Rutgers. 1988. *Ammonia volatilization from grazed pastures.* (CABO-Report 84. Report 64–2.) Centre for Agrobiological Research, Wageningen, The Netherlands. 37 p.

Villalobos, F. J. and E. Fereres. 1989. A simulation model for irrigation scheduling under variable rainfall. *Trans. ASAE* **32**:181–88.

Vince-Prue, D. 1975. *Photoperiodism in plants.* McGraw-Hill, New York. 444 p.

Wallace, D. H. 1985. Physiological genetics of plant maturity adaptation and yield. *Plant Breed. Rev.* **3**:21–167.

Walworth, J. L. and M. E. Sumner. 1987. The diagnosis and recommendation integrated system (DRIS). *Adv. Soil Sci.* **6**:149–88.

Wardlaw, I. F. 1990. Tansley review No. 27. The control of carbon partitioning in plants. *New Phytol.* **116**:341–81.

Wareing, P. F. and I. D. J. Phillips. 1981. *Growth and differentiation in plants.* Third edn. Pergamon Press, New York. 343 p.

Warren Wilson, J. 1959. Analysis of the spatial distribution of foliage by two-dimensional point quadrats. *New Phytol.* **58**:92–101.

Warren Wilson, J. 1960. Inclined point quadrats. *New Phytol.* **59**:1–8.

Warren Wilson, J. 1967. Stand structure and light penetration. III. Sunlit foliage area. *J. Appl. Ecol.* **4**:159–65.

Warrington, I. J. and E. T. Kanemasu. 1983. Corn growth response to temperature and photoperiod. I. Seedling emergence, tassel initiation, and anthesis. *Agron. J.* **75**:749–54.

Watson, D. J. 1952. Physiological basis of variation in yield. *Adv. Agron.* **4**:101–45.

Weir, A. H., P. L. Bragg, J. R. Porter, and J. H. Rayner. 1984. A winter wheat crop simulation model without water or nutrient limitations. *J. Agric. Sci. Camb.* **102**:371–82.

Weldon, C. W. and W. L. Slauson. 1986. The intensity of competition versus its importance: an overlooked distinction and some implications. *Quart. Rev. Biol.* **61**:23–44.

Wellings, S. R. and P. Bell. 1980. Movement of water and nitrate in the unsaturated zone of the upper Chalk near Winchester, Hants. *J. Hydrology* **48**:119–136.

White, J. 1981. The allometric interpretation of the self-thinning rule. *J. Theor. Biol.* **89**:475–500.

Whitfield, D. M. 1992. Effects of irrigation on $CO_2$ assimilation and light-use efficiency in wheat. *Field Crops Res.* (in press).

Whitfield, D. M., D. J. Connor, and P. J. M. Sale. 1980. Carbon dioxide exchanges in response to change of environment and to defoliation in a tobacco crop. *Aust. J. Plant Physiol.* **7**:473–85.

Whitfield, D. M., G. C. Wright, O. A. Gyles, and A. J. Taylor. 1986. Effects of stage growth, irrigation frequency, and gypsum treatment on $CO_2$ assimilation of lucerne (*Medicago sativa* L.) grown on a heavy clay soil. *Irrig. Sci.* **7**:169–81.

Whitson, R. E., R. D. Kay, W. A. LePori, and E. M. Rister. 1981. Machinery and crop selection with weather risk. *Trans. ASAE* **24**:288–91; 295.

Whittaker, R. H. 1975. *Communities and ecosystems.* Macmillan, New York. 387 p.

Williams, C. H. 1980. Soil acidification under clover pasture. *Aust. J. Exp. Agric. Anim. Husb.* **20**:531–67.

Williams, R. F. 1975. *The shoot apex and leaf growth.* Cambridge University Press. 256 p.

Wilson, D. and J. G. Jones. 1982. Effect of selection for dark respiration rate of mature leaves on crop yields of *Lolium perenne* cv. S23. *Ann. Bot.* **49**:313–20.

Wilson, J. R. (ed.). 1977. *Plant relations in pastures.* CSIRO, Melbourne. 425 p.

Wilson, J. R. (ed.). 1988. *Advances in nitrogen cycling in agricultural ecosystems.* CAB International, Wallingford, Oxon, UK. 451 p.

Wischmeier, W. H. and D. D. Smith. 1978. *USDA Handbook no. 537.* U.S. Government Printing Office, Washington D.C. 58 p.

Wolfe, M. S. 1985. The current status and prospects of multiline cultivars and variety mixtures for disease control. *Ann. Rev. Phytopath.* **23**:251–73.

Woodham-Smith, C. 1962. *The great hunger: Ireland, 1845–1849.* Harper and Rowe, New York. 510 p.

Woodruff, N. P. and F. H. Siddoway. 1965. A wind erosion equation. *Soil Sci. Soc. Am. Proc.* **29**:602–8.

Woodward, F. I. and J. E. Sheehy. 1983. *Principles and measurements in environmental biology.* Butterworth, London. 263 p.

Zadoks, J. C., T. T. Chang, and C. F. Konzak. 1974. A decimal code for the growth stages of cereals. *Weed Res.* **14**:415–21.

# Species list

Common and scientific names of species mentioned in the text.

| Common name | Scientific name |
| --- | --- |
| Alfalfa (lucerne) | *Medicago* spp. |
| Amaranth | *Amaranthus* spp. |
| Apple | *Malus* spp. |
| Banana | *Musa* spp. |
| Barley | *Hordeum vulgare* |
| Barley grass | *Hordeum leporium* |
| Bean | *Phaseolus, Vicia* spp. |
|   dry | *P. vulgaris* |
|   lima | *P. lunatus* |
|   navy | *P. vulgaris* |
|   broad, faba | *Vicia faba* |
| Big bluestem grass | *Andropogon gerardii* |
| Birdsfoot trefoil | *Lotus corniculatus* |
| Buckwheat | *Fagopyrum sagittatum* |
| Cabbage | *Brassica oleracea* |
| Canarygrass, annual | *Phalaris canariensis* |
| Carrot | *Daucus carota* |
| Cassava | *Manihot esculenta* |
| Chickpea | *Cicer arietinum* |
| Clover | *Trifolium, Melilotus* spp. |
|   berseem | *T. alexandrinum* |
|   red | *T. pratense* |
|   subterranean | *T. subterraneum* |
|   white | *T. repens* |
|   sweet | *Melilotus* spp. |
| Cocksfoot (orchard grass) | *Dactylus glomerata* |
| Coffee | *Coffea arabica* |
| Cotton | *Gossypium hirsutum* |
| Date palm | *Phoenix dactylifera* |
| Dry bean | *Phaseolus vulgaris* |

| Common name | Scientific name |
|---|---|
| Field pea | *Pisum arvense* |
| Flax | *Linum usitatissimum* |
| Kentucky bluegrass | *Poa pratensis* |
| Lettuce | *Latuca sativa* |
| Linseed | *Linum usitatissimum* |
| Lupin | *Lupinus* spp. |
|   narrow leaf | *L. angustifolius* |
| Maize (corn) | *Zea mays* |
| Medic | *Medicago* spp. |
|   barrel | *M. truncatula* |
| Melon | *Cucumis* spp. |
|   netted, muskmelon | *C. melo* |
| Millet | *Pennisetum, Setaria* |
|   pearl | *P. glaucum* |
| Oat | *Avena* spp. |
|   cultivated | *A. sativa* |
|   wild | *A. fatua* |
| Onion | *Allium* spp. |
| Orange | *Citrus sinensis* |
| Panic grass | *Panicum* spp. |
|   green | *P. maximum* |
| Paspalum grass | *Paspalum dilitatum* |
| Pea | *Pisum* spp. |
|   field | *P. arvense* |
| Peach | *Prunus persica* |
| Peanut | *Arachis hypogaea* |
| Pearl Millet | *Panicum glaucum* |
| Phalaris grass | *Phalaris aquatica* |
| Pineapple | *Ananas comosus* |
| Potato | *Solanum tuberosum* |
| Quinoa | *Chenopodium quinoa* |
| Radish | *Raphanus sativus* |
| Rape | *Brassica* spp. |
|   oilseed | *B. campestris* |
|   winter | *B. napus* |
| Rhodes grass | *Chloris gayana* |
| Rice | *Oryza sativa* |
| Rye | *Secale cereale* |
| Ryegrass | *Lolium* spp. |
|   annual, italian | *L. multiflorum* |
|   darnel | *L. temulentum* |
|   perennial | *L. perenne* |
|   wimmera | *L. rigidum* |
| Safflower | *Carthamus tinctorius* |

| Common name | Scientific name |
|---|---|
| Sorghum | *Sorghum vulgare* |
| Soybean | *Glycine max* |
| Sisal | *Agave sisalana* |
| Spinach | *Spinacia oleracea* |
| Strawberry | *Fragaria* spp. |
| Sudangrass | *Sorghum bicolor* |
| Sugarbeet | *Beta vulgaris* |
| Sugarcane | *Saccharum officinarum* |
| Sunflower | *Helianthus annuus* |
| Tea | *Thea sinensis* |
| Timothy grass | *Phleum pratense* |
| Tobacco | *Nicotiana tobacum* |
| Tomato | *Lycopersicon esculentum* |
| Vetch | *Vicia sativa* |
| Wheat | *Triticum aestivum* |
| Wheat grass | *Agropyron* spp. |

# Conversions and Constants Useful in Crop Ecology

## METRIC PREFIXES

Multiples of 1000 are preferred with SI units.

| | | | | | | |
|---|---|---|---|---|---|---|
| m | milli | $10^{-3}$ | | k | kilo | $10^3$ |
| μ | micro | $10^{-6}$ | | M | mega | $10^6$ |
| n | nano | $10^{-9}$ | | G | giga | $10^9$ |
| p | pico | $10^{-12}$ | | T | tera | $10^{12}$ |

## CONVERSIONS

| | *Metric* | *American* |
|---|---|---|
| Length: | 1 m = 39.37 in | 1 in = 25.4 mm |
| | 1 km = 0.62 mi (statute) | 1 foot = 0.305 m |
| Area: | 1 ha = 10 000 m² | 1 acre = 43 560 feet² |
| | 1 ha = 2.47 acre | 1 acre = 0.405 ha |
| | | 1 sq mi = 640 acre |
| Volume: | 1 l = 1000 cm³ | 1 acre-ft = 1233 m³ |
| | 1 m³ = 1000 l | 1 cu ft = 28.3 l |
| | 1 m³ = 35.3 cu ft | 1 bu (level) = 1.24 cu ft = 0.0352 m³ |
| | 1 m³ $H_2O$ = 1000 kg | 1 bbl (petroleum) = 42 gal |
| | | 1 gal (liq.) = 3.785 l |
| Mass: | 1 kg = 2.205 lb | 1 lb = 0.454 kg |
| | 1 t = 1000 kg | 1 ton = 2000 lb |
| | 1 t = 2205 lb | |
| Yield: | 1 kg ha$^{-1}$ = 0.89 lb acre$^{-1}$ | 1 lb acre$^{-1}$ = 1.12 kg ha$^{-1}$ |
| | 1 kg ha$^{-1}$ = 0.1 g m$^{-2}$ | |
| | 1 t ha$^{-1}$ = 0.45 ton acre$^{-1}$ | |
| Pressure: | 1 bar = $10^6$ dyne cm² | 1 atm = 1.013 bar |
| | 1 bar = 0.987 atm | |
| | 1 MPa = 10 bar | |

Energy:   $1 J = 10^7$ erg (dyne cm)      1 BTU = 252 cal
          $1 J = 0.239$ cal               1 cal = 4.184 J
          $1 J s^{-1} = 1$ Watt           1 HP = 0.75 kW
                                          1 HP = 2542 BTU $h^{-1}$

Radiation:  $1 W m^{-2} = 0.143$ mcal $cm^{-2}$ $min^{-1}$
            1 einstein = 1 mol quanta      1 cal $cm^{-2}$ $min^{-1}$ = 697 W $m^{-2}$

## CONSTANTS AND COEFFICIENTS

Avogadro's number                       $6.022 \times 10^{23}$
Gas constant                            $8.314$ J $mol^{-1}$ $K^{-1}$
  $RT$   (0°C)                           22.7 l bar $mol^{-1}$
  $RT$  (10°C)                           23.5 l bar $mol^{-1}$
  $RT$  (20°C)                           24.4 l bar $mol^{-1}$
  $RT$  (30°C)                           25.2 l bar $mol^{-1}$

Latent heat of fusion (0°C)             334 J $g^{-1}$
Latent heat of vaporization   (0°C)     2501 J $g^{-1}$
                             (10°C)     2477 J $g^{-1}$
                             (20°C)     2442 J $g^{-1}$
                             (30°C)     2430 J $g^{-1}$

Planck's constant                       $6.63 \times 10^{-34}$ J s
Saturation vapor pressure   (0°C)       6.11 mbar
  (see Eq. 6.14)            (10°C)       12.27 mbar
                           (20°C)       23.37 mbar
                           (30°C)       42.43 mbar

Solar constant                          1360 W $m^{-2}$ (currently 1370 W $m^{-2}$)
Specific heat of air      (0–40°C)      1.01 J $g^{-1}$ $C^{-1}$
Specific heat of water     (17°C)       4.184 J $g^{-1}$ $C^{-1}$
Speed of light (vacuum)                 $3.00 \times 10^8$ m $s^{-1}$
Stefan–Boltzmann constant               $5.67 \times 10^{-8}$ W $m^{-2}$ $K^{-4}$

# Index

Abbreviations used in this index: CAM, plants with crassulacean acid metabolism; $E_p$, transpiration; $E_s$, evaporation from soil; $E_o$, reference evapotranspiration; ET, evapotranspiration; PV, production value; $R_n$, net radiation; $R_g$ and $R_m$, growth-related and maintenance respiration, respectively; $T_a$ and $T_s$, temperature of air and soil, respectively; and $Y_g$, true growth yield.
The symbol '/' may be read as *and, or,* or *versus.*

acetylene
  assay for N fixation, 210
  production by nitrogenase, 207
acid rain and soil pH, 182
acid soil *see* soil acidity adaptation
  drought, 240–52
  temperature, 56, 71, 264–5, 270
adiabatic processes, 149, 157
advection, atmospheric, 153–4
agricultural chemicals
  concerns, 485, 486–7
  soil incorporation, 335
  *see also* biocides, fertilizer, herbicides, pests
agriculture
  continuum of society, 5
  energy and labor, 400–27
  land use, 83, 481, 482
  nations compared, 481–4
    food supply, 481
    soil resources, 482, 484
    workers in agriculture, 481
  objectives of, 409
  potential for increase, 483–4
  recent changes, 478–82
  relation to population, 31, 475–84
  soils used, 176
  sufficiency of, 475, 487
  technological/social change, 8, 64–6, 213–15, 450, 473, 487–92
  urban conflict, 484
  world statistics, 82–4, 479, 481
agricultural systems, 3–10
  competing regions, 451
  human resources, 79
  important attributes, 4–6
  maintenance of, 78–9
  modern agriculture, 482–3
    alternatives to, 221–2, 485–7
  *see also* low-input agriculture, organic farming
agroforestry, 287, 447

air *see* atmosphere, $CO_2$
air temperature ($T_a$)
  dew point, 148
  diurnal pattern, 145–6
  global trend, 162
  plant response, 55–6
    C3/C4 photosynthesis, 264–5
    diurnal, 189, 304–5
    flowering, 106–8, 112–14
    growth/photosynthesis, 264
    respiration, 292–3
    species classified, 56
  profile in canopy, 155
  sensible heat flux ($H$), 145–7
  wet bulb, 149
albedo, 144
alfalfa
  as feed, 24
  composition, 15
  energy cost of irrigation, 391, 392
  N nutrition, 210–11
  photosynthesis, 273–4, 276
  respiration, 298
  salinity tolerance, 383
  seed production, 98, 309
  synthetic cultivars, 92
  trap crop for lygus, 74
alkaline soil, 379–80, 396–7
allelopathy, 43
aluminum toxicity, 180, 448
amaranths, 84
amino acids, in human diet, 26, 27
ammonia
  deposition, 206
  fertilizer, 207, 329–30
  volatilization, 205–6
    from leaves, 206, 260
    from animal manures, 215, 219, 220, 466–7, 471
ammonification, 201–2